The Philosophy and Methodology of Economics
Volume II

The International Library of Critical Writings in Economics

Series Editor: Mark Blaug

Professor Emeritus, University of London
Consultant Professor, University of Buckingham
Visiting Professor, University of Exeter

This series is an essential reference source for students, researchers and lecturers in economics. It presents by theme an authoritative selection of the most important articles across the entire spectrum of economics. Each volume has been prepared by a leading specialist who has written an authoritative introduction to the literature included.

A full list of published and future titles in this series is printed at the end of this volume.

The Philosophy and Methodology of Economics Volume II

Edited by

Bruce J. Caldwell

Professor of Economics
University of North Carolina at Greensboro

An Elgar Reference Collection

Published by
Edward Elgar Publishing Limited
Gower House
Croft Road
Aldershot
Hants GU11 3HR
England

Edward Elgar Publishing Company
Old Post Road
Brookfield
Vermont 05036
USA

A CIP catalogue record for this book is available from the British Library

Library of Congress Cataloguing in Publication Data
The philosophy and methodology of economics/edited by Bruce J.
  Caldwell.
     p.   cm. – (The International library of critical writings in
  economics; 23) (An Elgar reference collection)
    Includes bibliographical references and index.
    1. Economics. 2. Economics–Philosophy. 3. Economics–
Methodology. I. Caldwell, Bruce J. II. Series. III. Series: An
Elgar reference collection.
HB34.P44 1993
330–dc20   92–33656
                                                                          CIP

ISBN 1 85278 385 0 (3 volume set)

Printed in Great Britain at the University Press, Cambridge

Contents

Acknowledgements

The editor and publishers wish to thank the following who have kindly given permission for the use of copyright material.

American Economic Association for articles: Wesley C. Mitchell (1925), 'Quantitative Analysis in Economic Theory', *American Economic Review*, **XV** (1), 1–12; Jack Hirshleifer (1985), 'The Expanding Domain of Economics', *American Economic Review Special Issue*, **75** (6), 53–68; George J. Stigler and Gary S. Becker (1977), 'De Gustibus Non Est Disputandum', *American Economic Review*, **67** (2), 76–90; Ronald Heiner (1983), 'The Origin of Predictable Behavior', *American Economic Review*, **73** (4), 560–95; Paul J.H. Schoemaker (1982), 'The Expected Utility Model: Its Variants, Purposes, Evidence and Limitations', *Journal of Economic Literature*, **XX**, 529–63; Vernon L. Smith (1989), 'Theory, Experiment and Economics', *Journal of Economic Perspectives*, **3** (1), 151–69.

Blackwell Publishers for articles: Adrian Pagan (1987), 'Three Econometric Methodologies: A Critical Appraisal', *Journal of Economic Surveys*, **1** (1), 3–24; Richard R. Nelson and Sidney G. Winter (1974), 'Neoclassical *vs.* Evolutionary Theories of Economic Growth: Critique and Prospectus', *Economic Journal*, **84** (336), 886–905.

Cambridge University Press for excerpt and article: Mary Morgan (1988), 'Finding a Satisfactory Empirical Model', in Neil de Marchi (ed.), *The Popperian Legacy in Economics*, 199–211; Paul J.H. Schoemaker (1991), 'The Quest for Optimality: A Positive Heuristic of Science?', *Behavioral and Brain Sciences*, **14** (2), 205–15.

Constitutional Political Economy for article: James M. Buchanan (1990), 'The Domain of Constitutional Economics', *Constitutional Political Economy*, Inaugural Issue, **1** (1), 1–18.

Elsevier Science Publishers B.V. for articles: Tjalling C. Koopmans (1947), 'Measurement Without Theory', *Review of Economic Statistics*, **XXIX** (3), 161–72; Rutledge Vining and Tjalling C. Koopmans (1949), 'Methodological Issues in Quantitative Economics', *Review of Economics and Statistics*, **XXXI** (2), 77–94.

Harper Collins Publishers for excerpt: T.W. Hutchison (1964), 'Types and Sources of Value-Judgments and Bias', *'Positive' Economics and Policy Objectives*, Chapter 2, 51–119.

Kluwer Academic Publishers for excerpt: Deborah Mayo (1981), 'Testing Statistical Testing', in J.C. Pitt (ed.), *Philosophy in Economics*, 175–203.

Prentice-Hall, Inc. for excerpt: Fritz Machlup (1969), 'Positive and Normative Economics: An Analysis of the Ideas', *Economic Means and Social Ends: Essays in Political Economics*, 99–129.

The American Scholar for article: Donald N. McCloskey (1988), 'The Limits of Expertise: If You're So Smart, Why Ain't You Rich?', *American Scholar*, 393–406.

University of Chicago Press for articles: Armen A. Alchian (1950), 'Uncertainty, Evolution, and Economic Theory', *Journal of Political Economy*, **LVIII**, 211–21; J. Hirshleifer (1977), 'Economics from a Biological Viewpoint', *Journal of Law & Economics*, **XX** (1), 1–52.

Every effort has been made to trace all the copyright holders but if any have been inadvertently overlooked the publishers will be pleased to make the necessary arrangement at the first opportunity.

In addition the publishers wish to thank the library of the London School of Economics and Political Science and The Alfred Marshall Library, Cambridge University for their assistance in obtaining these articles.

Part I
Estimation, Prediction and Testing

[1]

The

American Economic Review

VOL. XV MARCH, 1925 No. 1

QUANTITATIVE ANALYSIS IN ECONOMIC THEORY[1]

I

Eighteen years have passed since Dr. Alfred Marshall, addressing the Royal Economic Society, said that "qualitative analysis has done the greater part of its work" in economic science, and that the "higher and more difficult task" of quantitative analysis "must wait upon the slow growth of thorough realistic statistics."[2]

These dicta of the great teacher, to whom we owe so much, have an almost provocative ring. Were we like-minded with our predecessors of the 1880's, we might find the makings of new "Methodenstreit" in the saying that "qualitative analysis has done the greater part of its work." It is a cheering evidence of progress that no such futile disputation seems to be in progress or in prospect. We do not speak of qualitative *versus* quantitative analysis. We do not seek to prove even that one type should predominate over the other. Instead of dogmatizing about method at large, we are experimenting with methods in detail. In the measure of our proficiencies, we all practice both qualitative and quantitative analysis, shifting our emphasis according to the tasks we have in hand. And we are all eager to see our colleagues develop both types of analysis to the limits of efficiency in the tasks which they essay. Such differences of opinion as flourish among us turn chiefly on our expectations concerning the relative fruitfulness of qualitative and quantitative work in the near future—the future within which we and our associates can hope to be counted among the workers.

In discussing these expectations, I shall say little of qualitative analysis beyond making the obvious remark that it cannot be dispensed with, if for no other reason, because quantitative work itself involves distinctions of kind, and distinctions of kind start with distinctions of quality. The problematical and therefore interesting point is: What can we hope from quantitative, the less thoroughly proven type of analysis?

[1]Presidential address delivered at the Thirty-seventh Annual Meeting of the American Economic Association, held in Chicago, December 29, 1924.

[2]"The Social Possibilities of Economic Chivalry," *The Economic Journal* (March, 1907), vol. XVII, pp. 7, 8.

II

Since Dr. Marshall said that quantitative analysis "must wait upon the slow growth of thorough realistic statistics," the situation and outlook have changed in vital particulars.

In the United States, Canada, and somewhat less decisively in other countries, the "growth of thorough realistic statistics" has been accelerated. We may still fume about this growth as slow—it is slow in comparison with the demands of economic statisticians—but it is not as slow as it was before 1907. Quantitative analysis still waits upon the gathering of data in numerous fields; but in other fields the lack is of analysts—analysts with the imagination, technique and resources required to wring fresh knowledge from the accumulating masses of data. And the prospects seem bright that the recent rate of growth will be maintained. For the increasing complexity of economic organization makes more pressing our need of definite knowledge of our requirements and resources for meeting them.

Nor is it merely in the range and quality of the "realistic statistics" at their disposal that the prospects of the quantitative workers have grown brighter. A second gain is the steady improvement in the technical methods of statistical analysis. On this side, progress is not less rapid in other countries than in the United States.

In still a third respect prospects are improving. One of the chief obstacles in the way of quantitative analysis in economics has been the heavy burden of routine labor involved. A qualitative worker requires hardly any equipment beyond a few books and hardly any helper except a typist. A quantitative worker needs often a statistical laboratory, a corps of computers, and sometimes a staff of field workers. Few economists command such resources. But of late the endowment of economic research has begun on a scale which reduces this handicap upon quantitative research and promises to reduce it further in the near future. Numerous government agencies and large business enterprises have created research staffs which have considerable latitude in the choice of their problems, and so find opportunity to do work of scientific significance. Still freer to choose their own problems are the organizations created specifically to do research work, such as the Harvard Committee of Economic Research, the Pollak Foundation, the Institute of Economics, the National Bureau of Economic Research, the Food Research Institute, and the university bureaus of business or industrial research. The Social Science Research Council promises to become an agency through which important projects can obtain support. And there are signs that some of our universities presently will provide funds for aiding the researches of their faculties of social science.

III

Thus the economist of today has at his disposal a wider array of "thorough realistic statistics" than had the economist of yesterday, a more powerful technique, and more opportunities to get assistance. All this is recognized by everyone. But the crucial question remains: What use can we make of these data, this refined technique and these research assistants in solving the fundamental problems of economic science? Are not these the problems qualitative analysis has posed? When a theorist puts any one of his problems to a statistician, does the answer he gets ever quite meet his questions? And when a statistician attempts to test an economic theory, is his test ever conclusive? In fine, what evidence have we that quantitative analysis is taking over the task upon which qualitative analysis, with all its shortcomings, does make headway?

One view is that, despite all the gains it has made, quantitative analysis shows no more promise of providing a statistical complement of pure theory than it showed when Dr. Marshall pronounced his dicta. I think this view is correct, if the pure theory we have in mind is theory of the type cultivated by Jevons, or by Dr. Marshall himself. Indeed, I incline to go further and say that there is slight prospect that quantitative analysis will ever be able to solve the problems which qualitative analysis has framed, in their present form. What we must expect is a recasting of the old problems into new forms amenable to statistical attack. In the course of this reformulation of its problems, economic theory will change not merely its complexion but also its content.

Let me illustrate the reaction of methods upon problems by citing an example. In the course of his investigations into economic cycles, Professor Henry L. Moore needed to formulate "the concrete laws of demand for the representative crops." He approached this task by quoting Dr. Marshall's qualitative analysis of demand. But with Marshall's formulation of the problem it was impossible to get quantitative results. For Marshall treated the relation between demand and price on the assumptions (1) that the changes in the two variables are infinitesimal, (2) that the conditions remain constant, and (3) that the shape of the demand curve is known. Professor Moore, on the contrary, had to derive his curves of demand, and to deal with the real world where no factor is known to remain constant, and where changes in demand and price are finite. Attacking his problem by mathematical statistics, Moore obtained equations expressing the relations between the demands for and the prices of corn, hay, oats and potatoes; he determined the precision of these equations as formulas for predicting prices, and he measured the elasticity of demand for each crop. As he pointed out in concluding the discussion, his results do not solve Marshall's problem. But is not Moore's problem more significant theoretically, as well as more relevant to economic practice? If quantitative analysis can give us empirically valid demand curves and coefficients of elasticity for numerous commodities, shall we not have a better theory of demand than qualitative analysis can supply?[3]

From this concrete illustration of the reaction of quantitative method upon economic theory, we may pass to a broader range of considerations. Jevons preached that "The deductive science of Economics must be verified and rendered useful by the purely empirical science of Statistics." But the deductive theory for which Jevons wished a statistical complement was "based on a calculus of pleasure and pain."[4] Today there seems little likelihood that we shall have a quantitative proof—or disproof—of the calculus of pleasure and pain. That problem is passing off the stage.

Belonging to a younger generation than Jevons, Dr. Marshall formally repudiated hedonism; but he conceived of economic behavior as controlled by two opposing sets of motives, the motives which impel us toward consumption and the motives which repel us from labor and waiting. Money was to him "the center around which economic science clusters" because it is the economist's instrument for measuring the force of these motives.[5] One task which he hoped quantitative method would perform was that of rendering these measures more precise. Is there a better chance that we shall attain a statistical measurement of the force of motives than that we shall measure pleasures and pains?

I doubt it. For the quantitative data of the economist are limited to objective phenomena. Of course the theorist who so wishes may interpret these data in subjective terms, such as pleasure or the strength of desire. But these interpretations are something which the theorist adds to the data, not something which he draws out of them. In the present state of our knowledge of human nature, such interpretations smack more of metaphysics than of science. Economists who practice quantitative analysis are likely to be chary of deserting the firm ground of measurable phenomena for excursions into the subjective.

That such excursions are not imperative is readily shown. The theoretical purpose of Jevons' calculus of pleasure and pain, of

[3]Henry Ludwell Moore, *Economic Cycles: Their Law and Cause* (New York, 1914), ch. 4, "The Law of Demand."

[4]W. Stanley Jevons, *The Theory of Political Economy* (4th ed., London, 1911), pp. 22, 23.

[5]See book 1, ch. 2, in the later editions of Marshall's *Principles of Economics.*

Marshall's opposing sets of motives, and of the simultaneous equations used by the mathematical writers was to lay a foundation in the behavior of individuals on which could be built an explanation of mass phenomena. Of course the theorists have never supposed that any individual could really tell just how may units of one article he would give for successive units of another; but that mattered little, because the theorists have not been interested in the individuals as such. They presented the whole construction scrupulously as a conceptual device for getting insight into what happens in the real markets where the money incomes and costs of living of millions of men are fixed.

Now the quantitative workers derive their data directly from these real markets. They start with the mass phenomena which the qualitative analysts approached indirectly through their hypothetical individuals. With the fuller reports they are obtaining and the more powerful technique they are developing, properly equipped investigators can study the relations between the actual responses of prices to changes in supply and of supply to changes in prices. They can work out demand schedules which hold empirically within the ranges and periods covered by experience. They can trace the changes in the consumption of commodities by whole communities or by large groups. They can investigate the relations between monetary changes and "real" incomes, between saving and spending, between different forms of economic organization and production.

With all these fascinating problems and numberless others before them in shape for attack, it seems unlikely that the quantitative workers will retain a keen interest in imaginary individuals coming to imaginary markets with ready-made scales of bid and offer prices. Their theories will probably be theories about the relationships among the variables which measure objective processes. There is little likelihood that the old explanations will be refuted by these investigators, but much likelihood that they will be disregarded.

IV

If my forecast is valid, our whole apparatus of reasoning on the basis of utilities and disutilities, or motives, or choices, in the individual economy, will drop out of sight in the work of the quantitative analysts, going the way of the static state. The "psychological" element in the work of these men will consist mainly of objective analysis of the economic behavior of groups. Motives will not be disregarded, but they will be treated as problems requiring study, instead of being taken for granted as constituting explanations.

The obsolescence of the older type of reasoning in economics will be promoted by the change which is coming over our thinking about human nature. Psychologists are moving rapidly toward an objective conception and a quantitative treatment of their problems. Their emphasis upon stimulus and response sequences, upon conditioned reflexes; their eager efforts to develop performance tests, their attempts to build up a technique of experiment, favor the spread of the conception that all of the social sciences have a common aim—the understanding of human behavor; a common method—the quantitative analysis of behavior records; and a common aspiration—to devise ways of experimenting upon behavior.

This conception, that economics is one among a number of sciences all dealing with aspects of human behavior, need be no monopoly of the quantitative workers. But it will be especially congenial to their way of thinking. And it will put them in a better position than ever before to coöperate with quantitative analysts in other fields. What Jeremy Bentham's idea that all our actions are determined by pleasure and pain once did to provide a common program for jurists, economists, psychologists, penologists and educators, may be done again by the idea that all these groups together with the political scientists, sociologists, anthropologists, and historians, are engaged in the study of human behavior. On that basis the problems of each of these groups are significant for all the others, their technical methods are suggestive, their results pertinent.

The organizing influence of this conception will be felt inside of economics as strongly as in the whole program of the social sciences. Any objective study of economic behavior can find its place in this general scheme. In recent years many members of our Association have come to fear that economics may disintegrate into a number of specialties. This danger they combat by insisting that every young economist must receive "a thorough grounding in theory." The remedy seems inefficient, because the qualitative theory, in which we are commonly grounded, plays so small a role in our work as specialists in public finance and banking, in accountancy and transportation, in economic history and insurance, in business cycles, marketing, and labor problems. As economics becomes the study of objective behavior this breach between theory and the "practical" subjects will be narrowed. Specialization within economics will not be hampered, but it will become a process of "differentiation and integration" in Herbert Spencer's famous phrase, not a process of disintegration.

By this I do not mean that we can expect the rapid crystallization of a new system of economic theory built by quantitative analysis. Quite the contrary. The literature which the quantitative workers are due to produce will be characterized not by general treatises, but by numberless papers and monographs. Knowledge will grow by accretion as it grows in the natural sciences, rather than by the excogitation of new systems. Books will pass out of date more rapidly. The history of economic theory will receive less attention. Economists will be valued less on their erudition and more on their creative capacity. The advances will be achieved not only by conceiving new hypotheses, but also by compiling statistics from fresh fields, by inventing new technical methods, by refining upon old measures, and perhaps by devising experiments upon certain types of behavior. It will be harder for anyone to cover the whole field, perhaps quite impossible. From time to time some one will try to give a comprehensive survey of the results of quantitative research, but such books will not have the prestige won by the treatises by Adam Smith, Ricardo, Mill and Marshall.

V

Of the content of this quantitative economics we can form but uncertain surmises. One topic, however, is fairly sure to receive much attention—the topic defined twenty-four years ago at the thirteenth annual meeting of the American Economic Association by Dr. Veblen.[6] This is the relation between business and industry, between making money and making goods, between the pecuniary and the technological phases of economic life.

In qualitative analysis this problem has been sadly slurred over. The quantitative workers cannot so blink it. Much of their data will consist of two great groups of time series. One group shows variations in the output, stocks, shipment, or orders for economic goods expressed in physical units—bushels, pounds, yards, ton-miles, names on payrolls, hours of work, accident rates, labor turnover, and so on through a list that will grow with the growth of statistics. The second group of time series shows variations in quantities expressed in monetary units. The relations between these two groups of series will be an obvious problem of just the kind which quantitative workers enjoy attacking. They cannot content themselves by staying always on the money level of analysis, or always on the commodity level; and they cannot pass back and forth between the two levels without realizing what they are doing, as could the classical economists and their followers. Out of this technical characteristic of the statistical data we may expect to come a close scrutiny of the relations between our pecuniary institutions and our efficiency in producing and distributing goods. Such topics as the economic serviceability of advertising, the reactions of an unstable price level upon production,

[6] "Industrial and Pecuniary Employments," Thorstein Veblen. Publications of the AMERICAN ECONOMIC ASSOCIATION, Third series, vol. II. *Papers and Proceedings of the Thirteenth Annual Meeting, December, 1900,* pp. 190-235.

the effect of various systems of public regulation upon the services rendered by public utilities will be treated with incisive vigor as we become able to make the indispensable measurements. And investigations of this type will broaden out into a constructive criticism of that dominant complex of institutions known as the money economy—a constructive criticism which may guide the efforts of our children to make that marvelously flexible form of organization better fitted to their needs.

A bolder generalization may be hazarded. If our present beliefs are confirmed, that the human nature which men inherit remains substantially the same over milleniums, and that the changes in human life are due mainly to the evolution of culture, economists will concentrate their studies to an increasing degree upon economic institutions —the aspect of culture which concerns them. For whatever hopes we may cherish for the future of our race are bound up with the fortunes of the factor which certainly admits of change and perhaps admits of control. The quantitative workers will have a special predilection for institutional problems, because institutions standardize behavior, and thereby facilitate statistical procedure.

With the growing prominence of institutional problems, the fundamental issue of welfare is inextricably involved. What quantitative analysis promises here is to increase the range of objective criteria by which we judge welfare, and to study the variations of these criteria in relation to each other. The statistical worker is in no better position than any other student to specify what mankind should aim at; but in view of the multiplicity of our competing aims and the limitations of our social resources his help in measuring objective costs and objective results is indispensable to convert society's blind fumbling for happiness into an intelligent process of experimentation.

VI

In speaking of experimentation, I do not forget the difficulty of making experiments in the social sciences. That difficulty seems to me almost insuperable, so long as we hold to the old conceptions of human nature. But the behavioristic concept promises to diminish this handicap under which economics and its sister sciences have labored. For we can try experiments upon group behavior. Indeed, we are already trying such experiments. We have experimental schools, in which the physical and social environments of the children are made to vary, with the aim of studying the relations between the stimuli offered by the schools and the learning response. So, too, we experiment with different systems of remunerating labor, different forms of publicity, different organizations for distributing products, different price policies, different methods of supervising public utilities, and the like.

Of course, these experiments upon group behavior lack the rigor of the experimenting done in physical laboratories. The limits within which human beings can be manipulated are narrow; the behavior processes under scrutiny cannot be isolated from complicating processes, except as one applies the method of partial correlation to statistical records. Hence the work of experimenting in the social sciences requires a technique different from that of the natural sciences. The experimenter must rely far more upon statistical considerations and precautions. The ideal of a single crucial experiment cannot be followed. The experiments must be repeated upon numerous individuals or groups; the varieties of reactions to the stimuli must be recorded and analyzed; the representative character of the samples must be known before generalizations can be established. This whole procedure may have more in common with the quantitative study of data drawn from common experience than with the procedure of the man who deals with electric currents passing through a vacuum tube. But whatever approaches are made toward controlling the conditions under which groups act will be eagerly seized upon and developed with results which we cannot yet foresee.

In collecting and analyzing such experimental data as they can obtain, the quantitative workers will find their finest, but most exacting opportunities for developing statistical technique—opportunities even finer than are offered by the recurrent phenomena of business cycles. It is conceivable that the tentative experimenting of the present may develop into the most absorbing activity of economists in the future. If that does happen, the reflex influence upon economic theory will be more radical than any we can expect from the quantitative analysis of ordinary behavior records.[7] The most dazzling developments of the future may lie in this direction; but they are hardly more than a rosy glow upon the eastern horizon.

VII

So far my argument has run as follows: the increase of statistical data, the improvement of statistical technique, and the endowment of social research are enabling economists to make a larger use of quantitative analysis; in preparing for their work, the quantitative theorists usually find it necessary to formulate problems in a way different from that adopted by qualitative theorists; this technical necessity of restating problems promises to bring about radical changes in economic theory, in particular to make the treatment of behavior more objective,

[7]Compare Lawrence K. Frank, "The Emancipation of Economics," AMERICAN ECONOMIC REVIEW (March, 1924), vol. XIV, pp. 37, 38.

to emphasize the importance of institutions, and to promote the development of an experimental technique.

All this seems plausible as I reel it off; yet it runs counter to prevailing views. According to the classical concept of method, the business of the statistician is merely to verify conclusions established by deduction, and to discover disturbing causes which do not reveal themselves "to a reasoner engaged in the development of the more capital economic doctrines." Thus said Cairnes.[1] And even now some of the most distinguished statistical economists hold that their function is not to recast economic theory, but to provide a statistical complement for it. Professor Henry L. Moore, whose reformulation of Marshall's problem of the relations between demand and price I have cited, has taken this position.[2] What justification is there for a different opinion? Why should a freer use of quantitative analysis produce radical changes in economic theory?

I think there is a deeper-lying reason for my conclusion than is generally recognized. Our qualitative theory has followed the logic of Newtonian mechanics; our quantitative work rests on statistical conceptions. Between the mechanical type of theory and the statistical type of theory there are differences which will force changes in our fundamental conceptions as we shift our emphasis from one type to the other.

Let me expand this statement. In the hedonistic calculus which Jevons followed, man is placed under the governance of two sovereign masters, pain and pleasure, which play the same role in controlling human behavior that Newton's laws of motion play in controlling the behavior of the heavenly bodies. Dr. Marshall's conception of economic behavior as controlled by two opposing sets of motives is scarcely less mechanical in its logic. Indeed, any theorist who works by ascribing motives to men and arguing what they will do under guidance of these forces will produce a mechanical type of explanation.

Intermixed with speculation of this type in economics, there has usually been an element of broad observation upon average behavior. Quantitative work with statistics means the expansion and systematization of this element of observation. It has its counterpart in physics, introduced by Clerk-Maxwell, just as speculation about the force of motives has its counterpart in Newtonian mechanics. Expounding the statistical view of nature, Clerk-Maxwell wrote:

......those uniformities of nature which we observe in our experiments with quantities of matter containing millions of millions of molecules are

[1] *The Character and Logical Method of Political Economy,* by J. E. Cairnes (2d ed., 1875), Lecture iii, section 5.

[2] See his paper "The Statistical Complement of Pure Economics," *Quarterly Journal of Economics* (Nov., 1908), vol. XXIII, pp. 1—33.

uniformities of the same kind as those explained by Laplace and wondered at by Buckle, arising from the slumping together of multitudes of cases, each of which is by no means uniform with others." ". . . . . .if the molecular theory of the constitution of bodies is true, all our knowledge of matter is of a statistical kind.[10]

The difference between the mechanical and the statistical conceptions of nature has been clearly worked out in physics. The mechanical view involves the notions of sameness, of certainty, of invariant laws; the statistical view involves the notions of variety, of probability, of approximations.[11] Yet Clerk-Maxwell's "new kind of uniformity" was found to yield results in many physical problems which corresponded closely to results attained on mechanical lines.

Such a close correspondence between the results based on speculation and the results based on statistical observation is not to be expected in economics, for three reasons. First, the cases summed up in our statistics seldom if ever approach in number the millions of millions of molecules, or atoms, or electrons of the physicist. Second, the units in economic aggregates are less similar than the molecules or atoms of a given element. Third, we cannot approach closely the isolation practices of the laboratory. For these reasons the elements of variety, of uncertainty, of imperfect approximation are more prominent in the statistical work of the social sciences than in the statistical work of the natural sciences. And because our statistical results are so marked by these imperfections they do not approach so closely to the results of our reasoning on the basis of assumed premises. Hence the development of statistical method may be expected to make more radical changes in economic than it makes in physical theory.

Of course, this lack of close agreement between the results attainable on the statistical and the mechanical views of nature in economics might be advanced as a reason for holding more strictly to the mechanical type of work. But that would be a wrong conclusion, provided our aim in economics is to understand the world of which we are a part. On this proviso, we seem bound to argue: the mechanical type of speculation works with the notions of sameness, of certainty, of invariant laws. In economics these notions do not fit the phenomena closely. Hence we must put our ultimate trust in observation. And as fast as we can raise our observations to a scientific level we must drop the cruder, yet not wholly valueless, approximations attained by the mechanical type of work.

[10]Quoted by J. T. Merz from Campbell and Garnett, "Life of Clerk-Maxwell," *History of European Thought in the Nineteenth Century* (2d ed., London, 1912), vol. II, pp. 600, 601.

[11]Compare the admirable paper "On Measurement in Economics," by Fred C. Mills, in *The Trend of Economics*, edited by R. G. Tugwell (New York, 1924).

VIII

The growth of quantitative analysis which I foresee in economics, with its reformulation of old problems and its redistribution of emphasis, does not promise a speedy ending of the types of theory to which we are accustomed. For an indefinite time we shall probably have theorists who keep strictly to qualitative analysis and draw upon quantitative work merely for occasional illustrations of their propositions. Others meanwhile will be extending the range of problems conceived and discussed in quantitative terms. But even in the work of the most statistically minded qualitative analysis will keep a place. Always our thinking will cover a field larger than our measurements; the preconceptions that shape our ends, our first glimpses of new problems, our widest generalizations will remain qualitative in form. Indeed qualitative work itself will gain in power, scope and interest as we make use of wider, more accurate and more reliable measurements. And, to repeat what I said in the beginning, quantitative work cannot dispense with distinctions of quality. In the thinking of competent workers, the two types of analysis will coöperate with and complement each other as peacefully in economics as they do in chemistry.

Dr. Marshall's dicta, which I took as my text, hold out small hope of rapid progress in our science. If qualitative analysis has really "done the greater part of its work," and if the "growth of thorough realistic statistics" on which quantitative analysis "must wait" is slow, then Dr. Marshall's hope that his pupils will render his own work obsolete is not likely to be realized." I cherish a livelier optimism. With more abundant and more reliable data, more powerful methods, and more liberal assistance, the men now entering upon careers of research may go far toward establishing economics as a quantitative science. In so far as they accomplish this aim, they will in transforming the subject make obsolete not only the qualitative work of Dr. Marshall and others, but also the crude begnnings of quantitative work which their elders are now producing. All of us share in wishing them the fullest measure of success.

WESLEY C. MITCHELL.

Columbia University.

[14]Compare Dr. J. M. Keynes's charming memoir, "Alfred Marshall, 1842-1924," *Economic Journal* (Sept., 1924), vol. XXXIV, p. 866.

[2]

MEASUREMENT WITHOUT THEORY[1]

TJALLING C. KOOPMANS

THE EMPIRICAL APPROACH

WHEN Tycho Brahé and Johannes Kepler engaged in the systematic labor of measuring the positions of the planets, and charting their orbits, they started with conceptions and models of the planetary system which later proved incorrect in some aspects, irrelevant in others. Tycho always, and Kepler initially, believed in uniform circular motion as the natural basic principle underlying the course of celestial bodies. Tycho's main contribution was a systematic accumulation of careful measurements. Kepler's outstanding success was due to a willingness to strike out for new models and hypotheses if such were needed to account for the observations obtained. He was able to find simple empirical "laws" which were in accord with past observations and permitted the prediction of future observations. This achievement was a triumph for the approach in which large scale gathering, sifting, and scrutinizing of facts precedes, or proceeds independently of, the formulation of theories and their testing by further facts.

The book by Burns and Mitchell,[2] discussed here, approaches the problems of cyclical fluctuations in economic variables in the same empirical spirit. The book has two main purposes: first, a detailed exposition, with experimental applications, of the methods of measuring cyclical behavior, developed by the National Bureau of Economic Research; secondly, a search, with the help of these methods, for possible changes in cyclical behavior of economic variables over time, whether gradual, abrupt, in longer cycles, or otherwise.

The approach of the authors is here described as empirical in the following sense: The various choices as to what to "look for," what economic phenomena to observe, and what measures to define and compute, are made with a minimum of assistance from theoretical conceptions or hypotheses regarding the nature of the economic processes by which the variables studied are generated.

In fact, Burns and Mitchell are more consistently empiricist than Kepler was. The latter made no secret of his predilection for the principle of circular motion until observations spoke decisively for the elliptical orbit. He held other speculative views as to the role of the five regular solids and of musical intervals in the proportions of the planetary system, which now appear as irrelevant. Burns and Mitchell do not reveal at all in this book what explanations of cyclical fluctuations, if any, they believe to constitute plausible models or hypotheses.

The undertaking commands respect, and the precedent holds great promise: For, in due course, the theorist Newton was inspired to formulate the fundamental laws of attraction of matter, which contain the empirical regularities of planetary motion discovered by Kepler as direct and natural consequences. The terms "empirical regularities" and "fundamental laws" are used suggestively to describe the "Kepler stage" and the "Newton stage" of the development of celestial mechanics. It is not easy to specify precisely what is the difference between the two stages. Newton's law of gravitation can also be looked upon as describing an empirical regularity in the behavior of matter. The conviction that this "law" is in some sense more fundamental, and thus constitutes progress over the Kepler stage, is due, I believe, to its being at once more elementary and more general. It is more elementary in that a simple property of mere matter is postulated. As a result, it is more general in that it applies to all matter, whether assembled in planets, comets, sun or stars, or in terrestrial objects — thus explaining a much wider range of phenomena.

It appears to be the intention of Burns and

[1] This article will be reprinted as part of Cowles Commission Papers, New Series, No. 25. I am indebted to several friends, including Dr. A. F. Burns, for comments on an earlier draft. These comments have helped me to bring out more clearly the issues raised in this review, for which, of course, I remain exclusively responsible. T.C.K.
[2] Arthur F. Burns and Wesley C. Mitchell, *Measuring Business Cycles* (National Bureau of Economic Research, Studies in Business Cycles, No. 2, New York, 1946).

Mitchell — in any case it is the opinion of the present reviewer — that their book represent an important contribution to the "Kepler stage" of inquiry in the field of economics. It is concerned exclusively with cyclical fluctuations. Its hypotheses are concerned with the character of such fluctuations, rather than with the underlying economic behavior of man.

The auspicious precedent in the history of celestial mechanics suggests that this is a promising procedure, which may expect to be rewarded in due course by further development of theory. Nevertheless, this reviewer believes that in research in economic dynamics the Kepler stage and the Newton stage of inquiry need to be more intimately combined and to be pursued simultaneously. Fuller utilization of the concepts and hypotheses of economic theory (in a sense described below) *as a part of the processes of observation and measurement* promises to be a shorter road, perhaps even the only possible road, to the understanding of cyclical fluctuations. Such a course, in addition, promises as by-products greater insight into noncyclical and even nondynamic problems of economics.

While a systematic argument in support of this position would surpass the bounds of a review, I shall attempt to adduce some of the arguments in the course of this discussion of the book. It is then my duty to point out in what respects, in my opinion, the present state of business cycle analysis differs from the situation in which Tycho and Kepler approached the phenomenon of planetary motion. I hasten to add that the parallel with the classical problems of celestial mechanics is not mentioned by, and may not have been in the minds of, the authors. It is merely the best example, known to the reviewer, of a case where the empirical approach paved the way for the discovery of fundamental laws.

The example has been selected because it is favorable to the empiricist position. Needless to say, the history of science knows of many cases in which "fundamental" hypotheses, more or less integrated into a theory of the phenomena studied, have played a much larger role. However, the spectacular success, achieved in the case here chosen as an example, has set a pattern which has ever since, con-sciously or unconsciously, been in the minds of scientific workers in widely diverse fields.

MEASURES OF CYCLICAL "BEHAVIOR"

The authors formulate their objective in the following terms:

> Whatever their working concepts, ..., all investigators cherish the same ultimate aim — namely, to attain better understanding of the recurrent fluctuations in economic fortune that modern nations experience. This aim may be pursued in many ways. The way we have chosen is to observe the business cycles of history as closely and systematically as we can before making a fresh attempt to explain them (p. 4).

The point of departure is a definition of business cycles, derived from experience, and to be tested in the light of further experience:

> Business cycles are a type of fluctuation found in the aggregate economic activity of nations that organize their work mainly in business enterprises: a cycle consists of expansions occurring at about the same time in many economic activities, followed by similarly general recessions, contractions, and revivals which merge into the expansion phase of the next cycle; this sequence of changes is recurrent but not periodic; in duration business cycles vary from more than one year to ten or twelve years; they are not divisible into shorter cycles of similar character with amplitudes approximating their own (p. 3).

As is often the case in statistical work, a vast amount of data — represented here by (mostly monthly) observations of many economic variables over long periods — is to be reduced and summarized by computing a smaller number of "derived" measures, incorporating what is relevant and informative, omitting what is accidental or devoid of interest. The first eight chapters essentially consist in making reasoned choices as to what measures are relevant and informative. In that undertaking, the definition just quoted — itself the result of an earlier volume by Mitchell in the same series — is the main guide.

The *first* group of measures selected concerns location in time and duration. For each variable, lower and upper turning points are determined, as well as time intervals between them (expansion, contraction, trough-to-trough duration of *specific* cycles). In addition, turning points and durations are determined for

MEASUREMENT WITHOUT THEORY   163

reference cycles, i.e., points around which the corresponding specific cycle turning points of a great many variables are concentrated. Leads and lags are found as differences between corresponding specific cycle and reference cycle turning points. All turning points are determined after elimination of seasonal variation but without prior trend elimination, using as much as possible monthly or otherwise quarterly data.

The *second* group of measures relates to movements of one variable within one cycle, which may be either a cycle specific to that variable, or a reference cycle. For the computation of these measures, each variable is expressed in per cent of its mean over the cycle concerned — a procedure which eliminates intercycle trend but preserves intracycle trend. For each cycle, a pattern of nine successive "standings" is then computed, i.e., a sequence of nine averages, indicated by Roman numerals, of which I, V, and IX are generally three-month averages centered at successive trough, peak, and trough months, respectively, and those numbered II, III, IV, and VI, VII, VIII are averages arising from subdivision, into three approximately equal parts, of the intermediate periods of expansion and contraction, respectively. The result is a specific cycle pattern, or a reference cycle pattern, of the variable concerned, depending on what kind of turning points were employed. These patterns are plotted on a time scale reflecting whatever inequality there is in duration between expansion and contraction. For specific cycles the following measures of amplitude are considered: "rise" $(V - I)$, "fall" $(V - IX)$, and "rise and fall" $(2V - I - IX)$, both in absolute terms, and on a per month basis to indicate steepness of rise and fall. Reference cycle amplitudes are computed in a similar manner, but the three stages involved are not necessarily the reference stages I, V, IX, but rather such reference cycle stages (with constant Roman numeral) as are most frequently or closely coincident in timing with specific cycle stages I, V, IX.

The foregoing measures have been described for a single cycle. Averages of these measures for a sequence of cycles are likewise computed, and are qualified by presenting the average

deviation as a measure of variation between cycles.

The *third* group of measures expresses conformity of specific cycles of a variable to business cycles. These comprise ratios of average reference cycle amplitudes to average specific cycle amplitudes of the same variable, for expansions and contractions combined. They further comprise indexes of conformity expressing the proportion of all reference cycles covered in which the signs of $(V - I)$, of $(V - IX)$, and of $(V - I)$-per-month plus $(V - IX)$-per-month, respectively, are positive. In order to do justice to cases where specific cycles show regular lags or leads in relation to reference cycles, these measures are supplemented by similar conformity measures in which the reference cycle standings I, V, and IX are replaced by the three reference cycle standings described above, selected to reflect the average lag or lead shown by each type of specific turning point.

This somewhat lengthy, though still incomplete, enumeration of the various measures employed may serve to show the main preoccupation of the authors: faithful observation and summarizing of the cyclical characteristics of a large number of economic series. The toolkit of the theoretical economist is deliberately spurned. Not a single demand or supply schedule or other equation expressing the behavior of men or the technical laws of production is employed explicitly in the book, and the cases of implicit use are few and far between.

THE SPIRIT OF INQUIRY GROPING FOR GUIDANCE

As indicated above, I am here concerned mainly with evaluating this empiricist position taken by the authors, and with showing its implications and limitations. My *first argument*, then, is that even for the purpose of systematic and large scale observation of such a many-sided phenomenon, theoretical preconceptions about its nature cannot be dispensed with, and the authors do so only to the detriment of the analysis. It has already been mentioned that the later and more interesting part of the book (Chapters 9–12) is devoted to a search for possible changes in cyclical "behavior" over time, with a view to qualifying the meaning of average measures of cyclical "behavior" computed from a sequence of cycles. This analysis employs the following seven series, arranged here as classified on page 372:

Relating to	Series
Durable goods market	1. Pig iron production
	2. Railroad freight car orders
Money market	3. Yields of high-grade railroad bonds [a]
	4. Call money rates [a]
Stock market	5. Railroad stock prices [a]
	6. Number of shares traded [a]
Volume of payments	7. Deflated bank clearings

There is no systematic discussion of the reasons for selecting these particular variables as most worthy of study. As a justification for this choice the following few lines are given on page 384:

> These series cover processes that rank high among the activities stressed in theoretical studies of business cycles. Partly for this reason, partly because of the comparatively long stretch of time covered by these records, we regard our small sample as fairly satisfactory for the present purpose.

The choices made may have been the best possible ones. But "good" choices means relevant choices. What is relevant can only be determined with the help of some notions as to the generation of economic fluctuations, and as to their impact on society. In the light of such notions, wide fluctuations in call money rates may be unimportant if total employment is relatively stable. Fluctuations in the production of durable producers' goods would be less serious if they were approximately offset by opposite fluctuations in the production of consumers' goods. The choices as to what variables to study cannot be settled by a brief reference to "theoretical studies of business cycles." These issues call for a systematic argument to show that the best use has been made of available data in relation to the most important aspects of the phenomena studied.

Earlier in the book (pp. 71–76), some discussion is indeed devoted to the "meaning" of individual variables, in particular with a view to determining whether a single variable or

[a] Quoted on New York Stock exchange.

aggregate might be used to locate turning points of reference cycles. The shortness of the periods for which broad aggregates — like national income, an index of total production, or employment — are available rules out such series for all purposes requiring a long period of observation. But the use of a small number of aggregates is also warned against as being insufficient in principle. This question, it seems to me, admits of different answers in different cases, depending on the scope, the objective, and the underlying assumptions of each particular piece of analysis.

The lack of guidance from theoretical considerations is perceivable also in the choice of the measures computed from the variables selected. These are intended to be measures of cyclical "behavior." The use of the term "behavior" does not mean, however, that the authors intend to study the behavior of groups of economic agents (consumers, workers, entrepreneurs, dealers, etc.) whose modes of action and response, in the social organization and technological environment of the society studied, are the ultimate determinants of the levels of economic variables as well as their fluctuations. Instead, they study the "behavior" (in a more mechanical sense) of certain measurable joint effects of several of those actions and responses. This shift of attention from underlying human responses to their combined effects is a decisive step. It eliminates all benefits, described more fully below, that might be received from economic theory — by which I mean in this context the theoretical analysis of the aggregate effects of assumed patterns of economic behavior of groups of individuals. It also divorces the study of fluctuations from the explanation of the levels or trends around which the variables fluctuate, since such theoretical analysis is needed to bring out the common features in both groups of problems.

The rejection of the help that economic theorizing might give leaves a void. For now there is a need for some organizing principle to determine on what aspects of the observed variables attention should be concentrated. Here the definition of business cycles quoted above comes into operation. But it does not quite fill the gap. It does not become altogether clear why the cyclical forms of movement should receive such exclusive attention. With the great variety in types of movement in the real world, it is not even always clear what a cycle is. The gap left by the barring of explicit formal theory is thus filled with methodological quasi-theory concerned with delineating the object of study. There are lengthy discussions of questions like these: What is a turning point? When is a certain movement of a variable to be recognized as a specific cycle? (pp. 61–62). When are certain concurrent movements of a number of variables to be recognized as a business cycle? (pp. 87–94). In first instance the criteria employed are mechanical applications of clauses in the definition of business cycles quoted above, like limitations on the length of time between two successive turning points, or the rule that no "cycle" be divisible into shorter cycles with amplitudes approximating its own (even if those shorter cycles would escape recognition because of their shortness). Difficulties then arise in periods of war or important changes in economic policies. Reference is made to judgment and indeed to explanatory factors where those are clearly visible (tie-ups through weather or strike, economic effects of war, changing policies in the early "new deal" period). Arbitrary formal criteria are here combined with good though incidental pieces of causal analysis to answer what are, in frequent borderline cases, essentially irrelevant questions. The authors' insistence on seeing, counting, and measuring cycles before anything else reminds one of Kepler's preference for circular motion.

A similar group of questions, sometimes permitting only arbitrary answers, arises in deciding how to match the cycles specific to one variable with recognized business cycles, for certain comparisons. One of these questions is whether the variable concerned is to be treated on a positive (i.e., trough-to-trough cycle) or on an inverted (peak-to-peak) plan. We learn on page 115 the highly interesting fact that raw material stocks held by manufacturers tend to be positively related to business cycles, whereas stocks of finished products tend to be related invertedly. The authors do not at this stage ask for the motives or determining fac-

tors of this behavior of dealers or manufacturers. Instead they discuss formal rules to establish positive or inverted "behavior" of a variable on the basis of frequencies of concurrent or opposite directions of movement.

On the whole, the same measures are computed for all variables studied, irrespective of their economic nature. The importance of the economic phenomenon expressed by any particular variable is duly stressed (pp. 140–41) with reference to the interpretation to be placed on the measures computed, but is in general not permitted to influence the choice of measures used. An exception is found in the discussion of criteria for positive or inverted treatment, which contains hints of postulated behavior relationships (p. 117). This analysis would need to be made more explicit to remove the impression that somewhat scholastic distinctions are used in the discussion of how to relate specific and reference cycles (p. 118).

The notion of a reference cycle itself implies the assumption of an essentially one-dimensional basic pattern of cyclical fluctuation, a background pattern around which the movements of individual variables are arranged in a manner dependent on their specific nature as well as on accidental circumstances. (There is a similarity here with Spearman's psychological hypothesis of a single mental factor common to all abilities.) This "one-dimensional" hypothesis may be a good first approximation, in the same sense in which the assumption of circular motion provides a good first approximation to the orbits of the planets. It must be regarded, however, as an assumption of the "Kepler stage," based on observation of many series without reference to the underlying economic behavior of individuals. It is in this sense, I believe, that the authors refer (p. 3) to their definition of business cycles as "a tool of research, similar to many definitions used by observational sciences, and like its analogues subject to revision or abandonment if not borne out by observation." I believe that the authors would not object to the addition: "or by the logical consequences of observations of a wider range of phenomena."

SCANT GUIDANCE FOR MAKERS OF POLICIES

The examples given illustrate the authors' scientific "strategy," in which measurement and observation precede, and are largely independent of, any attempts toward the explanation of economic fluctuations. The plan of inquiry envisaged by the National Bureau is therefore to follow up the present methodological work by a series of monographs in which the techniques of measurement developed are applied comparatively to various industries, countries, or broad markets. Ultimately, it is intended to "weave the results established by the monographs together with existing knowledge into a theoretical account of how business cycles run their course." [4]

The wording of this statement of intentions still admits of the interpretation that even the ultimate objective of the authors is only a generalizing description of the typical course of a business cycle. However, I believe, and will assume for the purpose of this discussion, that more is meant, namely, a genuine explanation of economic fluctuations, i.e., an explanation in which only extra-economic phenomena are accepted as "data" without further inquiry, all relevant economic phenomena being subject to explanation in terms of assumed behavior patterns of men in a given institutional and technological environment. I am not sure whether a still further objective is included, which extrapolates the idea of explanation: the prediction, within the narrowest attainable limits of error, of the effects of stated hypothetical measures of economic policy on the level and movements of economic variables. However, I feel that such prediction is actually the most important objective of the analysis of economic fluctuations. The criterion of social usefulness of scientific analysis gives us the right to discuss the merits of any particular approach to the problem of economic fluctuation on the basis of the guidance it gives to economic policy, even if such guidance were not claimed by the authors.

Let us, then, now consider the question

whether the development that led from the empirical regularities observed by Kepler to the general theory of gravity discovered by Newton might find a counterpart in similar discovery of the laws of economic motion on the basis of carefully described regularities. I shall mention and discuss a few important differences between the two scientific situations.

Newton's achievement was based, not only on the regularities observed by Kepler, but also on the experiments conducted on the surface of the earth by Galileo. Economists are not in a position to perform experiments with an economic system as a whole for the sole purpose of establishing scientific truth (although deliberate changes in parts of the system have been undertaken at various occasions for other than scientific purposes, and have incidentally added to our information). It is therefore not possible in many economic problems to separate "causes" and "effects" by varying causes one at a time, studying the separate effect of each cause — a method so fruitful in the natural sciences.

On the other hand, economists do possess more elaborate and better established theories of economic behavior than the theories of motion of material bodies known to Kepler. These economic theories are based on evidence of a different kind than the observations embodied in time series: knowledge of the motives and habits of consumers and of the profit-making objectives of business enterprise, based partly on introspection, partly on interview or on inferences from observed actions of individuals — briefly, a more or less systematized knowledge of man's behavior and its motives. While much in these theories is incomplete and in need of reformulation and elaboration (particularly in regard to behavior over time under conditions of uncertainty), such theory as we have is an indispensable element in understanding in a quantitative way the formation of economic variables. For according to that theory the relevant economic variables are determined by the simultaneous validity of an equal number of "structural" equations (of behavior, of law or rule, of technology). The very fact that so many relations are simultaneously valid makes the observation of any one of them difficult, and sometimes even impossible. For any ob-

---

[4] P. 22. A less ambitious "preview" of this final volume is promised shortly under the title *What Happens During Business Cycles: A Progress Report*, by Wesley C. Mitchell.

served regularity between simultaneous and/or successive values of certain variables may have to be ascribed to the validity of several structural equations rather than any one of them. The mere observation of regularities in the interrelations of variables then does not permit us to recognize or to identify behavior equations among such regularities. In the absence of experimentation, such identification is possible, if at all, only if the form of each structural equation is specified, i.e., in particular, if we can indicate the set of variables involved in each equation, and perhaps also the manner in which they are to be combined. In each case, a preliminary study of the system of structural equations held applicable is required to decide whether the specifications regarding any particular equation are sufficiently detailed to permit its identification. Without such identification, measurement of the structural equation involved is not possible, and should therefore not be attempted.

One might object: why should measurement of the behavior equations of consumers, workers, entrepreneurs be necessary? If observed regularities are due to the simultaneous validity of several behavior equations, these regularities will persist as long as each of the underlying (unknown) behavior patterns persists. However, there are important arguments to counter this objection. Sheer scientific curiosity still urges us on to penetrate to the underlying structural equations. This curiosity is reinforced and justified (if you wish) by the awareness that knowledge of the behavior patterns will help in understanding or analyzing different situations, for instance, problems of secular trend, or cyclical problems in other countries or periods — in the same way (although one would not expect with the same exactness) in which the law of gravitation explains celestial and terrestrial phenomena alike. This point has particular relevance with regard to the different situations expected to arise in an impending future period of the same country that has been studied. Behavior patterns are subject to change: gradually through changing habits and tastes, urbanization and industrialization; gradually or unevenly through technological change; abruptly through economic policies or the economic

effects of political events. While one particular behavior pattern may be deemed fairly stable over a certain period, a much greater risk is involved in assuming that a whole system of structural equations is stable over time. An observed regularity not traced to underlying behavior patterns, institutional rules, and laws of production, is therefore an instrument of unknown reliability. The predictions it yields cannot be qualified with the help even of known trends in behavior or technology. It is of no help whatever in assessing the probable effects of stated economic policies or institutional changes.

There is no sign in the book of an awareness of the problems of determining the identifiability of, and measuring, structural equations as a prerequisite to the practically important types of prediction. Measurable effects of economic actions are scrutinized, to all appearance, in almost complete detachment from any knowledge we may have of the motives of such actions. The movements of economic variables are studied as if they were the eruptions of a mysterious volcano whose boiling caldron can never be penetrated. There is no explicit discussion at all of the problem of prediction, its possibilities and limitations, with or without structural change, although surely the history of the volcano is important primarily as a key to its future activities. There is no discussion whatever as to what bearing the methods used, and the provisional results reached, may have on questions of economic policy.

This, then, is my *second argument* against the empiricist position: Without resort to theory, in the sense indicated, conclusions relevant to the guidance of economic policies cannot be drawn.

CHANGES IN CYCLICAL "BEHAVIOR" OVER TIME

There is a highly interesting analysis in the last four chapters, already referred to, in which the following question is treated (phrasing by the reviewer): Is there evidence that such structural changes as have taken place during the period studied have led to changes in cyclical "behavior" of the variables studied? A search is made (Chapter 10) for secular changes, in duration, amplitude (absolute and per month) and timing of the specific cycles, and in the pattern of reference cycles, of the seven American variables selected for intensive study. A hypothesis by Mills linking durations of business cycles in various countries to stages of industrialization, and the hypothesis of a break in average duration and amplitude of specific cycles of the seven American series due to the first world war are tested. A search is also made (Chapter 11) for long cycles in cyclical charactersitics. Possible statistical connections with the long wave in building activity, and various long cycle hypotheses formulated by Wardwell, Kondratieff, Schumpeter, and Kitchin, respectively, are tested.

There appears to be a tendency in this chapter to select a hypothesis for testing because it has been stated in a scientific publication rather than on the basis of possible arguments in favor of it. Nevertheless, the hypotheses (granted that they concern the "behavior" of variables rather than of men) cover a wide range of possibilities. In particular the hypotheses of secular trend in cyclical characteristics, that of a break in structure due to war, and that of an influence of the long cycle in construction are of great theoretical and practical interest.

The most remarkable outcome of this whole group of tests is the extent to which mild traces of systematic change, of one type or another, in cyclical "behavior" are almost drowned by wide and apparently random variability between cycles. It is true that interesting particular changes are found. Money markets are found more susceptible to secular changes in cyclical behavior than industrial or security markets. The lead in the cyclical revival of pig iron production and freight car orders in early cycles is found to have disappeared in later cycles. The latter effect may be wholly or partly an automatical result of a diminishing rate of growth, given the fact that turning points are defined without prior elimination of secular trend.[5] It would indeed be interesting to determine whether the gradual decrease in cyclical lead would remain if turning points were determined after trend elimination. If so, there is a parallel phenomenon in the gradual decrease in the responsiveness of

demand for railway rolling stock to changes in traffic and profitability, in the United Kingdom during a period preceding the first world war, apparent from one of Tinbergen's investigations.[6]

One of the results interpreted as a possible sign of longer cycles in cyclical behavior might be merely the effect of considerable random variation between cycles, combined with correlation between the various characteristics of a cycle. I am referring to the differences found between average characteristics of the first and last cycles of groups of successive cycles separated by severe depressions. For such averages are obtained by a process of selection of cycles that start and end, respectively, in especially deep depressions. The authors stress this selection effect when they deal with Schumpeter's hypothesis that each Juglar cycle contains three Kitchin cycles, but do not seem to give it sufficient emphasis in relation to their own grouping of cycles just described.[7]

However this may be, any systematic effects present are found to be greatly obscured and dominated by random variation of the characteristics of individual cycles. The authors themselves express surprise (p. 413) at the slight manifestations of structural change (other than mere growth, largely eliminated by the use of relatives to cycle means) in data covering a period known to have witnessed thoroughgoing changes in economic organization. They state their intention to press the search for secular changes in cyclical behavior in subsequent studies concerned with particular industries or markets.

ISOLATING THE SOURCES OF RANDOM VARIATION

The presence of random variability in economic data gives rise to methodological requirements which do not arise in the study of planetary motion. In the latter case, the phenomenon studied can for all practical purposes be treated as a deterministic process, with some randomness entering into the data only through

[5] See the discussion in Chapter 7, Section III.

[6] J. Tinbergen, *Statistical Testing of Business Cycle Theories: I. A Method and Its Application to Investment Activity*, Graph V.2 on page 120.

[7] I do not understand the reasoning at the top of page 460, where evidence independent of selection is claimed.

MEASUREMENT WITHOUT THEORY

errors of measurement. In dynamic economics, the phenomenon itself is either essentially a stochastic process or needs to be treated as such because of the great number of factors at work.[8] Hence the analysis and interpretation of economic data call for the application of the methods of statistical inference.

The main problem of inference is the choice of "statistics," i.e., those functions of the observations — fewer in number than the observations themselves — which are to be used for estimation of parameters or for the testing of hypotheses. The question should therefore now be raised whether the authors' finding of strong domination of random variation over possible traces of systematic change in cyclical "behavior" is not at least partly due to the choice of the particular "statistics" studied. At the risk of becoming monotonous, I wish to state that explicit dynamic theory of the formation of economic variables is needed to throw light on this question. Most theories of this kind recently constructed have in common the attempt to describe the fluctuating economy by a complete system of structural equations which, as to their form, are stochastic difference equations. They are difference equations (embodying dynamic theory), in that they describe responses subject to time lags: past values of economic variables affect current actions of individuals. They are stochastic equations in that the behavior of any group of individuals, and the outcome of any production process, is determined in part by many minor factors, further scrutiny of which is either impossible or unrewarding. Such further scrutiny is not necessary provided that the analysis of each structural equation be pushed to the point where the joint effect of unanalyzed factors can indeed be regarded as random (if not necessarily independent) drawings from a reasonably stable probability distribution. To attain this end, it is often neces-

sary to introduce explicitly so-called "exogenous variables," representing the effects of wars, political events, population growth, economic policies, or technological developments which are not routine responses to economic conditions, etc.

Systems of this kind may possess a tendency for the variables to evolve in cyclical movements. Even if the random disturbances (or shocks) in individual equations possess a fairly stable distribution, however, there is no need for the ensuing cycles to be very regular or similar in duration or amplitude. Current values of economic variables are the cumulative effect both of a sequence of random shocks over the recent past, and of the impulses exerted by exogenous variables in the recent past.[9] Because of this tendency to cumulation of effects, relatively small shocks may have considerable effects over time on such "cyclical characteristics" as duration and amplitudes of cycles. Also, different impulses exerted successively by the same exogenous variables may produce different cycles of quite diverse appearance.

Now any rigorous testing of hypotheses according to modern methods of statistical inference requires a specification of the form of the joint probability distribution of the variables. In principle, such specification does not need to take on a "parametric" form, as when linear, parabolic or exponential functions, or normal distributions, are specified — although parametric assumptions usually admit more accurate estimation or more powerful tests whenever they are justified. In any case, however, it is necessary to hypothesize in what manner randomness enters into the formation of economic variables. It is for this reason that the form of each structural equation should be specified and/or determined to the point where at least a conceptual isolation of the random influences at work is attained.

The authors do not discuss randomness in terms of definite distributional hypothesis, although the idea of random factors as one of the determinants of economic variables is

[8] It has been stated by H. Hotelling ("Differential Equations Subject to Error and Population Estimates," *Journal of the American Statistical Association*, Vol. 22, 1927, pp. 283–314, quotation on p. 287), that celestial mechanics would for the same reason have developed as a statistical science, had the "solar" system to which the earth belongs contained several bodies of mass comparable to that of the sun. The full quotation is given and commented on by H. T. Davis, *The Analysis of Economic Time Series* (Bloomington, Indiana, 1941), see pp. 2–4.

[9] How long this "recent past" is to be taken depends on the degree of damping of the system, which in turn depends on the parameters or curves representing the several structural equations.

clearly in their minds.[10] They accordingly recognize (p. 392) that the analysis of variance tests applied by them to durations, amplitudes, time lags, are not rigorous, since such measures need not be independent in successive cycles. More important yet is the fact that those tests are not particularly powerful in discerning structural change under the welter of random variation. For on the one hand, these tests fail to take into account the influence of measurable exogenous variables, and to take advantage of the known time series of such variables — a possible advantage particularly important in periods of war or of new departures in economic policy. On the other hand, the basic cyclical measures they analyze are cumulative effects of random shocks, of which observations are limited to the number of cycles covered by the study. The additional information about the individual structural equations and the disturbances therein, contained in the more numerous original data, is thus lost.

In their defense of the application of analysis of variance, the authors mention that the original items of economic time series are even less independent serially than cycle durations or amplitudes. Probably they do not mean to imply a statement (which has often been fallaciously advanced) that the high serial correlation of economic time series precludes the use of such data (as distinct from "cyclical" measures derived therefrom) in any statistical tests or estimation procedures. Statistical theory is sufficiently flexible to face such situations. In the first place, it may be found that serial correlation in economic variables measured annually, say, is due only to their being determined by difference equations, with no serial correlation present in the disturbances (shocks) operating in individual equations — a situation which may be confirmed by tests based on the "residuals" obtained from fitting such equations. But even a situation of serially correlated disturbances — which is likely to prevail in any case in quarterly or monthly figures — is in principle equally amenable to statistical treatment. The mathematical and

computational difficulties inherent in such a situation pose technical problems which need to be overcome, to enable us to extract all information about the structure of our economy from statistical records.

The amplitudes, durations, and measures of conformity used by Burns and Mitchell are poor measures from this point of view. They waste an unknown but probably considerable amount of information contained in the original data. Their averages are unstable[11] because of the occurrence of borderline cases under the rules for recognizing cycles, because turning points are located without allowance for secular trend, and because of great variability between cycles.[12]

However, the extraction of more information from the data requires that, in addition to the hypotheses subject to test, certain basic economic hypotheses are formulated as distributional assumptions, which often are not themselves subject to statistical testing from the same data. Of course, the validity of information so obtained is logically conditional upon the validity of the statistically unverifiable aspects of these basic hypotheses. The greater wealth, definiteness, rigor, and relevance to specific questions of such conditional information, as compared with any information extractable without hypotheses of the kind indicated, provides the *third argument* against the purely empirical approach.

Let me wind up the argument with a statement combining exhortation and prophecy. In the monographs dealing with specific markets, in preparation or planned by the National Bureau of Economic Research, situations will frequently be encountered where the applicability of the behavior schedules of economic theory is more directly obvious, less beset with doubts on the score of unhomogeneity of commodities or individuals, and the connected difficulties of aggregation. Also, certain rela-

[10] This can be seen from the discussion of the causal interpretation of averages, particularly on page 506, where there is a groping for distinctions which only mathematical formulation can clarify.

[11] See the discussion of conformity indexes on pages 184–85.

[12] In two cases, on page 425 and page 433, the exclusion of the "exceptional" reference cycle 1927–33 from an average makes a sufficient difference to the test comparison being made to be mentioned (recommended?) in the test. Addition to the averages of the 1933–38 cycle (which is not included in the tests discussed above) might well have a similarly large effect.

MEASUREMENT WITHOUT THEORY

tionships between aggregates seem more strongly established *a priori* than others. The aggregate consumption function, a subject which the National Bureau is now investigating, so far stands on firmer ground than the investment schedule: consumption decisions are more of one kind than investment decisions. Among the latter decisions, inventory policies seem to be subject to a smaller number of considerations, more readily rationalized, than investment in productive equipment. Thus, the use of behavior schedules will inevitably force itself on the mind of an investigator dealing with some of the more specific partial subjects of dynamic economics. Such a development is both predictable and highly desirable. The combination of theoretical and statistical analysis into an explanation of cyclical fluctuations and an exploration of the means to influence them must necessarily proceed from detailed studies of individual relationships. Conversely, the statistical methods used in those detailed studies should recognize and take into account the fact that the specific relationship studied is part of a complete network of interrelations connecting the variables involved in many ways.

This already lengthy review could well end here. However, I cannot forego the opportunity to append a few brief comments on various specific points of method raised in the volume.

INDEX NUMBERS, TIME UNITS, SMOOTHING, SINE CURVES VERSUS TRIANGULAR PATTERNS

The authors' preference for the study of many individual series rather than index numbers doubtless derives from their basic decision to place the large-scale study of facts before theoretical concepts and hypotheses regarding the formation of economic variables. But their arguments provide a challenge to those who believe that the most relevant phenomena of economic fluctuation can fruitfully, or even better, be analyzed through aggregates or index numbers. To withstand critical examination, this belief needs to be argued more cogently than is usually done. It will be necessary to specify the purposes index numbers are required to serve, and to show theoretically

and statistically to what extent these purposes are actually served efficiently and without undue loss of relevant information.

The authors' views that quarterly or monthly data contain much information which is lost by reduction to annual averages deserves strong sympathy. It is true that several of the particular measures on which the National Bureau concentrates are especially vulnerable to such reduction, as the authors amply demonstrate. But also if the purpose is one of estimating the parameters of structural equations, the presence and dynamic importance of relatively small time lags in many equations, as well as the shortness of available time series, makes the use of at least quarterly figures an important objective of the analysis of economic fluctuations.

The authors' rejection of the use of smoothing formulae is similarly appropriate. One could add to their arguments that, if explicit mathematical formulation of the distribution of the observations is introduced to guide the choice of estimation or test procedures, smoothing is found both to be wasteful of information and to complicate mathematical treatment, because it mixes up the effects of successive disturbances as well as blurs the time-shape of exogenous variables. In fact, one of the reasons why business cycle analysis is a difficult undertaking is that the economic system itself is such an effective smoothing agent of the random shocks to which it is exposed. The analytical problem is one of de-smoothing rather than smoothing.

Exception must be taken to a statement appearing on page 369:

> When averages are struck for all cycles covered by a series, the erratic factors in the measures for single cycles have an additional opportunity to cancel out.

This is true generally, but is not applicable to the average standings at troughs (I, IX) and peaks (V). A selection effect is operative through the location of troughs and peaks at local minima and maxima of the curve, giving downward and upward biases to average trough and peak standings respectively, which will be especially pronounced if erratic disturbances persist for at least three months. This point is important because of the authors' statement

(p. 157) that a "triangular" cyclical pattern often gives a better approximation to reality than the sine-curve pattern (whose dominance in the literature the authors attribute particularly to the prevalent habit of smoothing time series before analysis (p. 343). An important theoretical question is involved: the rounded curve seems connected with the idea of a natural equilibrium level or trend line around which fluctuations take place; in particular, pure sine curves suggest linearity of the equations describing the economy, whereas less symmetric but still rounded curves are compatible with non-linear systems where no effective limits are placed on the range of the variables involved. However, the broken straight line pattern suggests one-sided movement as the natural condition of the economic system, reversed by capacity limits or other physical or incidental factors. Now the trough and peak standings are the crucial observations in making a choice between these two hypotheses. The selection effect mentioned produces a bias toward the triangular hypothesis, disqualifying average cyclical patterns as a means of testing the issue mentioned.

The authors are aware of the possibility of such bias,[13] but seem to feel that it will be unimportant except in series with pronounced erratic movements.[14] However, their graphs suggest a widespread occurrence of this bias. While all of the ten specific-cycle patterns in Chart 16 on page 56 show sharply defined kinks at the turning points, definite cusps are

[13] See page 334, footnote 30; page 346; and the third graph in the first column of Chart 47 on page 345.

[14] The authors refer on page 347 to an opposite bias due to the mild smoothing involved in the use of three-month averages for trough and peak standings. However, this bias is likely to be smaller than the bias due to selection, owing to the smallness of the three-month period compared with the average duration of cycles.

developed most clearly in the series most subject to erratic fluctuations (shares traded, total exports, sugar meltings). This does not mean that the issue between rounded curves and triangular patterns is to be decided in favor of the former. Other evidence, less marred by methodological doubts, is adduced to show that at least a substantial proportion of cycles have kinked peaks and troughs: slightly over two-thirds of the turning points in five American series are not shifted in time if determined after trend elimination instead of before (p. 277).

CONCLUSION

To sum up: the book is unbendingly empiricist in outlook. Granted this basic attitude, it shows great perseverance and circumspection on the part of the authors in handling a vast amount of statistical data. In the latter part of the book, hypotheses of theoretical and practical relevance, referring to the characteristics of cyclical movements of the economy as a whole, are tested. But the decision not to use theories of man's economic behavior, even hypothetically, limits the value to economic science and to the maker of policies, of the results obtained or obtainable by the methods developed. This decision greatly restricts the benefit that might be secured from the use of modern methods of statistical inference. The pedestrian character of the statistical devices employed is directly traceable to the authors' reluctance to formulate explicit assumptions, however general, concerning the probability distribution of the variables, i.e., assumptions expressing and specifying how random disturbances operate on the economy through the economic relationships between the variables.

[3]

The Review *of* Economics *and* Statistics

VOLUME XXXI   MAY, 1949   NUMBER 2

METHODOLOGICAL ISSUES IN QUANTITATIVE ECONOMICS *

KOOPMANS ON THE CHOICE OF VARIABLES TO BE STUDIED AND OF METHODS OF MEASUREMENT

Rutledge Vining

THE critical review by T. C. Koopmans of the recent review by T. C. Koopmans of the recent study by Burns and Mitchell [1] would apparently cast doubt on the efficiency of almost any method of analysis that is not essentially identical with the methods adopted and developed by Koopmans and his associates. While these methods are intriguing and the results of their application will be awaited with keen interest, they are as yet untested. Acceptance of them as the only, or the best, method for reaching economic truth must hinge on results, not on any advance statement, no matter how persuasive, of their potential merits. Until such evidence is available, they must be considered an exceedingly narrow class of methods, and an insistent appeal to use them, and them alone, as an invitation to put a strait jacket on economic research. I would therefore like to discuss some of the questions raised by Koopmans. Sometimes, it seems, a paper such as this one of Koopmans may be more referred to than read. It should be recorded somewhere that some of the points emphasized by Koopmans are more controversial than they appear as stated. I hope it will be clear from what follows that I am not attempting in this paper a critique of the particular methods adopted by Koopmans. It would be presumptuous of me to undertake such a task. Moreover, it follows from my general position that the only satisfactory test of the usefulness of these methods is their fruits, and these have not yet been attained, or if attained, have not yet been made generally available.

1. Koopmans classifies the stages of development of a theory into the "Kepler stage" and the "Newton stage" [2] — the analogy being the development of celestial mechanics from the systematic accumulation of measurements through the discovery of simple empirical laws to the formulation of Newton's law of gravitation. The book by Burns and Mitchell is regarded as a contribution to the Kepler stage. "Nevertheless," says Koopmans,

> this reviewer believes that in research in economic dynamics the Kepler stage and Newton stage of inquiry need to be more intimately combined and to be pursued simultaneously. Fuller utilization of the concepts and hypotheses of economic theory *as a part of the processes of observation and measurement* promises to be a shorter road, perhaps even the only possible road, to the understanding of cyclical fluctuations. . . .
>
> My *first argument*, then, is that even for the purpose of systematic and large scale observation of such a many-sided phenomenon, theoretical preconceptions about its nature cannot be dispensed with, and the authors do so only to the detriment of the analysis. . . .
>
> There is no systematic discussion [for example] of the reasons for selecting these particular variables as most worthy of study [in the search for possible changes in cyclical behavior over time]. . . . The choices made may have been the best possible ones. But "good" choices mean relevant choices. What is

* This entire paper, including the reply and the rejoinder, is to be included in Cowles Commission Papers, New Series, No. 29.

[1] T. C. Koopmans, "Measurement Without Theory," this REVIEW, XXIX (1947), pp. 161–72. This is a review article of the book by A. F. Burns and W. C. Mitchell, *Measuring Business Cycles* (National Bureau of Economic Research, New York, 1946).

[2] Tycho and Kepler are becoming fairly regular attenders of economic discussions nowadays.

relevant can only be determined with the help of some notions as to the generation of economic fluctuations, and as to their impact on society. . . . The choices as to what variables to study cannot be settled by a brief reference to "theoretical studies of business cycles." These issues call for a systematic argument to show that the best use has been made of available data in relation to the most important aspects of the phenomena studied.

His second argument is that,

The prediction, within the narrowest attainable limits of error, of the effects of stated hypothetical measures of economic policy . . . is actually the most important objective of the analysis of economic fluctuations . . . [and] without resort to theory, in the sense indicated, conclusions relevant to the guidance of economic policies cannot be drawn.

The third argument is explicitly a matter of statistical estimation.

Now any rigorous testing of hypotheses according to modern methods of statistical inference requires a specification of the form of the joint probability distribution of the variables. . . . [The measures used by Burns and Mitchell are poor measures in that] they waste an unknown but probably considerable amount of information contained in the original data. . . . The extraction of more information from the data requires that, in addition to the hypotheses subject to test, certain basic economic hypotheses are formulated as distributional assumptions, which often are not themselves subject to statistical testing from the same data. . . . The greater wealth, definiteness, rigor, and relevance to specific questions of such conditional information, as compared with any information extractable without hypotheses of the kind indicated, provides the *third argument* against the purely empirical approach.

The elaboration of these arguments introduces a somewhat new element into the discussion of the old controversy regarding the relation between theory and quantitative research. Briefly, Koopmans argues that without a theoretical framework having the *form* that he specifies (he doesn't really specify the content), statistical data cannot be used efficiently — this term being used in the sense given it by modern theoretical statistics. The discussion seems somewhat strained to me, and without defending the particular methodological procedures of the National Bureau or attacking the procedures of the Cowles Commission, I believe that one might raise the possibility that Koopmans' argument contains a misleading emphasis if not an error.

One need not doubt the importance of the statistical research going forward at the Cowles Commission in order to hold that a work that does not make use of the methods being developed there is not by that condition alone subject to criticism. It isn't that the work of the National Bureau on trade fluctuations is barren of results that are capable of development, for Koopmans refers to certain phenomena that these less elegant methods turned up as materials for further hypotheses. And Koopmans lays no claim that by his methods he has already reached these same results more "efficiently." Instead, he gives a preview of the potentialities of his new methods and proceeds to argue that the results that may be expected of his methods will be *better* results. But, surely, in arguing so, Koopmans has left the realm in which modern theories of tests of hypotheses provide criteria that are unambiguously applicable. The work of Burns and Mitchell that is being criticized purports to be a work of discovery and hypothesis-seeking, and it is not clear at all what meaning should be given to "efficiency" in this context. Statistical efficiency is an attribute of an estimation and testing procedure rather than of a procedure of "search," and problems of statistical efficiency may be trivial, or almost so, in the prospecting and probing phase of the development of the understanding of a phenomenon. Discovery has never been a field of activity in which elegance of conception and equipment is of prime consideration; and foreign to the nature of exploration is the confinement involved in the requirements that the procedure followed shall be characterized by theoretical preconceptions having certain prescribed forms and shall yield findings that are directly subject to the rather restricted tests provided by the ideas included in the Neyman-Pearson theory of estimation.

Koopmans, in arguing that the results yielded by the methods of the National Bureau are inferior to those that we may expect from his methods, takes a definite stand on the issue of the nature of the variation to be accounted for in the study of trade fluctuations. This step, I think, has always been the core of the controversy over what is generally referred to as the problem of the role of theory in quantita-

METHODOLOGICAL ISSUES IN QUANTITATIVE ECONOMICS

tive research. It would seem that we need not bother over whether or not a really discerning observer of phenomena approaches his materials with a theoretical or hypothetical framework in mind. We may take for granted that he does. The controversy might turn not so much upon assertions of the existence or absence of a hypothetical framework as upon the nature of the entity the behavior of which is to be accounted for. Koopmans presumably does not like the unit of analysis used in the Burns and Mitchell study — the "business cycle" of a given category of economic activity. I too feel that this unit of analysis is limited and, at least, should be regarded as strictly tentative — as it undoubtedly is regarded by these users; but I think that Koopmans' alternative unit — the individual economizing agent — is possibly even more fundamentally limited in the study of many aspects of aggregate trade fluctuations. But what we think will not settle these issues. We must try things to see.

A developing understanding of the population phenomenon of trade variation in its many aspects will of course draw upon many types of study. It seems unnecessary for us to accept the not infrequent assumption that a theoretical system based upon individual motivation and developed primarily for the discussion of welfare problems must also be *the* theoretical system to which we must turn in accounting for systems of variation representing the behavior of population phenomena. I believe that in our discussions of trade fluctuations, national and international, we deal with the behavior of an entity that is not a simple aggregate of the economizing units of traditional theoretical economics. I think that we need not take for granted that the behavior and functioning of this entity can be exhaustively explained in terms of the motivated behavior of individuals who are particles within the whole. It is conceivable — and it would hardly be doubted in other fields of study — that the aggregate has an existence apart from its constituent particles and behavior characteristics of its own not deducible from the behavior characteristics of the particles. We should work toward an explicit delineation of the entity itself — its structure and functioning — and the role that hypothesis and formal theory play in the earlier

stages of this growth of understanding is subtle and irregular.

I, therefore — primarily in defense of empiricism as a fundamental part of scientific procedure — shall offer three points counter to these arguments of Koopmans: First, his conception of the character or extent of the variation to be accounted for appears to be unduly narrow, and a broadening of this conception raises the question often posed as to whether economics, as a science of variation rather than as an argument in political philosophy, has approached any nearer than has biology to a state where a comprehensive mathematizing of knowledge of variation is feasible. This point does not question the crucial importance of mathematics in the investigation of special or subsidiary hypotheses. But a prime source of these ideas to be analyzed in the abstract is the explorative work such as this of Burns and Mitchell, who obviously do not proceed without the guidance of tentative hypotheses. Second, the position taken that present research is to be evaluated from the point of view of social action is entirely questionable. And, third, modern theories of statistical estimation and of tests of hypotheses with their emphasis upon distributional hypotheses, upon the extraction of maximum information, upon the power of a test, and the like, are almost beside the point in attempts to derive hypotheses, the exploratory stage that characterizes a great part of the work in all developing fields of knowledge.

2. With respect to the first point, Koopmans seems convinced that without our Kepler we have witnessed the emergence of what will pass as a first approximation to or a supporting framework for a Newtonian phenomenon. Some of his discussion suggests that we have already at hand a theoretical model that is a sort of social counterpart of Newtonian mechanics. But this is not asserted; rather, he argues that a way must be found (or has been found) to perform the Keplerian and Newtonian tasks together. Koopmans doesn't give his hypotheses specific economic content. He discusses the mathematical form that the model should (or must) take; and suggests the kind of content it should have in very general

terms, such as "the behavior of groups of economic agents," "underlying human responses," "knowledge of man's behavior and its motives." But apparently all he has to insist upon at present is the mathematical form, and from his discussion it appears not unfair to regard the formal economic theory underlying his approach as being in the main available from works not later than those of Walras. Once workers began to apply correlation methods to economic quantities and to rationalize or "identify" the resulting regression equations as demand or supply schedules, it was almost inevitable that before long someone would be computing as many such equations as the number of variables designated to be "explained." This of course was the general line followed in the work of Tinbergen published by the League of Nations some nine years ago. In connection with a particular detail, Koopmans remarks that:

> The mathematical and computational difficulties inherent in such a situation pose technical problems which need to be overcome to enable us to extract all information about the structure of our economy from statistical records.

In a sense, these are the only problems that have been attacked by this entire line of development — the problem of statistical estimation that would be presented by the empirical counterpart of the Walrasian conception. Add to Walras the simple notion of lagged effects (if it is not already there) and certain devices of the nature of the difference equation, and the problem is wholly statistical as contrasted with economic.

Now a formal theoretical model based upon postulated and fixed individual motives and transformation functions might be just the conception that we need for accounting for and analyzing the uniformities discoverable among human individual and population phenomena. But such has not been demonstrated and until evidence of the adequacy of this model is made available, it is an unnecessary restriction upon economic research to insist that the method used shall be essentially that adopted and developed by Koopmans and his associates. As indicated above, some of us may feel that the unit of analysis and the entity the behavior of

which it is of interest to study is not the individual economizer in his conscious, problem-solving state of mind.[3] I believe that much of

[3] With reference to this inclination on the part of some to regard a quantitative work that is not built upon the neo-classical theoretical model as being essentially without a theoretical foundation at all, there is a point of moderate interest to the modern history of economic doctrines. Not all of the neo-classical writers look upon this model as a particularly useful framework for quantitative studies. While there is all manner of subclassifications that could be contrived, the writings of F. H. Knight would be classed in general among those of the deductive schools of economics: the Marshallians, the Walrasians, the Austrians and Wicksellians. A school of statistical economics has sprung from this tradition, and "econometricians" have for some time been engaged in the statistical estimation of systems of demand, supply, and other relations formulated in Marshallian and Walrasian economics. This work is conceived of as being of the nature of a refinement, extension and quantitative expression of neo-classical economics, and it is in good color within the tradition; for it appears to have been the rule rather than the exception for economists of the classical school to look upon the ability quantitatively to predict responses of given economic variables resulting from known changes in other given factors as the ultimate objective of the development of their science. Rough and ready (and more or less casual) calculations demonstrating an alleged predictive value of certain theoretical formulations are found in almost all treatises on economic theory; and econometricians who profess an adherence to the classical tradition have made a point of giving references to passages in the works of the older writers such as Marshall, Pareto, Jevons, and the like in which this goal is expressed explicitly.

Knight, however, stands out against this conception of the role and prospective development of traditional theoretical economics. This latter is not even the beginning of the development of a social analogue for Newtonian mechanics, the knowledge represented being fundamentally different from the knowledge of relations between inert entities. The characteristically social and human problems are problems of freely establishing bases of agreement on the conditions of social organization, and the use of economic theory is instrumental in the discussion of the conditions under which an economic problem is to be solved. It purports to describe the results of economistic behavior under conditions that are fixed by postulate. As a basis for the discovery of predictive laws, as Newtonian mechanics, for example, is a basis for the derivation of differential equations describing the expected behavior of certain physical phenomena, it is fundamentally limited in that economistic behavior is "active" and developmental, in a sense that he discusses in detail, and not of the nature of phenomena that are subject to cause-and-effect explanation. The component of behavior that is positive is not motivated, and a model based upon conscious motivation would not be expected to be particularly relevant in the scientific search for "explanations" of uniformities and statistical regularities. The social analogue for Newtonian mechanics has yet to be developed, and perhaps it is biology that has the more cogent analogues anyway.

Institutionalism, following from or through the writings of Veblen, emphasizes this component of behavior that is positive and based upon non-deliberative, habitual behavior forms. Knight, I think, is critical of institutionalism, as a school of thought and as a social science to take the place

METHODOLOGICAL ISSUES IN QUANTITATIVE ECONOMICS   81

the statistical regularities that are to be observed in population phenomena and that are relevant for the discussion of economic problems involves the behavior of social organisms that are distinctly more than simple algebraic aggregates of consciously economizing individuals. I think that in a positive sense the aggregate has an existence over and above the existence of Koopmans' individual units and behavior characteristics that may not be deducible from the behavior of these component parts. This notion is of the nature of a postulate or hypothesis to be investigated, and I have sug-

of traditional economics, primarily because of the extremity of its positivism. Institutionalism does not touch upon what Knight regards as the distinctively "social" problems raised in the "active" seeking on the part of individuals for grounds of agreement and consensus. It has had a bias toward the development of instrumental knowledge for control purposes, the objectives being more or less taken for granted. Agreement on objectives, however, presents the real social problems for Knight, and traditional economics has developed to facilitate and improve the quality of social discussion. Knight, a traditional and deductive economist, is critical of institutionalism for its incomplete conception of the nature of a "social" problem, but at the same time he is as critical as the institutionalists are of the "scientism" and methods of the econometricians who base their work on the traditional economistic model. It would be of some interest to outline the basis for Knight's point of view and to note where Veblen's criticism of traditional economic theory as a framework of reference for the development of a positive social science has a good bit in common with this position. Both men classify human behavior and social phenomena into "active," deliberative, problem-solving *procedure* on the one hand and objective, passive, non-deliberative *process* on the other. Knight's emphasis is upon the philosophical or ethical problems involved in the first component in its impact upon matters of social organization that are subject to conscious deliberation. Veblen's emphasis is upon the instrumental knowledge of non-deliberative, unconscious process. To the extent that my reading and understanding has progressed, Veblen seems to me not strong on positive and constructive points of methodology in the study of this material, and Knight regards the study of this phenomena as outside his field of interest. But the writings of each would appear to imply that the search, in so far as it purports to be scientific, should be for rules of order and uniformities in space and time that are either absolutely invariant with respect to individual thought processes or that are subject to deliberate policy change if discovered and made known to society as a group. For Veblen's argument see, for example, *The Place of Science in Modern Civilization and Other Essays*, "Economics and Evolution," pp. 73 ff., and, "The Limitations of Marginal Utility," pp. 234 ff. (New York, 1919). For Knight's position see in particular, "Science, Philosophy, and Social Procedure," *Ethics*, Vol. 52 (1942), pp. 253–74; and "Fact and Value in Social Science," *Science and Man* (edited by Ruth Anshen, New York, 1942). Both essays are reprinted in *Freedom and Reform* (New York), 1947.

gested at another place [4] a fuller picture of a conception that I propose to investigate. I seek to view a great nation such as ours as an interlacing of definite population structures. An interspersing of population "clusters" exists with lines of union connecting these clusters. Along these lines flows of commerce may be observed in their concrete forms. Measures of the magnitudes and rates of change of these flows between and within these "clusters" suggest random and unruly variation. But patterns of behavior are suggested when these measures are observed as statistical distributions. This conception has reference to a population system, but the behavior described may nevertheless be regarded as "economic" if by that term we class together phenomena relevant in the discussion of socio-economic problems. The national series which we study in our business cycle inquiries may plausibly be interpreted as averages of measurements of such "organic" flows having a spatial dimension; and from this point of view the studies of Burns and Mitchell represent an accumulation of knowledge that may later play a part in a more complete account of a vast and immensely complex system of variation. An assertion that the development of Koopmans' methods is the best and simplest means by which we may account for the events *in space and time* that take place within the spatial boundary of such a system of population structures — and this is what an "understanding of cyclical fluctuations" might be broadened out to mean — seems to me a quite extraordinary statement in the present state of our knowledge. But if Koopmans should give a demonstration of the generality of his methods, then we would move awed and gladly on — or at least we *should* move gladly [5] — to unexplained fields of problems.

A more complete account of the philosophy or theory of the method of Koopmans' group

[4] "Measuring State and Regional Business Cycles," *Journal of Political Economy*, August, 1947, p. 350, and, "The Region as a Concept in Business Cycle Analysis," *Econometrica*, July, 1946, pp. 201–218.

[5] I recall a very telling passage in J. S. Mill's *Autobiography* giving an account of his introspection into how gladly he would have moved on if all the critical problems in which he had involved himself were suddenly solved. An acute depression of guilt, we are told, resulted from this introspective inquiry.

is to be found in Trygve Haavelmo's *The Probability Approach in Econometrics.*[6] This book appears to be an important piece of work that should somehow be presented in a form that would have more currency among economists than it now has. Haavelmo gives a rough fourfold classification of the main problems encountered in quantitative research: first, the construction of tentative theoretical models; second, the testing of theories; third, the problem of estimation; and fourth, the problem of prediction. It may be noticed that the first problem (possibly the second, depending upon one's interpretation) is the only one of the four that is not a problem of strictly modern statistical theory. He goes on to say that the "explanation" of phenomena "consists of digging down to more fundamental relations than those that appear before us when we 'stand and look.' " The more fundamental relations are those that have a great degree of invariance or autonomy with respect to the ordinary or reasonably expected changes in economic structure, and a theory is a construction of a system of autonomous relations. He illustrates the notion of an autonomous relation by considering the possibility of establishing a functional relationship between the distance of the accelerator from the floor of the automobile and the corresponding maximum speed of the car on a dry, flat road. Such a study might provide information sufficient to operate the car at a prescribed speed, but it would not tell us anything at all about the inner mechanism of an automobile. The relation depends on many other relations, some of which are transitory.

> On the other hand, the general laws of thermodynamics, the dynamics of friction, etc., etc., are highly autonomous relations with respect to the automobile mechanism, because these relations describe the functioning of some parts of the mechanism irrespective of what happens in some other parts.
>
> Let us turn from this analogy to the mechanism of economic life. Economic theory builds on the assumption that individuals' decisions to produce and to con-

sume can be described by certain fundamental behavioristic relations, and that, besides, there are certain technical and institutional restrictions upon the freedom of choice (such as technical production functions, legal restrictions, etc.).[7]

In statements of this sort there is no doubt but that these men are considering the vast and rich field of economic variation, where systematic classification and description has hardly begun, but where flows and movements of things may be observed — flows of objects within and between economic or social organisms. The functioning of the great supraorganisms which we see as population agglomerations, their growth and decline, their interdependencies, give rise to quantities having both a spatial and a temporal dimension. Are we ready to accept the particular list of economic relations given in the above quotation as *the* fundamental autonomous relations, sufficient for our purposes and not dependent on other relations transitory in character? Haavelmo mentions our faith in the existence of certain elements of invariance in relations between real phenomena, which are discoverable provided that we hit upon the right arrangement of our materials and ideas. But are we certain that those relations represent the right arrangement of ideas, and who has inquired into the degree of invariance exhibited by these relations?[8] Is it not something of a mighty jump to imply that the postulated preference function of an individual is in some sense analogous to the general laws of thermodynamics, the dynamics of friction, etc., etc.? Is the Walrasian conception not in fact a pretty skinny fellow of untested capacity upon which to load the burden of a general theory accounting for the events in space and time which take place within the spatial boundary of an economic system? When we think of the enormous body of factual knowledge digested and systematized in the other fields of variation and the meagerness of our own results from efforts to

---

[6] *Econometrica*, Vol. 12, Supplement, July, 1944. In connection with this matter of probability and phenomena of economic variation, this book seems to highlight a point of interest. Classical theoretical economics has drawn heavily for concepts upon classical mechanics, but the word "statistical" in *statistical economics* carries an entirely different connotation from the same word in *statistical mechanics*.

[7] *Ibid.*, p. 28.

[8] Where Haavelmo speaks of the invariance or autonomy of these behavioristic relations and technological restrictions, Veblen ends up a long discussion of these same relations with, "The wants and desires, the end and aim, the ways and means, the amplitude and drift of the individual's conduct are functions of an institutional variable that is of a highly complex and wholly unstable character." *Op. cit.*, pp. 242–43.

METHODOLOGICAL ISSUES IN QUANTITATIVE ECONOMICS   83

systematize, are we quite ready to leave Haavelmo's first problem and launch into the last three problems in estimation theory? When generations later and after vastly more systematic observation and taxonomic work has been done, is it a foregone conclusion that the hypotheses of Koopmans will be regarded as overwhelmingly more comprehensive in what they will be able to explain than those that must inhabit the minds of such workers as Burns and Mitchell as they choose their quantities and arrange their materials? Burns and Mitchell presumably are still on Problem 1. Koopmans has vaulted over, some would say hastily if the research is in the field of economics, to Problems 3 and 4. This is not to deny the very great interest that economic research has in the results of Koopmans' group on Problems 3 and 4. But it is to express the belief that, so long as a field of knowledge continues to develop, workers will be puttering around, and not in vain, within the unexplored expanses of Problem 1 — the searching for regularities and interrelations of regularities and the feeling around for interesting theoretical models. Not all of this work will find formal mathematics of immediate use, and much of it will be of such an explorative character as to render almost meaningless the notion of a planned maximization of information from given data.

3. I shall not argue the second point. The work of the National Bureau will bear comparison with the work of other research agencies from the point of view of social usefulness. But aside from this, easy illustrations may be cited of the unpredictability of the use of any given piece of knowledge, and it would appear unnecessary for us to put much stock in Koopmans' criterion of social usefulness in judging economic research. This insistence that research be pointed up to some topical problem of policy is put somewhat more baldly in the field of economics than seems to be the case with other fields of knowledge. J. B. S. Haldane makes certain comments regarding the conservatism with which scientific investigators should approach problems of public policy. Genetics has developed into a beautiful science, but this leading contributor to the development states: "I hold that a premature application of our rather scanty knowledge will yield little result, and will merely serve to discredit the branch of science in which I am working."[9] If knowledge in this field is scant, we have next to no knowledge at all in the field of economic variation. But we do not lack exponents of the application of knowledge in economics. Haldane, in denying that genetics as a science has been advanced far enough to provide knowledge upon which social policy might be based, offered the suggestion that while the relation between eugenics and genetics could only unfairly be regarded as similar to the relation between astrology and astronomy, the analogy provided in the history of the latter is not without point. Now, it would be clearly unjust and inappropriate to speak of the relation between economics as currently used in discussions of positive policy and economics as a study of a field of variation as being similar to the relation between astrology and astronomy. But fortune telling provided the principal support of many of the prominent early astronomers, and is fortune telling too hard an expression for much of what we do?

4. Regarding the third point, we may note that in those fields of investigation where modern statistics has found its greatest development there is much fundamental work done without assistance from theories of estimation and of tests of hypotheses of the Neyman-Pearson type. There are important schools of biology where statistics is not taught, and there are significant contributors to biological knowledge who make scarcely any use at all of modern theoretical statistics. To biology, microscopy is important no less than statistics. One of the more distinguished members of the University of Virginia faculty has spent the greater part of a fruitful scientific career studying the transparent tail of a tadpole — a ridiculous occupation to the lofty workers in our own field who occupy themselves with nothing less than the pathology of civilizations. But this person has succeeded in developing microscopic and photographic techniques by which the growth and functioning

[9] *Heredity and Politics* (London), 1938, pp. 8 and 175.

of living cells and organisms may be watched.[10] As I look at the motion pictures that he has succeeded in recording, the flows of identifiable objects, the motion of cells in action and cells in growth, the random, palpitating variation that somehow assumes form in the aggregate — all of this rich array of motion reminds me of what I think I can see reflected in the motion of economic quantities. Professor Speidel's contributions have been in the uncovering of knowledge not discernible by the unaided eye; that is, he has been engaged in Haavelmo's digging down process, finding more fundamental relations than those that appear when we merely "stand and look." But his tools include neither the Neyman-Pearson theory of estimation nor any mathematical formulation; and while modern principles of experimental design could perhaps be brought to bear in this work, such has not been done in its present stage. Mr. Speidel is not just a photographer. He is a highly regarded biologist, and as he arranges his materials for experiment and observation he obviously has in mind hypotheses or theories that are to be inquired into. No less do such workers as Burns and Mitchell have hypotheses in mind, and workers in neither field at this classificatory and descriptive level need be burdened down with the emphasis on an advanced and fascinating theory of estimation. There are numerous problems where modern statistics comes into full use — where quantities have been defined, where units of study or "organisms" have been tentatively delineated and their functioning described, where hypotheses regarding numerical aspects of relations have been formulated.[11] Koopmans presumably regards his work as in this stage. But it is not the stage of all economic research.

The excessive emphasis of modern statistics upon certain types of problems was stressed in a part of the discussion of a paper read by M.

G. Kendall a few years back.[12] Kendall had remarked that "the estimation of properties of a population from a sample is the most important practical problem in statistics and is long likely to continue so." Mr. Yule denied this proposition:

It never was, in my opinion, the most important practical problem in statistics, and so cannot continue to be that which it never was. The initial problem of the statistician is simply the description of the data presented; to tell us what the data themselves show. To this initial problem the function of sampling theory is in general entirely secondary or ancillary; to inform the investigator as to the limits within which his descriptive measures can be trusted, so far as fluctuations of simple sampling alone are concerned. The development of theory during my own lifetime followed at first the natural course suggested by this fact. Primarily it was new methods that were developed, and investigations of the "probable errors" involved only followed in their train. More recently methods, with few exceptions (time-series in economics, factor-methods in psychology), have been almost neglected, while there has been a completely lopsided development — almost a malignant growth — of sampling theory. I hope there may be a swing back towards the study of method proper, and as methods only develop in connection with practical problems, that means a swing back to more practical work and less pure theory. . . .

There are quite large fields of statistics into the discussion of which sampling theory hardly enters at all. . . . Even in the field of experimental work, if the investigator possesses caution, common sense and patience, those qualities are quite likely to keep him more free from error in his conclusions than the man of little caution and common sense who guides himself by a mechanical application of sampling rules. He will be more likely to remember that there are sources of error more important than fluctuations of sampling. . . . No: I cannot assign the place of highest importance to sampling theory — a high place perhaps, but not the highest.[13]

Mr. E. S. Pearson, whose name adorns one of the more important pieces of modern statistical apparatus, suggested that the following questions be put to mathematical statisticians:

How far do we practice what we preach in journal contributions, classroom or meeting-hall? Exactly how important a part do numerical probability measures play in the practical decisions following from our analysis of statistical data? Is our confidence in probability theory related to the simplicity of the

---

[10] For a description of this work see Carl C. Speidel, "Living Cells in Action," *American Scientist*, April 1948, pp. 237–57.

[11] For example, Frank L. Kidner's problem in his *California Business Cycles* is to some considerable extent a problem of estimation. See, e.g., a review article on this book, "Measuring State and Regional Business Cycles," *Journal of Political Economy*, August 1947.

[12] M. G. Kendall, "The Future of Statistics," *Journal of the Royal Statistical Society*, New Series, Vol. cv, Part II, pp. 69–72.

[13] *Ibid.*, pp. 83, *et seq.*

technique used? How often are we completely satisfied that the assumptions of randomness and so on
have been met? Frankly, for my part I do not know
the answers, and I see no way of obtaining them
except by attempting to keep a brief case-history of
every problem with which I am concerned in which
a numerical probability measure is calculated to
guide a practical decision.[14]

Kendall then went on to say that there was less
difference between Mr. Yule and himself than
might appear.

I would agree with Mr. Yule that, for practical purposes, a great deal of the modern developments of the
theory of sampling has taken place at the expense of
other and more important practical work. Perhaps
we have let mathematics run away with us a little.
It is interesting to see from Professor Pearson's remarks that he may feel something of the same kind
when he suggests that we should keep running records of the cases in which we make inferences from
data and note how often we really rely solely upon
the theory of probability and not intuitive judgments.[14]

Thus, I am not alone in feeling that an excessive emphasis is placed by modern statistics
upon the sampling problem. To be sure, Koopmans is an important contributor to new statistical method in the sense used by Yule — the
method of measuring simultaneous relations.
Yet, it appears to me that he emphasizes somewhat heavily the estimation aspects of his
problem. For example, his insistence upon a
"distributional hypothesis" is based upon estimation considerations rather than upon a primary interest in the distribution itself. Sampling and estimation theory is important to a
student of economic variation, but in a sense
it is secondary. A worker in this explorative
field might work in close contact with the statistical specialist in seeking a solution of his
sampling and estimation problems. But for the
basic work with his materials statistical theory
in its broader meaning is fundamental. At the
observational level it plays a role in economic
research similar to that played by microscopy
in biology. It must aid us in seeing our materials, and methods of arranging our data must be
discovered by which there will be revealed
any orderliness that exists in the welter of motion and confusion shown by the disorderly

units of the study. This latter point may be
extended beyond the meaning of mere method
of observation. The statistical point of view
is a conception of nature no less useful in the
study of economic variation than in the study
of physical phenomena. Much orderliness and
regularity apparently only becomes evident
when large aggregates are observed, and theoretical treatment involves a probability interpretation. Distributions of economic variates
in as large groups as can be obtained should
be studied and analyzed, and the older theories
of the generation of frequency distributions
should be brushed off, put to work, and further developed. That is to say, statistical economics is too narrow in scope if it includes just
the estimation of postulated relations. Probability theory is fundamental as a guide to an
understanding of the nature of the phenomena
to be studied and not merely as a basis for a
theory of the sampling behavior of estimates
of population parameters the characteristics of
which have been postulated. In seeking for
interesting hypotheses for our quantitative
studies we might want to wander beyond the
classic Walrasian fields and to poke around
the equally classic fields once cultivated by
such men as Lexis, Bortkiewicz, Markov, and
Kapteyn.

These are the roles that I should like statistics to play, and it seems to me that this is in
fair conformance with the views of Burns and
Mitchell. In any event, I should feel much
safer in bringing my little work before the
Commissar of Research if that chair were oc-
cupied by Burns or Mitchell than if Koopmans were the occupant. I would feel that the
first question put by Commissar Koopmans
would be, "Where are your difference equations?", and I would have to answer that I
did not have any to speak of. When the next
question was put, "Where is your argument
showing that the best use has been made of
available data in relation to the most important aspects of the phenomena studied?", I
would have to admit that I was still in a state
of puzzlement regarding the most important
aspect of the phenomena that I study. My
liquidation as an inquirer would be just preceded by the obvious reframing of the above
question, "Where is your assurance that in

[14] *Ibid.*, pp. 87, 90.

what you have done you have wasted no information?", for I would have to answer that I was fairly confident that I had in fact wasted worlds of it. There would clearly be no point in the Commissar going into the power of my tests. But such grounds for the liquidation of methods of research would, I think, be gravely

unfortunate. Most of us feel that we have got beyond a state of dilettantism, but, even so, dilettantes have played a quite remarkable role in the history of science and of ideas in general — and a reading of Koopmans' review may throw a little light upon why this might have been the case.

A REPLY

Tjalling C. Koopmans [1]

Questions of methodology are among the most difficult to reach agreement on or even to find a basis of discussion for. Undeniably, intuitive elements enter into our choice of scientific methods, and states of expectation or confidence affect our attitudes toward specific principles of scientific procedure. Equally obvious is the desirability to formulate explicitly and scrutinize rationally the assumptions and anticipations underlying these choices and attitudes. I fully agree with Vining that the only conclusive test of methods is results ultimately attained (postponing for further discussion under (c) below what is to be the meaning of the term "results"). In view of the insufficiency and inconclusiveness of "results" reached so far in quantitative economics, the only remaining criteria of choice are partly formal (logical clarity and consistency), partly empirical (analogies from other and older sciences that have attained more satisfactory results), and partly, indeed, intuitive.

It is unfortunate that some of the expressions employed by Vining might lead one to think that the issue before us is a dispute between two particular research institutions over their pet methods and procedures. The "econometric approach" to economic dynamics has been initiated and developed in many places by men like Fisher, Frisch, Tinbergen, Marschak, Kalecki, Ezekiel, Haavelmo, Tintner, Stone, Hurwicz, Klein, and others.[2] Similarly, the

"empiricist" position has been embraced by many a scholar outside the National Bureau of Economic Research.

The substance of Vining's criticism can perhaps be summarized in the following four sentences:

(a) To seek a basis for economic dynamics in the analysis of the economizing behavior of the individual agent may not be necessary or even particularly desirable.

(b) A narrow mathematical form has been imposed on a theoretical model for the study of economic dynamics.

(c) Social usefulness is hardly a relevant criterion in the evaluation of economic research.

(d) The present theories of statistical inference are of little help in a process of exploration and hypothesis seeking.

I shall attempt to explain why I remain in fundamental disagreement on the first point (a); that I believe (b) can be met by further clarification of my position; that I do not think we are far apart on (c); and that (d) points to important gaps and unsolved problems in the theory of statistical inference.

(a) With respect to the first statement, I cannot understand the meaning of the phrase that "the aggregate has an existence apart from its constituent particles and behavior characteristics of its own not deducible from the behavior characteristics of the particles." If a theory formulates precisely (although possibly in probability terms) the determination of the choices and actions of each individual in a group or population, in response to the

[1] I am indebted to my colleagues in the Cowles Commission for Research in Economics for valuable comments and criticism of an earlier draft of this reply.

[2] It is, therefore, embarrassing to me to see the methodological approach that resulted from the cumulative effort of these men referred to as "Koopmans' methods" or the "methods of Koopmans' group."

METHODOLOGICAL ISSUES IN QUANTITATIVE ECONOMICS 87

choices and actions of other individuals or the consequences thereof (such as prices, quantities, states of expectation), then the set of these individual behavior characteristics is *logically* equivalent to the behavior characteristics of the group. Such a theory does not have an opening wedge for essentially new group characteristics. Any deus ex machina who should wish to influence the outcome can only do so by affecting the behavior of individuals. This does not deny the existence of essentially social phenomena, based on imitation, such as fads and fashions, waves of optimism and pessimism, panics and runs; or based on power struggles, such as price wars, trust formation, lobbying; or based on a social code or sense of responsibility, such as the acceptance of personal sacrifice for a common objective. It is maintained only that such social phenomena are necessarily acted out by individuals [3] as members of a group.

The logical equivalence of group behavior to the set of individual behavior characteristics does not imply that the mathematical definition and derivation of aggregate behavior equations from individual behavior equations is a simple problem, or even a problem soluble with present mathematical tools. Neither should we exclude the possibility that group behavior will "look" surprisingly different from the individual behavior from which it is derived. On page 171 of my review [4] I have expressed some uneasiness at the lack of concern, in many econometric studies, with an explicit justification of aggregate behavior equations. The position has been taken by Arrow [5] that such aggregate equations are not even necessary for macro-analysis: the rele-

vant information can be conveyed by frequency distributions of individual behavior parameters in the group considered.

Neither does what I have said so far imply that for the analysis of group behavior it is necessary or even worth while to build on the foundation of individual analysis. Boyle established the (aggregate) gas laws by experiments before anyone worried about their derivation from hypothetical properties of molecules. However, on pages 166–67 of my review I have adduced what I believe to be strong arguments (not commented on by Vining) for the necessity of seeking a basis in theories of individual decisions. The first of these is the inavailability of experimentation to determine separately the relevant aggregate behavior equations (if I may continue in that terminology in spite of the doubts just expressed). The third (to interchange the order) is the necessity for identification [6] of separate aggregate behavior equations if the effect of policies is to be predicted — to that argument I shall return when discussing Vining's point (c). The second argument is the availability of direct knowledge about individual behavior. While it was long possible and sometimes tempting for physicists to deny the usefulness of the molecular hypothesis, we economists have the good luck of being some of the "molecules" of economic life ourselves, and of having the possibility through human contacts to study the behavior of other "molecules." Besides introspection, the interview or questionnaire, and even small scale experiments, are available as means of acquiring or extending knowledge about individual behavior. Thus we, indeed, have direct access to information already recognized as essential.

(b) The discussion now flows over into Vining's next point: that I am attempting to impose on the study of business fluctuations the strait-jacket of a narrow mathematical form. Vining correctly notes that I do not in the present context propose a definite content for the theory of individual behavior. The truth is that I am at this stage not even concerned with

---

[3] It is true that the choices of individuals are restrained by a framework of institutional rules enforced or adhered to by the government, the banking system and other institutions. These rules (tax schedules, reserve requirements, etc.) can to some extent be taken as given for the analysis of economic fluctuations. In a deeper analysis, these rules and the changes in them would need to be explained further from choices by individuals interacting, in various degrees of association with each other, through political processes.

[4] "Measurement Without Theory," this REVIEW, XXIX (1947), pp. 161–72. Also in Cowles Commission Papers, New Series, No. 25.

[5] In a paper "Summarizing a Population of Behavior Patterns" presented at the Chicago meeting of the Econometric Society, December 1947. An abstract of this paper appeared in *Econometrica*, Vol. 16, No. 2, April 1948.

[6] In another paper ("Identification Problems in Economic Model Construction," to be published in *Econometrica*, April 1949) I have given an exposition of this group of problems.

any very specific *mathematical* form of this theory. I am, for instance, quite unhappy about difference equations. They are clumsy instruments that treat time as if it comes in indivisible pieces of one year or one quarter each. The only excuses for their use are simplicity in exposition and the fact that statistical theory concerning the estimation of their parameters is further advanced than that for alternative, more realistic forms. I am hoping, however, that statisticians will soon teach us how to treat equation systems in which behavior responses are allowed to be subject to continously distributed lags and in which probability enters through "disturbances" that are stochastic processes of a continuous time variable. Similarly, I should be happy to follow Arrow's suggestion to scrap the notion of aggregate behavior equations, should he demonstrate that the notion of a frequency distribution of individual behavior parameters suffices for the objectives discussed under (c) below, and should we be able to collect the data relevant to the measurement of these concepts.

I do emphasize what might be called the *logical* form of a science of economic dynamics, or, if you like, its mathematical form in a very broad and general sense. At the basis: hypotheses regarding the behavior of individual consumers, laborers, entrepreneurs, investors, etc., in the markets indicated by these terms. In so far as we assume rational behavior, these hypotheses may be of the utility-maximizing or profit-maximizing type or, in situations involving strategy, of the type studied by Morgenstern and von Neumann.[7] Even then, time lags arise from the process of transmission of information and of decision taking. But we need not and should not confine ourselves to assuming rational behavior. What we need to measure is actual behavior, as shaped by habit, culture, ideals, imitation, advertising, prejudice and misinformation as well as by the narrower economic motives usually referred to as rational. Therefore, besides using deductions from the economic motive, we need to formalize and strengthen our knowledge of other motives of modern economic man, through observation, interview, and

[7] *Theory of Games and Economic Behavior* (Princeton, 1944).

sampling study, drawing on whatever results other social sciences have to offer.

The basic assumption is that the numerically measurable effects of the implementation of individual decisions have a relatively persistent relationship to the principal numerically measurable aspects of the information that has gone into the making of these decisions — persistent, if not for a given individual, then in some average or aggregate sense for a group of individuals. Since the relationship is between numerical entities, it is necessarily mathematical; since not all pieces of information relevant to the decision can be statistically traced and perhaps also because of basic erratic elements in all human behavior, the relationship has the form of a probability distribution of decision effects which depends on the decision data (some of which are exogenous, i.e., non-economic).

Not all economic variables are determined directly through individual decisions. Some are set by government or bank officials acting under law or conventional rule (as pointed out in footnote 3). Some are the outcome of productive processes, described by transformation functions possibly involving further time lags, new random elements and additional exogenous variables.

Whether or not the relationships of behavior, rule, and technology are sufficiently persistent to merit study, it must, I believe, be granted that they are a logically complete set of elements (building blocks) for explaining the formation of economic variables. If these relationships are valid, any other interesting relationships between the same variables or aggregates thereof must be dependent on (deducible from) these. So must, for instance, relationships between regional aggregates. Such aggregates are determined through behavior, rule, and technology in Virginia, Illinois, and other states, in interaction. That is, regional analysis does not enter as a new and independent principle of research. It directs interest to one particular (geographical) mode of aggregation.

(c) I have always felt that social usefulness as an objective should and does receive greater emphasis in economics than, for instance, in the natural sciences (other than technology).

METHODOLOGICAL ISSUES IN QUANTITATIVE ECONOMICS   89

But even physicists have become alarmed and worried at the thought that the social usefulness of their latest discoveries may well be negative. Political economy has traditionally sought justification for its speculations in the search of a scientific basis for public policy in economic matters.

However, this is clearly a matter of personal choice and emphasis. And even if the criterion of usefulness is adopted as the ultimate guide, this does not exclude in any way that a piece of knowledge obtained for knowledge's sake may some day turn out to have greater social usefulness than knowledge sought with a particular policy problem in mind. Indeed, the case for measurement of identifiable relationships expressing average economic behavior of individuals does not rest on the acceptance of a research criterion of social usefulness. It rests rather on the criterion that relevant knowledge should enable us to predict outcomes in not yet observed (future or past) situations. There has been a good deal of experience (Harvard barometer, etc.) to show that relationships between economic variables observed over a period of time but not traced to underlying behavior equations are unreliable as instruments for prediction. The reason, so excellently explained by Haavelmo in the study quoted by Vining, is that such apparent relationships may well depend for their validity on several behavior equations, and will fail even if only one of the latter fails, either because of a change in the response pattern itself or because some policy or exogenous variable affects the response. Changes in policies and in external conditions occur continually, and methods of prediction that fail whenever some such change occurs somewhere are of very limited use.[8]

Vining counters with the question whether even the most autonomous behavior equations can themselves be expected to have much persistence through time. Calling now on the criterion of social usefulness to reinforce an argument independent of it, I submit that this is an empirical question of great social importance. Suppose these behavior relationships are

so fickle and transitory as to escape measurement. Then the best we can expect from past observation is the type of information collected by Burns and Mitchell: statistical averages and frequency distributions of cyclical characteristics like the depth of depressions, the steepness of upswing or decline, etc. That is, assuming that for some unknown reason at least these averages and distributions possess stability over time, we can then form expectations as to what, on the average, the future has in store for us. But if some of this expected variety of events turns out to be detrimental to welfare, we shall then have no knowledge as to how to prevent or reduce the damage. Now, if we do not learn how to introduce greater stability in the economy by the indirect inducements of money supply, tax schedules, and other general incentives or deterrents to individual action — either because such knowledge is impossible or because we do not seek it — political processes and social necessities will make us move more to the method of direct administrative prescription of individual behavior. Thus, a question of social method and organization in which many non-economic issues and problems are involved may be decided in a particular way because lack of the quantitative knowledge of economic behavior required for one possible solution prevents an informed comparison of the alternatives before us.

(d) I am in agreement with much that is said by Vining under the last heading. Probability, randomness, variability, enter not only into estimation and hypothesis testing concerning economic behavior parameters. These concepts are an essential element in dynamic economic theory, in the model we form of the conditioning (rather than determination) of future economic quantities by past economic developments. I submit that the concept of an aggregate behavior equation, or of a frequency distribution of individual behavior parameters, is an excellent example of the "orderliness and regularity" which "only becomes evident when large aggregates are observed," referred to by Vining. I believe that his term "statistical theory in its broader meaning" is used in the same sense in which the econometricians speak of "model construction." It is the model itself, as

[8] See also J. Marschak, "Economic Structure, Path, Policy, and Prediction," *American Economic Review*, May 1947, pp. 81–84; especially Section III.

a more or less suitable approximation to reality, which is of primary interest. The problems of estimation of its parameters or testing of its features have a derived interest only. But this derived interest is strong: it has long been emphasized by Tinbergen and others, and recently again by Friedman,[9] that quantitative conclusions regarding cyclical movements and the influence of policies thereon depend critically on the numerical values of time lags and other response parameters.

I come now to the distinction between problems of "hypothesis-seeking" and problems discussed in the theory of estimation or in the Neyman-Pearson theory of "hypothesis-testing." This touches on unsolved problems at the very foundations of statistical theory, and I must confess that I do not see clearly through the issues involved. It is possible to take a formal view and argue that hypothesis-seeking and hypothesis-testing differ only in how wide a set of alternatives is taken into consideration. In the Neyman-Pearson theory a choice between only two alternatives (single or composite) is made. In estimation, a choice is made from an infinite number of alternatives which are neatly arranged in a continuous finite-dimensional space. Obviously these are only two special cases of a much broader problem. Statisticians are often compelled to use solutions to these special problems in situations requiring a broader approach (which has not yet been developed). For instance, we constantly take hints from the data regarding the choice of hypotheses to be tested from the same data — although we know that the degree of confidence to be placed in the test is affected by that practice. These and similar [10] difficulties can only be resolved by a theory or theories permitting choice of hypotheses from a wider range of alternatives than hitherto considered.

To the extent that hypothesis-seeking is an activity that can be formalized by such a theory, there is little doubt that the concept of statistical efficiency will remain relevant. It will also remain true, I believe, that choices between alternative hypotheses can be made with greater power of discrimination on the basis of explicit mathematical formulation of these alternatives, in the form of probability models describing the generation of the observations. However, there remains scope for doubt whether all hypothesis-seeking activity can be described and formalized as a choice from a preassigned range of alternatives. If not, there is further doubt whether the concept of statistical efficiency or discriminatory power of a method of selecting hypotheses can be given a definite meaning.

Having thus granted the principle of Vining's remark, I hasten to add that my criticism of the statistical measures used by Burns and Mitchell is not, I believe, affected thereby. On page 170 [11] of my review I indicated that these measures are found to be inefficient tools if the range of alternative hypothesis is restricted by the use of economic theory concerning the behavior patterns underlying the formations of economic variables. I adduced the availability of more efficient tools, and, indeed, of the yardstick of efficiency, as a strong reason for accepting such a restriction of alternatives, in order to attain greater sharpness of conclusion, at the price of attaining only a conclusion conditional on basic hypotheses not tested from the same data.

Arrow has pointed out to me in conversation that scientific progress has often been made in the past by narrowing down the range of alternatives in such a manner that a crucial experiment or test can be devised. He mentions as a striking example the historical dispute between corpuscular and wave theories of light. Progress was made just because this issue was believed settled in favor of the wave theory by experiments devised for the purpose, at a time when the synthesis of wave and corpuscular theory envisaged by modern quantum theory was not regarded as an available alternative. These and similar examples suggest a scientific strategy of not discarding basic theoretical notions and assumptions before they "cause trouble," that is, before observations are made which come in conflict with these basic notions and assumptions.

---

[9] Milton Friedman, "A Monetary and Fiscal Framework for Economic Stability," *American Economic Review*, June 1948, pp. 245–64; see especially Section IIIB.

[10] I discuss further limitations of present statistical theory in Section 6 of the article cited in footnote 6.

[11] In the middle of the second column.

It may be added that it becomes extremely difficult, if not impossible, to assess the appropriateness of any statistical technique if resort is not taken to some narrowing down of alternatives. If "hypothesis-seeking" means just looking for hypotheses which find some support in the data (without specifying what alternative hypotheses find less support) it will be hard to prove that tools as formal and elaborate as those employed by Burns and Mitchell are better than, as good as, or not greatly inferior to other possible measures or test criteria.

Vining's jocular remarks about a commissariat of research should, I am sure, have made me throw up my hands in horrified protest at the mere idea of such an anomalous office. Instead (I confess) they set me day-dreaming as to what questions I really would ask if for one day I were to be so installed (much like a schoolboy who is allowed to act as the mayor of the town for one whole day). I felt that my first official action would be to make available ample resources for the exploration of the basic principles of statistical inference. Then I would ask economists to overhaul their theories of individual behavior, modified in the light of sociology and social psychology, and express these theories in mathematical form. I would ask government economists for an enumeration and description of the possible instruments of policy, and welfare economists for a statement of (complementary or alternative) objectives of policy. Next I would ask mathematicians to perform such aggregations of individual behavior equations as would bring out the most important (aggregate) behavior parameters, knowledge of which would guide policy toward any of the relevant objectives. I would then ask statisticians to get ready for the collection of the necessary data (if not already available) and to devise methods to estimate these parameters. . . .

At this point disturbing thoughts occurred to me. What if I had forgotten some important link in the chain? What if each of these groups conceived of their tasks in such a way that their respective results could not be fitted together? These thoughts rather spoiled the day-dream, and I abandoned it before it could turn into a nightmare ending in my liquidation for inefficiency.

A REJOINDER

Rutledge Vining

Professor Koopmans has replied with patience and restraint, and one who has questioned his position cannot but appreciate his attitude. But his reply seems not to be a satisfactory resolution of our differences. Point (a) appears to me to be left somewhat in the air. Moreover, in the discussion of the other three points there are conveyed what I believe to be misconceptions. In my opinion, the attainments of the recent work in econometrics are primarily in the extension of the theory of regression, and on the basis of what has been published it seems misleading to imply that in this extension new truth has been discovered in the field of economic relations. Finally, I read from the reply what must surely be a misconception with regard to the type of empiricism represented by the work of Burns and Mitchell. I shall comment upon point (a) and upon the nature of the presumed misconceptions.

In his discussion of the appropriate unit of analysis, Koopmans is of course not maintaining that the effect of two or more "causes" acting together is necessarily equivalent to the sum of the individual "causes" acting independently. This kind of linearity, we are told by physicists, characterizes classical mechanics but not the phenomena stressed in modern physics. In this latter field the equation system is non-linear, and the effect of two or more causes acting jointly is not the sum of the individual effects. Neither is Koopmans intimating that anything at all can be inferred as *necessary* about the real world from first principles. The development of science has been a series of surprises. Mathematical systems and systems of logic contain no necessary truth about empirical phenomena. They are axiomatized systems of relations invented to deal with reality as found, and there is not just one algebra or one geometry.

Neither does he deny the *possibility* that an important component of motivated and problem-solving individual behavior is indeterminate and fundamentally unpredictable — in the sense that he would perhaps admit as unpredictable the outcome of his own problem-solving behavior. But he presumably does assert that a knowledge of all there is to know about individual behavior together with a mathematics with which the individual behavior equations may be combined would yield all of the parameters of group behavior relations, these latter in turn containing the properties of the structure of an economic system. He makes no claim that his present knowledge of the "individual behavior equations" is much more than trivial, and he states that the mathematics has perhaps not yet been invented.

One could quibble here. If individual behavior should have only a statistical stability and predictability, is the error term that is attached to the individual equations or the "expected value" of individual effects an attribute of a population or of the constituent individual? And is it the individual that Koopmans regards as the unit anyway? Perhaps his unit is the family or the firm, in some instances a grouping of families and in many instances a grouping of firms.

But the point at issue is more clear-cut than this. I maintain that it is gratuitous for anyone to specify any particular entity as necessarily the ultimate unit for the whole range of inquiry within some general and essentially unexplored field of study. Scientific procedure has involved working from observed regularities in space and time to logical inferences of other space-time relations. Theories, subject to test by observation, are developed in this process, the simplest theory accounting for observed phenomena being that which uses the least number of postulated and "unexplained" relations. What this implies with respect to the unit of analysis is an empirical matter. Koopmans in demonstrating the efficiency of his

choice among possible units must establish the relative simplicity of his empirically tested theory.

Koopmans presents his position in the form of a syllogism that is clearly faulty in its formulation. What he implies in his premise goes beyond what must necessarily be granted. There is implied that all actions and configurations associated with human beings are subject ultimately to individual determination. No room is left for the possibility of structural features and dynamic behavior characteristics that are invariant with respect to human decisions. His conclusion includes a term, "behavior characteristics of the group," which is not defined and which appears to be used in such a way that the statement is reduced to a tautology. No issue would be involved over the triviality that in moving a house one must move the constituent bricks; but no one would contend that from the properties of individual bricks one could infer all the properties of the house being constructed. There is more to the developing house than can be learned from the bricks. Whether or not this is the case with regard to human beings and the structural and functional characteristics of evolving societal forms is not a matter of logic, but rather a matter of fact.

These considerations seem so obvious that I am inclined to think that our differences are largely verbal. Koopmans' analogies are drawn primarily from physics, and he is thinking perhaps of "aggregate" in terms, say, of the total or joint effect of the bombardment of a screen by many atomic particles. I used the word "aggregate" or "population," following analogies drawn from biology, in the sense in which certain populations are regarded as fundamental biological entities. Certain aspects of a termite colony are studied by considering the entire organization as an integrated organism, just as the eye or the heart or the nervous system may be looked upon as a "population" of cells. These entities have structural and functional properties that are studied by observing the organism as a unit. Similarly, we may learn of structural and functional characteristics of human social forms by studying a social structure as a unit. From this point of view, Koopmans' conception of "structure" — as suggested by his use of "structural equations" and "structural coefficients" and by his reference to Arrow's comments — strikes me as being excessively formal; and his notion of the "aggregation problem" seems to me to be confined to the formal realm of arithmetic. A look at the older sciences, as Koopmans recommends, shows morphologists or their counterparts engaged in the study of the more concrete and "pictorial" aspects of structure and function in all the empirical sciences. To assume that *all* structural properties of an economic system may be expressed and most effectively studied as different modes of adding or combining "structural equations" appears to me not only to beg baffling questions but also to aspire to more generality than has been achieved in the "older sciences."

The point of the discussion, of course, has to do with where Koopmans thinks we should look for "autonomous behavior relations." He appeals to experience but in a somewhat oblique manner. He refers to the Harvard barometer "to show that relationships between economic variables . . . not traced to underlying behavior equations are unreliable as instruments for prediction." He might have gone back to a period prior to the Harvard barometer and been reminded of the research preceding the Federal Reserve Act which led to the reliably "planned" alteration of what was regarded as a socially undesirable extreme seasonality in the money markets. His argument would have been more effectively put had he been able to give instances of relationships that *have been* "traced to underlying behavior equations" *and* that have been reliable instruments for prediction. He did not do this, and I know of no conclusive case that he could draw upon. There are of course cases of economic models that he could have mentioned as having been *unreliable* predictors. But these latter instances demonstrate no more than the failure of the Harvard barometer: all were presumably built upon relations that were more or less unstable in time. The meaning conveyed, we may suppose, by the term "fundamental autonomous relation" is a relation stable in time and not drawn as an inference from combinations of other relations. The discovery of such relations suitable for the pre-

diction procedure that Koopmans has in mind has yet to be publicly presented, and the phrase "underlying behavior equation" is left utterly devoid of content.

In the lively exchange between Keynes and Tinbergen in 1939,[1] Keynes remarked that Tinbergen was anxious not to claim too much. "If only he is allowed to carry on, he is quite ready and happy at the end of it to go a long way towards admitting, with an engaging modesty, that the results probably have no value." But econometrics has faced up to its responsibilities since those faraway days, and Koopmans now confronts us with the awful portent of authoritarianism as the alternative to success in his venture. Keynes was heavily critical of the procedures used by Tinbergen. Econometricians have in general held that the criticisms were the conclusions of a sadly misinformed and misguided man. But I judge that with the arguments simply put, many economists today would agree with most of what Keynes had to say; and those points upon which he was misinformed they would regard as among the less important. Moreover, in my judgment, many economists, given a full account in simple terms of the theoretical and technical developments since Tinbergen's models of 1939, would find the present models as intellectually unsatisfying as the models of Tinbergen, and for the same basic cosmological reason. Many would simply remain unconvinced that the real thing is put together in any such fashion as is implied. They could be readily convinced of the validity of these procedures through empirical demonstrations. But many economists remain unimpressed by what has been made available.

Tinbergen's procedure amounted to a glorified multiple correlation project. He arranged to have a complete system of equations, "complete" being used primarily in an algebraic sense. His methods of estimating the parameters of these equations are now regarded as capable only of yielding biased estimates, the term "bias" being used in a sense defined in theoretical statistics. Statisticians have under-

[1] *Economic Journal*, Volume 49 and Volume 50.

standably found stimulation and interest in the hunt for unbiased methods of estimating the parameters of a system of equations. But my judgment is that many economists, while commending the reduction in bias of estimation, would be more impressed with the possibilities of biases introduced by the philosophical postulates of the "economic analysis." Tinbergen computed standard errors, but as then computed they are not regarded as valid measures of reliability. Confidence intervals, it is contended, may now be computed appropriate for the model adopted. But the meaning of "confidence" must be construed with care. It is not a confidence in the model for purposes of predicting the future. Nor is it a confidence in the model for purposes of predicting the effects of policy decisions. When Koopmans speaks of introducing "greater stability in the economy by indirect inducements" he has reference to a planned alteration of some of his estimated coefficients or to the "suppression of a structural equation." So far as I know, Koopmans has no practicable basis for feeling any confidence one way or another regarding such a refurbishing of his estimated equation system.

It is along these lines, I think, that the general economist can be misled by the econometricians' characterization of their own attainments. Econometricians, on the other hand, may apparently mislead themselves when they attempt to characterize the research efforts of economists. Consider, for example, Koopmans' characterization of the work of Burns and Mitchell. As the last resort for economists frustrated by failures in other efforts and as something, alas, inadequate for our stand against direct administrative prescription of individual behavior, he describes "the type of information collected by Burns and Mitchell: statistical averages and frequency distributions of cyclical characteristics." But this is a misconception. The book under review is not a terminal book and was explicitly designed to outline in detail certain methods of measure-

ment that have been adopted in an explorative study of economic variation. However uninspiring these particular procedures may seem to us, we have grounds for confidence in the investigators responsible for them. I would want the reader to refer back to Burns' *Production Trends in the United States since 1870*, and to pass judgment upon the nature of the knowledge provided in that book. To me, the book holds a magnificent portrayal of the dynamic growth of industrial America, implying an intricate theoretical structure. Perhaps this theoretical structure may be systematized in terms of simpler elements than those used, and maybe some later scholar will see in these evolutions of growth a generalizing principle. But having done our best towards systematizing, let a comparison be made between that which may be read from this book and the economic theory underlying one of Koopmans' models. This work should suggest expectations from the work on business cycles, even if a knowledge of Mitchell's work through the years had not already induced a confidence that an understanding of real processes would be furthered. Koopmans uses somewhat loosely the term "empiricist position" and associates it with the National Bureau. But, again, let the reader study the work of Friedman and Kuznets, *Income from Independent Professional Practice*, and answer whether or not economic and statistical theory are brought to bear and furthered. Or let him study the forthcoming volume on inventories by Abramovitz and answer whether or not the theory of the role of inventory investment in business fluctuations is furthered.

These are works that come to mind and of course others could be added. To some they evidence a growing understanding of the structure of an economic system, of how the variety of industrial behaviors are interwoven, and of the stresses and strains of a great economy in motion. In Koopmans' remarks there is no indication of a realization of this.

[4]

DEBORAH MAYO

TESTING STATISTICAL TESTING*

1. PHILOSOPHY OF STATISTICS AND PHILOSOPHY OF ECONOMICS

At a recent conference on problems in economics the following problem was raised:

Econometricians like to think of themselves as scientists, and their methods as scientific. Students of the philosophy of science, on the other hand, have not had any notable success in relating the formal concepts of scientific method or the logic of scientific explanation and theory construction to either the method or the theory of econometrics [3, p. 238].

This should not be taken to mean that the theory and practice of economics and econometrics is not scientific. It rather points to the need for a greater effort among philosophers to tie their analyses to actual scientific practice. More specifically, it indicates a need for philosophers of science to examine statistical theorizing in science, since inference and explanation in economics is often statistical in nature.

In building quantitative models of economic phenomena one may begin with an economic theory which is modelled mathematically, and then evaluate parameters of the model, or one may begin with a set of potentially relevant variables about which relationships are sought. In either case data must be gathered and values for the parameters of the model must be estimated or tested. The relevant consideration for our purposes is that whether it is due to the variability of the phenomena or the errors of observation and measurement, statistical methods are generally involved in evaluating this data. This raises questions about which statistical procedure to use and how its results bear upon the economic theory.

In the last 50 years or so a new battery of modern statistical techniques has become available, owing very heavily to the theories of Fisher [5] and Neyman and Pearson [21]. These techniques, often referred to as the *classical*, the *objective* or the *frequency* theory shall here be referred to as the *standard methodology* (SM). The application of statistics to economics gave birth to the science of econometrics. As with other scientists who applied statistics to their fields, workers in economics were more concerned with applying and absorbing statistical techniques into their science than with the foundational

175

J. C. Pitt (ed.), Philosophy in Economics, 175–203.

and philosophical questions associated with these methods. Perhaps this is as it should be for practitioners of science. It is, after all, the business of philosophers and not scientists to scrutinize the nature and epistemological basis of inference tools. With respect to statistical inference tools, this is the work of the philosophers of statistics.

Among those who were busy applying the SM, a growing controversy arose about which of the many new methods to use and how their results were to be interpreted. Several of those who searched for the valid basis for SM concluded that there was no valid basis. They claimed that the standard methods were misconceived and unable to perform the tasks for which they were being used in science. New inference philosophies arose which abandoned the principles of SM. Some were revivals of methods employed prior to modern developments, such as the Bayesian philosophy. This resulted in an even greater controversy over which methods to use. While the confusion and controversy has taken a number of turns, it is raging as strong as ever. As SM is increasingly being used in the sciences, it is increasingly coming under attack. With ever more vital decisions being based upon its methods the urgency in resolving the controversy is clear.

Given the close ties between economics and statistics, it is not surprising to find that problems concerning the evaluation of economic models are closely tied to controversies in the foundations and philosophy of statistics. By examining an important question in philosophy of statistics this paper hopes to be a contribution to the philosophy of economics.

The question upon which I shall focus is: What information is to be considered relevant for statistical inference? The particular sort of statistical inference to be focused on is *hypothesis testing*. The question has been such a major point of disagreement that the different testing philosophies may in general be distinguished on the basis of how they answer it. In particular, the standard and non-standard testing philosophies may be distinguished in this way.

The standard principles, that is, the principles of SM, deem relevant the manner in which data is generated and how various hypotheses to be evaluated by this data are specified. As a result, what would blithely be considered the same data and hypotheses may be treated differently according to how each was generated. In contrast, according to non-standard principles, in particular the likelihood principle, both the manner of generating data and specifying hypotheses are considered irrelevant for making inferences. It makes no difference to the result of a non-standard inference whether the hypothesis to be evaluated is specified *after the data* to be used in its evaluation

TESTING STATISTICAL TESTING 177

is generated (SAD) or whether it is specified *before the data* (SBD). Thus, the non-standard theorist sees as unjustified any requirement which demands that hypotheses be specified in advance of the experiment. And so, the non-standard theorist in effect is demanding that the SM theorist justify his requirement for SBD. But, how can such a requirement be justified, based as it is on a view that appears to make the very time at which a hypothesis is formulated logically relevant to the evaluation of the hypothesis?

I shall attempt to provide such a justification by showing how the requirement permits SM to guarantee the reliability and precision (size and power) of its tests. But the standard criteria of reliability and precision are based upon the *sample space*, something considered irrelevant on non-standard approaches. As a result, such non-standard approaches will be shown to permit drawing faulty inferences with high probability – in extreme cases with probability one. As an example of a non-standard theory of testing I will employ the likelihood approach of Ian Hacking as set out in his *Logic of Statistical Inference* [11]. I next consider how the problem of permitting hypotheses to be SAD bears upon a Bayesian philosophy. It is concluded that non-standard theories of testing require additional principles concerning the generation of data and hypotheses if they are to avoid objectionable inferences. Whether there exists any non-standard justification for such principles is unclear.

Having shown how requiring hypotheses to be SBD enables SM to uphold its principles of reliability and precision, I argue that the rationale for using tests which are reliable and precise differs from the one given in the accounts of standard tests. Typically, the rationale given is that such tests make relatively few faulty inferences in the long run. The purpose of statistical tests in scientific contexts, as I see it, is to detect certain discrepancies between hypotheses or between data and hypotheses. In this way it provides information in order to assess substantive scientific hypotheses. The goal of low error rates in the long run is not viewed as an end in itself for tests. The importance of tests with 'good-error characteristics' is the ability to use them to formulate tests which can detect all and only discrepancies of a certain size. Hence by requiring hypotheses be SBD, and thereby ensuring certain error rates, one is ensuring the test is providing the information it is supposed to. This constitutes the basis for the objectivity of tests built upon SM.

2. BACKGROUND

A brief look at the background of the problem of inductive inference provides clues as to how non-standard inference theories seem to have arisen. What is sometimes referred to as the 'old' problem of induction arose from the empiricist principle whereby the acceptance and rejection of theories is to be solely the result of observation and experiment, and the recognition by Hume that no finite amount of experimentation can logically justify general theories. As a result, people began to consider whether favorable observations could be seen as providing a certain degree of proof or confirmation to theories. This gave rise to the 'new' problem of induction which has typically been seen as finding a quantitative relation M which is to measure the evidential strength between data d and a generalization or hypothesis h.

Though one could not be logically certain of hypothesis h given data d, the possibility that one could consider h as having some degree of probability suggested itself. Hence, it was natural to use probability functions in setting up the quantitative relation M. There have been a number of attempts to erect a theory of inductive inference by setting up an evidential relation M. Typically, M is defined as measuring degrees of belief, confirmation, support, credibility, plausibility and the like. All such attempts will be referred to as *evidential relationship* or E—R approaches.[1] Confronted with the same data and hypothesis an identical measure of evidential relationship is obtained by applying measure M. Thus, for E—R views, the manner of data generation and the order in which the hypotheses are specified are irrelevant to the measure M and hence irrelevant to inference.

It is from this conception of inference, that sees the evidential import of data to be found in a measure of E—R, that the Likelihood Principle apparently arose. As both the Bayesian and Likelihood philosophies incorporate some form of Likelihood Principle, both of these non-standard philosophies may be seen as step-children of Hume and the empiricists. Not only do these E—R views enjoy the neatness of being based upon a single quantitative measure M, they also have the simplicity of having a single inference principle typically exhorting one to maximize or increase the measure M. For instance, Hacking, following Carnapian logic, employs the likelihood function to measure the degree of strength given data affords a hypothesis. He then obtains a measure of the relative support afforded to rival hypotheses h_0 and h_1 by calculating the ratio of the likelihoods of each. It is the likelihood ratio that serves as his measure M. The fundamental inference principle is to reject hypotheses having rivals with much greater likelihoods. Before examining such non-standard theories, however, let us consider an example of a standard theory of testing.

3. STANDARD TESTING: NEYMAN–PEARSON (NP) TESTS

In order to apply the mathematical apparatus of statistics to the results of an experiment it must be construed in terms of a *statistical model*. That is, the experiment is viewed as the observation of a random variable D whose possible values d_i make up the sample space X, and which has a certain probability distribution p_D. A statistical hypothesis is a statement about this distribution over X. Typically, the general form of p_D is assumed and the hypothesis is an assertion about the value of one (or more) of the parameters θ governing the distribution.[2]

A function of D, $T(D)$, called the *test statistic* is specified. The test consists of a rule which designates, before the experiment is carried out, which of the values of $T(D)$ will be taken to reject the hypothesis under test, that is the *test* or *null hypothesis* h_0. The set of observations yielding these values of $T(D)$ make up the *critical region* of the test. The critical region is specified so that $T(D)$ will have a given probability, called the *size* or the *significance level* of the test, of falling into the region if the null hypothesis is true. This is just the probability of making what is called the *type I error*, that is, falsely rejecting h_0.

In the NP theory, an alternative hypothesis h_1 is also specified before the experiment, and it is to be accepted just in case h_0 is rejected. Then a second type of error, the *type II error* may be specified. A type II error is committed when h_0 is accepted (i.e., not rejected) when it is actually false and the alternative h_1 is true. The probabilities of making type I and type II errors are denoted by α and β respectively:

$$P(\text{reject } h_0 / h_0 \text{ is true}) = \alpha$$
$$P(\text{accept } h_0 / h_1 \text{ is true}) = \beta$$

3.1. *Size and Power*

The smaller the size α the more reliable the test, but it must be balanced with a reasonable β. If β is too large, the test is said to have insufficient *power* (or precision) where power is defined as $1 - \beta$. By simply never rejecting h_0, α can be reduced to 0. But then h_1 is never accepted, so β is 1 and hence the power is 0. Such a test would literally have zero power to detect the truth of the alternative. An *optimal* NP test having a given size α is one which at the same time maximizes the power (i.e., minimizes β). The experimenter is construed as first specifying α to be the maximum proportion of times he can 'afford' to make a type I error, and then maximizing the power. The context is construed as a pragmatic, decision-theoretic one, although as I shall later argue it need not be.

Optimal NP tests typically take the form: reject h_0 iff $T(D) \geqslant t$ for some fixed value t. The associated critical region is $\{d : T(d) \geqslant t\}$. This form arises because it is often reasonable to suppose h_0 should be rejected when the value of D is too far (in one or another direction) from the value (or values) of θ hypothesized by h_0. For example, in testing a hypothesis h_0 about the mean θ of a distribution where h_0 is $\theta = \theta_0$, it is reasonable to conclude h_0 is false if the observed or sample mean is too far away from the hypothesized mean. If random variable D is the sample mean, the test may take the form: reject h_0 just in case $|D - \theta_0| \geqslant \delta$ for some positive value of δ. As distance is conveniently measured in units of *standard deviations*[3] of the observable D (i.e., σ_D's), δ may be written as $k\sigma_D$. A test of this form is appropriate if one is interested in rejecting h_0 when the true value of θ is either less than or greater than θ_0. This is the case when dealing with the composite alternative hypothesis h_1 of form: $\theta \neq \theta_0$, and yields what is called a *two-sided* test.

If the alternative hypothesis states that θ has a value greater than θ_0, then one would want to reject h_0 only when positive differences between the observed and hypothesized mean were detected. The appropriate test would then take the form: reject h_0 if and only if $(D - \theta) \geqslant k\sigma_D$, for some positive k. This is an example of a *one-sided* test. By letting the test statistic $T(D)$ be $\frac{(D - \theta_0)}{\sigma D}$ the above one and two-sided tests become: reject h_0 iff $T(D) \geqslant k$ and reject h_0 iff $|T(D)| \geqslant k$, respectively. Subtracting from D its mean and dividing by its standard deviation yields the *normalization* of D. Hence, $T(D)$ is here the normalization of D.

The virtue of using the normalization of D as the test statistic $T(D)$ is that $T(D)$ is known to have (approximately) a *normal* distribution with a mean of 0 and a standard deviation of 1 (i.e., it is *standard normal*) regardless of the distribution of D. By selecting $T(D)$ to be a statistic whose distribution is known without having to know the value of any unknown parameter, (such as the one under test) it is possible to calculate the probabilities of the two types of errors prior to the experiment. In this way it can be ensured that these probabilities are sufficiently small regardless of which hypothesis is true. The distribution of $T(D)$ is called the *sampling distribution*, and it is the basis for both formulating and evaluating standard tests. Considering an example of a commonly used test may help to illuminate the standard testing concepts.

EXAMPLE (3–1): In an experiment to determine whether the probability that a coin lands heads is 0.5 or 0.8, 100 tosses are made and the proportion of heads observed. Let the experiment be modeled as the observation of random variable D with a *binomial distribution*[4] where D is the proportion of heads observed, θ the probability of heads, h_0 is $\theta = 0.5$ and h_1 is $\theta = 0.8$, and $T(D) = \frac{(D - 0.5)}{\sigma_D}$. It is decided to reject h_0 iff the observed proportion differs from the hypothesized proportion by 2 or more standard deviation units. Then the test is:

Reject h_0 iff $T(D) \geqslant 2$.

The size of this test is

$$P(T(D) \geqslant 2/\theta = 0.5) = \alpha$$

and it may be easily calculated to be approximately 0.03 since $T(D)$ has the standard normal distribution. (The probability that *any* standard normal variable is greater than or equal to 2 is 0.03 regardless of the value of θ.) Being the area to the right of 2, 0.03 is called the *tail area* of the distribution. As $\sigma_D = 0.05$ under the assumption that $\theta = 0.5$ the test is equivalent to the rule:

Reject h_0 iff $D \geqslant 0.6$.

Then the probability of a type II error (i.e., accepting h_0 when the alternative is true) is

$$P(D < 0.6/\theta = 0.8) = \beta \approx 0.0000$$

and hence the power of the test is approximately 1. In Section 9 I shall discuss the import of this test in some detail.

4. NON-STANDARD TESTS: LIKELIHOOD TESTS

In contrast to the NP theory of testing is the non-standard theory of *likelihood tests*. As an example of such a theory I consider the one set out by Ian Hacking in [11]. The first notion to be defined is the *likelihood function* of a hypothesis h given observed data d. This is equal to the probability (or in the continuous case, the density) of d under the assumption that hypothesis h is true. That is

$$L(h/d) = P(d/h).$$

Likelihood functions differ from probability functions. The probability distribution of the result of observing random variable D with θ the fixed value of the relevant parameter, written $p(D/\theta)$, is a function over the space of possible results. As it defines a statistical distribution, summing over possible results (or integrating if D is a continuous variable), yields one. The likelihood function, in contrast, is a function of a statistical hypothesis (i.e., parameter) when the data is given. So now it is the data that is fixed as opposed to the parameter. This function does not define a statistical distribution and summing or integrating over possible hypotheses or parameters (even if these could be known) need not yield anything in particular — it clearly need not be one. The *likelihood ratio* of two hypotheses h_0 and h_1 given data d is defined as the ratio

$$L(h_1/d)/L(h_0/d)$$

and will be abbreviated as $r(d)$.

The basic intuition upon which likelihood inference is based is that the hypothesis with the greater support is the one having the greater likelihood on the data. This is formalized in the *law of likelihood* which states: Data d supports hypothesis h_0 better than hypothesis h_1 if the likelihood of h_0 given d is greater than that of h_1. In terms of relative likelihoods this becomes: Data d supports h_1 better than h_0 if $r(d) \geqslant 1$.

From the law of likelihood the theory of *likelihood tests* arises. According to Hacking

An hypothesis should be rejected if and only if there is some rival hypothesis much better supported than it is [11, p. 89].

Accordingly Hacking states [11, p. 90] that a simple hypothesis h_0 is *rejected at level c* in light of data d just in case there is a simple hypothesis h_0, consistent with the data, such that $r(d) \geqslant c$. For complex hypothesis H, d serves to reject H if for all simple hypotheses h_i in H, there is a hypothesis h_j that is consistent with the data such that $r(d) \geqslant c$.

The value of c in the likelihood test is the *critical ratio* (c-ratio) of the test and larger c values are taken to indicate more stringent tests. Associated with each likelihood test of hypothesis h_0 is a *rejection class* defined as [11, p. 90] the set of possible results for which there exists an alternative h_1 such that $r(d) \geqslant c$. The question as to what counts as "much better (or much less) supported" becomes a question as to what the appropriate c-ratio of a test is. According to Hacking, this is a matter of the quantity of evidence that is desired before rejecting a hypothesis. However, all c-ratios are not alike. Different tests having the same c-ratio can contain radically different quantities of evidence, and higher c-ratios need not mean more evidence. As a result, simply reporting that a hypothesis has been rejected at level c fails to provide sufficient information for comprehending an inference. Consider the following example.

EXAMPLE 4–1: Suppose 330 of the 1000 patients in hospital$_0$ and 990 of the 1000 patients in hospital$_1$ have disease X. A patient is randomly selected from three hospitals including these two, and it is observed whether or not he is suffering from X. The experiment may be described as the observation of a random variable D which takes on value d_1 if X is present, d_2 if it is not. Let θ be the probability of disease X. h_0 hypothesizes that the patient is from hospital$_0$ (i.e., $\theta = 0.330$) h_1, that he is from hospital$_1$ (i.e., $\theta = 0.990$).
The following chart summarizes the likelihoods for this experiment:

	d_1	d_2
$L(h_1/d_i)$	0.990	0.010
$L(h_0/d_i)$	0.330	0.670

Since $r(d_1) = 3$ a likelihood test rejects h_0 and accepts h_1 at this level. Having observed d_1 the likelihood statistician tells us to consider h_1 3 times better supported than h_0. However, such a statement is of questionable relevance for interpreting the result, as we would be told to favor h_1 at this level 33% of the time when in fact h_1 was false. This information shows up in the standard statistician's report that the size of the test is 0.33. In this way the rejection is distinguishable from other rejections at this level but where the size is much smaller. The likelihoodist, on the other hand, has no way of distinguishing this rejection from any other one at the same level. For him, any consideration of the probability of making certain errors is wholly irrelevant.

4.1. *Relevant Information*

Different attitudes towards inference give rise to different ideas as to what counts as relevant information. If information is processed solely by way of relative likelihoods, then what leaves them intact cannot contain information relevant for inference. This is embodied in the *likelihood principle* (LP), a notion about which statisticians admit confusion. In one of its weakest forms, the likelihood principle asserts that if two pieces of data yield proportional likelihoods for some hypothesis h, then they should compel the same statistical inference concerning h. A stronger version of the likelihood principle instructs us to look *only* at the likelihood function of observed data.

184   DEBORAH MAYO

Both the likelihood and the Bayesian schools of inference subscribe to versions of this principle. Briefly, for a Bayesian, the LP follows from the fact that given a prior distribution, outcomes having proportional likelihood functions result in the same posterior — and inference is by the way of such posterior probabilities. As Savage explains:

The evidential meaning of any experimental outcome is fully characterized by the likelihood function determined by the observations, without further reference to the structure of the experiment [23, p. 17].

While the present discussion is not specifically directed toward Bayesian inference, our criticism of likelihood inference bears upon Bayesian inference schemes as well. The manner in which it does will be discussed in Section 6.

The LP has the effect of rendering irrelevant considerations as to how the data were generated; that is, *sampling procedures, stopping rules*, as well as considerations of reliability (size), precision (power) and other criteria of SM, for the following reason. Inference according to the LP is conditional on the *particular realization d*. Unlike the SM, *d* is *not* viewed as one of several possible realizations of a random variable *D* (at least not for the purposes of making inferences from *d*). What might have happened is felt to be irrelevant for reasoning on the basis of what did happen. The reason, according to one Bayesian, is that "considerations about samples that have *not* been observed, are simply not relevant to the problem of how we should reason from the one that has been observed" [13, p. 200].

So, on this view only the particular sample observed is relevant, not the entire sample space. Accordingly, the sampling distribution which assigns probabilities to elements of the sample space is deemed irrelevant for inference. But each of the standard criteria (e.g., size and power) for formulating and evaluating inferences is based on the sampling distribution. Hence for followers of the LP each of these criteria is irrelevant. Lindley, one of the foremost Bayesians encapsulates this in the following remark:

It is methods that are not based on the likelihood function that are suspect. In particular, unbiased estimates, minimum variance properties, sampling distributions, significance levels, power, all depend on something more — something that is irrelevant in Bayesian inference — namely the sample space [15, p. 436].

While followers of the LP criticize SM for considering the method of data collection relevant for inference, a follower of SM likewise considers the inability to take the sampling or data-generating method into account a fundamental weakness of the LP schools. Such criticisms do little more than express the fundamental disagreement between the rival accounts. What is wanted is an argument concerning the relevance of the sample space that does not simply presuppose the correctness of the favored inference philosophy. I shall attempt to provide such an argument from which I conclude that the sample space is relevant, and that considerations about what could have happened are relevant for reasoning about what did happen. This is particularly true if one is interested in prediction. The argument will proceed by showing that ignoring the sample space prevents any check on the frequency of errors. This leads to inferences which are incorrect with high probability — in extreme cases with probability one!

5. SPECIFICATION AFTER DATA (SAD) VS. SPECIFICATION BEFORE DATA (SBD)

If only likelihoods or ratios of likelihoods after the experiment are relevant, then such things as when one decides to stop sampling and when one designates the hypotheses to be tested are going to be irrelevant. The reason is that the likelihoods are not affected. Hence, calculation of the E–R measure, which in the case of Hacking is $r(d)$, is unaffected. For example, suppose the experiment is one of tossing coins in order to test a hypothesis about the probability that the coin lands heads. Consider two different plans for the production of data: (1) It is decided in advance to keep tossing until 6 heads are obtained and it happens to take exactly 100 tosses. (2) It is decided in advance to toss the coin 100 times and calculate the number of heads, and say the result is 6 heads. The likelihood of getting 6 heads, given that θ is the constant probability of heads, is, in case (1): $\binom{99}{94} \theta^6 (1 - \theta)^{94}$ and in case (2): $\binom{100}{6} \theta^6 (1 - \theta)^{94}$. Since these two likelihoods are proportional, a follower of the LP deems both experiments evidentially equivalent.[5]

In contrast, for SM both of these are quite different experiments. In the first case, prior to performing the experiment what is uncertain is the number of trials it will take to produce 6 heads. In the second case it is known that 100 trials are to be performed and what is unknown is the number of heads which will result. Since each case involves a different set of possible outcomes, each has a different probability distribution.[6] It follows that each case gives rise to a different probability of wrong inferences. As SM differentiates experiments by their associated error probabilities, it follows that it will have to distinguish between these two cases.

As long as the rule for stopping the production of data (i.e., the stopping rule) is deemed irrelevant, it is perfectly acceptable to continue taking

186   DEBORAH MAYO

observations until a desired likelihood value is obtained. Suppose the rule S for stopping an experiment is the following:

S: Sample until obtaining a d such that $L(h_0/d) \leqslant 1/c$

for a given simple hypothesis h_0 and for a positive and arbitrarily large value for c. That is, we can make $L(h_0/d)$ as small as we like using this stopping rule. Such an experiment will always, (with probability one) yield $L(h_0/d)$ $\leqslant 1/c$, and so h_0 is given less than or equal to $1/c$ degree of support. In this way, as little support as is desired (for any c value of a likelihood test) may be assigned to h_0 even when h_0 is actually true! S in effect says

Continue sampling until h_0 is rejectible at level c.

The problem with this example is that the experiment which was to determine the degree of support for h_0 has h_0's support value built in through the stopping rule. This is a kind of likelihood version of the Liar's Paradox, and there is nothing in the likelihood approach to exclude such cases.

Now S permits h_0 to be rejected at any level c by a likelihood test since it is required only that there be *some* alternative (simple) hypothesis h_1 which is c times as likely on the data (i.e., $r(d) \geqslant c$). To serve as this alternative one can always choose the hypothesis which has the greatest likelihood on the data. This alternative will be one which says in effect that precisely what was observed had to have been observed. In other words, it will state that the data d arose from a process that had to produce d.

For example, if data d is the result of a coin tossing experiment, alternative h_1 may be that the probability of heads was 1 just on those tosses that resulted in a head. Using rule S we have $L(h_0/d) \leqslant 1/c$. Then, since the likelihood of this alternative h_1 given the data d is equal to 1, $r(d)$ is greater than or equal to $1/(1/c)$ which is just c. Having found a rival hypothesis at least c times as likely on the data as h_0, the likelihood test instructs us to reject h_0 and accept this alternative. The likelihood approach permits this since the ratio of likelihoods does not register a difference between cases where the hypotheses to test are SAD or SBD. It is possible to prove that stopping rule S permits the eventual rejection of *any* simple hypothesis h at any desired c-ratio in this manner, even if it is true.

There are two basic points which this goes to show. First, even a high c-ratio fails to provide information about which of two rival hypotheses is true, since hypotheses may be rejected by likelihood tests of *any* stringency in favor of some false hypothesis SAD. Hence likelihood inference can offer no guarantees about the reliability of its inferences. The second point concerns

SM. By insisting upon SBD, SM is able to guarantee it will not be wrong too often. In SAD cases, the logic of SM breaks down and no such guarantees can be claimed for its inferences. The following example will illustrate this. Here, it is seen that by permitting hypotheses to be SAD the probability of a false rejection is greater than the fixed size — indeed, it is equal to one. While the type of population is unusual, it must be remembered that the standard guarantee of a certain error rate is to hold regardless of the underlying population. So, in particular it should hold for this population.[7]

EXAMPLE 5–1 Imagine a population of 6 objects labelled a, b, c, d, e, f, each of which may possess some or all of 7 logically independent properties. Then we can talk about the proportion θ_i of the population that have property i where i ranges from 1 to 7. Let $P_i a$ express the claim that 'a has property i'. The true state Λ of this population is as follows:

$$
\begin{aligned}
\Lambda = \; & P_1 a \;\&\; P_2 a \;\&\; P_3 a && P_2 d \;\&\; P_4 d \;\&\; P_5 d \;\&\; P_6 d \\
& P_1 b \;\&\; P_3 b \;\&\; P_4 b && P_2 e \;\&\; P_4 e \;\&\; P_5 e \;\&\; P_7 e \\
& P_1 c \;\&\; P_5 c \;\&\; P_6 c \;\&\; P_7 c && P_3 f \;\&\; P_6 f \;\&\; P_7 f
\end{aligned}
$$

Suppose Λ is unknown and on the basis of a random sample of size 2 an inference about some property i is to be made. What is interesting about this population is that for any of the 15 possible samples of size 2 at least one of the properties is shared by both members of the sample, while in fact the true value of $\theta_i = 1/2$ for all i.

Having randomly selected 2 members of this population a SAD procedure may be: select a property i shared by both members and test the claim $\theta_i = 1/2$. To see how permitting the hypothesis to be SAD in this manner conflicts with standard tests, imagine an entire series of such experiments are made. While in each case the population may differ, suppose they each have the peculiar property that Λ has (i.e., each pair shares a property while $\theta_i = 1/2$ for all i). In each case the property i whose population proportion (θ_i) will be tested is specified as one for which the sample proportion is 1. Then, in each case the data is employed for evaluating a hypothesis for which it constitutes the most *misleading* evidence! That is, the chosen property i is that for which the observed proportion (1) differs most from the population (true) proportion, θ_i (1/2).

In contrast, an analogous standard test of $\theta_i = 1/2$ is to select a random sample and observe D_i, the proportion possessing a property i, where i is SBD. The set of possible outcomes of this experiment is the set of possible observed proportions of a preset property i in the pair selected, namely $\{0, 1/2, 1\}$.

In the SAD experiment above the set of possible outcomes is the set of *properties* $i(i = 1, 2, \ldots, 7)$ which may have a frequency of 1 in the observed sample. That a different experiment is involved from the SBD case does not show up in a likelihood test which reports only that $\theta_i = 1/2$ is only 1/5 as strongly supported as $\theta_i = 1$ (where i is the property selected SAD). The difference does show up, however, in a measure of the reliability (i.e., size) of the test, as this is sensitive to the difference in the sample space.

In each standard test of $\theta_i = 1/2$ (for each of the i SBD) a critical region is specified of the form: $\{d_i: D_i \geqslant 1/2 + \delta\}$. δ is specified so that D_i falls into this region with a preset probability α. One can then calculate the number of such experiments needed in order to ensure $\delta < 1/2$. Then, regardless of the distribution of D_i, the test will not wrongly reject $\theta_i = 1/2$ more than $(100)\alpha\%$ of the time. (This follows from the fact that D_i is within δ of θ_i with probability $1 - \alpha$.)

However if the property to test were permitted to be SAD in the manner above, then, since D_i always equals 1, it always falls into the rejection region of the standard test. But since in fact the claim $\theta_i = 1/2$ is true for all i, one is lead to falsely reject it not with probability α but with probability 1! Hence, when the hypotheses are SAD as in Example 5–1, the standard test can no longer uphold its guarantees of reliability. More generally, whenever the tested property depends on the statistical features of the sample, a series of experiments can be constructed where the probability of incorrect inferences differs from a preset probability. In the analogous standard experiments the preset error rate is guaranteed for all underlying universes, and hence also for these specially constructed cases. This establishes the inconsistency between SM and theories which permit SAD procedures.

In light of our results we must reject as untenable the following claim by Hacking which he puts forward as an 'obvious fact':

> If one hypothesis is better supported than another, it would usually be, I believe, right to call it the more reasonable [11, p. 28].

Although intuitively being well-supported seems like a desirable property for inferences to have, Hacking's notion of support does not embody our intuitive conception. For him, 'better supported' is equivalent to "more likely", but the best supported hypotheses SAD are generally false, and hence unreasonable. Even when dealing with two hypotheses neither of which is precisely true, the best supported hypothesis may not be the more reasonable.

For instance, it may be that a great deal of information about the underlying mechanism relating two quantities X and Y renders the hypothesis that

Y is some simple function of X correct within some small margin of error. Still, some other absurdly complex hypothesis may be more likely on the data although it contradicts theoretical background knowledge and as such is unreasonable. By advocating the acceptance of the hypothesis with the greatest likelihood on the data (or in general with the greatest E–R measure) one is advocating the most *ad hoc* hypothesis – that is, the one that differs least from the data. This is tantamount to suggesting that one not work with hypotheses at all but only with data!

But then what we have seems more useful for describing the data than for explaining it or for deriving predictions from it. If scientific models are to be used for predictions and explanations of phenomena as opposed to mere descriptions, then more than the specific data obtained must be taken into consideration. As a means of incorporating background information some likelihood theorists such as Edwards [4] make use of prior supports. The *Bayesians* make use of prior probabilities.

6. REMARKS ON BAYESIAN INFERENCE

It may be claimed that a follower of the Bayesian school of inference is not open to the kind of problems that SAD procedures pose for likelihoodists. Although both of these non-standard schools agree that likelihood functions exhaust the information from the experiment, the Bayesian also makes inferences dependent on something else; namely the *prior distribution* of the hypothesis. Without presenting the full theory of Bayesian testing, I shall now remark on how the problem of SAD bears upon Bayesian inference.

Bayesian inference proceeds by contemplating a (complete) set of hypotheses h_i, ... h_k and using the sample data to obtain the probability of h_i conditional on this data by way of *Bayes Theorem*. The theorem states:

$$P(h_i/d) = \frac{P(d/h_i)P(h_i)}{\sum\limits_{j=0}^{k} p(d/h_j)p(h_j)} \quad (i = 0, \ldots k).$$

It is seen that in order to calculate $P(h_i/d)$ one is required to have the values of $p(h_i)$ for all i. These are called the *prior probabilities*. The $p(h_i/d)$ are called the *posterior probabilities* – the basic E–R measure for Bayesians. One may use this measure to simply reject h_i if $P(h_i/d)$ is too small or to calculate a more elaborate test incorporating loses.[8]

The major controversy between Bayesians and non-Bayesians is not over the validity of this mathematically sound theorem, but over the use of prior probabilities of hypotheses. SM considers that the only sorts of things which have probabilities are events, such as the outcome 'heads' or '$D \geqslant d$'. SM does not assign probabilities to things considered fixed such as (i) random variables once their value has been observed, and (ii) hypotheses deemed either true or false and not able to be seen as the result of a probability experiment. When hypotheses can be construed as the result of a probability experiment, the relevant parameter θ may be construed as a random variable in contrast to its usual construal as a *fixed* value. In such cases, the standard methodologist has no qualms in applying Bayes Theorem.

An example of such a case is provided by Example 4–1. Suppose we have the additional information that all of the 1000 patients in the third hospital, hospital$_2$ have X. Hence $P(d_1/h_2) = L(h_2/d_1) = 1$, letting h_2 assert that the patient is from hospital$_2$ (i.e., $\theta = 1$). Then since there is an equal chance that the patient is from each of the 3 hospitals, θ may be viewed as a random variable taking on values 0.33, 0.99 and 1 with equal probability. Hence the priors $P(h_0) = P(h_1) = P(h_2) = 1/3$. Having observed d_1 the posterior $P(h_1/d_1)$ can be calculated using Bayes Theorem to be 0.43.

Typically, however, the hypothesis cannot be seen as the result of a probability experiment. Then the question as to what the prior probabilities mean and how they are to be obtained arises. The (subjective) Bayesian[9] sees the priors as measures of *degrees-of-belief* in hypotheses (in contrast to frequencies of occurrence of events). They are obtained by introspection or by cleverly considering how one would act in a series of bets. Lacking information about any of the hypotheses results in each being assigned an equal (or uniform) prior probability. This is known as the *principle of indifference*. Suppose in Example 4–1 one was not given the information that the patient was randomly selected from one of the three hospitals. Then, by virtue of one's ignorance, the 3 hypotheses would receive equal prior probability and the posterior $p(h_1/d_1)$ would still be 0.43. However, simply reporting this posterior (as a Bayesian would do) does not distinguish between the case where some random mechanism rendered the 3 hypotheses equiprobable and the case where one's ignorance does.

With respect to the problem of SAD two sorts of issues arise:

(1) *Priors SAD.* The Bayesian may argue that the sort of hypotheses SAD that result in objectionable inferences would be assigned a sufficiently small prior as to offset the high likelihood of h given d. But certainly there is no guarantee that all or even any Bayesian will happen to have a sufficiently low degree of belief in a hypothesis that happens to yield an objectionable

TESTING STATISTICAL TESTING   191

inference. Its objectionableness stems from the underlying population which presumably is unknown. This seems particularly true if priors are SAD and hence assigned (perhaps for several hypotheses) without knowing which the researcher plans to select, or for that matter, when. So while the Bayesian might avoid a high posterior in what turns out to be a false hypothesis SAD, it will be a matter of luck, and the Bayesian theory does not provide any means for distinguishing the lucky cases from the unlucky ones. The reason is that only the posterior is reported and not the prior nor the means by which the hypotheses, the data or the prior were generated.

In addition, there is nothing in the Bayesian philosophy itself to prevent the priors themselves from being SAD. The only principle is *coherency*, that is, not contradicting the probability axioms. It may be that if a Bayesian experimenter had been asked before the experiment for his prior probability for the claim: "all members of a random sample have a property *i*", that it would be quite low. However, once the experiment reveals a sample in which each element has the property *i*, he is likely to set his prior higher than he would have before the experiment. Then, the resulting posterior would be higher than if the prior were selected BD. Hence, if experimenting on the sort of population in Example 5–1, and both the hypotheses and the priors are SAD, the Bayesian continually assigns high posterior probabilities to false hypotheses.

It may be argued that one's prior degree of belief must always be SBD, but there seems to be nothing incoherent in having them be SAD. Indeed, there appears to be at least some cases in which Bayesians positively require that priors be SAD, such as when a subsequent observation indicates the prior is incorrect. As Lindley states, "Thus, if a prior leads to an unacceptable posterior then I modify it to cohere with properties that seem desirable in the inference" [15, p. 436]. However, Savage [23, p. 165] considers that a Bayesian who sets his prior AD on the basis of the very data which suggested the hypothesis is "in psychological danger of using the data twice." But it is still not clear that there are any strictly Bayesian grounds for ruling out double counting of data. (In the Lindley case it seems to be permitted.) In contrast, SM rules out such double use of data on the grounds that the probability of incorrect inferences is affected, as we have seen. But for a Bayesian any such consideration of error rates is irrelevant; his only official requirement is that one's total set of beliefs be coherent.

(2) *Hypotheses SAD*. Even if it is required that priors be SAD the Bayesian still appears to be open to the difficulties we have discussed concerning hypotheses SAD. Let us return to Example 5–1. Suppose that prior to the

experiment a Bayesian gives his priors for each property i for the claim: k out of the six have property i for $k = 0, 1, \ldots 6$. Suppose he has no information on the matter or for some other reason holds an equal degree of belief in each of the seven hypotheses for each i. (This could also be done using a continuous uniform prior.) As before, suppose it is decided to investigate claims about a property i shared by both members of a random sample selected from the six. The data d, the observed proportion having i is always (by the way i is selected) equal to 1. Having selected a sample, the Bayesian calculates the posteriors for the hypotheses about θ_i (the proportion that have property i), given $d = 1$.

For each i we have, $P(\theta_i = \frac{1}{2}/d) = 0.08$ and summing over the relevant hypotheses, $P(\theta_i > \frac{1}{2}/d) = 0.88$. So in each experiment the degree of belief assigned to H_i: $\theta_i > 1/2$ is 0.88. By repeating this type of experiment it is possible to evaluate hypothesis G_i: $P(\theta_i > 1/2) = 0.88$. If a sufficient number of repetitions are made, one's degree of belief in G_i continually increases towards one. This leads one to believe that in 88% of the experiments $\theta_i > 1/2$. In fact, however in 0 and not in 88% of the experiments is $\theta_i > 1/2$ (since $\theta_i = 1/2$). Thus one would be wrong about H_i many more times than expected.

It should be pointed out that less bizarre populations lead to the same sort of problem when hypotheses are SAD in the manner of Example 5–1, but with less dramatic results. Also, the above example may be elaborated upon to include utilities and thus bring it more in line with the typical type of Bayesian test.

I conclude that Bayesians, just as likelihoodists, should add to their philosophy some means for checking the rate of error or reliability of their inferences. Once reliability is seen to be relevant not only does the manner of data and hypotheses generation become relevant, but the manner of specification of priors as well.[10] Then each of these would have to be reported as information relevant to comprehending the experiment. If I am right, then this would have at least two undesirable consequences for the Bayesian philosophy. First, the Bayesian theory would forfeit one of its most attractive features: that of being a neat, simple, global account. Second, it would mean denying that a single probabilistic E–R measure, namely, the posterior distribution, is adequate for communicating all the relevant evidence for inference. This is to reject the LP. More specifically, to admit that the behavior of the E–R measure over different experiments is relevant, is to admit that not just the particular result of the particular experiment is relevant. In short, the one thing that the Bayesians insist is irrelevant (see p. 184) is admitted to be relevant, namely the sample space. This would seem to bring them closer to SM than most Bayesians would like.[11] However, I do not see how the Bayesian theory as it is presently formulated can provide means for testing the correctness of its tests.

I conclude that any purely formal attempt to relate data and hypotheses is inadequate. Behind such attempts seems to be the supposition that any *objective* inference scheme should lead from the same data and hypothesis to the same conclusion for any experimenter. This is precisely how the likelihood principle follows and with it the irrelevance of the data generation and order of hypotheses specification. From the standpoint of the formal quantitative E—R measure, it *is* irrelevant whether a hypothesis is SAD or SBD. It is not irrelevant, however, from the point of view of wanting hypotheses and theories that are at least approximately true and predictively reliable (to say nothing of interesting and informative).[12]

It should be pointed out that it is not that SBD methods are always more reliable than SAD ones. By formulating a suitable population it can be shown that the opposite is the case for that population. The real problem with SAD procedures, as I see it, is that whether or not they yield valid results is dependent upon which of the unknown hypotheses is true about the phenomena of interest. Hence a particular application of an SAD method cannot be identified as one of the cases resulting in a higher or a lower number of correct inferences. In contrast, by requiring SBD, SM can ensure a certain rate of error will not be exceeded regardless of which hypothesis is true. To my mind, it is this ability to guarantee validity that lies at the heart of an objective inference philosophy. This contrasts with E—R approaches which hold that objectivity is embodied in the requirement that the same data and hypothesis lead to the same conclusion.

7. VALIDATING THE EXPERIMENTAL MODEL

Even if the relevance of reliability and precision is granted, SM may be criticized as not being able actually to provide these guarantees. The standard test starts out with the assumption that we are observing a random variable that has a particular distribution and it remains only to determine the value of one of its parameters. But how do we know it actually has this distribution? The guarantees of reliability and precision hold only if the test statistic really has the assumed distribution, at least approximately.

This problem of validating the experimental model is shared by standard as well as non-standard philosophies. The likelihood function contains the relevant information from the data given a correctly specified statistical model, it does not contain all the information concerning the validity of this assumption. A separate test of the correctness of the underlying model is needed, ideally carried out before using it in a test based upon it.

Hacking admits [11, p. 222] that his theory is unable to test the underlying model. It cannot test claims before the data is in, nor can it test single hypotheses without alternatives. For a Bayesian to test whether an underlying model holds he is required to have a complete set of alternative hypotheses about how the model could fail as well as the necessary priors. It seems too much to require such detailed information be available at a stage where one is simply interested in whether a model is good enough to base an experiment upon.

Although the NP tests also involve alternative hypotheses, SM (despite what some people seem to think) does not consist solely of NP tests. Standard tests (e.g., Fisherian Significance Tests) are available to assess the 'goodness-of-fit' of a single hypothesis with data. Even NP tests do not require the specification of an alternative in order to run the test, but only to evaluate its power. As such, non-standard theorists may first find it useful to run certain standard tests in order to obtain reasonable alternatives as well as to explore with what sort of claims seem worth experimenting further. In addition to affording SM a means for building as opposed to only evaluating models, these single-hypothesis tests provide a means for testing the underlying model.

However, this seems to present a difficulty for SM. In order to test whether data follow a certain distribution one appears to be involved in testing a hypothesis based on the very data to be used in the test. But such hypotheses SAD were shown to prevent the guarantees of reliability. So it appears that in order to guarantee reliability (by validating the underlying model) the SM is required to carry out a procedure which precludes any such guarantees! Then, NP testing, which requires everything to be SBD, appears to be open to the following criticism by Rosenkrantz:

Neyman–Pearson theory implies that data provide no support for an hypothesis suggested by those same data and not thought of or specified in advance. But matters become awkward when the hypothesis in question specifies one of the many ways in which the underlying model of the experiment could fail. For then we find ourselves forced to accept the conclusions erroneously based on that experiment merely because it was not designed to test the pertinent assumption of the underlying model! [22, p. 319].

According to Rosenkrantz, then, if a standard methodologist has run a coin-tossing experiment where it was assumed the tosses were independent, the aim being to test some value for the probability of heads, and then the data makes him question whether the tosses were really independent after all, he cannot take this into account in assessing the conclusion from the experiment. I will argue that he is not at all forced to do this, and that he can test the claim "the tosses are independent" after looking at the data without being guilty of an illegitimate SAD. Nor are additional coin tosses needed.

The data from the experiment designed to test 'P (heads) $= p$' may be *remodelled* in order to serve as data for testing 'the tosses are independent'. In the first experiment the possible data may be the different possible proportions of heads in n tosses, and there are $n + 1$ of these. The random variable D in this experiment is the proportion of successes, the order of occurrence being irrelevant. In the second test for independence, the number of successes d would now be regarded as fixed and the different data sets would be the different orders in which this number of successes might have occurred. (This is of relevance even if it is already known which one actually occurred.) There are $\binom{n}{d}$ such data sets.

Then, the significance test one might carry out is one based on the number of runs of heads (i.e., the number of consecutive 'heads') called a *runs test*. What is relevant for our purposes is that the data used for the test of the probability of heads is distinct from the data used in the subsequent test of independence. Hence, no illegitimate double-use of data is required.

A follower of SM need not insist that data never be used to test a hypothesis suggested by the same data in any scientific problem. He insists only that if the hypothesis is SAD one not use a procedure appropriate only for hypotheses SBD — at least not if one wants the associated claims about the errors of the inference to be valid.

Having argued that SAD should be avoided in order to guarantee reliability and precision of inferences, I am not claiming that any test with good 'error characteristics' (e.g., low size and high power) is a good test. Nor do I think that reporting the result of a test ('accept' or 'reject') even together with a description of the experiment and the two error probabilities is sufficient for correctly interpreting statistical tests. SM is also in need of additional extra-statistical principles both to specify and interpret tests — something which it has been reluctant to provide, at least explicitly. In what follows I shall merely sketch the sort of supplements I have in mind. They are set out in more detail in [17].

8. THE RATIONALE OF TESTING

Much of the confusion and controversy concerning statistical methodologies stems from the fact that the formalism in which they are presented has little

bearing on how they are actually used to make informative scientific inferences. Neyman—Pearson tests are presented as a kind of recipe for making
'optimal' inferences. One simply fixes the size α of a test, finds the most
powerful test having a given size and then accepts or rejects. If asked why
anyone should find it desirable to do this the rationale given by Neyman (see
[21]) is this: If one 'behaves' in this way one will incorrectly reject h_0 not
more than 100α percent of the time and incorrectly accept h_0 not more than
100β percent of the time, (for α, β the probabilities of type I and type II
errors respectively).

However, Neyman's rationale may be criticized. Tests which are 'best' on
the standard criteria need not really be best.[13] One need not look further
than a simple coin-tossing experiment to find an example of such a test.

EXAMPLE 8–1: Test whether θ the probability of heads is $0.35(h_0)$ or
$0.10(h_1)$ by tossing a coin 4 times, and observing D, the proportion of heads.
Letting $d_i = i/4$, $i = 0, \ldots 4$, $d_0 - d_4$ are the five possible proportions. The
size α is set at 0.18. The likelihoods are as follows:

	d_0	d_1	d_2	d_3	d_4
$L(h_0/d_i)$	0.17	0.38	0.31	0.11	0.01
$L(h_1/d_i)$	0.65	0.29	0.04	0.003	0.001

The most powerful test of size 0.18 is test T_1 which instructs one to reject
h_0 iff d_0 or d_4 occurs. Yet if d_4 occurs (i.e., all heads) T_1 rejects $\theta = 0.35$
and accepts $\theta = 0.10$ although d_4 clearly makes the former more plausible.

A less powerful, but intuitively more satisfactory test is T_2 which rejects
h_0 iff d_0 occurs. However, to select text T_2 upon seeing it is more sensible
than T_1 is not strictly to follow NP test criteria. (While the size of T_2 is
slightly less than for T_1, T_1's greater power renders T_1 the best test of its
size.)

T_2 is a more sensible test as it is based on a more sensible test statistic,
namely one which measures the discrepancy between the observed proportion
d and the proportion hypothesized by h_0 (i.e., 0.35). A plausible basis for
choosing this discrepancy measure is that of (Euclidean) *distance*. Letting
$T(D)$ be $D - 0.35$ it is seen that only d_0 yields a value of $T(D)$ less than -0.1.
Hence test T_2 is equivalent to the rule: reject h_0 iff $T(D) < -0.1$ for $T(D)$ as
defined. This test statistic provides a plausible ranking of the observations in
order of how discrepant they are from h_0 (in the direction of h_1).

What I am claiming is that while tests with good error characteristics may coincide with good (or even best) tests, the error values are not themselves the reason for the test's goodness. It is only when the error rates are associated with a reasonable test statistic — one that is some sort of a measure of discrepancy — that good tests result. It is not low error rates in the long run that justify tests, since as critics of SM point out, one can do well in the long run but terribly in a particular case. Yet the rationale for NP tests according to Neyman is long run error rates alone. I would argue that the value of error rates is that combined with sensible test statistics they help ensure that the test will reject hypotheses just in case the data indicates the existence of a discrepancy from the null. One does this by ensuring that an extreme value of a test statistic (one leading to a rejection) be associated with a discrepancy of desired size.

Hence, the importance of being able to guarantee the reliability and precision (size and power) of an inference independently of unknown parameter values and of priors is not directly a concern with how often one will be right. Rather, the importance stems from a desire to guarantee that *this* test is picking up all and only discrepancies of a certain size. Ideally the discrepancies being detected will be of non-negligible size. However, even if this is not the case, the standard test need not yield faulty inferences as long as it is possible to ascertain after the experiment what sort of discrepancies were being detected. This is possible by guaranteeing that preset levels of reliability and precision are met. We have seen how SAD procedures permit actual error rates to differ greatly from preset ones. This has the effect of permitting the test to detect discrepancies of a size different from the intended one. Hence, from the present point of view SAD is objectionable in that it prevents one from objectively determining the type of discrepancy a test detects. In contrast, SM does permit such an objective determination and it would be desirable to report in addition to the reliability and precision, the type of discrepancies detected.

Standard tests are often criticized because with a large enough sample one can ensure reaching any designated size and power in rejecting a null hypothesis. This is because as sample size increases the standard deviation of the statistic observed decreases, being inversely proportional to the sample size. Hence, with a large enough sample, even a highly statistically significant difference may reflect a tiny discrepancy from the null. This leads to faulty inferences because typically statistical inferences are not distinguished from the subsequent scientific inferences based upon them. Upon distinguishing these two inferences one does not automatically interpret a rejection of a statistical hypothesis as the rejection of a substantive scientific hypothesis.

Tests should be supplemented with rules for interpreting the scientific or substantive significance of statistically significant results. What I have in mind may be illustrated by referring back to Example 3–1.

This test is a 'best' test for the given size 0.03 and it has extremely high power, practically one. Still, the question arises as to what information this test is providing. The following graphs indicate the relationship between the size and power of the tests:

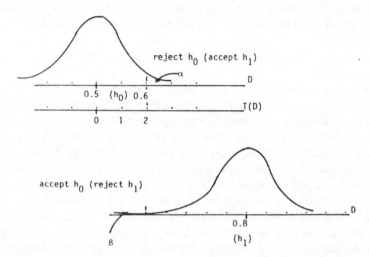

Since β is practically zero and is many times smaller than α, the test is sensitive to relatively small departures (in the direction of h_1) from h_0, and insensitive to large departures from h_1 (in the direction of h_0). In order to correctly test what information the test is providing one may calculate what I shall call the *effective discrepancy*. This is the size of the discrepancy that the test, in effect, is detecting. To obtain it one calculates for what alternative hypothesis the test would have the same probability of making a type I as it would a type II error. In this case it is approximately $\theta = 0.69$. This means that observations which typically arise given that $\theta = 0.69$ are taken as rejecting $\theta = 0.5$ and accepting $\theta = 0.8$ which may or may not be a desirable thing to do. The point is, instead of merely reporting the null was rejected, by a test with such and such size and power, the effective discrepancy should be reported. (A report of the sample size provides enough information together with the size and power to calculate the effective discrepancy but it is not itself as illuminating.)

TESTING STATISTICAL TESTING 199

Another way of correctly assessing the results of a test is to calculate the appropriate number of observations for which the test in question would be a fair one between the two given hypotheses. By a fair test I mean one where $\alpha = \beta$. In this case, had the sample size been only 35, the test would have been a fair test between $\theta = 0.5$ and $\theta = 0.8$. Hence, rejecting a test with this size and power given it had only 35 observations is actually more significant than rejecting it at this level with the 100 observations. This may seem counter-intuitive. Indeed, researchers typically believe that a rejection based on a larger sample size is more significant than one based on a smaller one. The reason stems from the fact that more instances of something is taken to provide more evidence. SM is sometimes criticized for seeming to go against this scientific principle, but in fact it does not do so. More instances do provide better evidence, but in adding to the sample size one is not adding instances but rather changing what counts as a *single* instance (e.g., the proportion of heads out of 35 as opposed to out of 100 tosses).

Having found the appropriate sample size to be smaller than the size of the sample actually made, should one simply throw out the extra data that is already available? No, the purpose of calculating the appropriate sample size even after the experiment is in order to comprehend the significance of the results obtained. By noting that the appropriate sample size is much smaller than the actual one it is seen that the test is detecting discrepancies which may be of negligible substantive importance. It is not part of the statistical test to decide what counts as a non-negligible discrepancy, but I do think it should provide the means for ascertaining the sort of discrepancy detected for two reasons: (1) for the sake of designing tests that detect discrepancies one is interested in and (2) for correctly evaluating the substantive significance of a test already made.

In other words, determining the effective discrepancy or the appropriate sample size provides a means for testing the appropriatness of statistical tests. In interpreting an inference one can argue that through inappropriate test specifications the test is rendered either too sensitive or too insensitive. However, even inferences based on tests with inappropriate sensitivity need not be illegitimate. If, for example, the test in Example 3–1 yields an inference not to reject h_0, the inference would be considered sound. The reason is that no discrepancy was detected by a test that had an abundance of power to detect relatively minor discrepancies. In general, if the sample size is so large as to discriminate an alternative closer to the test hypothesis than one that is scientifically interesting, and yet the null hypothesis is not rejected, the inference is sound (barring any other inadmissible moves). That is,

> If a test with an overabundance of power to detect a discrepancy fails to do so, then the conclusion is sound.

Similarly, if a sample size that is small relative to the appropriate sample size is used, and the test hypothesis is rejected in favor of the alternative, then the inference appears sound. That is,

> If a test which could not reasonably be expected to detect a discrepancy does detect one, then its conclusion is sound.

Under any other circumstances, however, inferences based on tests with incorrect sensitivities provide reason to question the relevance of the result. If an inference is based on a test with too many observations (relative to a balance between α, β and the alternative hypothesis) and the null is rejected, the reason for the rejection may be a trivial perturbation of the experiment. It may be the result of no real difference at all, or of one that is scientifically insignificant.

By viewing tests as tools for detecting discrepancies one is also lead to design tests with a view to having them detect all and only discrepancies of a certain size. It is up to the scientist to specify the kind of discrepancies about which he considers worth knowing. It is up to the test to detect all and only the sort of discrepancies it is commanded to detect. The value of the standard tests, I have argued, is that if used correctly they may be seen to function in this way. In short, they may be seen to provide objective standards for measuring discrepancies.

9. CONCLUSION

Our conclusion about what counts as a good test differs markedly from Hacking who claims

A good test for any hypothesis, statistical or otherwise, is one which rejects it only if another hypothesis is much better supported [11, p. 109].

We have seen that one can always find a hypothesis better supported in this sense (i.e., more likely) by selecting the most *ad hoc* hypothesis SAD. Instead, a good test for a statistical hypothesis is one which rarely fails to find a discrepancy of a given size (i.e., rarely accepts a hypothesis) unless no non-trivial discrepancy exists, and rarely finds a discrepancy of a given size (i.e., rarely rejects a hypothesis) unless a non-trivial discrepancy exists.

The reason for banning illegitimate SAD procedures is to guarantee claims about reliability and precision — but these are not ends in themselves, at least not in a scientific context. Their importance stems from a desire to check that a test is doing what it is supposed to be doing — that is, detecting discrepancies of a certain size. It provides a way of testing the validity of the test. Without such a means for testing statistical testing tests fail to be objective and to link up with truth.

Virginia Polytechnic Institute and State University

NOTES

* I am very grateful to I. J. Good and Joseph Pitt for useful comments on earlier versions of this paper, and to George Shapiro for mathematical advice.
[1] The most complete inference theory in this category is the one proposed by Carnap [3] and extended by his followers, most notably, Hintikka.
[2] I shall here omit consideration of cases where more than one unknown parameter exists.
[3] The standard deviation of D, σ_D is the square root of the average deviation (or *variance*) of D from its mean θ. The variance of D, σ_D^2 is

$$\sum_i (d_i - \theta)^2 \, P(D = d_i)$$

for D a discrete random variable with values d_i. (In the continuous case the summation is replaced by an integral.)
[4] This experiment may be modeled binomially provided that each toss (i) can yield only one of two results (heads, tails), (ii) is independent, (iii) has the same probability θ of landing heads.

The probability of getting k heads out of n tosses (i.e., $D = k/n$) is

$$\binom{n}{k} \theta^k (1 - \theta)^{n-k}$$

The standard deviation of D,

$$\sigma_D = \sqrt{\theta(1 - \theta)} / n$$

[5] That is, the likelihoodist considers the decision as to when to stop sampling irrelevant. This is referred to as the *irrelevance of optional stopping*.
[6] In case (1) the distribution is the *negative binominal* in case (2) it is the *binomial*.
[7] Populations of this sort are discussed more generally in [6] to make a similar point but concerning Bayesian estimation.
[8] In testing h_0: $\theta = \theta_0$ vs h_1: $\theta = \theta_1$ where the priors $p(h_0)$, $p(h_1)$ are given and a, b are the losses associated with a mistaken rejection and a mistaken acceptance of h_0 respectively, the Bayes test is to reject h_0 iff

$$\frac{a p(d/h_0) p(h_0)}{b p(d/h_1) p(h_1)} < 1$$

202   DEBORAH MAYO

given data *d*. Given any Neyman—Pearson test one can find losses and priors that make it equivalent to a Bayes test.

[9] While there are those who call themselves objective, or empirical Bayesians, I will here understand Bayesian to mean subjective Bayesian.

[10] In reporting the manner in which priors were specified it is not only relevant to report whether they were SAD or SBD. It is also relevant to the reliability of the result to know whether the priors have resulted from an experiment or from a prior degree of belief without an experiment. The former case appears more reliable.

[11] Possible exceptions would be those willing to hold a Bayesian philosophy which compromises between standard and non-standard views, most notably I. J. Good.

[12] Bayesians often admit that their philosophy is not about truth but simply provides a theory for personal decision making. As Lindley puts it, "The Bayesian Theory is about *coherence*, not about right or wrong" [16, p. 359].

[13] In criticizing Neyman's rationale Hacking [11, p. 96] gives an example of a test which is 'better' than some other test on NP criteria but which is clearly not better once the data is in. However this test is not the 'best' NP test and hence would not be recommended by the NP theory. As such his criticism does not present a problem for the NP theory. The example I present (Example 8—1) does.

                              REFERENCES

[1] Barnard, G. A., 'The logic of statistical inference', *British Journal of the Philosophy of Science* **23** (1972), 123—190.

[2] Carnap, R., *Logical Foundations of Probability*, 2nd edition, University of Chicago Press, Chicago, 1962.

[3] Cunnyngham, J., 'Econometric model construction and predictive testing', in *Problems and Issues in Current Econometric Practice*. Ed. K. Brunner, The Ohio State University, Ohio, 1972, pp. 238—261.

[4] Edwards, A. W. F., *Likelihood*, Cambridge University Press, Cambridge, 1972.

[5] Fisher, R. A., *Statistical Methods and Scientific Inference*, 2nd edition, Oliver and Boyd, Edinburgh, 1959.

[6] Giere, R. N., 'Bayesian statistics and biased procedures', *Synthese* **20** (1969), 371—387.

[7] Godambe, V. P., and Sprott, D. A. (eds.), *Foundations of Statistical Inference*, Holt, Rinehart and Winston of Canada, Toronto, 1971.

[8] Good, I. J., 'Probability or Support?', *Nature* **213** (1967), No. 5073, 233—234.

[9] Good, I. J., 'The Bayesian influence, or how to sweep subjectivism under the carpet', in [12], pp. 125—174.

[10] Goodman, N., *Fact, Fiction, and Forecast*, The Bobbs Merrill Company, Inc., New York, 1965.

[11] Hacking, I., *Logic of Statistical Inference*, Cambridge University Press, Cambridge, 1965.

[12] Harper, W. L., and Hooker, C. A. (eds.), *Foundations of Probability Theory, Statistical Inference, and Statistical Theories of Science*, Vol. II, D. Reidel Publishing Co., Holland, 1976.

[13] Jaynes, E. T., 'Confidence intervals vs Bayesian intervals', in [12], pp. 175—213.

TESTING STATISTICAL TESTING   203

[14] Lieberman, Bernhardt (ed.), *Contemporary Problems in Statistics*, Oxford University Press, New York, 1971.

[15] Lindley, D. V., 'The estimation of many parameters', in [7], pp. 435–447.

[16] Lindley, D. V., 'Bayesian statistics', in [12], pp. 353–362.

[17] Mayo, D., *Philosophy of Statistics*, Doctoral dissertation, University of Pennsylvania, 1979.

[18] Mood, A. M., Graybill, F. A., and Boes, D. C., *Introduction to the Theory of Statistics*, 3rd edition, McGraw-Hill, Inc., New York, 1963.

[19] Morrison, D. E. and Henkel, R. E. (eds.), *The Significance Test Controversy – A Reader*, Aldine Publishing Company, Chicago, 1970.

[20] Neyman, J., *First Course in Probability and Statistics*, Henry Holt, New York, 1950.

[21] Neyman, J. and Pearson, E. S., 'On the problem of the most efficient tests of statistical hypotheses', *Philosophical Transactions of the Royal Society* A231 (1933), 289–337.

[22] Rosenkrantz, R., 'The significance test controversy', *Synthese* 26 (1973), 304–321.

[23] Savage, L. J., *The Foundations of Statistics*, Wiley and Sons, Inc., New York, 1954.

[5]

THREE ECONOMETRIC METHODOLOGIES: A CRITICAL APPRAISAL [1]

Adrian Pagan

University of Rochester

Abstract. Three econometric methodologies, associated respectively with David Hendry, Christopher Sims and Edward Leamer have been advocated and practiced by their adherents in recent years. A number of good papers have appeared about each methodology, but little has been written in a comparative vein. This paper is concerned with that task. It provides a statement of the main steps to be followed in using each of the methodologies and comments upon the strengths and weaknesses of each approach. An attempt is made to contrast and compare the techniques used, the information provided, and the questions addressed by each of the methodologies. It is hoped that such a comparison will aid researchers in choosing the best way to examine their particular problem.

Keywords. Econometric methodologies; Hendry; Sims; Leamer; extreme bounds analysis; vector autoregressions; dynamic specification.

ι.ιethodological debate in economics is almost as long-standing as the discipline itself. Probably the first important piece was written by John Stuart Mill (1967), and his conclusions seem as pertinent today as when they were written in the 19th century. He observed that many practitioners of political economy actually held faulty conceptions of what their science covered and the methods used. At the same time he emphasized that, in many instances, it was easier to practice a science than to describe how one was doing it. He finally concluded that a better understanding of scope and method would facilitate the progress of economics as a science, but that sound methodology was *not* a necessary condition for the practice of sound methods. 'Get on with the job' seems the appropriate message.

It is interesting that it was not until the 5th World Congress of the Econometric Society in 1985 that a session was devoted to methodological issues. There are good reasons for this. Until the mid-1970's it would have been difficult to find a comprehensive statement of the principles guiding econometric research, and it is hard to escape the conclusion that econometricians had taken to Mill's injunction with a vengeance. Even the debate between 'frequentists' and 'subjectivists' that prevailed in statistics was much more muted in econometrics. It is true that there was a vigorous attempt to convert econometricians to a Bayesian approach by Zellner (1971) and the 'Belgian connection' at CORE (see Drèze and Richard, 1983). But this attempt did not seem to have a great impact upon applied research.

All of this changed after 1975. Causes are always harder to isolate than effects,

0950-0804/87/01 0003-22 $02.50/0
JOURNAL OF ECONOMIC SURVEYS Vol.1, No.1

4   PAGAN

but it is difficult to escape the impression that the proximate cause was the predictive failure of large-scale models just when they were most needed. In retrospect it seems likely that the gunpowder had been there for some time, and that these events just set it off. Most, for example, will know Ed Leamer's (1978, p. vi) account of his dissatisfaction with the gap between what he had been taught in books and the way practitioners acted, and it seems likely that many others had felt the same way about the type of econometrics then prevalent. But these misgivings were unlikely to have any impact until there was evidence that there was something to complain about.

Since 1975 we have seen a concerted attempt by a number of authors to build methodologies for econometric analysis. Implicit in these actions has been the notion that work along the prescribed lines would 'better' econometrics in at least three ways. First, the methodology would (and should) provide a set of principles to guide work *in all its facets*. Second, by codifying this body of knowledge it should greatly facilitate the transmission of such knowledge. Finally, a style of reporting should naturally arise from the methodology that is informative, succinct and readily understood.

In this paper we look at the current state of the debate over methodology. Three major contenders for the 'best methodology' title may be distinguished. I will refer to these as the 'Hendry', 'Leamer' and 'Sims' methodologies, after those individuals most closely *identified* with the approach. Generally, each procedure has its origins a good deal further back in time, and is the outcome of a research programme that has had many contributors apart from the named authors above. But the references—Hendry and Richard (1982), Leamer (1978) and Sims (1980a)—are the most accessible and succinct summaries of the material, and therefore it seems appropriate to use the chosen appellations. Inevitably, there has been some convergence in the views, but it will be most useful to present them in polar fashion, so as to isolate their distinct features.

1. The 'Hendry' methodology

Perhaps the closest of all the methods to the 'old style' of investigation is the 'Hendry' methodology. It owes a lot to Sargan's seminal (1964) paper, but it also reflects an oral tradition developed largely at the London School of Economics over the past two decades. Essentially it comprises four 'steps'.

(i)   Formulate a general model that is consistent with what economic theory postulates are the variables entering any equilibrium relationship and which restricts the dynamics of the process as little as possible.

(ii)   Re-parameterize the model to obtain explanatory variables that are near orthogonal and which are 'interpretable' in terms of the final equilibrium.

(iii) Simplify the model to the smallest version that is compatible with the data ('congruent').

(iv) Evaluate the resulting model by extensive analysis of residuals and predictive performance, aiming to find the weaknesses of the model designed in the previous step.

THREE ECONOMETRIC METHODOLOGIES   5

Steps (i) and (ii)

Theory and data continually interplay in this methodology. Unless there are good reasons for believing otherwise, it is normally assumed that theory suggests which variables should enter a relationship, and the data is left to determine whether this relationship is static or dynamic (in the sense that once disturbed from equilibrium it takes time to re-establish it).

It may help to understand the various steps of Hendry's methodology if a particular example is studied. Suppose that the investigator is interested in the determinants of the velocity of circulation of money. Let m_t be the log of the money supply, p_t be the log of the price level and y_t be the log of the real income. Theoretical reasoning suggests that, for appropriately defined money, $m_t - p_t - y_t$ should be a function of the nominal interest rate (I_t) along any steady state growth path. With $i_t = \log(I_t)$, we might therefore write $m_t^* - p_t^* - y_t^* = \delta i_t^*$ where the starred quantities indicate equilibrium values.

Of course equilibrium quantities are not normally observed, leading to the need to relate these to actual values. For time series data it is natural to do this by allowing the relations between the variables m_t, p_t, y_t and i_t to be governed by a dynamic equation of the form

$$m_t = \sum_{j=1}^{p} a_j m_{t-j} + \sum_{j=0}^{q} b_j p_{t-j} + \sum_{j=0}^{r} c_j y_{t-j} + \sum_{j=0}^{s} d_j i_{t-j}. \qquad (1)$$

The first step in Hendry's methodology sets p, q, r and s to be as large as practicable in view of the type of data (generally $p = q = r = s = 5$ for quarterly data), and to then estimate (1). This model, the general model, serves as a vehicle against which all other models are ultimately compared.

Now (1) could be written in many different ways, all of which would yield the same estimates of the unknown parameters, but each of which packages the information differently and consequently may be easier to interpret and understand. Generally, Hendry prefers to re-write the dynamics in (1) as an 'error correction mechanism' (ECM). To illustrate this point, the simple relation

$$x_t = ax_{t-1} + b_0 x_t^* + b_1 x_{t-1}^*, \qquad (2a)$$

where x_t^* is the equilibrium value of x_t, has the ECM

$$\Delta x_t = (a-1)(x_{t-1} - x_{t-1}^*) + b_0 \Delta x_t^* + (a - 1 + b_0 + b_1)x_{t-1}^*$$

$$= (a-1)(x_{t-1} - x_{t-1}^*) + b_0 \Delta x_t^*, \qquad (2b)$$

since steady-state equilibrium in (2a) implies $x = ax + b_0 x + b_1 x$ or $a + b_0 + b_1 = 1$. Although (2b) is no different to (2a), Hendry prefers it since Δx_t^* and $(x_{t-1} - x_{t-1}^*)$ are closer to being orthogonal and he is able to interpret its elements as equilibrium (Δx_t^*) and disequilibrium ($x_{t-1} - x_{t-1}^*$) responses.

Moving away from this simple representation we can get some feeling for the type of equation Hendry would replace (1) with by assuming that m_t adjusts within the period to p_t, making the log of real money $m_t - p_t$ the natural analogue of x_t in 2(a). The equilibrium value is then $x_t^* = y_t + \delta i_t$, and by appeal

6   PAGAN

to (2b) it is clear that a re-formatted version of (1) would involve terms such as Δy_t, Δi_t and $(x_{t-1} - x^*_{t-1}) = (m_{t-1} - p_{t-1} - y_{t-1} - \delta i_{t-1}) = (m_{t-1} - p_{t-1} - y_{t-1}) - \delta i_{t-1}$. Since $(m - p - y)_{t-1}$ is related to the lagged velocity of circulation, it may be easier to interpret this re-formulated equation. Terms such as $(m - p - y)_{t-1}$ frequently appear in studies of the demand for money by Hendry and his followers. For example, in Hendry and Mizon (1978), the following equation appears

$$\Delta(m - p)_t = 1.61 + 0.21\Delta y_t - 0.81\Delta i_t + 0.26\Delta(m - p)_{t-1}$$
$$- 0.40\Delta p_t - 0.23(m - p - y)_{t-1} + 0.61 i_{t-4} + 0.14 y_{t-4},$$

where I have replaced $\log(1 + i_t)$ with $- i_t$.

Thus, steps (i) and (ii) demand a clear statement of what the variables in the equilibrium relation should be, as well as a choice of parameterization. Hendry (1986) provides what is currently the most detailed explanation of his second step, but even a perusal of that source leaves an impression of the step being more of an art than a science, and consequently difficult to codify. To some extent the problem arises since Hendry tends to blur steps (ii) and (iii) in his applied work, with the re-formatted equation sometimes seeming to derive from an inspection of the parameter estimates in (1). In those cases (1) is both simplified and re-arranged at the same time.

The idea of beginning with a general model as the benchmark against which others might be compared seems only common-sense, but there is little doubt in my mind that it was a minority view in the 1960's (and may still be). One frequently saw (and sees) explicit rejection of this step on the grounds that it was impossible to do because economic variables were too 'collinear', with no attempt made to discover if there was even any truth in that assertion for the particular data set being used.[2] Over many years of looking at my own and students' empirical studies, I have found the rule of starting with a general model of fundamental importance for eventually drawing any conclusions about the nature of a relationship, and cannot imagine an econometric methodology that did not have this as its primary precept. As will be seen, all the methodologies analysed in this paper ascribe to that proposition.

Step (iii)

The first two steps in the methodology therefore seem unexceptionable. It is in the third that difficulties arise. These relate to the decision to simplify (1) and the reporting of this decision i.e. how to go from the large model implicit in (1) to one that is easier to comprehend but which represents the data just as well. Normally, in Hendry's methodology this step involves the deletion of variables from (1), but it could also involve choosing to set combinations of parameters to particular values. For convenience our discussion will centre upon model reduction via variable deletion. To simplify at all requires a *criterion function* and a *decision rule*; how to use and report inferences from such information are the difficult issues in this third step.

First, the decision stage. It is rare to find a criterion that is not based upon the log likelihood (or its *alter ego*, in regression models, the sum of squares). Frequently, it is something equivalent to the likelihood ratio test statistic, $- 2 \log (L_S / L_G)$ where L_S and L_G are the likelihoods of simplified and general models respectively. For regression models this is approximately the product of the sample size and the proportional change in the residual variance in moving from the general to simplified model. To know what is a 'big' change in the likelihood, it is common to select critical values from a table of the chi-square distribution by specifying a desired probability of Type I error. As is well known, one can think of this probability as indicating the fraction of times the simplified model would be rejected when it is true, given that the general model is re-estimated with data from many experiments differing solely by random shocks. Many see this myth as implausible in a non-experimental science such as economics, but myths such as this form the basis of many disciplines e.g. perfect competition in economics. What is important is that any framework within which analysis is conducted lead to useful results. If reliance upon the 'story' regularly causes error, it is then time to change it for something else.

On the whole, I believe that these concepts have served us well, but there are some suggestions of alternative decision rules that may prove to be more useful. Thus Akaike (1973) and Mallows (1973) derive decision rules that opt for the deletion of a variable in a linear model if the change in the residual variance is less than $\sqrt{2}$ times the inverse of the sample size.[3] Rissanen (1983), looking at the likelihood as an efficient way to summarize all the information in the data, formulates a decision rule that the change in residual variance must be less than a function of the sample size and difference in model dimensions. None of these is incompatible with the 'Hendry' methodology; to date they have not been used much, but that is a matter of choice rather than necessity.

Having made a decision what should be reported? My own attitude, summarized in McAleer *et al.* (1985), is that an exact description of the decisions taken in moving from a general to simplified model is imperative in any application of the methodology. Rarely does this involve a single decision, although it would be possible to act as if it did by just comparing the finally chosen simplified model and the original one, thereby ignoring the path followed to the simplified version. This is what Hendry seems to do in various applied studies; he normally only provides the value of a test statistic comparing the two models at each end of the path, with very little discussion (if any) of the route followed from one end to the other.

There seem to me to be some arguments against this stance. First, it is hard to have much confidence in a model if little is explained about its origin. Hendry's attitude seems to be that how a final model is derived is largely irrelevant; it is either useful or not useful, and that characteristic is independent of whether it comes purely from whimsy, some precise theory, or a very structured search (Hendry and Mizon, 1985). In a sense this is true, but it is cold comfort to those who are implementing the methodology or who are learning it for the first time. Reading Hendry's applied papers frequently leaves only puzzlement about how

8   PAGAN

he actually did the simplification. In Hendry (1986) for example, the transition from a model with thirty-one parameters to one with only fourteen is explained in the following way (p. 29):

> 'These equations.....were then transformed to a more interpretable parameterisation and redundant functions were deleted; the resulting parsimonious models were tested against the initial unrestricted forms by the overall *F*-test'.

It is true that confidence in the simplified model is partly a function of the value of the *F*-test, but by its very nature this evidence can only mean that *some* of the deleted variables don't matter. To see why, consider a general model with three regressors x_1, x_2 and x_3, all of which are orthogonal. Suppose the F statistic for the deletion of x_3 is 5 and that for x_2 is 0.5. Then the F statistic for the joint deletion of x_2 and x_3 is 2.75, and joint deletion is likely, even though it is dubious if x_3 should be deleted at all. Thus an adequate documentation of the path followed in any simplification process is desirable, rather than just accompanying any simplification with a vague statement about it. More than that, I do believe in the possibility of situations in which simplication may be done in a systematic way e.g. in choosing dynamics via COMFAC (as in Hendry and Mizon, 1978 or McAleer *et al.*, 1985), polynomial orders within Almon procedures and various types of demand and production restrictions that form a nested heirachy. As far as possible I am in favour of exploiting such well-developed strategies for simplification. Research should also be encouraged with the aim of developing new procedures or methods that require fewer assumptions.

Knowledge of the path may be important for another reason. As discussed above the critical value used in the decision rule is taken from the tables of the χ^2 or F distribution. But under the conditions of the story being used, this is only true if the simplification path consists of a single step. When there has been more than one step, the critical values cannot normally be taken from a χ^2 distribution, and it may be misleading if one proceeds as if it can. Some, for example Hill (1986), see this as a major flaw in the methodology, and others feel that the decision rule needs to be modified quite substantially in the presence of such 'data mining'. When the move from a general to a simplified model can be formulated as a nested sequence, adjustments can be made to obtain the requisite critical value (Mizon (1977) gives an account of this), but in the more common case where this is not possible theoretical analysis has made little progress. Nevertheless, numerical methods of Type I error evaluation, such as the bootstrap, do enable the tracing of Type I error for *any* sequence of tests and specified decision rules. Veall (1986) provides an application of this idea.

I am not certain that it is worthwhile computing exact Type I errors. Ignoring the sequence entirely produces a bias against the simplified model, but that does not seem such a bad thing. Moreover, the ultimate change in the criterion function is independent of the path followed. It is frequently the change in the criterion itself which is of interest, in that it displays the sensitivity of (say) the log likelihood to variation in parameter value for the deleted variables as these range from zero to the point estimates of the general model.

Step (iv)

Excellent accounts are available of the necessity of this step—Hendry and Richard (1982)—and the techniques for doing it—Engle (1984). Essentially, these procedures check if sample moments involving the product of specified variables with functions of the data (typically residuals) are zero. Very general treatments of diagnostic tests from this viewpoint have recently been given by Tauchen (1985) and Newey (1985).[4] These procedures fulfil a number of roles within the methodology. They are important within a modelling cycle for the detection of inadequate models, but they are also important in the reporting phase, where they provide evidence that the conventions underlying almost any modelling exercise are not violated by the chosen model. Routine examination of such items as the autocorrelation function and recursive estimation of parameters has proved to be indispensible to both my own modelling (Anstie *et al.*, 1983; Pagan and Volker, 1981) and to those of a large number of students studying applied econometrics at the Australian National University over the past decade (Harper, 1980; Kirby, 1981 for example). More than anything else, it is step (iv) which differentiates Hendry's methodology from that which was standard practice in the 1960's.

2. The 'Leamer methodology'

Providing a succint description of Leamer's methodology is a good deal more difficult than doing so for the Hendry variant. Basically, the problem lies in a lack of applications of the ideas; consequently it is hard to infer the general principles of the approach from any classic studies of how it is to work in practice. Despite this qualification, I have reduced Leamer's methodology to four distinct steps.

(i)   Formulate a general family of models.

(ii) Decide what inferences are of interest, express these in terms of parameters, and form 'tentative' prior distributions that summarize the information not contained in the given data set.

(iii) Consider the sensitivity of inferences to a particular choice of prior distributions, namely those that are diffuse for a specified sub-set of the parameters and arbitrary for the remainder. This is the extreme bounds analysis (EBA) of Leamer (1983) and Leamer and Leonard (1983). Sometimes step (iii) terminates the process, but when it appears that inferences are sensitive to the prior specification this step is only a warm-up for the next one.

(iv) Try to obtain a narrower range for the inferences. In some places this seems to involve an explicit Bayesian approach, but in others it seems just to involve fixing a prior mean and interval for prior covariance matrices. If the restrictions in this latter step needed to get a narrow range are too 'implausible', one concludes that any inference based on this data is fragile.

Collected as in (i)–(iv), Leamer's methodology seems to be just another sect in the Bayesian religion, and there is little point in my going over the debate in statistics concerning Bayesian procedures. Much of this is epistemological and I doubt if it will ever be resolved. In practice, the limited appeal of Bayesian methods to econometricians seems to have been based on the difficulties coming from a need to formulate high-dimensional priors in any realistic model, nagging doubts about the need to have precise distributional forms to generate posterior distributions, and the fact that many dubious auxiliary assumptions are frequently employed (for example, lack of serial correlation and heteroskedasticity in the errors). In theory, all of these doubts could be laid to rest, but the computational burden becomes increasingly heavy.

Viewed as basically an exercise in Bayesian econometrics, I have therefore very little to say about Leamer's method. It is not to my taste, but it may well be to others'. However, in attempting to sell his ideas, Leamer has produced, particularly in step (iii), an approach that can be interpreted in a 'classical' rather than Bayesian way, and it is this which one tends to think of as the 'Leamer methodology'. The reasons for such a belief lie in the advocacy of such ideas in Leamer's two most widely read articles, Leamer (1983) and Leamer and Leonard (1983), although it is clear from Leamer (1985, 1986) that he now sees the fourth step as the important part of his analysis. Nevertheless, applications tend to be of step (iii), and we will, therefore, analyse it before proceeding to (iv).

Returning to steps (i) and (ii), it is apparent they do not differ greatly from Hendry's methodology (HM); the main distinction is that in HM the emphasis is on building a model from which inferences will later be drawn, whereas Leamer focuses upon the desired inference from the beginning. Because of this concern about a particular parameter (or, more correctly, a linear combination of parameters), it is not clear if Leamer has a counterpart to the simplification step in Hendry's methodology. In published applications he always retains the complete model for inferences, but he has suggested to me that some simplification may be practised as an aid to communication or in the interest of efficient prediction.

Thus, cast in terms of (1) the essential distinction in these early steps between the two methodologies is that Leamer would want a clear definition of what the issues in modelling money demand are at the beginning. Suppose it was the question of the impact of interest rate variations on money demand, the question raised by Cooley and LeRoy (1981) in one of the best known applications of Leamer's ideas. Then either the size of individual d_j's or $(1 - \Sigma a_j)^{-1} \Sigma d_j$ (the long-run response) would be the items of interest, and the model would be re-parameterized to reflect these concerns. In Hendry's case it is rare to find a particular set of coefficients being the centre of attention; it is variable inter-relationships as a whole that seem to dominate. As in McAleer *et al.* (1985), questions about the magnitude of the interest rate response in (1) are answered after the final model is chosen.

Step (iii)

To gain a better appreciation of what is involved in step (iii), particularly as a contrast to HM, it is necessary to expose the link between them. Accordingly, take the general model

$$y_t = x_t\beta + z_t\gamma + e_t, \tag{3}$$

THREE ECONOMETRIC METHODOLOGIES   11

where z_t are a set of doubtful variables, and interest centres upon the point estimate of the first coefficient in the β vector, β_1. In terms of the variables in (1), x_t would relate to the interest rate variables while z_t would be the remainder. In step (iii) Leamer examines the extreme values of the point estimates of β_1 as all possible linear combinations of z_t are entered into regressions that always contain x_t (this being formally equivalent to diffuse priors upon β and arbitrary priors on γ). In McAleer *et al.* (1983, Appendix) it is shown that the absolute difference between these bounds, scaled by the standard deviation of the OLS estimate of β_1 from (3), is given by:[5]

$$\text{SD } (\hat{\beta}_1)^{-1} | \hat{\beta}_{1,\max} - \hat{\beta}_{1,\min} | = \phi \chi_D^2 \tag{4}$$

where $0 \leqslant \phi \leqslant 1$ and χ_D^2 is the chi-square statistic for testing if γ is zero.

Leamer refers to the left hand side of (4) as 'specification uncertainty'. Let us first take the extreme case that $\phi = 1$ and ask what extra information is provided by an EBA that is not available to someone following HM. In the latter, if χ_D^2 was small, the recommended point estimate of β_1 for someone following HM would be that from the model deleting z_t. From (4) an exactly equivalent statement would be that the 'specification uncertainty' is very small, and the point estimate of β_1 would not change very much as one moved from the general to the simplified model. This is to be expected since, following Hausman (1978), a large difference between $\hat{\beta}_1$ for the simplified and general models must mean evidence against any simplification. Thus the two approaches provide a different packaging of the same information, and share exactly the same set of difficulties. In particular, all the problems of nominating a critical value for χ_D^2 have their counter-part in Leamer's methodology as providing critical values for specification uncertainty. As observed in McAleer *et al.* (1985), there has been no agreement on the latter question by users of the EBA method, with a range of definitions being proposed. Another interesting concomitant of (4) is that if, $\gamma \neq 0$ in (3), $\chi_D^2 \rightarrow \infty$ as the sample size grows, and so, when $\phi \neq 0$, the range between the bounds tends to infinity. Thus Leamer's complaints about classical hypothesis testing apply also to his own methodology!

Now, in HM it is an *insignificant* χ_D^2 that is important, but this need not be *numerically small* if the dimension of z_t is large. Taking the previously cited example from Hendry (1986), where seventeen parameters were set to zero, $\chi^2(17, 0.05) = 27.59$, allowing a potentially enormous gap between $\hat{\beta}_{1,\min}$ and $\hat{\beta}_{1,\max}$; point estimates of the simplified model might therefore depart substantially from those based upon other ways of combining the z_t. *If it is point estimates of β_1* that are desired, it becomes very informative to perform an EBA (i.e. to compute ϕ); knowledge of χ_D^2 only sets an upper limit to the specification uncertainty, as it is the collinearity between regressors, reflected in ϕ, that determines the exact value of the 'specification uncertainty'.[6] Whenever a large number of variables are deleted in a simplification exercise, the provision of extreme bounds for any coefficients of interest seems desirable.

Where the two methodologies really part company is over the interpretation of a large χ_D^2. Followers of HM would argue that one should take point estimates of β_1 from the general model, concluding it would be an error to take them from

12   PAGAN

the simplified model, as the data clearly indicate that the z_t appear in the relationship.[7] Leamer would presumably conclude that 'Because there are many models which could serve as a basis for a data analysis, there are many conflicting inferences which could be drawn from a given data set' and therefore 'inferences from these data are too fragile to be useful' (Leamer and Leonard, 1983, p. 306). I confess that I cannot be convinced that our response to a situation where the data are clearly indicating that valid point estimates of β_1 will not be found by deleting z_t from (1) should be to conclude that the data are not informative about β_1!

There is no denying that there would be comfort in narrow bounds, as any conclusions that depend upon the precise value of β_1 would then be unchanged by variation in specifications. Some, for example Feldstein (1982), even see this as a desirable characteristic. But I think it hard to argue that the majority of modelling exercises can be formulated in terms of interest in the value of a single coefficient (or a linear combination of them). It is perhaps no accident that the examples Leamer provides in his articles do feature situations where single parameter inference is paramount, whereas Hendry's examples—money demand, consumption—are more concerned with the model as a whole. If the equation (3) was being developed as part of a policy model, or even to provide predictions, knowledge of χ_D^2 is important, as a large value would presumably imply that models which retained z_t would out-perform those that did not. Any model should be judged on all its dimensions and not just a few of them. One might argue for an extension of Leamer's methodology that chose 'β_1' as representative of many characteristics of a model. Since prediction errors can be estimated as the coefficients of dummy variables (Salkever, 1976) these might be taken as $\hat{\beta}_1$. Alternatively, why not look at the extreme bounds for the residual variance? But these must be the two estimates of σ^2 obtained by including and deleting all the z_t in (1), and so one is essentially re-producing the χ_D^2 statistics. Accordingly, once attention shifts from a single parameter to overall model performance EBA begins to look like a version of step (ii) of HM.

Step (iv)

The fourth step constitutes the clearest expression of Bayesian philosophy in Leamer's work. Until this step it is not mandatory to formulate a prior distribution, but now at least the mean and variance of it must be provided (only two moments are needed given the type of prior assumed in his SEARCH program). A proper Bayesian would then proceed to combine this prior knowledge with a likelihood, reporting the posterior distribution for the coefficient. If forced to give a point estimate of the coefficient, such an individual would probably give the mode, median or mean of the posterior distribution. That would then be the end of the exercise, the data and prior beliefs having been optimally combined to provide the best information possible about the parameter value. Consequently, when modelling money demand as in (1), a Bayesian would need to formulate a $(p + q + r + s)$-dimensional prior distribution upon the parameters of this model.

A daunting task, although some progress has been made in automating the process of prior elicitation in recent years, and Leamer (1986) is an excellent example of how to do this in a context similar to that in (1).

What differentiates Leamer from a standard Bayesian is his reluctance to follow the above prescription rigidly. Rather, he prefers to study how the mean of the posterior distribution changes as the prior variances change. In Leamer (1986) he stipulates a prior covariance matrix A, but them modifies it to V obeying the following constraint:

$$(1 - \lambda)A \leqslant V \leqslant \{1/(1 - \lambda)\} A \,(0 \leqslant \lambda \leqslant 1).$$

As λ ranges from zero to unity the precision of the prior information diminishes and, for any given value of λ, bounds for the posterior mean can be computed corresponding to each side of the inequality. What is of primary interest to Leamer is how these bounds change in response to variations in λ, rather than just the values at $\lambda = 0$. As he says in Leamer (1985), what he is concerned with is *sensitivity analysis*, and it is the question of sensitivity of inferences to variation in assumptions which should pre-occupy the econometrician.

If step (iv) is thought of as a tool to provide a Bayesian analyst with evidence of how important prior assumptions are for conclusions based on the posterior, it seems unexceptionable and useful. Is this also true for an investigator not operating within the Bayesian paradigm? What is of concern to that individual is the shape of the likelihood. Step (iv) can provide some information on this aspect. On the one hand, if the likelihood is completely flat the posterior and prior means would always coincide. On the other hand, if the likelihood was sharply defined around a particular point in the parameter space, changing λ would cause the posterior mean to shift from the prior mean to this point. Unfortunately, it is not entirely reliable as a guide to the characteristics of the likelihood, as can be seen in the case of the linear model. With the prior mean set to $\hat{\beta}_{OLS}$ and A proportional to $(X'X)^{-1}$, the posterior and prior means always coincide, so nothing is learnt about the likelihood as λ is varied.

From the above, the intention of step (iv) seems good, even if in execution it may leave something to be desired. I think it certainly true that workers in the HM tradition do not pay enough attention to the shape of the likelihood (see Note 7). The provision of second derivatives of the log likelihood (standard errors) gives some feel for it, but they can be very unreliable if problems are non-linear. Whether Leamer's procedure is the best response is a moot point; at the moment it is one of the few methods we have of discovering information about curvature in the likelihood, and its strategy to overcome the problems caused by a high dimensional parameter space (index it by a single parameter λ) may well be the best way to proceed. Certainly, we can use all the help we can get when it comes to the analysis of data.

My main reservation about step (iv), however, is that it does not do *enough* sensitivity analysis, being restricted to the parameters of the prior distribution. As exemplified in his SEARCH program, there are many conventions underlying the methodology (just as there were in HM), but those applying it have made

14   PAGAN

precious little attempt to query the validity of such conventions for the data set being analysed. This is odd since, in principle, there should be few difficulties in mimicking step (iv) of HM. Since most diagnostic tests can be formulated as measuring the sensitivity of the log likelihood to the addition of variables designed to detect departures from the conventions (Pagan, 1984) they should be readily adapted to Leamer's framework.[8] It seems imperative that this become part of the methodology. Leamer has indicated to me that he does see the need to examine the data for anomalies that suggest revision of the model space or of the initial prior distributions; the tools in this task ranging from unexpected parameter estimates and peculiar residual patterns to (possibly) goodness-of-fit statistics. But he emphasizes that adjustments must be made for any data-instigated revision of the model or prior. Because such adjustments are difficult his first preference is for an initial selection of prior and model extensive enough as to make any such revision unlikely. Nevertheless, when theory is rudimentary and underdeveloped, commitment to the original model and prior is likely to be low, and the need for revision correspondingly high.

3. Sims' methodology

Interdependence of actions is one of the characteristics of economic studies. Hence, it might be argued that the evaluation of policy will normally need to be done within a framework that allows for such interdependence. In fact, a good deal of analysis, and the econometrics supporting it, is done in a partial rather than general equilibrium way—see Feldstein (1982) for example, where the impact of taxes upon investment is assessed in a series of single equation studies. Traditionally, such questions were analysed with the aid of a system of structural equations:

$$By_t - Cx_t = e_t, \tag{5}$$

where y_t is a vector of endogenous variables, x_t a vector of predetermined variables, and e_t was the disturbance term. In (5), following the lead of the Cowles Commission researchers, both B and C were taken to be relatively sparse, so as to 'identify' the separate relations, i.e. it was assumed that an investigator could decide which variables appeared in which equations.

Both of the two previous methodologies would probably subscribe to this framework, aiming to calibrate the non-zero elements in B and C (Leamer might regard the exclusion restrictions as only approximately correct, but I know of nowhere that he has explicitly stated his preferred procedure). By contrast, the third methodology jettisons it. Sims (1980a) dissented vigorously from the Cowles Commission tradition, resurrecting an old article by Liu (1960), which insisted that it was 'incredible' to regard B and C as sparse. The argument touches a chord with anyone involved in the construction of computable general equilibrium models. If decisions on consumption, labour supply, portfolio allocations, etc. are all determined by individuals maximizing lifetime utility subject to a budget constraint, each relationship would be determined by the same set of variables. Consequently, theoretical considerations would predict no difference in the menu of variables entering different equations, although the quantitative importance of individual variables is most likely to vary with the type of decision.[9] Prescription of the zero elements in B and C therefore involves excluding variables with coefficients 'close' to zero. In this respect, the action is little different to what is done in any attempt to model reality by capturing the major influences at work. This was Fisher's (1961) reply to Liu, and I find it as pertinent now as when it was written.

Much more could be said about this issue of identifiability, but this is not the place to do so. One cannot help wondering, however, if it is as serious as Sims suggests. There do not seem many instances in applied work where identification is the likely suspect when accounting for poor results. Despite the large amount of attention paid to it in early econometrics, it is hard to escape the impression that issues of specification and data quality are of far greater importance.

Nevertheless, it would be silly to ignore these arguments if it was indeed possible to do analysis without such assumptions. Sims claims that it is. In the Cowles Commission methodology, 'structure-free' conclusions would have been derived from the reduced form:

$$y_t = B^{-1}Cx_t + B^{-1}e_t = \Pi x_t + v_t, \tag{6}$$

but Sims chooses instead to work with a vector autoregressive representation (VAR) for the endogenous and exogenous variables. Defining $z_t' = (y_t'\bar{x}_t')$, where $\bar{x}_t$ includes all members of x_t that are not lagged values of variables, this has the form:

$$z_t = \sum_{j=1}^{p} A_j z_{t-j} + e_t. \tag{7}$$

Although it is (7) that is estimated, two further manipulations are made for use in later stages of the methodology. First, (7) is inverted to give the innovations (or moving average) form:

$$z_t = \sum_{j=0}^{\infty} A_j e_{t-j} \tag{8}$$

where $\bar{A}_0 = \text{cov}(e_t)$. Since $\bar{A}_0$ is a positive definite matrix there exists a non-singular lower triangular matrix P such that $PA_0P' = I$, allowing the definition $\eta_t = Pe_t$, where η_t has zero mean and covariance matrix I. (8) may then be re-written in terms of η_t as:

$$z_t = \sum_{j=0}^{\infty} A_j P^{-1} Pe_{t-j} = \sum_{j=0}^{\infty} D_j\eta_{t-j}, \tag{9}$$

where the η_t are the *orthogonalized innovations*.

Having dispatched the preliminaries it is possible to summarize Sims' methodology in four steps.

(i)   Transform data to such a form that a VAR can be fitted to it.

(ii) Choose as large a value of p and $\dim(z_t)$ as is compatible with the size of data set available and then fit the resulting VAR.

(iii) Try to simplify the VAR by reducing p or by imposing some arbitrary 'smoothness' restrictions upon the coefficients.

(iv) Use the *orthogonalized* innovations representation to address the question of interest.

Step (i)

This is an important step. The idea that z_t can be expressed as a VAR has its origins in the theory of stationary processes, particularly in the Wold decomposition theorem. But that justification is not essential until the last step; until then the VAR might well have unstable roots. However, stable roots are indispensible to step (iv), as the coefficients $\bar{A}_j$ only damp out for a stable VAR, i.e. $z_t = a z_{t-1} + e_t$ (z_t a scalar) becomes

$$z_t = \sum_{j=0}^{\infty} a^j e_{t-j}$$

and $a^j \to 0 (j \to \infty)$ only if $|a| < 1$. If step (iv) is to be regarded as an essential part of the methodology, the question of the appropriate transformation to render z_t stationary must be faced at an early stage.

In Sims (1980a) and Doan *et al.* (1984), as well as most applications, this seems to be done by including time trends in each equation of the VAR. In the latter article the attitude seems to be that most economic time series are best thought of as a stationary autoregression around a deterministic trend: after setting up the prior that the series follow a random walk with drift (equation (3), p. 7) they then say:

> 'While we recognise that a more accurate representation of generally held prior beliefs would give less weight to systems with explosive roots.....'.

It is not apparent to me that this is a 'generally held prior belief', particularly given the incidence of random walks with drift in the investigation of Nelson and Plosser (1982) into the behaviour of economic time series. If the series are of the random walk type, placing deterministic trends into a regression does not suffice to induce stationarity, and an innovations form will not exist for the series in question. Of course, the sensible response to this objection would be to focus upon growth rates rather than levels for variables that are best regarded as ARIMA processes. I suspect that this makes somewhat more sense in many contexts anyway. In macroeconomic policy questions for example, interest typically centres upon rates of growth of output and prices rather than levels, and it therefore seems appropriate to formulate the VAR in this way. Consequently, the difficulties raised by the type of non-stationarity exhibited by many economic time series is not insurmountable, but it does suggest that much more care needs to be taken in identifying the format of the variables to be modelled than has been characteristic of past studies employing Sims' methodology.

Step (ii)

Both p and the number of variables in z_t need to be specified. The first parameter will need to be fairly large (the decomposition theorem sets it to infinity), and most applications of Sims' methodology have put p between four and ten. Doan *et al.* (1984, Footnote 3) indicate that, at least for prediction performance, conclusions might be sensitive to the choice of lag length. Stronger evidence is available that the selection of variables to appear in z_t is an important one—Sims' conclusions about the role of money in Sims (1980a) were severely modified in Sims (1980b) by expanding z_t to include an interest rate. Essentially step (ii) is the analogue of step (i) in the previous two methodologies, and the need to begin with a model that is general enough haunts all the methodologies. Perhaps the difficulties are greater in Sims' case, as he wants to model the reduced form rather than a single structural equation. To adopt such a position it would be necessary to respond to Sims' contention that structural equations should also contain a large number of variables, although what is really at issue is whether they are quantitatively more important to the reduced form analysis.

Step (iii)

Step (iii) is required precisely because of the fact that both p and $\dim(z_t)$ need to be large, and so the number of unknown parameters, $p \times \dim(z_t)$, can easily become too large to be estimated from the available data. In his original article Sims chose p via a series of modified likelihood ratio tests in exactly the same way as was done in step (ii) of Hendry's methodology. Because there are few degrees of freedom available in the most general model, this may not be a good way to select p. Accordingly, in Doan *et al.* (1984) a different approach was promoted that was 'Bayesian in spirit'. In this variant the A_j were allowed to vary over time as

$$\text{vec}(A^i_{j,t}) = \pi_8 \text{vec}(A^i_{j,t-1}) + (1 - \pi_8)\text{vec}(A^i_j) + v^i_{j,t}, \tag{10}$$

where the i indicates the ith equation and $v_{j,t}$ is a normally distributed random variable with covariance matrix V that is a function of $\pi_1 \ldots \pi_7$. Fixing the A^i_j in (10) (at either unity, if the coefficient corresponds to the first lag of the dependent variable of the equation, or zero otherwise), there remain eight unknown parameters. (10) describes an 'evolving coefficient model'. The likelihood for (9) and (10) was derived by Schweppe (1965) and can be written down with the aid of the Kalman filtering equations. Two of the π parameters were then eliminated by maximizing this likelihood conditional upon the fixed values of the others.

One might well ask what the rationale for (10) is; Doan *et al.* claim (p. 6):

> 'What we do thus has antecedents in the literature on shrinkage estimation and its Bayesian interpretation (for example, the works by...Shiller (1973)...'.

I would dispute this connection. In the Bayesian formulation of shrinkage estimators, shrinkage occurs only in a finite sample, since the prior information is dominated by the sample information as the sample size grows, i.e. changes in (say) the prior variance have a negligible effect upon the posterior distribution in large samples. This is not true for (10); changes in π always have an effect upon the likelihood, since the variance of the innovations is always a function of the π (see equation (10) of Doan *et al.*). Reference to Shiller's work seems even more misleading. Shiller allows the coefficients to be 'random' *across the lag distributions, not across time*, i.e. he would have

$$\text{vec}(A^i_{j,t}) = \pi_8 \, \text{vec}(A^j_{j-1,t}) + (1 - \pi_8)\text{vec}(A^j_j)$$

and not

$$\text{vec}(A^i_{j,t}) = \pi_8 \, \text{vec}(A^i_{j,t-1}) + (1 - \pi_8)\text{vec}(A^j_j).$$

Thus, as (10) is a model for coefficient evolution, and not the imposition of prior information, it is hard to see why this procedure is any less objectionable than that followed by the Cowles Commission; Malinvaud's (1984) reaction to the idea is easy to sympathize with.

Step (iv)

As step (iv) has been the subject of a number of excellent critiques, particularly Cooley and LeRoy (1985), little will be said about it. There are two major objections. First, the move from innovations to orthogonal innovations raises questions. With the exception of the first variable in z_t, the orthogonal innovations are hard to give any sensible meaning to; resort is frequently made to expressions such as 'that part of the innovation in money not correlated with the innovations in other variables'. In many ways the difficulty is akin to that in factor analysis; the mathematics is clear but the economics is not. Unfortunately, many users of the technique tend to blur the two concepts in discussion e.g. in Litterman and Weiss (1985) the 'orthogonalized' soubriquet is dropped.

A second query arises over the *use* of the orthogonalized innovations representation. As Cooley and LeRoy (1985) point out, to ascribe any meaning to impulse responses for these innovations, it is necessary that the latter be treated as exogenous variables, and that requires the imposition of prior restrictions upon the causal structure of the system in exactly the same fashion as was done by the Cowles Commission. The strong claims the methodology makes to being free of prior information therefore seem to be largely illusory.

As an aid to understanding the issues raised above it may help to return to (1) and the question of the response of money to interest rate variations. Sims would first choose a lag length and a set of variables to form the VAR. A minimal subset would be the variables m_t, p_t, i_t and y_t in (1), but because one is attempting to capture economy-wide interactions rather than just a money demand relation, extra variables that may need to be included could be world activity, the exchange rate, and fiscal policy variables. A lot of thought has to go into this choice. Making the set too small can seriously bias the answers, whereas making it too large renders the method intractable unless other restrictions are imposed upon the

VAR coefficients as in step (iii). Once the latter strategy is followed the 'clean-skin' appeal of VAR's begins to dissipate.

Granted that steps (i)–(iii) have provided a satisfactory VAR representation for m_t as in (7), it is then inverted to give the innovations representation (8) that expresses m_t as a linear function of the innovations in the interest rate $e_{i,t}$ and the other variables in the VAR: $e_{p,t}$, $e_{m,t}$, $e_{y,t}$, etc. The equation corresponding to m_t in (8) would be of the form

$$m_t = \bar{a}_{0,mm}e_{m,t} + \bar{a}_{0,mp}e_{p,t} + \bar{a}_{0,mi}e_{i,t} + \bar{a}_{0,my}e_{y,t} + \ldots\ldots$$

and the response of m_t to a unit innovation in the interest rate would be $\bar{a}_{0,mi}$. This is to be contrasted with the response of m_t to a unit innovation in the interest rate provided by (1)—$d_0\bar{a}_{0,ii}$—obtained by replacing i_t in (1) by $i_t = \bar{a}_{0,ii}e_{i,t}$ + ... (the interest rate equation in (8)). Therefore different answers to the question of the response of m_t to variations in i_t would be obtained from methodologies concentrating upon (1) alone from those that incorporate system responses; in (1) the response is estimated by holding prices and income constant, whereas Sims seeks the effects on the quantity of money without such *cet. par* assumptions. To some extent the methodologies are not competitive, as they frequently seek to answer different questions.

Sims aims to analyse a much broader set of issues than Hendry or Leamer normally do, but there are difficulties commensurate with this breadth. Making the set of variables to appear in the VAR large enough is one of these, and his fourth step illustrates another. To speak of the response of m_t to a unit innovation in the interest rate it must be possible to carry out that experiment without disturbing current prices, incomes, etc. But that means the innovations $e_{i,t}$ must be uncorrelated with all the other innovations. When they are not, Sims invokes artificial constructs, the orthogonal innovations, $v_{i,t}$, $v_{p,t}$, $v_{y,t}$, etc. These are linear combinations of $e_{i,t}$, $e_{p,t}$, $e_{y,t}$ designed to be orthogonal to one another, and hence capable of being varied independently of each other. Just like principal components, it is uncertain what meaning should be attached to these entities, leading to the controversy recounted above in discussion of step (iv).

4. Summing up

Our review of the methodologies now being complete, it is time to sum up. Ignoring the criticisms of details that have been offered, how effective are the methodologies in meeting the three criteria of 'goodness' listed at the beginning of this essay, namely the provision of general research tools, the codification and transmission of principles, and the reporting of results?

None of the methodologies claims to be completely general. Sims' explicitly deals only with time series, while many of Hendry's concerns are specific to such series as well. Leamer's techniques are heavily based upon the OLS estimator. All have the common deficiency of a failure to address explicitly the burgeoning field of microeconometrics. Whilst it is true that the philosophies underlying Hendry's and Leamer's work transfers (see, for example, Cameron and Trivedi

(1985)), the actual techniques employed would need extensive modification, particularly in light of the very large data sets that make traditional model selection methods inappropriate. There is clearly a lot to be done before any of the three methodologies provides a complete set of techniques for data analysis.

Part of the objective of this paper has been to try to set out the general principles of each methodology, so as to assist in the communication and teaching roles. But this was done at a high level of abstraction. When it comes to application many questions arise which currently seem to be resolved only by 'sitting at the feet of the master'. Hendry, for example, is very vague about how he manages to simplify his models, so little is learnt about how this is to be done by a reading of his articles. Leamer recommends formulating multi-dimensional priors, but provides little practical guidance on how (say) the covariance matrices featuring in them are to be selected. Sims' methodology seems clearest when it is applied to the big issues of macroeconomics such as the neutrality of money, but altogether vaguer when the question is of the much more prosaic kind such as the impact of a quota upon import demand. No doubt Sims would be able to handle such queries, but the personal ingenuity required seems a stumbling block to the transmission of knowledge.

What about reporting? Hendry's methodology seems to provide useful information in a concise form, although it is sometimes possible to be overwhelmed with the detail on the statistics presented when judging the adequacy of a model. Perhaps this just reflects a lack of familiarity and an early stage in learning about what are the most useful tests. Leamer's extreme bounds are easy to understand; however, the extensions in which prior variances are restricted become much harder to interpret. To my mind, it is Sims' methodology which is the worst when it comes to the reporting role, with pages of graphs and impulse responses being provided. Whether this reflects a transition stage, or the problems mentioned previously about step (iv), is still unclear, but a more consise method of reporting does seem to be needed.

Granted that no methodology has managed to obtain a perfect score, what have we learnt from all of this debate? First, a substantial clarification of the procedures of model selection and auxiliary concepts such as 'exogeneity'. Second, a pronounced recognition of the limits of modelling. Any reading of (say) Marschak (1953) makes it evident that the Cowles Commission researchers were not deficient in this respect (doubters might note the amount of space Marschak denotes to discussing the 'Lucas critique'), but somehow it got lost in the euphoria of the 1960s. The much more critical attitude towards econometrics that prevails today is generally a good thing, although there is a danger that the emergence of differing methodologies will be interpreted as a tacit admission of a complete failure of econometrics, rather than as constructive attempts to improve it.

What about the future? Constructing 'systematic theologies' for econometrics can well stifle creativity, and some evidence of this has already become apparent. Few would deny that in the hands of the masters the methodologies perform impressively, but in the hands of their disciples it is all much less convincing. It will be important to rid econometrics of the 'black box' mentality that always besets it. A poor modelling strategy is unlikely to give useful results, but a good one cannot rescue a project by rigidly following any methodology if it was badly conceived from the very beginning. What I see as needed is a greater integration of the different methodologies. Although it is convenient to draw demarcation lines between them in discussion, this should not blind a researcher to the fact that each methodology can provide insights that the others lack. Extreme bounds analysis is an important adjunct to Hendry's methodology if large numbers of parameters have been omitted in any simplification. Examining the residuals for model deficiencies should be as automatic in Leamer's and Sims' methodologies as it is in Hendry's. Checking if the restrictions imposed by a model selected by Hendry's or Leamer's methodologies upon the VAR parameters are compatible with the data should be part of any analysis involving time series. Our data are such that we cannot ignore the fact that the information therein may need to be extracted by a wide range of techniques borrowed from many different approaches.

Notes

[1] Much of this paper was presented in the symposium on 'Econometric Methodology' at the World Econometric Congress at Boston in August 1985. I am grateful to Ed Leamer for his extensive comments upon the paper.

[2] As is well known the importance of collinearity is a function of the parameterization used. Thus the data may be very informative about certain parameters e.g. long-run responses, but not others e.g. dynamics. It is not useful (or valid) to claim it is uninformative about everything.

[3] Problems emerge if a decision rule is employed based on keeping Type I errors constant—see Berkson (1938). As the test statistic is the product of the sample size by the proportional change in variance, even very small changes in the latter become large changes in the criterion when the sample size is large. Decision rules such as those in Rissanen (1983) and Schwartz (1978) overcome this, but it might be better to model formally the underlying conflict between Type I and Type II error as in Quandt (1980).

[4] Both papers treat only the case where the observations making up the sample moments are i.i.d., but it is clear that the analysis extends to the case where the 'orthogonality' relations follow a martingale difference process. This covers most cases of interest in econometrics. Note, however, that Tauchen's results require that the maintained model be estimated by maximum likelihood.

[5] Breusch (1985) has an elegant proof of this.

[6] This division shows that interpretations which see the differences between the methodologies as due to different attitudes to collinearity are incorrect. Bounds can be wide even if collinearity is weak (ϕ small).

[7] We have not dealt with the question of what inferences about β_1 might be then drawn from $\hat{\beta}_1$. Unfortunately, it is not uncommon in econometrics to see sharp conclusions drawn about the value of β_1 on the basis of a test of a sharp hypothesis such as $\beta_1 = 1$ or zero (Hall, 1978; Barro, 1977). All that can be concluded, however, is that a range of possible values for β_1 are compatible with $\hat{\beta}_1$, and this range is frequently found by examining $k\text{SD}(\hat{\beta}_1)$, where k is some selected constant. Traditionally, k was set by stipulating the Type I error to be sustained, but Don Andrews (1986) has recently suggested a way of incorporating power requirements into the determination of k.

[8] In Pagan (1978) I used CORE's Bayesian Regression Program to check for serial correlation. Lagged residuals were added to the model and the posterior distribution for the coefficient of that variable was then calculated.

[9] Even within these models the existence of governments means that (say) prices entering demand relations will be different from those in supply relations by the presence of indirect taxes, and this gives an external source of variation. It should be noted that Sims gives a number of other arguments against identifiability, some relating to expectations and others about our inability to specify the exact order of dynamics.

References

Akaike, H. (1973) Information theory and the extension of the maximum likelihood principle. In B. N. Petrov and F. Csaki (eds) *2nd. International Symposium on Information Theory* pp. 227–81. Budapest: Akailseonia-Kindo.

Andrews D. W. K. (1986) Power in econometric application. Mimeo, Yale University.

Anstie, R., Gray M. R. and Pagan A. R. (1983) Inflation and the consumption ratio. In P. K. Trivedi and A. R. Pagan (eds) *The Effects of Inflation: Theoretical Investigations and Australian Evidence*. Centre for Economic Policy Research, Canberra, Australia.

Barro, R. J. (1977) Unanticipated money growth and unemployment in the United States. *American Economic Review* 67, 101–15.

Berkson, J. (1938) Some difficulties of interpretation encountered in the application of the chi-square test. *Journal of the American Statistical Association* 33, 526–42.

Breusch, T. S. (1985) Simplified extreme bounds. University of Southampton Discussion Paper No. 8515.

Cameron, A. C. and Trivedi, P. K. (1986) Econometric models based on count data: comparisons and applications of some estimators and tests. *Journal of Applied Econometrics* 1, 29–54.

Cooley, T. F. and LeRoy, S. F. (1981) Identification and estimation of money demand. *American Economic Review* 71, 825–44.

—— (1985) Atheoretical macroeconometrics: a critique. *Journal of Monetary Economics* 16, 283–308.

Doan, T., Litterman, R. and Sims, C. (1984) Forecasting and conditional projection using realistic prior distributions. *Econometric Reviews* 3, 1–100

Drèze, J. H. and Richard, J. F. (1983) Bayesian analysis of simultaneous equation systems. In Z. Griliches and M. D. Intriligator (eds) *Handbook of Econometrics*. Amsterdam: North-Holland.

Engle, R. F. (1984) Likelihood ratio, Lagrange multiplier and Wald tests in econometrics. In Z. Griliches and M. D. Intriligator (eds) *Handbook of Econometrics*. Amsterdam: North-Holland.

Feldstein, M. (1982) Inflation, tax rules and investment: some econometric evidence. *Econometrica* 50, 825–62.

Fisher, F. M. (1961) On the cost of approximate specification in simultaneous-equation estimation. *Econometrica* 29, 139–70.

Hall, R. E. (1978) Stochastic implications of the life cycle—permanent income hypothesis: theory and evidence. *Journal of Political Economy* 86, 971–1007.

Harper, I. R. (1980) The relationship between unemployment and unfilled vacancies in Australia: 1951–1978. *Economic Record* 56, 231–43.

Hausman, J. A. (1978) Specification tests in econometrics *Econometrica* 46, 1251–72.

Hendry, D. F. (1986) Empirical modelling in dynamic econometrics. Applied Economics Discussion Paper No. 1. University of Oxford.

Hendry, D. F. and Mizon, G. E. (1978) Serial correlation as a convenient simplification, not a nuisance: a comment on a study of the demand for money by the Bank of England. *Economic Journal* 88, 549–63.

—— (1985) Procrustean econometrics. Discussion Paper. University of Southampton.

Hendry, D. F. and Richard, J. F. (1982) On the formulation of empirical models in dynamic econometrics. *Journal of Econometrics* 20, 3–33.

Hill, B. (1986) Some subjective Bayesian considerations in the selection of models. *Econometric Reviews* 4, 191–246.

Kirby, M. G. (1981) An investigation of the specification and stability of the Australian aggregate wage equation. *Economic Record* 57, 35–46.

Leamer, E. E. (1978) *Specification Searches*. New York: Wiley.

—— (1983) Let's take the con out of econometrics. *American Economic Review* 73, 31–44.

—— (1985) Sensitivity analyses would help. *American Economic Review* 75, 308–13.

—— (1986) A Bayesian analysis of the determinants of inflation. In D. A. Belsley and E. Kuh (eds) *Model Reliability* Cambridge, Mass.: M.I.T. Press.

Leamer, E. E. and Leonard, H. (1983) Reporting the fragility of regression estimates. *Review of Economics and Statistics* 65, 306–17.

Litterman, R. and Weiss, L. (1985) Money, real interest rates and output: a re-interpretation of postwar U.S. data. *Econometrica* 53, 129–56.

Liu, T. C. (1960) Underidentification, structural estimation, and forecasting. *Econometrica* 28, 855–65.

McAleer, M., Pagan, A. R. and Volker, P. A. (1983) Straw-man econometrics. Working Paper in Econometrics No. 097. Australian National University.

—— (1985) What will take the con out of econometrics? *American Economic Review* 75, 293–307.

Malinvaud, E. (1984) Comment to forecasting and conditional projection using realistic prior distributions. *Econometric Reviews* 3, 113–18.

Mallows, C. L. (1973) Some comments on C_p. *Technometrics* 15, 661–75.

Marschak, J. (1953) Economic measurements for policy and prediction. In W. C. Hood and T. C. Koopmans (eds) *Studies in Econometric Method (Cowles Commission Research Monograph No. 14)*. pp. 1–26. New Haven: Yale University Press.

Mill, J. S. (1967) On the definition of political economy and on the method of investigation proper to it. *Collected Works* Vol. 4. Toronto: University of Toronto Press.

Mizon, G. E. (1977) Model selection procedures. In M. J. Artis and A. R. Nobay (eds) *Studies in Modern Economic Analysis* Oxford: Basil Blackwell.

Nelson, C. R. and Plosser, C. I. (1982) Trends and random walks in macroeconomic time series: some evidence and implications. *Journal of Monetary Economics* 10, 139–62.

Newey, W. (1985) Maximum likelihood specification testing and conditional moment tests. *Econometrica* 53, 1047–70.

Pagan, A. R. (1978) Detecting autocorrelation after Bayesian regression. CORE Discussion Paper No. 7825.

—— (1984) Model evaluation by variable addition. In D. F. Hendry and K. F. Wallis (eds) *Econometrics and Quantitative Economics* Oxford: Basil Blackwell.

Pagan, A. R. and Volker, P. A. (1981) The short-run demand for transactions balances in Australia. *Economica* 48, 381–95.

Quandt, R. E. (1980) Classical and Bayesian hypothesis testing: a compromise. *Metroeconomica* XXXII, 173–80.

Rissanen, J. (1983) A universal prior for integers and estimation by minimum description length. *Annals of Statistics* 11, 416–31.

Salkever, D. S. (1976) The use of dummy variables to compute predictions, prediction errors and confidence intervals. *Journal of Econometrics* 4, 393–7.

Sargan, J. D. (1964) Wages and prices in the United Kingdom: a study in econometric methodology. In P. E. Hart, G. Mills and J. K. Whitaker (eds) *Econometric Analysis for National Economic Planning* London: Butterworth.

Schwarz, G. (1978) Estimating the dimension of a model. *Annals of Statistics* 6, 461–4.

Schweppe, F. C. (1965) Evaluation of likelihood functions for Gaussian signals. *I.E.E.E. Transactions on Information Theory* 11, 61–70.

Shiller, R. J. (1973) A distributed lag estimator derived from smoothness priors. *Econometrica* 41, 775–88.

Sims, C. A. (1980a) Macroeconomics and reality. *Econometrica* 48, 1–47.

—— (1980b) Comparison of interwar and postwar cycles: monetarism reconsidered. *American Economic Review* 70(1980), 250–7.

Tauchen, G. (1985) Diagnostic testing and evaluation of maximum likelihood models. *Journal of Econometrics* 30, 415–43.

Veall, M. R. (1986) Inferences on the deterrent effect of capital punishment: bootstrapping the process of model selection. Mimeo, University of Western Ontario.

Zellner, A. (1971) *An Introduction to Bayesian Inference in Econometrics* New York: Wiley.

[6]

Excerpt from *The Popperian Legacy in Economics*, 199–211.

CHAPTER 7

Finding a satisfactory empirical model

MARY MORGAN

It is commonplace criticism that econometricians never refute a model that they set out to "test" in the sense that they never reject the underlying theoretical model they have used. It has been argued that refutations cannot be expected from econometrics for various reasons of a logical or philosophical nature. The less kindly, more casual observer might note that econometricians sometimes blame the paucity of data or problems with the estimation method or computing power, rather than reject a theory; in other words that, as bad workers, they blame their tools.

Without wishing to detract from the sound philosophical arguments about the inability to test economic theories, and ignoring the unkind aspersions on econometricians, I want to argue from a different viewpoint – an historical viewpoint. This viewpoint suggests that although econometricians have described their activity as that of testing economic theories, this testing should not be understood in quite the same terms as methodological discussions about falsification and verification. In my view, econometricians have been primarily concerned with finding satisfactory empirical models, not with trying to prove fundamental theories true or untrue.

Historically, econometricians sought applied counterparts to theory that "worked" with reference to observed data. This involved not only the translation of theory into empirical models but also the parallel development of criteria for labeling empirical models "satisfactory." The range of criteria formed a sort of qualitative assessment with questions centered on the issue "How well does the empirical model work with reference to the data?" This chapter examines the problem of finding an empirical model and the development of testing criteria in the early history of econometrics. The quality control idea of testing that

My thanks go to the discussant and participants at the Klant conference and to Margaret Schabas for their helpful comments on the ideas expressed in this chapter. Much of the historical material in the chapter is drawn from an extended study of the history of econometrics, initially funded by a grant from the ESRC (Grant 6727) and reported in detail in Morgan (1984).

emerges in this "pre-Popper" period contrasts with the right or wrong, true or untrue, type of assessment that seems to pervade methodological debate on theory testing in economics.

I.   Empirical models

In the late nineteenth century, both in discussions about methodology and in economic practice, economists saw statistical and mathematical methods as two different tools operating in separate spheres. The role of mathematics was to aid in the task of deductive theorizing, whereas the role of statistics was to help in the empirical task of measuring economic laws, verifying or testing theories, and even suggesting theories.[1] Modern economic practice comes close to this original vision, with mathematical economists and econometricians operating in separate, or at least sequential, areas of interest. In contrast, between the early twentieth century and the 1950s, econometrics emerged as a distinct activity in which mathematical and statistical methods were united in a single practice within economics.

The initial aim of econometricians was to use mathematics and statistics to make economic theories "concrete" and measure the constant parameters of those laws. They were faced with immediate problems. First, theories were expressed in words, rather than in mathematical form; the relationships between the variables were often poorly defined, and the variables themselves might not be measurable. Second, although economic theories were taken to be fundamentally true, econometricians found that they were not necessarily readily applicable to any real data set. In response to these difficulties, econometricians of the 1920s and 1930s tried to bring about a closer correspondence, or matching, between theory and data (Morgan, 1984). Since the theoretical models themselves could not be measured, finding empirical models that could be subjected to measurement was the first task in this program. This required the translation of the theory into a more usable form and the development of the appropriate approximations to be applied to the basic economic theory for each particular set of circumstances.[2] Analogous problems and activities occur in all sciences; for example, in apply-

---

[1] While the methodological point of view is given, for example, by Keynes (1891), Jevons's work gives the prime practical example of the separation of the two tools.

[2] In discussing this aspect of empirical model building, I have been much influenced by Nancy Cartwright's provocative book *How the Laws of Physics Lie* (1983), in which she argues that the fundamental theoretical laws of physics are true in some fundamental sense but that for any given real circumstance, they are false.

ing Boyle's law, the chemist has to rely on a set of empirically derived approximations for each substance, and these have been gathered over the years by applied chemists. Similarly, engineers have developed the relevant approximations for physical theories to be applied, for example, in building a bridge.

In economics, finding an empirical model to match the theory involved making the theory operational in several ways:

1. Translating the verbal theory into mathematical form, and deciding in what form variables should be used and on the functional form for each theory.
2. Finding ways of dealing with the *ceteris paribus* clauses under which the theory is assumed to hold (for example, choosing homogeneous periods).
3. Finding the correct model for time and space: specifying the time adjustment/dynamic processes for each theory and taking into account local specific factors (e.g., institutional features such as price-setting mechanisms).

If we take as an example the development of demand studies in the interwar period (when the field of econometrics was young but developing fast), we see that the preceding three requirements were interwoven. Translating the simple downward-sloping law of demand into a mathematical equation linking price and quantity seemed easy enough, but before the coefficient of this "law of demand" could be measured, it was necessary to find some way of keeping the other disturbing factors constant in line with the *ceteris paribus* clauses of economic theory. This was, in turn, part of the need to deal with the gap between the theory, which was static, and the data, which were usually in the form of time series.

Econometricians initially dealt with the disturbing factors that changed over time (but were assumed constant in theory) by methods that preadjusted the data before the relationships of interest were fitted. One method was to adjust the quantities demanded to remove the effect of population growth before fitting a demand curve (Lehfeldt, 1914). Toward the end of the 1920s, it was suggested that it would be better to incorporate these disturbing variables in the empirical demand relationship because they were precisely the other variables that influenced demand (Smith, 1925; Schultz, 1928). This, in turn, was linked to the task of deciding which other variables of the many suggested by theorists were actually relevant in the empirical model: for example, which other prices from the "all other prices" of demand theory were the influential ones (Ezekiel, 1933).

At the same time in the late 1920s and the early 1930s, there was a discussion within econometrics about how to deal with the time dimension of the theoretical relationships in these models. Econometricians adopted different ways of introducing dynamic aspects into empirical models. One method involved introducing time lags of various lengths into the model to capture the delays between causes and effects. Another path was to add new forms of the theoretical terms into the model to capture a more complex behavior than simple response to current prices. These were not necessarily independent approaches; their use would often depend on whether the starting point was mathematical or statistical work.

The cobweb model provides a good illustration of the first path to dynamic models. In the cobweb model, price responds to this year's quantity demanded, while supply is determined by the previous year's price. This model was first used by Moore in 1925 to model what he called a "moving equilibrium" of demand and supply. Moore gave no particular reason for this choice of model, although he might have rationalized it on the basis of knowledge of the particular market. The model formulation was analyzed and applied again in the early 1930s in three different publications by Schultz, Leontief, and Tinbergen (Ezekiel, 1938). Tinbergen (1930), for example, expressed reservations about the model because he saw that under a certain range of parameter values the model implied a path diverging away from an equilibrium solution, giving an exploding cobweb pattern. The suggestion that such a divergent path could form the basis of a crisis model was made by Evans in 1931, and in 1938 Ezekiel proposed it as an alternative explanation of the malaise of the 1930s economies: that is, the economies had adjustment processes that led away from full employment. The lagged adjustments or responses in crucial relationships that characterized the cobweb model could also, in certain circumstances, produce cycles in the variables. This version of the model entered econometric business cycle literature in the early 1930s—for example, in Frisch's propagation and impulse model of 1933—and soon became an essential element in mathematical theories of the business cycle.

In this story, the cobweb model started off in the mid-1920s as an approximation for the time relationships of an empirical demand model, but by the mid-1930s it had become an essential element of empirical cycle models and thence of cycle theory. This rapid assimilation, from an empirical approximation to an essential element in theory, was no doubt due to the integrated nature of econometrics during this early period, when those who were undertaking empirical work were also responsible for developing satisfactory mathematical versions of verbal theories. It provides a good example of how econometric work played a role in theory development.

An example of the second way of formulating dynamic models is given by the work of Roos and Evans. Roos was an econometrician who became the director of economic research of the National Recovery Administration under the New Deal initiative in the United States and the first research director of the Cowles Commission (whose research program during the 1930s was purely econometric). He left academia in the late 1930s to form perhaps the first econometric consulting company. Evans was primarily a mathematician, and consequently his role was in the development of mathematical formulations and adaptations of economic theory. The mathematical demand models developed by Roos and Evans all involved quantity as the dependent variable and incorporated as explanatory variables a simple current price term, a term depicting the influence of past prices (the integral over past prices), a term incorporating the rate of change of prices (a differential term), and lastly, a linear time trend. They combined these terms in different ways: For example, the differential term was thought to be particularly appropriate in modeling speculative demand in wholesale markets, while the time trend was a commonly used approximation to cover influential trending variables. Roos adapted these to empirical models and applied them to individual commodities in a substantial monograph in econometrics entitled *Dynamic Economics* (1934). Roos's influence is less easy to trace than his career. Nevertheless, a study of the literature shows that the Roos–Evans equations were used in discussions of demand by Schultz (1938), whose work was highly influential, and by many others.

The use of past values and rates of change to help explain present values of variables and delayed responses within economic relationships was a fairly general development. Adjustment processes were used to model not only the past but also the future. Roos touched on the problem of expectations in his attempt to model speculators' demand by the rate of change of prices. Tinbergen (1933) attacked the problem of expectations more directly in trying to assess the planning horizons and reaction times of agents to unforeseen changes.

In general, the adaptations that econometricians made to verbal theories (whether justified by rationalizations of a semitheoretical kind or not) were designed to produce models with empirical relevance. This meant formulating a model that had the "correct" theoretical properties (e.g., equilibrium tendencies) but that also incorporated elements to

204   **Morgan**

make the model relevant to the particular real circumstances. The latter involved several possibilities. It could mean introducing elements to match some general observed features of data, such as cycles, or more specific observed features such as those seen in the market for a particular commodity. Above all, an empirical model must be one that is measurable. This translation of theories into empirical models that can be fitted to statistical data was described earlier as making theories "operational." This term was used deliberately, for Percy Bridgman was the only philosopher of science whose work was referenced by those involved in the econometric work of the period. Both Roos (1934) and Schultz (1938), important figures in econometrics, expressed admiration for Bridgman's ideas and used their books to try to introduce operationalism into economics. As Klant (1984) points out, Bridgman's ideas on operationalism had considerable influence on economists in the 1930s.[3]

These early econometricians were open and direct about their desire to translate theory into empirical models. Within the demand field, for example, there was some discussion about the relative roles of theorists (meaning nonmathematical economists) and of econometricians in developing such models. The econometricians blamed the theorists for their failure to develop adequate models to cope with the problem of time, and the consequent necessity for their own development of such models (Gilboy, 1930; Stigler, 1939). Some economists clearly resented what they saw as statisticians interfering in economic theory. For example, Keynes's famous critique (1939) of Tinbergen's work accused him of plucking lag lengths out of midair. Such criticisms were unfair, for as any econometrician of the period well knew, theorists just did not supply such information in their theories.

II.   Satisfactory models

Achieving a satisfactory level of correspondence between economic data and economic theory involved not only developing appropriate empirical (measurable) models but estimating these models (measuring the parameters of the relationships) and then deciding whether they were satisfactory or not. The assessment of models as "satisfactory" depends, of course, on the purpose of the empirical models. Early econometricians had many ideas about the purposes of their models and about assessing whether their models were satisfactory, but these ideas were rarely expressed clearly.

---

[3] For example, Klant reminds us that Samuelson's *Foundations of Economic Analysis* was written in 1937 under the title *The Operational Significance of Economic Theory*.

7 Finding a satisfactory empirical model   205

Their aims and criteria ranged over the following set of ideas:

1. To measure theoretical laws: Models must satisfy certain theoretical requirements (economic criteria).
2. To explain (or describe) the observed data: Models must fit observed data (statistical or historical criteria).
3. To be useful for policy: Models must allow the exploration of policy options or make predictions about future values.
4. To explore or develop theory: Models must expose unsuspected relationships or develop the detail of relationships.
5. To verify or reject theory: Models must be satisfactory or not over a range of economic, statistical, and other criteria.

Often econometric work covered several of these aims.

The main purpose of the earliest work, in the 1910s and 1920s, was to measure the parameters of empirical models based on theoretical laws that were assumed to be true. These were assessed by criteria based on economic theory. The primary criterion was whether the measured parameters had the "correct," that is, the expected, theoretical sign (Lehfeldt, 1915), and the size of the parameter was secondary. By the 1930s the purposes of empirical models and their assessment were widening. Other criteria were being developed, for example, parameter constancy when the empirical model was fitted over different time periods. Statistical criteria, which were external to economic theory and concerned with measures of fit to data, were introduced very gradually.

Two examples of applied work from the 1930s give an idea of how econometricians assessed whether their empirical models were satisfactory. These are not representative examples, for both economists were more coherent about their assessment strategies and used more criteria than most of their fellow econometricians of the period. Whitman (1936) was a product of the pragmatic U.S. school of econometricians; he developed the work of Roos and Schultz in the case of the demand for steel. His aim was not entirely clear, but he seemed to have been seeking a more detailed and applicable version of the theory of demand. He used the Roos–Evans empirical models (discussed previously) and estimated three models (rejecting Roos's integral variable as unmeasurable in favor of Evans's variable involving the sum of lagged prices). Each model was fitted for three different time periods, chosen because he believed that each period was reasonably homogeneous. He compared the models on the basis of (1) the "rationality" of the implied theoretical explanation; (2) the signs of the parameters (whether they were "correct"); (3) the sizes and stability of the parameters over the three time periods and their standard errors; and (4) the degree of statistical explanation achieved by the model (corrected R^2). He described the empirical models that were most satisfactory according to these criteria as "fairly good demand equations."

Whitman's comparison of alternative empirical models did not involve choosing between different fundamental theories but rather between different empirical models of the same theory involving different dynamic processes. He was not seeking to prove one of these models as the true one, but to find the most satisfactory of the different versions. His comparison used a relatively sophisticated assessment process for the period, for it tested the models' consistency with both theory and statistical data in a coherent way. Those that performed better on the tests were better models, but for Whitman they still held the interim status of "hypotheses" pending further econometric investigation.

Tinbergen was a product of the more mixed European tradition, also pragmatic in its way. In his macroeconometric modeling of the late 1930s (1937 and 1939) Tinbergen was, as always, modest and cautious in his work, though he did claim to "test" theories. He stated his belief on testing clearly: that statistical work cannot prove a theory correct, though it can go some way toward proving a hypothesis incorrect. Because of the difficulties involved in building and estimating a large macro-model, Tinbergen used graphic means to help choose the variables in the equations and assemble the empirical model. This method seemed to involve ad hoc adjustments and manipulations, but the work gained rather than lost from Tinbergen's willingness to be open about the problems involved. One of his aims was to use the final macro-model to simulate different policy options and to assess which policy would be most useful in reducing unemployment. He found that he could indeed use his empirical models for this task.

Tinbergen was one of the few econometricians to develop a well-defined testing program, using every possible criterion that had been developed in econometrics by the late 1930s to assess his empirical models. First, he considered the consistency of his results with economic theories in respect to the individual relationships and then in terms of the implied dynamic process of the system. He used statistical criteria to assess how well his model characterized the data set and to test whether assumptions about the technical properties required by the statistical method held true. (For example, he tested for constancy of the equations' parameters over different subperiods.) He also used historical criteria to see whether his empirical model explained certain peculiar historical features of the period such as the 1929 Great Crash. The information from these testing criteria was used to help him to reformulate his empirical model in an iterative process, for Tinbergen kept refining his model to find one that was more satisfactory than the last.

Consistency with theory, satisfactory fit to the data, sensible explanations of the history, and satisfactory fulfillment of the conditions and assumptions of the econometric method were the criteria that the empirical model must satisfy, and Tinbergen was sufficiently happy with the results of his assessment to claim "statistical verification." By this, he meant that his empirical model satisfactorily explained the statistical/historical data. During the process of building his model, Tinbergen had rejected some theories, or elements of theories, on the grounds that his empirical models of these theories did not explain the data. It was noticeable that formal ways of rejecting models using statistical tests were still lacking in econometrics. The introduction of more rigorous formal ideas of theory testing in econometrics was due to the work in the 1940s of Haavelmo, who introduced the probability approach into econometrics and placed the subject more firmly on its statistical foundations (Morgan, 1987). This change was established with the help of econometricians at the Cowles Commission.

Haavelmo (1944) stated that in the absence of an experimental framework in economics, econometrics must act on both the theory and the data, making adjustments on both sides in order to get satisfactory models. He also stated that a theory became a hypothesis that could be tested only when it was associated with a design of experiments that showed how to measure the variables and make the necessary approximations to get an empirical model. This was, of course, what econometricians in the 1920s and 1930s had already been doing in formulating empirical models. According to Haavelmo, all theories should also be formulated as probabilistic statements, for any theory formulated as an exact equation (one with no probabilistic or random element) was useless from the point of view of economics; it would always be rejected by observations (Haavelmo, 1943). What was required was some way of allowing true theories to be accepted most of the time and false theories to be rejected most of the time when they were tested against data. Probability theory, together with Neyman–Pearson testing methods, seemed to offer such a procedure. Using this framework, econometricians could throw out theories that often failed the statistical tests; but they might be left with many theories that were compatible with the same observed data set, and it was impossible to prove which of these theories were true. Since Haavelmo had already stated that tests could be made only after a theory had been formulated as a probabilistic empirical model, in effect he gave econometricians a formal procedure for rejecting empirical models.

Following Haavelmo's introduction of the probability approach to econometrics in 1944, a much fuller use of statistical techniques, and in particular Neyman–Pearson testing methods, came into econometrics. It is important to note the emphasis Haavelmo placed, not only on the probabilistic theory formulation and associated testing mechanism, but also on the "design of experiments" role of econometrics. The role of econometrics in designing the correct approximations or additions to theory is a strong current going back through the empirical work of the 1920s and forward to post–World War II econometrics.

III.   Testing

The testing developed by the early econometricians involved an idea of quality control and quality ranking. In the first place, a range of criteria were applied to empirical models to distinguish those that were satisfactory from those that were not. If the empirical model exhibited a basic set of qualities (satisfied the criteria), it was considered satisfactory. This set of qualities included both economic theory criteria and data criteria because the empirical models that econometricians worked with were a sort of halfway house, formed to capture the correspondence between theory and data, and thus needed to satisfy both sides. When empirical models failed to work according to the given set of quality indicators, the usual response of econometricians in the 1930s was to use a different set of approximations – that is, an alternative empirical model – rather than an alternative fundamental theory. In the second place, the tests provided a sort of ranking of empirical models: The model that performed best on the set of quality control indicators was considered the most satisfactory.

A study of the history of econometrics suggests that prior to Popper, there were ideas about testing in economics that were rather different in aim and meaning from the usual notions of refutation, confirmation, verification, or falsification. Present-day econometricians apparently focus their energies more explicitly on testing theories than earlier workers in the field, and the language of econometrics is now in a sense more Popperian, for models are typically rejected or not rejected. This change of emphasis and language in econometrics masks a continuity of both thought and practice with earlier work, for the testing notions adopted from the 1920s to the 1940s have naturally left a legacy.

It is easy to find examples of this legacy. In the process of finding satisfactory empirical models, the early econometricians built up a fund of empirical models or models with empirical relevance. Modern econometricians have continued this practice and now have access to a library of empirical models and approximations to which new ones may be added and from which old ones can be borrowed, applied, and comparisons made. For example, present-day econometricians can use one of a range of dynamic adjustment processes varying from the cobweb model or Irving Fisher's distributed lag model (both dating from 1925) to the more modern error correction models popularized by Davidson et al. (1978).[4] The presence of this set of ready-made approximations does not mean that any one of them will be automatically correct, but only that they have been found to work in similar circumstances. Indeed, such approximations go into the theory, as in the cobweb model, and sometimes become the source of theoretical argument in themselves – for example, whether expectations are adaptive or rational.

The quality control idea of testing can also be helpful in understanding and interpreting present practice in econometrics. For example, Gilbert (1986) compares British and American attitudes toward the presence of serial correlation. For both groups of economists, serial correlation is an unsatisfactory quality to find in an empirical model, but their response varies. Gilbert describes how the Americans see serial correlation as a "pathological" symptom of failure in the econometric model, whereas the British consider it an indication of how the empirical model needs to be reformulated to obtain a model with a better set of qualities. The latter approach shows that the notion of quality control testing is still to be found in the work of some current econometricians who, despite differences in language, share the same concerns as their predecessors.[5]

References

Cartwright, N. (1983). *How the Laws of Physics Lie*. Oxford: Clarendon Press.

Christ, C. (1966). *Econometric Models and Methods*. New York: Wiley.

Davidson, J.E.H., D.F. Hendry, F. Srba, and S. Yeo (1978). "Econometric Modelling of the Aggregate Time-Series Relationship between Consumers' Expenditure and Income in the United Kingdom," *Economic Journal* 88:661–92.

Evans, G.C. (1931). "A Simple Theory of Economic Crises," *Journal of the American Statistical Association* 26:61–8.

---

[4] See, for example, textbooks in econometrics, the survey article by Griliches (1967), or the recent listing of dynamic model formulations by Hendry and Richard (1982, Section 3).

[5] See, for example, Hendry (1983) for a very recent, relatively nontechnical discussion of empirical models and their evaluation that is close to the ideas discussed here. An earlier example of a similar approach is given by Carl Christ's text (1966).

210   **Morgan**

Ezekiel, M. (1933). "Some Considerations on the Analysis of the Prices of Competing or Substitute Commodities," *Econometrica* 1:172–80.

(1938). "The Cobweb Theorem," *Quarterly Journal of Economics* 52:255–80.

Fisher, I. (1925). "Our Unstable Dollar and the So-Called Business Cycle," *Journal of the American Statistical Association* 20:179–202.

Frisch, R. (1933). "Propagation Problems and Impulse Problems in Dynamic Economics," in *Economic Essays in Honour of Gustav Cassel.* London: Allen & Unwin.

Gilbert, C. (1986). "The Development of British Econometrics, 1945–85." Applied Economics Discussion Paper No. 8, Institute of Economics and Statistics, Oxford.

Gilboy, E.W. (1930). "Demand Curves in Theory and Practice," *Quarterly Journal of Economics* 44:601–20.

Griliches, Z. (1967). "Distributed Lags: A Survey," *Econometrica* 35:16–49.

Haavelmo, T. (1943). "Statistical Testing of Business Cycle Theories," *Review of Economics and Statistics* 25:13–18.

(1944). "The Probability Approach in Econometrics," *Econometrica* 12 (suppl.).

Hendry, D.F. (1983). "Econometric Modelling: The Consumption Function in Retrospect,"*Scottish Journal of Political Economy* 30:193–220.

and Richard, J.F. (1982). "On the Formulation of Empirical Models in Dynamic Econometrics," *Journal of Econometrics* 20:3–33.

Keynes, J.M., and Tinbergen, J. (1939 and 1940). "Professor Tinbergen's Method," *EJ* 49:558–68. Review of J. Tinbergen (1939): *Statistical Testing of Business Cycle Theories,* Vol. I. Geneva: League of Nations. "A Reply" by Tinbergben and "Comment" by Keynes, *Economic Journal* 50:141–56.

Keynes, J.N. (1891). *The Scope and Method of Political Economy.* London: Macmillan.

Klant, J.J. (1984). *The Rules of the Game.* Cambridge: Cambridge University Press.

Lehfeldt, R.A. (1914). "The Elasticity of the Demand for Wheat," *Economic Journal* 24:212–17.

(1915). "Review of H.L. Moore: *Economic Cycles: Their Law and Cause,*" *Economic Journal* 25:409–11.

Marschak, J. (1942). "Economic Interdependence and Statistical Analysis," O. Lange, F. McIntyre, and T.O. Yntema, eds., *Studies in Mathematical Economics and Econometrics – In Memory of Henry Schultz.* Chicago: University of Chicago Press.

Moore, H.L. (1925). "A Moving Equilibrium of Demand and Supply," *Quarterly Journal of Economics* 39:357–71.

Morgan, M.S. (1984). "The History of Econometric Thought," Ph.D. thesis, London School of Economics. Forthcoming as *The History of Econometric Ideas.* Cambridge University Press.

(1987). "Statistics without Probability and Haavelmo's Revolution in Econometrics," in L. Krüger, G. Gigerenzer, and M.S. Morgan, eds., *The Proba-*

bilistic Revolution, Vol. II: *Ideas in the Sciences.* Cambridge, Mass: MIT Press.

Roos, C.F. (1934). *Dynamic Economics.* Cowles Commission Monograph 1. Bloomington, Ind.: Principia Press.

Samuelson, P.A. (1947). *Foundations of Economic Analysis.* Cambridge, Mass.: Harvard University Press.

Schultz, H. (1928). *Statistical Laws of Demand and Supply with Special Application to Sugar.* Chicago: University of Chicago Press.

(1933). "A Comparison of Elasticities of Demand Obtained by Different Methods," *Econometrica* 1:274–308.

(1938). *The Theory and Measurement of Demand.* Chicago: University of Chicago Press.

Smith, B.B. (1925). "The Error in Eliminating Secular Trend and Seasonal Variation before Correlating Time Series," *Journal of the American Statistical Association* 20:543–45.

Stigler, G.J. (1939). "The Limitations of Statistical Demand Curves," *Journal of the American Statistical Association* 34:469–81.

Tinbergen, J. (1930). "Bestimmung und Deutung von Angebotskurven," *Zeitschrift für Nationalökonomie* 1:669–79. (English summary, 798–99.)

(1933). "The Notion of Horizon and Expectancy in Dynamic Economics," *Econometrica* 1:247–64.

(1937). *An Econometric Approach to Business Cycle Problems.* Paris: Hermann.

(1939). *Statistical Testing of Business Cycle Theories,* Vols. I and II. Geneva: League of Nations.

Whitman, R.H. (1936). "The Statistical Law of Demand for a Producer's Good as Illustrated by the Demand for Steel," *Econometrica* 4:138–52.

[7]

The Limits of Expertise

If You're So Smart, Why Ain't You Rich?

DONALD N. McCLOSKEY

AMERICANS SAY THEY DON'T HOLD MUCH WITH EXPERTS. Harry Truman said that the expert is someone who doesn't want to learn anything new because then he wouldn't be an expert. Europeans appear to need experts for a society of deference, to which the American response is a Bronx cheer. Though Nicholas Murray Butler made Morningside Heights an American refuge for experts, he said that they know more and more about less and less. The European next to him in the roll of remarks, Samuel Butler the Younger, had little respect for pretension in general but plenty for the pretension of experts: "The public do not know enough to be experts, yet know enough to decide between them." You don't say. The rhetoric of the New World abounds with deflations of pretense: "Look who's talking"; "Where do you get off?" "Who d'you think *you* are, Bub?" And from Maine to California the capitalistic, American democrat relishes that most American of sneers, that American Question: "If you're so smart, why ain't you rich?"

Well, why ain't you? The American scholar suffers taunts, unimaginable in Germany or France, for not meeting a payroll, for not coming down from the ivory tower, for not getting wet behind the ears of his arrogant egghead. But, if he's so gosh darn smart, why *hasn't* he gotten rich?

The question cuts deeper than most scholars care to admit. The test of riches is a fair one if the expertise claims to deliver the riches, in gold or in glory. At a minimum the American Question should constrain scholarship about gold, and the story can therefore begin with economics. It goes further, though. The Question embarrasses anyone claiming profitable expertise who cannot show a profit, the historian second-guessing generals, or the critic propounding a formula for art. He who is

⊘ DONALD N. McCLOSKEY is professor of economics and history at the University of Iowa. His recent books are *The Rhetoric of Economics*, *The Writing of Economics*, and *Econometric History*; he co-edited *The Rhetoric of the Human Sciences*. He claims that this essay was conceived and written before the recent stock-market crash.

so smart claims a Faustian knowledge, "Whose deepness doth entice such forward wits / To practice more than heavenly power permits."

I

Take it as an axiom of human behavior that people pick up five-hundred-dollar bills left on the sidewalk. The Axiom of Modest Greed involves no close calculation of advantage or large willingness to take a risk. The average person sees a quarter and sidles over to it; he sees a five-hundred-dollar bill and jumps for it. The axiom is not controversial. All economists subscribe to it, whether or not they "believe in the market" (as the shorthand test for ideology goes), and so should you. Yet it has a distressing outcome, a dismal commonplace of adult life, a sad little Five-Hundred-Dollar-Bill Theorem:

If the Axiom of Modest Greed applies, then there exists no sidewalk in the neighborhood of your house on which a five-hundred-dollar bill remains.

For proof, consider that if there had been a five-hundred-dollar bill lying there at one time, then, according to the axiom, someone would have picked it up before today.

From this scientific reasoning it is a short step to common sense. If a man offers advice on how to find a five-hundred-dollar bill on the sidewalk, for which he asks merely a nominal fee, the prudent adult declines the offer. If there really were a five-hundred-dollar bill, then the confidence man would pick it up himself.

Such common sense is so obvious that confidence games must clothe themselves in a false rhetoric of self-interest. In a trick called the Pigeon Drop, the victim (that is, the pigeon) is persuaded to part with his bank account as earnest money for a share in a bundle of money "found" on the sidewalk. He must be persuaded that the con men are asking for the earnest money only as self-interested protection against the pigeon himself absconding with the bundle (which, after the con men have disappeared with his bank account, turns out to be paper stacked between two ten-dollar bills). Even pigeons don't believe that someone will present them with five hundred dollars out of the goodness of his heart.

The leading case is the scheme to get rich quick. A letter arrives from Edward L. Green announcing: "The World's Greatest Secret! Now you can learn how to receive fifty thousand crisp five-dollar bills in the next ninety days. . . . A personal note from the originator of the plan." Green's surprising kindness is affirmed by Carl Winslow of Tulsa: "This is the

THE LIMITS OF EXPERTISE

only realistic money-making offer I've ever received. I participated because this plan truly makes sense!"

Common sense replies that the plan truly does not make sense, not any sense at all. Though the plan uses the rhetoric of mutual interest—believe me, fella, this deal's good for you and me both—it fails to turn the rhetoric on itself. If Mr. Green had the secret for receiving fifty thousand crisp five-dollar bills, he would clue you in only if your one crisp five-dollar bill was good for the chain and good for Edward L. Green. But you have no reason beyond Mr. Green's assurances to think you are early in the chain. If you are not, you send out money and get nothing in return. A child will subscribe to a chain letter—or a guaranteed investment in Civil War figurines or a set of presidential commemorative coins suitable for collectors—and expect to win; an adult will not. No one with experience of life believes Publisher's Clearing House when it writes, "*Ms. Z. Smithh*, you have just won $250,000." The adult does not expect fortune to come unbidden and asks prudently, "Why are they telling me this?" Prudence suspects an offer equivalent to picking up a five-hundred-dollar bill. Except to the flocks of optimistic Americans who invest daily in chain letters and prizewinning magazine subscriptions, this goes without saying.

Therefore, the bargains and hot tips and special deals for you alone offered by over-friendly men with clammy handshakes at dog tracks and used-car lots do not tempt the prudent adult. Yet similar offers made outside a Damon Runyon setting seem plausible to respectable if greedy folk. The high-class pigeons come flocking to the con, eager to believe that Mr. Expert is about to give them free advice on how to make a million.

Economists, for example, are routinely asked at cocktail parties what is going to happen to the interest rate or the price of housing or the price of corn. People think that asking an economist about the future is like asking the doctor at the party about that chest pain, getting an expert to do his job free. Take corn. Any agricultural economist·in the Midwest spends much of his television airtime delivering expert opinion on what will happen next month to the price of corn. Surely he, this expert, must know if anyone does. It would be depressing news to be told that, after all, no one does know.

An economist who claims to know what is going to happen to the price of corn, however, is claiming to know how to pick up five hundred dollars. With a little borrowing on the equity of his home or his reputation for sobriety, he can proceed to pick up five hundred thousand dollars, then five hundred million, then more. Nothing to it. If an agricultural economist could predict the price of corn better than the futures market, he would be rich. Yet he does not put his money where his mouth is. He is not rich. It follows that he is not so smart.

THE AMERICAN SCHOLAR

It may be objected that the profit making is risky and that professors of economics are cautious. Therefore, they do not put their money where their mouths are, even though their mouths are working fine. The objection has the problem that the bet on the price of corn can be hedged, which is insurance. It is no bet. Someone who can outsmart the market on average even a little can make a lot of money simply and safely. The opportunity to buy corn low and sell high, like the right to run a TV station in the 1960s or to import Toyotas in the 1980s, is like finding a five-hundred-dollar bill anytime you want.

It may be objected that the profit making is complicated and that professors of economics are elaborately trained experts in the complexities. Therefore the five-hundred-dollar bill is not available to just anyone, only to them. The wizards earn merely what they are worth, the normal return for years of studying wizardry. This objection, too, has problems. The first is that the wizards are telling us about the future price of corn or bonds or housing at cocktail parties and in the newspaper—for free. Why are they handing over to John Doe their just reward for going to wizard school? The second problem is that the wizardry claimed is systematic, formulaic, and, when you come right down to it, pretty simple. It involves the fitting of a few straight lines to scatters of points. Take a course in economic statistics, the promise goes, and become able to predict the future in profitable ways. The promise is hard to believe, because it sounds a lot like The World's Greatest Secret. Ordinary secrets and routine advice do flow from economics, and doubtless economists earn their keep. Unlimited wealth, however, cannot be expected to flow from a book or even from many years of concentrated study in economics. Compared to unlimited wealth, many years of study is like the trivial cost of reaching down to pick up a five-hundred-dollar bill. If someone knows a scholarly formula for predicting the price of corn, it would already have been exploited.

The same grim truth from the American Question applies to the stock market. Because the stock market is obviously a matter of expectations, about which we all know something, and because it is crowded with experts in handsome wool suits, the truth is hard to swallow. Hey, *Barron's* and "Wall Street Week" wouldn't kid me, would they? Surely all those analysts and pundits and technical elves know *something*.

No, unhappily, they surely do not. They truly do not make sense, not any sense at all. The reason they do not is the American Question and the Five-Hundred-Dollar-Bill Theorem: there exists no sidewalk in your neighborhood with five hundred dollars of stock-market profits lying on it. If a stockbroker were so smart, he would not be making his riches by selling stock tips to widows and orphans. In the style of the chain letter, the tipster divulges inside information for his gain and your loss. The

THE LIMITS OF EXPERTISE

rhetorical pose of stockbrokers and racetrack tipsters to be offering prudent advice is contradicted by their circumstances, a contradiction catalogued in rhetoric as the "circumstantial *ad hominem*." That is to say, "Being so smart, why don't you do it yourself, if it's such good advice?"

"A tout," said Damon Runyon, who knew the score on the economics of prediction, "is a guy who goes around a race track giving out tips on the races, if he can find anybody who will listen to his tips, especially suckers, and a tout is nearly always broke. If he is not broke, he is by no means a tout, but a handicapper, and is respected by one and all."

We know the force of the American Question and the Five-Hundred-Dollar-Bill Theorem as well as we know anything. If we know that the sun will rise tomorrow and that prime numbers are odd, we know that people who were so smart would be rich and that sidewalks that were so filled with five-hundred-dollar bills would be cleared. Therefore, a prediction about stocks—as distinct from mere current information about the market, a mere statement of the going odds, a mere consensus of public opinion, reflected in the price—is on average worthless.

It has been easy, therefore, to assemble statistical evidence that the Five-Hundred-Dollar-Bill Theorem is true about Wall Street: stock markets everywhere do in fact jiggle about in unpredictable ways. The evidence is by now overwhelming. In 1933 Alfred Cowles, the founder of the journal *Econometrica*, posed the question in a title, "Can Stock Market Forecasters Forecast?" "It is," he answered, "doubtful." Cowles himself had abandoned a forecasting business in 1931, ashamed of his failure to foresee the Great Crash. Burton Malkiel's *A Random Walk Down Wall Street* (1985) gives an accessible summary of the research since Cowles; one such study is P. H. Cootner, ed., *The Random Character of Stock Prices* (1964). The forecastability of stock prices continues to be at best doubtful.

It may be objected that sophisticated people do in fact buy stock-market advice. An economist (and only an economist) would conclude that something of value had been bought. A reply has been suggested by James Burk, a sociologist and former stockbroker, who found that the advice-giving industry sprang from legal decisions early in the century. The courts began to decide that the trustee of a pension fund or of a child's inheritance could be held liable for bad investing if he did not take advice. The effect would have been the same had the courts decided that prudent men should consult Ouija boards or the flights of birds. It was so at Rome: a consul who ignored the advice of the college of augurs was liable to prosecution after retirement. America decided through its judges that an industry giving advice on the stock market should come into existence, whether or not it was worthless. It did, and it was.

THE AMERICAN SCHOLAR

(Europe is not similarly blessed, because the law is different.) The industry can go out of existence the same way. The judge who first asks the American Question and rules a stockbroker liable for his unsuccessful advice will save many a widow and orphan from investment counseling.

It may be objected that, after all, a great deal of money is made in the stock market. This is true also at the track in Miami. Grandfather Stueland was offered Radio Corporation of America stock in the early 1920s and regretted later that he had invested in Stueland Electric instead. Some people did buy RCA; they must have known. But that some people win with the stockbroker or the hundred-dollar window at Hialeah does not mean that they were justified in their true belief. They could have won by luck rather than by a justifying technique. People win at slot machines, too, but cannot tell how, because they use no justifiable, inscribable, bookable technique. And even if some people *do* know they will win (God appears to them in a dream and tells them, maybe; or they have genuine inside knowledge), there is no way for the common pigeon to know that these alleged experts know. Why would they be telling you, Bub?

It may be objected at last that the economist or another seer in the stock or bond or housing market does not have access to the big loans to make big money. Yet consortiums do, and if the wisdom comes simply from being an economist, it ought to be easy to assemble them. A consortium of famous economists at Stanford and the University of Chicago in the early 1970s believed that interest rates, which were then at shocking, unprecedented highs (6, 6.5, my Lord, even 7.5 percent), just had to come down. The price of bonds, in other words, just had to go up. A good time to buy bonds. The economists complained at lunch that their bankers would not loan them money to exploit this sure thing, the world's greatest secret. But in the event, sadly, the bankers were right. Interest rates did not fall; they rose. The consortium of economists, relying on its collective expertise, lost its collective shirt.

The routine is the usual one. I myself have lost a shirt or two on real estate deals bound to succeed and on a consortium of economists speculating in the foreign exchanges. From John Maynard Keynes (who lost money regularly before breakfast) and Irving Fisher (who reduced Yale's endowment to half Harvard's by touting stocks in 1928) down to the latest scheme of some economist to make money from mathematical models of gold speculation, economists have not earned the confidence of bankers. As it was put by Paul Samuelson, a student of these matters, "It's a mug's game for a dentist—or an associate professor of econometrics—to think that he and the telephone can have an edge over those who count the cocoa pods in Africa and follow the minute-by-minute arrival of new information."

THE LIMITS OF EXPERTISE

The best-known counter-example among economists is said to be the late Otto Eckstein, a superb economist with much common sense who extended the large-scale econometric model into commercial use. He built Data Resources, Inc., into a company with revenues in 1984 of eighty-four million dollars. But Data Resources did not use its own predictions of prices and interest rates to speculate. It sold them to others, mainly to companies who wanted a myth of knowledge to comfort them in uncertainty and to answer wrathful stockholders: "We took the best advice." If Data Resources had believed its own predictions to the extent of speculating on them, and was correct in its belief, then it could have become fabulously richer than it was. To say that Otto Eckstein or Paul Samuelson or other honest purveyors of economic tips became in fact a little bit rich does not answer the American Question. Eckstein and Samuelson (and Louis Rukeyser of Wall Street and Hot Horse Herbie of Broadway) became rich by *selling* advice, in the form of models and statistical equations and other charming talk, not by using it.

Cato the Elder reported of the haruspices, who examined livers in Rome with an expertise approaching the econometric, that they could not but laugh on meeting one another. Economists know lots of similar gags about their inability to predict profitably: forecasting is very difficult, especially if it is about the future; an economist is an expert who can tell you tomorrow why the thing he predicted yesterday didn't happen today; the best I can hope for in a forecast is to be intelligently wrong or fortunately right.

Yet one must not get carried away. No one doubts that a well-informed economist can tell you a thing or two about the future, mainly from knowing the present well. As the economist Robert Solow re-marked about the predictions from Data Resources, "Every month it provides an orderly description of the data, organized in such a way that one's attention is called to events that seem to conform with a reasonable person's understanding of the economy." The American Question casts no doubt on predictions that offer little or no profit. A prediction makes no profit if it is a commonplace or if it does not offer a way to buy low and sell high. Predicting that the national income will not fall to zero next year is no more profitable than predicting that the sun will rise tomor-row.

Other people view economists as social weather forecasters. Econo-mists are not happy with that analogy, since they know they are not so smart. Weather forecasters and price forecasters could both earn a lot of money on a good forecast if they could keep it secret. Come to mention it, though, economists don't do much of a job as public forecasters. Victor Zarnowitz, the leading scholar in the field, makes only modest claims for the most promising method. A recent study by Zarnowitz and Geoffrey

Moore showed that "leading indicators," invented by Moore and now reported monthly in the press, can indeed predict business cycle peaks—but with leads, alas, ranging from one to nineteen months. "The economists are generally right in their predictions," Sidney Webb said once, "but generally a good deal out in their dates." Predicting the end of prosperity as coming somewhere in the next nineteen months is a little better than saying that, if it's August, then southern Florida has a fair chance after a while of getting a hurricane. Yet it is not so smart that the economic forecaster could retire to Miami. It is not good enough to be profitable; and if it were, it would already be discounted.

There are other ways of getting to the same doubt that economists can predict. For one thing, unlike humans, hurricanes are not listening. Humans react to economic predictions in ways that dampen or magnify the predictions. It would be as though the hurricane currently north of Cuba reacted to a forecast that tomorrow it was going to move to Miami by saying, "Hmm, I'd better turn around and go to Haiti instead." This is the point made by conservative economists suggesting that people have "rational expectations." One does not have to accept every notion in rational expectations to believe the more modest theorem proposed here. It would suggest, modestly, that the people are not so stupid that they are easy to surprise; if they are not easy to surprise, then the economy is not easy to manipulate, and its manipulators would not be rich.

Further and more deeply, the equations of fluid dynamics applicable to the weather do not include an equation that rules out cheap but profitable predictions. Economic models do. A person who was smart enough to know the solutions to the economic equations would be rich, unless profitable solutions were already anticipated and discounted by the model. But they should be discounted, according to the Five-Hundred-Dollar-Bill Theorem. If the model is a widely available piece of information, or if its essence were embodied in a widely held judgment, it would be useless for making anyone rich. Wise in retrospect, maybe; rich in prospect, no.

The American Question and the Five-Hundred-Dollar-Bill Theorem radically limit what economists and calculators can know about the future. No economist watches the TV program "Wall Street Week" without a vague sense that he is betraying his science. He should be pleased. His science proves its robustness by asserting confidently that the science cannot profitably predict—indeed, that no science of human-kind can profitably predict, even the science of stockbrokers. The economic theorem is so powerful that it applies to economists.

The post-modern economist is modest about profit-worthy detail, the detail from which he could buy low and sell high. He must be modest

THE LIMITS OF EXPERTISE

especially about the proud claim of economics in the 1960s, the claim to fine-tune the economy, making detailed adjustments to money and taxes to offset a depression just around the corner. As economists realize now after much tragedy sprung from hubris, if an economist could see around the corner, he would be rich. Fine-tuning violates the theorem: a fine-tuner would see dozens of five-hundred-dollar bills lying around his neighborhood. The economists go on relating impossibly detailed scenarios into the microphones of television reporters, but in their hearts they know they are wrong.

The American Question requires intellectual modesty in the economic expert, if he does not want people to laugh on meeting him. Hubris will need divine protection. Xenophon reported Socrates as saying: "Those who intend to manage [*oikesein*] houses or cities well are in need of divination. For the craft of carpenter . . . or economics [*oikonomikon*] . . . may be learned . . . ; but the greatest of these matters the gods reserve to themselves. . . . If anyone supposes that these [divinations] are not beyond reason, and nothing in them beyond our judgment, he is himself beyond reason." Socrates could turn to the oracles for divine supplementation of a craft. We have lost today the favor of the gods, and books on economic technique will not assuage our woe.

II

All this concerns economics; but there is more. The more leads back to the ancient and sensible doubt that critics can do as much in the way of art as artists can. The American Question mocks the hubris of the critic.

The critic's coin of profit need not be monetary. Political power is there on the sidewalk, too, waiting to be picked up if the 500,000-vote theorem is wrong. But of course the theorem is right. You cannot find a simple way, to be written down in a book, for getting 500,000 votes. If you think you can, well, why not try? Similarly, prestige in the local saloon would be cheaply available if the American Question did not also cast doubt on predictions of sporting events. But it does. The lineaments of the sporting future apparent to the average guy will be reflected in the sporting odds. Only fresh details give profits above average measured in money or prestige. Fresh details are hard to come by. Information, like steel, is costly to produce.

The American Question can be asked of all predictions of trends—in journalism, sociology, political science, commercial art, and elsewhere. It mocks the claims of predictors, social engineers, and critics of the social arts. The predictor who could get it usefully right would be a god incarnate, a diviner.

The reason is not that humans are too complicated or too changeable or too free. The humanistic criticisms of social science may be true but they are not telling; they are easy to make and easy to answer. The scientists answer, "Give us the money and we will finish the job." If humans are "ultimately" free, considered as individuals, they still can be predicted on average and in the mass. And if human masses are complex, they still can be predicted with another million dollars and another model. So long as humans are to be viewed as molecules bouncing against each other, the problem is merely to get the mathematics right. It is said that making predictions about human beings is bound to be more complicated than making predictions about planets or pigeons, but that is not true. It depends on what you are trying to predict. The heartbeat of a human is easier to predict than the twitching of the sixty-seventh feather on the pigeon's tail. It is a matter of how ambitious the prediction is. The "simple" problem of space flight, "merely" an application of Newton's laws, requires days of computation at high speed if the ambition is to put a rocket precisely *there* on Mars. For a given ambition, the complexity is only a matter of computer time.

The American Question puts more fundamental limits on what we humans can say about ourselves. It puts a limit on mechanical models of human behavior. It does not make the mechanical models useless for interesting history or routine prediction; it just makes them useless for gaining an edge about the future. If people were as predictable as naive behaviorism alleges, for instance, the psychologists would be rich and the personnel managers all-powerful. The field of industrial and managerial psychology was erected in the 1930s on just such a putative secret, but it led to miracles only on Thirty-fourth Street. To revert again to economics, the various "solutions" of bargaining problems have this flaw: that if the economist knew the solution, then so would the players, which would make the solution valueless. The Turing machine that could predict the next move of a competitor would sell for a lot of money. If Turing machines are cheap, no one can get rich by using them to outsmart others.

Likewise there are limits on the teachability of skills. It is paradoxical to claim that a Ph.D. qualifies one to teach "entrepreneurship," or even "excellence." The present content of the business school, with its burden of mechanical technique, undervalues the stories and moralities that make a business culture. Yet the humanities cannot be taught by machine, either. Gary Walton, an economist and dean of a business school, has written a book called *Beyond Winning* about "philosopher coaches," such as Woody Hayes in football or John Wooden in basket-

THE LIMITS OF EXPERTISE

ball. He is aware that, if coaching could be learned from a book, the woods would be full of Woodys and Woodens. If coaching were mechanical in its effects on the athletes, then East Germany would never lose an Olympic contest. The ability to teach exceptional performance is itself an exceptional performance. What can be said about the athletic case is what can be said about the scholarly case: that a great coach or a great scholar teaches not by instructing the students in a bookable technique but by exhibiting a way of life.

The limit on calculability and say-ability applies to language and rhetoric itself. If anyone could get his way by shouting, for example, then everyone would shout. H. P. Grice affixed an economic tag to the trumping of speech conventions: "exploitation." As Stephen Levinson put the point in his recent book *Pragmatics:*

There is a fundamental way in which a full account of the communicative power of language can never be reduced to a set of conventions for the use of language. The reason is that wherever some convention or expectation about the use of language arises, there will also therewith arise the possibility of the non-conventional *exploitation* of that convention or expectation. It follows that a purely conventional or rule-based account of natural language usage can never be complete.

A rhetorical analysis has this limit: that it can tell wisely and well how a speech has gone in the past, but cannot be expected to provide the world's greatest secret for the future. It can show how Cicero in *Pro Archia* exploited tricolon, how Descartes exploited rhetoric to attack rhetoric itself, or how Jane Austen in *Northanger Abbey* exploited an irony that was always intended, covert, finite, and stable. But rhetoric cannot be finished and formulaic, or else anyone could be a Cicero, Descartes, or Austen. The chimera of a once-finished formula for language must be left to Fregean philosophy or to magic.

Before Faust turns in vexation to magic he laments, "I see that we can know nothing! / It nearly breaks my heart." On reflection he amends this sweeping skepticism. The American Question does not imply literally that *wir nichts wissen können* but merely, as he then complains on behalf of his fellow men, that Faust can know nothing that betters mankind—*die Menschen zu bessern*. On reflecting a little more, however, he comes to the nub: his studies have taught him nothing that betters Dr. Faust, this very part of mankind. "And *I* have neither property nor money, / Nor honor and glory in the world: / No dog should go on living so"; "*Auch hab ich weder Gut noch Geld. . . .*" There lies the tragedy—at the impossibility of predictions profitable to *Faust* himself. He seeks the world's greatest secret for personal profit, which in due course he obtains, though not for free lying there on the sidewalk, *und hatte sowohl Gut als Geld.*

THE AMERICAN SCHOLAR

Lacking the Devil's bargain, science cannot predict itself. The paradox shows up in economics because economics so plainly must apply to itself, if it's so smart. But the paradox applies to any foreknowledge of new knowledge. The impossibility of self-prediction has become a commonplace in philosophy. You do not know today what you will decide tomorrow, unless you have already decided it, in which case it is not tomorrow but today that you decide it.

Prescience is an oxymoron, like cheap fortunes: pre-science, knowing before one knows. Prescience is required for central planning of science. Karl Popper and Alasdair MacIntyre among others have pointed out that knowing the future of science requires knowing the science of the future. It is not to be done. MacIntyre notes that the unpredictability of mathematical innovation is a rigorous case, resting on theorems concerning the incompleteness of arithmetic and the incalculability of certain expressions, proven by Gödel and Church in the 1930s. And "if the future of mathematics is unpredictable, so is a great deal else." If someone claims to know what method or lack of method would yield good science, why isn't he scientifically rich?

The other arts are similarly constrained. Some critics in the eighteenth century believed they had methods for assuring excellence in drama or painting. Nowadays no one would claim to have a formulaic, bookable method for constructing excellent paintings, except as a postmodern joke. The method would solve painting, in the sense that tic-tac-toe has been solved. This is not to say that rules of perspective or color harmonies cannot be constructed and applied. They can, the way a poet can check for agreement with the meter she has chosen or a dancer can check his fifth position. It says only that there is at present no routine, book-readable method for achieving artistic riches. The unusually profitable opportunities have been picked up, leaving normal returns to normal ability.

Each bit of the accumulated routine was once someone's personal and profitable trick. The genius has more tricks than the rest of us—tricks that become tomorrow's routines. The first Florentine businessman to use double-entry bookkeeping gained a control over his materials similar in value to the first Athenian sculptor's use of the slouch of standing bodies. In this age of iron, no one earns five hundred dollars from the mere idea of double entries or contrapposto. Any present day is an age of iron, because gold is picked up as soon as it appears.

The distinction between routine predictions and startling and profitable divination is analogous to the distinction between routine cooking and the profitable art of three-star cookery. In a peculiar little dialogue, the *Ion*, Socrates lampoons Ion, the performing Artist, who imagines he *knows* something. It is significant that, to mock Ion's claim to knowl-

THE LIMITS OF EXPERTISE

edge, Socrates uses the example of divining. As Plato and the American Question would say, the claim of divining to be an art, Greek *techne*, a mere bookable craft, is absurd.

Plato therefore wished to cage poetry, the god-possession that flatters men to think they know more than does the honest artisan, a technician in every sense. The followers of Plato down to the age of technique are enamored of knowledge as *techne*, a craft written down in books. They propose to cast books lacking such craft into the flames, as poetry and pretense, mere sophistry and illusion. The trouble is that their version of the fully rational life, the bookable final rules for language games, requires unusual prediction. And in human affairs a prediction beyond what earns merely usual returns is impossible, except by entrepreneurs, idiot savants, *auteurs*, and other prodigies of tacit knowledge. The notion that bookable knowledge can guide the world through its difficult moments, like the notion that central planning can guide an economy, is self-contradictory. If the philosopher kings and central planners were so smart, they, too, would be rich.

As indeed they are, for a reason other than their ability to predict. They live in a world ever hopeful that procedure, mechanism, calculation, bureaucracy, MBA degrees, and other social *techne* will keep us warm and safe. It will not, as the American Question reminds us so rudely, though the world is willing to pay for the illusion.

III

Nothing I have said implies that the project of acquiring systematic knowledge about the economy or about poems and paintings is worthless. Inside the margin, as economists say, it is worthful. The world runs on little else. Everyone needs to know how to write with an alphabet, though it took a Phoenician genius to think it up and make his fortune. No one afterwards, though, can expect to make a fortune by knowing the ABCs.

An economist examining the business world is like a critic examining the art world. Economists and other human scientists can reflect intelligently on present conditions and can tell useful stories about the past. These produce wisdom, which permits broad, conditional "predictions." Some are obvious; some require an economist; but none is a machine for achieving fame or riches.

The economist says, if a government shoots everyone with eyeglasses, the economy will not perform well. Or, if voluntary restrictions such as those in force a few years ago on Japanese automobile imports are reinstated, then the Japanese manufacturers will benefit by about $1,000 per car, and the American auto buyers will pay about $160,000 per year for each job saved in Detroit. Though useful as wisdom, and justifying the economist's role as critical theorist, neither of these predictions is bankable.

The argument is merely that, at the margin, where supernormal profits and reputations for genius are being made, the observer's knowledge is not the same as the doer's; the critic is no improvement as artist over the artist; the model of the future is no substitute for the entrepreneur's god-possessed hunch. The critics become ridiculous only when they confuse speaking well about the past with doing well in the future. Critics of art and literature stopped being ridiculous this way a long time ago. It would be a fine thing if critics of society would join them in their modest and sober sophistication.

No one is justly subject to the American Question who retains a proper modesty about what observation and recording and storytelling can do. We can observe the history of economies or the history of painting, and in retrospect tell a story about how security of commercial property or the analysis of vanishing points made for good things. An expert such as an economist is an expert on the past and an expert only about the future that can be known without divine and profitable possession. Human scientists and critics of human arts, in other words, write history, not prophecy.

Harry Truman had it about right. The expert as expert, a bookish sort consulting what is already known, cannot by his nature learn anything new, because then he wouldn't be an expert. He would be an entrepreneur, a statesman, or an Artist with a capital A. To these the expert critic can properly retort: if you're so rich, why aren't you smart? But, anyway, the bookish sort has to settle for low wages. Smartness of the scholar's sort cannot proceed to riches.

Part II
Value Judgements in Economics

[8]

Excerpt from *'Positive' Economics and Policy Objectives*, 51–119.

CHAPTER 2

Types and Sources of Value-Judgments and Bias

'What is proposed here is that objectivity for science lies at least in becoming precise about what value-judgments are being made and might have been made in a given enquiry.'

R. RUDNER
in *The Validation of Scientific Theories*
edited by P. G. Frank, 1961, p. 35.

'Discussion in general in this field is obscured by a reluctance of many writers who insist that valuations somehow seep into social analysis to state clearly where precisely this seepage occurs.'

P. STREETEN
Value in Social Theory
by G. Myrdal (edited and introduced by
P. Streeten), 1958, p. XXXVII.

(1) INTRODUCTION

The disagreements set out at the end of the previous chapter seem wide and deep. They relate both to economic theorizing and to discussions of policies. But it is impossible to tell just how wide and deep these differences are, because, as we have noted, so many of these sweeping pronouncements regarding economics and value-judgments have been thrown out *en passant* before some main substantial theme is taken up.

We are now going to try to set out, and examine in some detail, the types of value-judgment, or value-premiss, and of evaluative or persuasive statement, proposal or prescription, which economists make or have to make, or implicitly or explicitly assume. We shall try to indicate as precisely as we can the stages at which they occur or have to occur, and how far they conflict with or nullify claims to scientific objectivity, political and ethical neutrality, or 'Wertfreiheit'. We also examine where value-judgments play a part, often less explicitly and more insidiously, in the form of biased subjectivity and persuasiveness. From some sceptical critics one derives the impression that all economic and social enquiry is so inevitably

'Positive' Economics and Policy Objectives

impregnated, and almost unanalysably permeated, from start to finish, with value-judgments or persuasive biased statements of one kind or another, that any appearance of, or claim to, any measure of objectivity or neutrality, is bound to be spurious or naïve. But it is usually extremely difficult to find out from the generalizations of these sceptics exactly where and how the valuations creep in, their nature, and how far they are logically inevitable, or, on the other hand, due to conceivably avoidable errors or indiscipline, like false conclusions in logic or mathematics, the rules of which are not the less clear, or impossible to maintain, because they are frequently broken.

The disagreements mentioned in the last chapter as to how far value-premisses, and value-loaded or biased judgments and concepts, enter into economics, did not apparently turn on any significant differences, or on any inadequate clarity, regarding the nature of 'value-judgments' and ethical statements, or even on how these, or elements of these, when located, are to be distinguished from the theories and statements of 'positive' economics. We do not need, and it would take us much too far afield, to explore different theories of ethics, or the analysis of different kinds of value-judgment and ethical or evaluative statement or proposal, or the basis of their validity. For our purposes it suffices if we agree that these kinds of statement cannot be tested or refuted inter-subjectively in the same way as the 'positive' statements of science, and that a consensus regarding them cannot be reached of the same kind or in the same way. In marking off 'scientific' statements from 'non-scientific' statements and proposals (including ethical statements and value-judgments), we follow Popper's proposal of a 'demarcation criterion'. This is 'a fundamental proposal for an agreement or convention' to the effect that 'it must be possible for an empirical scientific system to be refuted by experience', that is, that scientific statements and theories must in principle be 'intersubjectively testable', and that their 'objectivity . . . lies in the fact that they can be intersubjectively tested'.[1] We do not need to insist on any particular precise or rigid view of the nature of ethical and evaluative statements and value-judgments. It suffices for our purposes that ethical and political value-judgments, value-premisses, 'proposals', prescriptions and persuasive judgments, can be broadly and adequately distinguished

[1] K. R. Popper, *The Logic of Scientific Discovery*, 1959, pp. 37, 41 and 44. For a further analysis by Popper of 'the dualism of facts and standards, or of propositions and proposals', the dissimilarities between them, and why in spite, also, of similarities 'they should be clearly and decisively distinguished', see *The Open Society and its Enemies*, 4th Ed., 1962, Vol. II, pp. 383–4. For the duality of 'propositions' and 'proposals', and for the nature of the latter, see L. J. Russell's paper, 'Propositions and Proposals', Library of the Tenth International Congress of Philosophy, Amsterdam, 1948, Vol. I, *Proceedings of the Congress*.

from the statements of an empirical science by such a 'demarcation criterion'. This is certainly not to say that ethical statements or value-judgments are 'nonsensical', or undiscussable, or beyond any rational examination. On the contrary, we shall argue that much more examination of them would often be helpful in discussions of economic policies. Often when some norm or objective for policy is urged—such as, for example, that price stability should be maintained—such a value-judgment will contain or imply a positive or descriptive element (such as that price stability will maintain a certain pattern of distribution). Further analysis can 'demarcate' or separate out for discussion the positive from the normative-evaluative elements in such a statement.

We shall be concerned mainly or entirely with two kinds of value-judgment, 'proposal', or value-premiss, and we emphasize the vital distinction between them with regard to the 'objectivity' of science. These are (1) the kind of value-judgments, 'proposals', or value-premisses involved (*a*) in choices of problems to be studied, and (*b*) in choice or adoption of the criteria or rules of procedure by which the problems are to be studied; and (2) ethical or political value-judgments and persuasive statements, overtly stated or latently implied, regarding the choices, objectives or 'ends' of policies in the widest sense. The first are logically inevitable in *any* science or study, and the second are logically necessary if policy recommendations are being put forward. We shall be concerned also (3) with biased subjectivity in positive empirical statements, and its possible points of entry and modes of operation in different parts of the scientific process, where political or ethical value-judgments can be said to have no logical or 'legitimate' place, but are nevertheless influencing and shaping hypotheses, theories, explanations and predictions.

(2) THE MAIN TYPES OF INEVITABLE 'PRE-SCIENTIFIC' VALUE-JUDGMENT

We start with the types of fundamental value-judgment or value-premiss which *have* to be made before any 'scientific' or disciplined intellectual process can begin, and which might, therefore, be called 'pre-scientific'. These value-judgments are logically inevitable, in a sense 'a priori', since they cannot possibly be avoided in any 'scientific' study of economic, social or any other problems, however detached, unbiased or cautious the scientist might be. There seem to be two main types:

(A) The acceptance of the presuppositions, rules of procedure and criteria of 'scientific' method and enquiry, involve a kind of value-judgment or 'proposal' in favour of engaging voluntarily in intellectual activity based on certain agreed conventions, or rules of the game, or of 'scientific' discipline or procedure. To set out these rules fully and precisely would require a whole treatise on scientific method. There is much broad agreement as to the general form these rules should take, though there are at the margin, and perhaps always will be, differences over particular rules and their interpretation, and controversial questions as to the best precise formulations of them. For example, we shall discuss below (Section 9) vaguenesses and differences regarding the rules of inductive inference and the precise limits of the function of the 'scientist' regarding decisions in conditions of uncertainty. We shall take as broadly accepted rules of scientific procedure the laws or conventions of logic and mathematics, the empirical testability of statements or theories and the readiness to expose them to critical, objective testing, and the obligation to try to avoid ambiguity, in particular normative-positive ambiguity, and to promote clarity in the use and interpretation of language. Such fundamental presuppositions, in whatever precise way they are formulated, are common to all 'sciences', and a kind of value-judgment or 'proposal' is made when such rules or criteria are proposed or accepted, or when the study of a subject is voluntarily pursued in accordance with such rules. The rules amount to a programme, or procedure, as to how a scientific consensus is to be attained (a consensus, of course, which is always provisional and subject to revision) and as to how theories and statements for which scientific status is claimed are to be arrived at, or selected.

It has been pointed out that the criteria of the scientific rules of the game have not always controlled the general acceptance or consensus regarding theories or the selection between conflicting theories and generalizations:

'Obviously, fitness to support a desirable conduct of citizens or, briefly, to support moral behaviour, has served through the ages as a reason for acceptance of a theory. When the "scientific criterions" did not uniquely determine a theory, its fitness to support moral or political indoctrination became an important factor for its acceptance. It is important to learn that the interpretation of a scientific theory as a support of moral rules is not a rare case but has played a role in all periods of history.'[1]

As a historical generalization this is undeniable and it is obviously illustrated throughout much of the history of economic thought. But this is only to say that the scientific criteria or rules have been widely disregarded, and still are sometimes disregarded, in spite of general

[1] P. G. Frank, 'The Variety of Reasons for the Acceptance of Scientific Theories', in *The Validation of Scientific Theories*, edited by P. G. Frank (paperback edition, 1961, p. 19).

Types and Sources of Value-Judgments and Bias   55

agreement as to what, broadly, the rules are, requiring, as they do, that 'every influence of moral, religious, or political considerations upon the acceptance of a theory'—or on its rejection—'is regarded as "illegitimate" by the so-called "community of scientists"—a view which 'certainly has had a highly salutary effect upon the evolution of science as a human activity'.[1]

We are concerned with economics as an enquiry or 'discipline' carried on in accordance with such rules or conventions, which most economists seem to claim their subject to be, even if the rules are not always obeyed or at some points even precisely agreed upon. A game of football remains a game of football even when the referee is frequently blowing his whistle for fouls, or even when there is no referee at all, or even when all the players do not completely know, or completely agree, as to every detail of the rules. At what precise point 'a game of football' ceases to deserve that description, and becomes 'a free-for-all', is a nice point of definition and judgment, of relevance, perhaps, to some debates between economists over economic policies.

Of course, nobody has to accept these procedures and rules, and the value-judgments underlying them, if he does not wish to do so.[2] He can, and some people do, more or less frankly, practise economics as a branch of political persuasion and propaganda, investigating problems and presenting explanations in the manner of party politicians before an election presenting their versions of recent economic history and critiques of future policies. Then, of course, propagandist victories and widespread *political* agreement may emerge, but not *scientific* consensus, or the kind of objective *scientific* status based upon it.

However, the main point we are concerned with here is simply that because value-judgments proposing or upholding scientific criteria, or a code of scientific ethics, are logically inevitable in any 'scientific' activity, the fact that this particular kind of value-judgment is, and has to be, made, does not nullify all claims to objectivity, value-neutrality, or *Wertfreiheit*, in the statements or theories arrived at by scientific enquiry.

(B) *Secondly*, and again this applies to *any* scientific enquiry, natural or social, the choice of problems for study depends on a kind of 'interest' or value-judgment. As one of the sceptical critics quoted above writes: 'The mere selection of economic problems for investigation involves value-judgments',[3] or, as Max Weber put it: 'The problems of the social sciences are selected by the value-

[1] P. G. Frank, *op. cit.*, p. 13.
[2] H. Albert, *Handbuch der empirischen Sozialforschung*, I Band, 1961, p. 48.
[3] A. Smithies, *Economics and Public Policy*, Brookings Lectures 1954, 1955, p. 2.

56   *'Positive' Economics and Policy Objectives*

relevance (*Wertbeziehung*) of the phenomena treated. . . . The very recognition of the existence of a scientific problem coincides, personally, with the possession of specifically oriented motives and values.'[1] Here again the kind of value-judgment involved could be described as 'pre-scientific', and, in any case, scientific objectivity or neutrality can be, and should only be, claimed regarding the *answers* to the problems selected.[2] The 'interest', relevance, or *Wertbeziehung*, which shapes the choice of problems for scientific study, or which ranks one problem as more important than another, may range from a relatively detached intellectual interest to the most immediate and selfish prospect of material gain, and it may well serve also as an indispensable driving force to scientific achievement. Certainly it is a major political and sociological problem how, in different societies, different kinds of questions come to be selected for study, regarding different methods of air defence, space travel, or consumers' tastes, for example; how research resources are raised and allocated, or how the estimates of the uncertain costs of different kinds of research are weighed against the uncertain prospective returns from them. Obviously the most fundamental clashes of interests and values may be involved, and the issues fought out as crude struggles for power. Moreover, social or political pressure, or the researcher's own prejudices or beliefs, may prevent certain questions, or whole areas of enquiry, from being investigated scientifically at all. The scientist also may voluntarily or involuntarily be the servant of political or commercial masters who may dictate to him the questions he is to investigate, and may exploit, pervert or suppress the answers he arrives at. But 'a betrayal of the criteria of science is only committed where the investigator not merely answers a dictated question, but supplies a dictated answer, that is, allows the particular practical aims of his client to influence his conclusions'.[3]

[1] Max Weber on *The Methodology of the Social Sciences*, translated and edited by E. A. Shils and H. A. Finch, 1949, p. 21 and p. 61.
[2] 'The rules of scientific method do not tell us what it is important to work on.' M. F. Millikan, in *The Human Meaning of the Social Sciences*, edited by D. Lerner, Meridian Books, 1959, p. 179.
[3] T. Geiger, *Ideologie und Wahrheit*, 1953, p. 119. Cf. also I. Berlin, *Philosophy, Politics and Society* (Second Series), edited by P. Laslett and W. G. Runciman, 1962, p. 6: 'The mere fact that value-judgments are relevant to an intellectual pursuit is clearly not sufficient to disqualify it from being a recognized science. The concept of normal health certainly embodies a valuation, and although there is sufficient universal consensus about what constitutes good health, a normal state, disease and so on, this concept, nevertheless, does not enter as an intrinsic element into the sciences of anatomy, physiology, pathology, etc. Pursuit of health may be the strongest sociological and psychological (and moral) factor in creating and promoting these sciences; it may determine which problems and aspects of the subject have been most ardently attended to; but it is not referred

Types and Sources of Value-Judgments and Bias   57

Furthermore, though there must be some preliminary selection of questions and problems to start from, their choice is not necessarily a once-and-for-all process but may be continually subject to revision, the questions being reformulated in the course of research. Sometimes only when an 'answer' has been propounded may it be seen precisely what question it is an answer to—perhaps quite a different one from that first posed. The historian faces special and weightier problems of selection (as we shall discuss very briefly below in Section 6 of this chapter), and he may seem to choose the detailed individual questions his history answers more or less as he goes along.

Nevertheless, the fundamental point remains valid that the *answers* to the questions eventually dealt with do not *necessarily* involve subjective valuations, and value-judgments and -premises, just because *the selection of the questions* does. Undoubtedly, 'the scientist decides what to study; he decides what model is adequate within which to pose his problem; he decides how, when, and where to make observations; he decides when to accept or reject a conclusion. As a decision-maker he is as much concerned with actions as is the executive.'[1] But, as a 'scientist' he has to take account of the rules and criteria of scientific procedure when making these decisions and choices, and, in any case, these are quite separate from the decisions and choices regarding, for example, which 'ends' and objectives of economic policies ought to be chosen or pursued.[2]

We thus have two basic types of value-judgment, choice and decision, which might be formulated, elaborated or sub-divided in different ways. They are involved in any scientific enquiry (natural, or social, or human), and are logically inevitable, or, in a sense, 'pre-scientific' or *a priori*, in that they cannot be avoided, in *any* science, even with the greatest, or most superhuman, measure of unbiased detachment or impartiality, or disciplined caution.

The economist is also involved with valuations, though not here in making a choice or decision, in that the social or human sciences (unlike, of course, the natural sciences) study people who are holding, expressing, projecting, fighting for, or living by, values of one

to in the science itself, any more than the uses of history or logic need be mentioned in historical or logical works.'

[1] C. W. Churchman, *Prediction and Optimal Decision*, 1961, p. 14.

[2] 'That scientific truth is a value worth pursuing is not a scientific truth but a value-judgment. And that X pursues knowledge for its own sake is the fruit of a fundamental valuation on his part according to which he puts scientific knowledge before many other objectives. It thus appears that a valuation by the will is somehow involved in every conceivable statement, and that all statements may be suspected of being value-loaded or ideological. The former conclusion is correct . . . the latter is not correct. . . .' T. Geiger, *Ideologie und Wahrheit*, 1953, p. 113.

kind or another. But claims for the 'objectivity' or neutrality of statements or theories *about* human activities are not invalidated by the fact that the activities themselves are expressive of, or impregnated with, values.

Moreover, the observers or enquirers are themselves 'bundles of prejudices' or 'masses of predilections' and impinge on, and are a part of, what they are observing or studying, though there is no necessity or inevitability in their coming to the subject as loaded with ideological and political prejudices as economists sometimes do, or that their loads should obstruct their entry even into what Pigou described as 'that first antechamber of knowledge' knowing that they do not know.[1] Also, as in the natural sciences, there is an interaction of observer and observed, which may be much more pervasive in the social sciences, but which does not involve value-judgments or presuppositions different in kind or principle from those of the natural sciences.[2] Of course, new empirical knowledge may have profound effects on values, attitudes and policies, whether in the 'natural' sphere, relating, say, to nutrition, disease or new forms of energy, or in the 'social' or 'human' sphere, where the example is frequently cited of Booth & Rowntree's new facts about poverty in England stirring the social conscience. But no empirical or factual knowledge necessarily entails an attitude, standard or policy, or a change therein, without the addition of a value-judgment, and because facts and standards are relevant to, and interact on, one another, it does not follow that they cannot be sharply distinguished.[3]

It is obvious then that the economist's subject-matter is essentially concerned with human beings and their values, and that he may himself come to the subject stiff with moral and political prejudices. The logical inevitability is also clear of the two types of 'preliminary' value-judgments involved in accepting a discipline, or rules of procedure, and in selecting questions and problems. It may, therefore, be misleading to claim that 'positive economics is in principle independent of *any* particular ethical position or normative judgments'.[4] But, on the other hand, having recognized these inevitable value-premisses, it seems a serious misconception to argue that the necessity of these types of value-judgment, or involvement in valuations and choices, disposes of *any* significant claims to scientific objectivity. Nearly fifty years ago, as pertinently as one might today, Max Weber complained bitterly of objections, on these grounds, to

[1] *Economics of Welfare*, 3rd Ed., 1929, p. VI.

[2] K. R. Popper, *The Poverty of Historicism*, 1961 edition, p. 12, et passim; and E. Grunberg and F. Modigliani, 'Predictability of Social Events', *Journal of Political Economy*, December 1954, pp. 465 ff. See also below, Section 8.

[3] Cf. K. R. Popper, *The Open Society and its Enemies*, 4th Ed., 1962, Vol. II, pp. 383–4.

[4] M. Friedman, *Essays in Positive Economics*, 1953, p. 4. (Italics added.)

Types and Sources of Value-Judgments and Bias   59

his defence of scientific objectivity or *Wertfreiheit*: 'In spite of all that I have said, the following "objections" have been raised in all seriousness: Science strives to attain "valuable" results, meaning thereby logically and factually correct results which are scientifically significant; and that further, the selection of the subject-matter already involves an "evaluation". Another almost inconceivable misunderstanding which constantly recurs is that the propositions which I propose imply that empirical science cannot treat "subjective" evaluations as the subject-matter of its analysis.'[1]

We are certainly not trying to prejudge the question to be examined throughout the rest of this chapter as to whether value-judgments or subjective, biased, persuasive or evaluative statements, must or do enter into economics at other points than these. But if, when it is stated, for example, that ' "a disinterested social science" has never existed and, for logical reasons, cannot exist',[2] this conclusion is based *simply* on the inevitability of the types of value-judgment and involvement in valuations which we have just discussed, then there can be no fundamental disagreement. We would simply complain regarding this statement, that if it is an analytical-tautological one, as it seems it might be, it might have been expressed as such more explicitly, and, furthermore, that the inclusion of the adjective 'social' is unnecessary and perhaps misleading. It seems logically essential for both social and natural 'sciences' that problems or questions have to be selected, that certain criteria and rules of the game have to be accepted in a 'scientific' discipline, and that the problems selected cannot be approached in a kind of mental vacuum, but inevitably with some 'load' of interests, values and preconceptions, if not with the cumbersome loads of political and ideological prejudice which are in fact frequently brought to bear.

(3) IDEOLOGY, 'VISION' AND POLITICAL PRESUPPOSITIONS

We have seen that the economist, like any 'scientist', is inevitably involved in kinds of value-judgment in selecting or accepting certain epistemological criteria or rules of his discipline, and in selecting his problems or questions. We have also noted that he starts, or may start, with something more than a mere detached intellectual interest in his question, but rather with a load of political presuppositions and prejudices. It is naïve empiricism, and the most suitable target for this common pejorative phrase, to suppose that a researcher can approach his problem with his mind a *tabula rasa*, and that his hypotheses and theories will, or can, emerge spontaneously from 'the facts', or automatically imprint themselves on this *tabula rasa*,

[1] Max Weber on *The Methodology of the Social Sciences*, translated and edited by E. A. Shils and H. A. Finch, 1949, p. 10.
[2] G. Myrdal, *Value in Social Theory*, ed. P. Streeten, 1958, p. 1.

or be 'given' simply by looking around him. To be able to make even a first tentative formulation of a question, in addition to some 'interest' in it, *some* initial equipment, however primitive and indefinite, is required, and this will include, or at any rate *may* include, various kinds of preconceptions, predilections, presuppositions or prejudices, as well as definitions, concepts and language, technical and 'everyday', which may, though not necessarily must, be heavily value-loaded. If it is necessary and inevitable to select questions and problems it is necessary and inevitable that there be some initial equipment or raw materials with which to formulate them.

In the first place, for example, the economist may approach his questions equipped more or less fully and intensively with an 'ideology', which may be regarded as a, or the, leading species of a large genus of preconceptions and presuppositions. We need not attempt a precise definition of ideologies, or of elements thereof. From one point of view they may be regarded as large-scale comprehensive explanations of the economic, social or political universe, infused with often passionately held value-judgments about it, and about the action that should be taken with regard to it; and they are often expounded with the aid of highly persuasive definitions, concepts and terminology.[1] Nor need we explore further how ideologies are formed, or the view that they may be conditioned by economic or social class. One usual feature is their systematic character, which fixes a limited exclusive framework within which questions can be formulated and answers propounded. Their comprehensive, large-scale, long-run character, involving sometimes whole historical epochs, tends to make them often practically impossible to test, or to frame in practically testable terms. It has been observed, incidentally, that the kinds of large-scale systematic ideologies, which flourished in the nineteenth and early twentieth centuries, seem today to be losing much of their influence on serious thinking in the western world, though it may be premature to conclude that they are disappearing for good.

However, ideology appears not only in comprehensive systems, but in bits and pieces as 'ideological' statements or elements. What we would regard as one of the main characteristics of 'ideology', whether in the form of some comprehensive system, or of a particular individual statement or theory, is the interweaving of normative and positive, the form or appearance of a positive empirical statement or theory being combined with, and shaped and biased to support (on the assumption of some widely held moral value-judgment), a more or less latent, crypto-normative, ethical or political component. The explicit moralist or preacher is not an 'ideologue' in this sense, and the explicitly moral or ethical statement has not, on this definition,

[1] See *Ideologie und Wahrheit* by Theodor Geiger, 1953.

Types and Sources of Value-Judgments and Bias   61

the ambiguity of an 'ideological' statement. For separating, in the interests of clarity, the positive empirical content from the latent value-judgment, enquiring how the proposition is to be tested, or could be refuted, seems a useful and indeed essential procedure.

Not clearly distinguishable, at the margin, from 'ideologies' are the social and political philosophies, ideals or 'principles', with which the economist may approach the formulation of his questions and hypotheses, and which may inspire his views as to the objectives of society and policies. These may be less comprehensive and historically large-scale than ideologies in the narrower sense, and initially they may be more explicitly normative, that is, not so closely and intensively interwoven with 'positive' analysis and 'scientific' pretensions, as are ideologies. These political ideals or principles may, however, take on more of the ambiguous characteristics of ideologies when 'rationalized' by economists. Quite a number of economists, either before, or very soon after, they began studying economics, seem to have adopted very definite political principles and values, in terms, for example, of 'freedom' on the one hand, or 'equality' on the other, and to have devoted much of their subsequent efforts as economists to working out a kind of economic justification or rationalization of them.[1] Their pronouncements on economic policies then tend to amount to dressing up their political predilections in esoteric jargon or technical patter. Perhaps—perhaps not—one could find more cases falling into this category than one could find of economists—like Pareto—who modified their political principles and programmes as a result of, or at any rate in the course of, their economic studies—though the bold generalization has been made that the study of economics has a broadly conservative effect.[2] Anyhow, the whole impetus to and initial interest in economic problems seems, in some cases, to have consisted in the buttressing and rationalizing of political views and principles. Of course, we are not for one moment suggesting that economists should not hold strong political principles or values. Our question rather is, what effects these *may* exercise on their would-be, or should-be, 'positive' hypotheses and theories about economic processes—not that these effects will necessarily or always be to render them false, though they *may* frequently seem to have distorting tendencies.

Schumpeter, who, among economists, has examined the role of

[1] 'If science is a straight line, economics is a spiral. In science new discoveries extend our knowledge: as new truth accumulates, old error is discarded. But in economics we go round and round: each new generation rediscovers old error at about the same rate as it absorbs truth. . . . Perhaps the reason lies not in economics, but in economists. In brash youth we take up our theoretical positions, and spend the rest of our lives selecting the facts to fit them.' (G. D. N. Worswick, *New Statesman and Nation*, August 30, 1963, p. 256.)

[2] G. J. Stigler, *Quarterly Journal of Economics*, November 1959, pp. 522 ff.

62   *'Positive' Economics and Policy Objectives*

ideology most acutely, uses the concept pretty broadly as the source of 'preconceptions about the economic process'[1] and of the 'visions', as he calls them, of the economic system, which have been the starting-point for the broader theorizing of great economists, in particular Smith, Marx and Keynes, of whose 'visions', and of whose subsequent scientific processing of their 'visions', he gives very interesting accounts. As Schumpeter says:

'Analytic work begins with material provided by our vision of things, and this vision is ideological almost by definition. It embodies the picture of things as we see them, and wherever there is any possible motive for wishing to see them in a given rather than another light, the way in which we see things can hardly be distinguished from the way in which we wish to see them.'[2]

As with comprehensive ideologies, the larger-scale and more comprehensive kinds of 'visions', which Schumpeter ascribes as their starting-points to Smith, Marx and Keynes, hardly have the same importance today. With increasing specialization and division of labour, the comprehensive book of *Principles*, or of *General Theory*, and the 'visions' of the economic cosmos which inspired them, or from which they started, have been to a large extent replaced by particular partial 'visions' and hypotheses about parts of the economic system, which are less difficult to 'process' and test scientifically, and in which, therefore, it should be less easy for ideological preconceptions and prejudices to survive—though, on the other hand, just because these are less blatant and systematic they may be more difficult to track down and neutralize or eradicate. Still, ideology and 'vision' may be drawn on for the answers to scientific questions, or the answers may be shaped by the desire to build up or strengthen ideology and 'vision'.

Sir Roy Harrod has claimed that 'experience suggests that many of those Englishmen who grew up to be professional economists, are born either little inflationists or little deflationists. It is something in the blood that they cannot get rid of.'[3] (Harrod claims that he himself was born, or is, a little 'flationist'.) Without taking over-seriously this theory of the biological determination, in one particular branch of economic analysis and policy, of English economists' ideological 'vision' of, or preconceptions about, economic processes, one may recognize how just is its emphasis on the profound and almost (but not quite) ineradicable extent to which economists' visions and preliminary hypotheses may be shaped pre-scientifically. Fifty to a hundred years ago many economists might have been

[1] *American Economic Review*, March 1949, p. 347.
[2] *History of Economic Analysis*, 1954, pp. 41–2.
[3] *Policy against Inflation*, 1958, p. VII.

Types and Sources of Value-Judgments and Bias   63

described, with some rhetorical exaggeration, as having been 'born' little free-traders or little protectionists. But the most general and important typological classification of economists' pre- or extra-scientific ideological visions, would be in terms of their views on the role of the state and central controls on the one hand, and of individualist enterprise and the market mechanism (and, in particular, the resulting distribution of income and the justice thereof) on the other hand. Some, perhaps many, economists would claim that they try, with Jevons, 'to judge each case upon its merits, interpreting with painful care all experience which can be brought to bear upon the matter'.[1] But in fact, to a considerable extent, many economists who pronounce on policy tend to bunch somewhat, or polarize or crystallize, into 'planners' or 'price-mechanists' of greater or less extremity. We must emphasize as strongly as possible that we are not attacking the maintenance of strong and definite political principles as such, or upholding expediency against principle. We are simply emphasizing the presence of these political principles, or elements of ideology, and how they *may* shape the selection of facts and factual generalizations about economic processes, which it is practically almost impossible to test conclusively, or only in the most tentative and uncertain way, and as to which no kind of scientific consensus has been reached. The economist coming with a more or less extreme belief in individual initiative and the price mechanism, on the one hand, and the economist believing, in a more or less extreme way, in socialist planning on the other hand, tend to assert as empirically valid widely differing and contradictory pictures of the economic world and of economic behaviour and its motivations. Their 'visions' and preconceptions shape, in turn, more specific and detailed hypotheses as to, for example, the effects of progressive taxation on the supply of effort, or of changes in interest rates on investment, or as to the extent of economies of large scale, or the diagnosis of inflation in terms of 'demand-pull' or 'cost-push', and as to a whole range of empirical questions about economic behaviour and processes. We discuss further examples in subsequent sections, drawing on a brilliant lecture by Lutz.[2]

In fact, wherever there is ignorance the gap is liable to be pseudo-scientifically filled in by ideology or biased 'vision', not merely left blank, thus obstructing entry even into that ante-chamber of knowledge, realization that one does not know. Edgeworth described as 'a peculiarity of our study':

'that in the race of the sciences we are as it were handicapped by

[1] W. S. Jevons, *The State in Relation to Labour*, 1882, p. 166.
[2] F. A. Lutz, 'Politische Überzeugungen und nationalökonomische Theorie', *Ordo*, Bd. IX, 1957. See Sections 5 and 7 below.

having to start at a considerable distance behind the position of mere nescience. An effort is required to remove prejudices worse than ignorance; a great part of the career of our science has consisted in surmounting preliminary fallacies.'[1]

And these 'preliminary fallacies' have not merely been those of the general public, but those introduced into the subject by economists' own ideologies and 'visions', and often tenaciously upheld without or against testing.

We have been concerned here with ideologies, 'visions' and elements thereof, at the 'pre-scientific' stage. They are in at the start, so to speak, or there is free and frequent entry for them. But it remains to be examined whether why and how they can and do survive the discipline of the scientific process, and how far their survival is inevitable.

(4) PERSUASIVE LANGUAGE AND VALUE-LOADED CONCEPTS

We have seen that economists, like other scientists, are inevitably involved in kinds of value-judgments regarding the choice of their problems and their epistemological criteria. We have seen also that, perhaps more than most other scientists, they come to their problems as 'bundles of prejudices', and that though it is not logically inevitable that they do so as heavily 'value-loaded' as they sometimes are, they cannot come in a mental vacuum, but must bring at least some minimum of pre-scientific interest, concepts or 'vision'. As they proceed to formulate their questions and answers more precisely, they have to choose also their language, concepts and definitions, a choice that certainly ceases to be pre-scientific and which could be said to involve a kind of value-judgment. In what sense, or how far, do such inevitable choices impair the objectivity or neutrality of 'scientific', or would-be 'scientific', theories and statements?

In recent years there has been much discussion of 'persuasive' definitions and 'value-loaded' concepts in economics.[2] Some of this discussion seems to confuse together questions of logic (or methodology) and questions of psychology. For the distinction sometimes seems not to be kept sufficiently clear between, on the one hand, the scientific criteria of the empirical testability and truth or falsity of statements, or, alternatively, their logical consistency; and, on the other hand, 'psychological' questions as to their effects on people's

---

[1] *Papers Relating to Political Economy*, 1925, Vol. I, p. 5.

[2] Cf. G. Myrdal, *Value in Social Theory*, edited by P. Streeten, 1958, p. 1: 'Our very concepts are value-loaded . . . they cannot be defined except in terms of political valuations.' Cf. also I. M. D. Little, *A Critique of Welfare Economics*, 2nd Ed., 1957, who states (p. 274) that his book 'might, in part, be described as a study of the usage of influential and persuasive language in economics'.

behaviour or their influence, or persuasiveness. It also sometimes seems almost to be suggested that claims to objectivity, or value-neutrality, *must* be false, because the making of *any* statement involves *choices* of concepts, definitions and language, and that these choices involve value-judgments.[1] To see what there is in these suggestions it is necessary to distinguish between different kinds of choice and to see how significant each kind is. Otherwise the suggestion might prevail that we are inevitably operating in an all-pervasive atmosphere of 'persuasiveness' and 'value-loaded' language. Let us then distinguish four kinds of choices with regard to language or definitions:

(1) In the first place a writer on any subject has to choose the language in which he is going to write or publish his statements, say English, German or Afrikaans, and whether he is going to use mathematical or literary symbols. Certainly a kind of value-judgment is involved here, and in some cases one which might have political relevance, but it is so obviously a pre- or extra-scientific one that we take it to be irrelevant to the issues we are concerned with.

(2) Secondly, for purposes of analysis economists have to define more precisely imprecise, everyday terms like 'wages', 'saving', 'income', 'rent', 'value', and so on; that is, they have to choose definitions. The history of economics has been full of confused controversies, and of a kind of terminological dogmatism, as to the 'right', 'real', 'essential' or 'best' definitions of words like 'value', 'welfare' and 'savings'. But such controversies would now be widely recognized as involving the fallacy of 'essentialism' (as Popper has called it), and it would be agreed that, subject to what is found to be generally convenient usage, all definitions should ultimately be tolerated, so long as the choice is clearly stated and consistently followed, and unless due warning is given. This represents simply a consensus and value-judgment in favour of clarity of communication and the rules of logic, and, as such, is preliminary or pre-scientific, though the 'convenience' of a definition may in turn depend on the pre-scientific choice of the question or theory in which the economist is interesting himself.

(3) Not essentially different, though rather more complex, is the frequent case where various choices for the measurement of a concept or the 'weighting' of index numbers are involved. The obvious point to make is almost the same as that in the previous paragraph. To imply that one particular index of 'national income',

---

[1] Cf. P. Streeten, 'Introduction' to *Value in Social Theory*, by G. Myrdal, 1958, p. XXI: 'The point is that the concepts and propositions of even the most purely empirical investigation derive their meaning and significance from a purpose, an interest, and involve choice and, therefore, valuation.'

for example, is the sole, real, uniquely significant measure, represents a kind of 'essentialist' dogmatism which might perhaps be 'persuasive' for the uninitiated public. But surely today it would be recognized by economists—though, of course, not by the general public—that, as the rules or conventions for the scientific use of language entail, there can be no one single, exclusively significant 'national-income' measurement, but only a series of indices which may at any moment be moving in different ways. Of course, which figure one gives more attention to, will, or may, depend more or less on one's pre-scientific interest, or choice of problem or theory. But the accuracy of any particular national income figure, for example, or of estimated changes in it, or of the effects of changes, are empirical, testable questions, and what the estimated figure or change entails is a logical one.

When indices of, say, 'national-income' come to be used in discussions of economic policies, or as policy objectives, goals or measures of 'progress', the danger of non-logical 'persuasiveness' obviously becomes more acute. There is often a tendency for what one is able, or had decided, to give a measure or index of (say 'real national income-per-head'), gradually, and perhaps more or less unconsciously, to take on a highly questionable normative significance.[1] Here the connection between terminology, or definitions and 'interest' goes further. But *simply* from '*scientific*' statements involving such indices, whether they are definitional as to how they have been composed, or empirical as to how they behave, or logical as to what their movements logically entail, no valid normative conclusions or recommendations can logically be drawn.

(4) When it is argued that some sorts of concepts or definitions are incompatible with scientific neutrality, or that there is a whole range of national-income definitions and measurements between which a choice has to be made, and a relative interest expressed, more is meant, presumably, than simply that any choice of words or definitions can be said to involve a value-judgment of some kind.[2] It is implied that there may be a more or less intentionally propagandist, persuasive or evaluative element in the terms, concepts and

[1] Andrew Shonfield has commented on how 'we' (Western economists) have 'wished . . . our own techniques for measuring economic progress on to the underdeveloped countries. . . . We had observed that they had responded by forcing the pace of those particular things we had decided to measure. . . . As so often happens, the devotion to the ideal of precision at all costs leads the technicians to attach inordinate importance to the factors that they happen to be able to measure—whereas the truth about these factors is often not that they are important but that they are just familiar to the people who have been responsible for setting up the conventional methods of measurement.' *Encounter*, December 1961, pp. 60–63.

[2] P. Streeten, Introduction to *Value in Social Theory* by G. Myrdal, 1958, p. xxi.

Types and Sources of Value-Judgments and Bias   67

definitions that are chosen, rendering the statements and theories in which they are used not merely, or purely, positive or descriptive, but, to some extent, also normative. This may be so. But the precise 'scientific' relevance of this point must be questioned, and the fundamental distinction insisted on between, on the one hand, questions of the empirically testable truth or falsity of statements, or their logical consistency or inconsistency, and of what they logically entail, and, on the other hand, their possible or actual effects, influence, or persuasiveness, or of the psychological reactions to them, or of the motives or suggestibility of those who discuss them. 'Scientific' criteria and rules of procedure are only concerned with the former and not with the latter questions, and only with the testable content or aspects of empirical statements and theories.

In any case, the concept of persuasive definitions, if it is not to be obfuscatory, must be sufficiently clearly defined and delimited, or the impression may be given that *all* definitions and concepts are, or may be, in some significant sense, impregnated with persuasive or evaluative overtones. As C. L. Stevenson, the inventor of the concept, makes clear, *any* definition expresses an interest, or a kind of value-judgment of the pre-scientific type involved in the choice of a problem for study, since it suggests that the concept, or what the concept refers to, is worth discussing.[1] All definitions must be 'persuasive' in this sense, but this is not enough to make them 'persuasive' in a significant moral or political sense.

Stevenson emphasized that merely because a definition (e.g. of national income) involves a choice and direction of interest, it is not thereby 'persuasive' in the sense he introduced:

'When a scientist introduces a technical term, in no matter how detached a manner, he indicates his interest in what he names—his estimation of the importance of talking about it, or of predicting its occurrence—and he often leads his readers to have a similar interest. It would be quite misleading to call all such definitions "persuasive".

'. . . The distinction depends on whether the term defined has a

[1] 'It will be obvious that no definition, however severely intellectual and detached it may be, can be wholly divorced from certain bearings, direct or indirect, upon human inclinations or purposes. Thus Russell, writing not of ethics but of logic and mathematics, has remarked: 'A definition usually implies (i.e. leads one to suspect) that the definiens is *worthy* of careful consideration. Hence the collection of definitions embodies our *choice* of subjects and our judgment as to what is more important." Now a choice of what is judged important or worthy of attention is a reflection of the speaker's attitudes, and may serve to redirect the attitudes of the hearer. If this is the usual effect of any technical definition (and Russell's observation seems beyond intelligent objection) then how are persuasive definitions to be distinguished from others?' C. L. Stevenson, *Ethics and Language*, 1945, p. 282.

strong emotive meaning, and upon whether the speaker employs the emotively laden word with dynamic purposes—with the predominating *intention* of changing people's interests. . . . When a definition is given mainly for the purposes of distinction or classification, when it is used to guide only those interests which (like *curiosity*) are involved in making the classification understood, and when it in no way suggests that this is *the one* legitimate sort of classification,then the definition will not be called "persuasive".'[1]

The sort of words, it has been pointed out, which mostly come in for definition,of this kind are 'those which have a relatively vague "conceptual" meaning but a very rich emotive meaning. . . . People seek to steal the good-will (or bad-will) which belongs to the word and use it for their own ends'.[2] Thus 'welfare', or 'economic welfare', has, or had, a fairly rich emotive meaning and a relatively vague conceptual meaning, but 'national income' has a relatively clear, (though far from fully precise), conceptual meaning, and not such a richly emotive meaning.

To be 'persuasive' in Stevenson's sense, therefore, a definition must influence more simply than the limited range of attitudes regarding what is judged important as a part of knowledge, and which, as we have seen, shape the scientist's preliminary choice of questions. They must influence what is judged important or desirable in other political or ethical respects. Above all, as Stevenson concludes, because the scientist is essentially involved in making definitions which inevitably involve judgments or evaluations of what is important or interesting knowledge, this does not mean, as he puts it, 'that science totters',[3] or is inevitably involved in evaluations as to what is politically or ethically desirable.

In any case, the influence, or persuasiveness of a sign, word, phrase or concept, depends on what happens to be the reactions of those who use or discuss it. To hold that any word is somehow *inherently* or *essentially* persuasive, normative or value-loaded, would be to profess a kind of terminological 'essentialism'. Economists, especially, can understand that a 'good' is not necessarily 'good'.

It is perhaps worth stressing further that it takes two to complete a process of persuasion, a persuader and a persuaded, and that to

[1] *Mind*, July 1938, p. 336.
[2] M. Warnock, *Ethics since 1900*, 1957, p. 101.
[3] *Op. cit.*, p. 290: 'There is unquestionably a possibility that interests in knowledge should be opposed, and lead to evaluative controversy, within science itself, about what is worth speaking of, or what classifications or distinctions are worth making. At times these issues are complicated enough to stand in the way of scientific agreement and must be debated by many of the methods that we have illustrated for ethics. But there is no occasion for philosophical fear, on this account, that science totters. The evaluative aspects of science involve only interests in knowledge.'

Types and Sources of Value-Judgments and Bias   69

the extent that economics is pursued as, or economic problems discussed in terms of, a 'scientific' discipline, economists are not concerned with persuading one another or being persuaded as to what is politically or ethically good, right, just, beneficial or desirable, to any extent beyond simply the implication that the subject or question is of some interest and importance, and worth studying in accordance with 'scientific' criteria. A rule of using and understanding language non-persuasively broadly coincides with the rules of procedure regarding empirical testing and testability and mathematical deduction. Of course, all these rules are constantly broken. But if one makes the preliminary claim or value-judgment, that it is worth practising economics as a 'scientific discipline', then there is an implied obligation to make a reasonable attempt to keep these rules, which, though some absolute ideal purity may, by definition, be unattainable, are not impossibly difficult to keep to within practicable human limits. Of course, if economists want to, and do, act as persuaders, hidden or open, as is certainly sometimes the case, then they are, of course, directly interested in propagandist effects and persuasiveness. Scientific rules or 'discipline' in the use and understanding of language, or the rules of logic and of testing and testability, then go by the board, or come a bad second.

Myrdal claims that in economics and the social sciences inevitably 'our very concepts are value-loaded'.[1] If these value-loads simply consist in the implication that the problems of economics and the social sciences, or, indeed, of any sciences, are of interest, or worth studying, then this is certainly true and is perhaps almost or actually a tautology, or, at any rate, a triviality. We could not or would not introduce or define concepts if we had not some 'interest' in them, or in what they referred to. If Myrdal means, on the other hand, that economists often, though not always and inevitably, approach their problems, and proceed to conceptualize them, very heavily and intensively loaded with political and ethical predilections, then this certainly seems a valid generalization, though one which one could imagine having to be mitigated at least to some extent. But, important though these considerations are, Myrdal might well be taken to imply a good deal more, and this, we think, must be rejected. The 'value-load' in that unfortunate term 'welfare' may be so heavy that

---

[1] *Value in Social Theory* by G. Myrdal, edited by P. Streeten, 1958, p. 1. Elsewhere, in a comprehensive omnibus statement on the subject, Myrdal writes: 'Valuations enter into social analysis, not only when conclusions concerning policy are drawn, but already in the theoretical endeavour to establish what is objectively true—in the choice of a field of enquiry, the selection of assumptions, even the decision as to what is a fact and what is a value. Our concepts are, therefore, "value-loaded".' See his contribution ' "Value-loaded" Concepts' in *Money, Growth and Methodology*, Essays in Honor of Johan Åkerman, 1961, p. 274.

it is practically impossible to unload it completely. But such unloading as is necessary is quite practicable with most of the main concepts of economics, and if it has not been achieved as thoroughly as it could (and should) have been in all cases, it is quite possible, and an outstanding analytical task, to push the unloading further—if it is desired to cultivate a disciplined subject, free, or as practicably free as possible, of value-loads. As regards Myrdal's example that 'economic integration' is a value-loaded term, because it 'carries the implication that the attainment of economic integration—in some sense—is desirable', there is certainly no logical implication here, and even the persuasive suggestion is rather tenuous, easily neutralizable, and highly questionable—and, in any case, it is scientifically irrelevant.

The argument we are attempting to present has been summarized with admirable trenchancy as follows:

'That everyday language is value-loaded and that the problems of the social sciences are rooted in everyday life and of vital interest to society is undeniable. But this also holds good for the natural sciences which have likewise only gradually freed themselves from normative elements. Why should this not be achieved in the social sciences? The vocabulary of modern sociology has to a considerable extent been practically neutralized. In cases of doubt the convention suffices for purposes of scientific discussion that the terminology in question is to be taken as neutral and free of valuations. Infringements of this rule, just like infringements of the rules of logical deduction, can immediately be corrected, as in fact often today occurs. The rules of the game in a positive science are certainly in other ways not very easy to follow. Circular definitions, false proofs, faulty deductions and contradictions are common. One can only rely for their elimination and correction on the institutionalized mechanism of sanctions which operates in scientific discussion, which can also see to it that the language of science is generally kept neutral and free of valuations. . . . That the valuations of other branches of culture may diverge (from those of the scientist) and that such conflicts of values may create personal difficulties where one and the same person seeks to combine the social role of the scientist with those of, for example, the politician, the business man, the teacher or the pastor, is undeniable. In the field of politics a value-loaded language can be more useful than neutralized, analytical conceptual tools. Implicit valuations and pseudo-objective arguments may well prove more effective than logical deductions from explicit value-premisses. The languages of political agitation and scientific argument diverge in opposite directions from that of everyday speech.'[1]

[1] H. Albert, *Schweizerische Zeitschrift für Volkswirtschaft und Statistik*, 1958, p. 339.

Types and Sources of Value-Judgments and Bias   71

The history of economics has been full of persuasive, value-loaded language and definitions, and indeed Stevenson himself took the majority of his examples from our subject: 'productive' and 'unproductive' labour, the 'sterile' class, definitions of 'value' (particularly in terms of labour), 'natural' values and incomes, 'equilibrium', 'exploitation' and, above all, 'welfare'. As we saw in the last chapter, J. E. Cairnes, in 1870, was complaining 'of the double meaning of such "passionate" terms as "principle", "value", "worth", "service" and the like', and that 'the economic vocabulary unfortunately lends itself only too readily to this sort of theorizing and few writers have entirely escaped illusion from this cause'.[1] To a modern economist it may possibly seem a little strange to find another economist describing such terms as 'value' and 'service' as 'passionate'. Although today in many contexts such words may be used 'passionately' or 'persuasively', in the context of economists' theorizing about value and the pricing of productive 'services', all, or nearly all, 'passion' has long been spent, all persuasiveness neutralized, and such terms are readily understood in a quite neutral, non-persuasive and non-evaluative sense — which illustrates that words or concepts are not inherently or essentially normative, persuasive or value-loaded, not even such words as 'value', 'goods' or 'services'. There is such a thing as 'progress' in logical and scientific analysis and an important element in this consists of the neutralizing of the value-loads or persuasiveness of the everyday language economists start from. In fact, today, increasing sophistication and awareness make it difficult for an economist to get away with persuasive usages for very long, or very far, *vis-a-vis* other economists. Of course, persuasive usages will continue to be perpetrated just as the rules of logic and mathematics will continue to be broken, but the scientific processes of critical analysis are not ineffective in checking them. An economist may well succeed in 'persuading' himself, or his immediate school or disciples, with his persuasive language, and, of course, in an extra-scientific context such as a letter to a newspaper or a broadcast talk, he may 'persuade' members of the general public unversed in the discipline of scientific usage. Graphical methods particularly offer scope for public 'persuaders' on television. Prices or G.N.P. can, according to taste, be made apparently to have rocketed up, or remained almost stationary, by choosing the appropriate scale. But in scientific or disciplined contexts neither verbal nor graphical persuasiveness is likely today to have a significant influence for any length of time.[2]

[1] J. E. Cairnes, *Essays in Political Economy*, 1873, p. 322.
[2] A recent example of a comparatively subtle use of a persuasive definition seems to have occurred in respect of the concept of equilibrium in international trade, according to which the presence of import restrictions entailed, by defini-

72   *'Positive' Economics and Policy Objectives*

The major recent example of a persuasive definition or concept is that of 'welfare' or 'economic welfare', and 'real national income' has also been cited.[1] But if we compare such a 'persuasive' statement as 'This policy will increase the welfare (or "real income") of the community' with such statements as 'This policy will increase the rate of growth' (or level of employment, or stability of prices), it is not obvious that there is inevitably and inherently something 'persuasive' about the former, and not about the latter, which certainly *can* be taken in a purely descriptive, positive sense.[2] It seems dogmatic to try to insist that the former statements (concerning 'welfare' and 'real income') *cannot*, or *must* not, be taken in the same positive mood as the latter, if this is made sufficiently clear, though certainly it might be urged that the terms had best be scrapped altogether.

Economists have often complained of the difficulties they are under in having to start with imprecise or ambiguous everyday language, and the normative-positive ambiguities in everyday language may be more dangerously confusing than purely positive ambiguities. It would be almost impossible to avoid *all* everyday words which started with some sort of persuasive overtones—'value', 'monopoly', 'equilibrium', and so on. But it was, of course, inviting normative-positive confusion to introduce such a highly-charged word as 'welfare' right into the centre of the discussion of economic policies, and to set it up as the main title and main concept of a whole branch of economics, as has been done over the last fifty years. On the whole, it would seem advantageous if the word 'welfare' was never uttered again by an economist, or, at any rate, never allowed out unless firmly shackled between inverted commas. It would surely be clearer simply to define a choice or efficiency criterion, or a movement in a particular national income index, without mentioning the word 'welfare'.

tion, 'disequilibrium', so that these had to be removed if 'equilibrium'—implicitly or explicitly suggested as the ideal—was to be reached. But this device was promptly exposed by other economists, who completely refused to be persuaded and neutralized its persuasiveness,—as they would have corrected it if it had been an error in logic or mathematics. Cf. F. Machlup, *Economic Journal*, March 1958, p. 23: 'The objections against persuasive definitions of equilibrium are not based on the fear that gullible people may actually be persuaded to stand up for the measures of policy "deduced" from arguments in which such an equilibrium concept is employed.'

[1] Cf. I. M. D. Little, *A Critique of Welfare Economics*, 2nd Ed., 1957, p. 275: 'Many economic statements, which appear at first sight to be merely descriptive, have value implications. Among the most important of such phrases are "increase of welfare" and "increase of real income".' J. de v. Graaff (*Theoretical Welfare Economics*, 1957, p. 2) states that 'we must place questions regarding "real income" in the normative division'. It is not clear what sort of 'must' this is.

[2] Cf. G. C. Archibald, 'Welfare Economics, Ethics and Essentialism', *Economica*, November 1959, p. 324.

Types and Sources of Value-Judgments and Bias   73

There has been much progress in recent decades in the rapid neutralization of persuasiveness, and a reasonable standard of observance of the rule of non-persuasiveness is not impossible to attain if there is a general, critical consensus in favour of it, in spite of the economist's handicap of having to use, or start from, everyday language. Persuasive language and concepts do not represent some kind of inevitable all-pervasive 'value-loadedness' in economics. As Popper says:

'Ordinary language is not rational, but it is our task to rationalize it, or at least to keep up its standards of clarity. . . . We ourselves and our ordinary language are, on the whole, emotional rather than rational; but we can try to become a little more rational, and we can train ourselves to use our language as an instrument not of self-expression (as our romantic educationists would say) but of rational communication.'[1]

At least this seems to be 'our task', and an inevitable value-premiss, if we are claiming to cultivate our subject 'scientifically', or arrogating to ourselves any 'scientific' objectivity. Of course, in so far as economists take on the role of political persuaders and ideologues —and quite a number of them do—such tasks and value-premisses do not arise.

(5) BIAS IN HYPOTHESES AND THEIR TESTING

When the scientific processes of critical analysis and testing get started, the analytical part of them will begin with wringing out imprecisions and ambiguities (including 'persuasive' ambiguities) in everyday language, so as to arrive at workably precise definitions permitting of workably precise questions and hypotheses. Relations between the more precisely defined concepts are then analysed deductively, definitional equations and taxonomies can be drawn up, and purely deductive models can be constructed on postulated conditions. Only the rules of logic and mathematics, and testing as to the observance of these rules, are involved here, and a good deal of —though not, of course, all—'theorising' in economics has been of this purely analytical kind. Logical consistency is the only test in this case, and empirical testing is irrelevant since, at this stage, only definitions and analytical statements, without empirical content, are being dealt with. At the same time, and more or less linked with this analytical work, empirical hypotheses may be set out, either taken over from extra-scientific ideologies or 'visions', or based on 'hunch',

---

[1] K. R. Popper, *The Open Society and Its Enemies*, 4th Ed., 1962, Vol. III pp. 278 and 357.

introspection, impressionism, casual empiricism, or more systematic empirical investigation, and these call for the essential scientific process of the empirical testing of hypotheses and the collection and examination of evidence to test them. The 'objectivity' of scientific statements depends on this inter-subjective testing.

We are now faced with the well-known difficulty of the critical and rigorous testing of hypotheses, theories and statements in the economic and social field.[1] The practical possibility of testing theories critically and significantly often hardly exists, and the strong wish to see the facts in one particular way, as expressed in an initial ideologically biased hypothesis, may mean that there is not even a will to test, in the sense of a genuine critical attempt to falsify. It is all too easy, even when the scientific process of refining, testing and attempting to falsify hypotheses has begun, for economists to retain their belief in what they want to believe.

Let us, however, consider a highly optimistic account of how ideological prejudices and subjective biases and preconceptions, and the disagreements they lead to, are purged away by the discipline of the scientific process of selection by inter-subjective testing. Under the heading 'The Objectivity of Economic Science', Oskar Lange wrote in a well-known essay:

'The statements of economic science have objective validity. This means that two or more persons who agree to abide by the rules of scientific procedure are bound to reach the same conclusion. If they start with the same assumptions, they are bound, by the rules of logic, to derive the same theorems. If they apply the same rules of identification and verification, they are bound to reach agreement as to whether the theorems should be accepted as "true" or rejected as "unverified" or "false". The test of verification decides whether the assumptions are adequate or not. In the latter case they have to be replaced by new ones which lead to theorems able to stand the

---

[1] Cf. M. Friedman, *Essays in Positive Economics*, 1953, pp. 10–11: 'Unfortunately, we can seldom test particular predictions in the social sciences by experiments explicitly designed to eliminate what are judged to be the most important disturbing influence. Generally, we must rely on evidence cast up by the "experiments" that happen to occur. The inability to conduct so-called "controlled experiments" does not, in my view, reflect a basic difference between the social and physical sciences. . . . The denial to economics of the dramatic and direct evidence of the "crucial" experiment does hinder the adequate testing of hypotheses; but this is much less significant than the difficulty it places in the way of achieving a reasonably·prompt and wide consensus on the conclusions justified by the available evidence. It renders the weeding-out of unsuccessful hypotheses slow and difficult. They are seldom downed for good and are always cropping up again. . . . One effect of the difficulty of testing substantive economic hypotheses has been to foster a retreat into purely formal or tautological analysis.'

Types and Sources of Value-Judgments and Bias   75

test of verification. The final verdict with regard to any statement of economic science is thus based on an appeal to facts, i.e. to empirical observations.'[1]

Lange traced disagreements between economists, which he admitted were many and profound, to three sources, which are 'all due to failure to abide by the rules of scientific procedure and can be resolved by strict application of these rules'. The first of these sources of disagreement consists of differences as to social objectives, which depend on differences in value-judgments, the remedy being to state these explicitly so that agreement can be reached on what particular measures promote, or fail to promote, different objectives. Next there may be disagreements owing to a failure to abide by the rules of logic—which have an obvious remedy. It is the disagreement described by Lange as 'disagreement about facts' with which we are concerned here and for which his remedy seems especially optimistic:

'Such disagreement can always be removed by further observation and study of the empirical material. Frequently, however, the empirical data necessary to resolve the disagreement are unavailable. In such cases the issue remains unsettled. The conclusion that the issue cannot be settled with the data available has interpersonal validity. Agreement is reached to withhold judgment.'[2]

Lange is describing how, in his terms, ideally, or 'on paper', the rules of the game 'should', or might be hoped to, operate. We can only emphasize how wide is the range of questions in economics, and particularly of policy questions, where 'the empirical data necessary to resolve the disagreement are unavailable'. We can only point out how much of the empirical content of economic theorizing remains untested, or even practically untestable, at any rate sufficiently significantly to remove disagreement, and how little disposed 'to withhold judgment' economists show themselves to be, especially when they feel the urge to discuss policy recommendations. As we have already noted, often when scientific criteria 'did not uniquely determine a theory, its fitness to support moral or political indoctrination became an important factor for its acceptance'.[3] Whether it is the effects of changes in interest rates on investment, income-tax

---

[1] 'The Scope and Method of Economic Science', reprinted from the *Review of Economic Studies*, No. 13, 1945–46, in *Readings in the Philosophy of Science*, edited by H. Feigl and M. Brodbeck, 1953, p. 748. It seems that Lange may subsequently have come to harbour reservations as to some of his arguments in this paper.

[2] *Op. cit.*, p. 749.

[3] Cf. P. G. Frank, 'The Acceptance of Scientific Theories', in *The Validation of Scientific Theories* (ed. P. G. Frank), paperback edition, 1961, p. 19.

rates on the supply of effort, levels of employment on price levels, levels of profits on the policies of firms, or the extent of possible economies of scale—just to begin what could be an almost endless list—the issues indeed 'remain unsettled', though it certainly does not follow that 'agreement is reached to withhold judgment'. Lange's conception of a smooth, rapid and almost automatic process to agreement is as far from the reality of economic controversy as a model of a smooth, rapid and almost automatic tendency to full long-term equilibrium throughout the economic system is from economic reality. In fact, it may be doubtful how significant it is to assume even a 'tendency' towards it. Nevertheless, Lange undoubtedly states the formula for agreement and scientific consensus, and this *could* be followed out if there was a will to do so, though clearly a great deal of 'withholding judgment' would be required.

Schumpeter also describes how the scientific process of analysis and empirical testing tends to crush out the influence of ideology:

'The rules of procedure that we apply in our analytic work are almost as much exempt from ideological influence as vision is subject to it. Passionate allegiance and passionate hatred may indeed tamper with these rules. In themselves these rules, many of which, moreover, are imposed upon us by the scientific practice in fields that are little or not at all affected by ideology, are pretty effective in showing up misuse. And, what is equally important, they tend to crush out ideologically conditioned error from the visions from which we start. . . . And if this process is allowed to work itself out completely, it will indeed not protect us from the emergence of new ideologies, but it will clear in the end the existing ones from error. It is true that in economics, and still more in other social sciences, this sphere of the strictly provable is limited in that there are always fringe ends of things that are matters of personal experience and impression from which it is practically impossible to drive ideology, or for that matter conscious dishonesty, completely. The comfort we may take from our argument is therefore never complete. But it does cover most of the ground in the sense of narrowing the sphere of ideologically vitiated propositions considerably, that is, of narrowing it down and of making it always possible to locate the spots in which it may be active.'[1]

Perhaps realizing that his emphasis here was slightly over-optimistic Schumpeter went on to add the following qualifications:

'We have had to recognize, on the one hand, that although there exists a mechanism that tends to crush out ideologies automatically, this may be a time-consuming process that meets with many resist-

[1] *History of Economic Analysis*, 1954, p. 43 and p. 44.

Types and Sources of Value-Judgments and Bias   77

ances and, on the other hand, that we are never safe from the current intrusion of new ideologies to take the place of the vanishing older ones.'

To say that the process of reaching agreement—including agreement to withhold judgment—is, in economics and the social sciences, a 'time-consuming' one 'that meets with many resistances', is certainly an understatement rather than an overstatement. It is not simply that the tests of a hypothesis, or of the evidence regarding it, may be so selective that it is only exposed to those which it will pass, that is, that they are no tests at all. There will often be an unwillingness simply to set out the evidence and accept its inconclusiveness. Rather an attempt will be made to weigh the evidence up, or interpret it in favour of the hypothesis, so that it is protected rather than tested. Alternatively, there may be a retreat into what Popper calls 'conventionalist stratagems' by elastically modifying the assumptions or definitions involved to protect the hypothesis against falsification, ultimately removing all falsifiable empirical content by reducing it to a tautology.[1]

An economist may come to an economic problem 'loaded' with ideological prejudices or political 'principles', the most important implications of which are the desirability of certain social objectives and of policies to promote them. It has been all too easy for such an economist to support his political and economic policy objectives by persisting in the assertion of those empirical propositions from which they can most easily be derived, that is, from which they follow on the basis of the most widely acceptable value-judgments. The process has been aptly described as follows:

'The question arises how to justify [policy] objectives by theoretical reasoning. Two ways are open to the theorist. One is faulty, i.e. elusive or contradictory reasoning; the other is the choice of suitable assumptions from which theoretical conclusions are logically deduced, supporting the political and economic objectives. The first way, though often followed, is theoretically less interesting. As to the second way, it is clear that if the choice of assumptions were free one could prove what one pleases. Actually, the choice is not free because assumptions which are obviously contrary to known facts cannot be used. But many facts in the field of economics are not known, about others only little is known, and many are controversial. Very often the quantitative significance of one or the other fact is debatable. If the theorist then attaches great significance to one fact and little to another his conclusions may well be in direct opposition to those at which he would have to arrive if he reversed his quantitative appraisal. It is here where the theorist has a wide field of

[1] v. K. R. Popper, *The Logic of Scientific Discovery*, 1959, pp. 82–4.

78   *'Positive' Economics and Policy Objectives*

activity where social ideals often determine, without difficulty from
the logical point of view, the "objective" conclusion.'[1]

Von Mering shows this process at work in contrasting theories of
interest, the history of which right down to the present day is rich
in instances of the influence of ideological and political preconceptions.[2] International trade, tax incidence and public debt are
other subjects where von Mering cites interesting examples, and the
'stagnation' thesis is another case.[3] Those with contrasting political
preconceptions—in favour, say, of economic individualism, on the
one hand, or socialist planning, on the other hand—do not merely
differ in their valuations of social and economic objectives, they tend
to uphold as valid quite different sets of factual generalizations about
economic behaviour and processes, and persist in upholding them
whether they have withstood testing or not.

The process of describing a situation, or diagnosing a disease, in
terms which suggest or imply that the kind of remedial measures
required—given certain fairly widely accepted value-judgments—
are ones which the doctor wished to have adopted *anyway*, can
probably be illustrated from the debate in the early and middle
'fifties as to whether inflationary processes in the British economy
came about through 'demand-pull' or 'cost-push'.[4] It was very

[1] O. von Mering, *Social Ideals and Economic Theory*, Kyklos, Vol. IV, 1950,
p. 175.

[2] O. Hobson (in *Not Unanimous*, edited by A. Seldon, 1960, p. 87), criticizing
the report of the Radcliffe Committee, writes: 'Its left-wing members started
with a fundamental antagonism to the idea that regulation of a modern industrial
community must hinge on control of its money supply. In the endeavour to meet
this antagonism, an alternative theory, which one may call the "liquidity structure theory", has been elaborated and adopted by the whole Committee.' The
process here described works, of course, both ways, from left to right, so to
speak, as well as from right to left. But we are not concerned with how far a
'tu quoque' may be justifiable regarding *'right*-wing' experts who 'started with a
fundamental antagonism' to central regulation and discretionary controls, and
were concerned to establish the theory of the effectiveness of acting on the
quantity of money. Our point is simply the pervasiveness of political bias and
latent value-premisses in theorizing about monetary processes and policies, the
desirability of making one's premisses much clearer and more explicit, and of
acknowledging the role of bias in the selection and weighting of evidence.

[3] 'Observation teaches us that liberal economists usually reject the assumption
of a deficiency of private investment opportunities, while economists sympathetic
to planning very willingly make use of it.' F. A. Lutz, 'Politische Überzeugungen
und nationalökonomische Theorie', *Ordo*, Bd. IX, 1957, p. 14. See below, Section 7 of this chapter.

[4] 'The economist may be tempted to stress one set of arguments because he
believes this supports a policy which is desirable in any case for other reasons.'
E. Devons, *Essays in Economics*, 1961, p. 44. The role of latent ideological or
political 'visions' or preconceptions in macro-economic theorizing has been
described as follows: 'Attitudes to inflation are coloured by very general, more
or less implicit, assumptions about how the economy works; and in particular

Types and Sources of Value-Judgments and Bias   79

difficult, if not practically impossible, to devise tests of whether it
was 'demand-pull' processes rather than 'cost-push', or *vice versa*,
which were predominantly at work in the actual inflationary situation. In fact, these two concepts were often not precisely defined or
delimited. On the empirical question as to which process was predominantly at work there was, for some years, no agreement and no
tests sufficient to eliminate one or other of the alternative answers.
On the contrary, one or the other formula was championed with
exclusivist fervour, and, to a considerable extent, it seemed, in accordance with preconceived political predilections. Those generally
favouring free markets and opposed to the extension of central
controls tended to favour the 'demand-pull' description, as this
implied that no essential expansion of central regulation or discretionary controls was necessary. The 'cost-push' description suggested or implied—given other widely supported policy objectives—
that a significant extension of the range of central controls was
necessary, and this tended to be supported by those who had
expressed an inclination—or no disinclination—to such extension,
for other reasons. Not that the mechanism, stressed by Schumpeter,
'that tends to crush out ideologies automatically', has not been
operative in gradually taking some of the exclusivist political sting
out of the controversy, but, as he said, it 'may be a time-consuming
process'.[1]

Another very broad and somewhat vague empirical generalization,
which seems liable to be shaped in opposite senses by conflicting
political preferences, concerns the extent of economies of scale in
modern industries. Socialistically inclined economists are apt to
emphasize the prevalence and growing importance of economies of
scale, and of a trend to widespread monopolistic conditions, as a
reason for nationalization or for public ownership or control. For
example, according to H. D. Dickinson:

about the degree to which it is sensitive to "market forces". It is difficult to
bring such general preconceptions to the test of evidence, without first making
them explicit.' (J. C. R. Dow, *Economic Journal*, September 1958, p. 613.) It still
remains very difficult to test them when they *are* made explicit.

[1] In his 1959 address to the Royal Economic Society, the then Economic
Adviser to H.M.G. stated: 'Economists have been, and to some extent still are,
broadly divided' as between the 'demand-pull' and 'cost-push' descriptions or
diagnoses. (*Economic Journal*, December 1959, pp. 647–8.) Two years later,
however, the effects of Schumpeter's 'time-consuming process' were, to some
extent, apparent in the form of a certain *détente* in expert opinion: 'The experts
. . . were at one time divided into two schools: one laid stress on the pull of
demand . . . ; the other stressed the upward push of negotiated rises in rates
of pay, initiating rises in cost. More recently the experts have found more common ground. There is now a wide measure of agreement that both "demand-
pull" and "cost-push" have been active.' (Fourth Report of the Council on
Prices, Productivity and Incomes, July 1961, p. 15.)

'In the early and middle period of capitalism, diminishing costs did not often occur . . . equilibrium was possible under competition. . . . But more recent times have seen the rapid growth of decreasing-cost industries. . . . What is needed, at any rate for the large-scale sector of the economy, is a system of production by public bodies . . . not obliged to make profits.'[1]

Jewkes, on the other hand, contradicts this generalization and asks 'Where is the evidence in support of the view that "indivisibilities" are of growing importance?' He asserts that 'we are not really confronted with the awkward choice between monopoly and inefficiency', and that 'it is difficult to believe that indivisibilities do really create a new situation in industry which now makes inapplicable the general case for a free economy'.[2] Of course, no proof can be offered that economists' political attitudes are liable to determine their beliefs about industrial technology, rather than that their beliefs about industrial technology shape their political beliefs. But, at least, the former seems not impossible.[3]

We must add here that the biased support of hypotheses and assumptions when the evidence is inadequate or disputed, may not always stem from *political* preconceptions. An economist, or school of economists, may see and weigh the evidence, as he or they want to see and weigh it, out of a determination to uphold his or its particular theory, without political preconceptions playing a part. Moreover, there is often a strong desire to come to *some* general conclusion, to have something reasonably succinct and coherent to say, rather than to have no definite conclusion to offer at all, and if the conclusion is unusual or novel so much the better.[4] Even if no political or ideological preconceptions and no policy issues are involved, there may be a tendency to selective simplification, or 'modellization', either quite independently of any political bias, or,

[1] *Humanitas*, Autumn 1946, quoted by J. Jewkes, *Ordeal by Planning*, 1948, p. 43.

[2] J. Jewkes, op. cit., pp. 42–3. An interesting reversal in the discussion of this issue has emerged in the debate over the economic gains or losses from Britain joining the Common Market. Socialistically inclined economists, who tended to be politically opposed to Britain joining, were to be found categorically denying the general significance of economies of scale: 'There is nothing in the argument that we need a larger internal market for such an improvement' (in investment and innovation). T. Balogh, *The Observer*, October 21, 1962. We are not accusing anyone of outright contradiction, but are simply suggesting that there may be a certain mutability of factual generalization—rather like Orwell's 'mutability of the past' in *1984*.

[3] See below the quotations from F. Lutz in Section 7 of this chapter.

[4] 'It is simply a fact that many of our best economists are irresponsible. They would as lief be wrong in an interesting way as be right along with the mob.' P. Samuelson, *Problems of the American Economy*, Stamp Memorial Lecture, 1961, 1962, p. 19.

Types and Sources of Value-Judgments and Bias   81

more probably, effectively reinforcing it. This process has been cogently analysed by H. G. Johnson, with reference to the theory of international trade:

'In order to choose between the impossible number of alternatives with which even a relatively simple analytical problem confronts him, the theorist is strongly tempted to eliminate some of the cases by prejudging the results of measurements he does not and perhaps could not make, either by illegitimately assuming that a number of qualitative statements can be added up into a quantitative fact, or by postulating an ideal world in which only the cases he chooses will exist. This temptation is particularly dangerous when questions of economic policy are involved, because then the desire for simplicity may be reinforced by personal preferences in prompting the exclusion of possible cases.'[1]

We wish to emphasize, however, that in spite of its well-known difficulties, and the deep and powerful psychological resistances at work, the mechanism of intersubjective testing often does its work of wringing out ideological prejudices and presuppositions, and of modifying 'visionary' hypotheses, at least sufficiently effectively to render complete and wholesale scepticism unjustifiable. It *could* be made to work more rapidly and efficiently. This does not mean that an attempt should be made to prohibit guess-work, particularly with regard to practical policy problems which cannot wait. It does mean that guesses, and particularly conflicting guesses, should, at least, be acknowledged as such, that is, as statements or theories that are untested or inadequately tested. When we discuss below (Section 8) predictions required for the elucidation of the choice of policies, we shall have to consider the controversial question of how far economists are 'entitled' to base these on various kinds or degrees of judgment or hunch.

We have seen that the economist has to select his questions or problems, and the scientific criteria or rules of the game by which he conducts his studies. He also selects, in a sense, his language, concepts and definitions. None of these kinds of selection or valuation, which are common to all sciences, need, or indeed should, be held to destroy scientific objectivity, or the possibility thereof, in any significant sense. We have also seen that whatever ideological or political prejudices or presuppositions he starts from, the scientist cannot, according to his rules of procedure, 'select' his theories, hypotheses, or answers to his questions, but must let the selection be settled in accordance with the rules of logic and mathematics, and of critical intersubjective empirical testing, which he himself has set

[1] *Economic Journal*, December 1951, p. 827.

F

up, preferably showing at least some disposition to admit that the evidence is inconclusive. That is the position we have reached so far. But we shall have to examine the view that the scientist does, and must, in the nature of his task, select causes and hypotheses. Let us first, however, briefly consider the problem of selection and bias in writing history.

(6) BIAS AND OBJECTIVITY IN HISTORY AND HISTORICAL SELECTION

We referred previously (in Section 2 above) to the problem of selection in history, and we must now enquire rather further as to whether, how far, and in what way, value-judgments may be involved in historical selection. We might avoid this problem, on which, of course, there is a large and controversial literature, by claiming that we are concerned simply with the premises and methods of economics, and with economic analysis and its application to policies, and not with economic history. But this would be something of an evasion. For economists are constantly concerned with questions of economic history, with the explanation of particular events and episodes, and especially with recent and contemporary history. They are constantly trying to establish conclusions, or illustrations, concerning longer or shorter periods of history, and they do this especially when discussing policies. Moreover, the frontier between economics and economic history, never in practice very clearly and explicitly marked or observed, has become much more frequented and blurred as more and more explicit attention has been given to the problems of economic growth and development. In fact, the study of economic growth, in general comprehensive terms, unless the questions are very cautiously formulated, offers an open invitation to 'historicist' ambitions, to the propounding of historical 'laws' and stages, and to the value-loaded teleology which often accompanies these efforts. But while we do not feel obliged to investigate at all thoroughly controversial issues of the methodology of history, such as the problem of historical objectivity, or the role of value-judgments in historical writing, we cannot neglect this frontier altogether.

A theoretical science is concerned both with general and particular statements, but especially with establishing general statements or laws, particular statements providing only test statements, or—and this is important—the specifications of the conditions (or 'assumptions') for applying a general law to a particular case for purposes of making a prediction. The historian, on the other hand, though inevitably using general statements and laws, is not concerned to establish these, but only particular, singular statements. Like the theoretical scientist he is involved in a kind of *a priori* value-judgment in accepting criteria for evidence and in selecting questions for study. But it may seem that the historian not merely has to select his questions but to some extent selects the answers he proposes, or selects what is relevant to an answer. It is argued, for example, that the historian cannot possibly give a *complete* account of an historical episode and all its antecedents, or reproduce it in its entirety, and that value-judgments are inevitably involved in his selection of what to include as relevant.

To some extent, at least, this argument can be countered by observing that if an historian does not start from a very precise question, as historians often do not, then what is relevant to his answer will be imprecise and will continually be requiring selection, involving a kind of value-judgment, as he goes along. If he does not make, *a priori*, the question selected (and the value-judgments involved) clear and precise, then these value-judgments will emerge in the answer he gives, and in the selection as to what is relevant which it reveals. If he starts out to write 'The History of Europe (or of Economic Thought) 1860–1960', he will have to select at some stage, or as he goes along, what, for him, 'the history of Europe (or of economic thought) 1860–1960' consists of. If he starts from a vague question such as 'What were the causes of the industrial revolution?' he will have to select the 'relevant' causes, or what is relevant to the 'causes'. On the other hand, if he starts from relatively precise questions such as 'Where, When and How did Hitler die?' or 'What was the increase in population, or steel output, in Britain between 1900 and 1950?' then what is 'relevant' will be comparatively clear-cut.

However, the peculiarly historical problem of selection arises from the absence of a standard of relevance of the kind which exists in theoretical sciences. Popper has pointed out that whereas theoretical sciences have laws and generalizations 'as centres of interest to which observations are related, or as points of view from which observations are made', there are no universal historical laws which can possibly fulfil this function:

'It must be taken over by something else. For undoubtedly there can be no history without a point of view; like the natural sciences, history must be *selective* unless it is to be choked by a flood of poor and unrelated material. . . . The only way out of this difficulty is, I believe, consciously to introduce a *preconceived selective point of view* into one's history; that is, to write that history which *interests us*. This does not mean that we may twist the facts until they fit into a framework of preconceived ideas or that we may neglect the facts that do not fit. On the contrary, all available evidence which has a bearing on our point of view should be considered carefully and objectively. . . . But it means that we need not worry about all those facts and aspects which have no bearing upon our point of view and which therefore do not interest us.'[1]

As Popper stresses, maintaining historical objectivity involves being conscious and critical of one's own selective point of view and its limitations. It is quite possible to maintain this to a reasonable, if not to some absolutely pure and ideal extent. To claim objectivity for an historical account, or that one account is more objective or less biased than another, is not just meaningless naïveté. One achieves a measure of 'objectivity' by stressing the 'subjective' elements in one's answers. We need hardly add that to uphold this possibility and practicability of reasonable objectivity is not to deny how much of economic history, and of the history of economic thought, has been written with a strong underlying desire to attack or defend particular economic policies and systems, or to suggest the need for particular sorts of policy.

The theoretical economist needs and uses economic history to provide examples of a particular theoretical model, or to suggest (given certain normative assumptions which may or may not be explicitly stated) the desirability of particular policies. Obviously the scope for bias in selecting and defining historical examples may be very wide, and the accuracy of statistical estimates used as examples may be highly questionable — as, for example, in discussions of 'the' rate of growth of the British economy where the dates of the period taken for measuring 'the' rate of growth make a significant difference.[2]

The difficulties of presenting an objective historical account become immense when an attempt has to be made to present historical facts not only for purposes of a discussion of policy, but sufficiently succinctly and graphically to be understood by the general public. For example, in its first report (1958), the Council on Prices, Productivity and Incomes stated:

'It has been our aim to present the relevant facts about the movements in recent years in prices, productivity and incomes in language intelligible not only to economists but to all who may be interested in these questions and to comment on those facts.'[3]

[1] *The Poverty of Historicism*, paperback edition, 1961, p. 150.
[2] See the controversy over '*the*' British rate of economic growth between C. G. Clark and F. W. Paish where, mainly as a consequence of taking different periods of years, they arrived at estimates 70 per cent apart (1.3 per cent and 2.2 per cent). See *The Listener*, July 6, 13, 20 and 27, 1961.
[3] Council on Prices, Productivity and Incomes, First Report, 1958, p. 1.

At different points it took its review back to 1850, 1938, 1946 and 1949. Historical selection, or value-judgments of a kind, were inevitable as to what, very roughly, was 'relevant' to the comprehensive and imprecise policy objectives set out in the terms of reference: 'the desirability of full employment and increasing standards of life based on expanding production and reasonable stability of prices'. What is 'relevant' is a vague question to which the answer must depend on one's interests. But that is quite a distinct question from that of the truth or falsity of whatever factual material is produced.

Historical explanation, furthermore, involves discovering and asserting the sufficient conditions for historical events. Often, or usually, these conditions are impossible to ascertain fully, and historians give, and can only give, what they hold to be the main, or most important, or fundamental causes. Here there is wide scope for subjectivity and bias—as one finds in debates over 'the causes' of particular wars and economic depressions—and sometimes not even a reasonable measure of objective consensus emerges. Statements assigning causal weights to different factors in historical processes, though not inevitably and in principle devoid of objective substance, are, in practice, often highly vague and subjective. As Nagel concludes:[1]

'Doubtless the basic trouble in this area of inquiry is that we do not possess at present a generally accepted, explicitly formulated, and fully comprehensive scheme for weighing the evidence for any arbitrarily given hypothesis so that the logical worth of alternate conclusions relative to the evidence available for each can be compared. Judgments must be formed even on matters of supreme practical importance on the basis of only vaguely understood considerations; and, in the absence of a standard logical canon for estimating the degree in which the evidence supports a conclusion, when judgments are in conflict each often appears to be the outcome of an essentially arbitrary procedure. This circumstance affects the standing of the historian's conclusions in the same manner as the findings of other students. Fortunately, though the range of possible disagreement concerning the force of evidence for a given statement is theoretically limitless, there is substantial agreement among men experienced in relevant matters on the relative probabilities to be assigned to many hypotheses. Such agreement indicates that, despite the absence of an explicitly formulated logic, many unformulated habits of thought embody factually warrantable principles of inference. Accordingly, although there are often legitimate grounds for

[1] See 'The Logic of Historical Analysis', by E. Nagel, reprinted in *Readings in the Philosophy of Science* edited by H. Feigl and M. Brodbeck, 1953, p. 700.

doubt concerning the validity of specific causal imputations in history, there appears to be no compelling reason for converting such doubt into wholesale scepticism.'

Among the 'other students', whose findings are put in doubt by these considerations, are students of economics, and Nagel's perhaps optimistic arguments lead on to our next problem as to the role or scope for subjectivity and value-judgments in analysing causal processes, and with regard to inductive inferences, prediction and the treatment of uncertainty.

(7) BIAS AND THE SELECTION OF CAUSES AND 'DETERMINANTS'

We have seen how the writing of history involves selection, and have noticed the problem of the 'weighting' of historical causes. It is arguable that the complex interdependence of economic, social and political phenomena, and the impossibility of isolating processes to test out the relative weights of 'causes' and 'effects' by laboratory experiments, means that the economist has, inevitably, more or less subjectively to select and 'weigh' causes. He can do this by simplificatory postulates in an abstract model, say, of the business cycle. But in *applying* any model to explaining or predicting in an actual historical case, the economist has to select or 'weigh' what he considers to be the actually important forces at work. Inevitable ignorance of the precise causal 'weights' to be assigned to different factors has to be, or at any rate often is, filled out by subjective impressionism, guesses and hunch, not in principle untestable, but practically not at the moment testable, or tested to the extent that some measure of consensus emerges. In the taking of practical decisions, which will not wait, this will often be unavoidable. But, of course, largely untested subjective guesses and hunch may be shaped by political and ideological bias and presuppositions. The problem has been well described by Lutz:

'Every change of an economic condition spreads its effects fan-wise throughout the whole system. Such a change in data sets off causal chains running in all directions. It is not possible for the theorist to follow out *all* of them completely and there is nothing for it but to leave aside some of them and take up the others under the never really valid assumption of *ceteris paribus*. He therefore has to make a judgment as to which causal chains he holds to be more important. But it is always at least conceivable that his judgment is quite unconsciously influenced by his political convictions. It must always be remembered that the theorist seldom detaches himself from the normative implications of his subject. So when he has followed out,

Types and Sources of Value-Judgments and Bias   87

purely analytically, some of the causal chains, he will always be thinking instinctively of how the effects he has analysed, if they seem to him unfavourable, can be counteracted or removed by policy measures. According to his attitude in principle to state intervention, he may, possibly, from the start, search for those causal chains which justify interventionist measures, or the reverse. One economist, for example, will emphasize unfavourable frictions which will obstruct the reaching of a new equilibrium when a change in data occurs. Another economist will make light of such frictional resistances and will push his analysis rapidly through to the new equilibrium condition in which everything is all right again.'[1]

An example of different or contrasting types of causal processes which have strong political implications is the somewhat misleadingly named division into 'short-period' and 'long-period' processes. The 'weighting' given to these two different types of process in general abstract economic theorizing, or in the explanation of particular historical processes, may be, and seems often to be, guided by political and ideological presuppositions. As Lutz says:

'The theorist is always free to interest himself solely in the short-period effects of a change or in the long-period effects. Keynes, for example, explicitly favoured the short-period treatment, as the assumptions underlying his system regarding given productive equipment clearly show. This choice between the short period and the long period leaves room for political presuppositions. The classics who always kept in view the beneficial long-period effects were non-interventionists, while today, economists who limit themselves to short-period effects—and these always consist of the unfavourable frictions before a new equilibrium is reached—appear rather to be interventionists. It remains an open question whether the classicals concentrated on the beneficial long-period effects because they rejected state intervention on the grounds of their political attitude regarding the role of the state, or whether they limited the economic role of the state as a result of their long-period treatment. The former seems to me by no means impossible.

'The same question arises regarding modern theorists who confine themselves to short-period effects . . . Whether an inclination to state intervention gives rise to short-period treatment, or the other way round, also remains an open question. Both are possible. I believe that the path is very often *from* the attitude regarding state intervention *to* the choice of short-period treatment, and not the reverse. My experience of theoretical discussions with colleagues has shown me that, nearly always, liberal economists are much more ready to apply

[1] F. A. Lutz, 'Politische Überzeugungen und nationalökonomische Theorie', *Ordo*, Bd. IX, 1957, p. 15.

long-period treatment than their opponents who incline to state intervention and put short-period disturbances in the forefront. . . .

'I cannot provide any concrete proofs because, of course, no economist will say straight out that he uses a short-period treatment because he favours state intervention, or a long-period treatment because he is opposed to it. These influences work at the sub-conscious level. But the possibility of this influence certainly exists and I personally have no doubt at all that it is actually at work in many cases.'[1]

Lutz goes on to cite an example of the selection of short-period and long-term causal processes in international trade theory.

The relation between the simplificatory selection of causes, and political bias, is also apt to be specially close in those mono-causal theories which used to be more influential than they are today (e.g. the labour theory of value and some versions of the marginal utility theory stressing 'consumers' sovereignty').[2] Sometimes, also, some elements will be stressed as 'causal' and others not, because the latter are held to be data which are unalterable, or which *should* not be altered. For example, if a country is in balance of payments difficulties those whose political attitude leads them to rule out devaluation will stress other elements, for example, perhaps wages, as the 'cause' of the difficulties, rather than an over-valued currency —or *vice versa*.[3] An analysis of causal responsibility or imputation is confused or combined with an analysis of moral or political responsibility, 'guilt', scapegoat-hunting, or with a kind of 'essentialist' dogmatizing as to what the 'real' cause is.

If the economist selects or assigns weights to different causes in a highly complex process, in partial ignorance of what these weights or the 'causes' at work actually are, on the basis of largely untested hunch or impressionism, agreement and consensus will be unlikely. The ideal—perhaps almost Utopian—recipe is Lange's formula of 'agreement to withhold judgment', or else guesses and hunches must be put forward as such, so that at least some measure of agreement to differ, pending further evidence, may be attainable.[4]

---

[1] F. A. Lutz, *op. cit.*, p. 16. Cf. also J. Viner's essay, 'The Short View and the Long in Economic Policy', in *The Long View and the Short*, 1958, pp. 103 ff. Viner holds that 'this habit of taking the long view is not only characteristic of the orthodox economic theorist, but in the discussion of matters of economic policy it is often the principal characteristic by which he can be distinguished from other professional economists or even from the intelligent layman' (p. 107).

[2] Cf. H. Albert, 'Die Problematik der Ökonomischen Perspektive', *Zeitschrift für die gesamte Staatswissenschaft*, .1961, p. 438 ff.

[3] Cf. H. Giersch, *Allgemeine Wirtschaftspolitik*, Grundlagen, 1960, p. 43.

[4] Cf. E. Devons, *Essays in Economics*, 1961, p. 46: 'There might be more understanding by the public of the issues involved if economists exercised self-restraint and confined themselves to attempting to explain the nature and complexity of the problems, rather than providing conflicting and widely divergent solutions.'

Types and Sources of Value-Judgments and Bias   89

(8) BIAS IN ECONOMIC PREDICTIONS

Our examination of how political prejudices and valuations get into and can survive in the shaping of economic theories and hypotheses, applies also as regards economic predictions. For a prediction, of a strictly scientific type, is, as we shall discuss below, simply one aspect, or implication, of a scientific theory. Scientific explanation is simply 'prediction written backwards'.[1] We are adding this discussion of prediction to what we have said about causation, because of the contradictory attitudes economists take about prediction, and for the further illustrations afforded of the operation of subjectivity and bias.

As with causal explanations, the difficulties of precise and critical testing make it easy for contradictory predictions to be maintained and even retrospectively to be defended. We cannot explain completely and we cannot predict completely, and our incompletenesses, or ignorance, are apt to be filled in according to bias and ideology. It may be that in some cases the predictions of economists have been so shaped by bias that they predict what they want to happen, as when a Marxist economist predicts a socialist revolution. But, more often, these events are predicted which are not so much wanted by the predictors for their own sakes, but because they will, on widely agreed normative assumptions, require, as remedial measures, policies which the predictors want anyway (e.g. that there will be inflation, and/or stagnation, unless there is much more central planning—or, alternatively, much less).[2]

Some economists stress prediction as the ultimate purpose of economic science, and perhaps a majority would broadly agree.[3]

[1] A. Marshall, *Industry and Trade*, 1919, p. 7, quoted by R. C. Tress, 'The Contribution of Economic Theory to Economic Prognostication', *Economica*, August 1959, p. 194.

[2] As Lord Robbins has observed (*Politics and Economics*, 1963, p. 111): 'The fact is, I suspect, that when it is a question of diagnosing what we believe to be present evils, we economists are particularly liable to the temptation to drive home our point by warnings which go considerably further than the circumstances of the case would in fact justify. The appendix to Sir John Sinclair's *History of the Public Revenue* (Third Edition, 1803) contains a most salutary list of unfulfilled predictions of imminent catastrophe by English economists; and it would be very easy indeed to bring it up to date.' The point is that all these dire warnings are not uttered out of a sheer delight in inspissated gloom for its own sake, but, very often, in order to persuade governments to adopt policies the predictors of catastrophe want *anyway*.

[3] Cf. M. Friedman, 'The Methodology of Positive Economics', in *Essays in Positive Economics*, 1953, p. 7: 'The ultimate goal of a positive science is the development of a "theory" or "hypothesis" that yields valid and meaningful (i.e. not truistic) predictions about phenomena not yet observed.' Also, G. J. Stigler, *Five Lectures on Economic Problems*, 1950, p. 23: 'The purpose of the study of economics is to permit us to make predictions about the behaviour of economic phenomena under specified conditions. *The sole test of the usefulness*

But others appear to reject economic prediction completely, or almost completely, though without holding, apparently, to a purely historical method and conception of the subject. For example, Jewkes holds 'that economists cannot without stepping outside their discipline predict in the sense of telling us what will happen in the future', and he rejects 'predictions as an activity proper to economic science'. By attempting predictions (or, at any rate, some kinds of predictions), Jewkes holds that economists may allow 'their authority completely to lapse by seeking to bluster a way into the ranks of the politicians through making bogus claims for the power of their science'.[1]

Jewkes supports his case by pointing out how often economists' predictions have been wrong ('the long list of appalling errors') and suggests that this may be due to the fact 'that economists, like other scientists, are biased', so that 'different economists looking at the same evidence frequently reach very different conclusions about the future'[2] (and about the present and the past, it might be added).

However, later on in his analysis, it appears that Jewkes's objections do not apply to *all* predictions of any and every kind (if they did, one might wonder what use there could be for economic knowledge). In fact, Jewkes argues that economists should have made *more* of *some sorts* of prediction, and complains that they 'have so frequently been reluctant to recommend the processes of the free market, the forces of supply and demand, as the most effective system for correcting economic maladjustments'. He indicates the kinds of prediction—surely very difficult—which he would like to see economists attempting—for example, with regard to the 'danger point' for progressive taxation.[3]

of an economic theory is the concordance between its predictions and the observable course of events.' (Italics added.)

[1] J. Jewkes, in *Economics and Public Policy*, Brookings Lectures, 1954, 1955, pp. 82 and 99. F. H. Knight also has very fundamental objections to prediction in economics: 'I must say, dogmatically if you like, that prediction or control, or both, do not and cannot apply in a literal sense to social science. . . . Science in this sense—knowledge used for prediction and control—simply does not apply in a society with freedom and equality.' *Intelligence and Democratic Action*, 1960, p. 69.

[2] J. Jewkes, *op. cit.*, pp. 85–6.

[3] *Op. cit.*, pp. 92 and 98. For a further statement of Jewkes's views see *Lloyds Bank Review*, April 1953, where he complains of 'this neurotic hankering after prediction', and holding that 'the purpose of a science is understanding and not the power to predict'. He states: 'It cannot be too strongly emphasized that there is nothing in economic science which enables us to foretell events. Those who claim otherwise are dragging their subject down to the level of astrology . . . for better or worse, in economic science we must, as Lecky put it, "endure the sufferings of suspended judgment" (pp. 24, 27 and 29). However, subsequently Jewkes has published an important prediction, or at any rate 'belief', that the entry of Britain into the Common Market 'will, over the next decade, be likely to put us in a better position than we will occupy if we stay out with all that that is likely to involve' (*The Times*, October 8, 1962).

Types and Sources of Value-Judgments and Bias   91

We wish strongly to emphasize the view at this point that the rational application of economic knowledge by way of making or discussing policy recommendations *must*, to some extent, or in some ways, involve prediction. We believe that the opposite view that economists can make, or advise as to, policy recommendations, without making or implying *some kinds of* prediction is dangerously confusing, since prediction is essentially involved in any kind of 'rational' choice. For example, it has been authoritatively denied that the economist's 'advisory power is confined within the narrow limits of his predictory power'.[1] The term 'advisory power' is a little imprecise. Of course, political persuasion and propaganda can be undertaken without any, or any clear, predictions being made. Gnomic maxims can be uttered to the effect that the welfare of the community should be maximized, or such vacuities as that a policy should be adopted if it makes at least one person better-off and nobody worse-off. Approved ideology can be purveyed, or political principles can be enunciated to the effect that no policy should be adopted if it diminishes freedom of choice on the one hand, or, alternatively, equality of distribution, on the other, or that '*laissez-faire* should be the general rule'.[2] But such utterances, however admirable—or the reverse—one holds them to be, should surely not be regarded as 'advice' based on economic knowledge, but as political maxims. Harrod went on to take the example of an import duty on wheat and claimed that the economist:

'may be able to say outright and with substantial authority that on the whole the individuals of the community will be in a worse position, *even although his power of predicting the actual course of prices and incomes is negligible.* Any definition of the economist's advisory scope which does not recognize this is unrealistic, and fails to do justice to the usefulness of the economist, even with his present limited powers.'[3]

[1] R. F. Harrod, 'Scope and Method of Economics', *Economic Journal*, September 1938, p. 390.

[2] Cf. J. S. Mill, *Principles of Political Economy*, Ashley's edition, 1909, Book V, Chapter XI, Section 7.

[3] R. F. Harrod, *op. cit.*, p. 391, italics added. Theoretical economists sometimes take the repeal of the Corn Laws in 1846 as the classic instance of a major policy decision being clinched or demonstrated by economic theorizing. Certainly Ricardo's general theorizing, a quarter of a century before, may have had some influence, though he advocated gradualness in repeal. But when it came to the point in the 1840s, of the four leading classical economists of the day, Torrens opposed repeal, J. S. Mill was dubious and almost silent, Senior was favourable but circumlocutory, and McCulloch was in favour of reduction but not complete repeal. Real and important policy issues can never be decided by a demonstration that one particular policy can, potentially, make some people better-off and nobody worse-off. (See W. D. Grampp, *The Manchester School of Economics*, 1960, Chapter 2.)

Harrod based this claim for the advisory power of the economist on his possession of 'his criterion of individual preference'. But, quite apart from the fact that it inevitably involves a not necessarily universally-shared value-judgment, a criterion is useless if there is nothing relevant to apply it to, and there can only be something relevant to which to apply a criterion if the effects of different policies are to some extent predicted.

As Harrod stressed, the power of prediction in economics at the present juncture is severely limited. It would be encouraging if the confidence and authority with which the economist could 'advise' the public was not restricted in this way. But we must repeat our view that there may be a misleading delusion here. Of course, the economist's predictions may be wide 'interval' predictions rather than 'point' predictions. Of course, they will be conditional, and yet still remain significant predictions with falsifiable predictive content, however difficult to test in practice. It seems, however, a questionable posture to deliver extremely conditional or hypothetical predictions and leave it entirely to the statesman, or decision-maker, to predict as to the applicability of *all* the conditions and hypotheses, *including all those concerned with economic processes.* Certainly 'the statesman' might be expected to predict regarding the more political contingencies (the result of the next election or international crisis).[1] But it is surely doubtful whether one should claim the status and authority of an expert adviser, while refusing to commit oneself to any non-trivial, falsifiable predictions whatsoever.

However, as there seem to be some pretty fundamental disagreements regarding prediction as a task for the economist, let us attempt some further clarification of what may be meant by 'prediction'.

Let us exclude altogether from 'predictions' analytical or empirically unfalsifiable statements such as 'If demand for exports is elastic a reduction in their prices will, other things being equal, result in an increase in receipts'. Such a statement, like any analytical statement, *might* be useful in elaborating the logical implications of a prediction, *if one were ventured,* to the effect, say, that the demand for exports was elastic. But it is not *itself* a prediction and has no predictive

---

[1] P. A. Samuelson, *Problems of the American Economy*, Stamp Memorial Lecture, 1961, 1962, p. 17: 'We laugh at students who, instead of answering the examination question as set, try to brazen it out by answering some quite different question. Some scholars are like that: when you ask them what would be the effects of a cut in personal income tax rates, they say you should be making a study of the effects on the balance of payments of an appreciation of the currency. Or they reply: "On the assumption of an *n*-person economy, with indifference curves that are homothetic and production functions that are homogeneous, and assuming workers save nothing and non-workers save all, tax rates enter merely as . . . blank, blank, blank . . . " — leaving you to decide how relevant is the answer and how it must be modified to give a tolerable approximation.'

content, since it is empirically unfalsifiable and remains true whatever happens.[1] It is often correctly—though sometimes rather uncritically—repeated that economic predictions, like all scientific predictions, are conditional. But the conditions have to be reasonably precisely stated, and leave some non-trivial, refutable content in the proposition, if it is to represent a significant prediction for policy-making.

Let us next make a two-fold division of 'predictions'—retaining the term for the two types together—into (*a*) 'scientific prognoses' based on tested scientific laws as to which a measure of scientific consensus has been reached; and (*b*) 'forecasts' which *may* make *some* use of scientific laws and theories, but which go beyond these in prophesying or forecasting what will happen, outside the range of tested scientific laws and theories.

This is certainly not a clear-cut distinction, or one as to which there would be immediate clarity and agreement as to just where the line between the two should be drawn. Exactly which statements deserve the description of 'scientific laws' or theories, and which do not, would not be immediately and clearly agreed in the social and economic sciences. We have also left vague the extent, and the manner in which, what we have called a 'scientific prognosis'—as contrasted with a 'forecast'—is 'based' on a scientific law or theory. But, though there is an ambiguous area on the frontiers between the two concepts, they are sufficiently distinct at their centres.

The nature of 'prognoses' based on scientific laws or theories has been set out very precisely by Popper, and he brings out very clearly the close relation between causal explanations, testing and prediction:

'I suggest that to give a causal explanation of a certain *specific event* means deducing a statement describing this event from two kinds of premisses: from some *universal laws*, and from some singular or specific statements which we shall call the *specific initial conditions*. For example, we can say that we have given a causal explanation of the breaking of a certain thread if we find that this thread could carry a weight of only one pound, and that a weight of two pounds was put on it. If we analyse this causal explanation, then we find that two different constituents are involved. (1) Some hypotheses of the character of universal laws of nature; in this case, perhaps: "For every thread of a given structure S (determined by its material, thickness, etc.) there is a characteristic weight W such that the thread will break if any weight exceeding W is suspended on it"; and "For every thread of the structure S_1, the characteristic weight W equals one pound". (2) Some specific (singular) statements—the initial

---

[1] Jewkes (*op. cit.*, p. 89) very cogently distinguishes 'economic logic' from prediction, i.e. such statements as 'If the supply of money increases by 100 per cent, everything else remaining equal, prices will rise'.

94   *'Positive' Economics and Policy Objectives*

conditions—pertaining to the particular event in question; in this case, we may have two statements: "This is a thread of structure S_1" and "The weight put on this thread was a weight of two pounds". Thus we have two different constituents, two different kinds of statements which together yield a complete causal explanation: (1) *Universal statements of the character of natural laws*; and (2) *specific statements* pertaining to the special case in question, called the *"initial conditions"*. Now from the universal laws (1) we can deduce, with the help of the initial conditions (2), the following specific statement (3): "This thread will break". This conclusion (3) we may also call a specific *prognosis*. The initial conditions (or, more precisely, the situation described by them) are usually spoken of as the *cause* of the event in question, and the prognosis (or, rather, the event described by the prognosis) as the *effect*; for example, we say that the putting of a weight of two pounds on a thread capable of carrying only one pound was the cause, and the breaking the effect.

'Such a causal explanation, will, of course, be scientifically acceptable *only if the universal laws are well tested and corroborated*, and if we have also some independent evidence in favour of the cause, i.e. of the initial conditions. . . . The use of a theory for *predicting* some specific event is just another aspect of its use for *explaining* such an event. And since we test a theory by comparing the events predicted with those actually observed, our analysis also shows how theories can be tested.'[1]

The difficulty in economics and the social sciences is, of course, that (1) there is not a substantial body of precise 'well-tested and corroborated' universal laws in the fields in which predictions are wanted, ventured or required to support rationally the policies adopted; and (2) the 'independent evidence' in favour of all 'the initial conditions' which are often so much more numerous, complex and difficult to isolate than in the natural world, is often practically impossible to ascertain with sufficient precision and reliability. That is, it is practically impossible to ascertain that the social and economic 'threads' are precisely of 'the given structure', and will remain so, undisturbed for the period of the prediction. For if predictions useful for practical policies are to be obtained, these initial conditions must themselves be reasonably precise, not too numerous, and themselves predictable.[2]

[1] K. R. Popper, *The Poverty of Historicism*, paperback edition, 1961, pp. 122–4. We have added the italics for the words *'only if the universal laws are well tested and corroborated'*.

[2] 'A typical law in the physical sciences is stated precisely, usually in mathematical terms, and is quite free of ambiguity. It has been tested repeatedly and has withstood the tests. The usual law in the social sciences, on the other hand, is ordinarily couched in Big Words and a great deal of ambiguity.' J. G. Kemeny,

Types and Sources of Value-Judgments and Bias   **95**

One of the most relied-on general laws, and the cornerstone of price theory, is broadly to the effect that, subject to conditions regarding tastes, expectations, incomes and other prices, a rise in the price of a good, other than a 'snob' or 'Giffen' good, will be followed by a fall in the quantity demanded. But the predictive usefulness of such a law or generalization is much impaired by the fact that the initial conditions with which it needs to be combined to yield a scientific prognosis in a specific case are numerous, complex and not easily ascertainable or predictable.

In fact, prediction in economics and the social sciences has often to be attempted not on 'well-tested and corroborated laws', but on tentative imprecise generalizations regarding trends and tendencies. In any case, no prediction, of course, can have absolute certainty. But most or many predictions based on the physical sciences can be corroborated by checking and re-checking the initial conditions and the law. But in economics and the social sciences only personal or subjective probability can usually be indicated.[1]

There is, in fact, a whole range of 'predictions' from, at one extreme, scientific 'prognosis', on the basis of physical or chemical laws, involved in engineering, or bridge or aeroplane building, through different types of medical prognoses, meteorological prognoses and detailed weather 'forecasting', population forecasting, the forecasts involved in insurance, economic forecasting of next year's G.N.P., stock-market forecasts and 'investment analysis', and the expert tips of horse-racing and football forecasters. There is something like a spectrum here in which a change of quality obviously takes place. This change turns on the degree of precise reliance on scientific laws, and is here described as moving from 'scientific prognoses' to 'forecasting'—though the transition is so gradual as to render rather arbitrary any clear-cut dividing line. Perhaps the spectrum can be continued through the 'hunch' and 'feel', or tradi-

---

A Philosopher Looks at Science, 1959, p. 244. This comparison does not seem seriously unfair, nor to be entirely refuted by Popper's perhaps rather optimistic list of examples of tentative 'sociological laws and hypotheses': 'You cannot introduce agricultural tariffs and at the same time reduce the cost of living.'—'You cannot, in an industrial society, organize consumers' pressure groups as effectively as you can organize certain producers' pressure groups.'—'You cannot have a centrally planned society with a price system that fulfils the main functions of competitive prices.'—'You cannot have full employment without inflation.' Popper gives further examples from the realm of power politics. See *The Poverty of Historicism*, paperback edition, 1961, p. 62.

[1] Jewkes (*op. cit.*, p. 88) lays down 'the golden rule' that 'the economic expert should be most scrupulous' in 'indicating the degree of probability that attaches to each' of his assumptions, when he attempts a prediction. But, however scrupulous the economist may be, he will usually only be able to give 'guess-timates' of the most subjective kind, regarding degrees of probability, from which those of other economists might widely diverge.

tional weather-wisdom, of sailors and farmers, on through non-rational superstitions, to astrology and fortune-telling. We have already noted the contrasting views economists take regarding economic prediction generally, and there would probably be much disagreement as to just where in this broad spectrum different kinds of economic predictions were to be placed. For example, by some, the use of economic statistics for the forecasting required for some types of policy is regarded as little better than a magic ritual or astrology.[1]

In the most important recent treatment of 'Economic Forecasts and Policy', Theil endeavours to lay down the requirements which predictions should meet if they are to merit 'the weighty adjective "scientific" '. But he does not seem able to make these requirements very precise or restrictive. His requirements simply are that predictions must be 'verifiable', which implies that they must be unambiguous as regards the concepts and timing they contain. But, however verifiable (or falsifiable) and unambiguous a prediction may be, it may merely be 'the result of the forecaster's imagination'. As Theil puts it:

'It is therefore not sufficient that the predictions themselves can be verified afterwards; it is, in addition to this, necessary that the line of thought which underlies the prediction can be verified. . . . It is not easy and even not fruitful to generalize about this point, but this at least can be said: the forecasting procedure must be based on theoretical considerations—however simple—and on empirical observations obtained beforehand—however scanty and crude.'[2]

In other words, it is impossible to mark off very strictly or clearly predictions which merit 'the weighty adjective "scientific" ' from those that do not. Samuelson appeals to what he calls 'loose' scientific

---

[1] Cf. E. Devons, *Essays in Economics*, 1961, p. 135: 'Decisions must be taken, and even if it is exaggerated confidence in the statistics which helps the Government to decide rather than dither, should we complain? Considered in this light there seem to be striking similarities between the role of economic statistics in out society and some of the functions which magic and divination play in primitive society.' See also J. Brunner, 'The Dash for Planning', *The Listener*, May 10, 1962, p. 796. After examining the forecasts of the Ridley Committee, 1951, Brunner concludes: 'Fuel forecasting is no more of a science than astrology. And if this is true in an industry where there is the maximum exchange of information, where there are hardly any exports, and where the nature of the product ensures a comparative stability of demand, how much more true is it of forecasting in more volatile industries.' Perhaps these sceptical quotations should be balanced with a quotation from Marshall (*Industry and Trade*, 4th Ed., 1923, p. 506): 'Greater risks are taken where no attempt is made to forecast the future, while considering methods of action or inaction that will largely affect the future, than by straining inadequate eyes in reading such faint indications of the future as can be discerned by them.'

[2] *Economic Forecasts and Policy*, 2nd Ed., 1961, pp. 11–14.

Types and Sources of Value-Judgments and Bias   97

method.[1] But it is just the inevitable scarcely definable 'looseness' which lets in subjectivity and bias. Moreover, a consensus of experts as to a prediction cannot necessarily be said to lend it a firm objectivity since, if aware of one another's predictions, they may be clustering together simply for mutual reassurance.[2] But certainly an economic prediction might seem to begin to take on some measure of objectivity and independence of political bias, if various economists agreed on it who were known to hold conflicting political viewpoints on the issue concerned. For example, if *both* those economists, who one had reason to believe were opposed to Britain entering the European Common Market on political grounds, *and* those who were politically in favour, agreed on an economic prediction as to one or other of the likely economic effects, say, that the resulting economies of scale were likely (or unlikely) to be of importance, then such an economic prediction would acquire at least a minimum basis of expert objective consensus (though, of course, it might be false). But this is often just what one does *not* get. Those politically opposed discover that economics of scale will be negligible, and those politically favourable tend to predict their importance.

Nevertheless, it might be argued that whichever methods of prediction or forecasting are adopted, *some* canons of expertise, and at least some measure of consensus regarding what is a respectable procedure for building a forecast, and what is not, do exist. It therefore seems impossible to accept the view that all forecasting, and even all prediction, should be banned as too dubious and disreputable for the 'scientific' economist. It is obviously much more deplorable to adopt such an austere attitude towards the predictions required for the kind of policies one dislikes, while urging more boldness as regards the predictions required—given widely accepted value-premisses—for the types of policies which one approves.

It seems clear that if the economist confined himself strictly to 'scientific prognoses', on the basis of 'well-tested and corroborated' scientific laws, he would be able to offer very little genuinely useful advice—though not absolutely none. But as regards most important realistic policy-issues, the scope of his advice would be extremely limited or negligible, unless he resorted to judgments and hunches on

[1] *Problems of the American Economy*, Stamp Memorial Lecture, 1961, 1962, p. 21.
[2] Cf. P. Samuelson, *op. cit.*, p. 28: 'Forecasters are if anything too homogeneous, too much in touch with one another, too sheep-like in their shifts of optimism. We have an apt saying: "Economic forecasters are like many eskimos crowded into the same bed. You can be sure of one thing, they will all turn over together." The reasons are not hard to find; what one fool can do, so can another; opinions mingle; finally it is safer to be wrong with the crowd than take the chance that you may not be right, all by yourself.' It must be emphasized that the eskimos' 'consensus' is not the same thing as genuine scientific consensus —however 'expert' eskimos they may be.

G

which different experts will often not agree, and which are inevitably liable, especially in the field of economic policy, to ideological prejudice or bias. To expect or suggest that in the vast majority of *realistic* policy issues an economist can or should 'demonstrate' the economic gains of one policy as compared with another—like the proof of a geometrical theorem, beyond all reasonable disagreement —is to indulge in intellectual delusion.[1] To state that there are significant economic gains from adopting one policy rather than another, one has to make predictions as to what the effects of the different policies will be. Logical, mathematical or geometrical 'demonstration' *may* illuminatingly analyse or elaborate a prediction when made. But in the majority of realistic cases it is the quality of the judgment in predicting or forecasting which is essential.[2]

The question arises then as to how far the economist's judgment or hunch is 'better', or more often 'right', than the non-economist's, with regard to economic predictions or forecasts; and how far he is entitled to claim or assume some measure of 'expert' authority for predictions in which subjective judgments are or may be present in differing degrees. In the case of one of the most important issues of British economic policy to be faced for many decades, admittedly a case involving extremely open, complex and long-term predictions, regarding the economic effects of Britain joining the Common

---

[1] 'It cannot be stated too emphatically that no economist of any standing in this country has alleged, much less demonstrated, that significant economic gains would accrue to this country on entering the Common Market.' E. J. Mishan, *The Times*, October 2, 1962. We are not concerned with what economists ('of any standing' or otherwise) *alleged* on this issue, but with the epistemological misconception of suggesting, even as a remote practical possibility, that any conclusions about economic gains or losses could be *'demonstrated'*—either from Britain entering or from her staying out of the Common Market.

[2] Cf. the classic pronouncement by Sir James Fitzjames Stephen: 'The one talent which is worth all other talents put together in human affairs is the talent of judging right upon imperfect materials, the talent if you please of guessing right. It is a talent which no rules will ever teach and which even experience does not always give. It often co-exists with a good deal of slowness and dullness and with a very slight power of expression. All that can be said about it is, that to see things as they are, without exaggeration or passion, is essential to it; but how can we see things as they are? Simply by opening our eyes and looking with whatever power we may have. All really important matters are decided, not by a process of argument worked out from adequate premisses to a necessary conclusion, but by making a wise choice between several possible views.' (*Liberty, Equality, Fraternity*, 2nd Ed., 1874, p. 352, quoted by A. S. Ashton, *Lloyds Bank Review*, October 1962, p. 30.) Stephen's recipe of 'simply . . . opening our eyes' may seem a little *simpliste*. But he is surely right that the 'batting averages' are not likely to be very high of the ideologue (with his 'passion') or the geometrician concentrating on processes of argument 'from adequate premisses to a necessary conclusion'. Unfortunately, so much economic education concentrates exclusively on these logical or geometrical processes as 'the one thing necessary', to the neglect of developing at least an awareness of the need for judgment—which itself may not be so completely unteachable as Stephen suggests.

Types and Sources of Value-Judgments and Bias   99

Market, one distinguished economist took the view that 'the only position for an economist with a respect for the facts is: . . . there is so much we don't know that it is a case of "your guess is as good as mine" '.[1] Rightly or wrongly not many other economists in Britain seemed to take such an austere view, suggesting usually that 'your' guess (whoever 'you' were) was not nearly as good as theirs (unless it agreed with it).

It is to this kind of large-scale, long-term, highly complex and 'open' prediction as to, say, the economic effects of Britain joining the Common Market that the following sceptical conclusion would apply (whether or not to the subjectivity, uncertainty and possible bias of the 'positive' predictions of the multifarious economic effects is added some large, if latent, value-judgment, striking a balance and weighing up the net outcome, as favourable or unfavourable). M. F. Millikan writes:[2]

'Our best formal models are still partial; they explicitly exclude consideration of some of the factors at work in any actual situation. The relative weight of the factors explicitly analysed can seldom be measured, and their combined influence seldom computed. Prediction of a sort is, of course, a necessary component of policy-making. Any decision to act must be based upon a judgment that the net consequences of the preferred course of action will be more favourable than those of some alternative. But in social situations such a judgment can seldom be effectively made by "scientific" procedures. If the policy-maker simply desires advice as to what he should do, he had better rely on the intuition of a man of wide experience and demonstrated understanding rather than on the intellectual skills and techniques of the social scientist. . . . A net predictive judgment in most human situations can be made more safely by the successful journalist, novelist, diplomat or businessman than by any social science research team.'

But there are many different kinds of economic, or politico-economic, predictions or forecasts, and, with regard to some, the sceptical conclusion that 'anybody's' guess will be as good as the economist's is less justified than with regard to others—though

[1] R. G. Lipsey, quoted in the *Observer*, October 14, 1962, p. 5. Lipsey was classified as regarding the economic arguments for and against Britain joining the Common Market as 'evenly balanced'. But there is, of course, a vital distinction between a confident belief on convincing evidence that the balance of advantages is about even, or is likely only to veer very slightly either way, and a belief that in view of the extensive ignorance of many of the factors affecting the various kinds of advantage and disadvantage involved, a fifty-fifty toss-up is as rational a method of decision as any other.

[2] *The Human Meaning of the Social Sciences*, edited by D. Lerner, Meridian Books, 1959, pp. 165–6.

economists can probably be found predicting with equal cheerfulness in both kinds of cases. In contrast with his colleague Millikan—the contrast being, perhaps, more apparent than real because they are probably dealing with different types of prediction—Samuelson has claimed that though economists *'cannot forecast well . . . they forecast the economy better than any other group thus far discovered.* Empirical statisticians, clairvoyants, down-to-earth businessmen, hunch-players—all these turn out to have a worse "batting-average" than government, academic and business economists'—though not, it seems, very much worse.[1] No one is better qualified to assert such a generalization than Samuelson, though it is not clear on how much systematic evidence he bases it, and it obviously holds only for some economists and not for all. Moreover, it should be noted that Samuelson's claim might be taken simply, or mainly, as covering, say, the forecasting of next year's G.N.P. for the United States, and not many other sorts of prediction (e.g. with regard to the economic effects of Britain joining the Common Market) which economists attempt.

Anyhow, a considerable complication regarding predictions in the social and economic field arises from the interaction of observer and observed, or the influence of the prediction on the predicted event—the 'Oedipus effect' as Popper calls it. It is as though meteorologists had to forecast the weather in conditions where private and/or governmental rain-making (as well as counter rain-making) agencies could, and did, frequently and effectively operate. But it has been shown that however much 'Oedipus' effects may complicate prediction they do not make it impossible, or render it, in the social field, completely different in principle from prediction in the natural sciences.[2] The problem, rather, which we are centrally concerned with here would be presented by a situation where some meteorologists were passionately interested financially and otherwise in outdoor activities, while others were passionately committed to indoor activities, and where these ideological prejudices and presuppositions affected their weather forecasts.

We conclude that because scientific 'prognosis' on the basis of 'well-tested and corroborated scientific laws' has, at any rate for the time being, a limited range, insufficient to support the wide policy

[1] P. A. Samuelson, *Problems of the American Economy*, Stamp Memorial Lecture 1961, 1962, p. 23. I. M. D. Little holds that it 'cannot be taken for granted' that 'economists are better at forecasting, and better at judging the economic consequences of alternative policies, than are administrators or bankers', but that their training does give them certain advantages. (*Lloyds Bank Review*, April 1957, p. 35, 'The Economist in Whitehall'.)

[2] v. K. R. Popper, *The Poverty of Historicism*, paperback edition, 1961, pp. 12–17; and E. Grunberg and F. Modigliani, 'Predictability of Social Events', *Journal of Political Economy*, December 1954, p. 465.

Types and Sources of Value-Judgments and Bias   101

ambitions of peoples and governments, much or most social and economic prediction *has* to consist of forecasting on the basis of hunch, judgment, guesswork and insufficiently tested generalizations, which may well be shaped by subjective optimism and pessimism stemming from political and ideological presuppositions. It does, however, seem reasonable to expect that one be given as clear indications as may be practicable as to how far the different elements —empirical generalizations, tendencies, hunches and 'guess-timates' —on which different predictions are based, consist of well-tested and corroborated laws and their initial conditions, on which a consensus exists, and how far they are untested and subjective, and therefore specially liable to bias. As we have already noted, we have the authority of Marshall for the view that 'economic studies are not to be limited to matters which are amenable to strictly scientific treatment'. He went on:

'Those conclusions, whether in detail or in general, which are based on individual judgments as to the relative desirability of different social aims, or as to matters of fact which lie beyond the scope of any individual's special studies, should be clearly distinguished from those which claim to have been reached by scientific method.'[1]

We would simply add that the conclusions 'based on individual judgments', which should be clearly distinguished from those claimed 'to have been reached by scientific method', should also include forecasts and predictions other than what we have called 'prognoses' firmly based on acknowledged scientific laws and generalizations; and should also include, as we shall discuss further below, attitudes to risk—of preference, aversion or neutrality— which are inevitably subjective.

The uncertainty and subjectivity of predictions and forecasts in economics leave a wide scope for the possible workings of bias and 'prejudice'. To some extent, and in no pejorative sense, a kind of prejudice may be inevitable in venturing a prediction as a basis for a policy recommendation. Just as, in Keynes's phrase, 'animal spirits', or 'a spontaneous urge to action rather than inaction', rather than reasonable calculation alone, is the basis of 'most, probably, of our decisions to do something positive, the full consequences of which will be drawn out over many days to come',[2] so a kind of intellectual high spirits prompting one to say something rather than nothing are the basis for some, if not many, kinds of predictions and forecasts. As Hazlitt said in his *Paragraphs on Prejudice*:

'Without the aid of prejudice and custom, I should not be able to

[1] *Industry and Trade*, 1919, p. 676.
[2] J. M. Keynes, *The General Theory of Employment Interest and Money*, 1936, p. 161.

find my way across the room; nor know how to conduct myself in any circumstances, nor know what to feel in any relation to life. Reason may play the critic, and correct certain errors afterwards, but if we were to wait for its formal and absolute decisions in the shifting and multifarious combinations of human affairs, the world would stand still. Even men of science, after they have gone over the proofs a number of times, abridge the process, and *jump at a conclusion*.'[1]

There is nothing wrong in stating one's 'prejudices' provided one makes it quite clear that that is what they are, not trying to pass them off as scientific conclusions with claims to what Popper has called 'the authority of objective truth'.[2]

(9) THE 'SELECTION' OF HYPOTHESES?

We now come to a more fundamental thesis as to the inevitability of value-judgments and subjectivity in science, whether natural or social. This thesis asserts that the scientist *has* to make value-judgments in having to assess evidence or accept or reject hypotheses. The leading statements of this thesis seem to have a strong pragmatist or even techno- (or sciento-) cratic flavour, and we had better say at once that we do not accept its central point or main assumptions. Nevertheless, it does focus attention on important problems and difficulties in keeping normative and positive distinct, which have not been faced by the more facile exponents of 'positive economics' and of a clear-cut distinction between positive theories and policy recommendations.

Here is a specially forthright statement of this thesis:

'Since no scientific hypothesis is ever completely verified, in accepting a hypothesis on the basis of evidence, the scientist must make the decision that the evidence is *sufficiently* strong or that the probability is *sufficiently* high to warrant the acceptance of the hypothesis. Obviously our decision with regard to the evidence and how strong is "strong enough" is going to be a function of the *importance*, in the typically ethical sense, of making a mistake in accepting or rejecting the hypothesis. Thus, to take a crude but easily manageable example, if the hypothesis under consideration stated that a toxic ingredient of a drug was not present in lethal quantity, then we would require a relatively high degree of confirmation or confidence before accepting the hypothesis—for the consequences of making a mistake here are exceedingly grave by our moral standards. In contrast, if our hypothesis stated that, on the basis of some sample, a certain lot of machine-stamped belt buckles was not defective, the degree of con-

[1] Quoted by Krsto Cviić, *The Listener*, December 13, 1962, p. 1008.
[2] *Conjectures and Refutations*, 1963, p. 375.

Types and Sources of Value-Judgments and Bias 103

fidence we would require would be relatively lower. *How sure we must be* before we accept a hypothesis depends on how serious a mistake *would be*.'[1]

We cannot accept Rudner's rather dramatic conclusion based on this argument that 'we are confronted with a first-order crisis in science and methodology'. But, certainly, important questions are being raised as to what precisely the rules and scope of scientific procedure are, particularly with regard to statistical hypotheses, and conclusions or decisions based on them, and as to what is, or should be, the demarcation line between the duties and functions of 'the scientific expert', and those of the choice-making customer or political authority, in conditions of uncertainty. In fact, the possibility of 'the involvement of inductive logic in evaluative considerations',[2] as it has been described, raises the question as to whether in practice, and if so how, or at what point, 'the decision-making animal' can, or should, be split up into a 'choice-animal' and an 'information animal' in conditions of uncertainty (that is, in most realistic conditions).[3]

The kind of decisions discussed by exponents of the thesis we are examining is, at any rate, realistic, in that it involves uncertainty. But the examples are drawn, on the one hand, from choices and decisions regarding the problems and costs of scientific research, or, on the other hand, are concerned with problems of pharmaceutical or industrial quality control. It could well be argued that the former may be classified as 'preliminary' or 'pre-scientific' (in the sense discussed in Section 2 above of this chapter), and that, as regards the latter, value-judgments are certainly and admittedly involved in, so to speak, 'post-scientific' applications in the form of policy recommendations about quality control.

There is no question as to the scientists' need to make choices and

[1] Cf. 'Value Judgments in the Acceptance of Theories', by R. Rudner, in *The Validation of Scientific Theories*, edited by P. Frank, paperback edition, 1961, p. 33. See also R. B. Braithwaite's lecture 'Moral Principles and Inductive Policies', 1950, and his *Scientific Explanation*, 1960, Chapter VII, 'The Choice between Statistical Hypotheses'. Also C. W. Churchman, *Prediction and Optimal Decision*, 1961, *passim*, and the discussion by R. C. Jeffrey and C. W. Churchman, in *Philosophy of Science*, July 1956, pp. 237 ff., and by I. Levi, *Journal of Philosophy*, May 1960, p. 345.

[2] R. B. Braithwaite, *Scientific Explanation*, paperback edition, 1960, p. 253.

[3] Cf. H. Theil, *Economic Forecasts and Policy*, 2nd Ed., 1961, p. 414: 'One of the problems in the decision-making process is the great diversity of tasks which the policy-maker has to face. He must not only make a choice (and bear the responsibility for it), but he must also be a forecaster. Naturally, the question arises whether it is possible to delegate at least the latter task to another man or to a staff, so that the "decision-making animal" is then split up into a "choice animal" and an "information animal".' Churchman (*op. cit.*) argues very strongly that this 'splitting up' is impossible—of course, not simply in economics.

decisions with regard to the projects they undertake and their possible costs. Rudner suggests that:

'. . . it would be interesting and instructive, for example, to know how high a degree of probability the Manhattan project scientists demanded for the hypothesis that no uncontrollable pervasive chain reaction would occur before they proceeded with the first atomic bomb detonation or even first activated the Chicago pile above a critical level. It would be equally interesting and instructive to know how they decided that the chosen probability value (if one was chosen) was high enough rather than one that was higher; on the other hand, it is conceivable that the problem, in this form, was not brought to consciousness at all.'[1]

It is not denying the immense importance of these decisions, or the significance of the values involved, to describe them, and the choices emphasized here, as 'preliminary' or 'pre-scientific'. No valuations or value-judgments enter into statements as to whether or how atomic explosions are possible, because of the crucial valuations and decisions involved in launching a Manhattan project and incurring the huge costs and possible risks. So when Churchman counters the thesis that 'science ends in summarizing its evidence, and it has no part in the evaluation of policies' with the argument that 'science obviously makes decisions of its own in both theoretical and applied science' and 'must decide to take certain steps in its procedures, and these steps must presumably be evaluated by science',[2] we can certainly agree with regard to the choice of research projects and of scientific criteria and rules of the game. But, so far, no conclusion follows at all that the scientist has to pass value-judgments regarding social and political policies, unless one simply asserts, in a question-begging way, that this is within his duties.

The other examples, taken from the field of medical and industrial quality control, might be described as *'post-scientific'*. For example, how highly probable, or virtually certain (because, of course, literally absolute certainty is out of the question), must the hypothesis be that a new drug does not have harmful effects of some kind or other before it is made publicly available? Such a decision only arises when there is an application of scientific knowledge to policy, and when particular policy objectives are being laid down. Then, in any case, a value-judgment is, indisputably, logically necessary, though one which is widely held to belong clearly with the 'choice animal'

[1] R. Rudner, 'Value Judgments in the Acceptance of Theories', in *The Validation of Scientific Theories*, edited by P. Frank, paperback edition, 1961, p. 33.

[2] C. W. Churchman, in *The Validation of Scientific Theories*, edited by P. Frank, paperback edition, 1961, p. 29.

rather than the 'information animal'. Anyhow, as pointed out, the strength of the evidence required might be very different depending on the policy objectives involved—or whether, for example, the drug being tested was intended for humans or animals. A parallel case with regard to social investigation would be the elaborateness of a sample, or the accuracy of a statistical estimate, being determined by the importance of the policy decisions and objectives to be based on the information it yielded. Certainly, here the functions of 'the choice animal' and 'the information animal' seem to merge together. But not, we would suggest, inextricably so, at any rate analytically.

Nassau Senior, for example, took the view of the scientist's functions that he 'does not presuppose any purpose beyond the acquisition of knowledge', and he ascribed to the distinct realm of 'art' that which 'is intended to influence the will' since 'it presupposes some object to be attained'.[1] In methodological programmes, though not so much in practice, this is a view for which much support could be found in the writings of 'orthodox' economists. To some, this view might seem rather too passive or quietist, but according to it the task for the scientist is simply to set out the evidence for and against different hypotheses as far as it goes, and not 'accept' or even 'reject' them in any stronger sense than this. Scientific investigation does not have 'to terminate with the replacement of doubt by belief'. Probabilities may be assigned to hypotheses and predictions, but in the economic and social field these will mostly be highly 'subjective' or 'personal' without often anything or much, of the 'objectivity' which a consensus of expert opinion might give, and therefore very liable to bias. Moreover, there are obvious practical difficulties in setting before the 'choice animal' or 'statesman' complicated probability distributions under numerous possible assumptions regarding the eventual decisions. As Theil puts it: 'The task of informing the "choice animal" about the stochastic consequences of his measures can easily become inconvenient and cumbersome. . . . Few policy-makers will appreciate their staffs providing them with information of such an elaborate and refined nature.'[2] However elaborate (or concise) may be the range of information which 'choice animals' or policy-makers 'appreciate', it is clearly their function to decide on action on the basis of *their* valuations of policy objectives and of the seriousness of mistakes.

In contrast with Senior's quietist view, a more activist scientocratic view may be urged on behalf of 'those who don't want science to stop just before it gives an answer'. Such a view may, of course, be held not only by scientific 'information animals' but by lay

[1] *Report of the British Association for the Advancement of Science,* 1860, pp. 183–4.

[2] Cf. H. Theil, *Economic Forecasts and Policy,* 2nd Ed., 1961, pp. 414–15.

'choice animals'. What the 'scientist' should or should not do, and how strictly he should confine himself, as Marshall put it, only to 'matters which are amenable to strictly scientific treatment', is, of course, a question of pre- or extra-scientific value-premisses. Certainly the application of these maxims, in particular practical cases, may inevitably turn on pretty fine shades of emphasis in the presentation of evidence for economic hypotheses and predictions that are being applied to policies.

There is, however, undoubtedly a kind of value-judgment arising out of risk and uncertainty, which is inevitably involved in policy decisions, and which seems to deserve more emphasis than it has received. The presentation of the evidence for prognoses or forecasts, and estimates of their probabilities, seem to lie in the field of 'the information animal', though often it will be impossible to eliminate subjectivity and thus the possibility of bias or prejudice. But, in any case, the attitude to risk and uncertainty, however these are presented or weighed up, involves a kind of value-judgment which definitely belongs to 'the choice animal' or political decision-maker, or is a part of his utility function. Even if the probability of a prediction could be formulated not merely in subjective personal terms, but in the precise, 'objective', quantitative terms of a gamble at roulette, which is surely quite unrealistic for most of the kinds of decisions involved in economic policy-making, and even if, also, the values of the outcomes or objectives, in terms of certainties, which (continuing to stretch the realism of the example) the political authority must be assumed to be clear about, there is an inevitable further value-judgment, or element of valuation, involved in the adoption of a particular attitude to risk, whether of risk-preference, risk-aversion or risk-neutrality. It is clearly for the 'choice-animal' to choose whether to adopt a more cautious 'minimax' type of attitude or a Bayesian or 'maximin' attitude. If two decision-makers take different attitudes of this kind in a similar situation, 'no one else, not even the scientists, can say which one is right when one adopts a Bayesian attitude and the other decides on the basis of pessimism'.[1]

It has been pointed out by Giersch that democratic governments may tend to an attitude of risk aversion, while oppositions may tend to urge attitudes of risk preference.[2] It is, in practice, often very difficult to distinguish the separate influences on a policy decision of the values or preferences of a decision-maker (as they would be between certainties) from his risk attitude: that is to distinguish between a high estimate of the possible costs of a possible unfavourable outcome of a policy—say an ambitious 'growth' policy—from a cautious, minimax risk-attitude to a choice between uncertainties; or,

---

[1] C. W. Churchman, *Prediction and Optimal Decision*, 1961, p. 166.
[2] *Allgemeine Wirtschaftspolitik*, Grundlagen, 1960, p. 336.

in the reverse case, to separate a high valuation of a possible out-standingly successful outcome from a bold attitude of risk preference. In fact, it is important to distinguish with regard to the concept of 'responsibility' in policy proposals, how far it signifies a particular pattern of valuations holding good for choices between certainties, and how far it relates rather to the attitude to risk. But, because of different risk-attitudes, two decision-makers could differ over and choose different policies, even if they were in agreement in their valuations of all choices between certainties, and also as regards all relevant 'positive' predictions and their probabilities.

However, the difficulty in distinguishing, in practice, between risk-attitudes and policy preferences does not matter for the problems of marking off analytically the functions of the 'choice-animal' from those of the 'information-animal'. For both the risk-attitudes, and the choices or valuations of objectives, are surely for the 'choice animal' to determine. Consequently, the scientist does not seem logically or inevitably to be involved in value-judgments simply because of the need for valuations or choices of risk-attitudes in conditions of uncertainty, any more than he needs to be involved in value-judgments because policy decisions, as between certainties, involve choices between, and valuations of, different outcomes or objectives. It is in the setting out of the evidence or 'probabilities' regarding the different possible outcomes of alternative policies that the vital frontier, with which we are concerned in this book, may become blurred, and a demarcation line between the functions of the 'information animal' and those of the 'choice-animal' may be difficult to ascertain precisely in practice.

The history of economic theorizing, of the more orthodox type at any rate, has been largely one of deductive theorizing and model-building, and of the analysis or logic of choice between certainties, whether for the individual consumer choosing consumption goods, or in the 'welfarist' logic of the choice of economic policies.[1] It has been mainly concerned with choice in 'transparent' conditions of 'perfect knowledge', with indifference curves and possibility lines, representing highly complex but *certain* knowledge and information, sweeping with smooth certainty across the page or blackboard. At least until comparatively recently the application and applicability to the actual world of conclusions arrived at by deductive logic were often left largely to impressionism, casual empiricism, or hunch.

[1] Cf. J. Buttrick's criticism (in *Theories of Economic Growth*, edited by B. Hoselitz, 1960, p. 160) of neo-classical theories: 'A model in the social sciences in which no stochastic elements are present, i.e. one in which relationships among variables are presumed to be exact and in which the variables themselves can be measured, is a model constructed for heuristic rather than "practical" (i.e. predictive) purposes.' Cf. also, T. W. Hutchison, *The Significance and Basic Postulates of Economic Theory*, 1938 and 1960, pp. 86–8.

As regards choices between certainties, the demarcation line between the functions of 'the choice animal' and 'the information animal' seems perfectly clear-cut. In fact, some of the more facile pronouncements and programmes regarding a clear-cut distinction between positive and normative seem, like so much of economic theory, to be assuming away uncertainty. But, in conditions of uncertainty, where decisions have to be taken on the basis of uncertain predictions, this demarcation line—though not, I would say, analytically impossible to draw—will often become in practice very difficult to ascertain, particularly if ideological and political value-loads may be shaping the predictions. The thesis we have examined in this section, whether or not one agrees with its assumptions about the scope of the scientist's functions, certainly draws attention to the problems of inductive and statistical inference, of the weighing of evidence and the uncertainty of predictions, which are the source of considerable practical difficulties in demarcating clearly in practice, in the social and economic field, the roles of the neutral, scientific expert and the political decision-making authority.

(10) 'MEANS' AND 'ENDS'

According to the conception of economics as a neutral, positive science, which might perhaps still just be called the 'orthodox' conception, not only can economic theories be kept free from value-judgments, subjective bias and 'persuasiveness', but, within a particular limiting framework, the discussion of economic policies can be also. This framework is often described in terms of the categories of 'means' and 'ends'. The 'scientific economist', it is held, should not, and indeed cannot 'as such', pronounce or advise on ends, but *given* the ends, by abstract assumption for the purposes of a particular model, or as laid down by a political authority, he can pronounce on the means which will promote them. The means-ends categories are thus regarded as providing a clear and precise formula for delimiting normative from positive and the frontier of positive economics. Means and ends are broadly treated as corresponding or parallel in discussing economic policies in the teleological mood, to 'causes' and 'effects' in the positive mood of economic theory.

In the first place, analysis in terms of means and ends is apt to suffer from the usual oversimplification of the 'certainty' assumption, treating the choice of 'ends' as a choice between known certainties, as discussed in the previous section. But it is a different line of criticism of the means-ends categories which we wish now to examine. The use of the means-ends categories has been criticized by several of those who are sceptical of the possibility of neutral positive economics. It is argued that it is not possible to mark off sharply 'means' from 'ends' so that the economist can clearly confine his pronouncements to the former. For example, Smithies writes: 'Attempts to draw sharp distinctions between means and ends can be misleading and dangerous. The means chosen to achieve particular ends today may alter the ends of tomorrow.'[1] Myrdal describes the common use of the means-ends categories as follows:

'The basic idea of this principle is this: By splitting economic processes into (1) a given initial situation, (2) alternative means, and (3) the hypothetical end, it should be possible to concentrate all value-judgments on the third link, viz. the purpose. This is particularly important for relativists. They can now discuss purely scientifically not only the initial situation, but also the means. They can conduct a teleological argument objectively. Values are attached to the means only indirectly, via the values attached to the end which the means can serve. In themselves, means are supposed to be neutral, value-free. . . .

'Now it is quite obvious that values are attached not only to "ends" but also to "means". Means are not ethically neutral. The value-judgment must compare and choose between alternative courses. Value-judgments thus refer always to whole sequences, not merely to the anticipated final outcome. . . . Moreover, as we have seen, by "end" we do not normally mean the *total* final situation (nor by "means" the total sequence), but only a relevant section of it. (Otherwise a discussion of alternative means would be impossible: only exceptionally do different means lead to precisely identical total results.) Therefore, even if it were possible to isolate means as neutral, we would still have to discuss the by-effects which may not be neutral. . . . The political value judgment refers not only to the end but to every component in all possible alternative sequences which are to be compared.'[2]

As Myrdal subsequently concluded:

'It is simply not true that only ends are the object of valuations and that means are valued only as instrumental to ends. In any human valuation means have, in addition to their instrumental value, independent values as well. The value-premiss which has to be introduced in order to allow policy conclusions to be reached from factual analysis has therefore to be a valuation of means as well as ends.'[3]

[1] *Economics and Public Policy*, Brooking Lectures 1954, 1955, p. 3.
[2] *Value in Social Theory*, by G. Myrdal, edited with an introduction by P. Streeten, 1958, pp. 210–11.
[3] *Op. cit.*, p. 49.

110 *'Positive' Economics and Policy Objectives*

Let us make a comment first on a purely definitional point. In elaborating and supporting Myrdal's argument, Streeten describes as a 'trick' the defining of anything to which value is attached as an 'end', leaving 'means' to be, by definition, neutral, with no values attached to them.[1] Such a definition hardly seems to us to amount to a 'trick', but to represent perhaps the most suitable, or 'correct', definition of the terms as they are widely understood. What seems criticizable is not so much defining 'means' as neutral, but including under 'means' what can only be considered neutral by an arbitrary value-judgment. But this point is mainly terminological. We would prefer to express the substantial point which Myrdal and Streeten are making, which is valid and important, as being that the means-ends categories are often misleadingly used because what are described as 'means', and as having by normal implication no intrinsic values attached to them apart from the ends they promote, are not 'means' or pure 'means', because they have, or may well be thought to have, their own intrinsic values. The means-end categories are only applicable, that is, to what may be called purely technical problems where the 'means' are generally agreed to be neutral. Otherwise the 'ends' are being incompletely stated and are spilling over into what are being misleadingly described as neutral 'means', so that hidden persuasion and concealed value-judgments, possibly of a highly controversial kind, are being inserted in implying that no value-premises are involved in the choice of 'means'. But in the social world policies and institutions cannot be treated as purely neutral 'means', except by the insertion of an often highly arbitrary value-judgment which may sometimes, when the means-end categories are used in the most crudely mechanical way, lead on to the tyrannical error of treating people and their ways of life as 'means' or 'human material'.[2]

This confusion is apt to originate from the definition of economic science as a relationship between ends and scarce means. Being neutral, the argument proceeds, economics does not choose between or pronounce value-judgments on different ends, and it is implied that no value-judgments are involved in recommending 'means' to

[1] *Op. cit.*, Introduction, p. XXI. For example, there does not seem to be any 'trick' involved in the following treatment of means as 'purely technical': 'Where ends are agreed, the only questions left are those of means, and these are not political but technical, that is to say, capable of being settled by experts or machines like arguments between engineers or doctors.' I. Berlin, *Two Concepts of Liberty*, 1958, p. 3.

[2] Cf. A. Huxley, *Ends and Means*, 1938, who observes: 'The end cannot justify the means, for the simple and obvious reason that the means employed determine the nature of the ends produced. . . . The means whereby we try to achieve something are at least as important as the end we wish to attain. Indeed they are more important. For the means employed inevitably determine the nature of the result achieved' (p. 9 and p. 52).

Types and Sources of Value-Judgments and Bias   111

given 'ends'. The point may then be illustrated by an example from the life of Robinson Crusoe where he has to choose between the 'ends' of warmth and protection in allocating his scarce means—a quantity of timber—between fires and fences;[1] or, alternatively, a housewife is described allocating her pennies between different household wants. Here the 'means' are represented by units of money or commodities. They can justifiably be assumed to be neutral and interchangeable means, having no intrinsic values of their own, except in so far as they promote the ends which are unambiguously and completely given by Crusoe's preferences for warmth and protection. The problems may be described as 'technical', and this use of the means-end categories *can* be, as far as it goes, unobjectionable. But these are not problems of social or political economy, and it is highly dangerous to extend this use of the means-end categories to questions of policies and institutions such as the choice between monetary and fiscal policies and the nationalization or de-nationalization of the steel industry. The 'means' here are not neutral (or rather are not pure 'means') and can only be assumed to be neutral by an arbitrary value-judgment, since the choice between them affects the whole distribution of powers, and ways of life, of the community.[2] The 'end', therefore, cannot be taken as unambiguously given—in terms simply of the stabilizing of prices or the efficient production of quantities of steel—except by a value-judgment regarding the neutrality of the 'means' which would not be widely agreed, even if it was explicitly inserted, but which in any case is often left implicit. The confusion is particularly serious in the discussion of problems of the economic development of poor countries whose institutions and ways of life are sometimes treated as purely neutral 'means' subordinate to the 'end' of 'economic growth', which is defined in terms of an index of real income-per-head. Max Weber was, in fact, dealing with an example from this field when he pointed out that 'strictly and exclusively empirical analysis can provide a solution only where it is a question of a means adequate to the realization of an absolutely unambiguously given end'.[3] It is just this absolutely

---

[1] Cf. L. Robbins, *Essay on the Nature and Significance of Economic Science*, 2nd Ed., 1935, p. 34.

[2] 'In every proposal of economic policy there lies an often undisclosed preference for a society integrated in one way rather than another.' M. Oakeshott, *Rationalism in Politics*, 1962, p. 37.

[3] Max Weber on *The Methodology of the Social Sciences*, translated and edited by E. A. Shils and H. A. Finch, 1949, p. 26; cf. also p. 37 and p. 45: 'The evaluations are unambiguous *only* when the economic end and the social context are definitely given and all that remains is to choose between several economic means, when these differ only with respect to their certainty, rapidity and quantitative productiveness, and are completely identical in every other value-relevant aspect. It is only when these conditions have been met that we evaluate a given means as "technically most correct", and it is only then that the evalua-

unambiguous statement of the ends, or objectives of policies, which in real-world policy discussions—as contrasted with abstract 'technical' models—is so difficult to achieve without arbitrariness and incompleteness.

The misuse of the means-ends classification and the confusions it perpetuates have played an important part in the perennial debates between those inclining to policies based on free markets and those favouring policies based on central controls and public ownership. Many examples could be cited from recent political debates, in particular from the Labour Party's reconsideration of its nationalization policies. We may take an example of a confusing and value-loaded use of the concept of 'means' from A. P. Lerner's *Economics of Control*. Lerner contrasts his concept of the 'controlled' economy with that of the 'mixed' economy:

'The term "mixed economy" is sometimes used to designate something like our controlled economy which has elements of collectivism as well as elements of private enterprise for profit. This is a very bad name because it suggests the absence of any single controlling principle but a confusion of different and perhaps contradictory principles. The fundamental point of the controlled economy is that it denies both collectivism and private enterprise as *principles* for the organization of society, but recognizes both of them as perfectly legitimate *means*. Its fundamental principle of organization is that in any particular instance, the means that serves society best should be the one that prevails.'

Anyone is—like Lerner—quite entitled to proclaim that he personally is indifferent as to whether there is a greater measure of public or social control or a greater measure of free individual enterprise in an economy; but he is not entitled to expect or imply that all 'rational' citizens will agree with his indifference. Nor is he entitled to argue that it is wrong or 'bad' to suggest that there is indeed a conflict of values and ends (or 'principles' as he calls them).[1] The

tion is unambiguous. In every other case, i.e. in every case which is not purely a matter of technique, the evaluation ceases to be unambiguous and evaluations enter which are not determinable exclusively by economic analysis. . . . It should be emphatically recalled that the possibility of the exact definition of the end sought for is a prerequisite to the formulation of this problem.'

[1] A. P. Lerner, *Economics of Control*, 1944, p. 4. See also the penetrating criticism by M. Friedman, *Essays in Positive Economics*, 1953, pp. 301 ff. Lerner is at one point (p. 85) prepared to take some marginal account of political values in admitting that 'anything that may contribute to the safeguarding of democracy is of great value'. He continues: 'The controlled economy may consider that even some sacrifice of efficiency in the allocation of resources is worthwhile as a contribution to the safeguard of democracy, though the kind of government that would take this into account could put up adequate safeguards even if it were 100 per cent collectivist.' What is misleading is treating different types of

Types and Sources of Value-Judgments and Bias　　　　113

whole task of economic analysis is surely to bring out conflicts of 'ends' or 'principles' and to elucidate the choice society has to make, and not to smother or obscure these by empty formulae about 'what serves society best'. There *are* conflicts between freedom and justice, progress and security, and so on, and all too often economists have tended to obscure the inevitable necessity of choice by obfuscatory formulae such as 'maximizing welfare' or 'utility'. Collectivism and private enterprise cannot be treated as purely neutral 'means', nor can fiscal policy and monetary policy be treated as purely neutral 'means' towards the 'end' of economic stability, without latent political value-judgments. Certainly, as Boulding has put it, 'publicness' has tended to become an end in itself among the socialists, 'privateness' among the libertarians, and such value-judgments may be explicitly questioned.[1] Certainly also, one may object to the Utopian dogmatism of some economists who present one system or the other as disposing of the problems of conflict and cost, and the need for choice, because *their* system realizes a maximum of *all* ends, freedom, distributive justice, stability, growth and everything else, while suggesting that what their system does not maximize or minimize is not worth bothering about. One does not clarify the issues by invoking a formula such as 'what serves society best', but by setting out explicit value-premises. As has been well said: 'In controversial matters there is always a tendency to conceal questions of ends and to pretend that every question is one of means only—as for instance in politics, where it is "claptrap" to announce portentously that we all desire the welfare of the community and to pretend that we differ only in our view of the best way of attaining it; what we really differ about is our ideas of the welfare of the community.'[2] In other words it is 'claptrap' to set up 'welfare' as the single 'agreed' end of policies and then discuss different kinds of policies, of very different significance in terms of political values, as purely neutral 'means'.

The means-ends categories are so often confusing and dangerous because in the social world there are few—or perhaps it might be said *no*—policies, institutions or arrangements which can be assumed to be purely neutral 'means' with no possible intrinsic value of their own.[3] The use of the distinction too often amounts to an

economy, say, 100 per cent, 50 per cent, and 5 per cent collectivist economies, simply as different machines, or pure techniques, for generating 'economic welfare', unless it is made quite clear that the analysis is strictly in terms of abstract models from which no policy conclusions are being, or can be, directly drawn.

[1] K. Boulding, *Principles of Economic Policy*, 1959, p. 138.

[2] N. Campbell, quoted by B. Wootton, in *Testament for Social Science*, 1960, p. 120.

[3] Cf. J. A. Passmore, 'Can the Social Sciences be Value-Free?' in *Readings in*

H

114   *'Positive' Economics and Policy Objectives*

incomplete and garbled statement of policy objectives or value-premisses, and hence the kind of inconclusive wrangling which results from crypto-normative and pseudo-neutral assumptions. We agree with Dahl and Lindblom when they hold that the means-ends framework is not necessarily always unusable. But, as they put it: 'Because most "ends" are themselves means in a lengthy chain of means-and-ends; because an end in one chain of means-ends may be a means in another chain of action; and because a means in one chain may be an end in another, sometimes the language of means-ends is slippery and cumbersome.'[1] They make use of a distinction between a 'prime' and an 'instrumental' goal, the former representing 'a direct source of satisfaction in itself', while the latter 'has value only because it facilitates the attainment of one or more prime goals'.[2]

Another useful distinction is Stevenson's between 'extrinsic' and 'intrinsic' values, the former values existing exclusively in the *consequences* of something, and the latter in the thing for its own sake. Apart from its consequences, Stevenson emphasizes that something, an institution, process or policy objective, can have both intrinsic and extrinsic value, the one reinforcing the other. For example, a decrease in unemployment *can* be regarded as, at the same time, both an end in itself and also as a means to a higher or better distributed national income. Of course, the same thing can be both 'means' and 'end' simultaneously, and can be an 'end' at one moment and a 'means' at another. Also, many, or most, so-called 'economic ends' are not, except for thoroughgoing materialists, at all *ultimate* 'ends' but rather 'instrumental goals'. In fact, that the pleonastic expression 'ultimate end' seems required points to the inadequacy in terminology.

Nevertheless, all this does not justify the view that means-ends statements are *inevitably* value-loaded and that the distinction cannot be drawn. It simply signifies that in the discussion of policies the

the *Philosophy of Science*, edited by H. Feigl and M. Brodbeck, 1953, p. 675: 'Scientists sometimes profess to be giving "merely technical advice" when in fact they are tacitly assuming a particular social policy. This gives encouragement to the view that "positive social sciences" are a sham. But, of course, genuine technical problems can also be found; they are contained within the sham sort; what the sham sort does is to include in the technical specifications factors which it does not mention.'

[1] Cf. R. A. Dahl and C. E. Lindblom, *Politics Economics and Welfare*, 1953, p. 26.

[2] C. W. Churchman deals with the point in terms of 'act-preference' (e.g. for buying in a favourite shop when the price of an 'identical' good is lower elsewhere): 'The dichotomy of the act and the goal (i.e. the means and the end) is primarily one of conceptual convenience, and there is no reason why a scientist might not want to make act-preference measures the inseparable components of goal values.' *Prediction and Optimal Decision*, 1961, p. 197.

Types and Sources of Value-Judgments and Bias   115

'ends' are often very nebulously and incompletely formulated, and that 'ultimate ends' and 'instrumental goals' or objectives are often not adequately distinguished and elaborated—not that they cannot be.[1] It also seems to point to the desirability of an alternative terminology. Valuable though it has been to expose these inadequacies, and the tendentious crypto-normative arguments based on them, the conclusion does not seem warranted, on this ground at any rate, that the economist must inevitably resort to value-judgments in discussing policies, or that he cannot separate quite clearly positive propositions about the consequences of policies from the assertion or assumption of value-judgments about the desirability of policy objectives (which latter can and will often include what have been mis-classified as 'means').[2]

What tend to get mis-classified as 'means' are often differing political or social institutions (e.g. free markets or controls, or the nationalized or private organization of an industry). The mis-classification involves making, inexplicitly, arbitrary political and social value-judgments. Moreover, what often seems to happen is that these inexplicit political presuppositions are shaping extremely speculative economic generalizations. But then by arbitrarily treating, explicitly or inexplicitly, the political choices of institutions as simply questions of 'means', the impression is given that crucial politico-economic issues can be and are being decided by purely economic expertise. It is a very similar procedure to that of the 'welfarist' economist pronouncing on 'economic welfare', while arbitrarily assuming, perhaps inexplicitly, that the non-economic effects—on 'other aspects of welfare'—are neutral, negligible, or generally move in the same direction as the economic effects. We are certainly not complaining that political value-judgments as to different political and social institutions and processes often seem to determine political preferences or decisions, but that they are not explicitly acknowledged as doing so. If the 'purely economic' effects of measures—of, say, monetary or fiscal policy—are very difficult to predict and weigh up, or even if they are not, it may be entirely reasonable and justifiable to decide the issue by political principle, or by preferences for particular kinds of political or social institution, or the distribution of power. But the pretence often seems to be made that preferences and decisions are in accordance with economic expertise, when in fact there is no well-tested or corroborated

---

[1] v. C. L. Stevenson, *Ethics and Language*, 1944, Chapter VII, pp. 174 ff.

[2] Myrdal himself says at one point that it is 'the essential character of science ... to make policy more rational ... by clarifying the causal relations between means and aims', which seems to imply that the means-ends formula *can* be legitimately employed. v. *Value in Social Theory*, edited by P. Streeten, 1958, p. 35.

116   *'Positive' Economics and Policy Objectives*

economic theory or generalization to support them, while latent
and arbitrary value-judgments are made treating political institutions
and principles as pure 'means'. The confusion is fostered by packing
all the many varieties of ends into a monistic hold-all such as 'maximum economic welfare'. It does not seem to be putting the point
right to argue that the difficulties and misuse of the means-ends
classification constitutes an *inevitable* source of value-judgments and
'value-loadedness' in the discussion of economic policies. But the
critics are, nevertheless, getting at a very real source of normative-
positive confusion in policy discussions, that is the difficulty of
stating even reasonably fully and precisely the objectives of policies.
This is the main topic of the second half of this book.

(11) SUMMARY AND CONCLUSIONS

This survey has wound to and fro through the preliminaries, processes, and boundaries of economic theorizing and its applications,
and we shall now try to summarize and review our conclusions. We
have tried to make reasonably complete this account of the different
types, sources and entry-points of value-judgments and bias in
economics. We think that the important types have been covered,
and that such as have not, could, in the main, be regarded as variants
or different formulations or combinations of the types with which
we *have* dealt.

The first distinction is between: (1) kinds of value-judgment or
'proposal' that are logically inevitable in any 'science' just as much
as in economics; and (2) value-judgments which are by no means
absolutely inevitable, but which logically have either to be postulated
or affirmed if policy recommendations are to be discussed; further,
(3) there are the questions of the sources and entry-points of subjectivity and possible bias in 'positive' statements, whether theories,
causal explanations or predictions.

As regards (1), in economics, as in all 'sciences', value-judgments
of a kind, or 'proposals', have to be made regarding (*a*) the choice
of problems to be studied, and (*b*) the choice of epistemological
criteria. But simply from a choice of problems or epistemological
criteria no value-judgments as to policy objectives or policy recommendations can ever *logically* follow. Nor can the choice of questions
make bias and dogmatism logically inevitable in the answers to
them.

(2) As regards those value-judgments which are certainly not
logically inevitable, but which may be introduced, these arise only,
or almost only, when policies, and therefore the more or less precise
objectives of policies, are being discussed. No value-judgments
inevitably have to be *asserted* even in discussions of policies, which

## Types and Sources of Value-Judgments and Bias					117

can always be treated in the perfectly 'positive' technical-hypothetical mood by simply *postulating* (not asserting) particular objectives, and examining to what extent different policy-measures attain them. Of course, if policy recommendations as to the objectives of policies *are* being made, then political or ethical value-judgments are inevitable. Logic and clarity require that as clear a distinction as possible be made between 'positive' theories, predictions or propositions, and political and ethical value-judgments regarding the effects or objectives of policies, if the latter are indulged in (though many authorities think they should not be).[1] Logic also requires that value-judgments regarding the objectives of policies, or policy-preferences, should be reasonably fully stated, not leaving camouflaged, for example, such political objectives as the widest possible operation of 'free' price mechanisms, on the one hand, or the maximum of 'social control' or distributive equality, on the other hand. The means-ends dichotomy, though it need not inevitably lend itself to this sort of partial camouflage, is liable to be misused in this way.

The inevitable value-judgments or 'proposals' of type (1), regarding choices of questions and criteria, come logically *before* the scientific process of analysis and testing, and might, therefore, be described as 'pre-scientific'. Value-judgments of type (2), relating to the choice of policies and policy objectives, come logically *after* the scientific process proper, and might, therefore, be described as 'post-scientific', since they arise only when theories are being 'applied', however loosely, to policies. As regards (3), subjectivity and possible bias, this operates in the scientific process itself—where no value-judgments are logically required, or, according to the rules, logically in order—by influencing the selection of 'positive' theories, explanations or predictions, which are asserted as empirically valid or unrefuted, when no adequate tests leading to a measure of consensus have been made.

The problems of bias, and the detection and neutralization of its devious workings, are more difficult than those of value-judgments. There is a strong initial drive and propensity to bias in the ideological prejudices and 'visions' with which economic problems are approached, and which often shape initial hypotheses about economic

---

[1] For a vigorous statement of the view that the 'scientist' should aim at making recommendations as to what *ought* to be done by developing methods of measuring the values of policy-objectives, see C. W. Churchman, *Prediction and Optimal Decision*, 1961. Churchman seems to be striving after something like the economist's choice-criterion of objectives or values—that people should do, or have, what they prefer. But he perceives the difficulty, as economists sometimes do not, that to serve as an adequate criterion, 'choice' must be 'adequately or fully informed choice', and that it is difficult to know what this would be when adequate or full information is not available, and even to define 'adequate' or 'full' information.

behaviour. When the scientific testing process gets started, the practicable tests are often inadequate, or too inconclusive, to promote consensus. Testing may narrow the range of hypotheses, but still leave a number of sharply conflicting competitors in the field, and, where tests fail to 'select', bias or prejudice (mostly more or less political), is free to, and often does, take over.

Though the biased 'selection' or use of persuasive value-loaded terminology and concepts has been prominent throughout much of the history of economic thought, this infringement of scientific procedure or criteria does not seem today to be more than a minor controversial nuisance *among economists*, and infringements are usually not difficult to detect and neutralize.

It is in historical evidence, causal explanations, and in predictions, particularly when a high degree of uncertainty is inevitable, as is most often the case, that selection by political bias, rather than by scientific criteria, becomes serious. Though it may not be difficult for the critical economist to detect it in the works of the more blatant propagandists and ideologues who write about economics and economic policy, it may, also, not be easy to tell just where it ends and some genuine positive insight may be beginning. When the propagandist element in one's own or other people's writings is not deliberate, the difficulties of detection may obviously be very great, especially when the evidence that would constitute an adequate test is not obtainable.

Moreover, bias may and does operate not only when policy proposals and objectives are under discussion but at the general theoretical level, for example with regard to short and long period treatment, theories of interest, and even of value, which may be shaped by ideological prejudices or political predilections for or against 'capitalism' or 'socialism', free markets or state regulation. In fact, though general theorizing only logically requires value-judgments or 'proposals' of type (1), and not those of type (2), which have either to be postulated or asserted in policy discussions, subjectivity and bias operate almost as pervasively in general theorizing as in policy discussions and decisions. Certainly, in the case of policy discussions, the pressure of prejudice is likely to be more acute, and the pretext of the need for rapid decision and action on uncertain evidence more effective. Indeed, when particular policy proposals, and the predictions involved, are being debated, flatly contradictory empirical generalizations may be asserted as valid (e.g. with regard to the presence of economies of scale in a larger European market).

Furthermore, in acting or in recommending action on uncertain predictions, a kind of value-judgment as to risk-attitudes is inevitably involved. Orthodox analysis of consumers' or policy choices in terms of certainties has encouraged too facile a separation of normative

Types and Sources of Value-Judgments and Bias 119

and positive. Though we are not prepared completely to agree with Churchman 'that knowledge and value are "inseparable" concepts',[1] they are intertwined much more deeply than may be realized by those who have concentrated on the choices between certainties.

Finally, the much more complex and often conflicting nature of policy objectives, discussed by economists and aimed at by governments in the last decade or two, has logically required, but has not been matched by, much more complex and precise value-judgments in the discussion of policies. For, apart from the inevitable 'preliminary' value-judgments and 'proposals' regarding choices of problems and criteria, it is policy objectives, in the broadest sense, that bias and value-judgments, latent or explicit, are mainly about. When it is reasonably, if optimistically, demanded that political value-judgments should be made clear and explicit, it is as clear and full statements, as reasonably possible, of policy-preferences, or reasonably full evaluations of different policy objectives, that are required.

---

[1] *Prediction and Optimal Decision*, 1961, p. 187.

[9]

Excerpt from *Economic Means and Social Ends: Essays in Political Economics*, 99–129.

6

FRITZ MACHLUP

POSITIVE
AND
NORMATIVE ECONOMICS
An Analysis of the Ideas

Although there are some economists who "can't be bothered" by such exercises in "philosophy" or "mere semantics," the distinction between positive and normative plays a considerable role in present-day economic discussion. And this has been true for more than 150 years. While for some the distinction refers to a boundary between two branches of a science, for others "normative science" is a contradiction in terms, the discourse of norms or values being by definition nonscientific. The question is, of course, semantic and philosophic, but this does not make it trivial or useless. An elucidation seems worth our while.

Such an elucidation should be both historical and analytical. In the interests of conserving space, I shall confine myself here, however, to a discussion of the analytic questions.[1] The reader

---

[1] When we distinguish analytical from historical semantics, we do not suggest that the former can be independent of the latter. Words have meanings because people have used them to express certain ideas, and the meanings in which words have been used are historical data—though they are derived by way of interpretation, not observation.

If meanings have changed over time and between different groups, historical semantics will present these changes. The task of analytical semantics is largely one of rearrangements: the historical evidence and the chronology are removed and the different meanings are ordered and grouped in a systematic fashion designed to exhibit significant contrasts and relationships,

who would care to pursue the matter on a historical level may, if he is patient, wait for the publication of the history of ideas I am preparing on the issues behind the concepts "positive" and "normative."

When we embark on a methodological analysis of the ideas of "positive" and other kinds of economics, we cannot dispense with semantics. Questions of semantics and methodology are difficult to disentangle.

This is easy to comprehend. If some authors, for example, expound the intricacies of welfare economics, old or new, and conclude that certain propositions are normative in character, whereas other authors have characterized the same propositions as positive, either the difference may be semantic or it may be a matter of methodological interpretation. Obviously, it makes a difference whether "normative" in this context is to mean prescriptive, advisory, persuasive, evaluative, ethical, emotive, instrumental, or political; and whether "positive" means expository, descriptive, explanatory, predictive, nonhypothetical, nonevaluative, nonmetaphysical, nonspeculative, operational, testable, verifiable, nonpartisan, or consistent with agreed premises. But even if authors agree on the meaning of the adjectives, they may still come to different judgments on the character of the propositions in question, for they may not agree on all that is involved.

We shall begin with a brief summary of findings from the historical survey.

THE MEANINGS OF "POSITIVE"

The adjective "positive" has been used, in the literatures of economics, of the social sciences in general, and of the philosophy of science, chiefly to modify the following nouns: economics, inquiry, science, theory, problems, propositions, premises, and conclusions. The meaning of the adjective, however, has varied considerably over time and among different authors. The following list presents a quick review of some of the meanings of "positive" as a modifier of relevant nouns, the nouns being shown in parentheses:

Incontrovertible, unconditional, not merely hypothetical	(conclusions)
Empirical, not arbitrary	(premises of empirical sciences)

and thus to aid in the understanding of the concepts in the contexts in which they are used.

Perhaps all this can be said more simply by prohibiting the analytical semanticist from acting like Humpty-Dumpty, whose program was, "When I use a word, it means just what I choose it to mean—neither more nor less." The semanticist may analyze, but not dictate.

Probably true	(conclusions, corresponding to "positive reality")
Free from metaphysical speculation	(stage of scientific development)
Unconcerned with ultimate efficient causes	(science)
Based on facts of immediate perception	(science)
Disregarding psychic and spiritual facts	(science)
Confirmable or at least conceivably testable	(propositions)
Not merely critical or negative	(theory)
Nonpolitical, nonethical	(problems)
Neither normative nor prescriptive	(inquiry)
Not concerned with ideals or precepts	(inquiry)

This list can be reduced to a few pairs of opposites:

Positive (constructive) versus negative (critical)
Positive (certain) versus uncertain
Positive (observable) versus nonobservable
Positive (confirmable) versus nontestable
Positive (descriptive) versus prescriptive
Positive (factual) versus normative

In addition, there are two terms that have been used sometimes as equivalents of positive and in other instances to denote the opposite of positive. One of these terms is *"speculative,"* which for practically all philosophical positivists stands for nonobservable, if not metaphysical, and hence nonpositive. For at least two authors, however (Sidgwick and Keynes), the word meant the opposite of normative–prescriptive and, hence, the equivalent of positive–theoretical. (Thus, they would not approve the pair of opposites used by philosophical positivists: positive versus speculative.)

The other term is *"natural."* In legal philosophy, it modifies "law" to mean norms dictated by reason, social necessity, or divine order, and imposing justice and ethical precepts. In contrast to this "natural law" (of metaphysical origin), "positive law" is formally laid down, artificially instituted, not derived from general principles of justice but formulated in accepted codes, anchored in statute or formal precedent. In scientific discourse, however, "natural law" has meant law of nature, empirically tested and therefore a part of positive science, in contrast to arbitrary construction, mere fiction, product of imagination—hence, metaphysical. (This would contradict the pair of opposites in the language of legal philosophers: positive versus natural.)

THE MEANINGS OF "NORMATIVE"

The semantic record of the adjective "normative" is less voluminous and less bewildering. This is clearly reflected in the dictionaries: *The Oxford Dictionary*, which lists thirteen meanings for "positive," gives only a single meaning for "normative": "Establishing norms or standards." But this overlooks some significant differences in the use of the word by different economists, social scientists, and philosophers.

The most important differences in the meanings of "normative" relate to the degree in which the statements in question are (1) explicit with regard to the norms (objectives, values) to which they refer; (2) focused on the problem of valuation, especially on the problem of comparing particular norms (objectives) with conflicting ones; and (3) concerned with the means and techniques of attaining certain stated norms (ends) which stand high in the value systems of some but not necessarily of the person making the statements.

There are writers who would use the word "normative" to denote all statements that are advisory or hortatory in effect or intent, regardless of whether the underlying values are concealed or clearly stated, the problem of conflicting values is raised, or the objective to be attained is assumed as given and independent of the adviser's personal system of values. Others, however, prefer to remove the tag "normative" from statements that merely describe the means and techniques by which given ends can be attained. And some would remove the tag as soon as the underlying values are made explicit and unambiguous.

"POSITIVE" VERSUS "NORMATIVE"

Disregarding for the moment all other meanings of "positive," and concentrating on "positive" as the antonym of "normative," we may think of two sets of ideas associated with this pair of opposites:

Positive	*Normative*
Description	Prescription
Explanation	Recommendation
Theory	Practice
Theory	Policy
Thought	Action
Laws (statements of uniformities)	Rules (statements of norms)
Science	Art
Factual judgments	Value judgments

Essay 6   FRITZ MACHLUP   103

| Statements in the indicative mood | Statements in the imperative mood |
| Testable propositions about facts | Nontestable expressions of feelings |

We shall not discuss all these pairs of opposites, some of which reflect misunderstandings, serious or trivial. We should not fail, however, to comment on the grounds on which "practice" and "art" were placed in the normative column.

Let us not forget that the writer most responsible for the wide adoption of the terms "positive economics" and "normative economics" really proposed a triple distinction, not a dichotomy. John Neville Keynes distinguished positive, normative, and practical economics, which are concerned, respectively, with uniformities, standards, and precepts. I find it expedient to follow this tripartite division, at least for some distance.

THE TRICHOTOMY AND THE CHOICE OF TERMS

According to Keynes, positive economics tells you "what is," normative economics tells you "what ought to be," and practical economics tells you "what you can do to attain what you want." [2]

The term "practical" in this context is ambiguous; it disregards two significant differences: the one between action and advice, and the other between general advice for typical situations and specific advice for concrete (unique) situations. If what is meant is advice of a more general nature ("precept"), a more self-explanatory term had better be sought. The frequently used term "prescriptive" is not of great help either. It may prescribe standards, and thus become synonymous with "normative," or it may prescribe actions, and thus be equivalent to "practical." In this case, it leaves open whether one prescribes according to one's own standards (values), those of one's client, or some other stipulated standards. In the first of these possibilities, "prescriptive" would be both normative and practical at the same time. Let us use the term favored by Adolph Lowe, "instrumental," to denote the task of describing and prescribing actions by means of which specified objectives can be obtained.

The term "normative" as one of the triad will be examined later in greater detail, but let us agree at this point that the norms to which it refers are not rules or precepts telling you what to do or not to do to

---

[2] The first two phrases between quotation marks are Keynes', the third is mine, designed to fit what Keynes intended to express.

achieve given ends, but instead ethical (or aesthetic) standards telling you what we consider good or bad, right or wrong. The term "evaluative," referring to systems of ethical (or aesthetic) values, would probably be more expressive of the idea. In any case, in the following discussion "normative" means "evaluative."

GRAMMATICAL FORMS

Positive, normative, and instrumental statements will now be characterized by simple relationships between events A and B, alternatively seen as causes and effects and as means and ends.

> Positive: If A, then B;
>   that is, B is the effect of the cause A.
> Normative: B is good;
>   that is, you ought to get (strive for) B.
> Instrumental: If you want B, A will get it for you;
>   that is, A will be the means for the end B.

Much has been made of the fact that normative sentences can (and ought to be) expressed in the imperative mood, whereas positive sentences would always be in the indicative mood. In the scheme above, both the positive and the instrumental propositions are stated in the conditional form, the positive one taking the cause (A) as the condition of achieving the effect (B), the instrumental one taking the end (B) as the condition for resorting to the means (A). The normative sentence can be translated in a variety of ways: it can be expressed in the indicative mood, in the imperative mood, and in conditional form.

> Indicative: B is good; indeed, B is the best.
> Imperative: Get B!!
> Conditional: (1) If you want the best, you ought to get B.
>   (2) If you don't get B,
>   (a) you don't know what's good for you;
>   (b) you are a fool or a coward; or
>   (c) you will be disliked, despised, or even punished.

It is questionable, however, whether these grammatical modifications are legitimate from a logician's point of view. Logical positivists deny the legitimacy of anything but the imperative mood. Rudolf Carnap, for example, contends that "actually a value statement is nothing else than a command in a misleading grammatical form. It may have effects upon the actions of men, and these effects may either be in accordance with our wishes or not; but it is neither true nor false. It does not assert anything and can neither be proved nor disproved."[3] The contention that the indicative mood is misleading because the value judgment "does not assert anything" is rather pretentious. After all, if I say that I value B, I do assert something about my likes and dislikes. But I know that this does not count for logical positivists; they are not interested in my or your tastes, maxims, or values. If I say, "Kate is the loveliest girl," they want me to express this in the imperative mood, such as, "Kiss me, Kate!"

The translations into the form of conditional statements do not fare much better. One should perhaps admit that forms 1 and 2a are merely attempts to express the value judgment in a more persuasive way. Form 2b tries to reinforce the persuasion by a threat which may influence the addressee by inducing fears of being regarded as a fool or a coward, at least by the maker of the statement. Form 2c goes farther by threatening the addressee with sanctions if he fails to accept the value judgment and to act accordingly. Incidentally, in this form it is not made clear just who entertains the valuation expressed: I; we; the majority of educated people, of voters, or of all people; the government; the prince; the dictator. But even without this specification, the statement seems to make an assertion; the predicted sanctions for nonconformists may in fact be imposed, and thus the statement can (at least conceivably) be tested and confirmed or disconfirmed. Perhaps, though, the statement in form 2c has been promoted from a value judgment to an indicative statement about the morals and codes of a group or society and to an instrumental proposition stating something like this: "If you want to avoid social or legal penalties, you will act to show that you too value B, and thus you will resort to A as the appropriate means for it." In this advisory proposition, B has become an intermediate end—namely, a means for avoiding the sanctions imposed on those who fail to conform with the value judgment in favor of B.

THE LANGUAGE OF THE COOKBOOK

Many discussions of normative science and technology refer to the cookbook or, more generally, to the book of recipes, as an analogy for prescriptive or normative statements. As a matter of fact, recipes in cookbooks (or technological handbooks) are commonly written in the imperative mood, and their authors thus seem to obey the logician's normative statement on the proper grammatical form of normative statements.

Some of the most frequently used imperatives in the cookbook are

---

[3] Rudolf Carnap, *Philosophy and Logical Syntax* (London: Kegan Paul, Trench, and Trubner, 1935), p. 24. Partially reproduced in Morton White, *The Age of Analysis* (3rd printing) (New York: Mentor Books, 1957), p. 217.

Have! Cut! Slice! Chop! Wash! Soak! Drain! Shake! Melt! Cook! Boil! Bake! Fry! Add!—all, of course, followed by quantities of victuals to which the prescribed operations are to be applied.

However, each of the sets of imperatives is under a heading, such as "Crab Cakes," "Cheese Omelet," or "Crêpes Suzette." From the logician's point of view, the heading is the premise of a hypothetical proposition, the premise stating the assumed objective. For example: "*If* you want to make a cheese omelet for n persons, *take* $2n$ eggs. . . ."

The imperatives of the cookbook are therefore in a grammatical form misleading for the beginning student of logic, though most helpful to the intermediate student of cooking. A logical cook could translate each recipe into a positive statement of cause and effect: "If you take $2n$ eggs . . . you will get a cheese omelet for n persons." But since the cookbook is organized and classified, not according to causes, but according to effects or ends, the more appropriate translation would be into instrumental statements about desired ends and required means. That is, to say as I said before, "If you want to make a cheese omelet for n persons, take $2n$ eggs. . . ."

This may be the point at which to digress for a discussion of whether a cookbook belongs to the science of cookery or to the art of cooking. The question is much broader, of course. Are instrumental propositions part of an "art"? Is "science" confined to positive propositions?

ART AND SCIENCE

Those who speak of cooking as an art do not mean to say that it is an art to read a cookbook and carry out its instructions, or to prepare without instruction the simple dishes commonly eaten by most of us. They refer, instead, only to the work of those rare cooks who prepare very special meals, using unusual imagination and a fine sense of taste, form, and color. The "art" in this activity lies precisely in their deviation from common practice and from common precepts.

This meaning of art, as a performance superior to that of most practitioners, is contrary to another meaning of art, as a body of precepts for practice; this is one of the dictionary definitions and has been widely used as an antonym of science. Art in this sense is, like science, systematic knowledge, but arranged in a different way, suitable for more immediate practical application. As John Stuart Mill has explained, science is a body of knowledge classified according to causes, and art is a body of knowledge classified according to effects, the causes of which are often the subject of several different sciences.

Bentham's aphorism, that science is knowledge while art is practice, places us right between the two meanings of art just contrasted. Clearly, not all knowledge is science and not all practice is art. Perhaps one may say that highly qualified knowledge (rather than common, everyday knowledge) is science,[4] while highly qualified practice (rather than common, everyday practice) is art. But since virtually all practice, and certainly all qualified practice, presupposes knowledge, it is quite possible, as some writers have proposed, to use "art" and "applied science" as synonymous terms.

Those who define art as practical knowledge have usually failed to differentiate various degrees of practicality and various degrees of practice. There are important differences between, say, a handbook of technology, technological advice in a concrete situation, actual instruction given for immediate activation, and the final, perhaps manual, execution of the instruction. Yet all four phases of practical knowledge, practical application of knowledge, and practice have indiscriminately been called art.[5] (Let us recall Menger's complaint about this confusion.)

An important idea in designating certain kinds of practical activity as art is, I submit, the recognition that these activities presuppose a combination of human qualities that cannot be obtained solely from books or lectures. These activities are "art" in that they call for judgment, intuition, inventiveness, and imagination; they call for skill in making the correct diagnoses and prognoses required for successful prescriptions and good performance. Here lies a real distinction from science, scientific knowledge, and even technology and general practical precepts.

To what extent can it be said that art is normative or contains significant normative elements? Let us recall our resolution to use "normative" as an equivalent of "evaluative"—that is, as referring to standards for judging things as good or bad, right or wrong—and not as rules helpful in the attainment of stated ends. In this sense, art is normative to the extent that the activity in question calls for judgments of value, ethical or aesthetic; it is neutral or nonnormative where no value judgments are involved. In other words, art cannot reasonably be put under the normative heading except after an examination of the value-content of the judgments employed.

That the fine arts and the performing arts presuppose commitment to aesthetic standards goes without saying. The medical arts and the engineering arts, however, may go a long way without giving up their basic

---

[4] See the discussion of the meanings of science by Joseph A. Schumpeter, *History of Economic Analysis* (New York: Oxford University Press, Inc., 1954), pp. 6–11. One of Schumpeter's definitions differentiates scientific knowledge from that of the layman and mere practitioner.

[5] The German word for art is *Kunst,* but the German language offers the compound nouns *Kunstlehre* (for art as a body of precepts, technology), *Kunstregel* (for art as a precept or rule for practical application), and *Kunstfertigkeit* (for art as technical skill).

value-neutrality. The art of making recommendations on economic policy, requiring diagnostic and prognostic skills as well as interdisciplinary intelligence, may likewise proceed on the basis of agreed ethical standards without any violation of the adviser's value-neutrality. The economic adviser practices an art, not because his recommendations serve certain ends desired by people committed to certain values, but rather because his recommendations presuppose so much more than economic science: politics, sociology, psychology, pedagogy, and diplomacy, as well as diagnostic judgment, prognostic flair, intuition, and inventiveness.

One other concept of art may be mentioned here, the one used in grouping the various academic disciplines taught by the nonvocational faculties of our universities. The "arts," in academic parlance, were originally the disciplines of the trivium (grammar, logic, and rhetoric) and the quadrivium (arithmetic, geometry, music, and astronomy). In a series of reorganizations, the universities have reassigned various disciplines among the faculties of arts and sciences. In some institutions the "reading departments" are considered as professing the arts subjects, the "laboratory departments" as professing the sciences. The adjective "normative" is not relevant to such a division of subjects. Sometimes the fields classified as the humanities are regarded as inseparable from commitments to unscientific value systems. This, too, is quite superficial, if not downright wrong. Studies in linguistics or paleography are not any less value-neutral than studies in acoustics or paleontology.

NORMS, VALUES, RULES, PRECEPTS, ADVICE, PERSUASION, AND COMMAND

Be it tedious repetition or proper reinforcement, it may be helpful to sort out, once again, the set of nouns that are related and yet differentiated in meaning: norms, values, rules, precepts, advice, persuasion, and command. (We could add many more, such as instruction, directives, recommendations, and guideposts.)

The idea common to all these nouns is that somebody's actions are to be directed: someone is told what to do or what not to do. Certain differences in connotation are not generally recognized in common parlance, and not always even in learned language analysis. Of course, the differences between advice, persuasion, and command are patent, but the difference between precepts and advice or the differences between norms, rules, and precepts are not.

Perhaps we can agree on the difference between the general or typical and the specific or concrete. Advice, persuasion, and command may refer to both, to typical as well as concrete situations (concrete as to time, space, and persons involved). Norms, values, rules, and precepts are always general, and their application in concrete cases is left to intelligent interpretation. Norms and values refer to systems of valuation which the acting individual or individuals may recognize as valid (cogent or imposed by sanctions) but may not necessarily accept as their own. (After all, persons frequently act in violation of legal, ethical, or religious norms, and in breach of social etiquette.) Precepts, on the other hand, are general advice, directing voluntary action in the interest of or toward ends desired by the decision-makers. Rules may be norms or precepts; the word has not acquired a special sense linking it to only one or the other. Norms, then, are rules of conduct, self-imposed or imposed by coercion or pressures of various sorts, which relate chiefly, though not exclusively, to social objectives, whereas precepts are rules of suitable conduct for the achievement of ends chosen by the decision-makers themselves.

These semantic explications will have justified our previous terminological decision to reserve the adjective "normative" for references to norms or value judgments, and to use the adjective "instrumental" for references to precepts that direct actions designed to attain explicitly stated objectives. In order to safeguard against misunderstandings, we should add that precepts may be used for individual or group action, and for the attainment of individual or group objectives. Thus, there are precepts for householders, telling them what to look out for in shopping, budgeting, borrowing, and so forth; and there are precepts for legislators, telling them what to look out for in drafting legislation to reduce unemployment, to alleviate poverty, to accelerate growth, and to achieve other national goals. A book of precepts is instrumental and not normative in that it tells what to do *if* certain things are wanted but does not say that these things are beneficial or worth their cost.

THE LOGICAL STATUS OF NORMATIVE STATEMENTS

From the survey of the philosophical literature, it has become apparent that normative statements, or expressions of value judgments, do not enjoy an unequivocal status in logic. They are, depending on which logician pronounces the verdict, empirical propositions, analytical propositions, or no propositions at all. The differences in the verdicts are not entirely due to the differences between logical schools, but are also due in part to semantic differences, since the meaning of "normative statement" is far from unambiguous.

There are several possible ways to show that a (supposedly) normative statement is an empirical proposition. "The policies of the United States between 1963 and 1967 indicate that the avoidance of large unemployment was regarded as more important than the removal of the deficit in foreign

payments." This is a statement about the system of values held or goals desired by the government (the Legislature as well as Administrations);
depending on the acceptance of certain definitional and theoretical relationships, the assertion can be tested and therefore represents an empirical
proposition. However, it may be denied that an assertion about values
held or shared by certain persons or groups is a normative statement.
That "full employment is more important than balance in foreign payments," would be a genuine value judgment. But that "full employment
is held to be more important than balance in foreign payments," or is
"more important to the government" or "to the majority of the people,"
is not a genuine value judgment.

"If a reduction in the payments deficit is desirable, but not at the price
of an increase in unemployment, then the Congress ought not to increase
the income tax." This looks really normative; it even employs the characteristic "ought." Yet, the statement merely asserts that a tax increase will
reduce both employment and the payments deficit. It also draws a correct
inference from an assumption about relative values. It does not try to
persuade anyone to accept this valuation. The opposite assumption might
be made, with the opposite inference, and the statement would make the
same assertion: "If a reduction in the payments deficit is desirable, even
at the price of increased unemployment, then an increase in the income
tax is not ruled out." (In this case, the "ought" cannot legitimately be used,
because it would presuppose, not only a comparison between the values
of reducing the deficit and increasing unemployment, but also a comparative evaluation of all other possible side effects of the tax increase.
The assumption in the "if"-clause has not gone that far.) The point is that
the (indirectly) asserted relationship between tax increase and payments
deficit makes the proposition empirical.

"The American people will resent an increase in unemployment and will
not regard it as a fair price to pay for a reduction in the deficit." If we
can agree on operational definitions for the feelings predicted in this
statement (take, for example, certain replies in an opinion poll), the
assertion is conceivably testable and the proposition can be characterized
as an empirical one. Thus, it may be denied that a value judgment was
expressed. A statement about people's reactions, even if these reactions
express their evaluations, is not regarded as normative by most logicians,
and surely not by radical empiricists. Indeed, when they speak of the
"science of ethics," what they have in mind is an empirical study of
observed or observable behavior in reaction to particular events.

That value judgments can be regarded as analytical propositions means
that they can be derived by logical inference from stated assumptions—
for example, from a convention or resolution about a definite system of
values. Given this convention with all its "axiological rules," to use Felix

Kaufmann's phrase, one can deduce whether 3 per cent unemployment with a payments deficit of two billion dollars is better or worse than 4 per cent unemployment with a deficit of only one billion dollars, all other things being equal. The value judgment is true "in terms of given axiological rules" if it was correctly deduced from the axiological system. The trouble with this position, in my opinion, is that there are an infinite number of such value systems, and we have no criteria for choosing among them in selecting the most appropriate "convention."

According to logical positivists, value judgments are no propositions at all. The sentences in which these judgments are expressed "say nothing." A sentence stating that "a reduction of the payments deficit from two billion dollars to one billion dollars is worth an increase in unemployment from 3 to 4 per cent" asserts nothing that can be true or false and, hence, is "meaningless," according to logical positivists. I submit that this formulation of the verdict against normative statements is unduly harsh. The condemned sentence makes perfectly good sense to me, and probably to many others, even if I readily admit that what it expresses cannot be proved or disproved. In order to show the difference between "meaningless" and "nontestable," I propose that we compare the sense of the indicted and condemned statement with that of the following: "A reduction of the deficit is greenish pink and much more erudite and farther east than an increase in unemployment." Even this sentence may make sense if there is a secret code to decipher those words that destroy the sense if they are given their ordinary meanings.

The assertion that a sentence expressing a nontestable judgment is meaningless cannot be tested either, and would therefore be meaningless itself by the standard it proposes. Speaking in a more reasonable language, I find the finding of "meaninglessness" against value judgments presumptuous and overdone. It suffices to say that pure value judgments cannot be tested by empirical procedures and therefore cannot be admitted into the body of positive science.

"POSITIVE" VERSUS "NONOBSERVABLE"

By giving the floor to logical positivists in the discussion of the logical status of "normative," we have unwittingly changed the meaning of "positive": From being the opposite of "normative" it has moved—because the normative is nonobservable and nontestable—to being the opposite of "nonobservable."

The logical positivist or radical empiricist will not recognize that there is a change of meaning involved: Normative equals metaphysical equals nonobservable equals nontestable equals meaningless. For me, these are

POSITIVE AND NORMATIVE ECONOMICS

quite different qualities and, hence, their opposites are different too. I
have many witnesses testifying in support of my position. Let me recall
a statement of Schumpeter's complaining about these qualifications;[6] the
pronouncements of John Neville Keynes, originator of the expression
"positive economics"; the comments of Milton Friedman in his essay on
the subject; and the remarks of Tjalling Koopmans in his methodological
discourses; to mention only a few. For none of these authors is positive
economics confined to propositions that are based solely on observable
premises and that assert nothing but observable relationships. Some if
not all of them would insist on "conceivable testability" as a criterion of
eligibility for positive economics; however, the tests may be indirect,
through rough correspondence of deduced consequences with observed
outcomes, rather than direct, through empirical confirmation of all assumptions, including the fundamental hypotheses.

Rather than expatiate on this issue, I may refer to several earlier statements of mine in which I have attempted to show that propositions in positive economics may—nay, must—be conceived in terms of purely mental
constructs, some of which do not even have operational counterparts.[7]
Thus, the "positive" in positive economics is definitely not the equivalent
of "observable."

"POSITIVE" VERSUS "NONTESTABLE"

I may repeat that many, perhaps most, economists nowadays insist on
conceivable testability of the propositions of positive economics, although
some are satisfied with indirect tests, applied to the conclusions, and do
not require direct tests of the premises.[8]

However, the insistence on empirical testing (as against merely logical
demonstration) is not implied in the designation "positive" economics.
The designation is given only to separate this body of knowledge from

---

[6] "The word 'positive' as used in this connection has nothing whatever to do with
philosophical positivism. This is the first of many warnings . . . against the dangers
of confusion that arises from the use, for entirely different things, of the same word
by writers who themselves sometimes confuse the things" [J. A. Schumpeter, *History
of Economic Analysis*, ed. E. B. Schumpeter (New York: Oxford University Press,
Inc., 1954), p. 8n].

[7] Fritz Machlup, "Operational Concepts and Mental Constructs in Model and
Theory Formation," *Giornale degli Economisti*, XIX (*Nuova Serie*) (1960), 553–582;
"Operationalism and Pure Theory in Economics," in *The Structure of Economic Science*, ed. Sherman Roy Krupp (Englewood Cliffs, N. J.: Prentice-Hall, Inc., 1966),
pp. 53–67; and "Idealtypus, Wirklichkeit und Konstruktion," *Ordo*, XII (1961), 21–57.

[8] In addition to the articles cited in the preceding footnote, see Fritz Machlup,
"The Problem of Verification in Economics," *The Southern Economic Journal*, XXII
(1955), 1–21; and "Rejoinder to a Reluctant Ultra-Empiricist," *The Southern Economic Journal*, XXII (1956), 483–493.

normative and perhaps also from practical or instrumental economics. In other words, the "positive" in positive economics is not meant to be synonymous with "testable."

THE ECONOMIST'S CONCERN WITH VALUES

It now seems well established that the "positive" in positive economics means nonnormative, nonevaluative. Moreover, the meaning of "normative," though perhaps not sufficiently cleanly defined, seems fairly well circumscribed. There is little danger, therefore, that a knowledgeable economist will confuse "value references," many of which he cannot avoid in his studies and reports, with "value judgments" incompatible with his value-neutrality and scientific objectivity. Noneconomists, however, including philosophers discussing the problem of "values" in scientific activity, may easily fall into error. Indeed, we could cite a good many confused dicta of philosophers of science reflecting on the supposed difficulties of purging the social sciences of nonscientific evaluations.

It may, therefore, be in order to examine the many kinds of values and value references with which the economist may have to concern himself. We must find out which ones, if any, are likely to lead him into making normative statements or expressing value judgments inadmissible in positive economics.

My list—may I be forgiven for my irrepressible propensity to produce lists?—has twelve items, referring to valuations by the economist, by those who produce the events he analyzes, by those for whom he makes his analyses, or by those whom he wishes to influence. More specifically, the values of possible concern to the economist are those of individuals as micro-economic decision-makers and micro-political decision-makers (items 1 and 2); of social groups or society as a whole (items 3 and 4); of the government (item 5); of the clients to whom the economist reports (item 6); of the symbolic clients whose "welfare function" he assumes as given (item 7); of his own values in his capacity as analyst (items 8–10); and of his own values in his capacity as adviser and persuader (items 11 and 12). Here is the list:

1. Values (estimates of utility, tastes, preferences) which the individuals, in the economist's models, are assumed to have and by which they are assumed to be guided as micro-economic decision-makers (household and business managers) in reaction to changes in their opportunities.
2. Values which individuals, acting alone or in groups, may reveal as micro-political decision-makers in voting for advocates of certain programs and for changes of constitutional provisions, in writing to

POSITIVE AND NORMATIVE ECONOMICS

newspapers and legislators, in lobbying, haranguing, demonstrating, or revolting.

3. Values which social groups or society as a whole, represented by writers, speakers, and preachers, leaders in schools, clubs, associations, parties, or communities, or any influential or vocal group, may express and by which the values of individuals as micro-economic decision-makers are shaped or influenced.

4. Values which society, as either anonymous group or political institution, expresses in the form of legal norms, ethical codes, or moral suasion and which operate as constraints on, or even prohibitions or suspensions of, individual preference systems and micro-economic decisions.

5. Values which guide the government (legislators and administrators) in its decisions affecting micro-economic decision-makers by changing through coercive measures or incentives the opportunities open to them.

6. Values of the economist's clients (business firms, trade or labor organizations, government agencies) which he takes as the basis for his analysis, leading to his recommendations of optimal policies to attain their objectives.

7. Values of the economist's symbolic client—the local community, nation, or world community—which he assumes to be given in the form of a "social welfare" function as a basis for his unsolicited policy recommendations designed to serve the public interest thus defined.

8. Values of the economist as analyst which influence him in the choice of his research projects, of the problems to be analyzed, and of the hypotheses to be entertained and examined.

9. Values of the economist as analyst which influence him in the choice of his research techniques and analytical procedures, in the weights he attaches to various types of evidence, in the elegance of his logical demonstrations, and in his eagerness to subject his findings to suitable empirical tests.

10. Values of the economist as analyst which influence him in the choice of his terminology and in the acceptance of available statistical data for purposes of measurement of magnitudes taken as operational counterparts of his theoretical constructs (such as national product at market prices, with the given distribution of income).

11. Values of the economist as adviser or persuader which influence him in substituting his own value judgments, chiefly those of the supposed interest of society, for those of his actual or symbolic clients, but without deliberate falsification of his data or conscious bias in his findings.

12. Values of the economist as adviser or persuader which influence him to use inappropriate or fabricated data, employ improper methods of calculation, and give false evidence, either in an attempt to secure material advantages for his clients and himself or, alternatively, in the hope of persuading people or governments to take political action in the supposed interest of society.

While the verdict is absolutely clear regarding the last item, we must ask which of the other values or value-concerns might contaminate the economist's product and violate his value-neutrality.

THE ECONOMIST'S SCIENTIFIC OBJECTIVITY

We need not feel nervous regarding the first five items. These values, either assumed or revealed through actual conduct, are part of the subject matter with which economists deal: they are data needed for the analysis of various kinds of problems.

Item 1, the values of household and business managers, which influence their decisions to buy, sell, hire, lend, borrow, and so forth, are "given" to the analyst, who employs models of decision-making and of supply and demand to explain changes in prices and quantities of goods and services. When the economist speaks of subjective-value theory, it is not his theory which is subjective. He deals objectively with the subjective values of the economic decision-makers whose actions or reactions produce observable changes which the economist has to explain. Whether the subjective values, the preferences of the acting decision-units, are (behaviorally) revealed or merely (postulationally) assumed is a question which may concern the radical empiricist (logical positivist), not because of any suspicion of a transgression into the normative domain, but only because of the nonempirical nature of merely assumed values.

Item 2 enters only rarely into economic analysis. It may become relevant in analyses of policy measures or of events likely to incite political reactions. The analysis of problems in which political reactions play a significant role can be perfectly objective, absolutely neutral with regard to the values behind the observed or predicted reactions.

Item 3 is important chiefly in problems with strong infusions of sociological elements, such as the effects of advertising, patriotic or educational campaigns, or changes in fashion or other habits (alcohol, smoking, drugs), to mention only a few social (moral) influences on people's preferences. Valuations that change valuations are subjects of study, and have in fact been studied, without inviting deviations from value-neutrality.

Item 4 hardly needs explanation. To give only one example, the effects of legal or ethical prohibitions upon decisions regarding production, employment, supply, and demand can be analyzed without any normative (evaluative) undertones or overtones.

Item 5 is quite similar. The "official" valuations which, for example, cause the U. S. Government to impose a tax on the purchase of foreign securities but exempt securities issued by less developed countries or by Canada and Japan are data which the analyst can accept and take into account without being deflected from his scientific objectivity.

Item 6 brings us closer to the danger zone, for we are now looking at an economist working on policy recommendations for government, special-interest organizations, business firms, or other clients. Of course, such recommendations cannot help being value-directed. Yet, if the values are not too complex and can be stated in the form of specific objectives, like the tasks assigned to an engineer, chemist, or physician, then the economist's analysis is not basically different from straight causal reasoning. Instead of inquiring for the effects of some action or measure, he has to inquire what actions or measures would cause the effect desired by the client. This procedure, which, following Adolph Lowe, we have called instrumental analysis, does not involve the analyst's value judgments and is not normative in character.

Item 7 is quite problematic, for in this case the "client"—a symbolic client—does not specify his objectives or value-function. The economist arrogates to himself the role of judge of what constitutes the public interest. To be sure, he has many clues that tell him that the community likes a larger income, more employment, faster growth, more equality of income and wealth, better schools, cleaner air and water, better roads, bigger parks, better fishing, and more freedom. If he had only one objective to worry about, he could do his instrumental analysis and maintain his innocent value-neutrality. But with a multitude of social objectives and no specification of an indifference map that would give him the community's marginal rates of substitution between competing goals, "objective" instrumental analysis is impossible. We conclude that this kind of economic analysis—welfare economics—is normative. But let us take this as a rebuttable conclusion, to be reconsidered in the next section.

Item 8 presents no problems to us, though only because the problems involved were authoritatively treated and definitely resolved by Max Weber sixty years ago. Since not every writer has studied and understood Weber's arguments, there have been occasional recurrences of suspicion. Myrdal, for example, thought he could reopen the case and renew the charges that the values which influence a scholar to become interested in a certain topic and particular problem, and to formulate his first hypotheses, would inevitably produce a bias in his analysis. These charges cannot be sustained unless the entire notion of scientific objectivity in any area of inquiry is to be discarded. For the same situation exists in all sciences, the physical and biological included. There is necessarily a valuation behind the choice of topic and problem, and a preconception behind the choice of preliminary hypotheses. But this does not imply anything concerning a lack of scientific objectivity in the analysis itself, in any of the sciences—physical, biological, or social.[9]

Item 9 is analogous to item 8. No scientist can help being influenced by his valuations of alternative methods of research and analysis. In many instances strong preferences for particular techniques, usually developed in the investigator's earlier training, may have a role even in his choice of problems to be researched. No doubt these values on the part of the analyst exist and may effectively influence the choice of his rules of procedure. To admit this, however, is not to admit any insincerity in his endeavor to reach correct solutions. To be sure, some of the favored techniques may hinder or prevent him from getting "true" findings, but this does not imply violation of his value-neutrality with respect to the results of his inquiries.[10]

Item 10 presents more difficult problems, chiefly because an economist's value judgments regarding choice of terminology and acceptance of available statistical data sometimes prevail over the analyst's zeal to obtain and report unbiased findings. The use of value-loaded language is perhaps less treacherous than the use of value-blended statistics, because any design to persuade with emotive or prejudicious words is more easily detected than an attempt to lie with statistics. However, the situation is not quite as serious as it may appear from these comments. The persuasive or emotive effects of value-loaded words may wear off with time or may be removed by proper cautions. And the use of value-blended statistical data may be disclosed or exposed by critical notes. (I am not referring here, incidentally, to fabricated data or to deliberately improper uses of data, both of which belong to item 12. The statistics referred to here as value-blended cannot be cleansed of their value contents. For example, any assemblage of goods, such as the national product, can be measured only in terms of prices or values; whether one uses current market prices, officially fixed prices, prices of some base period, hypothetical prices that would result with a different distribution of income, labor-cost prices, or another standard, some prices have to be used, and the decision may be influenced by value judgments concerning the "right" system.) [11] We

---

9 Professor Ludwig von Mises used to tell his students about the value judgment that induced chemists and biologists to do research on insecticides. The researchers' interest in these problems stemmed from an obvious bias: they were not impartial in siding with man and against the bugs. But this did not vitiate the scientific character of their endeavor. In the social sciences, research on means to preserve peace is guided by a preference for peace and a clear bias against war. Does this vitiate the research—apart from possible wishful thinking by some of the researchers?

10 For a good discussion of items 8 and 9, see T. W. Hutchison, *"Positive" Economics and Policy Objectives* (London: George Allen & Unwin, 1964), Chap. 2.

11 See Fritz Machlup, *The Political Economy of Monopoly* (Baltimore, Md.: The Johns Hopkins Press, 1952), pp. 459–461.

may conclude that transgressions into normative territory are possible on these counts, but that the implied threats to scientific objectivity are not serious enough to make even the purist fret and squirm.

Item 11 is closely related to item 7 in that the economic adviser (or pleader) often is not given sufficiently full specifications of the objectives to be attained and has to fill in with his own value judgments where the specifications leave blanks. The resulting bias may be, and usually is, unconscious, since most people innocently believe that they know what is wanted, either by their clients or by the community. The normative character of this sort of advice will be examined more closely in the next section.

Item 12 presents the most obvious instance of valuations leading to conscious bias and even deliberate fraud. To speak here only of a lack of scientific objectivity is unduly charitable. But let no one think that economists, or social scientists in general, have a monopoly on cheating. Hoaxes, fraud, biased testimonies, and cases of false evidence occur in all fields: in the physical and biological sciences, the engineering sciences, and even the humanities. I have supplied examples elsewhere.[12]

ADJUDICATING CHARGES OF BIAS

The point-by-point treatment of types of valuation calls for a brief summary, preceded by a restatement of the essential issue.

The issue is not whether value judgments *may* intrude into the economist's analyses and reports, or if they *may* impart a bias to his work, destroying his scientific objectivity. There is no question that this may happen and does happen. The real question is whether this is in the nature of all economic analysis or, perhaps, of certain kinds of economic analysis, and if it is therefore *unavoidable* in either all or some kinds of economic analysis.

The values or value-concerns enumerated in items 1–5 are quite irrelevant to the issue. While concern with valuations of this sort distinguishes the social sciences from the natural sciences, none of these value-concerns has any bearing on the issue of value-neutrality and bias.

The values described in item 6, the stated objectives assigned to the economist as an "engineer" in instrumental analysis, present no danger to his scientific objectivity in his work. He is given the task of solving certain problems and of reporting to his clients how they can get what they want.

---

12 Fritz Machlup, "Are the Social Sciences Really Inferior?" *The Southern Economic Journal*, XXVII (1961), 175–176. Reprinted in *Philosophy of the Social Sciences: A Reader*, ed. Maurice Nathanson (New York: Random House, Inc., 1963), pp. 163–164.

Whether he himself approves of their objectives or dislikes them may affect his work, but need not. Ethical conflicts may arise if he has qualms about the social desirability of his clients' or employers' objectives. I can even imagine some zealot supplying wrong answers in an attempt to thwart their "evil" designs. In such cases, however, it is the substitution of his own value judgments for those of his clients or employers that changes the character of his work, transforming it from instrumental into normative.

Almost the same problem arises in cases of incomplete specification of the objectives sought by the advisees—cases under item 11. The economic adviser, not having been given exact and complete instructions about the advisees' valuations of side effects, alternative means, and conflicting goals, has to use his own judgment. In this case, his value judgments are not substituted for those of his clients, but supplement them in more or less essential ways. Where he can do it in an explicit and unambiguous manner, he merely writes the missing part of the specifications of his assignment. If so, no harm is done to the scientific objectivity of his work. Often, however, the value system that supplements the simple set of objectives furnished by the clients or advisees is too complex to be unambiguously specified. In this case, the economist's analysis and report cannot help being colored by his hidden valuations and, thus, are no longer scientifically objective.

The suspicions and charges relating to items 8 and 9—concerning the choice of problem and preliminary hypotheses—were dismissed. Adjudicated long ago, they can worry only those who have not done their homework and have skipped the required reading.

Regarding item 10—value-loaded terms and value-blended figures—we merely advise caution on the part of both producers and consumers of economic reports. Where our language provides only value-loaded words and our statistics furnish only value-blended measurements, reports may have persuasive effects, intentional or unintentional. To deny the scientific objectivity of economics on these grounds would be a vast exaggeration.

This leaves the value problem of item 7 as the most sensitive of all. It is the problem of the normative nature of welfare economics, which we have resolved to consider once more.

THE NORMATIVE CHARACTER OF WELFARE ECONOMICS

Where the objectives are fully and unambiguously specified, the analysis of the best ways to attain the objectives is instrumental, not normative. But where there is any deficiency or ambiguity in the specification, the analyst cannot provide answers without (consciously or unconsciously) filling the gaps *ad hoc* according to value judgments he himself entertains at the moment. This is an undertaking that is hardly compatible with scientific objectivity. The findings of what is "better" or "best" for society under the circumstances become a function of the analyst's predilections.

We have to find out just what it means to have a full specification of social objectives. But before we try to answer this question, it will be helpful to show how a specified map of social preferences would be used in an analysis that determines the social optimum or, more modestly, an improvement of the given state of affairs.

If there were only two social goals, a two-dimensional map with in-difference curves would show the acceptable trade-offs between them. The trade-off rates, or marginal rates of acceptable substitution,[13] would of course be very different for different combinations of goal achievement. Assume, for example, that the two goals are "present consumption" and "rate of increase of growth of national product." The acceptable trade-off rates (represented by the slope of the indifference curve) in a range of low consumption and fast growth would be quite different from the acceptable trade-off rates in a range of high consumption and slow growth. Although this should be obvious to the trained economist, it does not tally with his frequent references to a "given hierarchy" of social goals.

The social indifference curves have to be brought together with social possibility curves for the same two goals. The slopes of these curves tell how much of each goal would have to be given up in order to get a little more of the other. In other words, they show the rates of required sacri-fice. Again, these rates will be quite different for different combinations of goal achievement. They can be regarded as marginal rates of potential substitution.

The social possibility curves are opportunity or transformation func-tions, showing the *required* trade-offs between alternative goal achieve-ments—that is, the *cost* of more of one in terms of less of the other. The social indifference curves are preference or welfare functions, showing the *acceptable* trade-offs between alternative goal achievements—that is, the *utility* of more of one in terms of less of the other. The optimum solu-tion would be that combination at which required and acceptable trade-off rates are equal.

To ascertain the required trade-off rates is one of the most important tasks of the economist. To pretend knowledge of the acceptable trade-off rates between social goals is the heroic assumption of welfare economics. Even for only two social goals, the assumption of knowing the acceptable trade-off rates for all possible combinations of goal achievement would

---

13 "Acceptable marginal rates of substitution" may be the preferred expression. I said "marginal rates of acceptable substitution" in order to indicate that all points on such a curve are equally acceptable, and that movement along such a curve repre-sents an "acceptable substitution."

be rather extravagant. To assume knowledge of all acceptable trade-off rates among a multitude of social goals for all possible combinations is well-nigh fantastic.

Even if we think only of the most commonplace menu of social goals offered to the voter in political platforms, we must be overwhelmed by the enormity of the task of imagining, let alone ascertaining, the trade-offs acceptable to just one representative citizen. For there are not only the full arrays of rates of employment, consumption, private investment, public expenditures, growth of GNP, foreign aid, income equality, and so forth—to mention only quantifiable goals—but there are also questions of the composition of these aggregate magnitudes. The same rate of employment may be the composite of several different distributions among regions, occupations, age groups, and racial and ethnic groups; the same rate of consumption may be the composite of different distributions among consumer groups (social groups, income groups) and among consumption items (food, housing, automobiles, entertainment, alcohol, tobacco); the same rate of investment may mean very different outlays in different sectors (agriculture, mining, manufacturing, public utilities, transportation); the same rate of public expenditures may comprise substantial variations in the appropriations for different purposes (defense, research, education, health, highways); and analogous illustrations could be given for each of the quantifiable goals.

If we think of the nonquantifiable objectives our agony increases, for there are innumerable combinations among all sorts of psychic income. Most important are the legal and institutional arrangements to increase or reduce various kinds of economic, political, intellectual, and religious freedoms, many of which conflict with one another as well as with other objectives, such as employment, production, investment, equality, etc. There are also activities to increase national prestige, with acceptable trade-offs against the achievement of other objectives.

The usual reflections on welfare economics have concentrated on measurable increases or decreases in total output or income, and on associated changes in the distribution of income. By making ingenious assumptions concerning side payments through which gainers would compensate losers, the relevance of income distribution for the evaluation of particular measures or changes was eliminated, and total income was made the sole determinant of economic welfare.

With a single social objective and a single constraint—increase in aggregate income with no reduction in any individual incomes—the problem of assessing alternative public policies became manageable. But as soon as one recognizes the existence of several partly conflicting objectives, the possibility of a unique solution, even the determination of the direction of change, disappears—unless the value system of one man can be represented as that of the community. That man can only be the economist himself, and the social optimum is then clearly a personal opinion which cannot be proved right or wrong. In addition, this Grand Arbiter of Social Welfare would probably be incapable of specifying his preference functions fully and in advance; many of his findings would be *ad hoc*, for particular occasions, improvised and not predictable.[14]

An illustration may help to make this clear. The Congress of the United States has been working on a new copyright law extending the term of protection to the lifetime of the author plus fifty years. Although it has not occurred to any legislator to ask for an economic appraisal of the effects of this provision, let us assume that an economist is commissioned to advise. He may be able to say something about the probable movement along the possibility function. He may predict that the increase in incentives for publishers and authors will lead to the publication of additional books (including five novels per year, eight mystery stories, six books on sex, and seven new textbooks, two of which will be on elementary economics with poor chapters on welfare economics); that the prices of books, especially those published long ago but still selling in considerable quantities, will go up by 10 per cent; that private consumer spending on books will be only slightly affected, as consumers will buy fewer books with a somewhat larger outlay of money, but that the budgets of public libraries and libraries of educational institutions will have to be increased; that the appropriations to education departments of states and public-school districts will have to be raised because of the higher prices of most textbooks; that these expenditures will be met partly by raising taxes and partly at the expense of other educational outlays, including teachers' salaries; that expenditures for lawyers' fees and court costs will go up because of the increase in litigation of copyright cases; and that the chief redistributive effects will be from book readers, researchers, teachers, and taxpayers to the grandchildren of the authors of the (very few) successful books. Now all this is on the possibility or transformation side of the prediction. What about the evaluation of the changes involved?

The welfare economist will have to decide how much "society" will delight in the publication of the additional titles (including those on sex and economics); how much "society" will resent paying higher taxes; how much it will appreciate the decrease in teachers' salaries and increase in lawyers' incomes; and, especially, how much it will relish the thought that

---

[14] This can also be said of particular decisions on problems of individual households and firms, but with different implications. It means only that their reactions cannot always be correctly predicted and, unless odd decisions cancel out, predictions of reactions of aggregate supply and demand may be less than accurate. The problem is quite different with regard to a single Grand Arbiter of Social Welfare.

some fortunate heirs of authors will receive royalties on the literary products of their late grandfathers or great-aunts.

The use of value-loaded language in the exposition of this piece of applied welfare economics may have revealed the value judgments of the present writer. Whether these judgments agree with those of the majority of the people or of the legislators in Congress is not known, but is quite unlikely. The best that I can say in support of my value judgment is that I presume that most other people would agree with me if, but only if, they thought about the problem hard enough.

The point of my illustration, however, was not that my valuations may be peculiar prejudices not shared by others; what I intended to show was that my value system could not possibly have been specific on the merits or demerits of potential gifts to unknown grandchildren of authors of books that still enjoy sales long after their publication. This spot on my social-welfare function was completely blank until the problem arose and I had to fill in the relevant valuations for the occasion. I could, of course, assert that my appraisal of the legislative action represents a logical inference from my value system and that I can *now* give the necessary specification for others to check my logic. I still doubt that this will meet the objections that the whole procedure is "unscientific."

One more difficulty should be considered: the welfare economist's valuations of future benefits derived from present sacrifices, and of present benefits obtained at the cost of future sacrifices. Some welfare economists are very generous toward future generations and are prepared to give away much of the income of their own contemporaries. Others are quite stingy and resent making sacrifices for the yet unborn great-grandchildren of their friends and fellow taxpayers. ("Why should I do so much for posterity? What has posterity done for me?") Any social indifference map presupposes given sets of rates of time preference (generosity or stinginess *vis-à-vis* future generations), and thus is the result of entirely subjective inclinations.

It may seem that a way out of this and all similar difficulties would be not to specify just one social-value system, but to give the client or advisee (that is, the representatives of society) a large set of alternative systems from which to choose. This is not really practicable, however, simply because there are an infinite number of possible preference systems. It is not feasible to propose a sufficiently large number of alternative value systems to do justice to the existing variety of tastes and preferences. It is not feasible to tell those in the seats of government that they have a choice among millions of different value systems and that, corresponding to each, there may be a different answer to their specific questions. The welfare economist, if he is very conscientious, will at best specify a small sample of alternative welfare functions and, in limiting the open choices in this way, will again have engaged in normative economics.

STAYING PURE VERSUS COMING CLEAN

Having concluded that welfare economics is normative in character, the purists among us may cry, "Unclean! Unclean!" whenever they see a piece of welfare analysis. This would be unfortunate. Even if welfare economics is impure, it is a necessary part of our work.

The recent fashion for "cost-benefit analysis" represents a healthy recognition of the danger of choosing blindly and of the advantages of making choices on the basis of a rational consideration of alternatives. It is true that the considerations include estimates of benefits that rest on more or less arbitrary valuations, but this does not imply that we would be better off if we avoided all "unscientific" estimates and made our decisions without considering what the effects might be and how we would like them.

Honesty demands that we be frank about the evaluative nature of our appraisals and recommendations. But this does not mean that we must write long methodological introductions to each and every policy memorandum. If we did, we would only increase the percentage of memoranda reaching their final destination—the files—without being read by those to whom they were addressed. This would be too bad. A great deal needs to be done to improve the quality of economic policy advice. We can meet the demands of honesty by discussing and justifying the value assumptions made in the analysis and, even better, by showing how the findings would be affected if we varied the value assumptions. As a rule, we probably will indicate which value position we regard as the most "reasonable." Most of us will do this in a rather unmistakable way, since we are usually convinced that our own ethical values are more ethical than others.

SOME THOUGHTS ON LOWE'S INSTRUMENTALISM

Now that I am through with the analytical semantics of the terms and the methodological analysis of the issues involved, I may take up Dr. Lowe's commitment to instrumentalism and examine it in the light of my findings.

In order to guard against misunderstandings, it may be well to say that Dr. Lowe's instrumentalism is neither identical with nor closely related to John Dewey's philosophical position by the same name, which is usually regarded as a species of pragmatism. Nor is Dr. Lowe's instrumentalism related to that of Adolf Lampe, the late economist of the

University of Freiburg, who thought of it as advocacy of an economic system that would evolve as a compromise between liberalism, the economic system steered by free-market prices, and socialism, the centrally directed economy. Dr. Lowe's instrumentalism is meant to be a type of analysis, differentiated from both positive and normative analyses.

The trichotomy—positive, normative, instrumental—follows the proposal of John Neville Keynes, except that Keynes used "practical," not "instrumental," to denote the third type of economics. For Keynes, moreover, the third type was firmly based on the results of positive and normative economics. Dr. Lowe, on the other hand, views instrumental analysis as independent of positive analysis, which he distrusts as inapplicable to the industrial economies of our time, and independent also of normative analysis, which he regards as meta-scientific.

THE INSTRUMENTAL INFERENCES

The scheme of things in the framework of Dr. Lowe's analytical setup, in a form in which the knowns are stated as premises and the unknowns as questions, looks like this:

1. If you are in macro-state A (the "initial" state), and
2. If you want to *move* to macro-state Z (the "macro-goal"), and
3. If L, R, and G are general laws, rules, and empirical generalizations, respectively,

then

1. What *path* is suitable to that movement?
2. What *patterns of micro-behavior* are appropriate to keep the system on that path?
3. What *micro-motivations* are capable of generating suitable behavior?
4. What political *control* can be designed to stimulate suitable motivations?

Most economists, unacquainted with Dr. Lowe's work, would see in this arrangement of premises and questions nothing that is different from their own procedures in applied economics. The second premise, stating the macro-goal, is evidently the result of normative economics, and the third premise comprises the results of positive economics—the general laws, the institutional rules and constraints, and the empirical generalizations. This, however, is not what Dr. Lowe has in mind. Although he admits that macro-goals are "the results of normative judgment,"[15] he does not tell us how such judgments are justified, which would be norma-

---

[15] See pp. 18, 24.

tive economics. And the third premise, according to Dr. Lowe, does not state the results of positive economics but only those of natural sciences, engineering, and psychology. For in Dr. Lowe's framework, my notation L stands for "laws of nature," R represents "engineering rules," and G stands for empirical generalizations "concerning sociopsychological relations." [16] Thus, Dr. Lowe's instrumental analysis, as he sees it, is not based on either normative or positive economics. He holds that "only after reality has been transformed through such [Control] action" (namely, "measures of public Control suitable to bring about that conformance" of structural, behavioral, and motivational conditions which assure goal attainment) "can the instrumental inferences serve as major premises in a deductive syllogism." [17]

I submit that these contentions cannot be sustained. As soon as there are several goals and several paths toward their attainment, instrumental analysis needs normative economics, because the choices among the alternative paths and the many possible combinations of goal attainments cannot be made without complex systems of values (preferences) which cannot be assumed as objective data given to the instrumentalist. Likewise, the questions regarding the "suitable" path toward goal attainment, the "appropriate" patterns of micro-behavior, the micro-motivations "capable" of generating the required behavior patterns, and the political controls designed to stimulate the right motivations cannot be answered except on the basis of full knowledge of theoretical laws, institutional rules, and empirical generalizations about economic relations—that is, on the basis of positive economics.

THE NEED FOR POSITIVE AND NORMATIVE ANALYSES

Judgments about what is suitable, adequate, capable, and so forth, imply predictability, which in turn presupposes either law statements (positive theory) or firmly established correlations (significant regression coefficients). It is logically impossible to infer the suitable instruments from the "given" goals if there exists no reliable positive knowledge of the type, "If A, then B," which is the type commonly found in positive economics. (This says nothing about the way such knowledge was acquired. More often than not it may have been by way of a search for the unknown cause, A, of an observed effect, B. But this need not be "instrumental analysis.")

The inevitability of normative economics within (and not only before)

---

[16] *OEK*, p. 143.
[17] *OEK*, p. 311.

instrumental analysis is a consequence of the impossibility of knowing in advance the choices that have to be made among alternative paths, alternative behavior patterns, alternative control measures. It is not just a matter of postponing decisions until we have to "cross the bridge"; it is rather complete ignorance of what bridges there may be to cross. The instrumentalist—the political economist—cannot possibly know what benefits and sacrifices may have to be compared, what compromises to be made, and therefore what values to be applied to the choices among alternative "instruments." Hence, he does not arrive at the many bridges with a ready-made evaluation kit or social-preference map for guidance in the necessary choices. The relevant preferences will have to be mapped out and justified *ad hoc* at every one of the indefinite number of questions whose existence is unknown to the chooser of the best or second-best instruments.

One may ask whether there really are quite that many alternatives to choose from for one's policy recommendations. Things would be easy if there were only one path to the desired macro-state (or even none), or perhaps only two or three, with foreseeable cost-and-benefit comparisons for which all the needed value data can be read off the prepared preference map. Such simplicity cannot be expected; I have always been able to think of countless alternatives in any problem of economic policy with which I have been concerned. For example, when the removal or reduction of the U. S. payments deficit was "given" as a very urgent macro-goal, I enumerated forty-one different types of measures capable of steering behavior along suitable paths—with an indefinite number of variations in degree of application and of possible combinations—each of them restricting to some extent the attainment of other macro-goals. And I doubt that any two of the consultants had the same comparative evaluations of the benefits that would be secured or sacrificed by the alternative courses of action. In other words, justification of values—normative economics—is part and parcel of the job of the policy adviser, the man engaged in instrumental economics.

THE CRITICAL BOUNDARY

The reader, or *this* reader at least, repeatedly frightened out of his wits by all the talk of goal-choosing and control-imposing by the authorities, is finally reassured: Dr. Lowe has us "restrict the choice of our substantive goals to such states and processes as can be brought into agreement with the strivings of the large majority of micro-units." [18]

---

[18] *OEK,* p. 318.

He explains this by accepting the old liberal tenet that "micro-autonomy is vindicated if it is suitable to promote political freedom, and if such freedom takes precedence over any conceivable principle according to which production and distribution can be organized." [19] However, "it is the *well-understood interest* of the micro-units that must agree with the macro-goal, rather than their crude strivings. To enlighten the individual marketer about his true interests by reducing expectational uncertainty and by suitably patterning action directives is the very function of manipulative controls." [20]

We are now definitely in normative territory. Alas, "however hard we may try to avoid choices based on value judgments pure and simple, we cannot run away from an ultimate decision as to the relative significance of the economic and the political sphere or as to the ranking of rivalling political goals." [21] Dr. Lowe justifies the invasion of normative territory by granting that "liberty . . . must be adopted as a 'provisional value' if those among us who believe in absolute values are to be allowed to continue fighting for them." [22]

Dr. Lowe thinks he crossed the boundary into normative or evaluative economics only when he granted priority to political freedom over some "economic" goal or goals. This may strike us as rather strange, since he has again and again allowed some chosen macro-goal to overrule and restrain the wishes of the "micro-units." Perhaps he relies on the widely held thesis that goals and values are subjects of value judgments only when they are compared with other goals and values or when they remain concealed, but are admitted as legitimate data in positive analysis as long as they are clearly stated and are examined only in relation to the means suitable for their attainment.

The trouble with this view is that not only the choice among alternative techniques of control but also the unquestionable "plurality of macro-goals" will always force us to engage in value judgments. The preference scales (or indifference maps) of macro-goals in the value systems of the

---

[19] *OEK*, p. 319.

[20] *OEK*, p. 320.

[21] *OEK*, p. 320.

[22] *OEK*, p. 322. I cannot help setting Dr. Lowe's view in juxtaposition to a statement made by Frank H. Knight, many years before Lowe's plea for instrumental economics: "In the field of social policy, the pernicious notion of instrumentalism . . . is actually one of the most serious of the sources of danger which threaten destruction to the values of what we have called civilization. Any such conception as social engineering or social technology has meaning only in relation to the activities of a super-dictatorship, a government which would own as well as rule society at large, and would use it for the purposes of the governors" [Frank H. Knight, "Fact and Value in Social Science," in *Science and Man*, ed. Ruth Anshen (New York: Harcourt, Brace & World, Inc., 1942); reprinted in Frank H. Knight, *Freedom and Reform* (New York: Harper & Row, Publishers, 1947), pp. 225–226].

Goal Selectors cannot be identical and cannot be fully specified. The elasticities of substitution among additional tenths of per cents of unemployment, total output, total consumption, growth, and all the rest, are too complex and too unstable to be admissible as a "given" assumption of a supposedly scientific "instrumental analysis."

At several points Dr. Lowe tries to escape the normative task of instrumental analysis by making "the implicit assumption that the different aspirations of a goal-setter are mutually compatible and can be translated into a consistent and realizable set of targets." [23] The assumption of a given "hierarchy of goals," where some goals may become means for other goals but where "the precise nature of these interrelations poses a genuinely scientific problem unencumbered by any value judgment or norm," [24] serves the same purpose. But these assumptions are legitimate only as part of a logical demonstration designed to show (1) under what conditions instrumental analysis *would* be nonevaluative, and (2) that these conditions are contrary to fact. Dr. Lowe's hope that the tasks of goal-setting and policy-choosing can be separated and that those engaged in instrumental analysis need not as a rule—except where possible infringements of political freedom are involved—cross over the "critical boundary" [25] into the territory of normative analysis is, in my opinion, not justified.

However, I am neither apprehensive nor critical in any way of such crossings of the border between the Domain of the True or False and the Domain of the Good or Bad. I would do away with all prohibitions, customs duties, and passport requirements between the domains. Of course, I would want all imported or produced values to be declared rather than concealed. But, and this is my point in this context, I do not believe that an honest declaration at the frontier of instrumental analysis would be at all possible or helpful. The customs officer may ask the traveler—the peripatetic political economist—the usual question: "Have you anything to declare? Have you any values or norms in your bag?" And the traveler may declare all the values and norms he is aware of having brought with him; however, he cannot declare those values that he will work out or develop only long after settling down, when he finds that he has to make choices for which none of the evaluations that he has ever thought about are relevant.

---

[23] See p. 19.
[24] *OEK*, p. 316.
[25] *OEK*, p. 321.

Part III
The Scope and Boundary of Economics

A
Framing the Issues – The Economist as Imperialist

[10]

The Expanding Domain of Economics

By Jack Hirshleifer*

Definitions of economics are legion. Two familiar ones will be particularly appropriate for my purposes:

> . . .ECONOMICS is a study of mankind in the ordinary business of life; it examines that part of individual and social action which is most closely connected with the attainment and with the use of the material requisites of wellbeing.
> — Alfred Marshall [1920, p. 1]

> Economics is the science which studies human behavior as a relationship between ends and scarce means that have alternative uses.
> — Lionel Robbins [1962, p. 16]

As to Marshall, how terribly narrow, dull, bourgeois! Must we economists limit our attention to the ordinary, the crassly material business of life? While equally prosaic, Robbins' "relationship between ends and scarce means" does open the door wider. After all, the ends that men and women seek include not just bread and butter but also reputation, adventure, sex, status, eternal salvation, the meaning of life, and a good night's sleep — the means for achieving any of these being, too often, notably scarce.

In dealing with economics as an expansive imperialist discipline (see Gerard Radnitzky and Peter Bernholz [1985]), a geopolitical metaphor may be illuminating. Our heartland is an intellectual territory carved off by two narrowing conceptions: (1) of *man* as rational, self-interested decisionmaker, and (2) of *social interaction* as typified by market exchange. However, the logic of ideas irresistibly draws economists beyond these core areas. Rational self-interested choice plays a role in many domains of life other than markets, for example in politics, warfare, mate selection, engineering design, and statistical decisions. Conversely, even within the domain of market behavior, economists can hardly deny that what people want to buy and sell is influenced by cultural, ethical, and even "irrational" forces more customarily studied by social psychologists and anthropologists. And how people go about their dealings in the market touches upon issues also involving law and sociology.

Responding to these intellectual attractions, the rhetoric of an economic imperialist like Gary S. Becker is notably more muscular:

> The combined assumptions of maximizing behavior, market equilibrium, and stable preferences, used relentlessly and unflinchingly, form the heart of the economic approach. . .
> [1976a, p. 4]

*University of California, Los Angeles.

It is this approach that has powered the imperialist expansion of economics into the traditional domains of sociology, political science, anthropology, law, and social biology — with more to come.

Space constraints rule out any attempt to review here the detailed intellectual histories of these various imperialist invasions, or to assess their overall success or failure. I will have to omit, apart possibly from occasional remarks, a vast array of important and exciting subjects such as: the substantivist vs. formalist controversy in anthropology; in political science the design of optimal constitutions, the stability of voting equilibria, and the balance of power among pressure groups; crime and its deterrence in sociology and law; and a host of interdisciplinary topics like optimal foraging, the division of labor by sex or age or caste, and patterns of fertility and marriage.[1] Instead, I shall reverse the emphasis to concentrate upon a necessarily idiosyncratic selection of lessons that these imperialist forays have for economists about the validity of our image of economic man and about the relative roles of market vs. non-market interactions.

I will emphasize two central themes. First, that it is ultimately impossible to carve off a distinct territory for economics, bordering upon but separated from other social disciplines. Economics interpenetrates them all, and is reciprocally penetrated by them.[2] *There is only one social science.* What gives economics its imperialist invasive power is that our analytical categories — scarcity, cost, preferences, opportunities, etc. — are truly universal in applicability. Even more important is our structured organization of these concepts into the distinct yet intertwined processes of optimization on the individual decision level and equilibrium on the social level of analysis. Thus economics really does constitute the universal grammar of social science. But there is a flip side to this. While scientific work in anthropology and sociology and political science and the like will become increasingly indistinguishable from economics, economists will reciprocally have to become aware of how constraining has been their tunnel vision about the nature of man and social interactions. Ultimately, good economics will also have to be good anthropology and sociology and political science and psychology.

[1] A few selected references (the products of economic imperialists, or else "native" writings with an explicit or implicit economic orientation) are: on the substantivist vs. formalist controversy, Richard Posner [1980, pp. 2-3]; on optimal constitutions, James M. Buchanan and Gordon Tullock [1962, Ch. 6], on majority-voting equilibrium Dennis C. Mueller [1979], and on pressure-group equilibrium, Gary S. Becker [1983]; on optimal foraging, Eric L. Charnov [1976] and Eric Alden Smith [1983]; on the division of labor in insect societies, E.O. Wilson [1978b]; on monogamous vs. polygamous marriage, Wilson [1975, pp. 327-331] and Amyra Grossbard [1980].
[2] Thus I cannot agree that the other social sciences are, in any useful sense, "contiguous" to economics as contended by Ronald H. Coase [1978].

53

54　　　　　　　　　　THE AMERICAN ECONOMIC REVIEW　　　　　　　　　DECEMBER 1985

The second underlying theme was succinctly expressed by Marshall:

> But economics has no near kinship with any physical science. . .It is a branch of biology broadly interpreted. [1920, p. 772]

That economics is an aspect of a broader biological "economy of nature" would not have seemed strange to Adam Smith who, in the *Moral Sentiments,* sounded a near-Darwinian note:

> The economy of nature is in this respect exactly of a piece with what it is upon many other occasions. . . . Thus self-preservation, and the propagation of the species, are the great ends which nature seems to have proposed the formation of all animals. Mankind are endowed with a desire of those ends, and an aversion to the contrary.
> [1976 (1759), p. 152]

It is no new idea that the social sciences (including economics) must rest to some degree upon the biological constitution of the human species. But there is a sense in which, I will argue, economics and biology are uniquely intertwined.

I. Economic Man

Economic man is characterized by *self-interested goals* and *rational choice of means.* On both scores, this image of the human animal has been the object of grumbles. After all, men and women do sometimes seek the welfare of others, and they are sometimes led astray by thoughtlessness and confusion. How should our profession respond to these complaints? (1) A kind of answer, one with which I have little patience, is to use a verbal trick so as to redefine all goals as self-interested, and all choice of means as rational. (2) More defensibly, our profession might adopt a self-denying ordinance, setting aside non-self-interested goals and non-rational choice of means as "non-economic." Economists could then modestly claim that the hypothesis of rational self-interested man, though admittedly inaccurate, has proved to have great explanatory power *in the areas where we apply it.*

There is always something to be said for modesty. But the scientific enterprise demands more. When the phenomenon of radioactive decay refuted the principle of conservation of mass, it would have been modest but unproductive for physicists to decide henceforth to limit their investigations to those processes for which mass was indeed conserved. And similarly, if the hypothesis of economic man fails in any field of application, the correct scientific response is not modest retreat but an aggressive attempt to produce a better theory.

The history of imperialist economics illustrates that the model of economic man has indeed been productive, but only up to a point. Each of our expansionist invasions has typically encountered an initial phase of easy successes, where postulating rational self-interested behavior in a new field of application has yielded sudden sharp results. In the field of politics it was like a breath of fresh air when Anthony Downs boldly proposed as "axioms" that men seek office solely for income, prestige, and power and that every political agent acts rationally to achieve goals with minimal use of scarce resources [1957, p. 137]. Or in the field of crime when Gary S. Becker [1968] and Isaac Ehrlich [1973] chose to set aside the possibly "deviant" personalities of criminals and instead treat them as individuals rationally responding to opportunities in the form of punishment and reward. These, and similarly oriented explorations into domains of study such as law, marriage and the family, and war and conflict, have led to a rapid intellectual flowering of exciting results.

But then comes a second phase, when doubts begin to emerge. In the partially conquered new territories some of the evidence persists in remaining intractable, difficult to square with the postulate of rational self-interested behavior. In politics these include the fact of voting, the willingness to provide public goods, the grip of ideology. As to crime, it remains true that faced with the same incentives some people commit offenses while others respect the law. So more than a suspicion remains that, after all, criminals are to a degree "deviant" personalities. In some of the fields of imperialist extension of economics we are still in the first phase, reaping easy results. But my emphasis will be upon the more interesting second stage, and what we can learn from the difficulties encountered.

In what follows I will examine what our imperialist explorations have taught us about the two crucial aspects of economic man — *self-interest* (Sec. II) and *rationality* (Sec. III). I will then take up the topic of *conflict* (Sec. IV) to illustrate what economics can say about this most important of the nonmarket interactions that humans engage in. The final Sec. V analyzes the biological underpinnings of all these patterns.

II. Self-Interest

Adam Smith, as usual, said it best:

> We are not ready to suspect any person of being defective in selfishness.
> [1976 (1759), p. 482]

And of course there are his famous lines:

> It is not from the benevolence of the butcher, the brewer, or the baker that we expect our dinner, but from their regard to their own interest.
> [1937 (1776), p. 14]

From the neoclassical era a characteristically strong statement comes from F.Y. Edgeworth:

> The first principle of Economics is that every agent is actuated only by self-interest.
> [1881, p. 16]

And finally, a modern quotation from Richard Posner, the celebrated legal scholar who — like the convert more Catholic than the Pope — has become one of the most outstanding of our economic imperialists:

> Economics. . .explores and tests the implications of assuming that man is a rational maximizer of his ends in life, his satisfactions — what we shall call his "self-interest."
>
> [1977, p. 3]

There is a problem here, which Posner promptly raises. Suppose a person's ends in life include the well-being of others. If so, do *their* interests become his "self-interest"? Posner, like many others, answers in the affirmative — an evasion that robs the concept of self-interest of any distinguishable content. But it is not so easy to separate "self-interested" satisfactions from the psychic sensations generated by the experiences of others.

A distinction proposed by Amartya K. Sen illustrates the nature of the difficulty:

> If the knowledge of torture of others makes you sick, it is a case of sympathy; if it does not make you feel personally worse off, but you think it is wrong. . ., it is a case of commitment. . . . [B]ehavior based on sympathy is in an important sense egoistic, for one is oneself pleased at others' pleasure and pained at others' pain, and the pursuit of one's own utility may thus be helped by sympathetic action. It is action based on commitment rather than sympathy which would be non-egoistic in this sense.
>
> [1977, p. 327]

Thus Sen would count the emotion of sympathy as self-interested, leaving only an abstract intellectualized moralism as non-egoistic — which does not seem a very appealing categorization. For present purposes, the following commonsense interpretation (consistent, I believe, with David Collard [1978, p. 7]) will serve: someone is non-self-interested to the extent that he or she attaches utility to the impact of events upon the bodies or psyches of other parties. When my mother says, "Drink your milk," that is her benevolent concern for my bodily well-being. And if I drink it only to please her, that is my benevolent concern for her psychic comfort. (Ultimately, as will be seen below, the difficulty can be resolved only in the light of bioeconomic considerations which allow us to separate the *motivational* from the *functional* aspects of self-interest.)

It is important to distinguish motivations, aspects of individuals' utility or preference functions, from *actions*. (Even entirely egoistic individuals, we economists know, may be led to engage in mutually helpful actions by an appropriate set of penalties and rewards.) Self-interested or egoistic motivations represent an intermediate point on a spectrum that has benevolence at

one extreme and malevolence at the other.[3]

In what follows I will be showing how imperialist economics has cast light upon the nature and extent of self-interest. In some cases, furthermore, new models and approaches suggested by these explorations promise to be useful even in traditional heartland economics.

1. Political behavior and the split-Smith model

Can political behavior be explained solely in terms of self-interest? The issue has been debated from the beginnings of political thought. As Roger Masters describes it:

> In ancient Greece, the question was therefore already posed with clarity. The pre-Socratics developed a frankly egoistic or hedonistic theory of human nature. . . .Best known from the speeches of Thrasymachus in Plato's *Republic,* this hedonistic view treats human laws or customs as "restraints" on nature. . . .
>
> Both Plato and Aristotle, following the tradition apparently inaugurated by Socrates, contest this position. For example, when Aristotle asserts that man is by nature a "political animal," he directly challenges the Sophists' assertion that human society rests on contractual or conventional obligations among calculating individuals. Aristotle's view rests on a developmental or evolutionary account of social cooperation.
>
> [1978, pp. 59-60]

The recent irruption of economists into political science has been almost entirely based upon the postulate of self-interest — the Sophist position. This approach, rigorously and unflinchingly pursued, has had its triumphs. But the analytically uncomfortable (though humanly gratifying) fact remains: from the most primitive to the most advanced societies, a higher degree of cooperation takes place than can be explained as a merely pragmatic strategy for egoistic man. The social contract seems to maintain itself far better than we have any right to expect, given the agency and free-rider problems involved in enforcing the contract against overt or covert violations. Or putting the emphasis the other way, the workings of the social system appear to be lubricated by individuals who are willing to act voluntarily *pro bono publico.*

Consider voting. Explanations in terms of rational self-interest do carry us a certain distance. As one

---

[3] The term "benevolence" (from the Latin "to wish well") is less ambiguous than the commonly encountered "altruism". This latter word has become a source of confusion for the very reason mentioned above: while some authors (like Collard [1978]) carefully use it only in its original and proper motivational sense, others loosely characterize as altruistic any *action* which has beneficial effects on others — even if selfishly motivated. Biologists, for example, use the expression "reciprocal altruism" for what is often a merely self-interested *exchange* of benefits.

56 THE AMERICAN ECONOMIC REVIEW DECEMBER 1985

instance, a self-interested individual would be more likely to incur the costs of going to the polls in a race expected to be close — since his chance of casting the deciding ballot is greater. And larger turnouts have in fact been observed in close elections.[4] Such evidence is consistent with the self-interest assumption in the *comparative* sense: the behavioral response to variations in self-interest parameters is in the direction anticipated. But in *absolute* terms it remains difficult to rationalize self-interested voting at all, so long as there are costs associated with casting a ballot. The chances of any single voter being decisive are usually far too remote to be worth considering.[5]

An even greater "scandal" is the extent of voluntary private provision of public goods. For concreteness, suppose that individual i's utility function is such that at any income level he would devote, if he were the sole contributor, a fraction k of his income to the public good. Then in the specific case where $k = .1$ it turns out that, for a community of N individuals like i, as N rises toward infinity the community in the limit would spend only 10% more *in aggregate* upon the public good than any single member would have spent alone![6] Evidently, individuals' voluntary provisions for public goods go far beyond what can be satisfactorily explained on the self-interest hypothesis.

Howard Margolis [1982] drives home this point with a thought-experiment, of which a modified version is as follows. In the light of his own circumstances and his beliefs as to what others will contribute, Smith has decided to give exactly $50 to a public good — specifically, to the annual United Fund charitable campaign. Just as he is about to make out his check he learns that Jones, from whom no contribution had been anticipated, has in fact just given $50. According to the standard analysis, Smith would now drastically scale back his intended donation. For example, if (as in the example used previously) Smith in isolation would have spent 10% of his income on the public good, he should now reduce his own contribution from $50 to $5.[7] Everyday observation tells us that this would not happen, that Smith would scale back his own contribution very little if at all.[8] I will use Margolis' proposed resolution of the paradox as my first illustration of new models or approaches arising from the difficulties encountered in the expanded domains of economics.

Let us suppose that within Smith's breast there are really two personalities, Smith$_1$ and Smith$_2$. Smith$_1$ has ordinary selfish motivations; he is concerned only for the well-being of the physical Smith. Smith$_2$ has broader horizons, but he is not exactly unselfish either: Smith$_2$ does derive satisfaction from making contributions, but only via his own "participation utility" rather than through any direct gratification from the actual benefits conferred upon others.

If Smith were *truly* benevolent to some degree, his utility function might take a form like:

$$U^S = U^S(x_S; x_A, x_B, \ldots) \tag{1}$$

where x_S is his own consumption vector and $x_A, x_B, \ldots$ are the consumption vectors of other members of the community (all the marginal utilities being positive).[9] But our Smith's preferences have the form:

$$U^S = U^S(x_S, y_S) \tag{2a}$$

where y_S refers to his own "participation" expenditures. And more specifically, suppose that (2a) can be written:

$$U^S = W u^S{}_1(x_S) + u^S{}_2(y_S) \tag{2b}$$

Here $u^S{}_1$, the Smith$_1$ utility component, is a function of Smith's consumption while $u^S{}_2$ is a function of Smith's participation expenditures — both components being characterized by positive but diminishing marginal utility. W is a weighting factor, which can be taken as a constant parameter[10] describing the "balance of power" at any moment between the two personalities. We would expect that this internal balance of power would generally differ from person to person and possibly change with age and external circumstances.[11]

Using this model, the public-goods paradox — that Jones' donations, being in traditional theory a near-perfect substitute for Smith's contributions, should displace the latter almost one-for-one (but do not) — can be resolved. For, Jones' contributions are no substitute at all for Smith's *participation expenditures*. Furthermore, if we specify that consumption utility is more easily saturated than participation utility — that u'_1 falls faster than u'_2 — we obtain the additional observed consequence that wealthier individuals will spend relatively more upon such contributions. The model also suggests that investigations into how to measure the weighting factor W, and the interpersonal and circumstantial determinants thereof, may be fruitful. One other point which will have some bearing upon what follows: our human inconsistencies in decisions or occasional seeming "irrationality" may be due to internal switches of command between our Smith$_1$ and Smith$_2$.[12]

4 See, for example, Barzel and Silberberg [1973].

5 Some computations on this score are provided by G. Chamberlain and M. Rothschild [1980], as described in Fred Thompson [1982].

6 The theorem underlying this remarkable result is apparently due initially to Martin McGuire [1974], but its importance was first recognized by Howard Margolis [1982, p. 21].

7 Having been in effect enriched by $50 owing to Jones' contribution, Smith would now like to have $5 more of the public good than he originally planned, or a total of $55 more. But towards this amount Jones has already provided $50, so Smith need spend only $5.

8 But see Russell D. Roberts [1984] for evidence supporting a somewhat opposed view.

9 Alternatively a benevolent Smith's utility function might take the form:

$$U^S = U^S(x_S; U^A[x_A], U^B[x_B], \ldots)$$

Here Smith takes pleasure in others' *utilities* rather than in their *consumptions of goods*. (The difference is that the text formulation (1) would allow Smith to have "meddlesome" preferences as to his beneficiaries' consumptions.) This distinction will not be pursued here; for further discussion see Collard [1978], pp. 7-8.

10 Margolis makes W also a function of the ratio x_S/y_S, but this seems a needless complication if (as he assumes) each separate utility component is characterized by diminishing marginal utility.

11 As discussed in detail by Thomas C. Schelling [1980]. Notice also the affinity with the Freudian tripartite division of the personality among id, ego, and superego.

12 This point is emphasized in Schelling [1980]. For somewhat

VOL. 75 NO. 6   *HIRSHLEIFER: THE EXPANDING DOMAIN*   57

2. Benevolence in the family and the Rotten-Kid Theorem

In the sphere of politics it may still be possible to argue the thesis of exclusively self-interested motivations. But in the domain of the family no-one can seriously deny that benevolence plays an overwhelming role. Even here, however, economists would expect and have indeed shown that *comparative* predictions can be made on the basis of self-interest. Other things equal, pro-natalist subsidies that reduce parents' cost of child-bearing can be expected to increase the birth rate.[13] And we would expect parents to take children out of school earlier in rural rather than urban environments, since young children can be relatively more helpful on the farm than in the city.

Benevolence among family members thus falls short of complete submergence of the individuals' separate interests. Nevertheless, the family typically displays strong cohesive tendencies, as if the benevolence present had a certain "contagious" property. It is this phenomenon that Gary Becker [1976b] explained in terms of the "Rotten-Kid Theorem" — which will serve as my second example of a new model generated to explain the phenomena in the expanded domains of imperialist economics.

In Figure 1 the Rotten Kid is self-interested; he simply wants to maximize his material income x_K without regard to Daddy's income x_D. Daddy, however, has a degree of benevolence leading to a normal-looking preference map (as represented by the solid indifference curve U_D) on x_D, x_K axes. Let us suppose that Kid chooses the productive solution along a joint productive opportunity locus QQ, after which Daddy may transfer income on a 1:1 basis to Kid along the 135° line TT. If Kid were *shortsightedly* selfish, he would simply maximize his own income at R* along QQ. But *enlightened* self-interest would direct Kid to maximize family income at J* along QQ. He can count on the fact that, starting from J*, Daddy's benevolent motivations would lead to transfers of income along TT up to position A* in the diagram. Since x_K is greater at A* than at R*, Kid is better off. This alone is not the remarkable result; it has always been known that enlightened self-interest can be more rewarding than shortsighted piggishness. The remarkable part of the theorem is that *Daddy* is better off at A* than at R*, even in terms of sheer material income x_D. Thus, it seems, Golden-Rule motivations can be functionally profitable!

I will mention here three conditions that have to be met for this result to hold. *First*, Kid's family-income-maximizing productive choice J* along QQ must provide Daddy with enough preponderance of income to induce the transfer. *Second*, Daddy's benevolence must surpass a certain threshold. If his benevolence were in fact weaker, as suggested by the dashed indifference curve U'_D in Figure 1, the transfers he would make from J* to B* would not suffice to induce Kid's cooperation, and so the parties would end up at R*. *Third*, Daddy has to have the "last word." If Daddy's benevolent transfer had to precede Kid's choice along QQ, Kid would assuredly not make the productive decisions that maximize family income.[14]

The Rotten-Kid Theorem, and the limitations thereon, help us understand a wide variety of phenomena within the family, of which I will mention only one. Outside public assistance to some family members, for example to a handicapped child, has less of an effect upon the beneficiary than might at first be anticipated — because benevolent parents, having already been transferring resources to such a child, would now rationally cut back their own transfers.[15] Finally, the "contagious" property of benevolence, when the conditions for the Rotten-Kid Theorem are met, may help explain the extent of non-self-interested behavior even in domains other than the family.[16]

3. Gifts, status, and the "rat-race"

The importance of gifts and other "redistribution institutions" in nearly all observed societies may at first suggest widespread benevolence. However, the central tradition of anthropological explanation is in accord with the model of economic man. Gifts among primitive

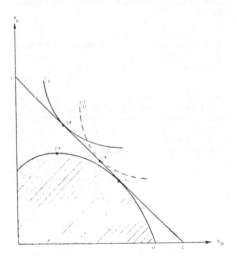

Fig. 1: The Rotten-Kid Theorem

[14] This discussion and diagrammatic representation are based on Hirshleifer [1977]. See also Gordon Tullock [1977].
[15] See Becker [1981], pp. 124-126.
[16] For a discussion of the extent to which government can serve as a big Daddy to induce cooperation among self-interested citizens, see Bruce R. Bolnick [1979].

parallel discussions see Sen [1977] and Albert O. Hirschman [1985].
[13] See Stephen P.Coelen and Robert J. McIntyre [1978].

58   THE AMERICAN ECONOMIC REVIEW   DECEMBER 1985

peoples are interpreted as really a form of social exchange; if not reciprocated, the gift will be revoked (or even severer penalties applied). What appears to be benevolence is but indirect or disguised self-interest. Thus Marcel Mauss contends that such "prestations" are:

> . . .in theory voluntary, disinterested and spontaneous, but are in fact obligatory and interested.
> [1954 (1925), p. 1]

But this established tradition[17] leaves open the question: Why go to the trouble of disguising what is really exchange as a gift? There is no point to simulation, absent a real thing to be simulated. So we are led to ask: What is being simulated by these pretended gifts? I will anticipate my biological discussion somewhat to respond along the following lines. In very primitive times, voluntary resource transfers took the form only of sharing within a kin-group (as exemplified by Daddy's transfers in the Rotten-Kid model). The biological basis for such benevolence is immediately evident. With widening scope and extent of interactions, actual kinship among transacting parties diminished. But familial sharing remaining the mental image, as a useful fiction one's trading partners became "adopted" as quasi-kin. This fiction became less and less credible as the social distance among transactors increased — so that, in the limit, truly impersonal exchange among strictly self-interested parties was approximated. Still, a residue of quasi-kinship sentiments aids us even in the "ordinary business of life" (Marshall) of modern times. Some willingness to forego selfish advantage, some element of genuine trust between trading partners or among business associates, almost always remains a necessity in the world of affairs.

In contrast with the foregoing, Friedrich A. Hayek [1979, pp. 153-176] rather paradoxically contends that human social organization could not have advanced beyond the small band to settled communities and civilized life until cultural evolution taught men to *overcome* their biological "innate instincts to pursue common perceived goals." (See also E.O. Wilson [1978a].) At times Hayek appears almost to claim, contra Adam Smith, that the natural man is indeed "defective in selfishness".[18] But a fairer interpretation of Hayek's point, I believe, is that the primitive social ethic of kin-

ship sharing had to be replaced by an alternative social ethic — centered upon fair dealing and reciprocity — appropriate to the market order. While Hayek emphasizes that this latter ethic is culturally learned, an ingrained human predisposition may also have evolved to help support reciprocity as a social norm. (I have argued [1980] that social evolution has instilled in man elements of at least three distinct social ethics: one associated with the Golden Rule of sharing, a second with the Silver Rule of private rights and reciprocity, and a third with what might be called the Iron Rule of dominance and subordination.)

Returning to gifts, the economic imperialist Richard Posner [1980] (together with a number of anthropologists) interprets them as essentially a device for mutual insurance. A hunter with a good catch today will help out a less fortunate colleague because he knows that tomorrow the circumstances are likely to be reversed. This explanation cannot be regarded as fully satisfactory, for at least two reasons: (1) Some individuals will be systematically better hunters than others, hence the "insurance" payments and receipts will not balance out over time. (2) In the absence of a formal insurance contract there will be widespread openings for opportunistic behavior: shirking, deferred or slighted repayment, etc.[19]

Nevertheless, to an important extent *reciprocal giving* does approximate self-interested exchange among equals. But what about one-sided or *redistributive giving?* Paradoxically, anthropologists commonly regard the motivation here as not even neutral but often actively hostile — the underlying aim being to enhance or assert status. According to Claude Lévi-Strauss the purpose is:

> . . .to surpass a rival in generosity, to crush him if possible under future obligations which it is hoped he cannot meet, thus taking from him privileges, titles, rank, authority, and prestige.
> [1957 (1964), p. 85]

A very well-known example is the "potlatch" institution of certain Pacific Coast Indian societies, in which (allegedly, at least) resources were consumed or even deliberately destroyed in grand feasts designed to shame less affluent rivals.

Rank-oriented motivations are intrinsically malevolent, since one person's rise is another's fall — the process is a zero-sum game. As the desire for status notoriously pervades all human activities,[20] it is quite remarkable that economists up to quite recently have

---

[17] See articles in the *International Encyclopedia of the Social Sciences* [1968] under such titles as "Exchange and Display," "Interaction: Social Exchange," and "Trade, Primitive". A somewhat different point of view is that of Marshall D. Sahlins [1972, Ch. 4-5] who emphasizes the pacifying effect of gift exchange upon parties otherwise likely to war for resources.

[18] Starting from a very similar evolutionary orientation, Donald T. Campbell in his Presidential address to the American Psychological Association [1975] argues a position almost the opposite of Hayek's. To wit, that biologically innate selfishness always threatens to subvert the social order, which is defended only by rather fragile culturally evolved moral traditions. Campbell points out that the sins decried by such moral traditions — "selfishness, stinginess, greed, gluttony, envy, theft, lust, and promiscuity" — are in fact behaviors that "come close to biological optimization" [p. 1119].

[19] For evidence on a number of these points see Hillard Kaplan and Kim Hill [1985].

[20] One example is provided by surveys of self-reported "happiness." Reported happiness correlates with higher income at any moment of time, as would be expected, but as income has trended upward *over time* there has been no corresponding upward trend in self-estimates of happiness (see Richard Easterlin [1974]). The most natural explanation is that happiness is more powerfully affected by relative income status than by absolute income; the poor are richer than before, but still at the bottom of the heap.

VOL. 75 NO. 6   *HIRSHLEIFER: THE EXPANDING DOMAIN*   59

so signally failed to incorporate this phenomenon into their models.[21]

Rank *may* however be only a proximate and not an ultimate concern — for example, if income is generated by a "contest" process with rank-determined payoffs. In a footrace or a war, even if your goal is only to win a material prize you still have to outmatch your opponent. Income-generating processes with highly progressive rank-determined rewards lead to the "superstar" phenomenon recently noticed in the literature (Sherwin Rosen [1981]). But our interest here is where rank enters into the *utility function,* so that:

$$U^i = U^i(x_i, R_i) \qquad (3)$$

where x_i is individual i's income and R_i may be interpreted as the percent of the comparison group falling below i on the basis of the status-determining criterion. One interesting implication of (3) is that such a person would be most actively malevolent toward his immediate neighbors along the rank ladder, and be essentially neutral to those far above or below him. Thus, concern for status may be distinguished from sheer *envy* of the well-being of all others.[22]

When status is conferred by conspicuous consumption there is a double payoff to income — greater consumption *plus* higher prestige. From this stems the "rat-race" phenomenon analyzed in the recent book by Robert H. Frank [1985]. As novels about modern suburbia tell us, the rat-race grows ever worse with increasing levels of income. The reason is that as individuals become richer they attempt to purchase both more consumption and more status. Status being socially in absolutely fixed supply, its marginal desirability relative to consumption steadily rises — inducing ever more intense efforts to achieve it, efforts that in aggregate must fail.[23]

If on the other hand the status-determining condition is distinct from income, the latter can often be traded off against rank. What makes some societies successful may be a suitable rank-determining criterion. A tribe facing fierce enemies is more likely to survive if status is earned by bravery in battle. And redistribution institutions, whereby prestige is earned by liberal generosity, tend to moderate rat-race competitions for income. In such societies high income can be used to support consumption or to generate prestige, but not both.

III. Rationality

When it comes to rationality, economics as an imperialist discipline finds itself in an unwontedly defensive position. Damaging attacks upon rational man

have come from the direction of psychology. But this is all to the good if, as I have maintained, economics must ultimately become coextensive with all of social science. Generalized economics will have to deal with man as he really is — self-interested or not, fully rational or not.

Rationality is an *instrumental* concept. In the light of one's goals (preferences), if the means chosen (actions) are appropriate the individual is rational; if not, irrational. "Appropriate" here refers to *method* rather than *result.* Rational behavior is action calculated on the basis of the rules of logic and other norms of validity. Owing to chance, good method may not always lead to good result.

Few real men and women behave rationally all the time, and many of us scarcely any of the time. How then can economics maintain the postulate of rationality? Several answers can be given, in parallel with the responses offered when the self-interest postulate was challenged: (1) We could redefine all choice as rational. ("If I chose to do X, I must have thought that X was best.") This gets us nowhere. (2) We could retreat to a fallback position, asserting that the rationality postulate yields useful predictions in the field *where economists customarily apply it*— to wit, in market decisions. Such modesty, as argued above, is an improper evasion of the scientific challenge.[24] Ultimately we must be ready to abandon the rationality paradigm to the extent that it fails to fit the evidence about human behavior.

Rationality may fail in two quite distinct ways. First, individuals often commit errors in logical inference even when doing their best to reason logically. Second, what is quite a different matter, actions are often "unthinking"; when governed by habit or passion, people do not even attempt rational self-control. (I will be suggesting below that such failures of rationality, like violations of the self-interest postulate, may have proved functionally adaptive in the genetic and cultural evolution of the human species.)

1. On lapses of logic

To reason in accordance with the canons of formal logic is no easy task. I will discuss three different categories of logical lapses.

First are straight violations of the laws of inference. In the following example (adapted from Leda Cosmides [1985]), experimental subjects were instructed somewhat as follows:

> In a card-sorting task there is one rule: "Every card marked with an 'A' on one side should have a '1' on the other." Indicate whether you need to

---

[21] The early discussion by Thorstein Veblen [1953 (1899)] is more satiric than analytical. Models incorporating one or more aspects of the drive for status have been offered by Becker [1971], Reuven Brenner [1983], and Robert H. Frank [1985].

[22] On envy see Helmut Schoeck [1969 (1966)] and Becker [1971, pp. 1088-1090].

[23] *Time* also becomes increasing scarce, relatively speaking, as income rises. Status and time constraints reinforce one another to help produce the phenomenon of the "harried leisure class" (see Becker [1965] and Staffan B. Linder [1970]).

[24] An interesting issue, however, is why the rationality postulate so often remains a useful social predictor despite its lack of validity on the individual level. One reason is *aggregation:* since rational behavior is systematic and purposive, whereas irrational behavior tends to be random and erratic, after aggregation even a limited degree of rationality tends to dominate the social totals. Another reason is *selection via competition,* to be discussed in more detail below.

60   THE AMERICAN ECONOMIC REVIEW   DECEMBER 1985

inspect the reverse side of the following cards to detect violation of the rule: (1) A card showing an 'A'; (2) A card showing a 'B'; (3) A card showing a '1'; (4) A card showing a '2'.

In a large preponderance of cases, while the subjects correctly realized the need to inspect the reverse of card #1, they failed to notice that they should do the same for card #4.

What is instructive, however, is that the results were quite different for a formally identical problem presented as follows:

You are the bouncer in a Boston bar, concerned to enforce the following rule: "Anyone who consumes alcohol on the premises must be at least 20 years old." Indicate whether you need more information about any of the following individuals to detect violation of the rule: (1) An individual drinking whisky; (2) An individual drinking Coke; (3) An individual aged 25; (4) An individual aged 16.

Here almost everyone perceived the need for more information about individual #4 as well as individual #1. The author's suggested explanation is biological: however imperfect our mental capacities are at formal logic, Darwinian natural selection has made us efficient at detecting cheating or violations of social norms — a factor entering into the second but not the first experiment.

More familiar to economists is a relatively large literature, most notably associated with the psychologists Amos Tversky and Daniel Kahneman,[25] on errors people make in probability judgments. Tversky and Kahneman indicate that:

. . .people rely on a limited number of heuristic principles which reduce the complex tasks of assessing probabilities. . .to simpler judgmental operations. In general, these heuristics are quite useful, but sometimes they lead to severe and systematic errors.

[1974, p. 1124]

Among the many examples of such errors are: (1) a tendency to overestimate on the basis of psychological salience (someone who has seen a house burning down usually assesses a higher probability to such an event than someone who has only read about it), and (2) a tendency to attribute excessive representativeness to small samples (thus, people do not seem to intuitively appreciate that average word lengths in successive lines of a given text vary more than average word lengths in successive pages). As a general conclusion, it appears that the human mind employs rules of thumb that work well most of the time, but which can

lead to certain systematic classes of errors.[26]

What psychologists term "cognitive dissonance" has received some attention from economists (see George Akerlof and William T. Dickens [1982]). This phenomenon is not so much a lapse of logical reasoning as its perversion. Suppose someone has chosen an employment generally regarded as excessively risky. To reduce his mental discomfort, he is likely to revise his beliefs and kid himself into thinking that his job is not so risky after all! What is involved here is known in more old-fashioned terminology as *rationalization.* When a person is made aware of a disharmony between his actions and his preferences and beliefs, the economist would expect him to revise his choice of action — but the cognitive dissonance theorist predicts that he is likely instead to modify his preferences or beliefs.

The basic premise here is that a person always tries to present to the world (and to himself) a picture of his own behavior that fits an integrated rational pattern. Observed discrepancies call for correction, but the correction may take either the *rational* or the *rationalizing* form. An elaboration of this idea distinguishes between "underjustification" and "overjustification." Cognitive dissonance is an example of the former. If a subject is made aware of having done something without adequate *extrinsic* justification in the form of reward or constraint, he rationalizes by manufacturing an intrinsic reason (revising his goals or beliefs). "Overjustification" consists of making the subject aware that there is a strong extrinsic reason for his behavior, from which he is likely to infer an *absence* of intrinsic reason. For example, it has been alleged, if children in a classroom are led to expect that reading achievements will be rewarded by gold stars, they are likely to actually reduce their reading activity afterward, when gold stars are no longer offered.[27]

While these processes of belief revision may not always be totally absurd,[28] they tend to violate the reality principle. Suppose a military commander learns that his left flank is dangerously weak. The economist, expecting a *rational* response, predicts that the general will reinforce his left. The cognitive-dissonance theorist rather expects a *rationalizing* response instead, in which the general chooses to believe that the enemy will not attack him on the left. Environmental selection

25 A useful collection is the volume edited by Kahneman, Paul Slovic and Tversky [1982].

26 For a related analysis, which emphasizes the strengths rather than weaknesses of commonsense inference, see Harold Kelley [1973].

27 For discussions see Edward L. Deci [1971] and Mark R. Lepper, David Greene, and Richard E. Nisbett [1973]. Notice that "overjustification" is in opposition to the better-known *conditioning* theory, which predicts that patterns of behavior induced by reward (e.g., Pavlov's famous salivating dog) will persist to some extent even after withdrawal of the reward.

28 A child who observes that a certain activity receives extrinsic social compensation might well infer, for example, that people in general find the activity onerous or distasteful. Since we are all always learning from others, the apparent weight of others' judgments should reasonably have some impact upon our own estimates of what we ought to like or dislike.

will always be tending to eliminate such inappropriate responses, as will be discussed further below.

2. On non-rational (or "boundedly rational") decision processes

At least as important as failure to reason correctly is the fact that, in some contexts people do not even attempt to think rationally at all (or do so only in a very limited way). *Habit* is surely a way of economizing on scarce reasoning ability. Indeed, in many contexts habit may be faster and more accurate than thinking; no-one can play the piano or drive a car effectively without engaging in a host of complex unthinking actions. But I am not aware of any studies of the psycho-economics of habit.

Under the heading of "bounded rationality", Herbert A. Simon [1955, 1959] has contended that a person faced with a complex mental task will not attempt to strictly optimize but will be content instead merely to "satisfice". That is, he aims to find not the best but a good solution — one which achieves a given proximate target or aspiration level. Simon argues that:

> Models of satisficing behavior are richer than models of maximizing behavior, because they treat not only of equilibrium but of the method of reaching it as well. . .(a) When performance falls short of the level of aspiration, search behavior. . .is induced. (b) At the same time, the level of aspiration begins to adjust itself downward until goals reach levels that are practically attainable. (c) If the two mechanisms just listed operate too slowly to adapt aspiration to performance, emotional behavior — apathy or aggression, for example — will replace rational adaptive behavior.
>   [1959, p. 263]

Simon's steps (a) and (b), it might at least be argued, constitute a valid successive-approximation technique for optimization that economizes on humans' limited information and reasoning ability. Only step (c), the emotional response to frustration, seems clearly dysfunctional in terms of rational adaptation. However, it can be shown, even "irrational" emotions may serve a useful adaptive function.

Specifically, an individual's uncontrollable anger/ gratitude response[29] to another's hurtful/helpful activity can induce cooperation in much the same way as the Rotten-Kid Theorem. Figure 2 is similar to Figure 1. But in addition to the "transfer lines" T,T',T" that describe once again how a grateful Daddy can transfer income to Kid on a 1:1 basis, here there are also "punishment lines" D,D',D". These indicate that an angry Daddy can deprive Kid of income, but again only on a 1:1 basis — that is, Daddy loses one unit himself for each unit penalty imposed on Kid. (This assumption reflects the fact that anger, like gratitude, can be expressed only at a

[29] This development is based upon Hirshleifer [1984].

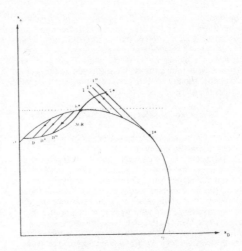

Fig. 2: The Anger/Gratitude Response (AGR) Curve

cost.) Then the rational self-interested first-mover, Kid, in selecting a productive vector along QQ does so in the light of the final positions attainable along Daddy's Anger/Gratitude Response (AGR). The pictured shape of the AGR curve reflects the reasonable assumption that Daddy becomes decreasingly grateful (or increasingly angry) the more selfish is Kid's productive choice along QQ. The final Figure 2 solution at point V* is an efficient outcome, quite analogous to the Figure 1 solution at point A*. In Figure 1 it was Daddy's benevolence that guaranteed his implicit promise to reward a self-interested Kid for cooperative behavior; in Figure 2, the same function is served by Daddy's passionate "loss of control" in response to Kid's good or bad behavior.

The possibility of achieving the efficient outcome through the AGR effect is premised upon a number of special assumptions, very much in parallel with those required for the initial Rotten-Kid model. Once again, Daddy must "have the last word" in the interaction. And the overall result is somewhat dependent upon the specific location and shape of the AGR curve. If Daddy is strongly predisposed to be angry (so that the AGR curve lies almost entirely below QQ), he may even be able to extort income from Kid — i.e., to achieve a distributive gain at Kid's expense. But Daddy's propensity to anger, if carried too far, may lead Kid to settle for a very inefficient productive outcome: one in which both parties are so impoverished that Daddy cannot (or will not want to) inflict further punishment.

I will conclude this discussion of the psychology of rationality on a properly aggressive imperialist note. Economists, for example Akerlof and Dickens [1982] and David Alhadeff [1982], to my mind have been over-respectful of what psychology is supposedly able to tell us. While rich in data, on the theoretical level psychology remains a confusing clamor of competing categories; there is no integrating theoretical structure. I will be so bold as to predict that such a structure, when achieved, will be fundamentally economic — or more specifically bioeconomic — in nature. That is, it will show how mental patterns have evolved as optimizing solutions subject to the constraints of scarcity and competition.[30]

3. Environmental selection and "as if" rationality

Even if individuals commit any or all of the reasoning errors discussed above, to some extent decisions will still be disciplined by competitive selection processes in the economy. Armen A. Alchian [1950] argued that even if a business firm's choices were completely random, the environment would select for survival those decisions that were relatively correct in meeting the minimum standard of viability. Expanding on this, Stephen Enke [1951] argued that competition would ensure that all policies save the truly optimal would in time fail the survival test. As those firms pursuing relatively successful policies expand and (owing to imitation) multiply, a higher and higher standard of achievement becomes the minimum criterion. In the long run, viability dictates optimality. Consequently, for long-run predictive purposes, in competitive situations the analyst is entitled to assume that firms behave "as if" they were truly engaged in rational optimization.

This model has to be inaccurate at least in one respect: in describing the *approach to equilibrium.* Actual economies, though falling short perhaps of the rational ideal, surely avoid the profligate waste (abandonments, bankruptcies, and the like) that would ensue from merely random behavior (see Edith Penrose [1952]). Another serious flaw is that, as shown initially by Sidney G. Winter [1964, 1971], the selectional-evolutionary process will not necessarily always lead to the same long-run equilibrium outcome "as if" firms actually optimized. In this connection Richard R. Nelson and Winter [1982] have explored the consequences of a process wherein boundedly rational firms choose among "organizational routines" while competitive environmental selection is simultaneously operating to change the representation of these alternative routines in the population. And John Conlisk [1980] has examined a process where, with optimization costly relative to mere *imitation,* in general the ultimate "natural selection" equilibrium will be a mixture of the two types. A somewhat parallel analysis, emphasizing that imitation can be regarded as cultural inheritance, appears in Robert Boyd and Peter J. Richerson [1980].

While economists have been working on the environmental selection of firms and their business routines, evolutionary anthropologists have developed strikingly similar models for the natural selection of cultural practices like group size, birth spacing, and land tenure arrangements among primitive peoples.[31] What the anthropologists have been doing here is an instance of a more general (and somewhat controversial) quasi-economic evolutionary modelling principle known as *the adaptationist hypothesis* or *the optimization theory:* that morphology and behavior, on both the individual and social levels, can be explained "as if" chosen to maximize the chances of evolutionary success.[32] Especially on the social level, a number of difficulties have been encountered owing mainly to the fact that what is best for the individual may not be best for the group. Economists could make important contributions here, having already systematically explored the bases for such "fallacies of composition" — e.g., divergent interests, differences of beliefs, and externalities. But I would now like to call attention to another, less familiar yet enormously important reason for disparities between private and social adaptation: the role of *conflict* in determining patterns of social organization.

IV. Conflict

Vilfredo Pareto said:

> The efforts of men are utilized in two different ways: they are directed to the production or transformation of economic goods, or else to the appropriation of goods produced by others.
> [1971 (1927), p. 341]

Pareto is suggesting, as I believe will be proved to be correct, that aggressive behavior aimed at the appropriation of goods will ultimately provide as rich and fruitful field for the application of economic reasoning as our traditional topics of production and markets. While appropriation can be undertaken to some extent by lawful means, for example via redistributive politics or what has become known as "rent-seeking,"[33] its most dramatic and indeed characteristic form involves conflict. At any moment of time a rational self-interested person will strike an optimal balance between achieving his ends through production and voluntary exchange on the one hand or through force, extortion, and fraud on the other. In fact, even if he has no intention of using the latter techniques himself, he would be well-advised to devote some of his resources to defense against invasions by others. The final social equilibrium will integrate the destructive and invasive as well as the constructive and cooperative efforts of humans in all of their interactions with one another.

I can briefly allude only to three topics under this vast

---

[30] A psychology text with such an orientation is J.E.R. Staddon [1983].

[31] Surveyed in Eric A. Smith [1985]. The anthropologists are analytically ahead of the economists in tying the environmental selection of institutions to more ultimate evolutionary considerations — the reproductive survival of human beings.

[32] The diverging views of evolutionary theorists on this more general issue are illustrated by John Maynard Smith [1978], Richard C. Lewontin [1979], and Richard Dawkins [1982, Ch. 3].

[33] See Anne O. Krueger [1974].

heading — one concerned with the *causes* of conflict, the second with the *conduct and technology* of conflict, and the last with the social *consequences* of conflict.[34]

1. On the causes of conflict

Involved in a rational decision to engage in conflict, economic reasoning suggests, will be the decision-maker's *preferences, opportunities*, and *perceptions*. These three elements correspond to traditional issues debated by historians and political scientists about the "causes of war": Is war mainly due to hatred and ingrained pugnacity (hostile preferences)? Or to the prospects for material gain (opportunities)? Or is war mainly due to mistaken perceptions, on one or both sides, of the other's motives or capacities?

In the simplest dyadic situation, and setting aside complications such as those associated with group choices,[35] Figures 3 and 4 are alternative illustrations of how preferences, opportunities, and perceptions jointly influence decisions. In each diagram the curve QQ bounds the peaceful possibilities or "settlement opportunity set" — drawn on axes representing Blue's income I_B and Red's income I_R. Points P_B and P_R indicate the parties' respective *perceptions* of the outcome of conflict. And the families of curves labelled U_B and U_R are the familiar utility indifference contours.

Figure 3 shows a relatively benign situation: settlement opportunities are complementary, preferences

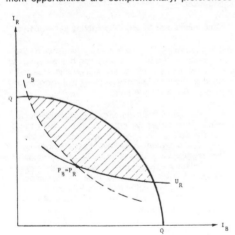

Fig. 3: Statics of Conflict — Large Potential Settlement Region

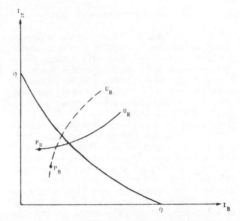

Fig. 4: Statics of Conflict — Small Potential Settlement Region

display benevolence on each side, and perceptions of returns from conflict are conservative and agreed (P_B and P_R coincide). The "Potential Settlement Region" PSR (shaded area in the diagram), the set of income partitions such that *both* parties regard themselves as doing better by settling than by fighting, is large — which plausibly implies a high probability of coming to an agreement. Figure 4 shows a less pleasant situation: antithetical opportunities, mutually malevolent preferences, and divergently optimistic estimates of the returns from conflict. The PSR is therefore small, and the prospects for settlement much poorer.

Such a summary presentation is of course little more than a way of organizing ideas, so as to direct attention to the forces underlying and determining the parties' opportunities, preferences, and perceptions. I can only mention a few specifics here. Whether or not peaceful *opportunities* are harmonious may depend upon Malthusian pressures, upon the economics of increasing returns and the division of labor, and upon the possibility of enforcing agreements. *Preferences* (benevolence or malevolence) may be a function of kinship and shared cultural heritage. And *perceptions* will be influenced by communications, including threats and bluffs, and by each party's demonstrated prowess in past and ongoing hostilities.[36]

But even when these static considerations tend to favor peaceful settlement, the dynamics of the negotiation process may prevent the parties from achieving a mutually beneficial accommodation. In the famous Prisoners' Dilemma, for example, inability to make a binding agreement traps the players in a mutually unsatisfactory outcome.

---

[34] This discussion is based largely upon Hirshleifer [1987 (forthcoming)].

[35] Some of the problems of group organization in a military context are analyzed in Geoffrey Brennan and Gordon Tullock [1982].

[36] Some of the problems involved in the relation between perceptions and conflict are discussed in Donald Wittman [1979].

2. On the technology of conflict

Conflict is a kind of "industry" in which different "firms" compete by attempting to disable opponents. Just as the economist without being a manager or engineer can apply certain broad principles to the processes of industrial production, so, without claiming to replace the military commander he can say something about the principles governing how desired results are "produced" through violence.

Battles typically proceed to a definitive outcome — victory or defeat. *Wars* may be less conclusive, often ending in compromise. These historical generalizations reflect the intertwined working of increasing versus decreasing returns applied to the production of violence: (1) Within a sufficiently small geographical region such as a battlefield, increasing returns to military strength apply — a small military superiority is typically translated into a disproportionately favorable outcome. The reason is that, at any moment, the stronger side can inflict a more-than-proportionate loss upon the opponent, thus becoming progressively stronger still (Frederich William Lanchester [1976 (1916)]). (2) But there are decreasing returns in projecting military power away from one's base area, so that it is difficult to achieve superiority over an enemy's entire national territory (see Kenneth E. Boulding [1962], pp. 227-233). The increasing-returns factor explains why there is a "natural monopoly" of military force *within* the nation-state. The diminishing-returns factor explains why a multiplicity of nation-states have remained militarily viable to this date. (However, there is some reason to believe, the technology of attack through long-range weapons has now so come to prevail over the defense that a single world-state is indeed impending.)

3. Efficiency as consequence of conflict

Struggle and conflict are obviously costly, inefficient processes. Yet might it be the case that struggle masks a deeper harmony of interests? Some observers have professed to see, for example, a profound beneficent wisdom underlying conflict in Nature. Thus the leopard is admired for his helpfulness to prey, in controlling their numbers and eliminating the infirm and unfit. And the head-butting of male rams, fighting for sexual access, is said to improve the breed. These arguments, and their analogs on the human level, are to my mind rather fatuous. Conflict, unlike exchange, can rarely benefit all participants.

Somewhat more defensible is the contention that conflict leads, ultimately at least, to *efficiency*. That is, as a consequence of struggle, resources will end up under the control of those parties able to turn them to best use. Such a model has been offered by economic imperialists to explain the evolution of law.

Imagine a situation where mutually advantageous exchanges of entitlements are partially or wholly unfea-

sible. Then the Coase Theorem (Ronald H. Coase [1960]) does not apply, and the effective assignment of property rights will make a real efficiency difference. The various parties at interest may contend for resources, among other ways, by lawsuits. Then, the proposition is, those individuals and groups for whom a particular entitlement or legal rule is worth more will ultimately win because they can bring more pressure to bear than their opponents. One model of this process, due to Paul H. Rubin [1977], emphasizes *relitigation*. Since precedents are never absolutely binding, attempts will be made repeatedly to overturn an inefficient one. So long as there is a random element in judicial decisions, even apart from any possible learning factor, the efficient rule will eventually be hit upon — and, being efficient, it will be a relatively stable precedent. In an alternative model, those standing to benefit from the more efficient decision can afford to make greater investments (for example, to hire better lawyers) and thus are more likely to win the contest (John C. Goodman [1978]).

Finally, this efficiency-through-strength model is by no means limited to the arena of common-law litigation. With minimal modifications the same logic could be extended to statute law and constitutional interpretation. For that matter, since the process is essentially one of "trial through combat," why not apply it also to civil wars and international conflicts? Clearly the argument that conflict generates efficiency can have only limited validity, but I will have to break off at this interesting point.

V. Economics and Biology: Competing Imperialisms?

While economics has been expanding *horizontally*, so to speak, a simultaneous invasion has been taking place *vertically* as evolutionary biology has asserted a claim to be the foundation of all the social sciences. As argued by Edward O. Wilson:

> For every discipline in its early stages of development there exists an antidiscipline. . .With the word *antidiscipline* I wish to emphasize the special adversary relation that exists initially between the studies of adjacent level of organization. . . .[B]iology has now moved close enough to the social sciences to become their antidiscipline. . . .Many scholars judge this core [of social theory] to be the deep structure of human nature, an essentially biological phenomenon.
> [1977, p. 127]

This development, though controversial in some respects,[37] should not disturb economists. The influence

---

[37] Unfortunately, "sociobiology" has become the object of ideological attack on the part of some scientists and publicists concerned to minimize the genetic as opposed to the cultural sources of social behavior and organization. But no-one can seriously deny that mor-

VOL. 75 NO. 6   HIRSHLEIFER: THE EXPANDING DOMAIN   65

of Malthus and of Adam Smith upon Charles Darwin's thought is well-known.[38] And whereas Alfred Marshall declared that economics is a branch of biology, the biologist Michael Ghiselin [1978] would make *universal economy* the more general discipline. Under this broad heading, biologists can be regarded as studying *natural economy* while the socially regulated behavior of humans constitutes *political economy*.[39] In short, these two colliding imperialisms can say, with the comic-strip character Pogo, "We have met the enemy, and he is us!"

I could defend this assertion by pointing to fundamental common concepts like competition and specialization, or to terminological pairs like species/industry, mutation/innovation, evolution/progress, etc., or most explicitly by setting up parallel systems of equations describing equilibrium states and paths of change. But I must limit myself to a few specific points that bear upon issues discussed above.

1. As to self-interest, a number of paradoxes are resolved when it is appreciated that in biology *there are two levels of self* — the organism and the gene. The gene is a "selfish gene" (Richard Dawkins [1976]). But sometimes it is profitable for a selfish gene to program its carrier organism to be benevolent (or malevolent) to other organisms. Non-self-interested motivations on the level of the organism may therefore be *functionally* self-interested on the level of the gene.

2. Just as firms and other social groupings are alliances of individuals, so the organism is in a sense an alliance of genes. Certain remarkable phenomena, such as functionless or "parasitic" DNA, reveal that free-riding and other alliance problems occur even within organisms. Thus some of the forces that limit the achievement of social efficiency or harmony also impair the optimal adaptation of individual organisms to their environments.

3. In the game of Darwinian natural selection, *reproductive survival* (RS) or *fitness* can be regarded metaphorically as the "goal" of the gene. But since one's kin have calculable chances of carrying the same gene, it is possible to quantify the degree of benevolence an organism should display toward relatives. In particular, what might be called the first law of bioeconomics (due to W.D. Hamilton [1964]) says that an animal will help another without reward if and only if:

$$b/c \geq I/r \qquad (4)$$

Here b is the benefit to the recipient and c the cost to the donor, both in RS units, while r is the degree of relatedness between the parties. An individual should be willing to sacrifice one unit of RS, for example, for two RS units of benefit to a brother or sister (since r = 1/2 between full siblings). Translating from RS to income units, and assuming the equivalent of diminishing marginal utility, we can obtain a normally curved benevolent-toward-kin preference map (like Daddy's in Figure 1).

4. Of course, Hamilton's formula is valid only in an "other things held equal" sense. As a consequence of generational timing, for example, in RS terms parents are more motivated to help children then children to help parents. More generally, behavior depends not only upon preferences (relatedness) but upon opportunities. In very competitive environments there may be sharp conflict not only between male and female parents but even between parents and offspring, or among siblings competing for parental aid.[40]

5. As Darwin emphasized, natural selection does not choose on the basis of an absolute standard of performance, but rather on how well an organism does in comparison with its closest competitors — for example, in the reproductive competition among males for access to females. This is perhaps the ultimate source of our seemingly ingrained concern for dominance and rank.

6. Darwin argued that, in primitive times, human groups whose members were "courageous, sympathetic, and faithful" would have a selective advantage. But he already appreciated that a free-rider problem would be at work: *individual selection* for effective pursuit of self-interest would tend to subvert *group selection* for benevolent traits. Furthermore, the consensus among biologists has been that individual selection is almost always the more potent. However, many modern biologists follow Darwin in making an exception at least for man. Exceptionally rigorous group selection, especially through conflict and warfare, together with the mental abilities of humans[41] that make it possible to identify and punish subversively selfish behavior, have led to the evolution of a degree of group-oriented benevolence.[42]

7. This development has strongly xenophobic implications. Other things equal an organisms would "treat as 'enemies', harming them when he could, all individuals having less than average relationship" to him (W.D. Hamilton [1970, p. 1219]). Thus the impartial or universalistic benevolence of our moral philosophers finds no counterpart in evolutionary biology.

8. Finally, however, the mental hyperdevelopment of mankind has made us the only species able to "rebel against the tyranny of the selfish replicators" — our genes (Dawkins [1976], p. 215). Recognizing our ingrained behavioral drives, we can train ourselves to oppose them — just as we can amend our bodily shape or internal biochemistry through surgical or medical

---

phology and biochemistry play *some* role in social behavior, just as no "sociobiologist" of repute has ever ruled out the influence of cultural determinants. (Furthermore, the human capacities for culture, of which language is the most notable, are themselves of genetic origin.) While individual sociobiologists may have constructed faulty theories or misread the evidence on particular issues, such errors cannot condemn the entire scientific enterprise of searching for the biological underpinnings of behavior.

38 On this see especially S.S. Schweber [1978].

39 I have attempted to develop this distinction in Hirshleifer [1978].

40 On these issues see Robert L. Trivers [1972, 1974].

41 These mental qualities themselves very likely evolved by stringent selection of human strains in warfare (Roger Pitt [1978]).

42 See, for example, Richard D. Alexander [1979], especially Ch. 4.

66					THE AMERICAN ECONOMIC REVIEW					DECEMBER 1985

interventions. While this fact cuts against theories of simplistic genetic determinism, certain ultimate principles like scarcity and opportunity cost, and the universal bioeconomic processes of competition and selection, will always remain valid for analyzing and predicting the course of human behavior and social organization.

I must conclude very briefly. In pursuing their respective imperialist destinies, economics and sociobiology have arrived in different ways at what is ultimately the same master pattern of social theory — one into which the phenomena studied by the various social sciences to some extent already have been, and ultimately will all be, fitted.

REFERENCES

Akerlof, George A. and William T. Dickens, "The Economic Consequences of Cognitive Dissonance," *American Economic Review,* v. 72 (June 1982), 307-19.

Alchian, Armen A., Uncertainty, Evolution, and Economic Theory," *Journal of Political Economy,* v. 58 (1950).

Alexander, Richard D., *Darwinism and Human Affairs,* (Seattle: U. of Washington Press, 1979).

Alhadeff, David, *Microeconomics and Human Behavior: Toward a Synthesis of Economics and Psychology* (Berkeley: U. of California Press, 1982).

Barzel, Yoram and Eugene Silberberg, "Is the Act of Voting Rational?", *Public Choice* v. 16 (Fall 1973).

Becker, Gary S., "A Theory of the Allocation of Time," *Economic Journal,* v. 75 (1965), 493-517.

_____, "Crime and Punishment: An Economic Approach," *Journal of Political Economy,* v. 76 (Mar./Apr. 1968), 169-217.

_____, "A Theory of Social Interactions," *Journal of Political Economy,* v. 82 (Nov./Dec. 1971), 1063-93.

_____, *The Economic Approach to Human Behavior* (Chicago: U. of Chicago Press, 1976).

_____, "Altruism, Egoism, and Genetic Fitness: Economics and Sociobiology," *Journal of Economic Literature,* v. 14 (September 1976).

_____, *Treatise on the Family* (Cambridge, MA: Harvard U.P., 1981).

_____, "A Theory of Competition Among Pressure Groups for Political Influence," *Quarterly Journal of Economics,* v. 98 (Aug. 1983), 371-400.

Bolnick, Bruce R., "Government as a Super Becker-altruist," *Public Choice,* v. 34 (1979), 499-504.

Boulding, Kenneth E., *Conflict and Defense: A General Theory* (New York: Harper & Brothers, 1962).

Boyd, Robert and Peter J. Richerson, "Sociobiology, Culture and Economic Theory," *Journal of Economic Behavior and Organization,* v. 1 (June 1980), 97-122.

Brennan, Geoffrey and Gordon Tullock, "An Economic Theory of Military Tactics," *Journal of Economic Behavior and Organization,* v. 3 (1982), 225-42.

Brenner, Reuven, *History — The Human Gamble* (Chicago: U. of Chicago Press, 1983).

Buchanan, James M. and Gordon Tullock, *The Calculus of Consent* (Ann Arbor: U. of Michigan Press, 1962).

Campbell, Donald T., "On the Conflicts Between Biological and Social Evolution and Between Psychology and Moral Tradition," *American Psychologist,* v. 30 (Dec. 1975), 1103-22.

Chamberlain, G. and M. Rothschild, "A Note on the Probability of Casting a Decisive Vote," Social Systems Research Institute, U. of Wisconsin-Madison (1980).

Charnov, Eric L., "Optimal Foraging: The Marginal Value Theorem," *Theoretical Population Biology,* v. 9 (1976), 126-36.

Coase, Ronald H., "The Problem of Social Cost," *Journal of Law and Economics,* v. 3 (Oct. 1960), 1-45.

_____, "Economics and Contiguous Disciplines," *Journal of Legal Studies,* v. 7 (June 1978).

Coelen, Stephen P. and Robert J. McIntyre, "An Econometric Model of Pronatalist and Abortion Policies," *Journal of Political Economy,* v. 86 (Dec. 1978), 1077-1101.

Collard, David, *Altruism and Economy* (New York: Oxford U.P., 1978).

Conlisk, John, "Costly Optimizers versus Cheap Imitators," *Journal of Economic Behavior and Organization,* v. 1 (Sept. 1980), 275-93.

Cosmides, Leda, "Deduction or Darwinian Algorithms: An Explanation of the Elusive Content Effect on the Wason Selection Task," unpublished Harvard University Ph.D. thesis (1985).

Dawkins, Richard, *The Selfish Gene* (New York: Oxford U.P., 1976)

_____, *The Extended Phenotype* (New York: Oxford U.P., 1982).

Deci, Edward L., "Effects of Externally Mediated Rewards on Intrinsic Motivation," *Journal of Personality and Social Psychology,* v. 18 (1971), 105-15.

Downs, Anthony, "An Economic Theory of Political Action in a Democracy," *Journal of Political Economy,* v. 65 (April 1957), 135-50.

Easterlin, Richard, "Does Economic Growth Improve the Human Lot? Some Empirical Evidence," in Paul David and Melvin Reder, eds., *Nations and Households in Economic Growth: Essays in Honor of Moses Abramovitz* (New York: Academic Press, 1974)

Edgeworth, F.Y., *Mathematical Psychics* (London: C. Kegan Paul & Co., 1881).

Ehrlich, Isaac, "Participation in Illegitimate Activities: A Theoretical and Empirical Investigation," *Journal of Political Economy,* v. 81 (May/June 1973), 521-65.

Enke, Stephen, "On Maximizing Profits: A Distinction Between Chamberlin and Robinson," *American Economic Review,* v. 41 (Sept. 1951), 566-78.

Frank, Robert H., *Choosing the Right Pond* (New York: Oxford U.P., 1985).

Ghiselin, Michael T., "The Economy of the Body," *American Economic Review,* v. 68 (May 1978).

Goodman, John C., "An Economic Theory of the Evolution of the Common Law," *Journal of Legal Studies,* v. 7 (1978), 393-406.

Grossbard, Amyra, "The Economics of Polygamy," in J. Simon and J. DaVanzo, eds., *Research in Popula-*

tion Economics, v. 2 (Greenwich, CT: JAI Press, 1980).

Hamilton, W.D, "The Genetical Evolution of Social Behavior, I," Journal of Theoretical Biology, v. 7 (1964).

_____, "Selfish and Spiteful Behaviour in an Evolutionary Model," Nature, v. 228 (Dec. 19, 1970), 1218-20.

Hayek, Friedrich A., The Political Order of a Free People, v. 3 of Law, Legislation, and Liberty (Chicago: U. of Chicago Press, 1979).

Hirschman, Albert O., "Against Parsimony: Three Easy Ways of Complicating Some Categories of Economic Discourse," Economics and Philosophy, v. 1 (1985, forthcoming).

Hirshleifer, J., "Shakespeare Versus Becker on Altruism: The Importance of Having the Last Word," Journal of Economic Literature, v. 15 (June 1977).

_____, "Natural Economy Versus Political Economy," Journal of Social & Biological Structures, v. 1 (Oct. 1978).

_____, "Privacy: Its Origin, Function, and Future," Journal of Legal Studies, v. 9 (Dec. 1980).

_____, "On the Emotions as Guarantors of Threats and Promises," UCLA Economics Dept. Working Paper #337 (Aug. 1984).

_____, "Conflict and Settlement," in The New Palgrave; A Dictionary of Economic Theory and Doctrine (London: Macmillan, 1987 [forthcoming]).

International Encyclopedia of the Social Sciences, David L. Sills, ed. (New York: Macmillan and Free Press, 1968).

Kahneman, Daniel, Paul Slovic, and Amos Tversky, Judgment Under Uncertainty: Heuristics and Biases (Cambridge: Cambridge U.P., 1982).

Kaplan, Hillard and Kim Hill, "Food Sharing Among Aché Foragers:Tests of Explanatory Hypotheses," Current Anthropology, v. 26 (1985, forthcoming).

Kelley, Harold, "The Processes of Causal Attribution," American Psychologist, v. 28 (February 1973), 107-28.

Krueger, Anne O., "The Political Economy of the Rent-Seeking Society," American Economic Review, v. 64 (June 1974), 291-304.

Lanchester, Frederick William, Aircraft in Warfare: The Dawn of the Fourth Arm, (London: Constable, 1916). Extract reprinted in James R. Newman, ed. The World of Mathematics, v. 4 (New York: Simon and Schuster, 1976), 2138-57.

Lepper, Mark R., David Greene, and Richard E. Nisbett, "Undermining Children's Intrinsic Interest with Extrinsic Reward: A Test of the 'Overjustification' Hypothesis," Journal of Personality and Social Psychology, v. 28 (1973), 129-37.

Lévi-Strauss, Claude, "The Principle of Reciprocity," in Lewis A. Coser and Bernard Rosenberg, eds., Sociological Theory (New York: Macmillan, 1964).

Lewontin, Richard C., "Fitness, Survival, and Optimality," in D.J. Horn, R.D. Mitchell, and G.R. Stairs, eds., Analysis of Ecological Systems (Columbus: Ohio State U.P., 1979).

Linder, Staffan B., The Harried Leisure Class (New York: Columbia U.P., 1970).

Margolis, Howard, Selfishness, Altruism, and Rationality (Cambridge: Cambridge U. Press, 1982).

Marshall, Alfred, Principles of Economics, 8th ed. (London: Macmillan, 1920).

Masters, Roger D., "Of Marmots and Men: Animal Behavior and Human Altruism," in Lauren Wispé (ed.), Altruism, Sympathy, and Helping: Psychological and Sociological Principles (1978).

Mauss, Marcel, The Gift: Forms and Functions of Exchange in Archaic Societies (Free Press, 1954; original French publication, 1925).

Maynard Smith, John, "Optimization Theory in Evolution," Annual Review of Ecology and Systematics, v. 9 (1978), 31-56.

McGuire, Martin, "Group Size, Group Homogeneity, and the Aggregate Provision of a Pure Public Good Under Cournot Behavior," Public Choice, v. 18 (Summer 1974).

Mueller, Dennis C., Public Choice (Cambridge: Cambridge U.P., 1979).

Nelson, Richard R. and Sidney G. Winter, An Evolutionary Theory of Economic Change, (Cambridge, MA: Harvard U.P., 1982).

Pareto, Vilfredo, Manual of Political Economy, tr. Ann S. Schwier (New York: A.M. Kelley, 1971). [Original French publication 1927].

Penrose, Edith T., "Biological Analogies in the Theory of the Firm," American Economic Review, v. 42 (1952).

Pitt, Roger, "Warfare and Hominid Brain Evolution," Journal of Theoretical Biology, v. 72 (1978), 551-75.

Posner, Richard A., The Economic Analysis of Law, 2nd ed. (Boston: Little, Brown and Co., 1977).

_____, "A Theory of Primitive Society, with Special Reference to Law," Journal of Law and Economics, v. 23 (April 1980), 1-53.

Radnitzky, Gerard and Peter Bernholz, eds., Economic Imperialism: The Economic Approach Applied Outside the Traditional Areas of Economics (New York: Paragon House, 1985 [forthcoming]).

Robbins, Lionel, The Nature and Significance of Economic Science (London: Macmillan, 1962).

Roberts, Russell D., "A Positive Model of Private Charity and Public Transfers," Journal of Political Economy, v. 92 (Feb. 1984), 136-48.

Rosen, Sherwin, "The Economics of Superstars," American Economic Review, v. 70 (1981), 845-58.

Rubin, Paul H., "Why Is the Common Law Efficient?", Journal of Legal Studies, v. 6 (1977), 51-63.

Sahlins, Marshall D., Stone Age Economics (Chicago: Aldine-Atherton, Inc., 1972).

Schelling, Thomas C., "The Intimate Contest for Self-Command," Public Interest, No. 60 (Sept. 1980).

Schoeck, Helmut, Envy: A Theory of Social Behaviour, tr. Michael Glenny and Betty Ross (New York: Harcourt, Brace and World, 1969). [Original German publication 1966].

Schweber, S.S., "The Genesis of Natural Selection — 1838: Some Further Insights," BioScience, v. 28 (May 1978).

Sen, Amartya K., "Rational Fools: A Critique of the Behavioral Foundations of Economic Theory," Philosophy and Public Affairs, v. 6 (1977), 317-44.

68   THE AMERICAN ECONOMIC REVIEW   DECEMBER 1985

Simon, Herbert A., "A Behavioral Model of Rational Choice," *Quarterly Journal of Economics,* v. 69 (Feb. 1955), 99-118.

——————, "Theories of Decision-Making in Economics and Behavioral Science," *American Economic Review,* v. 49 (June 1959), 253-83.

Smith, Adam, *The Theory of Moral Sentiments,* E.G. West ed. (Indianapolis: Liberty Classics, 1976). [Original publication 1759].

——————, *Wealth of Nations,* Modern Library edition (New York: Random House, 1937). [Original publication 1776].

Smith, Eric Alden, "Anthropological Applications of Optimal Foraging Theory: A Critical Review," *Current Anthropology,* v. 24 (Dec. 1983), 625-51.

——————, "Optimization Theory in Anthropology: Applications and Critiques" (April 1985).

Staddon, J.E.R., *Adaptive Behavior and Learning* (Cambridge: Cambridge U.P., 1983).

Thompson, Fred, "Closeness Counts in Horseshoes and Dancing. . .and Elections," *Public Choice,* v. 38 (1982), 305-16.

Trivers, Robert L., "Parental Investment and Sexual Selection," in Bernard G. Campbell, ed., *Sexual Selection and the Descent of Man 1871-1971* (Chicago: Aldine, 1972).

——————, "Parent-Offspring Conflict," *American Zoologist,* v. 14 (1974).

Tullock, Gordon, "Economics and Sociobiology: A Comment," *Journal of Economic Literature,* v. 15 (June 1977), 502-06.

Tversky, Amos and Daniel Kahneman, "Judgment under Uncertainty: Heuristics and Biases," *Science,* v. 185 (27 Sept. 1974), 1124-1131.

Veblen, Thorstein, *The Theory of the Leisure Class,* rev. ed. (New York: New American Library, 1953). [Original publication 1899].

Wilson, Edward O., *Sociobiology: The New Synthesis* (Cambridge, MA: Harvard U.P., 1975).

——————, "Biology and the Social Sciences," *Daedalus* (Fall 1977).

——————, "Altruism," *Harvard Magazine,* v. 81 (Nov.-Dec. 1978).

——————, "The Ergonomics of Caste in the Social Insects," *American Economic Review,* v. 68 (December 1978).

Winter, Sidney G. Jr., "Economic 'Natural Selection' and the Theory of the Firm," *Yale Economic Essays,* v. 4 (1964).

——————, "Satisficing, Selection, and the Innovating Remnant," *Quarterly Journal of Economics,* v. 85 (1971).

Wittman, Donald, "How a War Ends: A Rational Model Approach," *Journal of Conflict Resolution,* v. 23 (Dec. 1979).

[11]

De Gustibus Non Est Disputandum

By Georgealdo —

By George J. Stigler and Gary S. Becker*

The venerable admonition not to quarrel over tastes is commonly interpreted as advice to terminate a dispute when it has been resolved into a difference of tastes, presumably because there is no further room for rational persuasion. Tastes are the unchallengeable axioms of a man's behavior: he may properly (usefully) be criticized for inefficiency in satisfying his desires, but the desires themselves are *data*. Deplorable tastes—say, for arson—may be countered by coercive and punitive action, but these deplorable tastes, at least when held by an adult, are not capable of being changed by persuasion.

Our title seems to us to be capable of another and preferable interpretation: that tastes neither change capriciously nor differ importantly between people. On this interpretation one does not argue over tastes for the same reason that one does not argue over the Rocky Mountains—both are there, will be there next year, too, and are the same to all men.

The difference between these two viewpoints of tastes is fundamental. On the traditional view, an explanation of economic phenomena that reaches a difference in tastes between people or times is the terminus of the argument: the problem is abandoned *at this point* to whoever studies and explains tastes (psychologists? anthropologists? phrenologists? sociobiologists?). On our preferred interpretation, one never reaches this impasse: the economist continues to search for differences in prices or incomes to explain any differences or changes in behavior.

The choice between these two views of the role of tastes in economic theory must ultimately be made on the basis of their comparative analytical productivities. On the conventional view of inscrutable, often capricious tastes, one drops

the discussion as soon as the behavior of tastes becomes important—and turns his energies to other problems. On our view, one searches, often long and frustratingly, for the subtle forms that prices and incomes take in explaining differences among men and periods. If the latter approach yields more useful results, it is the proper choice. The establishment of the proposition that one may usefully treat tastes as stable over time and similar among people is the central task of this essay.

The ambitiousness of our agenda deserves emphasis: we are proposing the hypothesis that widespread and/or persistent human behavior can be explained by a generalized calculus of utility-maximizing behavior, without introducing the qualification "tastes remaining the same." It is a thesis that does not permit of direct proof because it is an assertion about the world, not a proposition in logic. Moreover, it is possible almost at random to throw up examples of phenomena that presently defy explanation by this hypothesis: Why do we have inflation? Why are there few Jews in farming?[1] Why are societies with polygynous families so rare in the modern era? Why aren't blood banks responsible for the quality of their product? If we could answer these questions to your satisfaction, you would quickly produce a dozen more.

What we assert is not that we are clever enough to make illuminating applications of utility-maximizing theory to all important phenomena—not even our entire generation of economists is clever enough to do that. Rather, we assert that this traditional approach of the

---

*University of Chicago. We have had helpful comments from Michael Bozdarich, Gilbert Ghez, James Heckman, Peter Pashigian, Sam Peltzman, Donald Wittman, and participants in the Workshop on Industrial Organization.

[1]Our lamented friend Reuben Kessel offered an attractive explanation: since Jews have been persecuted so often and forced to flee to other countries, they have not invested in immobile land, but in mobile human capital—business skills, education, etc.—that would automatically go with them. Of course, someone might counter with the more basic query: but why are they Jews, and not Christians or Moslems?

economist offers guidance in tackling these problems—and that no other approach of remotely comparable generality and power is available.

To support our thesis we could offer samples of phenomena we believe to be usefully explained on the assumption of stable, well-behaved preference functions. Ultimately, this is indeed the only persuasive method of supporting the assumption, and it is legitimate to cite in support all of the existing corpus of successful economic theory. Here we shall undertake to give this proof by accomplishment a special and limited interpretation. We take categories of behavior commonly held to demonstrate changes in tastes or to be explicable only in terms of such changes, and show both that they are reconcilable with our assumption of stable preferences and that the reformulation is illuminating.

I. The New Theory of Consumer Choice

The power of stable preferences and utility maximization in explaining a wide range of behavior has been significantly enhanced by a recent reformulation of consumer theory.[2] This reformulation transforms the family from a passive maximizer of the utility from market purchases into an active maximizer also engaged in extensive production and investment activities. In the traditional theory, households maximize a utility function of the goods and services bought in the marketplace, whereas in the reformulation they maximize a utility function of objects of choice, called commodities, that they produce with market goods, their own time, their skills, training and other human capital, and other inputs. Stated formally, a household seeks to maximize

$$(1) \qquad U = U(Z_1, \ldots Z_m)$$

with

$$(2) \quad Z_i = f_i(X_{1i}, \ldots X_{ki}, t_{1i}, \ldots t_{\ell i}, S_1, \\ \ldots S_\ell, Y_i), \quad i = 1 \ldots m$$

[2]An exposition of this reformulation can be found in Robert Michael and Becker. This exposition emphasizes the capacity of the reformulation to generate many implications about behavior that are consistent with stable tastes.

where Z_i are the commodity objects of choice entering the utility function, f_i is the production function for the ith commodity, X_{ji} is the quantity of the jth market good or service used in the production of the ith commodity, t_{ji} is the jth person's own time input, S_j the jth person's human capital, and Y_i represents all other inputs.

The Z_i have no market prices since they are not purchased or sold, but do have "shadow" prices determined by their costs of production. If f_i were homogeneous of the first degree in the X_{ji} and t_{ji}, marginal and average costs would be the same and the shadow price of Z_i would be

$$(3) \qquad \pi_i = \sum_{j=1}^{k} \alpha_{ji} \left(\frac{p}{w_1}, \frac{w}{w_1}, S, Y_i \right) p_j \\ + \sum_{j=1}^{l} \beta_{ji} \left(\frac{p}{w_1}, \frac{w}{w_1}, S, Y_i \right) w_j$$

where p_j is the cost of X_j, w_j is the cost of t_j, and α_{ji} and β_{ji} are input-output coefficients that depend on the (relative) set of p and w, S, and Y_i. The numerous and varied determinants of these shadow prices give concrete expression to our earlier statement about the subtle forms that prices take in explaining differences among men and periods.

The real income of a household does not simply equal its money income deflated by an index of the prices of market goods, but equals its full income (which includes the value of "time" to the household)[3] deflated by an index of the prices, π_i, of the produced commodities. Since full income and commodity prices depend on a variety of factors, incomes also take subtle forms. Our task in this paper is to spell out some of the forms prices and full income take.

II. Stability of Tastes and "Addiction"

Tastes are frequently said to change as a result of consuming certain "addictive" goods. For example, smoking of cigarettes, drinking of alcohol, injection of heroin, or close contact with some persons over an appreciable period of

[3]Full income is the maximum money income that a household could achieve by an appropriate allocation of its time and other resources.

time, often increases the desire (creates a craving) for these goods or persons, and thereby cause their consumption to grow over time. In utility language, their marginal utility is said to rise over time because tastes shift in their favor. This argument has been clearly stated by Alfred Marshall when discussing the taste for "good" music:

> There is however an implicit condition in this law [of diminishing marginal utility] which should be made clear. It is that we do not suppose time to be allowed for any alteration in the character or tastes of the man himself. It is therefore no exception to the law that the more good music a man hears, the stronger is his taste for it likely to become . . . [p. 94]

We believe that the phenomenon Marshall is trying to explain, namely that exposure to good music increases the subsequent demand for good music (for some persons!), can be explained with some gain in insight by assuming constant tastes, whereas to assume a change in tastes has been an unilluminating "explanation." The essence of our explanation lies in the accumulation of what might be termed "consumption capital" by the consumer, and we distinguish "beneficial" addiction like Marshall's good music from "harmful" addiction like heroin.

Consider first beneficial addiction, and an unchanging utility function that depends on two produced commodities:

$$(4) \qquad U = U(M, Z)$$

where M measures the amount of music "appreciation" produced and consumed, and Z the production and consumption of other commodities. Music appreciation is produced by a function that depends on the time allocated to music (t_m), and the training and other human capital conducive to music appreciation (S_m) (other inputs are ignored):

$$(5) \qquad M = M_m(t_m, S_m)$$

We assume that

$$\frac{\partial M_m}{\partial t_m} > 0, \frac{\partial M_m}{\partial S_m} > 0$$

and also that

$$\frac{\partial^2 M_m}{\partial t_m \partial S_m} > 0$$

An increase in this music capital increases the productivity of time spent listening to or devoted in other ways to music.

In order to analyze the consequences for its consumption of "the more good music a man hears," the production and consumption of music appreciation has to be dated. The amount of appreciation produced at any moment j, M_j, would depend on the time allocated to music and the music human capital at j: t_{m_j} and S_{m_j}, respectively. The latter in turn is produced partly through "on-the-job" training or "learning by doing" by accumulating the effects of earlier music appreciation:

$$(6) \qquad S_{m_j} = h(M_{j-1}, M_{j-2}. \ldots, E_j)$$

By definition, the addiction is beneficial if

$$\frac{\partial S_{m_j}}{\partial M_{j-v}} > 0, \text{ all } v \text{ in (6)}$$

The term E_j measures the effect of education and other human capital on music appreciation skill, where

$$\frac{\partial S_{m_j}}{\partial E_j} > 0$$

and probably

$$\frac{\partial^2 S_{m_j}}{\partial M_{j-v} \partial E_j} > 0$$

We assume for simplicity a utility function that is a discounted sum of functions like the one in equation (4), where the M and Z commodities are dated, and the discount rate determined by time preference.[4] The optimal allocation of consumption is determined from the equality between the ratio of their marginal utilities and the ratio of their shadow prices:

$$(7) \qquad \frac{MU_{m_j}}{MU_{z_j}} = \frac{\partial U}{\partial M_j} \bigg/ \frac{\partial U}{\partial Z_j} = \frac{\pi_{m_j}}{\pi_{z_j}}$$

The shadow price equals the marginal cost of adding a unit of commodity output. The marginal cost is complicated for music appreciation M by the positive effect on subsequent music human capital of the production of music

---

[4] A consistent application of the assumption of stable preferences implies that the discount rate is zero; that is, the absence of time preference (see the brief discussion in Section VI.)

appreciation at any moment j. This effect on subsequent capital is an investment return from producing appreciation at j that reduces the cost of production at j. It can be shown that the marginal cost at j equals[5]

$$(8) \quad \pi_{m_j} = \frac{w \partial t_{m_j}}{\partial M_j} - w \sum_{i=1}^{n-j} \frac{\partial M_{j+i}}{\partial S_{m_{j+i}}} \bigg/ \frac{\partial M_{j+i}}{\partial t_{m_{j+i}}}$$

$$\cdot \frac{dS_{m_{j+i}}}{dM_j} \cdot \frac{1}{(i+r)^i}$$

$$= \frac{w \partial t_{m_j}}{\partial M_j} - A_j = \frac{w}{MP_{t_{m_j}}} - A_j$$

where w is the wage rate (assumed to be the same at all ages), r the interest rate, n the length of life, and A_j the effect of addiction, measures the

[5]The utility function

$$V = \sum_{j=1}^{n} a^j U(M_j, Z_j)$$

is maximized subject to the constraints

$$M_j = M(t_{m_j}, S_{m_j}); \quad Z_j = Z(x_j, t_{z_j})$$

$$S_{m_j} = h(M_{j-1}, M_{j-2}, \ldots, E_j)$$

$$\sum \frac{px_j}{(1+r)^j} = \sum \frac{wt_{w_j} + b_j}{(i+r)^j}$$

and $t_{w_j} + t_{m_j} + t_{z_j} = t$,

where t_{w_j} is hours worked in the jth period, and b_j is property income in that period. By substitution one derives the full wealth constraint:

$$\sum \frac{px_j + w(t_{m_j} + t_{z_j})}{(1+r)^j} = \sum \frac{wt + b_j}{(1+r)^j} = W$$

Maximization of V with respect to M_j and Z_j subject to the production functions and the full wealth constraint gives the first-order conditions

$$a^j \frac{\partial U}{\partial Z_j} = \frac{\lambda}{(1+r)^j} \left(\frac{pdx_j}{dZ_j} + \frac{wdt_{z_j}}{dZ_j} \right) = \frac{\lambda}{(1+r)^j} \pi_{z_j}$$

$$a^j \frac{\partial U}{\partial M_j} = \frac{\lambda}{(1+r)^j} \cdot \left(\frac{w \partial t_{m_j}}{\partial M_j} + \sum_{i=1}^{n-j} \frac{wdt_{m_{j+i}}}{dM_j} \cdot \frac{1}{(1+r)^i} \right)$$

$$= \frac{\lambda}{(1+r)^j} \pi_m,$$

Since, however,

$$\frac{dM_{j+i}}{dM_j} = 0 = \frac{\partial M_{j+i}}{\partial S_{m_{j+i}}} \frac{dS_{m_{j+i}}}{dM_j} + \frac{\partial M_{j+i}}{\partial t_{m_{j+i}}} \frac{dt_{m_{j+i}}}{dM_j}$$

then

$$\frac{dt_{m_{j+1}}}{dM_j} = -\frac{\partial M_{j+i}}{\partial S_{m_{j+i}}} \bigg/ \frac{\partial M_{j+i}}{\partial t_{m_{j+i}}} \cdot \frac{dS_{m_{j+i}}}{dM_j}$$

By substitution into the definition of π_{m_j}, equation (8) follows immediately.

value of the saving in future time inputs from the effect of the production of M in j on subsequent music capital.

With no addiction, $A_j = 0$ and equation (8) reduces to the familiar marginal cost formula. Moreover, A_j is positive as long as music is beneficially addictive, and tends to decline as j increases, approaching zero as j approaches n. The term w/MP_{t_m} declines with age for a given time input as long as music capital grows with age. The term A_j may not change so much with age at young ages because the percentage decline in the number of remaining years is small at these ages. Therefore, π_m would tend to decline with age at young ages because the effect on the marginal product of the time input would tend to dominate the effect on A. Although π_m might not always decline at other ages, for the present we assume that π_m declines continuously with age.

If π_z does not depend on age, the relative price of music appreciation would decline with age; then by equation (7), the relative consumption of music appreciation would rise with age. On this interpretation, the (relative) consumption of music appreciation rises with exposure not because tastes shift in favor of music, but because its shadow price falls as skill and experience in the appreciation of music are acquired with exposure.

An alternative way to state the same analysis is that the marginal utility of time allocated to music is increased by an increase in the stock of music capital.[6] Then the consumption of music appreciation could be said to rise with exposure because the marginal utility of the time spent on music rose with exposure, even though tastes were unchanged.

The effect of exposure on the accumulation of music capital might well depend on the level of education and other human capital, as indicated by equation (6). This would explain why educated persons consume more "good" music (i.e., music that educated people like!) than

[6]The marginal utility of time allocated to music at j includes the utility from the increase in the future stock of music capital that results from an increase in the time allocated at j. An argument similar to the one developed for the price of music appreciation shows that the marginal utility of time would tend to rise with age, at least at younger ages.

other persons do.

Addiction lowers the price of music apprecia-tion at younger ages without any comparable effect on the productivity of the time spent on music at these ages. Therefore, addiction would increase the time spent on music at younger ages: some of the time would be considered an investment that increases future music capital. Although the price of music tends to fall with age, and the consumption of music tends to rise, the time spent on music need not rise with age because the growth in music capital means that the consumption of music could rise even when the time spent fell with age. The time spent would be more likely to rise, the more elastic the demand curve for music appreciation. We can express this result in a form that will strike many readers as surprising; namely, that the time (or other inputs) spent on music apprecia-tion is more likely to be addictive—that is, to rise with exposure to music—the more, not less, elastic is the demand curve for music appre-ciation.

The stock of music capital might fall and the price of music appreciation rise at older ages because the incentive to invest in future capital would decline as the number of remaining years declined, whereas the investment required simply to maintain the capital stock intact would increase as the stock increased. If the price rose, the time spent on music would fall if the demand curve for music were elastic. Conse-quently, our analysis indicates that the observed addiction to music may be stronger at younger than at older ages.

These results for music also apply to other commodities that are beneficially addictive. Their prices fall at younger ages and their con-sumption rises because consumption capital is accumulated with exposure and age. The time and goods used to produce an addictive com-modity need not rise with exposure, even though consumption of the commodity does; they are more likely to rise with exposure, the more elastic is the demand curve for the commodity. Even if they rose at younger ages, they might decline eventually as the stock of consumption

capital fell at older ages.

Using the same arguments developed for beneficial addiction, we can show that all the re-sults are reversed for harmful addiction,[7] which is defined by a negative sign of the derivatives in equation (6):

$$(9) \qquad \frac{\partial S_j}{\partial H_{j-r}} < 0, \text{ all } v \text{ in (6)}$$

where H is a harmfully addictive commodity. An increase in consumption at any age reduces the stock of consumption capital available sub-sequently, and this raises the shadow price at all ages.[8] The shadow price would rise with age and exposure, at least at younger ages, which would induce consumption to fall with age and expo-sure. The inputs of goods and time need not fall with exposure, however, because consump-tion capital falls with exposure; indeed, the inputs are likely to rise with exposure if the commodity's demand curve were inelastic.

To illustrate these conclusions, consider the commodity "euphoria" produced with input of heroin (or alcohol or amphetamines.) An in-crease in the consumption of current euphoria raises the cost of producing euphoria in the fu-ture by reducing the future stock of "euphoric capital." The effect of exposure to euphoria on the cost of producing future euphoria reduces the consumption of euphoria as exposure con-tinues. If the demand curve for euphoria were sufficiently inelastic, however, the use of heroin would grow with exposure at the same time that euphoria fell.

Note that the amount of heroin used at younger ages would be reduced because of the negative effect on later euphoric capital. Indeed, no heroin at all might be used only because the harmfully addictive effects are anticipated, and discourage any use. Note further that if heroin

---

[7] In some ways, our analysis of beneficial and harmful addiction is a special case of the analysis of beneficial and detrimental joint production in Michael Grossman.

[8] Instead of equation (8), one has

$$\pi_{h_j} = \frac{w}{MP_{t_j}} + A_j$$

where $A_j \geq 0$

were used even though the subsequent adverse consequences were accurately anticipated, the utility of the user would be greater than it would be if he were prevented from using heroin. Of course, his utility would be still greater if technologies developed (methadone?) to reduce the harmfully addictive effects of euphoria.[9]

Most interestingly, note that the use of heroin would grow with exposure at the same time that the amount of euphoria fell, if the demand curve for euphoria and thus for heroin were sufficiently inelastic. That is, addiction to heroin—a growth in use with exposure—is the *result* of an inelastic demand for heroin, *not,* as commonly argued, the *cause* of an inelastic demand. In the same way, listening to music or playing tennis would be addictive if the demand curves for music or tennis appreciation were sufficiently elastic; the addiction again is the result, not the cause, of the particular elasticity. Put differently, if addiction were surmised (partly because the input of goods or time rose with age), but if it were not clear whether the addiction were harmful or beneficial, the elasticity of demand could be used to distinguish between them: a high elasticity suggests beneficial and a low elasticity suggests harmful addiction.[10]

We do not have to assume that exposure to euphoria changes tastes in order to understand why the use of heroin grows with exposure, or why the amount used is insensitive to changes in its price. Even with constant tastes, the amount used would grow with exposure, and heroin is

---

[9]That is, if new technology reduced and perhaps even changed the sign of the derivatives in equation (9). We should state explicitly, to avoid any misunderstanding, that "harmful" means only that the derivatives in (9) are negative, and not that the addiction harms others, nor, as we have just indicated, that it is unwise for addicts to consume such commodities.

[10]The elasticity of demand can be estimated from the effects of changes in the prices of inputs. For example, if a commodity's production function were homogeneous of degree one, and if all its future as well as present input prices rose by the same known percentage, the elasticity of demand for the commodity could be estimated from the decline in the inputs. Therefore the distinction between beneficial and harmful addiction is operational: these independently estimated commodity elasticities could be used, as in the text, to determine whether an addiction was harmful or beneficial.

addictive precisely *because* of the insensitivity to price changes.

An exogenous rise in the price of addictive goods or time, perhaps due to an excise tax, such as the tax on cigarettes and alcohol, or to restrictions on their sale, such as the imprisonment of dealers in heroin, would have a relatively small effect on their use by addicts if these are harmfully addictive goods, and a relatively large effect if they are beneficially addictive. That is, excise taxes and imprisonment mainly transfer resources away from addicts if the goods are harmfully addictive, and mainly reduce the consumption of addicts if the goods are beneficially addictive.

The extension of the capital concept to investment in the capacity to consume more efficiently has numerous other potential applications. For example, there is a fertile field in consumption capital for the application of the theory of division of labor among family members.

III. Stability of Tastes and Custom and Tradition

A "traditional" qualification to the scope of economic theory is the alleged powerful hold over human behavior of custom and tradition. An excellent statement in the context of the behavior of rulers is that of John Stuart Mill:

> It is not true that the actions even of average rulers are wholly, or anything approaching to wholly, determined by their personal interest, or even by their own opinion of their personal interest. . . . I insist only on what is true of all rulers, viz., that the character and course of their actions is largely influenced (independently of personal calculations) by the habitual sentiments and feelings, the general modes of thinking and acting, which prevail throughout the community of which they are members; as well as by the feelings, habits, and modes of thought which characterize the particular class in that community to which they themselves belong. . . . They are also much influenced by the maxims and traditions which have descended to them from other rulers, their predecessors; which maxims and traditions have been known to retain an ascendancy during long periods, even

82   THE AMERICAN ECONOMIC REVIEW   MARCH 1977

in opposition to the private interests of the rulers for the time being. [p. 484]

The specific political behavior that contradicts "personal interest" theories is not clear from Mill's statement, nor is it much clearer in similar statements by others applied to firms or households. Obviously, stable behavior by (say) households faced with stable prices and incomes —or more generally a stable environment—is no contradiction since stability then is implied as much by personal interest theories as by custom and tradition. On the other hand, stable behavior in the face of changing prices and incomes might contradict the approach taken in this essay that assumes utility maximizing with stable tastes.

Nevertheless, we believe that our approach better explains when behavior is stable than do approaches based on custom and tradition, and can at the same time explain how and when behavior does change. Mill's "habits and modes of thought," or his "maxims and traditions which have descended," in our analysis result from investment of time and other resources in the accumulation of knowledge about the environment, and of skills with which to cope with it.

The making of decisions is costly, and not simply because it is an activity which some people find unpleasant. In order to make a decision one requires information, and the information must be analyzed. The costs of searching for information and of applying the information to a new situation are such that habit is often a more efficient way to deal with moderate or temporary changes in the environment than would be a full, apparently utility-maximizing decision. This is precisely the avoidance of what J. M. Clark termed the irrational passion for dispassionate rationality.

A simple example of economizing on information by the habitual purchase from one source will illustrate the logic. A consumer buys one unit of commodity X in each unit of time. He pays a price p_t at a time t. The choices he faces are:

1. To search at the time of an act of purchase to obtain the lowest possible price $\hat{p}_t$ consistent with the cost of search. Then $\hat{p}_t$ is a function of the amount of search s (assumed to be the same at each act of purchase):

$$(10) \qquad \hat{p}_t = f(s), f'(s) < 0$$

where the total cost of s is $C(s)$.

2. To search less frequently (but usually more intensively), relying between searches upon the outcome of the previous search in choosing a supplier. Then the price p_t will be higher (relative to the average market price), the longer the period since the previous search (at time t_o),

$$p_t = g(t - t_o), g' > 0$$

Ignoring interest, the latter method of purchase will have a total cost over period T determined by

1) K searches (all of equal intensity) at cost $K \, C(s)$.

2) Each search lasts for a period T/K, within which $r = T/K$ purchases are made, at cost $r \, \bar{p}$, where $\bar{p}$ is the average price. Assume that the results of search "depreciate" (prices appreciate) at rate δ. A consumer minimizes his combined cost of the commodity and search over the total time period; the minimizing condition is[11]

[11] The price of the ith purchase within one of the K search periods is $p_i = \hat{p}(1 + \delta)^{i-1}$. Hence

$$\bar{p} = \frac{1}{r} \sum_{i=1}^{r} \hat{p}(1 + \delta)^{i-1} = \hat{p}\,\frac{(1 + \delta)^r - 1}{r\delta}$$

The total cost to be minimized is

$$TC = Kr\bar{p} + KC(s) = K\hat{p}\,\frac{(1 + \delta)^r - 1}{\delta} + KC$$

By taking a second-order approximation to $(1 + \delta)^r$, we get

$$TC = T\left\{\hat{p}\left[1 + \frac{(r - 1)\delta}{2}\right] + \frac{C}{r}\right\}$$

Minimizing with respect to r gives

$$\frac{\partial TC}{\partial r} = 0 = T\left(\frac{\hat{p}\delta}{2} - \frac{C}{r^2}\right)$$

or

$$r = \sqrt{\frac{2C}{\delta\hat{p}}}$$

$$(11) \qquad r = \sqrt{\frac{2C}{\delta \hat{p}}}$$

In this simple model with r purchases between successive searches, r is larger the larger the amount spent on search per dollar spent on the commodity $(C/\hat{p})$, and the lower the rate of appreciation of prices (δ). If there were full search on each individual act of purchase, the total cost could not be less than the cost when the optimal frequency of search was chosen, and might be much greater.

When a temporary change takes place in the environment, perhaps in prices or income, it generally would not pay to disinvest the capital embodied in knowledge or skills, or to accumulate different types of capital. As a result, behavior will be relatively stable in the face of temporary changes.

A related situation arises when an unexpected change in the environment does not induce a major response immediately because time is required to accumulate the appropriate knowledge and skills. Therefore, stable preferences combined with investment in "specific" knowledge and skills can explain the small or "inelastic" responses that figure so prominently in short-run demand and supply curves.

A permanent change in the environment, perhaps due to economic development, usually causes a greater change in the behavior of young than of old persons. The common interpretation is that young persons are more readily seduced away from their customs and traditions by the glitter of the new (Western?) environment. On our interpretation, young and old persons respond differently, even if they have the same preferences and motivation. To change their behavior drastically, older persons have to either disinvest their capital that was attuned to the old environment, or invest in capital attuned to the new environment. Their incentive to do so may be quite weak, however, because relatively few years remain for them to collect the returns on new investments, and much human capital can only be disinvested slowly.

Young persons, on the other hand, are not so encumbered by accumulations of capital attuned

to the old environment. Consequently, they need not have different preferences or motivation or be intrinsically more flexible in order to be more affected by a change in the environment: they simply have greater incentive to invest in knowledge and skills attuned to the new environment.

Note that this analysis is similar to that used in the previous section to explain addictive behavior: utility maximization with stable preferences, conditioned by the accumulation of specific knowledge and skills. One does not need one kind of theory to explain addictive behavior and another kind to explain habitual or customary behavior. The same theory based on stable preferences can explain both types of behavior, and can accommodate both habitual behavior and the departures therefrom.

IV. Stability of Tastes and Advertising

Perhaps the most important class of cases in which "change of tastes" is invoked as an explanation for economic phenomena is that involving advertising. The advertiser "persuades" the consumer to prefer his product, and often a distinction is drawn between "persuasive" and "informative" advertising.[12] John Kenneth Galbraith is the most famous of the economists who argue that advertising molds consumer tastes:

> These [institutions of modern advertising and salesmanship] cannot be reconciled with the notion of independently determined desires for their central function is to create desires—to bring into being wants that previously did not exist. This is accomplished by the producer of the goods or at his behest.—Outlays for the manufacturing of a product are not more important in the strategy of modern business enterprise than outlays for the manufacturing of demand for the product. [pp. 155–56]

---

[12]The distinction, if in fact one exists, between persuasive and informative advertising must be one of purpose or effect, not of content. A simple, accurately stated fact ("I offer you this genuine $1 bill for 10 cents") can be highly persuasive; the most bizarre claim ("If Napoleon could have bought our machine gun, he would have defeated Wellington") contains some information (machine guns were not available in 1814).

We shall argue, in direct opposition to this view, that it is neither necessary nor useful to attribute to advertising the function of changing tastes.

A consumer may indirectly receive utility from a market good, yet the utility depends not only on the quantity of the good but also the consumer's knowledge of its true or alleged properties. If he does not know whether the berries are poisonous, they are not food; if he does not know that they contain vitamin C, they are not consumed to prevent scurvy. The quantity of information is a complex notion: its degree of accuracy, its multidimensional properties, its variable obsolescence with time are all qualities that make direct measurement of information extremely difficult.

How can this elusive variable be incorporated into the theory of demand while preserving the stability of tastes? Our approach is to continue to assume, as in the previous sections, that the ultimate objects of choice are commodities produced by each household with market goods, own time, *knowledge,* and perhaps other inputs. We now assume, in addition, that the knowledge, whether real or fancied, is produced by the advertising of producers and perhaps also the own search of households.

Our approach can be presented through a detailed analysis of the simple case where the output x of a particular firm and its advertising A are the inputs into a commodity produced and consumed by households; for a given household:

$$(12) \qquad Z = f(x, A, E, y)$$

where $\partial Z/\partial x > 0$, $\partial Z/\partial A > 0$, E is the human capital of the houshold that affects these marginal products, and y are other variables, possibly including advertising by other firms. Still more simply,

$$(13) \qquad Z = g(A, E, y)x$$

where $\partial g/\partial A = g' > 0$ and $\partial^2 g/\partial A^2 < 0$. With A, E, and y held constant, the amount of the commodity produced and consumed by any household is assumed to be proportional to the amount of the firm's output used by that household.[13] If the advertising reaching any household

[13]Stated differently, Z is homogeneous of the first degree in x alone.

were independent of its behavior, the shadow price of Z, the marginal cost of x, would simply be the expenditure on x required to change Z by one unit. From equation (13), that equals

$$(14) \qquad \pi_z = \frac{p_x}{g}$$

where p_x is the price of x.

An increase in advertising may lower the commodity price to the household (by raising g), and thereby increase its demand for the commodity and change its demand for the firm's output, because the household is made to believe— correctly or incorrectly—that it gets a greater output of the commodity from a given input of the advertised product. Consequently, advertising affects consumption in this formulation not by changing tastes, but by changing prices. That is, a movement along a stable demand curve for commodities is seen as generating the apparently unstable demand curves of market goods and other inputs.

More than a simple change in language is involved: our formulation has quite different implications from the conventional ones. To develop these implications, consider a firm that is determining its optimal advertising along with its optimal output. We assume initially that the commodity indirectly produced by this firm (equation (12)) is a perfect substitute to consumers for commodities indirectly produced by many other firms. Therefore, the firm is perfectly competitive in the commodity market, and could (indirectly) sell an unlimited amount of this commodity at a fixed commodity price. Observe that a firm can have many perfect substitutes in the commodity market even though few other firms produce the same physical product. For example, a firm may be the sole designer of jewelry that contributes to the social prestige of consumers, and yet compete fully with many other products that also contribute to prestige: large automobiles, expensive furs, fashionable clothing, elaborate parties, a respected occupation, etc.

If the level of advertising were fixed, there would be a one-to-one correspondence between the price of the commodity and the price of the firm's output (see equation (14)). If π_z were given by the competitive market, p_x would then also be given, and the firm would find its optimal output in the conventional way by equating marginal cost to the given product price. There is no longer such a one-to-one correspondence between π_z and p_x, however, when the level of advertising is also a variable, and even a firm faced with a fixed commodity price in a perfectly competitive commodity market could sell its product at different prices by varying the level of advertising. Since an increase in advertising would increase the commodity output that consumers receive from a given amount of this firm's product, the price of its product would then be increased relative to the fixed commodity price.

The optimal advertising, product price, and output of the firm can be found by maximizing its income

$$(15) \qquad I = p_x X - TC(X) - Ap_a$$

where X is the firm's total output, TC its costs of production other than advertising, and p_a the (constant) cost of a unit of advertising. By substituting from equation (14), I can be written as

$$(15') \qquad I = \pi_z^0 g(A)X - TC(X) - Ap_a$$

where π_z^0 is the given market commodity price, the advertising-effectiveness function (g) is assumed to be the same for all consumers,[14] and the variables E and y in g are suppressed. The first-order maximum conditions with respect to X and A are

$$(16) \qquad p_x = \pi_z^0 g = MC(X)$$

$$(17) \qquad \frac{\partial p_x}{\partial A}X = \pi_z^0 Xg' = p_a$$

Equation (16) is the usual equality between price and marginal cost for a competitive firm, which continues to hold when advertising exists and is a decision variable. Not surprisingly, equation (17) says that marginal revenue and marginal cost of advertising are equal, where

[14]Therefore, $p_x X = \pi_z^0 g \sum_{i=1}^{n} x_i$

where n is the number of households.

marginal revenue is determined by the level of output and the increase in product price "induced" by an increase in advertising. Although the commodity price is fixed, an increase in advertising increases the firm's product price by an amount that is proportional to the increased capacity (measured by g') of its product to contribute (at least in the minds of consumers) to commodity output.

In the conventional analysis, firms in perfectly competitive markets gain nothing from advertising and thus have no incentive to advertise because they are assumed to be unable to differentiate their products to consumers who have perfect knowledge. In our analysis, on the other hand, consumers have imperfect information, including misinformation, and a skilled advertiser might well be able to differentiate his product from other apparently similar products. Put differently, advertisers could increase the value of their output to consumers without increasing to the same extent the value of the output even of perfect competitors in the *commodity* market. To simplify, we assume that the value of competitors' output is unaffected, in the sense that the commodity price (more generally, the commodity demand curve) to any firm is not affected by its advertising. Note that when firms in perfectly competitive commodity markets differentiate their products by advertising, they still preserve the perfect competition in these markets. Note moreover, that if different firms were producing the same physical product in the same competitive commodity market, and had the same marginal cost and advertising-effectiveness functions, they would produce the same output, charge the same product price, and advertise at the same rate. If, however, either their marginal costs or advertising-effectiveness differed, they would charge different product prices, advertise at different rates, and yet still be perfect competitors (although not of one another)!

Not only can firms in perfectly competitive commodity markets—that is, firms faced with infinitely elastic commodity demand curves—have an incentive to advertise, but the incentive may actually be greater, the more competitive the commodity market is. Let us consider the case of a finite commodity demand elasticity.

The necessary conditions to maximize income given by equation (15'), if π_z varies as a function of Z, are

$$(18) \quad \frac{\partial I}{\partial X} = \pi_z g + X \frac{\partial \pi_z}{\partial Z} \frac{\partial Z}{\partial X} g - MC(X) = 0,$$

or since $Z = gX$, and $\partial Z / \partial X = g$,

$$(18') \quad \pi_z g \left(1 + \frac{1}{\epsilon_{\pi_z}}\right) = p_x \left(1 + \frac{1}{\epsilon_{\pi_z}}\right)$$

$$= MC(X)$$

where ϵ_{π_z} is the elasticity of the firm's commodity demand curve. Also

$$(19) \quad \frac{\partial I}{\partial A} = X \frac{\partial p_x}{\partial A} - p_a =$$

$$\pi_z \frac{\partial Z}{\partial A} + \frac{\partial \pi_z}{\partial Z} \cdot \frac{\partial Z}{\partial A} \cdot Z - p_a = 0$$

or

$$(19') \quad X \frac{\partial p_x}{\partial A} = \pi_z g' X \left(1 + \frac{1}{\epsilon_{\pi_z}}\right) = p_a$$

Equation (18') is simply the usual maximizing condition for a monopolist that continues to hold when there is advertising.[15] Equation (19') clearly shows that, given $\pi_z g' X$, the marginal revenue from additional advertising is greater, the greater is the elasticity of the commodity demand curve; therefore, the optimal level of advertising would be positively related to the commodity elasticity.

This important result can be made intuitive by considering Figure 1. The curve DD gives the firm's commodity demand curve, where π_z is measured along the vertical and commodity output Z along the horizontal axis. The firm's production of X is held fixed so that Z varies only because of variations in the level of advertising. At point e^0, the level of advertising is A_0, the product price is p_x^0, and commodity

$$\epsilon_{\pi_z} = \frac{dZ}{Z} \bigg/ \frac{d\pi_z}{\pi_z} = \epsilon_{\nu_x} = \frac{dX}{X} \bigg/ \frac{dp_x}{p_x}$$

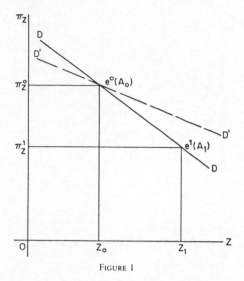

FIGURE 1

output and price are Z_0 and π_z^0, respectively. An increase in advertising to A_1 would increase Z to Z_1 (the increase in Z is determined by the given g' function). The decline in π_z induced by the increase in Z would be negatively related to the elasticity of the commodity demand curve: it would be less, for example, if the demand curve were $D'D'$ rather than DD. Since the increase in p_x is negatively related to the decline in π_z,[16] the increase in p_x, and thus the marginal revenue from the increase in A, is directly related to the elasticity of the commodity demand curve.[17]

The same result is illustrated with a more con-

[16]Since $\pi_z g = p_x$,

$$\frac{\partial p_x}{\partial A} = \pi_z g' + g \frac{\partial \pi_z}{\partial A} > 0$$

The first term on the right is positive and the second term is negative. If g, g', and π_z are given, $\partial p_x / \partial A$ is linearly and negatively related to $\partial \pi_z / \partial A$.

[17]Recall again our assumption, however, that even firms in perfectly competitive markets can fully differentiate their products. If the capacity of a firm to differentiate itself were inversely related to the elasticity of its commodity demand curve, that is, to the amount of competition in the commodity market, the increase in its product price generated by its advertising might not be directly related to the elasticity of its commodity demand curve.

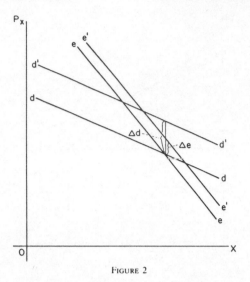

FIGURE 2

ventional diagram in Figure 2: the firm's product output and price are shown along the horizontal and vertical axes. The demand curve for its product with a given level of advertising is given by *dd*. We proved earlier (fn. 15) that with advertising constant, the elasticity of the product demand curve is the same as the elasticity of its commodity demand curve. An increase in advertising "shifts" the product demand curve upward to $d'd'$, and the marginal revenue from additional advertising is directly related to the size of the shift; that is, to the increase in product price for any given product output. Our basic result is that the shift is itself directly related to the elasticity of the demand curve. For example, with the same increase in advertising, the shift is larger from *dd* to $d'd'$ than from *ee* to $e'e'$ because *dd* is more elastic than *ee*.

This role of information in consumer demand is capable of extension in various directions. For example, the demand for knowledge is affected by the formal education of a person, so systematic variations of demand for advertisements with formal education can be explored. The stock of information possessed by the individual is a function of his age, period of residence in a community, and other variables, so systematic

patterns of purchase of heavily and lightly advertised goods are implied by the theory.

V. Fashions and Fads

The existence of fashions and fads (short episodes or cycles in the consumption habits of people) seems an especially striking contradiction of our thesis of the stability of tastes. We find fashions in dress, food, automobiles, furniture, books, and even scientific doctrines.[18] Some are modest in amplitude, or few in their followers, but others are of violent amplitude: who now buys an ouija board, or a bustle? The rise and fall of fashions is often attributed to the fickleness of people's tastes. Herbert Blumer, the distinguished sociologist, gave a characteristic expression of this view:

> Tastes are themselves a product of experience, they usually develop from an initial state of vagueness to a state of refinement and stability, but once formed they may decay and disintegrate. . . .
> The fashion process involves both a formation and an expression of collective taste in the given area of fashion. The taste is intially a loose fusion of vague inclinations and dissatisfactions that are aroused by new experience in the field of fashion and in the larger surrounding world. In this initial state, collective taste is amorphous, inarticulate, and awaiting specific direction. Through models and proposals, fashion innovators sketch possible lines along which the incipient taste may gain objective expression and take definite form. [p. 344]

The obvious method of reconciling fashion with our thesis is to resort again to the now familiar argument that people consume commodities, and only indirectly do they consume market goods, so fashions in market goods are compatible with stability in the utility function of commodities. The task here, as elsewhere, is to show that this formulation helps to illuminate our understanding of the phenomena under dis-

---

[18] "Fashion" indeed, does not necessarily refer only to the shorter term preferences. Adam Smith says that the influence of fashion "over dress and furniture is not more absolute than over architecture, poetry, and music" (p. 283).

cussion; we have some tentative comments in this direction.

The commodity apparently produced by fashion goods is social distinction: the demonstration of alert leadership, or at least not lethargy, in recognizing and adopting that which will in due time be widely approved. This commodity—it might be termed *style*—sounds somewhat circular, because new things appear to be chosen simply because they are new. Such circularity is no more peculiar than that which is literally displayed in a race—the runners obviously do not run around a track in order to reach a new destination. Moreover, it is a commendation of a style good that it be superior to previous goods, and style will not be sought intentionally through less functional goods. Indeed, if the stylish soon becomes inferior to the unstylish, it would lose its attractiveness.

Style, moreover, is not achieved simply by change: the newness must be of a special sort that requires a subtle prediction of what will be approved novelty, and a trained person can make better predictions than an untrained person. Style is social rivalry, and it is, like all rivalry, both an incentive to individuality and a source of conformity.

The areas in which the rivalry of fashion takes place are characterized by public exposure and reasonably short life. An unexposed good (automobile pistons) cannot be judged as to its fashionableness, and fashions in a good whose efficient life is long would be expensive. Hence fashion generally concentrates on the cheaper classes of garments and reading matter, and there is more fashion in furniture than in housing.

Fashion can be pursued with the purse or with the expenditure of time. A person may be well-read (i.e., have read the recent books generally believed to be important), but if his time is valuable in the market place, it is much more likely that his spouse will be the well-read member of the family. (So the ratio of the literacy of wife to that of husband is positively related to the husband's earning power, and inversely related to her earning power.)

The demand for fashion can be formalized by assuming that the distinction available to any person depends on his social environment, and his own efforts: he can be fashionable, give to

approved charities, choose prestigious occupations, and do other things that affect his distinction. Following recent work on social interactions, we can write the social distinction of the ith person as

$$(20) \qquad R_i = D_i + h_i$$

where D_i is the contribution to his distinction of his social environment, and h_i is his own contribution. Each person maximizes a utility function of R and other commodities subject to a budget constraint that depends on his own income and the exogenously given social environment.[19] A number of general results have been developed with this approach (see Becker), and a few are mentioned here to indicate that the demand for fashion (and other determinants of social distinction) can be systematically analyzed without assuming that tastes shift.

An increase in i's own income, prices held constant, would increase his demand for social distinction and other commodities. If his social environment were unchanged, the whole increase in his distinction would be produced by an increase in his own contributions to fashion and other distinction-producing goods. Therefore, even an average income elasticity of demand for distinction would imply a high income elasticity of demand for fashion (and these other distinction-producing) goods, which is consistent with the common judgement that fashion is a luxury good.[20]

If other persons increase their contributions to their own distinction, this may lower i's distinction by reducing his social environment. For distinction is scarce and is to a large extent simply redistributed among persons: an increase in one person's distinction generally requires a reduction in that of other persons. This is why people are often "forced" to conform to new fashions. When some gain distinction by paying

---

[19]The budget constraint for i can be written as

$$\Pi_{R_i} R + \Pi_z Z = I_i + \Pi_{R_i} D_i = S_i$$

where Z are other commodities, Π_{R_i} is his marginal cost of changing R, I_i is his own full income, and S_i is his "social income."

[20]Marshall believed that the desire for distinction was the most powerful of passions and a major source of the demand for luxury expenditures (see pp. 87–88, 106).

attention to (say) new fashions, they lower the social environment of others. The latter are induced to increase their own efforts to achieve distinction, including a demand for these new fashions, because an exogenous decline in their social environment induces them to increase their own contributions to their distinction.

Therefore, an increase in all incomes induces an even greater increase in i's contribution to his distinction than does an increase in his own income alone. For an increase in the income of others lowers i's social environment because they spend more on their own distinction; the reduction in his environment induces a further increase in i's contribution to his distinction. Consequently, we expect wealthy countries like the United States to pay more attention to fashion than poor countries like India, even if tastes were the same in wealthy and poor countries.

VI. Conclusion

We have surveyed four classes of phenomena widely believed to be inconsistent with the stability of tastes: addiction, habitual behavior, advertising, and fashions, and in each case offered an alternative explanation. That alternative explanation did not simply reconcile the phenomena in question with the stability of tastes, but also sought to show that the hypothesis of stable tastes yielded more useful predictions about observable behavior.

Of course, this short list of categories is far from comprehensive: for example, we have not entered into the literature of risk aversion and risk preference, one of the richest sources of *ad hoc* assumptions concerning tastes. Nor have we considered the extensive literature on time preference, which often alleges that people "systematically undervalue . . . future wants".[21]

---

[21]This quote is taken from the following longer passage in Böhm-Bawerk:

We must now consider a *second* phenomenon of human experience—one that is heavily fraught with consequence. That is the fact that we feel less concerned about future sensations of joy and sorrow simply because they do lie in the future, and the lessening of our concern is in proportion to the remoteness of that future. Consequently we accord to goods which are intended to serve future ends a value which falls short of the true intensity of their future marginal utility. *We systematically undervalue our future wants and also the means which serve to satisfy them.* [p. 268]

The taste for consumption in say 1984 is alleged to continue to shift upward as 1984 gets closer to the present. In spite of the importance frequently attached to time preference, we do not know of any significant behavior that has been illuminated by this assumption. Indeed, given additional space, we would argue that the assumption of time preference impedes the explanation of life cycle variations in the allocation of resources, the secular growth in real incomes, and other phenomena.

Moreover, we have not considered systematic differences in tastes by wealth or other classifications. We also claim, however, that no significant behavior has been illuminated by assumptions of differences in tastes. Instead, they, along with assumptions of unstable tastes, have been a convenient crutch to lean on when the analysis has bogged down. They give the appearance of considered judgement, yet really have only been *ad hoc* arguments that disguise analytical failures.

We have partly translated "unstable tastes" into variables in the household production functions for commodities. The great advantage, however, of relying only on changes in the arguments entering household production functions is that *all* changes in behavior are explained by changes in prices and incomes, precisely the variables that organize and give power to economic analysis. Addiction, advertising, etc. affect not tastes with the endless degrees of freedom they provide, but prices and incomes, and are subject therefore to the constraints imposed by the theorem on negatively inclined demand curves, and other results. Needless to say, we would welcome explanations of why some people become addicted to alcohol and others to Mozart, whether the explanation was a development of our approach or a contribution from some other behavioral discipline.

As we remarked at the outset, no conceivable expenditure of effort on our part could begin to exhaust the possible tests of the hypothesis of stable and uniform preferences. Our task has been oddly two-sided. Our hypothesis is trivial, for it merely asserts that we should apply standard economic logic as extensively as possible. But the self-same hypothesis is also a demanding challenge, for it urges us not to abandon opaque and complicated problems with the easy suggestion that the further explanation will perhaps someday be produced by one of our sister behavioral sciences.

REFERENCES

G. S. Becker, "A Theory of Social Interaction," *J. Polit. Econ.*, Nov./Dec. 1974, 82, 1063–93.

H. C. Blumer, "Fashion," in Vol. V, *Int. Encyclo. Soc. Sci.*, New York 1968.

Eugen von Böhm-Bawerk, *Capital and Interest*, vol. 2, South Holland, IL 1959.

John K. Galbraith, *The Affluent Society*, Boston 1958.

M. Grossman, "The Economics of Joint Production in the Household," rep. 7145, Center Math. Stud. Bus. Econ., Univ. Chicago 1971.

Alfred Marshall, *Principles of Economics*, 8th ed., London 1923.

R. T. Michael and G. S. Becker, "On the New Theory of Consumer Behavior," *Swedish J. Econ.*, Dec. 1973, 75, 378–96.

John S. Mill, *A System of Logic*, 8th ed., London 1972.

Adam Smith, *Theory of Moral Sentiments*, New Rochelle 1969.

[12]

BEHAVIORAL AND BRAIN SCIENCES (1991) 14, 205–245
Printed in the United States of America

The quest for optimality:
A positive heuristic of science?

Paul J. H. Schoemaker
Center for Decision Research, Graduate School of Business, University of
Chicago, Chicago, IL 60637
Electronic mail: fac_paul@gsbacd.uchicago.edu

Abstract: This paper examines the strengths and weaknesses of one of science's most pervasive and flexible metaprinciples: *optimality* is used to explain utility maximization in economics, least effort principles in physics, entropy in chemistry, and survival of the fittest in biology. Fermat's principle of least time involves both teleological and causal considerations, two distinct modes of explanation resting on poorly understood psychological primitives. The rationality heuristic in economics provides an example from social science of the potential biases arising from the extreme flexibility of optimality considerations, including selective search for confirming evidence, ex post rationalization, and the confusion of prediction with explanation. Commentators are asked to reflect on the extent to which optimality is (1) an organizing principle of nature, (2) a set of relatively unconnected techniques of science, (3) a normative principle for rational choice and social organization, (4) a metaphysical way of looking at the world, or (5) something else still.

Keywords: adaptation; biases; causality; control theory; economics; entropy; evolution; explanation; heuristics; homeostasis; optimization; rationality; regulation; sociobiology; variational principles

Most scientists seek to *explain* as well as describe and predict empirical regularities.[1] Often such explanations involve *optimality arguments*, ranging from "least effort" principles in physics to "survival of the fittest" in biology or economics. This paper suggests that the use of optimality in science is a powerful heuristic (i.e., a mental shortcut) for describing existing phenomena as well as predicting new ones. As with any heuristic (Tversky & Kahneman 1974), however, the optimality approach is prone to systematic biases, which the paper identifies.

First, a brief review is offered of the pervasiveness of optimality arguments in various sciences. The concept of optimality is then examined as a model bound notion, involving intentional and teleological perspectives. Fermat's principle of least time is used to examine the difference between teleological and causal theories, followed by a discussion of modes of scientific explanation. The paper closes with an examination of the rationality assumption underlying economics. Both the power of the optimality heuristic and its inherent biases are highlighted.

1. Optimality principles

Whenever a behavior or other empirical phenomenon is explained as maximizing or minimizing some objective function (subject to well-defined constraints), an optimality principle is implicitly or explicitly adduced. This paper examines the scientific use of such optimality principles, a key characteristic of which is that the empirical phenomenon of interest is viewed as a necessary consequence of optimizing some well-specified objective function. The following are examples of such optimality

principles in various fields of inquiry. To develop the argument, we will equate extremum principles with optimality principles (although some readers may find this objectionable).

1.1. Economics. Among the social sciences, economics is most closely wedded to the optimality approach, especially at the microlevel. Individual consumers as well as business organizations are presumed to be maximizing entities who calculate with lightning speed their optimal consumption patterns and output levels. Cournot (1838), Pareto (1897), and others (such as Edgeworth, Slutsky, Walras, and Marshall) introduced mathematics with great vigor (and controversy) into economics, and Paul Samuelson (1946) set the standard for subsequent generations regarding the use of formal analysis. Today optimality models abound in economics, ranging from Pareto optimality to the optimal designs of incentive structures and contracts in firms.

Current theories of finance, as a branch of microeconomics, offer a good example of the approach (Fama 1976). Firms are presumed to issue stock and debt in ratios that minimize the total cost of capital. Investors assess stock prices by rationally projecting dividends and discounting them for time and risk. The latter concerns only the so-called systematic risk component (i.e., covariance with the market) as most firm-specific risk can be diversified away via portfolios. Investors are assumed to hold only *efficient* portfolios, that is, those having minimum risk for a given level of expected return. New information immediately gives rise to new expectations concerning dividends (via Bayes' theorem), so that stock prices follow Martingale distributions or random walks (see Fama & Miller 1972). Although no claim is made that

Schoemaker: Optimality

anyone actually solves the complex equations involved, it is nonetheless argued (in the tradition of positivism) that such "as if" assumptions closely predict aggregate real-world behavior.

Several authors have examined optimality parallels between economics and physics (Magill 1970; Samuelson 1970; Tinbergen 1928) as well as economics and biology (Alchian 1950; Cooper 1987; Ghiselin 1974; Hirshleifer 1977; Houthakker 1956; Maynard Smith 1978). In economics, either expected utility or economic profit is maximized; in biology, mean fitness or reproductive survival of genes or organisms (Lewontin 1974).[2] In the latter case (as in physics and chemistry), the optimization argument is clearly advanced "as if," since biological entities lack the conscious striving and foresight characteristic of humans. Thus, the justification for the optimality heuristic seems, a fortiori, stronger in economics than in the life or physical sciences, although some consider even economic rationality no more than "as if" (Friedman 1953).

1.2. Physics. Maupertuis's (1744) principle of least action is perhaps the first major use of a formal optimality argument in science (see von Helmholtz 1886). It holds that a mechanical system moves along the path of least resistance (i.e., minimal mechanical action). In optics, this law was known earlier (ca. 1657) as Fermat's principle of least time (assuming total energy remains constant). Both principles were later generalized, following Euler (1744) and Lagrange (1788), by Hamilton (1834; 1835) to systems without conservation of energy. Hamilton's principle of least action has become one of the major unifying concepts of theoretical physics.

The application of Hamilton's principle involves the calculus of variations and can be illustrated by considering the trajectory a ball will follow when thrown away in the air. In a constant gravitational field, without other forces operating, the trajectory of the ball will be a parabola. This is derivable from the least action principle as follows. Let $\frac{1}{2}mv(x)^2$ be the kinetic energy at a given point x along the trajectory and mgx its potential energy (where m is mass, v velocity and g the gravitational constant). If we "sum" the differences between kinetic and potential energy along the trajectory, the following function obtains:

$$\text{Action} = \int_{t_1}^{t_2} [\frac{1}{2}mv(t)^2 - mgx(t)]dt \quad \text{where } x = f(t)$$

$$\text{and } v = \frac{dx}{dt}$$

To find the path of least action, perturbation analysis can be used along a presumed optimal path $x(t)$. This method, familiar in the calculus of variations, will yield a parabolic function as the solution (see Hylleraas 1970).

Similar calculus of variation models are found in relativity theory, where the optimal path (in curved space) corresponds to that of minimum length. In membrane physics, the minimum energy principle translates into liquid films enveloping a given volume (e.g., droplet) with minimum surface area. In electrostatics it predicts that the potential between two conductors adjusts itself so

that electrostatic energy is minimal. Similarly, an electric current will distribute itself through a material so as to minimize heat generation (assuming Ohm's law holds). As Feynman et al. (1964, Chapter 19, p. 13) noted, Hamilton's law is a cornerstone principle of both classical and modern physics, which offers "excellent numerical results for otherwise intractable problems."

1.3. Chemistry. Apart from its use of physics, chemistry has developed optimality principles of its own (although fewer than physics). Perhaps the most general one is the equilibrium concept in chemical kinetics. Equilibrium seeking can be viewed and expressed as minimizing a difference function defined on the actual and ideal states. Le Chatelier's principle, for example, predicts that solutions in equilibrium will react chemically to counter the cause of any change that might be introduced (see Brescia et al. 1966, pp. 341–43). Another example in chemistry/physics is Hund's rule of maximum multiplicity, which describes how electrons fill up orbits around atoms (Brescia et al. 1966, p. 189).

A second major principle in chemistry (and physics) is that of entropy maximization in closed systems. When two gases are mixed, this principle predicts that their configuration will tend toward maximum chaos. The entropy concept is closely linked to that of maximum likelihood, which features prominently in statistical mechanics and physical chemistry (e.g., the Maxwell-Boltzmann distribution law for molecular velocities in a gas; see Tipler 1969, pp. 66–78). In contrast to the least effort principle, chemistry advanced in the late nineteenth century the Thomsen-Berthelot principle of *maximum* work or heat to explain chemical reactions between solids (see Partington 1964). Later, this principle was restated in terms of free energy and entropy.

1.4. Biology. Although biology seems qualitatively different from physics and chemistry in that it examines mutable living systems, many links exist. The equilibrium-seeking laws of chemistry and physics find expression in dissipative structures as the principle of homeostasis. The latter causes the cells or organism to maintain certain chemical balances and tree leaves to position themselves for optimal sun intake. Homeostasis may also underlie various allometric laws, which describe optimal relationships between form and function (d'Arcy Thompson 1917; Varela 1979). For example, stable log-linear relationships can be found between head (or tail) length of fish and total length; or when plotting trunk width against trunk length in adult mammals. The presumption is that these ratios reflect optimal design and biological autonomy.[3]

The presumed driving force behind such biological optimality is natural selection. Whenever a population possesses (1) variance in genotype, (2) inheritability of genotype, and (3) natural selection, evolution is predicted toward the fittest (in the reproductive sense). Much evidence exists for such evolution, which in stable environments might bring forth optimal adaptation. For example, the shark, barracuda, and dolphin exhibit remarkable similarity of form (for such different vertebrates), suggesting that their common environment has evolved an "optimal" design. Similarly, it has been mathematically argued that our vascular system has evolved into an optimal network when examining at what angles arteries branch, how often they branch, and how diameters narrow further down the supply lines (Rosen 1967).

Ecology or population biology is especially drawn to the optimality approach. Various analytic and empirical studies have claimed optimal sex ratios in species (Bull 1983; Karlin & Lessard 1986), optimal foraging (Charnov 1976; Fantino & Abarca 1985; Rodman & Cant 1984) and predator switching (Rapport 1971) in animals, optimal division of labor among social insects (Wilson 1975), or optimal mating behavior in animals (Maynard Smith 1982). Strong parallels exist, in these models, with those of economics where selection occurs at the organizational as well as individual level. In biology, selection is presumed to operate at the species, organism, as well as genome levels.

1.5. Other disciplines. Most other sciences seem not as permeated with optimality principles as economics, physics, chemistry, and biology. No doubt differences in the use of mathematical modeling explain much of this, although biology is not an especially mathematical discipline (for exceptions see Lotka 1956 or Barigozzi 1980). Whenever striving or competition is involved, the optimality perspective seems plausible. Nonetheless, sociology or anthropology generally do not claim (either quantitatively or qualitatively) that their societies, structure or processes are, in a general sense, optimal. Exceptions exist, however.

Wilson (1975), a sociobiologist, has used ergonomic theory to show that certain caste systems among social insects are optimal in their division of labor. In mature colonies, he argues, caste ratios approach an optimal mix in the sense of maximizing the rate of production of virgin queens and mates (given its size). Similarly, Becker (1976), an economist, developed formal models of marriage, discrimination, capital punishment, and so on, that rest on utility maximization. In psychology, signal detection theory, learning, operant conditioning, and choice theory have been formally expressed in optimization terms (Coombs et al. 1970). In sociology, in contrast, few formal optimization arguments are encountered, even though a flourishing subfield of mathematical sociology exists that is concerned with quantitative models of change and network structures (Coleman 1990; Sorenson 1978). Functional explanations in sociology and anthropology (Elster 1982) – such as social institutions serving the greater good – can also be construed as qualitative optimality arguments (e.g., Elster 1983 for a discussion of maximization in art).

Optimality arguments are also used in other physical sciences besides physics and chemistry. In geology, the paths of rivers have been shown to afford maximum throughput of water per time unit relative to the constraints of the terrain (Press & Siever 1974). In meteorology, weather systems are commonly found to equilibrate or dissipate in optimal fashion (Paltridge 1975). Last, cybernetics (Ashby 1956; Shannon & Weaver 1949; Wiener 1961) often models feedback and control systems in optimality terms. Furthermore, in the sciences of the artificial (Simon 1981), explicit attempts are made to design optimal systems. If the design problems are too complex for mathematical solution, analog models can sometimes be used to let nature solve them. For exam-

ple, Kirkpatrick et al. (1983) used simulated physical annealing to optimize otherwise intractable combinatorial problems in computer design.

This section has established, at some length, the pervasive use of the optimality or at least extremal principles across a wide range of sciences. It is surprising, however, that most scientific texts fail to mention optimality in their indices. Whereas epistemological aspects of optimality have been extensively examined (Canfield 1966; Nagel 1953; Rosenberg 1985; Woodfield 1976), the concept is absent from the eight-volume index of the *Encyclopedia of Philosophy* (Edwards 1972), although it does contain a brief section on extremal principles. Optimality is also not mentioned, as a distinct philosophical entry, in *The New Palgrave: A Dictionary of Economics* (Eatwell et al. 1988). This paper seeks to redress this imbalance by asking scientists to clarify to what extent they deem optimality (in their own discipline) to be in the eye of the beholder as opposed to part of nature.

2. The concept of optimality

The use of optimality arguments in science involves a mathematical as well as an empirical component. The mathematical component is essentially a test of internal validity: Is the proposed solution indeed optimal (either locally or globally) relative to the criterion function and permissible domain? Although such questions can be complex, especially regarding the existence, uniqueness, and identifiability of a solution, the formal meaning of the optimality concept is well-defined. The real difficulty concerns the model's external validity: Does it correctly describe the phenomenon of interest? Three factors will be discussed as potentially troublesome concerning the empirical component: (1) Can anything be modeled as being optimal (given sufficient degrees of freedom)? (2) How comprehensive can our perceptions of nature be, given that they are species-specific constructions of reality? (3) Are nature's optimality principles, as uncovered across fields, mutually compatible?

Concerning the first point, the optimality concept can be easily trivialized as follows. Take any empirical law $y = f(x)$; express it as the first-order condition $y - f(x) = 0$; find an integrand $F = F \cdot x \cdot y$ and boundary conditions such that $dF/dx = (\delta F/\delta y)(dy/dx) + \delta F/\delta x = y - f(x)$. Of course, the maximand F must be plausible, and so must the boundary conditions. The issue is by no means trivial (see Bordley 1983), however, especially in a field such as economics, where the permissible degrees of freedom concerning (1) the objective function, (2) the decision variables, and (3) the constraints are less well specified (e.g., unobservable budget constraints, transaction costs, information sets, cost of thinking, etc.). In the hands of a capable mathematical economist, a disturbingly large number of behaviors can be rationalized as being optimal, attesting to the dangerous and seductive flexibility of this heuristic. In Schoemaker (1982), such ex post facto use of optimality was referred to as *postdictive*, in contrast to predictive or positivistic models, which are falsifiable at least in principle.[4]

Similarly, in population ecology, foraging or mating behavior can easily be modeled as being optimal, which in turn has prompted various essays (Dupre 1987; Kings-

Schoemaker: Optimality

land 1985; Maynard Smith 1984; Oster & Wilson 1978; Rachlin 1985) as to who is optimizing: the scientist or nature? Gould and Lewontin (1979), for example, particularly criticized panselectionists for their quick-footedness in proposing new selectionist explanations once old ones were discredited. Here is a sample of their criticism:

If one adaptive argument fails, try another. Zig-zag commissures of clams and brachiopods, once widely regarded as devices for strengthening the shell, become sieves for restricting particles above a given size. . . . A suite of external structures (horns, antlers, tusks) once viewed as weapons against predators, become symbols of intraspecific competition among males. . . . The eskimo face, once depicted as 'cold engineered' . . . , becomes an adaptation to generate and withstand large masticatory forces. . . . We do not attack these newer interpretations; they may all be right. We do wonder, though, whether the failure of one adaptive explanation should always simply inspire a search for another of the same general form, rather than a consideration of alternatives to the proposition that each part is 'for' some specific purpose [i.e., the product of natural selection]. (Gould & Lewontin 1979)[5]

A second reason for being suspicious of grand optimality principles, such as Hamilton's least effort principle, Darwin's survival of the fittest,[6] or Smith's invisible hand (as a way of maximizing social welfare or at least allocative efficiency)[7] is that they were posited by creatures who themselves are part of the world they seek to describe (Whitehead 1920). Through our sense-awareness we presumably obtain just one of several possible representations of outside reality. In the case of vision, our normal range is limited from three to about eight thousand angstroms. And even within this narrow window we actively attend to less than 2% of the visual field. In addition, the eye is hardly an objective camera with cables, lenses, and screens (Hubel & Wiesel 1979), but part of a highly specialized information processing system that acts on prior categorization and expectations (Chomsky 1980; Hess 1973).

Our sense of there being just one reality (the one we all perceive) presumably stems from a uniformity within our species as to our mental primitives and pattern recognition.[8] Nonetheless, even our own limited window on the world is not always coherent. Optimal illusions remind us of the approximate nature of our perceptions. The notion that we can objectively perceive the surrounding world has proved untenable, especially in quantum mechanics (d'Espagnat 1979). In addition, nature has hardly proved to be commonsensical: Current conceptions of space (Callahan 1976) and time (Layzer 1975) are beyond most intelligent lay people and more than stretch our imagination. As Haldane (1927) noted, "The universe is not only queerer than we suppose, but queerer than we can suppose." Although researchers' bounded rationality (Simon 1957) is a caveat for all scientific theories, it especially applies to those claiming to have uncovered Nature's deepest or grandest principles.

The third concern is that optimality principles may be postulated which collectively do not add up to a coherent whole. Is the principle of least action, for instance, compatible with that of maximum chaos? (Most physicists would say yes, but not all; see Prigogine & Stengers

1984.) Can a natural selection principle, which operates reactively and with lags, ever lead to optimal adaptation in a changing world? Is evolution and the complexification of dissipative structures (Prigogine & Stengers 1984) compatible with the principles of entropy and chaos? Is *constrained* optimization (e.g., maximizing economic utility subject to a budget constraint) a contradiction in terms if the constraints can be relaxed (at a nonzero shadow price)?

What guarantees can we have that the infinite regression problem inherent in relaxing or (tightening) constraints at various metalevels will converge toward a stable solution (see Mongin & Walliser 1987)? How could we have argued that economic man was optimal 10 or 20 years ago, when by today's standards these past optimality models are simplistic and incomplete? Especially in the economics of information, the early optimization models made such strong assumptions as fixed search rules (Stigler 1961), whereas later models introduced "more optimal" variable rules (Rothchild 1973; 1974). Future generations will presumably consider our current optimality models unduly constrained and simplistic (Bounds 1987).[9]

Although the social sciences may suffer more from the fact that optimality is a moving target, conscious striving may be a condition favorable to optimality arguments. (Note, however, that consciousness and choice also open the door for suboptimal decisions.) [See also Libet: "Unconscious Cerebral Initiative and the Role of Conscious Will in Voluntary Action" *BBS* 8(4)1985; and Searle: "Consciousness, Explanatory Inversion, and Cognitive Science" *BBS* 13(4)1990.] Animals are less deliberatively purposive (McFarland 1977; although see Griffin 1981), whereas plants and lower organisms are mostly passive participants in the process of natural selection. Nonetheless, they do undergo selection (by the environment). In contrast, physics, the most sophisticated of the optimality sciences, has the fewest a priori arguments in its favor. The laws of nature do not seem to have been selected for, nor do they appear mutable. Only appeals to a grand designer (God) or viewing optimality as a heuristic can justify the prominence of optimality theories in physics. To assess the extent to which physics' use of optimality involves teleology or metaphysics, Fermat's principle of least time is examined next.

3. The principle of least time

When we place a stick in the water, it seems that the angle above water is different from that below. This refraction phenomenon was extensively examined by the Greeks (especially Claudius Ptolemy) who constructed various tables of ingoing (or incident) and outgoing (or refracted) angles between air and water. However, it was not until the seventeenth century that an algebraic law was discovered (by the Dutch scientist Willebrord Snell) linking incident (θ_1) and outgoing (θ_2) angles. Snell's well-known law is $\sin \theta_1 = n \sin \theta_2$, in which n is a constant specific to the media involved. Although the task of science may seem completed when such laws are discovered, the French scientist Pierre Fermat (1601–1665) took it one step further (as is common in science; see Nagle 1961).

In going from A to B, he argued, light does not

necessarily travel the path of minimum distance but rather that of shortest time (see Figure 1a). Suppose A is a point on the beach, and B a point in the ocean. What will be the quickest way to rescue someone drowning in the water at B when starting from point A? Ideally, one should angle the point of entry into the ocean (point X in Figure 1a) so that more time is spent in the faster medium (the beach), relative to the straight line route, and less in the slower medium (water). The optimal angle directly depends on the relative velocities in the two media, and corresponds to n in Snell's law.

Snell's law can be derived directly from the geometric puzzle discussed above. As light travels from point A to B in Figure 1a, its refraction at the border between air and water will be such that $\sin \theta_1 = (v_1/v_2) \sin \theta_2$. This, as proved in the Appendix, guarantees the shortest path in time. Fermat's ingenious principle generated a host of new hypotheses in optics, many of which proved correct. For instance, the least time principle predicts symmetry when reversing direction of propagation. It also predicts that light travels faster in air (v_1) than water (v_2), and that $n = v_1/v_2$. Thus, Fermat took Snell's law far beyond the original phenomenon of interest, deducing the shape needed for perfectly converging lenses as well as how light behaves with multiple lenses. No doubt Fermat's principle was very productive. But does it mean that nature optimizes?

The eminent physicist Richard Feynman expressed well the concern many feel when confronted with such principles as Fermat's. In his words:

> The following is another difficulty with the principle of least time, and one which people who do not like this kind of a theory could never stomach. With Snell's theory we can "understand" light. Light goes along, it sees a surface, it bends because it does something at the surface. The idea of causality, that it goes from one point to another, and another, and so on, is easy to understand. But the principle of least time is a completely different philosophical principle about the way nature works. Instead of saying it is a causal thing, that when we do one thing, something else happens, and so on, it says this: we set up the situation, and *light* decides which is the shortest time, or the extreme one, and chooses the path. But *what* does it do, *how* does it find out? Does it *smell* the nearby paths, and check them against each other? The answer is, yes, it does, in a way. (Feynman et al. 1964, Chapter 26, p. 7)

As Feynman explains, there is a quantum-mechanical view of Snell's law that gives considerable justification to Fermat's principle. Consider shining a flashlight into a rectangular water basin at an angle so that an underwater image appears on the back wall of the basin (as in Figure 1b). Why will the image be lower than expected from a straight line viewpoint (i.e., below point C)?

If light is viewed as photons (i.e., particles), the brightest image on the back wall occurs where the most photons strike. The probability of a photon striking is directly proportional to the number of pathways from point A (the origin) to some point B (on the back wall). Each pathway has a complex vector associated with it, whose angle is proportional to the travel time of that path. The overall probability of striking is obtained by adding all these complex vectors for a given point B and taking the squared length of the sum. The brightest point on the

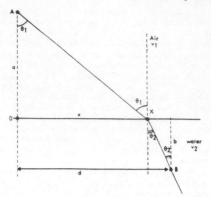

Figure 1a.   Geometric illustration of Fermat's principle

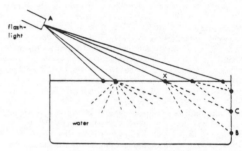

Figure 1b.   Photon view of light refraction

back wall will be that for which the various pathways are aligned in terms of vector angles as opposed to cancelling.

The path of least time has the mathematical property that nearby paths will differ little from it in travel time, thus reinforcing the total vector length. In the language of the calculus of variations, the least time path is one for which first-order deviations from the path have only second-order effects on the time function. Only at a minimum or maximum do small deviations make no difference as a first-order approximation (e.g., in a Taylor series expansion).

Fermat was ingenious to have formulated a principle that accords so well with a deeper reality that was unrecognized at the time. His principle injected science with a metaphysical perspective, however. Whereas Fermat may have been inspired by the prevailing view that God designed a perfect universe, modern use of optimality stems more from a pragmatic (i.e., it works) than a religious belief. Nonetheless, the teleological nature of optimality arguments, especially in physics, sets them apart from causal theories. The next section contrasts teleological with causal explanations, and argues that both rest on psychological primitives that are only partly understood.

Schoemaker: Optimality

4. Scientific explanations

Of the many objects. organisms. behaviors. and systems around us. two classes might be distinguished depending on how we talk about them. If we attribute no inner purposes. needs. or intentions to them. they are non-teleological (e.g.. a stone. fire. air. or stars). The other class. in contrast. is characterized by the presumption of intention. goal directedness. or plasticity (i.e.. the ability to reach a goal from multiple directions or initial conditions). Humans. animals. and many lower organisms fall into this second. teleological class. The distinction is useful as it influences the types of scientific explanations deemed appropriate for each class. Causal explanations are typically expected for the nonteleological class. whereas intentional and causal ones are appropriate for the teleological class. Let us examine each type.

When asked. "Why did x occur." one acceptable answer is to identify a causal pathway from a set of plausible initial conditions to x (see Bromberger 1970). Many pathways (or causes) may exist. however. When a house burns down is it because of (1) a match being dropped. (2) the flammability of the carpet. (3) the failure of the sprinkler system. (4) the slowness of the fire department. or still other causes? Mackie (1980) defined an acceptable cause as being "an insufficient but nonredundant part of an unnecessary but sufficient condition." This view implies that causal explanations are usually not unique and depend on the expectational field of the observer. Objects and events in the world exhibit correlation. temporal antecedence. and contiguity (in space and time). but *not* logical necessity. The latter. as Hume (1888) emphasized. is a construction of the mind based on subjective conceptions and expectations. Indeed. Russell (1959) felt strongly that causality should be dropped entirely from our scientific dictionary. Nonetheless. nonteleological reasoning about scientific phenomena often rests on a primitive "causation" that is rather metaphysical and remains ill-understood in both psychology (Einhorn & Hogarth 1986) and philosophy (Bunge 1979: Davidson 1986: Kim 1981).

An alternative mode of scientific explanation is to ascribe purposes and intentions. In a sense. teleological explanations are the opposite of causal ones in that they reverse the temporal order. A proper cause. it might be argued. precedes its effect in time. When we say that birds build nests to lay eggs. however. a future (desired) state is alleged to govern the action. As such. the distinguishing feature of teleological explanations is not so much temporal order as the emphasis on goals and purposes (Wright 1976). Although purpose and intentionality may suggest notions of intelligence. consciousness. or even free will. the coexistence of physical determinism and purposiveness has become less problematic since Hobbes (1909) and Hume (1888) (see also Dennett 1978 or Schlick 1939). [10] Thus. teleological explanations (such as water seeking its lowest level) need not be metaphysical (see Woodfield 1976). [See also Dennett: "Intentional Systems in Cognitive Ethology: The 'Panglossian Paradigm' Defended" *BBS* 6(3)1983: and Schull "Are Species Intelligent?" *BBS* 13(1)1990.]

Teleological explanations seem especially appropriate when dealing with

1. cybernetic systems involving feedback (Rosenblueth et al. 1943).
2. homeostatic systems that try to maintain an equilibrium (Nagel 1953). or
3. ill-understood systems. [See Toates: "Homeostasis and Drinking" *BBS* 2(1)1979.]

Examples of each type are (1) a target-seeking missile. (2) a thermostat. and (3) animals. humans. or nature. In the latter case. the teleological approach often entails anthropomorphism. When a child is thrown over by a gust of wind. it will probably say the wind tried to hurt it (Piaget & Inhelder 1975). To children and adults. random or unexplained occurrences often assume personal meaning. Similarly. scientists may explain puzzling phenomena by imputing intentions. When asked why a balloon is round. we might say it chooses this form over others to equalize interior pressure. Such an explanation makes balloons lawful and predictable. while suggesting new avenues for exploration (e.g.. what happens when you squeeze it or partly submerge it in water). [11]

Because of its metaphoric nature. the teleological approach can stimulate the mind to explore new avenues more effectively than the causal approach. As with causality. however. it rests on a primitive. namely. the concept of purpose or intention. which remains philosophically problematic (Canfield 1966: Chisholm 1956: Wimsatt 1972) and. according to some. unnecessary in our scientific lexicon (e.g.. Skinner 1969). [See *BBS* special issue on the work of Skinner *BBS* 7(4)1984.] Psychologically. this primitive involves notions of forethought (i.e.. a future orientation). assent (i.e.. wish or desire). potency (i.e.. the ability to affect the world). and consciousness of self (Warren 1916). Both causation and purpose appear to be psychological primitives that we naturally use to make sense of our surrounding world. It remains unclear which of these two crucial concepts is epistemologically more objective or valid (Braithwait 1966).

5. The rationality heuristic

Saying that people are rational. narrowly defined. implies that they use reason (*ratio*. Latin) to select means that maximize a well-defined end. [12] This assumption seems especially plausible in humans. who consciously strive to better their situation and must often do so in a competitive environment. This section examines both the pitfalls and promises of the optimality heuristic when applied to market behavior via the rational-economic man assumption. Economists generally assume that when the stakes are high enough people will act rationally for markets to reach equilibrium and be efficient. The argument rests on arbitrage opportunities being competed away by economic agents who possess (1) well-defined preferences. (2) comprehensive perceptions of the available options. (3) rational expectations concerning consequences (admittedly a thin theory of rationality: see Elster 1983). and (4) the ability to calculate which option has the highest subjective worth (e.g.. expected utility). These premises are usually presumed to be "as if" assumptions and built into economic models to predict (rather than explain) real-world behavior. Several concerns exist. however.

about the rationality heuristic (which is the primary optimality principle in social science).

First, rationality (in the sense of optimal behavior) is only operationally defined in limited circumstances. In the case of certainty or risk (i.e., known probabilities), near consensus exists among experts on what is meant by rational behavior. Under certainty, it means maximizing a utility function reflecting well-behaved preferences (i.e., those that are transitive, connected, etc.) subject to given constraints. Under objective risk, it is usually defined by economists as obeying the Von Neumann-Morgenstern (1947) axioms and maximizing expected utility (Keeney & Raiffa 1976). When outcomes are uncertain or ambiguous however (i.e., no agreed-upon probabilities exist), expert consensus breaks down and a variety of choice procedures are encountered, ranging from pessimism or regret minimization to *subjective* expected utility (see De Finetti 1975; March 1978; Milnor 1954; Schoemaker 1984; Shepard 1964).

In decision making under conflict, a similar absence of consensus is found (Luce & Raiffa 1957). Game theory offers numerous solutions, but only for the simplest of cases is a strong prescription found (such as the maximin principle, i.e., the notion that in certain zero-sum games one is best off pursuing a strategy offering the highest [max] return under the worst [min] possible countermove). In addition, group decision theory is plagued with a variety of impossibility theorems, making it difficult in most cases to identify the rational group decision (Arrow 1951; Satterthwaite 1975). Finally, intertemporal choice theory rests on a less solid axiomatic foundation than one would like. Discounted utility models, for instance, require Koopman's (1972) stationarity axiom, meaning that preferences are invariant under deletion or addition of time periods involving the same consumption levels. This axiom in turn forbids wealth effects and intertemporal synergies (see also Loewenstein 1987). Thus, although rationality may be well defined in the abstract, its operationality (in the sense of decisiveness) is often limited in scope.

A second concern is that for those instances where rationality is clearly defined, a growing body of laboratory and field studies suggests that people do *not* act according to the axiom (Einhorn & Hogarth 1981; Elster 1979; Hershey et al. 1982; Kahneman & Tversky 1979; Schoemaker 1982; Tversky & Kahneman 1981). Three defenses are usually invoked by economists concerning this counterevidence. One is that positive models need not be realistic in their underlying assumptions, as long as their predictions are accurate (Friedman 1953). Second, laboratory studies fail to provide the incentives and learning opportunities encountered in the real world. Third, in markets only a subset of the economic agents need to be rational (i.e., those trading at the margin or arbitraging) for the theory to work. It is usually not specified how many agents are enough, however, nor how quickly convergence to equilibrium should occur. Although the individual evidence against the rationality assumption is formidable, it remains an open question whether under aggregation (in real-world markets) the suboptimalities cancel, diminish or magnify (see Hogarth & Reder 1986). This question is especially crucial for such fields as policy or corporate strategy, where many of the interesting issues vanish when hyperrationality is assumed (see Schoemaker 1990).

A third concern regarding the rationality hypothesis is that it may be nonfalsifiable. The inconclusiveness of rationality principles in such crucial domains as conflict and group decisions, along with our limited understanding of the links among individual, firm, market, and macroeconomic behavior, permits a wide range of phenomena. In addition, such unobservables as transaction costs or the psychological cost of thinking introduce ill-specified frictional forces that allow considerable departures from the ideal. For example, Simon's (1957) theory of bounded rationality, according to which people satisfice rather than optimize, could be viewed as optimal once taking into account search costs, limited knowledge, and information processing limits. Of course, if all behavior can be argued to be optimal, the concept loses empirical content and falsifiability.

Nonetheless, the rationality heuristic has flourished in economics. In microeconomics it gave rise to equilibrium theories and theorems about comparative statics; in the macro realm it spawned rational expectations theory. Moreover, the rational economic approach has expanded beyond its traditional domain into animal economics (Battalio et al. 1981 [see also Rachlin et al.: "Maximization Theory in Behavioral Psychology" *BBS* 4(3)1981]; Mazur 1981), crime, marriage, and fertility (Becker 1976), public policy (Buchanan & Tullock 1962; Downs 1957), law (Posner 1973), conflict and war (Schelling 1960; Boulding 1962), and theories of organization form (Barney & Ouchi 1986). This wide scope speaks to the great power of the rationality heuristic. In the absence of detailed knowledge of the situation (e.g., about a firm or a marriage), ordinal predictions can be made (e.g., about direction of change) when varying certain parameters. This generality, however, is also the Achilles heel of economics: the precision and specificity of the hypotheses lessen as the theory's reach is extended.

6. The optimality heuristic and its biases

Given the wide use of the optimality heuristic, let us try to characterize its general nature and provide a brief summary of its potential biases. The following eight features characterize the optimality heuristic in general terms, with Fermat's example shown in parentheses.

1. *Posing a why question (or explanandum)*: An unexpected or intriguing state of nature needs to be explained (e.g., Why is light refracted?).

2. *Bounding the domain of inquiry*: What are the problem's boundary conditions? What are the variables and what are their permissible ranges (e.g., light travels in straight lines; all refraction angles between 0 degrees and 180 degrees are *a priori* permitted)?

3. *Selection of salient features*: What aspect of the phenomenon can be anthropomorphized or examined via other metaphors (e.g., viewing light as traveling)?

4. *Teleological description of the system*: The phenomenon is modeled as seeking a desired end state, subject to certain constraints (e.g., light wishing to travel in the least amount of time).

5. *Search for the optimal solution*: Mathematical tools

Schoemaker: Optimality

are used to solve the optimization problem defined in step 4 (e.g., the time function is differentiated with respect to the angle of entry).

6. *Empirical comparisons:* The optimum solution obtained in step 5 is compared with the observed state in step 1 (e.g., Is the first-order condition that $\sin \theta_1 = (v_1/v_2) \sin \theta_2$ observed empirically?).

7. *Further refinement of the model:* If the predicted solution does not accord well with reality, the constraints or objective function might be adjusted to improve the model (e.g., under a very flat angle light may not refract but simply reflect).

8. *Generation of new hypotheses:* Does the teleological principle imply new predictions that can be tested empirically (e.g., What shape would be required for a perfectly converging lens?)?

The value of any particular optimality model depends in large measure on its plausibility (features 3–4) and the new insights it generates (features 7–8). If aspect 7 is highly contorted or arbitrary, for example, when the empirical phenomenon is force-fit into an optimality mold, the approach loses appeal and value. Whenever the underlying teleological principle is plausible and general (as with the law of least action), the associated metaphoric reasoning can be a powerful shortcut to new insights and solutions (Oppenheimer 1956). As is the nature of all heuristics, however, the optimality approach may be prone to various inferential biases (Kahneman et al. 1982). Not all of these are unique to optimality models, but each could seriously undermine their value, given the highly flexible nature of this heuristic.

6.1. Attribution bias.
When scientific data fit some optimality model (ex post facto), it does not necessarily follow that nature or the agent therefore optimizes. To a large extent, optimality is in the eye of the beholder. It is the observer who is optimizing rather than nature (see Kitcher 1985). Nonetheless, in such fields as economics or ecology, agents' behavior is often deemed optimal whenever it can be accounted for by some optimality model. This, in my view, is a systematic and serious attribution error. As Ernest Mach (1883; see also Bradley 1971), Heisenberg (1955), and many others have emphasized, reality is the nexus between our mind and a presumed outside reality. The latter can hardly be understood independent of the observer (although see Schroedinger 1954; 1967).

6.2. Confirmation bias.
Another inherent danger of the optimality heuristic is that its proponents may search more vigorously for confirming than disconfirming evidence. Falsificationism (Lakatos 1970; Popper 1968) would encourage such questions as, "How might we prove that light (or people) are suboptimal?" to appreciate better the limits of Fermat's (or economic) theory. In the case of light, we might ask how it would behave if it could travel in curved rather than straight lines, or if it minimized energy expended rather than travel time.

The confirmation bias may also slip in when reviewing the historical track record of the optimality heuristic. We remember well the names of Pierre Fermat, Charles Darwin, or Adam Smith, who were highly successful champions of the optimality principle. We hardly recall those who searched in vain for optimality or other aesthetically pleasing principles. One can only wonder what additional insights Einstein's formidable mind might have generated had he not stalked for more than 30 years the elusive unified theory of the (then) four basic forces of nature. Thus, the optimality heuristic may appear more successful in hindsight than a complete historical accounting would indicate.

6.3. Excessive rationalization.
A third and related bias is that the optimality heuristic can result in tortuous rationalization. If one's prior belief in the value of the optimality heuristic is upwardly biased by the attribution and confirmation biases, it may seem productive to pursue it relentlessly. The attendant danger, however, is that the heuristic degenerates into the kind of thinking parodied in Voltaire's (1759) *Candide.* Reacting against the prevailing view that God had created a perfect world, Voltaire describes Candide's life as one disaster and mishap after another. Yet, amidst all the war, rape, famine, and suffering, each chapter reiterates that "this is the best of all possible worlds." By taking the argument to its extreme, Voltaire highlights the danger of Leibnitz's axiomatic commitment to a worldview steeped in optimality.[13] Economics, ecology, and sociobiology are some of the disciplines that have been criticized precisely because of their remarkable propensity to rationalize away anomalies.[14]

6.4. Illusion of understanding.
A final important bias of the optimality heuristic is that it may create an illusion of understanding by describing rather than explaining. In Molière's play *Le Malade Imaginaire,* a doctor is asked to explain the tranquilizing effect of a drug. He tries to do so by attributing it to its "dormative faculty." Especially when phrased in Latin, such relabeling may instill an illusion of understanding (see Bateson 1979, p. 98). It fails as an explanation, however (as well as description), because it predicts nothing new and offers no further insight. Saying that light is refracted because it optimizes something is certainly more than relabeling (as new predictions were generated); however, it does fail to offer a process or causal account.

The positivist view that only prediction matters is fundamentally unsatisfying, and optimality principles consequently suffer from being too paramorphic. Does Fermat's principle really *explain* why and how light refracts? Do economic models predicting consumer reactions to price changes or equilibrium behaviors really explain how people behave? When ecologists argue that animals engage in optimal foraging, leaving one patch of land for another when the benefit/cost ratio gets too low, do they really explain how animals search for food? [See also Fantino & Abarca: "Choice, Optimal Foraging, and The Delay-reduction Hypothesis" *BBS* 8(2)1985; Houston & McNamara: "A Framework for the Functional Analysis of Behaviour" *BBS* 11(1)1988; Clark: "Modeling Behavioral Adaptation" *BBS* 14(1) 1991.] Each optimality principle, it seems, begs for an associated process explanation that describes causally, within the constraints of an organism or system, how it operates.

7. Conclusions

The optimality heuristic appears to be a very powerful principle of scientific explanation and inquiry. It is encountered in almost all sciences that are mathematical, and even in those that are not. Survival of the fittest, which is perhaps the grandest of all optimality principles, was formulated as a qualitative, conceptual cornerstone in Darwin's (1859) theory of evolution. Entropy and least action principles are other broad optimality laws, applicable to systems that do not overtly strive or compete (e.g., nonliving systems). Equilibrium notions and homeostatic behavior can also be interpreted as general optimality principles, covering wide domains of application. The issue arises, however, whether or not such optimality is solely in the eye of the beholder.

It was argued that for fields such as physics or chemistry the optimality principle is metaphysical unless viewed as a heuristic. As illustrated with Fermat's principle of least time, the refractive behavior of light can be viewed teleologically (i.e., light *choosing* the quickest route) or causally (i.e., photons following discrete paths that interfere or magnify). Although the causal view may seem more scientific, both modes of explanation rest on psychological primitives (i.e., the notions of causation and purpose) that remain ill-understood. Indeed, the teleological approach, owing to its metaphoric nature, can offer parsimonious summaries of physical laws while often suggesting new hypotheses. Especially in the physical sciences, the optimality approach (as a teleological principle) seems to have worked well (starting with Newton's laws of motion).

In the life sciences, the optimality heuristic has similarly been quite powerful. Formal applications are found in population biology, ecology, and medicine (e.g., mathematical models of the heart or knee). Because of natural selection, the justification for optimality principles seems stronger in the life than physical sciences. Nonetheless, adaptive systems can at best be optimal relative to a past condition (because of lags) and it will be hard to assess for optimality without explicit knowledge of the range of genetic variation. Furthermore, if random (i.e., nonadaptive) mutations are introduced, the range of potentiality becomes even harder to assess, and evolution may be neutral (Kimura 1979; 1983). Thus, the reactive nature of natural selection, the gradient climb toward local optima, and the unknown forward potential of mutations would appear to limit the appeal of optimality as an evolutionary principle. As emphasized by Jantsch and Waddington (1976), evolving systems are usually (1) imperfect, (2) in disequilibrium, and (3) unpredictable.

In human systems, however, a forward looking dimension is encountered. Humans are presumed to deliberate their future by learning from the past. Hence here the case would seem strongest a priori for the use of optimality arguments. Yet, with the exception of economics, the social sciences have hardly embraced the optimality heuristic (although see Zipf 1949). Not all of this can be attributed to the lack of mathematical modeling. In part it reflects a reluctance (possibly based on introspective evidence) to ascribe too much optimality to ourselves. As the anthropologist Eric Smith (1987, p. 205) claimed, "The bias in most of the social sciences [is]

against reducing social institutions and processes to the action of self-interested individuals." Our inner complexity, as well as that of social aggregates, defies characterization in optimality terms without considerable simplification. Economics appears to be willing to pay the price of simplification; most psychologists prefer to render more detailed process descriptions (see Newell & Simon 1972; Sayre 1986) with fewer grand, unifying principles (such as utility maximization). Both approaches have their merit and reflect more than differences in mathematical sophistication.

Overall, the optimality heuristic has proved to be a powerful heuristic of science. Ironically, it is used most systematically and successfully in the physical sciences where its case is weakest a priori, and least in the social sciences (with the exception of economics), where its case is strongest prima facie (because of the conscious striving of people and the presence of competition and selection). The heuristic is powerful because it can offer an efficient summary of a system's behavior (Teller 1980) as well as suggesting new hypotheses. Its limitations, however, are that it can be too flexible, which may in turn lead to attribution errors, confirming rationalizations, and the confusion of prediction with explanation. Since its plasticity seems to be higher in the social than the physical sciences (owing to agents' consciousness, presumed free will and numerous unobservables), it is perhaps not surprising that optimality arguments are less eagerly embraced in the social realm.

The overall appeal of optimality arguments rests in part on our desire for simplicity and elegance in scientific theories. This was forcefully expressed by physicist Leon Lederman when he received the 1988 Nobel Memorial Prize for his work on subatomic particles. "My goal is to someday put [the basic laws of nature] all on a T-shirt . . ." he said. "We physicists believe that when we write this T-shirt equation it will have an incredible symmetry. We'll say: 'God, why didn't we see that in the beginning? It's so beautiful. I can't even bear to look at it'" (*Chicago Tribune* 1988). Symmetry, simplicity, and elegance appear to rank with optimality as among the most important driving forces in scientific inquiry (Chandrasekhar 1987). Our commitment to them, however, seems as much metaphysical as it does scientific, and is therefore in need of continual scrutiny.

In closing, I should emphasize that this paper is by no means an exhaustive treatment of the optimality heuristic. Given the broad range of issues involved, cutting across the physical, biological, and the social sciences, as well as philosophy, I humbly acknowledge my relative ignorance. Consequently, the ideas presented here should be viewed as personal reflections, aimed at inviting criticism and improvement. I leave it to each commentator and reader to decide what optimality really is: (1) an organizing principle of nature, (2) a set of philosophically unrelated techniques of science, (3) a normative principle for individual rationality and social organization, or (4) a metaphysical way of looking at the world. If the latter, we should strive to understand better when and how this root metaphor (Pepper 1942) enhances rather than obstructs scientific inquiry. As to my personal view, I consider the extremity principles encountered across sciences to represent both a common

Schoemaker: Optimality

mathematical tool kit and a deeper assumption about nature's economy and elegance. My overall concern is that optimality principles reflect heuristic metastrategies for scientific inquiry that are prone to significant, often unrecognized, biases. The biases enumerated may be stronger in the social and biological sciences than the physical sciences because of the former's greater complexity and larger degrees of freedom.

8. Appendix

Derivation of Snell's law of refraction. Assume we start at point A and wish to reach point B as soon as possible with a travel speed of v_1 above the horizontal line in Figure 1a and a velocity of v_2 below this horizontal line. Our decision variable is x, the point on the horizontal border where we change relative velocities. To solve this problem, we must first define the travel time $T(x)$ as a function of x, and then differentiate with respect to x to find an extremum.

$$T(x) = \frac{AX}{v_1} + \frac{XB}{v_2}, \text{ where } AX = \sqrt{a^2 + x^2}$$

$$\text{and } BX = \sqrt{(d - x)^2 + b^2}$$

$$\text{or } T(x) = \frac{\sqrt{a^2 + x^2}}{v_1} + \frac{\sqrt{(d - x)^2 + b^2}}{v_2}$$

$$\text{Thus, } \frac{dT(x)}{dx} = \frac{2x}{2v_1\sqrt{a^2 + x^2}} + \frac{2(d - x)(-1)}{2v_2\sqrt{(d - x)^2 + b^2}} = 0$$

$$\text{or } \frac{x}{\sqrt{a^2 + x^2}} v_2 = \frac{d - x}{\sqrt{(d - x)^2 + b^2}} v_1$$

or $\sin \theta_1 = n \sin \theta_2$ with $n = v_1/v_2$.

ACKNOWLEDGMENT

Thanks to George Constantinides, the late Hillel Einhorn, Jon Elster, Eugene Fama, Victor Goldberg, Robin Hogarth, Paul Kleindorfer, David Lindley, George Loewenstein, Laurentius Marais, Stanley Martens, Merton Miller, Phillipe Mongin, Alex Orden, Alexander Rinnooy-Kan, J. Edward Russo, George Stigler, and William Wimsatt for helpful comments on earlier drafts.

NOTES

1. Scientists' high regard for theory and explanation (as opposed to classification or mere description) is clearly reflected in Luis Alvarez's remark about paleontologists: "They are not really very good scientists; they are really more like stamp collectors." Description, in my sense, occurs at the level of observation (e.g., Snell's refraction law in optics). Explanation involves reductionism or some appeal to other, possibly nonobservable, constructs (as in Fermat's principle of least time). Prediction concerns the ability to generalize beyond the original domain of inquiry in empirically correct ways. As Friedman (1953) argues, prediction need not involve description nor explanation. I sympathize, however, with those who dislike black box positivism (e.g., Samuelson 1963). Also, the earlier distinction between description and explanation is rejected by many (e.g., Bridgman 1948; Mach 1883/1942); however, see also Kuhn (1962) and Quine (1969).

2. More specifically, the currency in most optimal foraging models is the expected net rate of energy expended in foraging (Smith 1987). More complex currencies might be multidimensional (reflecting key nutrients), and include risk measures such as variance.

3. Immanuel Kant wrote: "In the natural constitution of an organized being, that is, one suitably adapted to life, we assume as an axiom that no organ will be found for any purpose which is not the fittest and best adapted to that purpose" (Kitcher 1987, p. 78).

4. Note that Boland (1981) in general refutes the falsifiability of utility maximization by resorting to Popper's 1968 view that "all and some" statements are not refutable. For a counterargument, see Mongin (1986).

5. Adapted from Gould & Lewontin (1979, p. 586) as quoted in Beatty (1987, p. 53) who critically reviews Mayr's (1983) counterargument that the strategy of trying another hypothesis when an initial one fails is common to all branches of science. The key issue, however, concerns the level at which the reformulation occurs and how many falsifications are needed before the underlying theory or paradigm is questioned. See also Kitcher (1985).

6. This phrase was actually Herbert Spencer's but captures well the spirit of Darwin's remarkable and sweeping theory.

7. The presumed optimality of the free market system has evolved much beyond Adam Smith's (1776/1976) insight that voluntary exchange is mutually advantageous and ultimately utility-maximizing for the parties involved. Coase (1960) emphasized that, under free exchange, property rights and resources eventually end up in the hands of those for whom they are most valuable (i.e., optimal allocation and usage) *independent* of initial distributions or endowments. This insight is in turn exerting an influence on the design and function of our institutions and our legal system (Posner 1977). For more detail see Hirshleifer (1987, Chapter 9).

8. Although sense organs differ markedly across species – with humans experiencing the world mostly through vision, bats or dolphins relying much more on hearing, dogs or rats using smell, certain fish and eels sensing electric fields, and spiders or scorpions registering primarily vibrations – Shepard (1987) has argued that all share the same three-dimensional Euclidean world in terms of internal representation. He hypothesizes that "our deepest wisdom about the world has long ago been built into our perceptual systems at a level that is relatively automatic and unconscious. If this is so, we may all be smarter than we 'think' – that is, smarter than our more recently acquired processes of articulate thought" (Shepard 1987, p. 267). This view further vitiates the notion that we could consciously comprehend nature's optimality, if any.

9. Many economists would argue that economic man is indeed optimal, but that our attempts to model economic man are not, and thus undergo continual improvements (analogous to physicists' improved models of the atom). The paradox here, for economics, is that these bright scientists acknowledge their own suboptimality in the fiercely competitive game of model building while attributing perfect rationality to their lesser brethren in the game of economic life.

10. Lenoir (1982) offers a fascinating insight into teleological versus mechanical views among nineteenth century German biologists when Darwin's ideas gained currency. Although the Darwinian view won out, biological language is still replete with teleological terms, from selfish genes to survival instinct.

11. When plunged into water, the balloon will change in size and shape, but not instantly. As physicist David Lindley noted: "Air inside the balloon will bounce around and oscillate until the new stable shape is assumed. The significance of this is that the bouncing around represents a physical and entirely causal way by which the air in the balloon literally tries out other configurations before reaching the one dictated by least energy" (personal communication, Nov. 9, 1988).

12. A broader definition would include the rationality or moral worth of the ends as well, and would perhaps reduce the emphasis on the use of explicit reasoning (see Elster 1989).

13. I am referring here to Leibnitz's principle of perfection, according to which "God selects that universe for which the amount of perfection is a maximum" (Rescher 1979, p. 26).

Leibnitz viewed this principle as a moral rather than a logical necessity, stemming from the choice of the best.

14. Recent candidates in financial economics include attempts to rationalize dividend policies of firms (Miller 1986), and to explain away high volatility of stock prices (Kleidon 1986; Shiller 1981) including the stock market crash of October 1987 (Roll 1989; Malkiel 1989). In the area of preference theory, interesting rationalizations can be found regarding utility theory anomalies (Cohen 1981; Loomes & Sugden 1982; Machina 1982; Schoemaker 1982), and the so-called preference reversal phenomenon (Grether & Plott 1979; Slovic & Lichtenstein 1983). Of course, whether these are "true" rationalizations or standard scientific defenses is largely a matter of opinion.

B
Economics and Biology

[13]

UNCERTAINTY, EVOLUTION, AND ECONOMIC THEORY

ARMEN A. ALCHIAN[1]

University of California at Los Angeles

A MODIFICATION of economic analysis to incorporate incomplete information and uncertain foresight as axioms is suggested here. This approach dispenses with "profit maximization"; and it does not rely on the predictable, individual behavior that is usually assumed, as a first approximation, in standard textbook treatments. Despite these changes, the analytical concepts usually associated with such behavior are retained because they are not dependent upon such motivation or foresight. The suggested approach embodies the principles of biological evolution and natural selection by interpreting the economic system as an adoptive mechanism which chooses among exploratory actions generated by the adaptive pursuit of "success" or "profits." The resulting analysis is applicable to actions usually regarded as aberrations from standard economic behavior as well as to behavior covered by the customary analysis. This wider applicability and the removal of the unrealistic postulates of accurate anticipations and fixed states of knowledge have provided motivation for the study.

The exposition is ordered as follows: First, to clear the ground, a brief statement is given of a generally ignored aspect of "profit maximization," that is, where foresight is uncertain, "profit maximization" is *meaningless* as a guide to specifiable action. The constructive development then begins with an introduction of the element of environmental adoption by the economic system of a posteriori most appropriate action according to the criterion of "realized positive profits." This is illustrated in an extreme, random-behavior model without any individual rationality, foresight, or motivation whatsoever. Even in this extreme type of model, it is shown that the economist can predict and explain events with a modified use of his conventional analytical tools.

This phenomenon—environmental adoption—is then fused with a type of individual motivated behavior based on the pervasiveness of uncertainty and incomplete information. Adaptive, imitative, and trial-and-error behavior in the pursuit of "positive profits" is utilized rather than its sharp contrast, the pursuit of "maximized profits." A final section discusses some implications and conjectures.

I. "PROFIT MAXIMIZATION" NOT A GUIDE TO ACTION

Current economic analysis of economic behavior relies heavily on decisions made by rational units customarily assumed to be seeking perfectly optimal situations.[2] Two criteria are well known—profit maximization and utility maximiza

---

[1] I am indebted to Dr. Stephen Enke for criticism and stimulation leading to improvements in both content and exposition.

[2] See, e.g., J. Robinson, *Economics of Imperfect Competition* (London: Macmillan), p. 6, for a strong statement of the necessity of such optimal behavior. Standard textbooks expound essentially the same idea. See also P. Samuelson, *Foundations of Economic Analysis* (Cambridge: Harvard University Press, 1946).

tion.[3] According to these criteria, appropriate types of action are indicated by marginal or neighborhood inequalities which, if satisfied, yield an optimum. But the standard qualification usually added is that nobody is able really to optimize his situation according to these diagrams and concepts because of uncertainty about the position and, sometimes, even the slopes of the demand and supply functions. Nevertheless, the economist interprets and predicts the decisions of individuals in terms of these diagrams, since it is alleged that individuals use these concepts implicitly, if not explicitly.

Attacks on this methodology are widespread, but only one attack has been really damaging, that of G. Tintner.[4] He denies that profit maximization even makes any sense where there is uncertainty. Uncertainty arises from at least two sources: imperfect foresight and human inability to solve complex problems containing a host of variables even when an optimum is definable. Tintner's proof is simple. Under uncertainty, by definition, each action that may be chosen is identified with a *distribution* of potential outcomes, not with a unique outcome. Implicit in uncertainty is the consequence that these distributions of potential outcomes are overlapping.[5] It is worth emphasis that each possible action has a *distribution* of potential out-

[3] In the following we shall discuss only profit maximization, although everything said is applicable equally to utility maximization by consumers.

[4] "The Theory of Choice under Subjective Risk and Uncertainty," *Econometrica*, IX (1941), 298–304; "The Pure Theory of Production under Technological Risk and Uncertainty," *ibid.*, pp. 305–11; and "A Contribution to the Nonstatic Theory of Production," *Studies in Mathematical Economics and Econometrics* (Chicago: University of Chicago Press, 1942), pp. 92–109.

[5] Thus uncertainty is defined here to be the phenomenon that produces overlapping distributions of potential outcomes.

comes, only one of which will materialize if the action is taken, and that one outcome cannot be foreseen. Essentially, the task is converted into making a decision (selecting an action) whose potential outcome *distribution* is preferable, that is, choosing the action with the *optimum distribution*, since there is no such thing as a *maximizing* distribution.

For example, let each of two possible choices be characterized by its subjective distribution of potential outcomes. Suppose one has the higher "mean" but a larger spread, so that it might result in larger profits or losses, and the other has a smaller "mean" and a smaller spread. Which one is the maximum? This is a nonsensical question; but to ask for the optimum distribution is not nonsense. In the presence of uncertainty—a necessary condition for the existence of profits —there is no meaningful criterion for selecting the decision that will "maximize profits." The maximum-profit criterion is not meaningful as a basis *for selecting* the action which will, in fact, result in an outcome with higher profits than any other action would have, unless one assumes nonoverlapping potential outcome distributions. It must be noticed that the meaningfulness of "maximum profits —a realized outcome which is the largest that could have been realized from the available actions"—is perfectly consistent with the meaninglessness of "profit maximization"—a criterion for selecting among alternative lines of action, the potential outcomes of which are describable only as distributions and not as unique amounts.

This crucial difficulty would be avoided by using a preference function as a criterion for selecting most preferred distributions of potential outcomes, but the search for a criterion of rationality and choice in terms of pref-

UNCERTAINTY AND ECONOMIC THEORY 213

erence functions still continues. For example, the use of the mean, or expectation, completely begs the question of uncertainty by disregarding the variance of the distribution, while a "certainty equivalent" assumes the answer. The only way to make "profit maximization" a specifically meaningful action is to postulate a model containing certainty. Then the question of the predictive and explanatory reliability of the model must be faced.[6]

II. SUCCESS IS BASED ON RESULTS, NOT MOTIVATION

There is an alternative method which treats the decisions and criteria dictated by the economic *system* as more important than those made by the individuals in it. By backing away from the trees—the optimization calculus by individual units—we can better discern the forest of impersonal market forces.[7] This approach directs attention to the interrelationships of the environment and the prevailing types of economic behavior which appear through a process of economic natural selection. Yet it does not imply that individual foresight and action do not affect the nature of the existing state of affairs.

In an economic system the realization of profits is the criterion according to which successful and surviving firms are selected. This decision criterion is applied primarily by an impersonal market system in the United States and may be completely independent of the decision processes of individual units, of the variety of inconsistent motives and abilities, and even of the individual's awareness of the criterion. The reason is simple. Realized positive profits, not *maximum* profits, are the mark of success and viability. It does not matter through what process of reasoning or motivation such success was achieved. The fact of its accomplishment is sufficient. This is the criterion by which the economic system selects survivors: those who realize *positive profits* are the survivors; those who suffer losses disappear.

The pertinent requirement—positive profits through relative efficiency—is weaker than "maximized profits," with which, unfortunately, it has been confused. Positive profits accrue to those who are better than their actual competitors, even if the participants are ignorant, intelligent, skilful, etc. The crucial element is one's aggregate position relative to actual competitors, not some hypothetically perfect competitors. As in a race, the award goes to the relatively fastest, even if all the competitors loaf. Even in a world of stupid men there would still be profits. Also, the greater the uncertainties of the world, the greater is the possibility that profits would go to venturesome and lucky rather than to logical, careful, fact-gathering individuals.

The preceding interpretation suggests two ideas. First, success (survival) accompanies relative superiority; and, second, it does not require proper motivation but may rather be the result of fortuitous circumstances. Among all competitors, those whose particular conditions happen to be the most appropriate of those offered to the economic system for testing and adoption will be "se-

---

[6] Analytical models in all sciences postulate models abstracting from some realities in the belief that derived predictions will still be relevant. Simplifications are necessary, but continued attempts should be made to introduce more realistic assumptions into a workable model with an increase in generality and detail (see M. Friedman and L. Savage, "The Utility Analysis of Choices Involving Risks," *Journal of Political Economy*, LVI, No. 4 [1948], 279).

[7] In effect, we shall be reverting to a Marshallian type of analysis combined with the essentials of Darwinian evolutionary natural selection.

lected" as survivors. Just how such an approach can be used and how individuals happen to offer these appropriate forms for testing are problems to which we now turn.[8]

III. CHANCE OR LUCK IS ONE METHOD OF ACHIEVING SUCCESS

Sheer chance is a substantial element in determining the situation selected and also in determining its appropriateness or viability. A second element is the ability to adapt one's self by various methods to an appropriate situation. In order to indicate clearly the respective roles of luck and conscious adapting, the adaptive calculus will, for the moment, be completely removed. All individual rationality, motivation, and foresight will be temporarily abandoned in order to concentrate upon the ability of the environment to *adopt* "appropriate" survivors even in the absence of any adaptive behavior. This is an apparently unrealistic, but nevertheless very useful, expository approach in establishing the attenuation between the ex post survival criterion and the role of the individual's adaptive decision criterion. It also aids in assessing the role of luck and chance in the operation of our economic system.

Consider, first, the simplest type of biological evolution. Plants "grow" to the sunny side of buildings not because they "want to" in awareness of the fact that optimum or better conditions prevail there but rather because the leaves that happen to have more sunlight grow

faster and their feeding systems become stronger. Similarly, animals with configurations and habits more appropriate for survival under prevailing conditions have an enhanced viability and will with higher probability be typical survivors. Less appropriately acting organisms of the same general class having lower probabilities of survival will find survival difficult. More common types, the survivors, may appear to be those having *adapted* themselves to the environment, whereas the truth may well be that the environment has *adopted* them. There may have been no motivated individual adapting but, instead, only environmental adopting.

A useful, but unreal, example in which individuals act without any foresight indicates the type of analysis available to the economist and also the ability of the system to "direct" resources despite individual ignorance. Assume that thousands of travelers set out from Chicago, selecting their roads completely at random and without foresight. Only our "economist" knows that on but one road are there any gasoline stations. He can state categorically that travelers will *continue* to travel only on that road; those on other roads will soon run out of gas. Even though each one selected his route at random, we might have called those travelers who were so fortunate as to have picked the right road wise, efficient, foresighted, etc. Of course, we would consider them the lucky ones. If gasoline supplies were now moved to a new road, some formerly luckless travelers again would be able to move; and a new pattern of travel would be observed, although none of the travelers had changed his particular path. The really possible paths have changed with the changing environment. All that is needed is a set of varied, risk-taking

[8] Also suggested is another way to divide the general problem discussed here. The process and rationale by which a unit chooses its actions so as to optimize its situation is one part of the problem. The other is the relationship between changes in the environment and the consequent observable results, i.e., the decision process of the economic *society*. The classification used in the text is closely related to this but differs in emphasizing the degree of knowledge and foresight.

UNCERTAINTY AND ECONOMIC THEORY   215

(adoptable) travelers. The correct direction of travel will be established. As circumstances (economic environment) change, the analyst (economist) can select the types of participants (firms) that will now become successful; he may also be able to diagnose the conditions most conducive to a greater probability of survival.[9]

IV. CHANCE DOES NOT IMPLY NONDIRECTED, RANDOM ALLOCATION OF RESOURCES

These two examples do not constitute an attempt to base all analysis on adoptive models dominated by chance. But they do indicate that collective and individual random behavior does not per se imply a nihilistic theory incapable of yielding reliable predictions and explanations; nor does it imply a world lacking in order and apparent direction. It might, however, be argued that the facts of life deny even a substantial role to the element of chance and the associated adoption principle in the economic system. For example, the long lives and disparate sizes of business firms and hereditary fortunes may seem to be reliable evidence of consistent foresighted motivation and nonrandom behavior. In order to demonstrate that consistent success cannot be treated as prima facie evidence against pure luck, the following chance model of Borél, the famous French mathematician, is presented.

Suppose two million Parisians were paired off and set to tossing coins in a game of matching. Each pair plays until the winner on the first toss is again

[9] The undiscerning person who sees survivors corresponding to changes in environment claims to have evidence for the "Lysenko" doctrine. In truth, all he may have is evidence for the doctrine that the environment, by competitive conditions, selects the most viable of the various phenotypic characteristics for perpetuation. Economists should beware of economic "Lysenkois m."

brought to equality with the other player. Assuming one toss per second for each eight-hour day, at the end of ten years there would still be, on the average, about a hundred-odd pairs; and if the players assign the game to their heirs, a dozen or so will still be playing at the end of a thousand years! The implications are obvious. Suppose that some business had been operating for one hundred years. Should one rule out luck and chance as the essence of the factors producing the long-term survival of the enterprise? No inference whatever can be drawn until the number of original participants is known; and even then one must know the size, risk, and frequency of each commitment. One can see from the Borél illustration the danger in concluding that there are too many firms with long lives in the real world to admit an important role to chance. On the contrary, one might insist that there are actually too few!

The chance postulate was directed to two problems. On the one hand, there is the actual way in which a substantial fraction of economic behavior and activity is effected. On the other, there is the method of analysis which economists may use in their predictions and diagnoses. Before modifying the extreme chance model by adding adaptive behavior, some connotations and implications of the incorporation of chance elements will be elaborated in order to reveal the richness which is really inherent in chance. First, even if each and every individual acted in a haphazard and nonmotivated manner, it is possible that the variety of actions would be so great that the resulting collective set would contain actions that are best, in the sense of perfect foresight. For example, at a horse race with enough bettors wagering strictly at random, someone will win on all eight races. Thus individual random behavior does not eliminate the likelihood of observing "appropriate" decisions.[10]

Second, and conversely, individual behavior according to some foresight and motivation does not necessarily imply a collective pattern of behavior that is different from the collective variety of actions associated with a random selection of actions. Where there is uncertainty, people's judgments and opinions, even when based on the best available evidence, will differ; no one of them may be making his choice by tossing coins; yet the aggregate *set* of actions of the entire group of participants may be indistinguishable from a set of individual actions, each selected at random.[11]

Third, and fortunately, a chance-dominated model does not mean that an economist cannot predict or explain or diagnose. With a knowledge of the economy's realized requisites for survival and by a comparison of alternative conditions, he can state what types of firms or behavior relative to other possible types will be more viable, even though the firms themselves may not know the conditions or even try to achieve them by readjusting to the changed situation if they do know the conditions. It is sufficient if all firms are slightly different so that in the new environmental situation those who have their fixed internal conditions closer to the new, but unknown, optimum position now have a greater probability of survival and growth. They will grow relative to other firms and become the prevailing type, since survival conditions may push the observed characteristics of the set of survivors toward the unknowable optimum by either (1) repeated trials or (2) survival of more of those who happened to be near the optimum—determined ex post. If these new conditions last "very long," the dominant firms will be different ones from those which prevailed or would have prevailed under other conditions. Even if environmental conditions cannot be forecast, the economist can compare for given alternative potential situations the types of behavior that would have higher probability of viability or adoption. If explanation of past results rather than prediction is the task, the economist can diagnose the particular attributes which were critical in facilitating survival, even though individual participants were not aware of them.[12]

Fourth, the bases of prediction have been indicated in the preceding paragraph, but its character should be made explicit. The prediction will not assert that every—or, indeed, any—firm necessarily changes its characteristics. It asserts, instead, that the characteristics of the new *set* of firms, or possibly a set of new firms, will change. This may be

[10] The Borél gamblers analogue is pertinent to a host of everyday situations.

[11] Of course, the economic units may be going through a period of soul-searching, management training, and research activity. We cannot yet identify mental and physical activity with a process that results in sufficient information and foresight to yield uniquely determinate choices. To do so would be to beg the whole question.

[12] It is not even necessary to suppose that each firm acts as if it possessed the conventional diagrams and knew the analytical principles employed by economists in deriving optimum and equilibrium conditions. The atoms and electrons do not know the laws of nature; the physicist does not impart to each atom a wilful scheme of action based on laws of conservation of energy, etc. The fact that an economist deals with human beings who have sense and ambitions does not *automatically* warrant imparting to these humans the great degree of foresight and motivations which the economist may require for his customary analysis as an outside observer or "oracle." The similarity between this argument and Gibbsian statistical mechanics, as well as biological evolution, is *not* mere coincidence.

UNCERTAINTY AND ECONOMIC THEORY 217

characterized by the "representative firm," a purely statistical concept—a vector of "averages," one dimension for each of the several qualities of the population of firms. A "representative firm" is not typical of any one producer but, instead, is a set of statistics summarizing the various "modal" characteristics of the population. Surely, this was an intended use of Marshall's "representative firm."

Fifth, a final implication drawn from consideration of this extreme approach is that empirical investigations via questionnaire methods, so far used, are incapable of evaluating the validity of marginal productivity analysis. This is true because productivity and demand analyses are essential in evaluating relative viability, even though uncertainty eliminates "profit maximization" and even if price and technological changes were to have no consciously redirecting effect on the firms. To illustrate, suppose that, in attempting to predict the effects of higher real wage rates, it is discovered that every businessman says he does not adjust his labor force. Nevertheless, firms with a lower labor-capital ratio will have relatively lower cost positions and, to that extent, a higher probability of survival. The force of competitive survival, by eliminating higher-cost firms, reveals a population of remaining firms with a new average labor-capital ratio. The essential point is that individual motivation and foresight, while sufficient, are not necessary. Of course, it is not argued here that therefore it is absent. All that is needed by economists is their own awareness of the survival conditions and criteria of the economic system and a group of participants who submit various combinations and organizations for the system's selection and adoption. Both these conditions are satisfied.[13]

As a consequence, only the method of use, rather than the usefulness, of economic tools and concepts is affected by the approach suggested here; in fact, they are made more powerful if they are not pretentiously assumed to be necessarily associated with, and dependent upon, individual foresight and adjustment. They are tools for, at least, the diagnosis of the operation of an economic system, even if not also for the internal business behavior of each firm.

V. INDIVIDUAL ADAPTING VIA IMITATION AND TRIAL AND ERROR

Let it again be noted that the preceding extreme model was designed to present in purest form only one element of the suggested approach. It is not argued that there is no purposive, foresighted behavior present in reality. In adding this realistic element—adaptation by individuals with some foresight and purposive motivation—we are expanding the preceding extreme model. We are not abandoning any part of it or futilely trying to merge it with the opposite extreme of perfect foresight and "profit maximization."

Varying and conflicting objectives motivate economic activity, yet we shall here direct attention to only one particular objective—the sufficient condition of realized positive profits. There are no implications of "profit maximization," and this difference is important. Although the latter is a far more extreme objective when definable, only the former is the sine qua non of survival and success. To argue that, with perfect competition, the two would come to the same thing is to conceal an important difference by means of a very implausible as-

[13] This approach reveals how the "facts" of Lester's dispute with Machlup can be handled with standard economic tools.

sumption. The pursuit of profits, and not some hypothetical undefinable perfect situation, is the relevant objective whose *fulfilment* is rewarded with survival. Unfortunately, even this proximate objective is too high. Neither perfect knowledge of the past nor complete awareness of the current state of the arts gives sufficient foresight to indicate profitable action. Even for this more restricted objective, the pervasive effects of uncertainty prevent the ascertainment of actions which are supposed to be optimal in achieving profits. Now the consequence of this is that modes of behavior replace optimum equilibrium conditions as guiding rules of action. Therefore, in the following sections two forms of conscious adaptive behavior are emphasized.

First, wherever successful enterprises are observed, the elements common to these observable successes will be associated with success and copied by others in their pursuit of profits or success. "Nothing succeeds like success." Thus the urge for "rough-and-ready" imitative rules of behavior is accounted for. What would otherwise appear to be merely customary "orthodox," nonrational rules of behavior turns out to be codified imitations of observed success, e.g., "conventional" markup, price "followship," "orthodox" accounting and operating ratios, "proper" advertising policy, etc. A conventionally employed type of behavior pattern is consistent with the postulates of the analysis employed, even though the reasons and justifications for the particular conventions are not.[14]

Many factors cause this motive to imitate patterns of action observable in past successes. Among these are: (1) the absence of an identifiable criterion for decision-making, (2) the variability of the environment, (3) the multiplicity of factors that call for attention and choice, (4) the uncertainty attaching to all these factors and outcomes, (5) the awareness that superiority relative to one's competitors is crucial, and (6) the nonavailability of a trial-and-error process converging to an optimum position.

In addition, imitation affords relief from the necessity of really making decisions and conscious innovations, which, if wrong, become "inexcusable." Unfortunately, failure or success often reflects the willingness to depart from rules when conditions have changed; what counts, then, is not only imitative behavior but the willingness to abandon it at the "right" time and circumstances. Those who are different and successful "become" innovators, while those who fail "become" reckless violators of tried-and-true rules. Although one may deny the absolute appropriateness of such rules, one cannot doubt the existence of a strong urge to create conventions and rules (based on observed success) and a willingness to use them for action as well as for rationalizations of inaction. If another untried host of actions might have been even more successful, so much the worse for the participants who failed, and even for those who missed "perfect success."

Even innovation is accounted for by imitation. While there certainly are those who consciously innovate, there are those who, in their imperfect attempts

[14] These constructed rules of behavior should be distinguished from "rules" which, in effect, do no more than define the objective being sought. Confusion between objectives which motivate one and rules of behavior are commonplace. For example, "full-cost pricing" is a "rule" that one cannot really follow. He can try to, but whether he succeeds or fails in his objective of survival is not controllable by following the "rule of full-cost pricing." If he fails in his objective, he must, of necessity, fail to have followed the "rule." The situation is parallel to trying to control the speed of a car by simply setting by hand the indicator on the speedometer.

UNCERTAINTY AND ECONOMIC THEORY   219

to imitate others, unconsciously innovate by unwittingly acquiring some unexpected or unsought unique attributes which under the prevailing circumstances prove partly responsible for the success. Others, in turn, will attempt to copy the uniqueness, and the imitation-innovation process continues. Innovation is assured, and the notable aspects of it here are the possibility of unconscious pioneering and leadership.

The second type of conscious adaptive behavior, in addition to imitation, is "trial and error." This has been used with "profit maximization," wherein, by trial and ensuing success or failure, more appropriate actions are selected in a process presumed to converge to a limit of "profit maximization" equilibrium. Unfortunately, at least two conditions are necessary for convergence via a trial-and-error process, even if one admits an equilibrium situation as an admissible limit. First, a trial must be classifiable as a success or failure. The position achieved must be comparable with results of other potential actions. In a static environment, if one improves his position relative to his former position, then the action taken is better than the former one, and presumably one could continue by small increments to advance to a local optimum. An analogy is pertinent. A nearsighted grasshopper on a mound of rocks can crawl to the top of a particular rock. But there is no assurance that he can also get to the top of the mound, for he might have to descend for a while or hop to new rocks. The second condition, then, for the convergence via trial and error is the continual rising toward some *optimum optimorum* without intervening descents. Whether decisions and actions in economic life satisfy these two conditions cannot be proved or disproved here,

but the available evidence seems overwhelmingly unfavorable.

The above convergence conditions do not apply to a changing environment, for there can be no observable comparison of the result of an action with any other. Comparability of resulting situations is destroyed by the changing environment. As a consequence, the measure of goodness of actions in anything except a tolerable-intolerable sense is lost, and the possibility of an individual's converging to the optimum activity via a trial-and-error process disappears. Trial and error becomes survival or death. It cannot serve as a basis of the *individual's* method of convergence to a "maximum" or optimum position. Success is discovered by the economic system through a blanketing shotgun process, not by the individual through a converging search.

In general, uncertainty provides an excellent reason for imitation of observed success. Likewise, it accounts for observed uniformity among the survivors, derived from an evolutionary, adopting, competitive system employing a criterion of survival, which can operate independently of individual motivations. Adapting behavior via imitation and venturesome innovation enlarges the model. Imperfect imitators provide opportunity for innovation, and the survival criterion of the economy determines the successful, possibly because imperfect, imitators. Innovation is provided also by conscious wilful action, whatever the ultimate motivation may be, since drastic action is motivated by the hope of great success as well as by the desire to avoid impending failure.

All the preceding arguments leave the individual economic participant with imitative, venturesome, innovative, trial-and-error adaptive behavior. Most conventional economic tools and concepts are still useful, although in a vastly different analytical framework—one which is closely akin to the theory of biological evolution. The economic counterparts of genetic heredity, mutations, and natural selection are imitation, innovation, and positive profits.

VI. CONCLUSIONS AND SUMMARY

I shall conclude with a brief reference to some implications and conjectures.

Observable patterns of behavior and organization are predictable in terms of their relative probabilities of success or viability *if* they are tried. The observed prevalence of a type of behavior depends upon both this probability of viability and the probability of the different types being submitted to the economic system for testing and selecting. One is the probability of appearance of a certain type of organization (mutation), and the other is the probability of its survival or viability, once it appears (natural selection). There is much evidence for believing that these two probabilities are interrelated. But is there reason to suppose that a high probability of viability implies a high probability of an action's being taken, as would be implied in a system of analysis involving some "inner directed urge toward perfection"? If these two probabilities are not highly correlated, what predictions of types of action can the economist make? An answer has been suggested in this paper.

While it is true that the economist can define a profit maximization behavior by assuming *specific* cost and revenue conditions, is there any assurance that the conditions and conclusions so derivable are not too perfect and absolute? If profit maximization (certainty) is not ascertainable, the confidence about the predicted effects of changes, e.g., higher taxes or minimum wages, will be dependent upon how close the formerly existing arrangement was to the formerly "optimal" (certainty) situation. What really counts is the various actions actually tried, for it is from these that "success" is selected, not from some set of perfect actions. The economist may be pushing his luck too far in arguing that actions in response to changes in environment and changes in satisfaction with the existing state of affairs will converge as a result of adaptation or adoption toward the optimum action that should have been selected, if foresight had been perfect.[15]

In summary, I have asserted that the economist, using the present analytical tools developed in the analysis of the firm under certainty, can predict the more adoptable or viable types of economic interrelationships that will be induced by environmental change even if individuals themselves are unable to ascertain them. That is, although individual participants may not know their cost and revenue situations, the economist can predict the consequences of higher wage rates, taxes, government policy, etc. Like the biologist, the economist predicts the effects of

---

[15] An anomalous aspect of the assumption of perfect foresight is that it nearly results in tautological and empty statements. One cannot know everything, and this is recognized by the addendum that one acts within a "given state and distribution of the arts." But this is perilously close, if not equivalent, to saying either that action is taken only where the outcome is accurately foreseen or that information is always limited. The qualification is inserted because one might contend that it is the *"constancy* of the state and distribution of arts" that is necessary as a *ceteris paribus.* But even the latter is no solution. A large fraction of behavior in a world of incomplete information and uncertainty is necessarily directed at increasing the state of arts and venturing into an unknown sphere. While it is probably permissible to start with a prescribed "distribution of the knowledge of the arts," holding it constant is too restrictive, since a large class of important and frequent actions necessarily involves changes in the state and distribution of knowledge. The modification suggested here incorporates this search for more knowledge as an essential foundation.

environmental changes on the surviving class of living organisms; the economist need not assume that each participant is aware of, or acts according to, his cost and demand situation. These are concepts for the economist's use and not necessarily for the individual participant's, who may have other analytic or customary devices which, while of interest to the economist, serve as data and not as analytic methods.

An alternative to the rationale of individual profit maximization has been presented without exorcising uncertainty. Lest isolated arguments be misinterpreted, let it be clearly stated that this paper does not argue that purposive objective-seeking behavior is absent from reality, nor, on the other hand, does it indorse the familiar thesis that action of economic units cannot be expressed within the marginal analysis. Rather, the contention is that the precise role and nature of purposive behavior in the presence of uncertainty and incomplete information have not been clearly understood or analyzed.

It is straightforward, if not heuristic, to start with complete uncertainty and nonmotivation and then to add elements of foresight and motivation in the process of building an analytical model. The opposite approach, which starts with certainty and unique motivation, must abandon its basic principles as soon as uncertainty and mixed motivations are recognized.[16] The approach suggested here is intellectually more modest and realistic, without sacrificing generality. It does not regard uncertainty as an aberrational exogenous disturbance, as does the usual approach from the opposite extreme of accurate foresight. The existence of uncertainty and incomplete information is the foundation of the suggested type of analysis; the importance of the concept of a class of "chance" decisions rests upon it; it permits of various conflicting objectives; it motivates and rationalizes a type of adaptive imitative behavior; yet it does not destroy the basis of prediction, explanation, or diagnosis. It does not base its aggregate description on individual optimal action; yet it is capable of incorporating such activity where justified. The formalization of this approach awaits the marriage of the theory of stochastic processes and economics—two fields of thought admirably suited for union. It is conjectured that the suggested modification is applicable to a wide class of events and is worth attempts at empirical verification.[17]

[16] If one prefers, he may believe that the suggestions here contain reasons why the model based on certainty may predict outcomes, although individuals really cannot try to maximize profits. But the dangers of this have been indicated.

[17] Preliminary study in this direction has been very convincing, and, in addition, the suggested approach appears to contain important implications relative to general economic policy; but discussions of these are reserved for a later date.

[14]

NEOCLASSICAL *vs.* EVOLUTIONARY THEORIES OF ECONOMIC GROWTH: CRITIQUE AND PROSPECTUS[1]

THE relationship between technical change and economic growth has recently been reviewed in four major articles: by Nadiri in the *Journal of Economic Literature* (Nadiri, 1970), Pavitt for OECD (1971), Mansfield in *Science* (1972) and Kennedy and Thirlwall in the ECONOMIC JOURNAL (1972). It is our contention in this paper that there is a sharp inconsistency between the two bodies of research surveyed in these articles—the macro growth literature and the micro literature on technological change *per se*—that calls into question the basic tenets of neoclassical theory. In Section I we discuss neoclassical growth theory, and the nature of its inconsistency with the micro studies of technological change. We also consider the apparent attractiveness of the Schumpeterian alternative to neoclassical theory.

The basic elements of an evolutionary growth theory are discussed in Section II. It is proposed that this theory provides the framework for a rigorous and rich analysis of the processes of technical change and dynamic competition, encompassing several of the Schumpeterian ideas. Section III describes a particular evolutionary model and discusses some simulation results. Acceptance of the view that growth is an evolutionary, not a neoclassical, process involves a number of important changes in perspective and interpretation, and these are discussed in Section IV.

I. ECONOMIC GROWTH THEORY: THE NEOCLASSICAL STRUCTURE AND THE SCHUMPETERIAN ALTERNATIVE

In economics (as in physics) what we refer to as a theory is more a set of basic premises—a point of view that delineates the phenomena to be explained and modes of acceptable explanation—than a set of testable propositions. The theory points to certain phenomena and key explanatory variables and mechanisms, but generally is quite flexible about the expected conclusions of empirical research, and a wide class of models is consistent with it. Inadequate or incomplete explanations or even contradictions with the data, generally are interpreted as puzzles and problems to be worked on within the broad framework proposed by the theory, rather than grounds for its rejection. Thus it clearly is a delicate business to "evaluate" a particular

[1] The authors are professors of economics at Yale University and The University of Michigan respectively. We are indebted to Carlos Diaz-Alejandro and Robert Evanson for useful comments on an earlier draft, and to the editors and two anonymous referees for comments which led to a significant improvement of the version first submitted to the ECONOMIC JOURNAL. Herbert L. Schuette figured importantly in the development of the simulation model to which we make frequent reference. Financial support for this research was provided by the Institute of Public Policy Studies at Michigan, and by the National Science Foundation under Grant GS-35659; this support is gratefully acknowledged.

theory or, even, to state precisely what the theory is, and what it is to "explain".

We take it that there is at least rough agreement among economists on what growth theory is to explain. The minimal set of phenomena to be explained are the time paths of output, input and prices. Nations have grown at various rates over time, and in given eros nations have grown at different rates. Once we disaggregate the growth experience of particular countries it is apparent that certain sectors have developed much more rapidly than others, and that the sectoral pattern of growth has varied over time. While different theories may define and delineate these central phenomena somewhat differently, and may also divide on questions of the relevance of data of other types (*e.g.* productivity differences among firms), almost all economists would agree that a satisfactory growth theory must be able to explain the above phenomena.

We also take it that most economists would agree that the following are essential elements of the neoclassical explanation. The dominant theme derives from the theory of the firm and production in a competitive industry. At any time firms are viewed as facing a set of alternatives regarding the inputs and outputs they will procure and produce. Firms choose so as to maximise profit or present value, given external conditions facing the firm. The sector is assumed to be in equilibrium in the sense that demand and supply are balanced on all relevant markets and no firm can improve its position given what other firms are doing. If we think of a "macro" economy with one sector and with no Keynesian difficulties, growth occurs in the system because over time factors of production expand in supply and production sets are augmented; in an "industry" growth model, changes in demand must be considered as well. The time paths of output, input, and prices are interpreted as the paths generated by maximising firms in a moving equilibrium driven by changes in product demand, factor supply, and technological conditions.

As a glance at the recent survey articles (or at Solow's recent (1970) volume) testifies, the theory comprises a variegated family of specific models. The empirical work generated by the theory is similarly diverse. Various neoclassical econometric models have "explained" growth reasonably well on the basis of input growth and technical change, if the criterion is a high R^2. Growth accounting has proceeded apace and has provided an intellectual format for enriching our understanding of the factors which have influenced growth.[1] Thus the theory has been robust in the sense that it continues to survive and to spawn a considerable amount of research which has enhanced our understanding of economic growth. This is a strong plus for neoclassical theory.

However, neoclassical explanations have run into difficulties. To a considerable degree the success of the calibration and testing work alluded to

---

[1] For a critique of the growth accounting literature, see Nelson (1973).

above has been due to the *ad hoc* flexibility of the theory. Thus in the early days of growth accounting, the "residual"—which was as large as the portion of growth explained by increases in the factors of production then considered— was simply labelled technical change, and the theory thereby preserved. We are still doing roughly the same thing when we try to explain growth by improvement in the quality of different factors (however measured) without giving an explicit account of how these quality improvements came about or explaining in a persuasive way how these factors affect growth. In our view, and that of the authors of the survey articles, research of this type has served principally to establish the need for a richer analysis of the sources and effects of technical advance and of factor quality improvements.

In fact, such an analysis is to some extent available in the body of research on technological change done by economic historians, researchers within the industrial organisation tradition, and scholars interested in invention and innovation *per se*. Studies by historians like Usher, Landes, Habakkuk, David, Temin, Rosenberg, and by students of industrial organisation and technical change like Schmookler, Jewkes, Sawers and Stillerman, MacLaurin, Peck, Griliches, Mansfield, and Freeman have revealed extremely interesting facts about the technological change process.[1] However, while some of these are in harmony with neoclassical themes, others are quite discordant. We have, for example, much evidence of the role of insight in the major invention process, and of significant differences in ability of inventors to "see things" that are not obvious to all who are looking. The same pattern apparently obtains in innovation. Relatedly, there are considerable differences among firms at any time in terms of the technology used, productivity and profitability. While these studies show clearly that purpose and calculation play an important role, the observed differences among persons and firms are hard to reconcile with simple notions of maximisation, unless some explicit account is taken of differences in knowledge, maximising capabilities, or luck. The role of competition seems better characterised in the Schumpeterian terms of competitive advantages gained through innovation, or early adoption of a new product or process, than in the equilibrium language of neoclassical theory.

The difficulties can be seen most sharply by considering the major role of the concepts of innovation and imitation in the literature on technical change referred to above, and the awkwardness of these concepts within neoclassical theory. The concept of innovation carries the connotation of something novel, and clearly is not adequately characterised in terms of an induced change in choice within a given and constant choice set. Nor does a more or less mechanical treatment of the expansion of the choice set, whether spontaneously or as a result of R and D, capture the nature of

---

[1] Rather than providing specific references to the illustrative sample of works, it seems appropriate to refer to the broad bibliographies in the aforementioned survey articles. See also the bibliography in R. Nelson, M. J. Peck and E. D. Kalachek (1967).

innovation, as it has been analysed in the literature not bound by neoclassical terms. Similar difficulties affect the concept of imitation. It is apparent that the fact that one firm imitates another often reflects a tacit admission that the other firm was doing a better thing. The fact that lagging firms often fail suggests the futility of dealing with this challenge to the assumptions of neoclassical theory by arguing that the lagging firm may have been opti-mising because it saved on R and D costs.

The problem here is more than inability of the theory, at least in simple form, to be useful to certain kinds of research, and goes beyond the fact that there are some interesting data that are difficult for the theory to digest. Research within the neoclassical theory now acknowledges the centrality of technical change in the growth process. The "indigestible" phenomena appear—the minute the neoclassical blinkers are removed—to be basic characteristics of the technical change process.

The recent survey articles do not confront this problem squarely. Nadiri sidesteps it largely by ignoring the micro literature on technological advance, despite the importance he attributes to technical change. Pavitt ignores the macro literature. Mansfield leaves the tension between the two literatures unanalysed. However, the organisation of the recent article by Kennedy and Thirlwall does make the division explicit. The analytic structure used in the first part of the survey, on the effect of technical change, is predominantly neoclassical growth theory. There is an explicit or implicit commitment to the assumptions of faultless maximisation and equilibrium. Very few of the studies of the second part of the review, concerned with the processes of technical change, employ these assumptions. Several of these studies (for example, the models of diffusion) implicitly deny them.

In another recent article appraising the state of growth theory there is sharper awareness of the problems. Nordhaus and Tobin remark:

> "The (neoclassical) theory conceals, either in aggregation or in the abstract generality of multi-sector models, all the drama of the events—the rise and fall of products, technologies, and industries, and the accompanying transformation of the spatial and occupational distribu-tions of the population. Many economists agree with the broad outlines of Schumpeter's vision of capitalist development, which is a far cry from growth models made nowadays in either Cambridge, Mass. or Cambridge, England. But visions of that kind have yet to be transformed into theory that can be applied to everyday analytic and empirical work." (1972, p. 2.)

But much of the research within the economic history and industrial organi-sation traditions has been concerned with just that drama.

We would concede, of course, that recent theoretical developments have considerably broadened the scope of neoclassical theory. Various models have been proposed that explicitly dispense with the perfect information assumption. Some of these view the firm as searching for the best alternative, balancing the costs of search against the expected benefits. Models of investment and employment expansion incorporate distributed lag and other adaptive behaviour structures. These developments are steps in the direction of a richer theory that can encompass some of the phenomena currently proving indigestible. However, they pose the question of what remains of the theory if they are accepted. They drastically alter the characterisation of the choice set over which the firms are supposed to maximise and raise some questions regarding the very meaning of maximisation.[1] Equilibrium tends to be preserved as a characterisation only of steady state conditions which are not assumed generally to obtain.

It seems obvious that research on economic growth within the neoclassical theory is creating new intellectual problems more rapidly than it is solving them. One can continue to search for solutions to these problems guided by the assumptions of neoclassical theory. Or, one can try a new tack.[2]

As the Nordhaus–Tobin quote remarks, it is apparent that many economists studying growth are much attracted to the perspective sketched out by Schumpeter 60 years ago in Chapter 2 of his *Theory of Economic Development* (1934, original publication 1911).

The core ideas of Schumpeterian theory are of course quite different from those of neoclassical theory. For Schumpeter the most important firms are those that serve as the vehicles for action of the real drivers of the system—the innovating entrepreneurs. Firms (and entrepreneurs) may seek profit, and may innovate or imitate to achieve higher profit. However, the emphasis on careful calculation over well-defined choice sets is absent. The competitive environment within which firms operate is one of struggle and motion. It is a dynamic selection environment, not an equilibrium one. The essential forces of growth are innovation and selection, with augmentation of capital stocks more or less tied to these processes.

What accounts for the fact that this highly plausible interpretation has been relatively neglected in theoretical discussion? As Nordhaus and Tobin suggest, the likely explanation is that the neoclassical approach has held sway because of its apparently greater susceptibility to *formal* modelling. Fuller assimilation of the Schumpeterian contribution may be achieved if an appropriate formal framework for it can be developed.

---

[1] In particular, there is a serious question whether it is possible to construct an internally consistent theory involving optimising actors for whom *all* information and computation is costly—as opposed to theories in which the perfect information assumption is merely shifted back a stage or two in the logic. See the discussion of this point in S. Winter (1964).

[2] The Keynesian revolution is the obvious example of a crisis in economics which led to such a "new tack". Perhaps another crisis is building now; there has occurred in the last few years a remarkable surge of authoritative grumbling about the state of the discipline, particularly in presidential addresses. See Phelps Brown (1972); Hahn (1970); Leontief (1971); Worswick (1972).

II. ELEMENTS OF AN EVOLUTIONARY THEORY OF ECONOMIC GROWTH

In this section we introduce the elements of an evolutionary theory of the behaviour of firms and economic sectors.[1] Many of the specific concepts and orientations presented are, we believe, of broad applicability. They are relevant not only to the problems of economic growth and technical change but also, for example, to the dynamics of inflation and the control of monopolies. Indeed, we consider them applicable to some systems in which government bureaucracies replace business firms as key actors. However, since our present focus is on growth, and technical change, we will present the ideas in a manner appropriate to that area of inquiry, and draw illustrative examples from it. In the following section, we reduce the scope of the discussion still further. The simulation model discussed there represents a particular case within the evolutionary theory in the same sense that a model with a Cobb-Douglas production function, neutral technical change, exogenous labour force growth, and savings proportional to income represents a particular member of the class of neoclassical models.

The first major commitment of the evolutionary theory is to a "behavioural" approach to individual firms. The basic behavioural premise is that a firm at any time operates largely according to a set of decision rules that link a domain of environmental stimuli to a range of responses on the part of firms. While neoclassical theory would attempt to deduce these decision rules from maximisation on the part of the firm, the behavioural theory simply takes them as given and observable. The plausibility of this approach has, we think, been adequately established by previous work on the behavioural theory of the firm.[2] For purposes of theoretical analysis, we deal with abstract decision rules stated in the language of mathematics or a computer programme.

The particular rules considered, and the manner of their description, will vary from case to case depending on the purpose of the inquiry. If the focus is on the decisions of a single large firm, the descriptions may be quite detailed. If it is on the historical development of a sector or an entire economy, considerations of tractability and information availability will dictate a very

---

[1] Space limitations prevent us from exploring here the parallels and divergences between our proposal and theories of biological evolution; we also omit a full discussion of the relationship of our work to the many previous uses of biological analogies in the economic literature. However, some brief references to the latter are in order. A particularly influential article was Alchian's "Uncertainty, Evolution and Economic Theory" (1950). It should be noted that Alchian comes much closer to treating the evolutionary approach as a serious alternative theory than does Friedman in his famous methodological essay (1953). For a critique of use of evolutionary arguments as a crutch for orthodoxy, see Winter (1964). Still more recently, M. Farrell has taken the evolutionary approach seriously in "Some Elementary Selection Processes in Economics" (1970); his purposes are, however, somewhat narrower than our own, and he makes more direct use of the available mathematical models in biological theory.

[2] The basic reference is Cyert and March (1963). In an interesting recent paper, Baumol and Stewart attempt a replication of a portion of the empirical work reported in the Cyert and March volume, with reasonably satisfactory results (1971).

892 THE ECONOMIC JOURNAL [DECEMBER

simple and stylised characterisation of individual firm rules. For example, in our simulation study and in other work we have identified the "production decision rule" of the individual firm with a list of coefficients characterising the unit level of operation of a single productive technique. This treatment reflects, but in a highly stylised way, what we believe to be a fact about firm behaviour, namely, that commitments to routinised production methods are maintained for fairly long periods and adjustment to changing conditions is sporadic rather than continuous.

The assumption of short-run stability in the decision rules provides an essential element of continuity on which to base an evolutionary analysis. Firm decision rules are not immutable, however, and the processes of change are as basic to the evolutionary story as the sources of continuity. While an assumption of constancy in decision rules may be a good approximation for purposes of relatively short-range predictions, understanding of longer-term trends must be based on analysis of the mechanisms that operate to modify both the rules applied in individual firms and the relative importance of different rules in determining economic outcomes at a more aggregate level.

Prominent among the processes of rule change in the individual firm are those that involve deliberate, goal-oriented "search" or "problem-solving" activity. Such activity takes a wide variety of forms and can occur at different "levels" in a hierarchical structure of decision rules. For example, a firm's R and D policy may commit it to a certain level and pattern of search for new products and productive techniques, but also the R and D policy itself may be regarded as a decision rule subject to change by higher-order search processes. Regardless of the particular rule involved, however, a theoretical model of the search process must comprise answers to the following questions: (i) What goals of the firm are operative in the search process, and how do they affect it? (ii) What determines the intensity, direction and strategy of search activity? (iii) What is the field of search, *i.e.* the set from which possible rules are drawn, and how are the likely search outcomes distributed in it?

Our general answers to these questions do not represent irrevocable commitments; neither are they as complete as we would like. Tentatively, we adhere to the orthodox view that some form of the profit motive is the dominant motivational consideration; however, the logic of the evolutionary approach is equally consistent with a "managerialist" emphasis on growth or "the quiet life". On the question of the intensity of search, one appealing hypothesis is that search is stimulated by adversity, or by perceived "problems" or "exceptions" arising with the existing decision rules. On the other hand, it is clear that firms institutionalise at least some forms of search activity, *e.g.* in R and D or operations research programmes, and thus continue searching even when things are going well. The influences on the direction and strategy of search are obviously complex, but among the major considerations which one would certainly want to include are market prices, information concerning the decision rules of other firms (the basis for imitative behaviour), and exogenous changes in relevant knowledge. Finally, the modelling of the set of possible decision rules will be specific to the purposes of the inquiry. When the concern is with the evolution of productive technique, we may, as noted above, identify rules with vectors of technical coefficients. The set of possible rules then bears a superficial resemblance to a production set—superficial because the production set characterises *known* techniques whereas we are concerned with the set of (physically) *possible* techniques.

Evolutionary theory involves, finally, explicit analysis of the economic selection mechanism—the change in the weighting of different decision rules that comes about through the expansion of firms using profitable rules and the contraction of firms using unprofitable ones. The first step in such analysis is to delineate the set of actual and potential firms whose behaviour is to be studied; depending on the purpose of the inquiry this set may include the firms of an entire economy, of a large sector, or of a narrowly defined industry. The nature of the decision rules that determine entry or exit, expansion or contraction, must be specified. Next, the "selection environment" must be characterised. This involves specification of, at a minimum, the following: (i) the conditions of supply and demand for current inputs and outputs, (ii) the functioning of the financial and capital goods markets facing the firms of the sector. Thus, the selection environment is at once the medium through which exogenous influences (*e.g.* shifts in input supply curves) are transmitted to the firms in the sector; and the medium through which the firms of the sector influence each other (*e.g.* the expansion of one firm resulting in higher input prices to the others as well as to itself). And, of particular importance to an evolutionary analysis, the selection environment determines the way in which these influences impinge on the investment decisions of firms.

The general logic of the selection mechanism may now be described. The current decision rules of firms determine their input and output decisions, and hence, collectively, the prevailing market prices. Prices determine profitability and in conjunction with firm investment rules and capital market rules, the rates of expansion or contraction of individual firms. With the sizes of the firms thus altered, the firm decision rules yield different input and output decisions, hence different price and profitability signals, and so on. By this process, clearly, aggregate input and output and price levels for the sector would undergo dynamic change, even if search processes did not modify the individual firm decision rules.

But individual firm rules *do* change, and the phenomena of search and selection are simultaneous, interacting aspects of the evolutionary process. The same prices that provide selective feedback also influence the directions of search. Through the joint action of search and selection, the firms evolve over time, with the condition of the industry on each day bearing the seeds of its condition on the day following.

The conceptual scheme just set forth has distinct advantages over neo-classical theory as a basis for interpreting the phenomena of economic growth. First of all, it offers a natural definition of innovation—change of existing decision rules. It is far easier to make use of a term that has the connotation "new" or "novel" in a theory that explicitly relies on notions of routine behaviour than in one that presumes flexible maximising behaviour always. Secondly, and relatedly, explicit introduction of the concepts of profit-motivated search and problem-solving behaviour provides a basis for the discussion of a distinctive entrepreneurial function. By contrast, the neo-classical over-emphasis on consistent maximising behaviour by one and all renders entrepreneurship otiose (a point well made by Baumol, 1968). Thus the proposal offers a systematic framework for a Schumpeterian analysis of the competitive process. However, acceptance of the evolutionary point of view need not imply a complete loss of contact with orthodox conclusions— the equilibrium theorem of Winter (1971) shows, for example, how the two may be reconciled in the (hypothetical) long run.

III. A SIMULATION STUDY

The theoretical structure just set forth is obviously very roomy; a large family of specific models could be established within it. As yet, we have been able to familiarise ourselves with only a few of those models, and these few are far from ideal representatives. They do not, for example, draw on specific descriptive information of firm decision processes to the extent that we consider desirable. Both the decision rules imputed to firms and the characterisa-tions of rule-change processes are extremely simple and must be considered to be in the nature of temporary expedients. In spite of these deficiencies, and the attendant danger that the flaws of the exemplars may be (wrongly) imputed to the general approach, we describe one of these primitive models here. This should serve to establish that there is at least some reasonable prospect of developing a formal counterpart for our appreciative theory.

The model we use for illustrative purposes here is described in much greater detail in another paper (Nelson, Winter and Schuette, 1973).[1] In its quantitative, empirical aspects it is based on the data employed by Solow in his classic 1957 article "Technical Change and the Aggregate Production Function" (1957); it provides an evolutionary parable as an alternative to Solow's neoclassical one. In its formal, mathematical aspects the model is a

---

[1] This report is available from the Institute of Public Policy Studies, The University of Michigan, Ann Arbor, Michigan 48104, USA, at a price of $1.00 per copy. A detailed documentation of the computer programme is also available at the same price. We would be happy to arrange to transfer the programme itself to anyone who wished to experiment with it and had access to appropriate equipment for doing so. Winter (1971) and Nelson (1974) contain mathematical analyses of closely related models.

Markov process in a set of "industry states"; this seems to be a highly convenient framework for evolutionary analysis and one that we are continuing to employ, although in more complex formulations, in our current work. In various aspects of its structure and operation, the model illustrates the possibility of developing precise analytical counterparts for some of the concepts introduced in the preceding section of this paper.

The model involves a number of firms, all producing the same homogeneous product by employing two factors—labour and physical capital. In a particular time period a firm is characterised by its production technique—described by a pair of input coefficients, (a_L, a_K)—and its capital stock, K. A firm's production decision rule is simply to use all its capacity to produce output, using its current technique—no slowdown or shutdown decision is allowed for. A *firm state* is a triple (a_L, a_K, K), indexed by time and the identification number for a particular firm. The *industry state* at time t is the (finite) list of firm states at time t. Given the basic behavioural assumption, aggregate output and labour demand are directly determined by the industry state. The cost of capital (required dividend payout) is taken to be exogenous and constant. The wage rate is endogenous, and is determined in each time period by reference to a labour supply curve. Thus, given these factor price determination mechanisms, the industry state also implies aggregate and firm values of profits, labour share, *etc.*

Changes in the industry state are generated by applying probabilistic transition rules, independently, to the individual firm states. Technique changes by individual firms are governed, first of all, by a satisficing mechanism. If the firm's rate of return on capital exceeds a target level, the firm retains its current technique with probability one. Otherwise a probabilistic search process generates a possible alternative technique. The probability distribution governing search outcomes is constructed in a manner that reflects the influence of "closeness" and of "imitation". The alternatives turned up are likely to be characterised by input coefficients close to those currently in use by the firm, or to be techniques that currently account for a large proportion of output by other firms in the industry. Finally, a test is applied to determine if the technique turned up by the search process is actually less costly, at the prevailing wage rate, than the one the firm currently uses. If the answer is yes, the firm changes technique.

A simpler rule governs the change in the individual firm's capital stock. The capital stock is first reduced by a random depreciation process, and then augmented by "gross profit"—defined as the excess of revenue over the sum of the wage bill and the required dividend payout. This assumption is the most direct way possible of introducing the selection mechanism into the picture. Apart from the randomness in depreciation, the growth rate of a firm is made to conform to its rate of excess return on capital. Clearly, this assumption cannot be regarded as a serious theory of the financing of aggregate investment. The model involves no personal saving, no taxation of corporate profits or personal incomes, no government surplus or deficit, and no financial intermediation. It is immune to Keynesian difficulties, since gross saving and gross investment are both equal to gross profit, firm by firm. Thus, following the dubious tradition of neoclassical growth theory, the model ignores the problems of short-run adjustment. The implicit *long-run* theory of the level of aggregate investment is that it accommodates population growth and the labour-saving bias of technical change.

The simulation model is linked to Solow's data, and to United States economic growth, in the following ways. First, the set of one hundred techniques used in the simulations was chosen, randomly, from a region that brackets the values in Solow's time series for the period 1909–49. A simulated time period corresponds to a year, and wage rates are quoted in 1929 dollars per man-hour. The model's labour supply curve shifts to the right at 1·25 % per year, a rate roughly comparable to the rate of labour force growth in the United States. The depreciation rate in the model is 0·04, and critical rate of return in the satisficing mechanism is 0·16. Initial conditions for the simulations were established by giving the firm's initial techniques in the vicinity of the 1909 aggregate input coefficient values, and capital stocks of a convenient size from a computational point of view. The labour supply curve was positioned so as to yield, at the initial level of aggregate labour demand, approximately the 1909 wage rate.

The model has a number of other features, which we will mention only in passing. There are special assumptions governing "entry", *i.e.* firms making transitions from zero to positive capital stocks. The general rate of technical change in the model is controllable by a programme parameter that determines how local the local search is, *i.e.* how tightly the search outcome distribution is concentrated around current technique. It is also possible to introduce factor-saving bias into the local search mechanism, and to alter the relative weights of imitation and local search.

In summary, then, the model comprises a number of very simple firms interacting in an equally simple selection environment. Technically advanced firms reinvest their profits and expand, thereby driving up the wage rate facing other firms. Firms with low rates of return look for better techniques, sometimes finding them and sometimes not: but since they reject technical regress in favour of the *status quo*, progress is achieved on the average. Imitation helps to keep the technical race fairly close, but at any given time there is considerable cross-sectional dispersion in factor ratios, efficiency and rates of return.

How do the quantitative results look? In a word, the answer is: plausible. In Table I the Solow data, and the results of a simulation run, are displayed side by side. There is, of course, no reason to expect agreement between the real and simulated data on a year to year basis. The simulation run necessarily reflects non-historical random influences. But more than that, and of particular importance to this comparison, the simulation model (unlike

TABLE I

Selected Time Series from Simulation Run 0001, Compared with Solow Data, 1909–49

Year	Q/L Sim.	Q/L Solow	K/L Sim.	K/L Solow	W Sim.	W Solow	S_K Sim.	S_K Solow	A Sim.	A Solow
1909	0·66	0·73	1·85	2·06	0·51	0·49	0·23	0·34	1·000	1·000
1910	0·68	0·72	1·84	2·10	0·54	0·48	0·21	0·33	1·020	0·983
1911	0·69	0·76	1·83	2·17	0·52	0·50	0·25	0·34	1·040	1·021
1912	0·71	0·76	1·91	2·21	0·50	0·51	0·30	0·33	1·059	1·023
1913	0·74	0·80	1·94	2·23	0·51	0·53	0·31	0·33	1·096	1·064
1914	0·72	0·80	1·86	2·20	0·61	0·54	0·15	0·33	1·087	1·071
1915	0·74	0·78	1·89	2·26	0·56	0·51	0·24	0·34	1·108	1·041
1916	0·76	0·82	1·89	2·34	0·60	0·53	0·21	0·36	1·136	1·076
1917	0·78	0·80	1·93	2·21	0·59	0·50	0·23	0·37	1·159	1·065
1918	0·78	0·85	1·90	2·22	0·62	0·56	0·21	0·34	1·169	1·142
1919	0·80	0·90	1·96	2·47	0·57	0·58	0·29	0·35	1·190	1·157
1920	0·80	0·84	1·94	2·58	0·64	0·58	0·19	0·32	1·192	1·069
1921	0·81	0·90	2·00	2·55	0·61	0·57	0·25	0·37	1·208	1·146
1922	0·83	0·92	2·02	2·49	0·65	0·61	0·21	0·34	1·225	1·183
1923	0·83	0·95	1·97	2·61	0·70	0·63	0·17	0·34	1·243	1·196
1924	0·86	0·98	2·06	2·74	0·64	0·66	0·26	0·33	1·274	1·215
1925	0·89	1·02	2·19	2·81	0·59	0·68	0·33	0·34	1·293	1·254
1926	0·87	1·02	2·07	2·87	0·74	0·68	0·15	0·33	1·288	1·241
1927	0·90	1·02	2·16	2·93	0·67	0·69	0·25	0·32	1·324	1·235
1928	0·91	1·02	2·18	3·02	0·70	0·68	0·23	0·34	1·336	1·226
1929	0·94	1·05	2·27	3·06	0·68	0·70	0·28	0·33	1·370	1·251
1930	0·98	1·03	2·47	3·30	0·62	0·67	0·37	0·35	1·394	1·197
1931	0·99	1·06	2·46	3·33	0·70	0·71	0·29	0·33	1·408	1·226
1932	1·02	1·03	2·57	3·28	0·69	0·62	0·32	0·40	1·435	1·198
1933	1·02	1·02	2·46	3·10	0·85	0·65	0·16	0·36	1·452	1·211
1934	1·04	1·08	2·45	3·00	0·85	0·70	0·19	0·36	1·488	1·298
1935	1·05	1·10	2·44	2·87	0·87	0·72	0·17	0·35	1·500	1·349
1936	1·06	1·15	2·51	2·72	0·82	0·74	0·22	0·36	1·499	1·429
1937	1·06	1·14	2·55	2·71	0·83	0·75	0·22	0·34	1·500	1·415
1938	1·11	1·17	2·74	2·78	0·76	0·78	0·32	0·33	1·543	1·445
1939	1·10	1·21	2·66	2·66	0·88	0·79	0·20	0·35	1·540	1·514
1940	1·13	1·27	2·75	2·63	0·84	0·82	0·25	0·36	1·576	1·590
1941	1·16	1·31	2·77	2·58	0·90	0·82	0·23	0·38	1·618	1·660
1942	1·18	1·33	2·78	2·64	0·95	0·86	0·20	0·36	1·641	1·665
1943	1·19	1·38	2·79	2·62	0·93	0·91	0·22	0·34	1·652	1·733
1944	1·20	1·48	2·80	2·63	0·97	0·99	0·20	0·33	1·672	1·856
1945	1·21	1·52	2·82	2·66	0·97	1·04	0·20	0·31	1·683	1·895
1946	1·23	1·42	2·88	2·50	0·96	0·98	0·22	0·31	1·694	1·812
1947	1·23	1·40	2·89	2·50	0·98	0·94	0·21	0·33	1·701	1·781
1948	1·23	1·43	2·87	2·55	1·01	0·96	0·18	0·33	1·698	1·809
1949	1·23	1·49	2·82	2·70	1·04	1·01	0·15	0·33	1·703	1·852

Q/L Output (1929 dollars per man-hour; Solow data adjusted from 1939 to 1929 dollars by multiplying by 1·171 = ratio of implicit price deflators for GNP).

K/L Capital (1929 dollars per man-hour).

W Wage rate (1929 dollars per man-hour; Solow data adjusted from 1939 to 1929 dollars).

S_K Capital share (= 1 — labour share)

A Solow technology index. (Recalculation on the basis of figures in other columns will not check exactly, because of rounding of those figures. Solow figures shown for 1944–49 are correct; the values originally published were in error.)

Solow's analysis) generates its own input history on the basis of very simple assumptions about behaviour and institutional structure. The period in question involved episodes of depression and war, and while these episodes might be considered as historical random events, the simulation model is not prepared to deal with them realistically. The same trend in the labour force, the same Say's Law assumption, the same link of investment to retained earnings, persists year by year. Since the model's historical accuracy is so sharply limited by these considerations we have not attempted to locate parameter settings that would, in any sense, maximise similarity to the real time series. For example, it would have been easy to assure better match of initial conditions. A less obvious case is this. In the run shown we assumed no factor-saving bias in the search process and a "required dividend" of 2 % of capital; for reasons we shall discuss shortly, it seems likely that we could have matched better certain aspects of the real data if we had modified these assumptions somewhat. Thus, the history generated by the simulation model reflects the workings of long-run mechanisms built into the model, without any contact with the reality of particular years, and with simplifying assumptions that in any case would preclude mimicking reality in detail. Comparisons of actual and simulated data must therefore focus on general patterns.

So considered, the simulation is quite succesful. The historically observed trends in the output–labour ratio, capital–labour ratio and the wage rate are all visible in the simulated data; as in the historical data the movements are far from monotone. The column headed A in the table shows the Solow-type index of technology, computed data on the neoclassical hypotheses of constant returns to scale, marginal productivity pricing, and Hicks-neutral technical change.[1] The simulated average rate of change in this measure is about the same as in the Solow data (indicating, essentially, that we have chosen an appropriate value for our localness-of-search parameter). It is interesting to note, however, that our relatively "chaotic" world of simple-minded firms generates somewhat *smoother* technical progress than Solow found in the real data for the United States. For example, our series shows only five instances of negative technical progress, whereas Solow's series shows eleven—and the run shown is typical in this respect.

Pursuing further the neoclassical analysis of our simulated data, we have estimated production functions from the aggregate time series produced by the simulation model. The fits are typically excellent, with R^2 usually exceeding 0·99; the parameter estimates are typically, though not consistently, satisfactory. When a Cobb-Douglas function is fitted to the Table I data[2] by regressing log Q on log K, log L and T(ime), it yields an R^2 of 0·999 and the three coefficients are respectively, 0·34, 0·65, and 0·012. If this is the sort

[1] The A values shown are the rounded results of computations involving more decimal places than are displayed in Table I. Hence an attempt to replicate the calculation using the data shown will lead to A values slightly different from those shown.

[2] The data used in the regression were more exact than those shown.

of result that represents "success" for neoclassical theory, then the world clearly does not have to be very neoclassical for such success to occur.

Perhaps the most noticeable discrepancy between Table I and the historical data is that our series for non-wage income (s_K) runs lower and is more volatile than the historical series; also, the capital–labour ratio grows somewhat too fast. Both the s_K problem and the K/L problem are a reflection of the fact that our required dividend rate of 2% is too low. This diagnosis is confirmed by our other experiments with the model. However, it is still not clear whether, without assuming labour-saving bias in local search, one can generate both a plausible share series and plausible behaviour of the capital–labour ratio in the same run (see Nelson, Winter and Schuette (1973) for more extensive discussion).

The excessive volatility of the capital share series is quite typical of our experimental results. In part, this is probably an artifact—though it is not clear whether the most important artifacts are in our simulations or in the firm accounting procedures and statistical estimation methods that underlie the "real" data. We conjecture, however, that much of the volatility problem may be traceable to one highly unrealistic assumption of the model: the labour market always clears. If it did not, period-to-period changes in the demand for labour would be reflected more in the unemployment rate and less in the wage rate; very likely the result would be smaller fluctuation in the non-wage share. To explore this conjecture properly one would have to build a model not only with a more realistic labour market, but also with more realistic treatment of aggregate demand and of short-term capacity utilisation decisions. (We do not, of course, have to apologise to neoclassicists for our failure properly to integrate these considerations into our growth model.)

IV. Changes in Perspective

The results of the simulation study described above indicate that a model within an evolutionary theory is quite capable of generating aggregate time series with characteristics corresponding to those of economic growth in the United States. One does not have to extrapolate the performance of evolutionary theory very far beyond the present primitive level in order to conclude that neoclassical models are unlikely to be decisively superior in this area. Nor is it reasonable to dismiss the evolutionary theory on the grounds that it fails to provide a coherent explanation of these macro phenomena. Indeed, many of the familiar mechanisms have a place in the evolutionary framework, and their specific characterisation in that framework may be more persuasive to many people than the neoclassical formalisation.

Consider, for example, the empirically observed nexus of rising wage rates, rising capital intensity and increasing output per worker. Our simulation model generated data of this sort. In that model, as in the typical neoclassical one, rising wage rates move firms in a capital intensive direction.

When firms check the profitability of alternative techniques that their search processes uncover, a higher wage rate will cause certain techniques to fail the "more profitable" test that would have "passed" at a lower wage rate, and enable others to pass the test that would have failed at a lower wage rate. The former will be capital intensive relative to the latter. Thus a higher wage rate nudges firms to move in a capital-intensive direction compared with that in which they would have gone. Also, the effect of a higher wage rate is to make all technologies less profitable (assuming, as in our model, a constant cost of capital) but the cost increase is proportionately greatest for those that involve a low capital–labour ratio. Since firms with high capital–labour ratios are less adversely affected by high wage rates than those with low capital–labour ratios, capital-intensive firms will tend to expand relatively to labour intensive ones. For both of these reasons a higher wage rate will tend to increase capital-intensity relatively to what would have been obtained: and output per worker will be increased; a more capital-intensive technology cannot be more profitable than a less capital-intensive one unless output per worker is higher.

Perhaps it is the familiar sound of accounts like the foregoing that provokes a reaction we have frequently encountered, namely that our "story" is really just what sophisticated neoclassicists have believed all along. Or, alternatively, it is a neoclassical model with unusually strong assumptions concerning the costs of information and adjustment. We do not think, however, that a devout neoclassicist should insert our model into his book of acceptable scripture until he has scrutinised it very closely for signs of heresy.

Although the firms in our simulation model respond to profitability signals in making technique changes and investment decisions, they are not maximising profits in any fundamental sense. Their behaviour could be rationalised equally well (or poorly) as pursuit of the quiet life—since they relax when they are doing well, and typically make only small changes of technique when they do change—or of corporate growth—since they maximise investment subject to a payout constraint. Neither does our model portray the economy as being in equilibrium. At any given time, there exists considerable diversity in techniques used, and in realised rates of return. The observed constellations of inputs and outputs cannot be regarded as optimal in any Paretian sense—there are always better techniques not being used because they have not yet been found, and laggard firms using technologies less economic than current best practice. And, of course, there is no reason to suppose that rates of discovery and diffusion of new techniques in our model world could not be favourably influenced by policy tools.

It is our position that these differences (and others yet to be mentioned) are essential. And while we can applaud the ecumenical spirit that leads people to nod their agreement to these doctrines, such tolerance tends to deepen the mystery of where the basic neoclassical commitments are to be found.

On our reading, at least, the neoclassical interpretation of long-run productivity change is sharply different from our own. It is based on a clean distinction between "moving along" an existing production function and shifting to a new one. In the evolutionary theory, substitution of the "search and selection" metaphor for the maximisation metaphor, plus the assumption of the basic improvability of procedures, blurs the notion of a production function. In the simulation model discussed above there was no production function—only a set of physically possible activities. The production function did not emerge from that set because no assumption was made that firms used the most efficient activities. The exploration of the set was treated as an historical, incremental process in which non-market information flows among firms played a major role.

We argue—as others have before us—that the sharp "growth accounting" split made within the neoclassical paradigm is bothersome empirically and conceptually. Consider, for example, whether it is meaningful to assess the relative contribution of greater mechanisation versus new technology in increasing productivity in the textile industries during the Industrial Revolution, scale economies versus technical change in enhancing productivity in generation of electrical power, or of greater fertiliser usage versus new seed varieties in the increased yields associated with the Green Revolution.[1] In the Textile Revolution the major inventions were ways of substituting capital for labour, induced by a situation of growing labour scarcity. It could plausibly be argued that in the electric power case, various well-known physical laws implied that the larger the scale for which a plant was designed, the lower the cost per unit of output it should have. However, to exploit these latent possibilities required a considerable amount of engineering and design work, which became profitable only when the constellation of demand made large-scale units plausible. Plant biologists had long known that certain kinds of seed varieties were able to thrive with large quantities of fertilisers, and that others were not. However, until fertiliser prices fell, it was not worth while to invest significant resources in trying to find these varieties. In all of these cases patterns of demand and supply were evolving to make profitable different factor proportions or scales. But the production set was not well defined in the appropriate direction from existing practice. It had to be explored and created.[2]

[1] There obviously are many references on each of these developments. The ones that bring out our point most nicely are, on textile mechanisation, D. Landes (1970), on electrical power, W. Hughes (1971), on the fertiliser-seed interaction, Hayami and Ruttan (1971).

[2] We are simply elaborating here our earlier point that a theory of induced innovation blurs the distinction between moving along a production function and a "technological advance". For an earlier discussion of this point see Nelson, Peck and Kalachek (1967, Chapter 2). There is clearly some resemblance between our approach to technical change and the "technical progress function" employed by Kaldor (1957) and Kaldor–Mirrlees (1962). More generally, there is a substantial overlap between our concerns and those involved in the "Cambridge controversies". Within that area of overlap, our position seems to be closer to the English Cambridge than the American one. Nevertheless, there are pronounced differences between our complaints about the neoclassical theory and the complaints made in the English Cambridge, and even more pronounced differences in

The question of the nature of "search" processes would appear to be among the most important for those trying to understand economic growth, and the evolutionary theory has the advantage of posing the question explicitly. In the simulation model we assumed technical progress was the result strictly of the behaviour of firms in the "sector" and that discovery was relatively even over time. However, it is apparent that the invention possibilities, and search costs, for firms in particular sectors change as a result of forces exogenous to the sector. Academic and governmental research certainly changed the search prospects for firms in the electronics and drug industries, and for aircraft and seed producers. In the simulation, the "topography" of new technologies was relatively even over time. However, various studies have shown that often new opportunities open up in clusters. A basic new kind of technology becomes possible as a result often of research outside the sector. After a firm finds, develops, and adopts a version of the new technology, a follow-on round of marginal improvements becomes possible. This appears to be the pattern, for example, in petroleum refining equipment and aircraft. However, this pattern does not show up in cotton textiles, after the industrial revolution, or in automobiles, where technical advance seems to have been less discrete. The search and problem-solving orientation of an evolutionary theory naturally leads the analyst to be aware of these differences and to try somehow to explain or at least characterise them.

The perspective on the role of the "competitive environment" is also radically different in the evolutionary theory, and leads one to focus on a set of questions concerning the intertwining of competition, profit, and investment within a dynamic context.[1] Is the investment of a particular firm strictly bounded by its own current profits? Can firms borrow for expansion? Are there limits on firm size, or costs associated with the speed of expansion? Can new firms enter? How responsive are "consumers" to a better or cheaper product? How long can a firm preserve a technically based monopoly? What kind of institutional barriers or encouragements are there to imitation? The answers to these questions are fundamental to understanding the workings of the market environment. The dynamics of their treatment, like that of the nature and topology of "search", is an empirical issue within our theory.

Sectors clearly differ sharply. Consider Phillips' (1971) description of competition in the industry that produces aircraft for commercial airlines. This is a sector in which firms are able to borrow money from the outside and are not limited to their own financial resources. It also is an industry in which firms are able to expand capacity rapidly but in which it is costly and

---

the theoretical prescriptions offered. In particular, we are much more concerned about the neglect of the details of technical advance, adjustment and firm decision making. It would take us much too far afield to try to sort these issues out completely—judging by experience in the Cambridge controversies, it may be impossible to do so..

   [1] Our intellectual debts to F. Knight (1921), as well as to Schumpeter (1934, 1950) should be obvious.

time-consuming to imitate another company's successful product. In this institutional regime a company that comes up with a superior product has a great advantage over its competitors. Because of the lags and costs of imitation, other firms may simply be out of luck. The selection environment here is obviously vastly different from that in agriculture. In agriculture it is very difficult for a successful firm to expand rapidly, because of the costs and complexity of purchasing particular pieces of adjacent land. Conversely, an elaborate subsidised mechanism has been established to disseminate widely among farmers information regarding the best new techniques; imitation is easy. Thus one farmer is unable to inflict serious hardship on others because of a technological advantage, and new technological departures are easy to mimic.

V. SUMMARY AND CONCLUSIONS

We return now to our opening theme—the tension between the micro and macro literatures concerned with technical change and economic growth. It is obvious that a great deal of diversity and change is hidden by the neoclassical macro approach based on aggregation, maximisation and equilibrium. Indeed, the principal virtue of those tools is the gain in analytic tractability and logical coherence that has been obtained precisely by abstracting from all that diversity and change. No one would claim that this gain has been costless.

The question is, how high is the price? For us, the evidence is compelling on a number of points that are either denied or obscured by neoclassical orthodoxy. Firms pursue profits (and perhaps other goals), but their choice sets are not sufficiently static and well defined to make profit *maximisation* descriptively plausible. For the individual firm, technical change is an aspect of the pursuit of profits. There are significant rewards for solving problems, or for guesses made early and correctly. Corresponding penalties exist for being wrong or late. These rewards and penalties are not mere conjectural possibilities, they actually occur, and the occurence helps to shape the future course of events. This is because the firms are *not* all alike, and the situation is *not* one of moving equilibrium. The extent of the rewards and penalties, and the rates of introduction and diffusion of new techniques, depends on a complex of environmental and institutional considerations that differs sharply from sector to sector, country to country, and period to period. And the aggregates are what you get by adding up.

In short, the diversity and change that are suppressed by aggregation, maximisation and equilibrium are not the epiphenomena of technical advance. They are the central phenomena.

Still, if facing up to that diversity and change meant turning one's back on analytic tractability and logical coherence, it might be a hard choice. This, we have argued, is not the case. Theorists can work analytically with dynamic systems in which the abstract individual firms differ significantly from one another. The choice of assumptions can be informed by what is known of actual firm behaviour, the micro processes of technical change, and the characteristics of selection environments. This solves at a stroke the problem of squaring the theory with the known micro details. And if we want to discuss aggregates, we can—as in our simulation study—obtain them by adding up. An evolutionary theory is a real alternative.

RICHARD R. NELSON
SIDNEY G. WINTER

Yale University
University of Michigan
Date of receipt of final typescript: July 1974.

REFERENCES

Alchian, A. A. (1950). "Uncertainty, Evolution and Economic Theory," *Journal of Political Economy*, Vol. 58 (June).

Baumol, W. J. (1968). "Entrepreneurship in Economic Theory," *American Economic Review*, Vol. 58 (May).

—— and Stewart, M. (1971). "On the Behavioural Theory of the Firm," in R. Marris and A. Wood (eds.), *The Corporate Economy: Growth, Competition and Innovative Potential*, Cambridge: Harvard University Press.

Cyert, R. & March, J. (1963). *A Behavioural Theory of the Firm*, Prentice Hall, Inc., Englewood Cliffs, N.J.

Farrell, M. J. (1970). "Some Elementary Selection Processes in Economics," *Review of Economic Studies*, Vol. 37.

Friedman, M. (1953). "The Methodology of Positive Economics," chap. 1 in *Essays in Positive Economics*, University of Chicago Press.

Hahn, F. H. (1970). "Some Adjustment Problems," *Econometrica*, Vol. 38 (January).

Hayami, Y. & Ruttan, V. (1971). *Agricultural Development, An International Perspective*, Johns Hopkins Press, Baltimore.

Hughes, W. R. (1971). "Scale Frontiers in Electric Power", chap. 4 in W. Capron (ed.), *Technological Change in Regulated Industries*, Brookings Institution, Washington.

Ijiri, Y. & Simon, H. A. (1971). "The Relative Strength of Middle-Sized Firms and the Curvature in Firm-Size Distributions," paper presented to the Econometric Society, December.

Kaldor, N. (1957) "A Model of Economic Growth", ECONOMIC JOURNAL, Vol. 87 (December).

—— and Mirrlees, J. A. (1962). "A New Model of Economic Growth," *Review of Economic Studies*, Vol. 29 (June).

Kennedy, C. & Thirlwall, A. P. (1972). "Surveys in Applied Economics: Technical Progress," ECONOMIC JOURNAL, Vol. 82 (March).

Knight, F. (1921). *Risk, Uncertainty and Profit*, Houghton Mifflin Company, New York.

Landes, D. (1970). *The Unbound Prometheus*, Cambridge University Press.

Leontief, W. (1971). "Theoretical Assumptions and Non-observed Facts," *American Economic Review*, Vol. 61 (March).

Mansfield, E. (1972). "Contribution of R and D to Economic Growth in the United States," *Science*, Vol. 175 (February).

—— (1962). "Entry, Gilbrat's Law, Innovation, and the Growth of Firms," *American Economic Review*, Vol. 53 (December).

Meyer, J. & Kuh, E. (1957). *The Investment Decision*, Harvard University Press.

Nadiri, M. I. (1970). "Some Approaches to the Theory of Total Factor Productivity: A Survey," *Journal of Economic Literature*, Vol. 8 (December).

Nelson, R. (1972). "Issues and Suggestions for the Study of Industrial Organization in a Regime of Rapid Technical Change," in V. R. Fuchs (ed.), *Policy Issues and Research Opportunities in Industrial Organization*, National Bureau of Economic Research, New York.

—— (1973). "Recent Exercises in Growth Accounting: New Understanding or Dead End?" *American Economic Review*, Vol. 63 (June).

—— (1974). "The Effects of Factor Price Changes in an Evolutionary Model," Mimeo. (March).

—— Peck, M. and Kalachek, E. (1967). *Technology, Economic Growth and Public Policy*, Brookings Institution, Washington, D.C.

Nelson, R., Winter, S. and Schuette, H. (1973). "Technical Change in an Evolutionary Model," University of Michigan Institute of Public Policy Studies, Discussion Paper No. 45.

Nordhaus, W. and Tobin, J. (1972). "Is Growth Obsolete?" in R. Gordon (ed.), *Economic Research: Retrospect and Prospect, Economic Growth*, National Bureau of Economic Research, New York.

Pavitt, K. (1971). "Conditions of Success in Technological Innovation," OECD, Paris.

Phelps Brown, E. H. (1972). "The Underdevelopment of Economics," ECONOMIC JOURNAL, Vol. 82 (March).

Phillips, A. (1971). *Technology and Market Structure: A Study of the Aircraft Industry*, D. C. Heath and Co., Lexington, Mass.

Schumpeter, J. A. (1934). *The Theory of Economic Development*, Harvard University Press.

—— (1950). *Capitalism, Socialism and Democracy*, 3rd ed., Harper and Brothers, New York.

Solow, R. (1957). "Technical Change and the Aggregate Production Function," *Review of Economics and Statistics*, Vol. 39 (August).

—— (1970). *Growth Theory*, Oxford University Press.

Winter, S. G. (1964). "Economic 'Natural Selection' and the Theory of the Firm," *Yale Economic Essays*, Vol. 4 (Spring).

Winter, S. G. (1971). "Satisficing, Selection and the Innovating Remnant," *Quarterly Journal of Economics*, Vol. 85 (May).

Winter, S. G. (no date). "An SSIR Model of Markup Pricing" (mimeo.).

Worswick, G. D. N. (1972). "Is Progress in Economic Science Possible?" ECONOMIC JOURNAL, Vol. 82 (March).

[15]

ECONOMICS FROM A BIOLOGICAL VIEWPOINT*

J. HIRSHLEIFER
University of California, Los Angeles

I. ECONOMICS AND BIOLOGY

THE field variously called population biology, sociobiology, or ecology is concerned to explain the observed interrelations among the various forms of life—organisms, species, and broader groupings and communities—and between forms of life and their external environments. The subject includes both material aspects of these interrelations (the geographical distributions of species in relation to one another, their respective numbers, physical properties like size differences between the sexes) and behavioral aspects (why some species are territorial while others flock, why some are monogamous and others polygamous, why some are aggressive and others shy).

From one point of view, the various social sciences devoted to the study of mankind, taken together, constitute but a subdivision of the all-encompassing field of sociobiology.[1] The ultimately biological subject matter of economics in particular has been recognized by some of our leading thinkers.[2] There is however a special link between economics and sociobiology over and above the mere fact that economics studies a subset of the social behavior of one of the higher mammals. *The fundamental organizing con-*

---

* Thanks for comments and suggestions, far too numerous and important to be fully responded to here, are due to: Armen Alchian, Shmuel Amir, Edward C. Banfield, Gary Becker, Eric L. Charnov, Ronald Cohen, Harold Demsetz, Michael Ghiselin, Joel Guttman, Bruce Herrick,, Gertrude Himmelfarb, David Levine, John G. Riley, Vernon L. Smith, Robert Trivers, and James Weinrich.

[1] See chapter 27 of E. O. Wilson's authoritative text Sociobiology (1975) [hereinafter cited as Sociobiology], and also *id.*, Biology and the Social Sciences, Daedalus (forthcoming).

[2] "But economics has no near kinship with any physical science. It is a branch of biology broadly interpreted." Alfred Marshall, Principles of Economics 772 (9th Variorum ed. 1920). See also Kenneth E. Boulding, A Reconstruction of Economics ch. 1 (1950). Also relevant, of course, are the famous passages in The Wealth of Nations where Adam Smith attributed the emergence of the division of labor among mankind, and its failure to develop among animal species, to a supposedly innate human "propensity to truck, barter, and exchange." Adam Smith, An Inquiry into the Nature and Causes of the Wealth of Nations 15-18 (Edwin Cannan ed. 1937).

cepts of the dominant analytical structures employed in economics and in sociobiology are strikingly parallel.[3] What biologists study can be regarded as "Nature's economy."[4] Oswald Spengler perceived (and regarded it as a serious criticism) that Darwin's contribution represented "the application of economics to biology."[5] Fundamental concepts like scarcity, competition, equilibrium, and specialization play similar roles in both spheres of inquiry. And terminological pairs such as species/industry, mutation/innovation, evolution/progress, mutualism/exchange have more or less analogous denotations.

Regarded more systematically, the isomorphism between economics and sociobiology involves the intertwining of two levels of analysis. On the first level, acting units or entities choose strategies or develop techniques that promote success in the struggle or *competition* for advantage in given environments. The economist usually calls this process "optimizing," the biologist, "adapting." The formalizations involved are equations of constrained maximization. The second, higher level of analysis examines the social or aggregate resultant of the interaction of the striving units or agents. The formalizations here take the form of equations of equilibrium. (In more general versions, the static solutions may be embedded in "dynamic" equations showing the time paths of approach to solution states.) The solutions on the two levels are of course interdependent. The pursuit of advantage on the part of acting units takes place subject to opportunities and constraints that emerge from the social context, while the resulting social configuration (constituting at least part of the environment for each separate agent) depends in turn upon the strategies employed by the advantage-seeking entities.

Among the methodological issues that might arise at this point are two with somewhat opposed thrusts: (1) Given the validity of a sociobiological outlook on human behavior, are we not claiming too much for economics? What role is there left for the other social sciences if economics can be regarded as essentially coextensive with the sociobiology of human behavior? (2) But alternatively, are we not claiming too little for economics (and a fortiori for the other social sciences) in adopting the reductive interpretation of human behavior implicit in the sociobiological approach? May it not be the case that the cultural evolution of the human species has carried it into a realm where biological laws are determinative of only a minor fraction of behavioral phenomena? (Or perhaps economics is the discipline that regards

[3] A somewhat similar argument is made in the very recent paper by David J. Rapport & James E. Turner, Economic Models in Ecology, 195 Science 367 (1977).

[4] Michael T. Ghiselin, The Economy of Nature and the Evolution of Sex (1974).

[5] Gertrude Himmelfarb, Darwin and the Darwinian Revolution 396 (1959).

ECONOMICS FROM A BIOLOGICAL VIEWPOINT   3

mankind as merely sociobiological in nature, while the other social sciences treat of the higher aspects of human culture?)

Consideration of the second group of questions will be reserved for the concluding sections of this paper. With regard to the first—a seeming claim that the domain of economics is coextensive with the total sphere of all the social sciences together—a unified social-science viewpoint is adopted here, in which economics and other social studies are regarded as interpenetrating rather than compartmentalized. The traditional core area of compartmentalized economics is characterized by models that: (a) postulate rational self-interested behavior on the part of individuals with given preferences for material goods and services, and (b) attempt to explain those interactions among such individuals that take the form of market exchanges, under a fixed legal system of property and free contract. That only a very limited portion of human behavioral association could be adequately represented under such self-imposed analytical constraints has often been pointed out to economists by other social scientists. In recent years economics has begun to break through these self-imposed barriers, to take as subject matter all human activity that can be interpreted as goal-directed behavior constrained by and yet, in the aggregate, determinative of resultant social configurations. Significant innovative instances of the application of techniques of economic analysis to broader social issues include Schelling and Boulding's works on conflict and warfare, Downs and Buchanan and Tullock on political choice, and Becker on crime and marriage.[6] And each of these efforts has been followed by a growing literature, in which both economists and other social scientists have participated.[7] The upshot is that (at least in their properly scientific aspect) the social sciences generally can be regarded as in the process of coalescing. As economics "imperialistically" employs its tools of analysis over a wider range of social issues, it will *become* sociology and anthropology and political science. But correspondingly, as these other disciplines grow increasingly rigorous, they will not merely resemble but will *be*

[6] Thomas C. Schelling, The Strategy of Conflict (1960); Kenneth E. Boulding, Conflict and Defense (1962); Anthony Downs, An Economic Theory of Democracy (1957); James M. Buchanan & Gordon Tullock, The Calculus of Consent (1962); Gary S. Becker, Crime and Punishment: An Economic Approach, 76 J. Pol. Econ. 169 (1968); *id.*, A Theory of Marriage: Part I, 81 J. Pol. Econ. 813 (1973).

[7] In the earlier "classical" era the compartmentalization of economics within such narrow boundaries had not yet taken place. Adam Smith in particular discussed law, government, psychology, and the biological instincts promoting and hindering social cooperation—as well as economics in the narrow sense—throughout his works. See R. H. Coase, Adam Smith's View of Man, 19 J. Law & Econ. 529 (1976); Leonard Billet, The Just Economy: The Moral Basis of the Wealth of Nations, 34 Rev. Soc. Econ. 295 (1976). In a sense, then, economics is in the process of returning to the classical view of the whole man.

4   THE JOURNAL OF LAW AND ECONOMICS

economics. It is in this sense that "economics" is taken here as broadly synonymous with "social science."[8]

One of the obvious divergences between economics and sociobiology, it might appear, is that men can consciously optimize—or so we often like to think—whereas, for all but a few higher animals, the concepts of "choice" or "strategy" are only metaphorical. What happens in the biological realm is that, given a sufficiently long run, *natural selection* allows survival only of entities that have developed successful strategies in their respective environments. So the result is sometimes (though not always, as we shall see) *as if* conscious optimization were taking place. The idea that selective pressure of the environment can do the work of conscious optimizing (thus freeing us of any need to postulate a "rational" economic agent) has also received some controversial discussion in the economics literature. This topic will be reviewed in Section III.

After these preliminaries, the central portions of the paper will survey some of the main parallels and divergences in economic and sociobiological reasoning. Since this is written by an economist with only an amateur interest in the biological sciences, attention will be devoted to "what message sociobiology has for economics" rather than to "how we can set the biologists straight."

II. SOME MUTUAL INFLUENCES

The most famous example of the influence of an economist upon biological thought is of course the impact of Malthus upon Darwin and Wallace. The codiscoverers of evolution each reported that Malthus' picture of the unremitting pressure of human population upon subsistence provided the key element leading to the idea of evolution by natural selection in the struggle for life.[9] Malthusian ideas of compounded growth also play a role in modern

---

[8] Marx's "economic interpretation of history" can be regarded as an earlier instance of intellectual imperialism of economics, but its connection with this modern development is limited. Marx's economic interpretation was a *materialistic* one. He contended that the essentially autonomous progress of the methods and organization of material production was decisive for shaping the entirety of social relationships in every era. True or false, this is a *substantive* proposition essentially independent of the *methodological* stance of modern economic imperialists. The latter analyze marriage, fertility, crime, law, revolution, etc., with the tools of economic analysis without necessarily asserting that these patterns of social interaction are determined by "materialistic" considerations (such as the ownership of the means of production) as contended by Marx.

[9] Oddly enough, this example is not really a valid one, for the borrowing was already from biology to economics in Malthus' own thought! Malthus drew his ideas about human populations from a biological generalization attributed to Benjamin Franklin on the first page of the Essay on the Principles of Population: "It is observed by Dr. Franklin that there is no bound to

ECONOMICS FROM A BIOLOGICAL VIEWPOINT   5

biological theory. The "Malthusian parameter," as defined by biologists, represents the exponential rate at which a population will grow as limited by its genetic capabilities and constrained by the environment.[10]

In the very recent period a number of biologists have come to make significant use of tools and approaches of economics. Michael T. Ghiselin[11] has urged fellow biologists to adopt the "methodological individualism" of economics in preference to the open or disguised "teleologism" of assuming optimizing behavior on the part of higher-level groupings and species. A few instances of recent biological optimization studies that seem to be consciously modelled upon economic analytical techniques can be cited: (1) Rapport[12] showed that the extent of "predator switching" from one prey species to another in response to changes in relative abundance could be expressed in terms of shapes of the predator's indifference curves and opportunity frontier; (2) Gadgil and Bossert[13] interpreted various characteristics of organisms' life histories—such as the timing and scale of reproductive effort and the determination of survival probabilities at various ages—as the resultant of a balance between "profit" (that is, gain) and "cost" (that is, foregone gain or opportunity cost) in choosing strategies to maximize the Malthusian parameter of population growth. (3) Trivers[14] demonstrated that several aspects of parental behavior, in particular the differing extent in various species of male versus female "investment" in care of offspring, could be explained in terms of differences in the selectional return on investment to the male and female parents (that is, in terms of the comparative propagation of their respective genetic endowments); (4) Cody[15] examined the conditions determining the relative competitive advantages of "generalist" versus "specialist" strategies in the exploitation of a mixed-resource environment. (5) E. O. Wilson[16] employed linear programming models to

the prolific nature of plants or animals but what is made by their crowding and interfering with each other's means of subsistence." See Gertrude Himmelfarb, *supra* note 5, at ch. 7.

[10] The classical definition by R. A. Fisher, The Genetic Theory of Natural Selection, ch. 2 (2nd rev. ed. 1958) as applied by him to a population of mixed ages, corresponds to what the economist would call the *internal rate of return* on investment (the growth rate of invested capital). Fisher, in fact, uses the metaphor of a business loan to explain the concept.

[11] Michael T. Ghiselin, *supra* note 4. See also the review by Harold Demsetz, On Thinking Like an Economist, 1 Paleobiology 216 (1975).

[12] David J. Rapport, An Optimization Model of Food Selection, 105 Am. Naturalist 575 (1971).

[13] Madhav Gadgil & William H. Bossert, Life-Historical Consequences of Natural Selection, 104 Am. Naturalist 1 (1970).

[14] Robert L. Trivers, Parental Investment and Sexual Selection, in Sexual Selection and the Descent of Man, 1871-1971, at 136 (B. Campbell ed. 1972).

[15] Martin L. Cody, Optimization in Ecology, 183 Science 1156 (1974).

[16] Sociobiology, *supra* note 1, at ch. 16.

determine the optimal number and proportion of castes in the division of labor among social insects. (6) Charnov[17] develops an optimality theorem for foraging animals, in which the forager terminates exploitation of a given food patch when the marginal energy intake falls to equality with the average return from the habitat.

But the more significant intellectual influence has been in the other direction, from biology to social science. The success of theories of evolution and natural selection in the biological realm led quickly to the body of thought called "Social Darwinism"—the most characteristic figures being the philosopher Herbert Spencer in England and the economist William Graham Sumner in America. On the scientific level Social Darwinism represented an attempt to explain patterns of social stratification as the consequence of the selection of superior human types and forms of organization through social competition. To a considerable extent, its exponents went on to draw the inference that such existing stratification was therefore ethically *justified*. The political unpalatability of this conclusion has led to an exceptionally bad press for Social Darwinism—at the hands of other social scientists, jurists, and philosophers, as economists after Sumner have scarcely discussed the question. The Social Darwinists, or some of them at least, did confuse descriptive with moral categories so as to attribute excessive beneficence to natural selection on the human level. In the real world, we know, success *may* sometimes be the reward of socially functional behavior, but also sometimes of valueless or disruptive activities like monopolization, crime, or most of what is carried on under the heading of politics.

It would be incorrect to assume that Darwinism is necessarily conservative in its social implications. The implications would seem to be radical or conservative according as emphasis is placed upon the necessity and importance of mutability and change (*evolution*) or upon final states of harmonious adaptation as a result of selection (*equilibrium*).[18] Similarly, racist and imperialist theories, on the one hand, and pacifist and universalist theories, on the other hand, could both be founded on Darwinian ideas.[19] The first would emphasize the role of ongoing struggle, and the latter the role of social instinct and mutual aid, in promoting selection of human types. And even among those for whom the key lesson of Darwinism is the competitive struggle for survival, there are a variety of interpretations, ranging from individualistic versions of Spencer and Sumner to a number of collectivist

[17] Eric L. Charnov, Optimal Foraging: The Marginal Value Theorem, 9 Theoret. Pop. Biology 129 (1976).

[18] On this see R. C. Lewontin, 5 Int'l Encycl. Soc. Sci., Evolution: The Concept of Evolution 202 (1968).

[19] See Richard Hofstadter, Social Darwinism in American Thought ch. 9 (rev. ed. 1955) and, especially, Gertrude Himmelfarb, *supra* note 5, at ch. 19.

versions: the idea of superior or fitter social classes (Karl Marx), or systems of law and government (Bagehot),[20] or of course racial groups.[21]

In the spectrum of opinion that went under the name of social Darwinism almost every variety of belief was included. In Germany, it was represented chiefly by democrats and socialists; in England by conservatives. It was appealed to by nationalists as an argument for a strong state, and by the proponents of laissez-faire as an argument for a weak state. It was condemned by some as an aristocratic doctrine designed to glorify power and greatness, and by others, like Nietzsche, as a middle-class doctrine appealing to the mediocre and submissive. Some socialists saw in it the scientific validation of their doctrine; others the negation of their moral and spiritual hopes. Militarists found in it the sanction of war and conquest, while pacifists saw the power of physical force transmuted into the power of intellectual and moral persuasion.[22]

But the too-total rejection of Social Darwinism has meant a lack of appreciation of its valid core of scientific insights: (1) that individuals, groups, races, and even social arrangements (democracy versus dictatorship, capitalism versus socialism, small states versus large) are in never-ending competition with one another, and while the results of this competition have no necessary correlation with moral desert, the competition itself is a fact with explanatory power for social phenomena; (2) that the behavior of mankind is strongly influenced by the biological heritage of the species, and that the forces tending toward either cooperation or conflict among men are in large part identical with phenomena observable in the biological realm.

The sweeping rejection of biological categories for the explanation of human phenomena, on the part of social scientists, is strikingly evidenced by the concluding paragraph of Hofstadter's influential and penetrating study:

Whatever the course of social philosophy in the future, however, a few conclusions are now accepted by most humanists: that such biological ideas as the "survival of the fittest," whatever their doubtful value in natural science, are utterly useless in attempting to understand society; that the life of man in society, while it is incidentally a biological fact, has characteristics that are not reducible to biology and must be explained in the distinctive terms of a cultural analysis; that the physical well-being of men is a result of their social organization and not vice versa; that social improvement is a product of advances in technology and social organization, not of breeding or selective elimination; that judgements as to the value of competition between men or enterprises or nations must be based upon social and not allegedly biological consequences; and, finally, that there is nothing in nature or a naturalistic philosophy

---

[20] Walter Bagehot, Physics and Politics (1st Borzoi ed. 1948) (1st ed. 1875).

[21] Gertrude Himmelfarb, *supra* note 5, at 407. The subtitle of the Origin of Species is "The Preservation of Favoured Races in the Struggle for Life," and there is no doubt that Darwin himself applied this conception to the competition among races of mankind.

[22] *Id.* at 407.

of life to make impossible the acceptance of moral sanctions that can be employed for the common good.[23]

This statement is on solid ground in rejecting attempts to draw moral claims from biological premises. But it promotes confusion in confounding these claims with—and therefore rejecting out of hand—the entirely scientific contention that man's biological endowment has significant implications for his social behavior.

Following Nicholson,[24] Darwinian evolution involves four main factors: the occurrence of *variations*, some mechanism of *inheritance* to preserve variations, the Malthusian tendency to *multiplication* (leading sooner or later to *competition* among organisms), and finally environmental *selection*. From this broad point of view it is clear that there may be cultural evolution even apart from any biological change. Hofstadter seems to regard the forms of human association and the patterns of human social and cultural change as almost entirely free of biological determinants—apart, presumably, from permanent human characteristics like degree of intelligence which determine and constrain the *possibilities* of cultural advance. In contrast, the sociobiological point of view is that cultural and biological change cannot be so totally dichotomized; cultural tracking of environmental change is a group-behavioral form of adaptation, which interacts in a variety of ways with genetic and populational responses.[25] There is cultural evolution even in the nonhuman sphere, as animals discover successful patterns of behavior which then spread by learning and imitation. Apart from the direct implications for population composition (those individuals who succeed in learning more efficient behavior survive in greater numbers), there may be genetic consequences in that the behavioral changes may modify the conditions of selection among genetic mutations and recombinations.[26]

Along this line, the anthropologist Alland[27] emphasizes that culture itself should be regarded as a kind of biological adaptation. And there is a long tradition among biologists which encourages attention to the implications of human biological origins for social behavior and institutions. Among the important recent instances are J. Huxley, Fisher, Dobzhansky, Lorenz, Tiger and Fox, and of course E. O. Wilson.[28] On the more popular level are

[23] Richard Hofstadter, *supra* note 19, at 204.

[24] A. J. Nicholson, The Role of Population Dynamics in Natural Selection, in 1 Evolution After Darwin: The Evolution of Life 477 (S. Tax & C. Calender eds. 1960).

[25] See Sociobiology, *supra* note 1, at 145.

[26] Ernst Mayr, The Emergence of Evolutionary Novelties, in 1 Evolution After Darwin, *supra* note 24, at 349, 371.

[27] Alexander Alland, Jr., Evolution and Human Behavior ch. 9 (1967).

[28] Julian S. Huxley, The Living Thoughts of Darwin (rev. ed. 1958); R. A. Fisher, *supra* note 10; Theodosius Dobzhansky, Mankind Evolving (1962); Konrad Lorenz, On Aggression (Mar-

such works as Ardrey (1961 and 1970) and Morris.[29] But these ideas have won relatively little acceptance among social scientists.

Turning now to economics, the relevance of quasi-biological (selectional) models has been the topic of controversial discussion since Alchian's paper in 1950.[30] Alchian argued that environmental selection ("adoption") could replace the traditional analysis premised upon rational profit-maximizing behavior ("adaptation") as a source of verifiable predictions about visible characteristics of business firms. This discussion, which has interesting parallels within biology proper, will be reviewed next.

III. BIOLOGICAL MODELS OF THE FIRM: OPTIMIZATION VERSUS SELECTION

Alchian contended that optimization on the part of the business firm (profit maximization in the traditional formulation) was an unnecessary and even unhelpful idea for purposes of scientific explanation and prediction. While profit is undoubtedly the firm's goal, the substantive content of profit *maximization* as a guiding rule erodes away when it is realized that any actual choice situation always involves profit as a probability distribution rather than as a deterministic variable.[31] And even if firms never attempted to *maximize profit* but behaved purely randomly, the environment would nevertheless select ("adopt") relatively correct decisions in the sense of meeting the *positive realized profit* condition of survival.[32] Without assuming profit maximization, therefore, the economist can nevertheless predict that relatively correct (viable) adaptations or decisions will tend to be the ones observed—for example, the employment of low-skilled workers becomes less viable a practice after imposition of a minimum-wage law.

Enke[33] expanded on Alchian's discussion, with a significant shift in point of view. He suggested that, *given sufficient intensity of competition,* all policies save the optimum would in time fail the survival test. As firms pursuing successful policies expand and multiply, absorbing a larger fraction of the market, a higher and higher standard of behavior becomes the mini-

---

jorie Wilson trans. 1966); Lionel Tiger & Robin Fox, The Imperial Animal (1971); Sociobiology, *supra* note 1.

[29] Robert Ardrey, African Genesis (1961); *id.,* The Social Contract (1970); Desmond Morris, The Naked Ape (1967).

[30] Armen A. Alchian, Uncertainty, Evolution, and Economic Theory, 58 J. Pol. Econ. 211 (1950), reprinted in Armen A. Alchian, Economic Forces at Work 15 (1977).

[31] *Id.* at 212.

[32] *Id.* at 217.

[33] Stephen Enke, On Maximizing Profits: A Distinction Between Chamberlin and Robinson, 41 Am. Econ. Rev. 566, 571 (1951).

mum criterion for competitive survival. *In the long run, viability dictates optimality.* Consequently, for long-run predictive purposes (under conditions of intense competition), the analyst is entitled to assume that firms behave "as if" optimizing.

"As if" optimization is of course what the biologist ordinarily has in mind in postulating that organisms (or, sometimes, genes or populations) "choose" strategies leading to evolutionary success. Two levels of the optimization metaphor in biology may be distinguished. First, there are axes along which the organism can be regarded as having a degree of actual choice (what size of territory to defend, how much effort to devote to the struggle for a mate, what intensity of parental care to confer upon offspring). Here we speak only of "as if" optimizing because we do not credit the animal with the intelligence necessary for true (nonmetaphorical) optimization. Secondly, there are axes along which the organism cannot exercise choice in any meaningful sense at all (whether or not to be an unpalatable insect, whether or not to be a male or a female). Nevertheless, such is the power of selection that the optimization metaphor often seems workable for "choice" of biological characters even on this second level.

There is, however, a serious problem here not yet adequately treated in either economics or biology. If, as applies in almost all interesting cases, the strategic choice is *among probability distributions*, what is the "optimum"? According to what criterion does natural selection select when strategies have uncertain outcomes?

In evolutionary theory, the "as if" criterion of success (the maximand) is generally postulated to be *fitness*: the ratio of offspring numbers to parent numbers at corresponding points in the generational life cycle.[34] In a deterministic situation, no doubt it is better adaptive strategy to choose higher fitness over lower. (Or, translating from metaphorical to literal language, in the long run the environment will be filled by those types of organisms who have developed and passed on to descendants traits permitting higher multiplication ratios.) But what if the situation is not deterministic, so that some or all of the strategies available generate probability distributions rather than definite deterministic numbers for the fitness ratio? In such circumstances the strategy that is optimal in terms of *mean* fitness—that yields the highest mathematical expectation of offspring per parent—might be quite different from the strategy that rates highest in terms of viability (that minimizes the probability of extinction). Where such a conflict arises, some biologists have suggested that viability considerations dominate over mean fitness.[35]

[34] See R. A. Fisher, *supra* note 10, at 37; Edward O. Wilson & William H. Bossert, A Primer of Population Biology 51, 73-76 (1971).

[35] See, for example, George C. Williams, Adaptation and Natural Selection 106 (1966).

No solution to this general problem in evolution theory will be offered here.[36] The point to be underlined is that Enke envisaged a situation where the outcome of each alternative policy option for the firm is *objectively* deterministic, although *subjectively* uncertain from the point of view of the firm's decision-maker (acting under limited information). Under these conditions there really does exist an objectively optimum course of action leading to maximum profit, which intense competition (even in the absence of knowledge) ultimately enforces—in Enke's view—upon all surviving firms. Alchian sometimes seems to have the same idea.[37] In saying that *maximum* realized profits is meaningful while *maximizing* profit is not, he means that one cannot "maximize" a probability distribution representing subjective uncertainty about profit, but there is nevertheless a deterministic or objective "maximum" of profit that could be attained if the knowledge were available. Usually, however, Alchian seems to have in mind the quite different case in which the outcomes are intrinsically or *objectively* probabilistic, rather than merely subjectively uncertain because of imperfect knowledge. Here there does not exist any unequivocal optimum, and Enke's argument does not apply. For Alchian, it is in such an environment that viability (positive realized profit) becomes the relevant success criterion.

Independent of Alchian's introduction of the viability argument, but parallel in its implications, was Herbert A. Simon's contention[38] that firms are better regarded as "satisficing" than as optimizing. Starting from a psychological rather than evolutionary orientation, Simon contended that decision-makers are conservative about modifying established routines yielding satisfactory results—unless forced to do so by exogenous changes that threaten unacceptable outcomes. The reason given was informational: the

---

[36] A number of the complex issues involved may be briefly alluded to. In balancing extinction probability against multiplication ratio, a long-term (multi-generational) point of view must be taken. In any such long-term comparison there will be some prospect of changes in the external environment and even in the genetic constitution of the organism's descendants over time. Even if a high-mean-fitness strategy pays off, the extinction risk being avoided, eventually diminishing-returns constraints (what the biologists call "density-dependent effects") are likely to be encountered—so that the one-generation high-multiplication ratio cannot be indefinitely maintained. On both these grounds the probability distribution for "fitness" measured in terms of a *single* generation's multiplication ratio may give misleading results. A high extinction probability is more acceptable if descendants will spread into a number of different environments or otherwise diversify so that the extinction risks have a degree of independence of one another. In this case, while many lines of descent may be extinguished, others are likely to survive and multiply. Finally, flexibility is an important consideration; a very advantageous strategy might include a capacity to mutate between high-mean-fitness and low-extinction-probability characters over time.

[37] Armen A. Alchian, *supra* note 30, at 212.

[38] Herbert A. Simon, A Behavioral Model of Rational Choice, 69 Q. J. Econ. 99 (1955); *id.*, Theories of Decision-Making in Economics and Behavioral Science, 49 Am. Econ. Rev. 253 (1959).

decision-maker who recognizes the inadequacy of his knowledge, or the costs of performing the computations necessary for determining optimality even if he had all the relevant data, does not find that it pays even to attempt to optimize.[39] Simon did allow for a long-run approach toward optimization under stationary conditions in the form of a gradual shift of the decision-maker's "aspiration level" toward the best outcome attainable. But, he emphasized, business decisions take place in a context of ever-recurring change; the process of gradual approximation of optimality can never progress very far before being confounded by events. Thus, for Simon as for Alchian, the environment primarily plays a selective role in rewarding choice of *viable* strategies. Simon, in contrast with Alchian, chooses to emphasize how this process has in effect been internalized into the psychology of decision-makers.

A closely related aspect of the optimizing-selection process is the question of "perfection." It is possible in evolutionary models alternatively to emphasize the *achieved state of adaptation*, or the *process of adaptive change* toward that state. In the biological realm a high state of perfection on the organismic level has been attained: ". . . organisms in general are, in fact, marvellously and intricately adapted, both in their internal mechanisms, and in their relations to external nature."[40] The high degree of perfection is evidenced by the fact that the vast majority of mutations, which follow a random law, are harmful to the organism rather than beneficial. An important and less obvious consequence of the high degree of perfection is that the environment, as it changes under a variety of random influences, is always (from the organism's viewpoint) tending to deteriorate. So even relatively well-adapted organisms, or particularly such organisms, require the ability to track environmental changes. In the economic sphere, in contrast, we do not—though perhaps we should—think in terms of a very high degree of perfection in the adaptations of individuals or firms.[41] The argument in terms of perfection has been at the heart of much of the critical discussion of the biological model in economics.

---

[39] Of course, behavior might be optimized *subject to these informational constraints*. While it seems possible to adopt such an interpretation, there may be operational or even logical difficulties in calculating "the optimal amount of departure from optimality" See Sidney G. Winter, Optimization and Evolution in the Theory of the Firm, in Adaptive Economic Models 73, 81-85 (Richard H. Day & Theodore Graves eds. 1975).

[40] R. A. Fisher, *supra* note 10, at 44.

[41] But note that a high degree of such "selfish" adaptation, on the part of private economic agents, need not imply optimality of the Invisible-Hand variety on the *social* level. Similarly in the biological domain, perfection on the level of the organism does not imply that the entire biota, or even smaller aggregates like single species, have been optimally adapted to the environment. See Gordon Tullock, Biological Externalities, 33 J. Theoret. Biology 565 (1971); Michael T. Ghiselin, *supra* note 4. This point will be discussed further below.

ECONOMICS FROM A BIOLOGICAL VIEWPOINT   13

Penrose[42] criticized Alchian by contending, in effect, that the achieved state of economic adaptation is generally *too perfect* to be accounted for by merely random behavior on the part of businessmen. Although high states of adaptation are indeed attained in the biological sphere even without rational optimizing, that is due, she argued, to the extreme intensity of competition forced by organisms' innate urge to multiply—the Malthusian principle. This urge being lacking in the economic sphere, and competition therefore less intense, the businessman's purposive drive to make money is required to supply the analogous driving force.[43]

Of course, the *desire* to make money is not enough. The key point of the Penrose criticism is that this desire must, for the most part, be realized. Businessmen must expect to be successful if they are to enter the competitive arena. And any such expectation would be too regularly refuted to persist if actual outcomes realized were no better than would ensue from random action. So the Penrose image is one of a changing environment (else there would not be much in the way of profit opportunities) very effectively tracked by rationally optimizing businessmen.

The selectional processes of Nature, driven by random variation and Malthusian competition, are profligately wasteful of life and energy.[44] An implication of the Penrose thesis is that the wastage cost of economic selection should be considerably less than that of biological selection.[45] Quantitative estimates of the selectional wastage cost (bankruptcies, abandonments, etc.) would be of interest, therefore, in providing some measure of the prevalence and success of rational optimization.[46]

While Penrose argued that the observed degree of adaptation in the econ-

[42] Edith Tilton Penrose, Biological Analogies in the Theory of the Firm, 42 Am. Econ. Rev. 804, 812 (1952); *id.*, Biological Analogies in the Theory of the Firm: Rejoinder, 43 Am. Econ. Rev. 603 (1953).

[43] Edith Tilton Penrose, Biological Analogies in the Theory of the Firm (1952), *supra* note 42, at 812.

[44] See J. B. S. Haldane, The Cost of Natural Selection, 55 J. Genetics 511 (1957); William Feller, On Fitness and the Cost of Natural Selection, 9 Genetical Research 1 (1967).

[45] Not all biological adaptive mechanisms are random in their working, however. Mutations and genetic combinations are completely random, but patterns of activity (for example, feeding, mating) often are not. Even lower animals display simple purposive behavior, such as escape maneuvers when threatened. And there is a great deal of adaptive *learning* on the nonhuman level.

[46] To some extent, market experiments—while failing to capture the full richness and variety of economic environments—do provide insights as to the rapidity of convergence to optimal solutions. Vernon L. Smith, Experimental Economics: Induced Value Theory, 66 Am. Econ. Rev., pt. 2, at 274 (Papers & Proceedings, May 1976), in surveying such experiments is generally quite impressed by the ability of experimental subjects to approximate optimal (rather than merely viable) behavior. Experiments on economic choices even on the part of animals provide evidence of a considerable degree of "rationality". John H. Kagel, Howard Rachlin, Leonard Green, Raymond C. Battalio, Robert L. Basmann & W. R. Klenn, Experimental Studies of Consumer Demand Behavior Using Laboratory Animals, 13 Econ. Inquiry 22 (1975).

omy is *too perfect* to be accounted for by blind environmental selection, Winter's critique[47] is based on the opposite contention—that the state of adaptation is *too imperfect* to be accounted for by a process that leads to the same outcomes "as if" firms actually optimized. His argument is therefore directed against Enke's extension of the selectional model, against the idea that in the long run viability requires optimality, rather than against Alchian's original version. The main evidence of imperfection cited by Winter is the prevalence in business practice of conventional rules of thumb (for example, a pricing policy of fixed percentage markups) even where seemingly in conflict with profit-maximizing behavior.[48]

Winter contributed interesting suggestions about the nature of *inheritance* and *variation* in economic selectional models. For Alchian, the inherited aspect of the firm was described as "fixed internal conditions"[49]—in effect, simple inertia due to the fact that the firm is more or less the same from one day to the next. Variation was attributed to imitation of successful firms,[50] or simply to trial-and-error exploration. For Winter the inherited element, analogous to the biological genotype, is represented by certain more permanent aspects of the firm (its "decision rule"). This is to be distinguished from the specific decision made in a given context, which is analogous to the biological phenotype. What the environment selects is the correct action, even though it be the chance result of a rather inferior decision rule. In natural selection as well, well-adapted and less well-adapted genotypes might be represented at a given moment by the same phenotype. But, over a number of generations, natural selection working together with the Mendelian laws of inheritance will tend to fix the superior genotype in the population.[51] The economic mechanism of repeated trials is somewhat different, as no genetic recombination is involved. But surely we can expect that, as a variety of selectional tests are imposed over time, those firms providing a merely lucky action-response to a particular environmental configuration will tend to be selected against as compared with those following a more correct decision rule.[52]

[47] Sidney G. Winter, Jr., Economic "Natural Selection" and the Theory of the Firm, 4 Yale Econ. Essays 225 (1964); *id.*, Satisficing, Selection, and the Innovating Remnant, 85 Q. J. Econ. 237 (1971); *id.*, *supra* note 39.

[48] Sidney G. Winter, Jr., Satisficing, *supra* note 46, at 241.

[49] Armen A. Alchian, *supra* note 30, at 216.

[50] And "innovation" to imperfect imitation that happens to be successful!

[51] Suppose a dominant allele *A* at a certain gene locus is the superior type, and the recessive allele *a* is inferior. Then the heterozygote *Aa* will be represented by the same phenotype (and so be subjected in the current generation to the same selection) as the homozygote *AA*. But in the next and succeeding generations, the descendants of *AA* will on the average do better than those of *Aa*—ultimately extinguishing the inferior allele.

[52] Winter appears to doubt this. Sidney G. Winter, *supra* note 39, at 97; *id.*, Economic "Natural Selection", *supra* note 46, at 257-58.

In his first article Winter employed the term "organization form" for what his later papers call "decision rule" or "rule of action." While the intended referent is the same, and is indeed better described by the words "decision rule" or "rule of action," the initial term had interesting implications that might well have been pursued. "Organization form" would ordinarily be understood to mean something like corporation or partnership, large firm or small, etc. This is a more visible and operational concept than "decision rule." Since even the best decision rule (in the usual sense of that term) might not make possible survival of a firm with an ill-adapted organization form, we should really think of three levels of selection—action, decision rule, and organization form.[53]

The broadly similar views of Alchian and Winter represent, it might be noted, a Lamarckian evolutionary model. Lamarck believed (as did Darwin) that acquired characters can be inherited, and also that variations tend to appear when needed. Failure-stimulated search for new rules of action (Winter), taking in particular the form of imitation of observed success (Alchian), is—if the results are assumed to be heritable—certainly in the spirit of Lamarck. The Lamarckian model is inapplicable to inheritance and variation (whether somatic or behavioral) mediated by the *genetic* mechanism, but it seems to be broadly descriptive of *cultural* evolution in general, and of economic responses in particular.[54]

Perhaps Winter's most important contribution in this area is his actual modelling of possible *selectional equilibrium* situations. Space does not permit adequate exposition or review of these formulations here, but the following summary may be suggestive:

Those organization forms which have the lowest zero growth price are viable, others are not. Or, to put the matter another way, price will tend to the lowest value at which some firm's organization form still yields non-negative growth. Firms whose organization forms result in decline at that price will approach zero scale as time goes on, leaving the firms which have the minimum zero growth price to share the market.[55]

This language suggests the "long run zero-profit equilibrium" of the competitive industry, reinterpreted in terms of the biologists' population equilibrium condition of zero growth. But Winter is at pains to show that even a

[53] George J. Stigler, The Economies of Scale, 1 J. Law & Econ. 54 (1958) employed, though without placing any emphasis upon biological analogies, a selectional model called *the survivor principle* to draw inferences about efficient plant and firm sizes in a variety of industries. The same method could evidently be applied to other firm characteristics that could be described as "organizational forms."

[54] Since behavioral changes, by modifying the conditions of selection, may *lead* to changes in genetic compositions of populations, to a degree Lamarckism plays a role even in the modern theory of genetic evolution. See C. H. Waddington, The Nature of Life ch. 4 (1961).

[55] Sidney G. Winter, Economic "Natural Selection", *supra* note 46, at 253.

firm with the lowest possible zero-growth price (lowest minimum of Average Total Cost curves) might—as a result of using an inappropriate decision rule—not actually be a survivor in selectional equilibrium. So the traditional competitive equilibrium might not be generated, or, once generated, might not respond in the standard way to changes in exogenous determinants.[56] One reason for this divergence from the traditional result, however, is that Winter's model is limited to the single adjustment mechanism of *firm growth*. Among the factors not considered, *entry pressure* on the part of new firms and (a more surprising omission in view of the previous emphasis) *failure-stimulated search* on the part of unsuccessful existing firms would tend to force a progressively higher state of adaptation upon survivors.

In his 1971 article Winter indicates that in order to achieve the optimality properties of the standard competitive model an "innovating remnant" is needed. This category consists of firms that are, for unexplained reasons, inveterate searchers who will ultimately hit upon any as-yet-undiscovered superior decision rules.[57] But new entrants, upon whom standard theory relies to discipline firms already in the industry, can also serve this exploratory role. A fruitful approach, consistent with biological observation, would be to recognize that one of the many possible survival strategies adopted by organisms (firms) is a tendency to search—and at any moment of time there will be a balance between organisms searching for new niches and organisms adapting to existing ones. (This point will come up again when competitive strategies are discussed below.)

It is a rather odd accident that biological models entered into economic thought in connection with the theory of the *business firm*—a highly specialized and consciously contrived "cultural" grouping. To some extent, as just seen, evolution theory is applicable to firms: inheritance, variation, competition, selection, adaptation—all play roles in explaining the observed patterns of survivorship and activity. Still, if biological models were being explored afresh for possible relevance to economic behavior, one's first target for consideration would naturally be the *individual* together with the *family*—entities of direct biological significance. Without any preconceived limitation of attention to the business firm, several aspects of economic theorizing will now be examined from a biological orientation: the nature and provenance of preferences; the evolution of patterns of competition, cooperation, and conflict; and resulting tendencies toward equilibrium, cycles, and progressive change.

[56] In a more recent work, Richard R. Nelson & Sidney G. Winter, Neoclassical vs. Evolutionary Theories of Economic Growth: Critique and Prospectus, 84 Econ. J. 886 (1974) have developed simulation models of growth in which firms and industries evolve over time by a selectional process, one not describable as a path of moving equilibrium.

[57] Sidney G. Winter, Satisficing, *supra* note 46, at 247.

ECONOMICS FROM A BIOLOGICAL VIEWPOINT   17

IV. Elements of Economic Theorizing: A Biological Interpretation

The contention here is that the social processes studied by economics, or rather by the social sciences collectively, are not mere analogs but are rather *instances* of sociobiological mechanisms—in the same sense in which chemical reactions have been shown to be a special class of processes following the laws of physics.[58] For this to be in any way a useful idea, it remains to be shown that a more general sociobiological outlook can in fact provide social scientists with a deeper and more satisfactory explanation of already-known results, or better still can generate new ones.[59]

A. *Utility, Fitness, and the Provenance of Preferences— Especially, Altruism*

Modern neoclassical economics has forsworn any attempt to study the source and content of preferences, that is, the goals that motivate men's actions. It has regarded itself as the logic of choice under conditions of "given tastes." But many of the great and small social changes in history have stemmed from *shifts* in people's goals for living. The very terminology used by the economist—preferences, wants, tastes—tends not only to trivialize these fundamental aims and values, but implies that they are arbitrary or inexplicable (*de gustibus non est disputandum*). Nor have the other social sciences, to whom the economists have unilaterally delegated the task of studying preferences, made much progress in that regard. The healthy aggrandizing tendency of modern economics requires us, therefore, to overstep this boundary like so many others.

No doubt there is a large arbitrary element in the determination of wants. Individuals are idiosyncratic, and even socially influenced preferences may reflect chance accidents in the histories of particular societies. But it is equally clear that not all preferences for commodities represent "mere taste." When we learn that Alabamans like cooling drinks more than Alaskans do, it is not hard to decipher the underlying physiological explanation for such differences in "tastes." Unfortunately, the refusal of modern economics to examine the biological functions of preferences[60] has meant that the bridge

---

[58] Compare Alexander Alland, Jr., *supra* note 27, at 194-97 and Edward O. Wilson, Biology and the Social Sciences, *supra* note 1.

[59] And, of course, it is possible that the more general science of sociobiology might benefit from results independently achieved in the special fields of the human sciences.

[60] Recent reformulations of consumer theory by Kelvin J. Lancaster, A New Approach to Consumer Theory, 74 J. Pol. Econ. 132 (1966) and Gary S. Becker, A Theory of the Allocation of Time, 75 Econ. J. 493 (1965) treat commodities as packages of more fundamental characteris-

between human physiology and social expressions of desires has been studied
by no one (except, perhaps, by practitioners of empirical "human engineering").

On a very abstract level, the concept of *homeostasis* has been put forward
as the foundation of wants: the individual is postulated as acting to maintain
vital internal variables within certain limits necessary for optimum functioning, or at least for survival.[61] But homeostasis is too limited a goal to
describe more than very short-run human adaptations. And in any case, the
internal "production function" connecting these internal variables with external social behavior has somehow fallen outside the domain of any established field of research.

Of more critical importance to social science than tastes for ordinary
commodities are preferences taking the form of attitudes toward other humans. Anger and envy are evidently antisocial sentiments, while benevolence and group identification promote socialization. Socially relevant attitudes differ from culture to culture: in some societies hierarchical dominance is a prime motive for action, in others not; in some, marital partners
value fidelity highly, in others promiscuity is regarded as normal; in some
cultures people cluster closely together, in others they avoid personal contact. The programmatic contention here is that such preference patterns,
despite seemingly arbitrary elements, have survived because they are mainly
adaptive to environmental conditions. (No strong emphasis will be placed
upon the issue of whether such adaptations are cultural or genetic in origin,
in line with the argument above that the ability to evolve cultural traits is
itself a kind of genetic adaptation.) This contention will surely not be always
found to hold; in the biology of plants and animals as well, it is often unclear
whether a particular morphological or behavioral trait is truly adaptive or
merely an accidental variation. Nature is unceasingly fertile in producing
random modifications. But if a trait has survived, as a working hypothesis
the biologist looks for an adaptive function.[62]

As a nice example, in a famous passage in *The Descent of Man* Darwin
asserted that for hive bees the instinct of maternal hatred rather than maternal love serves an adaptive function. He went on to generalize that, for
animals in general (and not excluding mankind), "sentiments" or social attitudes are but a mechanism of adaptation.[63] The anthropologist Ronald

tics which constitute the true desired entities. But without a biological interpretation, this
reformulation merely pushes the arbitrariness of tastes one step farther back.

[61] Richard H. Day, Adaptive Processes and Economic Theory, in Adaptive Economic Models, *supra* note 39, at 1.

[62] Though whether the function is adaptive to the individual only, or alternatively to some
larger social group to which he belongs, may remain subject to controversy.

[63] Michael T. Ghiselin, *supra* note 4, at 218-19. Adam Smith, it might be noted, argued that

ECONOMICS FROM A BIOLOGICAL VIEWPOINT   19

Cohen[64] has similarly pointed to variations among cultures in degrees of "affect" (that is, of interpersonal emotional attachment) as adaptive responses to environmental circumstances.

The biological approach to preferences, to what economists call the utility function, postulates that all such motives or drives or tastes represent proximate aspects of a single underlying goal—fitness. Preferences are governed by the all-encompassing *drive for reproductive survival.* This might seem at first absurd. That all humans do not solely and totally regard themselves as children-making machines seems evidenced by phenomena such as birth control, abortion, and homosexuality. Or, if these be considered aberrations, by the large fractions of income and effort devoted to human aims that compete with child-rearing—among them entertainment, health care beyond the childbearing age, personal intellectual advancement, etc. Yet, all these phenomena might still be indirectly instrumental to fitness. Birth control may be a device leading *on net balance* to more descendants rather than fewer; health care beyond the childbearing age may more effectively promote the survival and vigor of children or grandchildren. And, as we shall see shortly, even a childlessness strategy *may* be explicable in fitness terms!

In any attempt to broaden the application of economic reasoning, to make it a general social science, a key issue is the problem of altruism (the "taste" for helping others): its extent, provenance, and determinants. Old-fashioned, narrow economics was often criticized for employing the model of economic man—a selfish, calculating, and essentially nonsocial being.[65] Of course, it was impossible to postulate such a man in dealing with that essential social grouping, *the family.* Neoclassical economics avoided the difficulty by abandoning attempts to explain intrafamily interactions! Some economists formalized this evasion by taking the household rather than the individual as the fundamental *unit* of economic activity; in effect, they postulated total altruism within and total selfishness outside the family.

Modern economic "imperialists" have been dissatisfied both with the excessively restrictive postulate of individual selfishness and with the exclusion of intrafamily behavior from the realm of economic analysis. The modern view postulates a generalized preference or utility function in which selfishness is only the midpoint of a spectrum ranging from benevolence at one extreme to malevolence at the other.[66] But, standing alone, this is really

---

the desires (or passions, appetites, or sentiments) driving men have been implanted (as by a wise Providence) to promote the survival of the species. See R. H. Coase, *supra* note 7.

   [64] Ronald Cohen, Altruism: Human, Cultural or What?, 2 J. Soc. Issues, No. 3, at 39, 46-51 (1972).

   [65] A criticism quite inapplicable, as already observed, to Adam Smith's view of man. See note 7, *supra*.

   [66] See, for example, Gary S. Becker, A Theory of Social Interactions, 82 J. Pol. Econ. 1063 (1974).

an empty generalization. Where any individual happens to lie on the benevolence-malevolence scale with regard to other individuals still remains a merely arbitrary "taste." And yet we all know that patterns of altruism are not merely arbitrary. That a parent is more benevolent to his own child than to a stranger's is surely capable of explanation.

From the evolutionary point of view the great analytical problem of altruism is that, in order to survive the selectional process, altruistic behavior must be profitable in fitness terms. It must somehow be the case that being generous (at least sometimes, to some beneficiaries) is selectively more advantageous than being selfish!

A possible semantic confusion arises here. If altruism were defined simply as accepting injury to self in order to help others, without countervailing benefit of any kind, then indeed natural selection would quickly eliminate altruist behavior. When biologists speak of altruism they do not mean to rule out offsetting or redeeming mechanisms making unselfish behavior profitable in some sense; indeed, their analysis requires that such exist.[67]

The redeeming mechanisms identified by biologists seem to fall into two main categories. In the first, altruistic behavior survives because, despite initial appearances, a fuller analysis shows that *the preponderance of benefit or advantage is really conferred on the self*. We may, though paradoxically, call such behavior "selfish altruism"; being ultimately selfish, such altruism does not require compensation or reciprocity to be viable. In the second class of redeeming mechanism compensation does take place; Trivers[68] has termed such behavior "reciprocal altruism." Reciprocal altruism, apart from motivation, approaches what economists would of course call *exchange*. It will be discussed, in connection with that topic, in Section B following.

The clearest cases of selfish altruism, of behavior only seemingly unselfish, stem from the fact that *in the biological realm there are two levels of self*. On one level is the morphological and physiological constitution of the organism (the phenotype); on the other level the organism's genetic endowment (the genotype). The genetic constitution may contain recessive genes that are not expressed in the phenotype; perhaps even more important, the phenotype is subjected to and modified by environmental influences that leave the genotype unaffected. "Unselfish" action defined as behavior that injures the organism's phenotypical well-being may yet tend to propagate the organism's genotype. Indeed, since all living beings eventually die, ultimately

---

[67] Still another semantic difficulty is suggested by a remark like the following: "If an individual's utility function has the well-being of another party as argument, there need be no conflict between (selfishly) maximizing utility and (unselfishly) helping the other." Here maximizing utility is taken as the *definition* of selfish behavior, a verbal device that only evades the real substantive issue: to explain *how* it is that aiding others can viably enter an individual's utility function.

[68] Robert L. Trivers, The Evolution of Reciprocal Altruism, 46 Q. Rev. Biology 35 (1971).

ECONOMICS FROM A BIOLOGICAL VIEWPOINT   21

the only way to achieve a payoff in fitness terms is to help certain other organisms—most notably, of course, one's offspring—carry one's genetic endowment beyond the death barrier.

The mechanism rewarding this type of altruist behavior is called *kin selection.*[69] Maximization of fitness from the point of view of the genotype often dictates a degree of altruism from the point of view of the phenotype—not only to offspring, but more generally to close relatives. Setting aside a number of qualifications, we might say that any individual should be willing to give his life to save two of his brothers (since full sibs have at least half their genes in common), or four half-brothers, or eight cousins, etc. Put another way, the "as if" maximand governing choice of evolutionary strategy is not the organism's *own* fitness but its *inclusive* fitness—the reproductive survival, with appropriate discounting for distance of relationship, of all those organisms sharing its genetic endowment.

Before proceeding to draw out some of the implications of altruism motivated by kin selection, a word of caution: actual behavior always represents the *interaction* of two determining factors—on the one side preferences, on the other side opportunities (constraints). We cannot directly infer altruistic preferences from cooperative behavior; in some environments the limited opportunities available may dictate that even enemies cooperate in the interests of selfish survival. Nor can we directly infer malevolence from hostile behavior; in some environments even brothers may be impelled to fight one another for survival.

Compare parent-to-offspring altruism with sib-to-sib altruism. Parental altruism is behaviorally much the more evident, and yet the degree of kinship (proportion of shared genes) in the two cases is exactly the same! The reason for the difference is that brothers and sisters are ordinarily in much closer *competition* with one another than parents are with children.[70] Why then the famed maternal hatred and sisterly altruism among ants? The explanation is remarkable. Due to the unusual method of sex determination called haplodiploidy, sisters in ant colonies (the queen and worker castes) are more closely related to one another than they are to their own offspring (or would be, if they had offspring)![71] The notoriously lazy male drones, on the other hand, have only the ordinary degree of kinship with other colony members.

Yet it must not be assumed that parents and offspring never compete.

[69] W. D. Hamilton, The Genetical Evolution of Social Behavior I, 7 J. Theoret. Biology 1 (1964).

[70] For many species, the struggle for food or shelter among members of a litter is a matter of life or death.

[71] Robert L. Triver & Hope Hare, Haplodiploidy and the Evolution of the Social Insects, 191 Science 249 (1976).

Each offspring's selfish interest lies in having its parents' full devotion. But the parent aiming at reproductive survival strives for an optimal allocation of care and protection over *all* his or her offspring—past, present, and future. One nice implication is described by Trivers.[72] Intergenerational conflict occurs during the period when additional parental care, still desirable from the offspring's point of view, is no longer optimal for the parent (who must consider his opportunity cost in the form of the potential fitness gain in caring for a new batch of offspring). But the *intensity* of such "weaning conflict" is a function of the offspring's expected degree of relationship with his sibs of the later batch. If an offspring in a promiscuous species foregoes maternal care, his sacrifice will probably operate to the benefit of mere half-sibs; in permanently mating species, to the benefit of full sibs. Hence the prediction, which is in fact confirmed, that offspring will be somewhat less "selfish" (weaning conflict will be less intense) in species following the stable-family pattern.[73]

Another point of interest: why are parents generally more altruistic to offspring than offspring to parents—since the degree of relationship is the same? The reason turns on their disparate *opportunities* for helping one another. The offspring may initially require care simply in order to survive, while the parents usually have energy available over their own immediate survival needs. As the offspring develop self-sustaining capacity over time, parental devotion diminishes. Still another factor is the asymmetry in time. In terms of fitness comparisons, offspring generally have greater "reproductive value," that is, offspring are more efficient at producing future descendants for parents than parents are in producing future relatives (sibs and their descendants) for offspring.[74] This is of course clearest when parents have entirely completed their reproductive activity. And, as seen above, the sibs are likely anyway to be pretty close competitors. Yet, in appropriate biological environments, offspring sometimes do curtail personal reproduction to help parents rear sibs.[75]

What of altruism *within* the parental pair? From the biological viewpoint, alas, the parental partner is just a means to the end of selfish reproductive survival. He or she is undoubtedly to be valued, but only as a kind of specialized livestock! Trivers[76] has explored in detail the mixed cooperative-competitive incentives for parents. Each requires the other to achieve reproductive survival, yet each is motivated to load on to the other

[72] Robert L. Trivers, Parent-Offspring Conflict, 14 Am. Zoologist 249 (1974).

[73] In human polygamous families, full sibs reputedly display greater mutual altruism than half-sibs. But I am unaware of any hard evidence on this point.

[74] R. A. Fisher, *supra* note 10, at 27-30.

[75] Sociobiology, *supra* note 1, at 125.

[76] Robert L. Trivers, *supra* note 14.

ECONOMICS FROM A BIOLOGICAL VIEWPOINT   23

a disproportionate share of the burden. The relatively smaller male investment in germ cells (sperm vs. egg) tends to lead to desertion, promiscuity, or
to polygyny as ways for males to maximize numbers of descendants. The
female, having already made a substantial somatic commitment in each
reproductive episode, is less well placed than her mate to refuse additional
parental commitment. (Females sometimes have means of cheating through
cuckoldry, however.) The actual expression of one or more of these nonaltruistic tendencies depends upon the specific opportunities provided by the
environmental situations of each species. There are situations in which parental pairs are models of mutual devotion, most notably in difficult environments where the survival of offspring requires full concentrated team-
work on the part of both parents.[77]

Let us now go beyond the kin-selection mechanism favoring altruism
directed at close relatives. Wynne-Edwards[78] propounded the broader view
that altruistic behavior may be favorably selected because it promotes the
good of the species as a whole even though adverse to individual fitness—an
example being voluntary restriction of number of offspring in times of food
scarcity. Or, more generally, it has been argued that in environments where
within-group altruism strongly promotes group success (as will often be the
case), altruism tends to evolve through a process of *group selection*. For
example, ant colonies that cooperate more efficiently will thrive and multiply, in comparison with colonies whose altruism is not so fully developed.

But biologists recognize a serious difficulty here, equivalent to what economists call a "free-rider problem." To wit, the bearer of a gene dictating
altruistic behavior tends to be negatively selected *within* his group as against
fellow group members who are nonaltruists. Thus, *individual* selection
opposes *group* selection; the altruistic groups may thrive, but always tend to
become less and less altruistic while doing so. Even if the altruist groups
drive all others to extinction, they themselves tend to end up nonaltruistic.

One important consideration might make it appear, at first sight, that the
argument for selection of *kin-directed* altruism (that it is really selfish behavior, genotypically speaking) extends with almost equal force to broader
within-group altruism—and indeed, even to cooperation on the level of the
species as a whole. There is a strong degree of relationship (in the sense of
correlation of genetic endowments) even among "unrelated" members of the
same species. At many, or even the great majority of loci, genes are *fixed* in
any given species;[79] everyone has both genes in common at any such locus.
So even individuals chosen at random in a species may well share 70 or 80
per cent of their genetic endowments.

[77] *Sociobiology, supra* note 1, at 330.

[78] V. C. Wynne-Edwards, Animal Dispersion in Relation to Social Behavior (1962).

[79] R. A. Fisher, *supra* note 10, at 137.

This fact would seem to imply a very heavy "selfish" payoff, genotypically speaking, for altruistic behavior toward any conspecifics whatsoever. (And, of course, the correlation will tend to be closer, and so the payoff greater, within localized social groupings having any degree of inbreeding.) The flaw in this argument is that group selection for altruistic behavior is not governed by *overall* correlations of genetic endowments, but by the presence or absence of the *specific* gene or genes determining altruist behavior. The "free-rider problem" operates equally effectively to favor noncarriers of the altruist gene, whether or not the individuals concerned otherwise have high or low correlations of genetic endowments. The altruist gene, metamorphically speaking, only "wants" to help *its* close relatives—organisms likely to be bearing the same specific gene. Given that the altruist gene is initially rare, it is highly unlikely that both parents carry it. Thus there is only a 50 per cent chance that one's full brother is a fellow carrier, and essentially no chance that a random conspecific is.

Still, it remains true that, from the point of view of the organism's overall genotype, altruism has a higher value for promoting fitness the higher the genetic correlation with the beneficiary. The mechanism governing the spread of the specific altruist gene might be thought of as the "supply" factor, with the overall genotypical benefit as the "demand" factor, in the process. The idea is that the free-rider problem is more likely to be overcome the greater the benefit from doing so.[80]

Two different types of process for overcoming the free-rider problem seem to have been identified by biologists: genetic drift, and group dispersal-reassortment. Genetic drift refers to variation of gene frequencies due simply to random fluctuations in the process of genetic recombination associated with mating. It may so happen that, despite the free-rider factor acting systematically to reduce within-group frequency of the altruist gene, by sheer random fluctuation the gene may nevertheless become fixed in the group.[81] Once every member of the mating group possesses *only* altruist genes, there can be no within-group selection against altruists (unless the nonaltruist gene is reintroduced by mutation or by entry of outsiders.) Such a development is highly improbable, unless the group is very small. And yet, Nature's experiments over time have been so unimaginably numerous that the improbable does happen from time to time. The improbability is sharply reduced for colonial species that "bud off" mating pairs to found new colonies.[82] Here the altruist gene need only become fixed from time to time in a minimally-sized group—a mating pair. Such a pair may then found a colony

---

[80] I am indebted to Joel Guttman for this point.

[81] J. Maynard Smith, Group Selection and Kin Selection, 201 Nature 1145 (1964).

[82] R. C. Lewontin, The Units of Selection, 1 Ann. Rev. Ecology & Systematics 1, 13-14 (1970).

which will be favorably group-selected in competition with other colonies. With successive "buddings off" from such a thriving colony, the altruist genes may spread and eventually preponderate.

The second process, often mixed with the first, involves regular dispersal and reassortment of groups having larger and smaller proportions of altruist genes.[83] *Within* each of the two classes of groups, prevalence of the altruist gene is progressively reduced by individual selection. Yet, if the collective advantage of altruist behavior is sufficiently large, it may be that groups with larger altruist representation increase in numbers so much relative to the others that the *overall* representation of the altruist gene increases in the population at large. If the groups regularly disperse and reassort themselves at some stage in the life cycle, this process can continue. (Failing dispersal and reassortment, on the other hand, individual selection will ultimately tend to drive out the altruist genes.)

A quite different sort of altruistic behavior, not necessarily involving close kin or even fellow carriers of the altruist gene, still falls into the selfish category. An instance appears in the development of alarm calls in birds.[84] A caller who alerts the flock to a predator, it is hypothesized, is thereby subjected to a higher risk (by attracting attention to itself). This behavior can be viable in fitness terms in certain circumstances, provided that it is only *comparatively* (not absolutely) disadvantageous to the caller. Thus, the altruism is merely *incidental* to selfish behavior. (The alarm may discourage the predator entirely or at least reduce his efficiency, so that the caller benefits on balance.) Still, under such "incidental altruism" even the *comparative* disadvantage tends to lead to elimination of the altruistic caller types by natural selection in favor of other group members (free riders). The saving feature here is that flocks are fluid, ever-changing aggregations. The caller gets only a small benefit, but gets it every time; the noncaller occasionally gets a big benefit from a free ride, but otherwise loses by refraining from calling. This tends to lead to an interior solution with a mixed population of callers and noncallers, for as the callers increase in numbers, the marginal advantage of being a noncaller (receiving more free rides) increases.[85]

Incidental altruism of the alarm-call type is an instance of what economists would term the *private provision of a public good*. Olson[86] argues that

[83] David Sloan Wilson, A Theory of Group Selection, 72 Proc. Nat'l Acad. Sci. USA 143 (1975).

[84] Robert L. Trivers, *supra* note 67, at 43-44.

[85] Eric L. Charnov & John R. Krebs, The Evolution of Alarm Calls: Altruism or Manipulation, 109 Am. Naturalist 107 (1975) [letter to the ed.].

[86] Mancur Olson, Jr., The Logic of Collective Action ch. 1 (Harv. Econ. Stud., vol. 124, 1965).

such a provision is more likely to be found in small groups, and particularly so where there are size or taste disparities within the group. (The larger members, or of course the more desirous ones, are the most motivated to provide the public good; the smaller, or the less desirous, are more likely to be the free riders.) Buchanan[87] has a somewhat different analysis, showing that substantial amounts of the public good might be provided even without such disparities. For Buchanan the main factor is the wealth enhancement that each group member derives from the purchase of the public good by others. On the one hand such purchases by others impel him to cut back his own purchases (the free-rider effect), but on the other hand the wealth enhancement stops him from cutting back all the way to zero (income effect).

Summing up, we have seen how altruistic behavior may prove to be viable in selectional terms even in the absence of any reciprocation. Over the course of human and pre-human evolutionary development, drives or instincts promoting such behavior have evolved and ultimately taken the form that the economist so inadequately calls preferences. And what is true for the specific "taste for altruism" holds in considerable degree for preferences in general—that these are not arbitrary or accidental, but rather the resultants of systematic evolutionary processes. This does not mean that such attitudes are now immutable. On the contrary, the inbuilt drives themselves contain the capability of expressing themselves in diverse ways depending upon environmental circumstances, which will in turn be modified by cultural evolution. The main lesson to be drawn, therefore, is not that preferences are biologically determined in any complete way—but rather, that they are scientifically analyzable and even in principle predictable in terms of the inheritance of past genetic and cultural adaptations together with the new adjustments called for by current environmental circumstances.

B. Exchange and Other Competitive Strategies

Exchange, the sole form of social interaction traditionally studied by economists, is a particular competitive strategy in the great game of life—one involving a mutually beneficial relation among two or more organisms. It fits into the more general category called "mutualism" by biologists, of which there are both interspecific and intraspecific examples. Among the former are the symbiosis of alga and fungus that constitutes a lichen, the pollination-nectar exchange between bees and flowers, the presence of nitrogen-fixing bacteria on the roots of leguminous plants, and the resident protozoa in the gut of the termite that facilitate digestion of cellulose. Particularly interesting are the complementary associations among somewhat higher animals, which can be regarded as involving a degree of conscious-

[87] James M. Buchanan, The Demand and Supply of Public Goods (1968).

ness and discretionary choice. Here mutualism approaches the economic concept of exchange.

In the absence of legal enforcement of compensation for acts conferring advantages on others, such patterns of mutual aid in the biological realm may represent instances of altruism on the part of one or more of the participants.[88] A nice example of what Trivers[89] called reciprocal altruism is the interaction wherein certain fish species feed by grooming other, larger species—who in return refrain from eating their cleaners.

The key question for the selectional advantage of such reciprocal aid (in economic terms, for the viability of a pattern of exchange or "market") is control of cheating. As Trivers points out, this is a Prisoner's Dilemma—a special case of the more general public-good situation. However great the advantage jointly to the trading pair of establishing a reciprocal relationship, it pays each member to cheat if he can. The big fish, once having been properly groomed, would seem to be in a position to profit by snapping up his helper. (The little cleaner fish often does his work actually within the mouth of his client.) On the other side of the transaction, mimics have evolved that imitate the characteristic markings of the true cleaners. Upon being permitted to approach the big fish, the mimic takes a quick bite and then escapes!

The problem here is essentially the same as the cheating, sale of "lemons," or "moral hazard" that arises in a number of market contexts.[90] While these phenomena threaten market viability, given the mutual advantage of trade the market can tolerate *some* slippage through cheating, provided it is kept within bounds.[91] A number of devices have evolved, in both market and biological contexts, to limit the degree of slippage. The market cheater may be punished by law, the mimic cleaner fish by being (with some probability) caught and eaten. Noncheaters in markets establish personal reputa-

---

[88] But even in human interactions, exchange very often takes place without legally enforceable contracts. This is true not only for trading among primitive peoples, but for highly sophisticated transactions under the most modern conditions. Stewart Macaulay, Non-contractual Relations in Business: A Preliminary Study, 28 Am. Sociol. Rev. 55 (1963). And in the sphere of "social exchange" among humans (George C. Homans, Social Behavior as Exchange, 63 Am. J. Sociol. 597 (1958)) legal enforcement is ordinarily out of the question.

[89] Robert L. Trivers, *supra* note 67. Trivers also classes alarm calls in birds under reciprocal altruism. But, as argued above (and in line with his detailed analysis), the benefit to the calling bird in no way depends upon reciprocation in the form of self-sacrificing behavior on the part of other birds. Alarm calls appear to represent incidental altruism, under the more general heading called "selfish altruism" in the previous section.

[90] See George A. Akerlof, The Market for "Lemons": Qualitative Uncertainty and the Market Mechanism, 84 Q. J. Econ. 488 (1970); Michael R. Darby & Edi Karni, Free Competition and the Optimal Amount of Fraud, 16 J. Law & Econ. 67 (1973).

[91] Richard Zeckhauser, Risk Spreading and Distribution (Aug. 1972) (Discussion paper No. 10 Kennedy Sch. Harv. U.).

28   THE JOURNAL OF LAW AND ECONOMICS

tions and brand names, while cleaner fish develop (so it is claimed) a regular clientele of satisfied customers.

Mutually advantageous exchange is facilitated by altruistic motivations; the emotions of affection and sympathy have evolved, Trivers contends, because they provide a better guarantee of reciprocity than any mere calculated advantage of doing so. Put another way, altruism economizes on costs of policing and enforcing agreements.[92]

Becker[93] has contended that sympathetic motivation may be required *only on one side* of reciprocal-altruism interactions. The other party can be quite selfish in his aims, yet may still find cooperative behavior advantageous. Consider a selfish beneficiary of a parent's benevolence: a "rotten kid." The key proposition is that the rotten kid may still act benevolently toward the parent, simply in order to maximize the latter's capacity to bestow benefits upon him. And, in these circumstances, the mutual advantage of cooperative behavior may be such that even the "unselfish" parent ends up *selfishly* better off than he would if he were not altruistic! Consequently, in biological terms, no loss of fitness on either side is involved. This altruistic "contagiousness"—unselfish motivation on one side breeding cooperative behavior on the other side—would seem to promote the evolution of mutual aid patterns. Let one party be so motivated, for whatever reason (for example, altruism on the part of the parent could evolve simply from kin selection), and we will tend to observe reciprocity and mutual aid.[94]

More generally, Trivers argues that human evolution has developed a balance between the abilities to engage in and to detect and suppress subtle cheating while participating in reciprocal interactions. The sense of justice, what Trivers calls "moralistic aggression," is an emotion that involves third parties as additional enforcers to punish cheaters. Finally, the selectional advantage of these emotions has led to evolution of the ability to simulate or mimic them—to hypocrisy. Note once again how these emotional qualities, absent from the makeup of "economic man," turn out to have an important place in the biological economy of human relationships. Economics can, as the economic imperialists allege, deal with the whole human being, and indeed *must* do so even to explain the phenomena in its traditional domain of market behavior.

----

[92] See also Mordecai Kurz, Altruistic Equilibrium (Stan. U. Inst. for Math. Stud. in Soc. Sci., Econ. Ser., Rep. No. 156, 1975).

[93] Gary S. Becker, Altruism, Egoism, and Genetic Fitness: Economics and Sociobiology, 14 J. Econ. Lit. 817 (1976).

[94] There is one important limitation, however. The benevolent party must be in a position to have the last word, the last move in the interaction. If "rotten kid" has the last free choice of action, he may ruthlessly destroy his parent (Shakespeare's Regan and Goneril in relation to King Lear), so that the interaction would not be viable in selectional terms. See J. Hirshleifer, Shakespeare vs. Becker on Altruism: The Importance of Having the Last Word, 15 J. Econ. Lit. 5 (1977).

The chief biological example of *intraspecific* exchange is of course mating interaction. Here vying for trading partners, sexual competition, not only has market parallels but is of course an important economic phenomenon in its own right. In some human societies marriage partners are explicitly sold, but more generally the marriage relationship constitutes a form of "social exchange."[95] The competition for mates in the biological realm displays many familiar and some unexpected parallels with market phenomena.

Health and vigor in sexual partners are obviously desirable qualities, correlated with the probability of generating and rearing viable offspring. As a means of demonstrating these qualities (that is, of advertising), sexual displays, combats, and rituals have developed.[96] There is a nice analogy here with recent economic theories of "competitive signalling."[97] Some characteristics may be acquired by economic agents not because they *confer* competitive superiority, but only because they *demonstrate* a preexisting superiority (in potential for mutually advantageous exchange). Just as success in display or combat, even in cases where biologically useless in itself, may signal sexual vigor—so educational attainment, even where of itself useless in contributing to productivity, may yet be a signal of useful qualities like intelligence.

Another desirable quality in a mate is possession of territory, generally by the male.[98] This is advertised in birds by the call. Presumably it is not the artistic excellence of the male's call that attracts the female, but the mere announcement effect—since the quality of the product (of the territory) is evident on inspection.[99] But for goods whose quality can be determined only by experience, the main message conveyed by advertising is simply that the product is worth the effort of advertising![100] Sexual displays seem to fall in this category.

Sexual competition also provides parallels with what is sometimes called

---

[95] An economic analysis quantifying some of the determinants of polygynous marriages appears in Amyra Grossbard, Economic Analysis of Polygyny: The Case of Maiduguri, 17 Cur. Anthrop. 701 (1976).

[96] "Advertising" is also observed in some interspecific exchanges, for example, showy flowers and fragrances designed to attract the attention of pollinating insects.

[97] See Michael Spence, Competitive and Optimal Responses to Signals: An Analysis of Efficiency and Distribution, 7 J. Econ. Theory 296 (1974); Joseph E. Stiglitz, The Theory of "Screening": Education and the Distribution of Income, 65 Am. Econ. Rev. 283 (1975); John G. Riley, Information, Screening and Human Capital, 66 Am. Econ. Rev., pt. 2, at 254 (Papers & Proceedings, May 1976).

[98] While the most obvious illustrations of sexual competition involve male competition for females, females compete for males as well. This is reasonably evident in the human species.

[99] It seems, however, that there may be some selection for excellence in the call. The reason appears to be that well-developed calls are correlated with age which is a good indicator of ability in birds. (Personal communication from M. Cody.)

[100] On this see Phillip Nelson, Information and Consumer Behavior, 78 J. Pol. Econ. 311 (1970), and especially *id.*, Advertising as Information, 82 J. Pol. Econ. 729 (1974).

"excessive" or "destructive" competition for trade. Cheating is once again a factor, as it pays males to mimic vigor by convincing displays even if they do not actually possess it. (The "coyness" of the female is said to have evolved to prevent premature commitment of her limited reproductive capacity to males with only a superficially attractive line.)[101] Sexual combats may go beyond mere demonstration and actually harm the vanquished party, or sometimes the victor as well. Biologists have devoted considerable attention to cases like the peacock, where the extreme development of sexual ornaments appears to be disfunctional to the species or even to the individual. The explanation seems to be that positive *sexual selection* can to a degree overcome a disadvantage in terms of *natural selection*—the peacock with a splendid tail does not survive so well or so long but is more likely to find a mate. Such a development requires that male ornamentation and female preference evolve in parallel, which when carried to an extreme degree may represent a rather unstable equilibrium.[102]

In economic exchange, another mechanism of competition is *entry and exit*—variation of numbers to equalize on the margin the net advantages of the various types of activity. This also operates in sexual competition; the sex ratio varies to equalize the advantage of being a male or a female! Other things equal the equilibrium male/female sex ratio is 1/1. Taking any offspring generation, exactly half its genetic endowment is provided by male parents and half by female parents. Hence, if one sex were scarcer than the other in the parent generation at mating age, its *per capita* representation in the offspring generation's genes (genetic fitness) would be greater. If the disproportion persisted, it would pay in fitness terms to have offspring of the scarcer sex, and an adaptive response in this direction would correct the disparity. Even such practices as disproportionate infanticide of females will not affect the equilibrium 1/1 ratio. (This outcome displays the power of individual as opposed to group selection, since a 1/1 ratio is not the most "efficient" from the point of view of species growth. In terms of group selection it would generally be much more desirable to have a larger proportion of females.)

One factor that does distort the equilibrium sex ratio has been described by Trivers and Willard.[103] It is nearly universal among mammals that male parents have a higher *variance* in number of offspring than female parents. (A single male can father hundreds or even thousands of offspring, but the female's reproductive capacity is much more severely limited.) Also, healthy, vigorous parents tend to have healthy, vigorous offspring and physically

---

[101] See Sociobiology, *supra* note 1, at 320.

[102] R. A. Fisher, *supra* note 10, at 152.

[103] Robert L. Trivers & Dan E. Willard, Natural Selection of Parental Ability to Vary the Sex Ratio of Offspring, 179 Science 90 (1973).

weak parents, weak offspring. Taken together, these two considerations imply that it pays stronger parents to have *male* offspring; strong male children will tend to engender a relatively larger number of descendants. Conversely, it pays weaker parents to have *female* offspring, to minimize exposure to this variance. Thus an explanation is provided for the otherwise mysterious tendency of the human male/female sex ratio to rise with socio-economic status[104] (since status tends to be correlated with health and vigor). More generally, the normally higher early male mortality is explained. Prenatal and postnatal mechanisms discriminating against males permit stronger parents (who will suffer relatively less early mortality among their offspring) to end up with relatively more male children and weaker parents with relatively more female children.

Even *interest,* Trivers[105] suggests, ultimately has a biological origin. *Reproductive value* (the average number of offspring an organism will engender in the future) declines with age in the childbearing life phase. A loan today involves a cost to the lender in fitness terms; since his reproductive value upon repayment will be less, the repayment would have to be proportionately greater to make up the difference.

So exchange in a variety of forms, and with many familiar implications, exists in the biological realm. But what does seem to be a specifically human invention is the *organized* market, a form of exchange involving "middlemen" specialized to trading activity. This must have been what Adam Smith really had in mind in his otherwise too-sweeping assertion that "the propensity to truck, barter, and exchange" is specifically associated with the human species.[106] Sexual competition and cleaning symbioses provide sufficient evidence to the contrary. And associations such as pack membership also undoubtedly involve "social exchange."

But competition for trading partners remains only one very special type of biological competition. The more general concept used by biologists is illustrated in Figure I.[107] Let N_G and N_H signify numbers of two populations G and H. Then if $\dot{N}_G$, the time-derivative of N_G, is a negative function of N_H, and N_H of N_G, the two populations are called competitors. In the diagram we

[104] Sam Shapiro, Edward R. Schlesinger & Robert L. Nesbitt, Jr., Infant, Perinatal, Maternal, and Childhood Mortality in the United States (1968).

[105] Robert L. Trivers, *supra* note 67.

[106] "It is common to all men, and to be found in no other race of animals, which seem to know neither this nor any other species of contracts." Adam Smith, *supra* note 2, at 15-18. Simmel, who adopted a broad view of exchange as equivalent to *compromise,* also regarded the process as a human invention. Georg Simmel, Conflict 115 (Kurt H. Wolff trans. 1955). But compromise surely occurs in nonhuman interactions.

[107] These curves have already been expounded and analyzed in the economic literature by Kenneth E. Boulding, A Reconstruction of Economics, *supra* note 2; *id.,* Conflict and Defense, *supra* note 6.

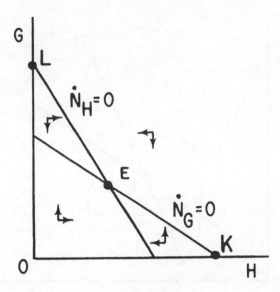

FIGURE I
Two Competitive Populations, Stable Coexistence Equilibrium

can draw for population G what the economist would call a "reaction curve" showing the population levels for which $\dot{N}_G = 0$, and similarly for population H. Since the populations are competitors, the reaction curves have negative slope. Their intersection will be a state of equilibrium. (Whether the equilibrium is stable or unstable depends upon the relative slopes at the point of intersection—as will be explored further in the next section.) If the reaction curves are *positively* sloped as in Figure II, the two populations are complementary rather than competitive. (Again, depending upon the relative slopes, the intersection point may be stable or unstable.) Finally, there is a mixed case, typified by predator-prey interactions, where the reaction curve of the predator has $\dot{N}_G$ as an increasing function of the prey population N_H, while $\dot{N}_H$ is a falling function of N_G. (Again the equilibrium at the intersection may or may not be stable.)

Competition in the general sense exists because some resource of relevance for two or more organisms is in scarce supply. The consequent *universality of competition* (the "struggle for existence") was of course the main message Darwin drew from Malthus. The ecologists speak of an organism's "fundamental niche" as the volume of abstract resource space in which it can exist—and of the "realized niche" as the volume which it actually occupies. Where niches overlap, there is competition. These considerations have one very essential implication: *that competition is generally more severe the more similar the organisms*. The more similar the organisms, the greater the niche

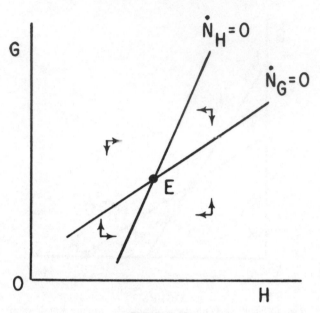

FIGURE II
Two Complementary Populations, Stable Coexistence Equilibrium

overlap. In particular, *intra*species competition tends to be more intense
than *inter*species competition.[108] For example, territorial birds exclude conspecifics but to a greater or lesser extent tolerate birds of other species. And,
we have seen, competition tends to be particularly severe within families and
especially among litter-mates; the high correlation of genetic endowments
and of positions in the generational life cycle, plus physical proximity, make
for near identity of resource requirements (niches).

There are two opposing forces which together constitute what might be
called the "dilemma of sociality." On the one hand, altruistic preferences or
motivations stem mainly from degree of relationship (from correlation of
genetic endowments), not only among close kin but extending to more dis-
tant relatives. And even, perhaps, to a degree over the entire species. (Other
things equal, a man's genes would tell him to favor his fellowman fighting
with a bear.) This is the main socializing force. On the other hand, competition, which opposes socialization, tends to be most intense precisely where
degree of relationship is closest. (The other man will often be a closer competitor than the bear.) In consequence, as organisms strike some balance

[108] Charles Darwin, The Origin of Species ch. 3 (Mentor ed. 1958) (1st ed. 1859). In exceptional cases, however, as when population density is held down by other forces such as predation, intraspecies competition may not be very severe.

between cooperative and competitive strategies, there is an element of instability in the outcome. The degree of conflict or of social cooperation is not a simple function of closeness of relationship, but depends upon the specific details of kinship as related to the environmental situation.

Competition-limiting strategies range over a spectrum, from minimal patterns of "holding back" to full cooperation. "Holding back" means that the economic unit or biological organism merely competes somewhat less intensely for resources than short-run selfish interest would dictate. An obvious economic example is cartelization, but more praiseworthy forms of holding back—for example, refraining from blowing up your competitor's premises—also fall into this category. In human societies the institutions of government and law provide reinforcers for what might otherwise be the too-frail force of altruism in limiting the extent of destructive forms of competition. Unfortunately, as evidenced most strikingly by the phenomenon of war, human genetic and cultural evolution have not progressed as far in this direction as might be desired.

Limits on competition have also evolved in the biological realm. In what is called "exploitation competition" organisms scramble to utilize resources but ignore competitors, whereas, in "interference competition," they gain resources precisely by hampering competitors.[109] Interference may take the milder form, as in territoriality, of fighting only as necessary to deny a limited zone of resource access to others. But more aggressive versions also exist, of direct attack upon conspecifics—even of cannibalism, where the competitor himself is converted into a resource. This is relatively rare, however. Presumably, extreme forms of interference strategies have mainly proved disfunctional to the groups or species evolving them, and have therefore been selected against. (*Group* selection need not be involved here, as there is a fitness loss to the individual to the extent that his own descendants are inclined to eat one another up.) Biologists have observed that interference competition is more likely to evolve when resource limitations are particularly severe. In economic affairs as well, "cut-throat competition" is a product of hard times. When organisms are occupying unfilled environments, on the other hand, or firms are interacting in a growing market, competition takes place mainly through the externality of resource depletion (in economic terms, bidding up prices of inputs or driving down prices of products).

Another important means of limiting competition is *specialization*. It is useful to distinguish the specialization that results from competitive pressure, on the one hand, from the kind of cooperative specialization more

---

[109] S. J. McNaughton & Larry L. Woolf, General Ecology ch. 11 (1973); Sociobiology, *supra* note 1, at chs. 11, 12.

properly called *the division of labor*. Unfortunately, there has been some confusion on this score. The valuable pioneering study on biology and economics by Houthakker[110] confounds the two categories. The very important analysis by the biologist Ghiselin,[111] on the other hand, distinguishes what he calls the *competitive* division of labor (represented by the subdivision of ecological niches in the biological sphere, corresponding to product or locational differentiation in the economy) from the *cooperative* division of labor. In the former case (which, preferably, ought to be termed simply competitive specialization) there is no mutual dependence or complementarity among the entities. Each would be better off if the others were to vanish. The latter type of differentiation, the division of labor proper, is associated with true alliance—to achieve a common end, or at least for mutual benefit where a degree of complementarity exists.

In competitive specialization in the biological realm, each of the contending species is forced away from the zone of resource overlap—not only in locational terms, but in the form of divergent evolution of characters. This process of character displacement, resulting in an equilibrium *separation distance* between the species,[112] is completely parallel to the economic mechanisms described in our textbooks under the heading of product-differentiation competition and locational competition ("monopolistic competition"). But on the other hand, the biologists emphasize, such specialization is constrained by the possibility that a generalist of intermediate character might outcompete the set of specialist types.[113] Relative abundance and certainty of resources favor specialists; relative scarcity and unpredictability favor generalists.

Biologists, having developed a more subtle and elaborate approach to this question of specialization/generalization strategies than economists, recognize a variety of different dimensions of "generalist" competition against specialists. Individuals of a species might tend to a common intermediate character, able to make tolerably good use of a range of resources. Or the *individuals* might be specialized, yet the *species* show enough interindividual variety to generalize its command over resources. Still another form of generalization is *plasticity,* whereby the species is enabled to change its character in response to environmental shifts.[114] Such plasticity might be genetically determined if the population maintains a reserve of variety in the

[110] Hendrik S. Houthakker, Economics and Biology: Specialization and Speciation, 9 Kyklos 181 (1956).

[111] Michael T. Ghiselin, *supra* note 4, at 233-40.

[112] S. J. McNaughton & Larry L. Woolf, *supra* note 108, at 312-24.

[113] Martin L. Cody, *supra* note 15.

[114] See the discussion of "adaptability" in George J. Stigler, The Theory of Price 129-30 (3rd ed. 1966).

form of a largely heterozygotic genetic composition. Or failing this, it may have evolved a high mutation rate as a way of tracking the environment. Finally, even with a fixed genetic constitution the capability for learning and *behavioral* adaptation may exist to a greater or lesser extent. The human species, of course, has concentrated upon becoming a generalist of this last type.

Turning now to cooperation in the true sense, we arrive at what is properly called the division of labor. Since competition is most intense when organisms are all attempting to do the *same* thing (to occupy the same niche, to use the same resources), one way out is for individuals or groups to cooperate by doing *different* things. For the group, or rather for each member thereof, command over resources is thereby extended.

The division of labor in Nature penetrates profoundly into the deepest aspects of the differentiation of living matter. In multicelled organisms the parts unselfishly cooperate to serve the whole, which is of course warranted by the fact that all the cells of an individual organism are genetically identical (save the germ cells, of course). Sexual differentiation also represents an evident instance of the cooperative division of labor in the interests of reproductive survival. Here altruism is less perfect, in that each member of the parental team is altruistic toward the other only to the extent necessary for promoting the reproductive survival of his or her own genetic endowment.[115] Nevertheless, the mechanism works well enough to have won out, for the most part, over asexual reproduction. Going beyond this most elemental social unit—the male-female pair—the *family* involves a related type of role differentiation: that associated with the generational life cycle. This provides a temporal division of labor; each generation plays its role, in due course, in promoting the reproductive survival of the parent-offspring chain. While altruism between generations is by no means unlimited, as seen above, the differentiation of tasks ties together the interests of the family group.

For larger cooperative associations, necessarily among more remotely related organisms, specialization through the division of labor with its concomitant of social exchange must, to be viable, become compensatingly productive as the force of altruism is diluted. Traditional economics, epitomized by Adam Smith, demonstrated the economic advantage of the division of labor even for a group of entirely selfish individuals. The sociologist Durkheim,[116] in contrast, claimed that the division of labor generates a kind of superorganismic "solidarity." He argued that the economic

[115] Robert L. Trivers, *supra* note 14.

[116] Emile Durkheim, On the Division of Labor in Society 39-229 (George Simpson trans. 1933).

benefits of the division of labor are picayune compared to this solidarity, a union not only of interests but of sentiments (as in the case of friends or mates). As so often occurs in social analysis, however, Durkheim fails to distinguish properly between desires (preferences) and opportunities. If there is any superorganismic tie among individuals, it can only be (according to the hypothesis accepted here) their sharing of genetic endowments. Yet in many important instances of the division of labor (for example, bees and flowers) there is no genetic association at all. The cooperative division of labor in such cases is no more than an alliance for mutual benefit. With genetic sharing it is no doubt easier for cooperation to evolve, but superorganismic ties are not sufficient causes and certainly not necessary consequences of the division of labor.

The human species, of course, has carried the division of labor to extraordinary lengths. The extent to which this represents genetic versus cultural evolution is not a simple matter to resolve. The regulation of cheating, necessary to make exchange and therefore the division of labor possible, has, as we have seen, been achieved in Nature to some degree. Even emotional supports for exchange, like the sense of justice ("moralistic aggression") may represent genetically evolved characters. On the other hand, human culture has evolved institutional supports for exchange and the division of labor—property, law, and government.

Analysis on the part of economists of the determinants of the division of labor has gone little beyond Smith's famous proposition: ". . . That the division of labour is limited by the extent of the market."[117] Houthakker,[118] taking the standpoint of the individual, views him as the potential beneficiary of a number of activities some or all of which may however be disharmonious if undertaken together. The choice to be made is for individuals either to act as nonspecialists and incur costs of internal coordination, or else to separate and distribute the activities via a division of labor that entails costs of external coordination. Here Smith's "extent of the market" is taken as the inverse of inter-individual transaction costs, the absence of which would facilitate specialization with external coordination. Stigler's analysis[119] is fundamentally similar, though concentrating on firms as decision units rather than individuals. Again there are a number of activities, all desirable or even essential in the production of output, but diverging mainly in offering economies or diseconomies of *scale*. The firms would do better to divest themselves of at least the increasing-returns activities, if a specialized external supplier were available. As the *industry* expands, such specialized

[117] Adam Smith, *supra* note 2, at 17-21.

[118] Hendrik S. Houthakker, *supra* note 109.

[119] George J. Stigler, The Division of Labor is Limited by the Extent of the Market, 59 J. Pol. Econ. 185 (1951).

suppliers become economically viable entities. Thus, for Stigler, "extent of the market" signifies *aggregate* scale of output.

The discussion by the biologist Ghiselin[120] provides many apt illustrations: for example, that an insect colony must reach a certain size before it pays to have a specialized soldier caste. But Ghiselin is inclined to stress that there are important advantages of nonspecialization, such as the existence of complementarities among certain activities (for example, teaching and research). In addition, there may be sequential rather than individual specialization, as when members of an ant colony all progress through a common series of different productive roles in the course of the life cycle.

Following up a suggestion by Ghiselin, it might really be better to think in terms of "combination of labor" rather than "division of labor." Division is the first step; it is the combination (external coordination) that produces the result. Apart from the division of labor as a form of *complementary combination* of individuals undertaking different specialized tasks, there is also the possibility of *supplementary combination* whereby individuals reinforce one another in performing the *same* task. A simple example would be men tugging on a rope to move a load; such "threshold phenomena" are quite important and widespread. Wherever scale economies for a given activity dictate a minimum efficient size greater than the full output of a single individual, we would expect to see a mixture of complementation and supplementation, of specialization and multiplication of numbers, in the general process of cooperation through the combination of labor.

A number of other dimensions of choice have been explored by biologists. One such is between "K-strategies" and "r-strategies." K symbolizes the carrying capacity of the environment, that is, the species number N^* at which the time-rate of change $\dot{N} = 0$. The symbol r signifies the maximum rate of Malthusian growth, which obtains under conditions where the environment is not constraining. The r-strategists are opportunist species, who pioneer and settle new unfilled environments. The K-strategists are solider citizens, who compete by superior effectiveness in utilizing the resources of relatively saturated environments. The r-strategists thus make their living from the recurrence of disequilibrium situations (entrepreneurial types, we would say). But their success can only be transient; ultimately they will be displaced by the more efficient K-strategist species. The r-strategists tend to be characterized by high early mortality, as they must continually disperse and take long chances of finding new unsaturated habitats. A high birth rate is therefore a necessity. Among other tendencies are rapid maturity, small body size, early reproduction, and short life. K-strategists, in contrast, tend to develop more slowly, have larger body size, and longer life.[121] Their

[120] Michael T. Ghiselin, *supra* note 4, at 233–47.
[121] Sociobiology, *supra* note 1, at 101.

inclination is to produce a smaller number of more carefully optimized off-spring.[122]

Analogs in the world of business exist for a number of these strategies. In the high-fashion industry we observe high birth rates and death rates of firms, in public utilities the reverse. In general, pioneering strategies tend to be more suitable for small firms—which survive better in highly changeable environments.

But as applied to *firms*, as emphasized previously, biological reasoning is only a metaphor. In particular, firms do not follow the reproductive laws of biology: small firms do not give birth to other small firms, and firms of one "species" (industry) may transfer to another. By way of contrast, human individuals, families, races, etc. *are* biological entities which may be re-garded as choosing competitive strategies. Martial races may concentrate on success through politics, conflict, or violence ("interference strategy"); others may have proliferated and extended their sway through high birth rates; others through lower birth rates but superior efficiency in utilizing resources ("exploitation strategy"). The *r*-strategist pioneering human type was pre-sumably selected for in the early period of American history—a period long enough for genetic evolution, though cultural adaptation may have been more important. This type was not entirely antisocial; altruist "pioneer" virtues such as mutual defense and sharing in adversity can emerge under *r*-selection. In the present more crowded conditions the preferred forms of altruism represent "urban" virtues of a negative rather than positive sort: tolerance, nonaggressiveness, and reproductive restraint.[123] Even today it seems likely that a suitable comparison of populations in environments like Alaska on the one hand and New York City on the other would reveal differential genetic (over and beyond merely cultural) adaptations.[124]

C. *The Results of Social Interaction—Equilibrium Versus Change*

Equilibrium in biology has one striking feature with no close counterpart in economics: a dualism between processes taking place simultaneously on the level of *organisms* and on the level of *genes*.

In dealing with the interactions of *organisms* the biologist generally uses a partial-equilibrium model, taking genetic compositions as fixed. He then

---

[122] Compare the discussion of "high-quality" and "lower quality" children in Gary S. Becker, An Economic Analysis of Fertility, in Demographic and Economic Change in Developed Countries ([Univ.] Nat'l Bur. Econ. Res., 1960); Marc Nerlove, Household and Economy: Toward a New Theory of Population and Economic Growth, 82 J. Pol. Econ. 200 (1974).

[123] Sociobiology, *supra* note 1, at 107-08.

[124] Many such associations of human genetic types with historical and geographical deter-minants are elaborated in Ellsworth Huntington, Mainsprings of Civilization (1945). While his work remains highly controversial, and not all of his instances are convincing, that some racial characters are indeed adaptive (for example, the dark skin of Africans, the body shape of Eskimos) is evident.

asks such questions as: (1) For a given species G, what will be the limiting population number in a particular environment (the "carrying capacity" of the environment for that species)? (2) Or, with two or more interacting populations, G and H, what will be their respective equilibrium numbers N_G and N_H. And, in particular, will one drive the other to extinction, or might they even *both* become extinct? (The last possibility may seem surprising. Yet a predator might conceivably be so efficient as ultimately to wipe out its prey, in which case its own extinction may follow.) (3) Where new species may enter an environment by migration, thus offsetting loss of species from extinction, what is the equilibrium number of distinct species, and how do the species partition the total biomass?

To take up the second of these three questions, it was remarked above that the intersection of the two reaction curves of Figure I (two competitive populations) might be a stable or an unstable equilibrium point. It will be evident, by consideration of the nature of the interaction (as illustrated by the arrows showing the directions of change of the two populations from any N_G, N_H point in the positive quadrant), that the intersection equilibrium as shown is stable. Thus, we have here a coexistence solution at point E. If the labels on the reaction curves were reversed, however, it may be verified (by making appropriate changes in the arrows showing the directions of change) that the coexistence equilibrium would be unstable. Depending upon the initial situation, population H would drive G to extinction at point K, or population G would drive H to extinction at point L.

A similar analysis of the complementary populations in Figure II will show that the coexistence equilibrium at point E is again stable. But if the labels on the reaction curves were reversed, the populations would jointly (depending upon the starting point) either decay toward zero or explode toward infinity. (Of course, in the latter case another branch of at least one of the reaction curves would eventually be encountered, beyond which the rate of change of population would again become negative.)

The arrows of directional change in the predator-prey diagram of Figure III show that a kind of spiral or cobweb exists around the intersection point E. Depending upon the slopes of the curves, the cobweb could: (a) repeat itself indefinitely, (b) converge to the coexistence equilibrium at E, or (c) oscillate explosively. In the latter case the result may be extinction of the predator (if the spiral first hits the prey axis, since the prey can continue to survive without the predator), or the extinction of both (if the spiral first hits the predator axis, in the case where the predator cannot continue to survive without prey). The theoretical tendency of predator-prey interactions toward cycles in population numbers has in fact been confirmed in empirical observations.[125]

[125] S. J. McNaughton & Larry L. Wolf, *supra* note 108, at ch. 10.

ECONOMICS FROM A BIOLOGICAL VIEWPOINT   41

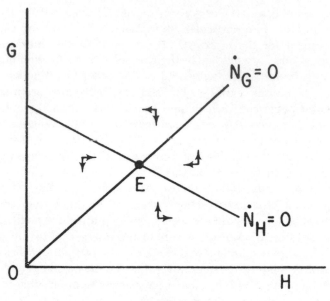

FIGURE III
Predator-Prey Interaction

These models have rather direct analogies with a number of processes in the realm of the human sciences. The reaction-curve format closely parallels Lewis F. Richardson's models of arms races[126] and Lanchester's equations of combat.[127] Economists will of course recognize the duopoly solutions associated with Cournot.[128]

Biological models of equilibrium on the *genetic* level are again of a partial-equilibrium nature, since they typically involve only processes within a single population. The simplest version of such models is known as the Hardy-Weinberg Law. If at a particular gene locus two alleles A and a exist, under sexual reproduction there are three possible genotypes: AA, Aa, and aa. With random mating, if selective and other pressures determine the proportions p and q (where $p + q = 1$) for the prevalence of alleles A and a respectively, then the equilibrium proportions for the genotypes will be p^2 for AA, $2pq$ for Aa, and q^2 for aa. This equilibrium is reached extremely

---

[126] Lewis F. Richardson, Variation of the Frequency of Fatal Quarrels with Magnitude, 43 J. Am. Stat. A. 523 (1948). See, on this, Anatol Rapoport, Fights, Games, and Debates ch. 1 (1960). Some extensions are provided in Kenneth E. Boulding, Conflict, *supra* note 6, at chs. 2, 4, 6. Kenneth E. Boulding, Reconstruction, *supra* note 2, proposed that these models serve as the core of an "ecological" reorientation of economics.

[127] See F. W. Lanchester, Aircraft in Warfare (1916); Philip M. Morse & George E. Kimball, Methods of Operation Research (1951).

[128] See R. G. D. Allen, Mathematical Analysis for Economists 200-04 (1938).

rapidly, in fact—apart from random fluctuations—in the first filial generation.[129]

The proportions p and q will not in general remain stable, however. They are affected by mutation (A may change into a, and vice versa), by gene flow due to migration, by random fluctuation ("genetic drift"), and most importantly by natural and sexual selection associated with differing fitnesses of the three genotypes.

Selection operates on the gene proportions through differential survival of the phenotypes. A *dominant* deleterious (low-fitness) gene will tend to be extinguished relatively rapidly, in terms of generational time. But a *recessive* deleterious allele expresses itself as a phenotype only in the case of the *aa* genotype, and so tends to be eliminated only slowly. There may be other complicating features. For example, the allele causing human sickle-cell anemia is a recessive lethal in the homozygote (*aa*) form, but tends to confer a degree of immunity against malaria in the heterozygote (*Aa*) form. Where malaria is a serious cause of reduced fitness, the *a*-type allele will not be eliminated.[130]

"Genetic drift" occurs because the actual numbers of the phenotypes *AA, Aa,* and *aa* will differ stochastically to a greater or lesser degree from the respective mean values p^2, $2pq$, and q^2. The most important consequence is a tendency toward the loss of heterozygosity, that is, genetic drift tends ultimately to fix a single allele in the population. Genetic drift operates more powerfully upon smaller populations, of course, and elimination obviously is much more likely to occur for an allele that is already rare. Note that even a superior-fitness allele, if sufficiently rare, might well be eliminated by stochastic fluctuations. (It was genetic drift that was called on above to explain the occasional fixing of low-individual-fitness "altruist" genes in some populations.)

Somewhat tenuous analogies exist between genes and ideas, between mutation and invention, etc.[131] A human population might increase fitness by "mutations" like a new form of social organization or the invention of a new tool or weapon. And ideas, like genes, are subject to the selectional test of competition. But the laws of the generation and propagation of ideas are so different from those of genes that the comparison does not really seem fruitful.

Some broader parallels might still be of interest, however. Sexual reproduction may be interpreted as a device that (among other things) provides populations with a *reserve of variability of characters*. Heterozygosity makes

---

[129] 1 William Feller, An Introduction to Probability Theory and its Applications 94-95 (1950).

[130] Edward O. Wilson & William H. Bossert, *supra* note 34, at 68-70.

[131] See Kenneth E. Boulding, *supra* note 2, at 7.

a range of different phenotypes available for selection in each generation, thus permitting the tracking of environmental shifts while delaying the loss of potential characters that might turn out to be useful in the future. Asexual organisms, lacking this reserve of variability, are more vulnerable to environmental shifts. In effect, sexual reproduction provides species with "memory," though at the cost of some loss of efficiency. In each generation, as was seen above, each of the combinations *AA, Aa,* and *aa* will generally be "recalled" and tried again—so long as $0 < p < 1$. And in actuality, more than two alleles are often "stored" at a given locus, and in addition there may exist other, more complex forms of genetic recombination or recall. The widened opportunities provided by sexual reproduction are related to the issue of satisficing versus optimizing discussed at several points previously. In the absence of "memory" of alternative possibilities, a biological entity could not successfully stray very far from any current combination that leads to even minimally satisfactory outcomes—since it cannot remember anything old, it can scarcely afford to learn something new. The mental development of the human species, culminating in speech and writing, has permitted the vast development of *cultural* memory independent of genetic storage of variability, thus widening the ability to explore alternatives and approach closer to true optimization.

Another feature that operates to store variety in the economic system is *the law of diminishing returns*, in its various forms. Rising marginal cost tends to lead to interior or coexistence solutions; entities or forms of organization that are favored by environmental changes tend to increase in prevalence, but not ordinarily so totally as to drive out all others. Thus, a capacity for rapid response to change tends to be preserved.[132] The concept corresponding to diminishing returns in biology is called "density dependence," though biologists tend to call upon this mainly to explain why single populations do not increase without limit.[133] With respect to competing populations the biologists have a proposition that seems to run counter to diminishing returns in economics—Gause's Exclusion Principle. The idea is that no two species that fill the same ecological niche can permanently coexist.[134] Here, at least, it would seem that the biologists can learn from us. Because of diminishing returns to any form of expansion (density-dependent effects), coexistence equilibria in the same niche should be perfectly possible. Ultimately, the same forces preventing a single *organism* from monopolizing a

---

[132] On the other hand, the less stringent inheritance process in economics—the ability of a "mutation" to spread by mere imitation—means that storage of alternative productive techniques or forms of organization is not so vital.

[133] Edward O. Wilson & William H. Bossert, *supra* note 34, at 106-09.

[134] *Id.* at 156-58.

niche against conspecifics also tends to control the expansion of the species as a whole against its competitors.[135]

Biologists, as compared with economists, seem to devote relatively more effort to the description of processes of ongoing *change* as opposed to processes leading to *equilibrium* in the sense of stationary states. This is historically understandable, in that modern biology was faced at the outset with the great polemical problem of winning public acceptability for the fact of evolutionary change. In consequence, perhaps, biologists do not seem to have developed (or at any rate do not pay much attention to) concepts of *general* equilibrium. They do not seem, to cite one example, to have felt the need for integrating the two partial-equilibrium developments described above—one on the level of population numbers, the second on the level of genetic composition. On the other hand, they have developed models showing the working of a rich variety of mechanisms of change—mutation and recombination, selection and migration, learning, genetic drift, etc.—as well as useful generalizations concerning the extent and prevalence of certain patterned responses to change such as mimicry, convergence, character release, speciation, and the like.

Related to the intellectual problem of the relative importance of equilibrium versus change is an issue that has concerned both disciplines—the question that biologists call teleology. In Panglossian terms, is this the best of all possible worlds? Or, if not the best just yet, does our world at least progress toward such a desirable goal?

In biology, the teleological theme seems to underlie the concluding sentence of *The Origin of Species*:

Thus, from the war of nature, from famine and death, the most exalted object which we are capable of conceiving, namely, the production of the higher animals, directly follows. There is grandeur in this view of life, with its several powers having been originally breathed by the Creator into a few forms or into one; and that, whilst this planet has gone cycling on according to the fixed law of gravity, from so simple a beginning endless forms most beautiful and most wonderful have been, and are being evolved.[136]

Darwin's language suggests, though it does not quite say, that evolution is directed by some higher force and that its results represent in some sense progress. Herbert Spencer and others went further to develop an evolutionist ethics—moral conduct is *defined* as that which contributes to better adaptation and progress toward higher forms. T. H. Huxley, Darwin's great sup-

---

[135] While the law of diminishing returns makes coexistence equilibrium *possible,* corner solutions are not necessarily ruled out.

[136] Charles Darwin, *supra* note 107.

ECONOMICS FROM A BIOLOGICAL VIEWPOINT   45

porter, declared: "The absolute justice of the system of things is as clear to me as any scientific fact."[137]

The alternative mechanistic view, that evolution is an entirely undirected process, is almost universally and emphatically postulated by modern biologists.[138] Ghiselin[139] contends further that hidden teleology lurks wherever adaptation is explained in such terms as "the good of the species" or "the good of the community." But this accusation does not seem warranted. The scientific question is simply whether the mechanistic processes of evolution can lead to the emergence of characters benefiting larger groups although harming the individual bearer. That this is at least possible, as in the devotion of parents to offspring, can scarcely be denied. More generally, the genetic-relationship argument for altruism (kin selection) shades gradually in diluted form to groups up to the level of the species, and possibly beyond. Since Nature does select simultaneously on both the organism and the gene level—and on higher population and community levels as well— and since groups of genes or groups of individuals may become coadapted in a variety of ways and so coselected, it would seem that some of Nature's productions could validly be interpreted as responding to "the good of the group" rather than solely of the organism (or the gene).

Yet, it is evident, the argument of "perfection" does not hold with any force above the organism level. The many forms of destructive competition in Nature—from sexual combats within species to predation between species—preclude any inference of a universal harmonious adaptation to the nonliving environment.[140] Still, it seems that there may be at least some slow long-run pressure in this direction.[141]

A related question is the degree to which *cultural* evolution, which necessarily concerns group rather than individual traits, is adaptive. Again, one can hardly make any strong arguments for perfection of cultural adaptation. And yet, selection processes are certainly at work which tend to destroy societies that have somehow evolved seriously maladapted cultures.[142]

[137] Quoted in Gertrude Himmelfarb, *supra* note 5, at 382. Huxley was later to totally reverse his position, going on to argue that ethical progress required *combating* the natural tendency of the cosmic processes. *Id.* at 385.

[138] Mechanism is not, any more than its opposite (the postulate of design or purposiveness) a scientifically provable proposition. It is a working hypothesis.

[139] Michael T. Ghiselin, *supra* note 4.

[140] See Gordon Tullock, *supra* note 41.

[141] H. E. Frech, III, Biological Externalities and Evolution: A Comment, 39 J. Theoret. Biology 669 (1973). One possible instance is the tendency of disease parasites to evolve in the direction of reduced virulence (Sociobiology, *supra* note 1, at 116). It is sometimes contended that the beneficial bacteria living within our bodies have evolved from harmful ones.

[142] See Alexander Alland, Jr., *supra* note 27, at 171; Sociobiology, *supra* note 1, at 560;

The main classical tradition in economics has similarly been subjected to criticism on grounds of teleology. Adam Smith's view,[143] that under laissez-faire an "invisible hand" leads to a kind of *harmony* of private interests, has been attacked as apologetics for the capitalist system—as a tendentious attempt to prove that what exists is indeed the best of all possible worlds. Setting questions of motivation aside, it is indeed true that much of the intellectual effort of modern theorizing has gone into proving social optimality—in the very special sense of *Pareto-optimality*—of idealized versions of the laissez-faire capitalist economy. (Or, in some cases, of the welfare-state or even the socialist economy!) More specifically, what has been shown is that the equilibrium outcome under an unregulated economy with fully defined property rights is a social optimum in the sense that it would not be possible to improve the situation of any individual (in his own eyes) without harming one or several individuals (in their own eyes).

However, these results might equally well be interpreted as anti-apologetics. For, the idealized conditions necessary to make them valid evidently do not fully apply to any actual capitalist (or welfare-state or socialist) economy. And in fact, economists have devoted major energy to examination of forces leading to failures of Pareto-optimality—natural monopoly, oligopoly, externalities, and public goods being leading examples.

The lack of the institution of *property*—founded, in turn, upon the larger institutions of *law* and *government*—in the economy of Nature is an important element explaining the "imperfection" of social adaptations in the biological realm. Some observers have regarded animal *territoriality* as closely analogous to property, but this is incorrect. Territory in Nature is held only so long as it is continuously and effectively defended by the force of its possessor. Property does sometimes need to be defended by force, but what makes it property is the availability of impersonal enforcement through the law of the community.[144] To the extent that the property system is effective, a degree of progressive cultural adaptation tends to take place over time. Individuals need not expend energy in combat or other contests for possession, but are instead motivated to search out mutually advantageous ways of employing property so as to achieve a more complete division of

---

Ronald Cohen, *supra* note 63; William H. Durham, Resource Competition and Human Aggression, Part I: A Review of Primitive War, 51 Q. Rev. Biology 385 (1976).

[143] "By pursuing his own interest he frequently promotes that of the society more effectually than when he really intends to promote it." Adam Smith, *supra* note 2, at 423.

[144] Melvin C. Fredlund, Wolves, Chimps and Demsetz, 14 Econ. Inquiry 279 (1976) claims to have found that property in this sense does exist, at least in primitive form, in some animal communities.

ECONOMICS FROM A BIOLOGICAL VIEWPOINT   47

labor. In particular, they are motivated to find ways around the failures of Pareto-optimality mentioned above.[145]

Yet, lest this seem too unguardedly hopeful, it must be pointed out that the institutions of law and government are powerful mechanisms that may be employed to achieve many private or group ends quite apart from Pareto-optimality. Law and government may destroy some individuals for the benefit of others, may penalize rather than promote the division of labor, may undermine rather than support the institution of property. Nor can we say on scientific grounds that law and government "ought not" do so. But to the extent that they do not, the progress of adaptation to the environment will be hampered or even reversed.

V. POINTS OF COMPARISON—A TABULAR VIEW

Tables 1 and 2 have been designed as a way of pulling together, without undue repetition, the strands of the preceding discussions. The first table is an attempt to systematize, in a comparative way, the entities or units of action as viewed by biologists and by economists. The second table is intended to display, again in a comparative way, the *processes* of action and interaction involving these entities.

For the economist the fundamental acting unit or agent is of course the *individual*. Individuals organize into many types of composite units for purposes of joint action—these are the "Cooperative Groups" in Table 1. A useful though somewhat rough distinction can be made between "unselfish" groupings, whose dominant feature is the existence of altruistic preference functions connecting the goals of the members, and "selfish" aggregations where cooperative action is motivated only by mutual anticipation of selfish gain.

The family is of course the standard example of a supposedly "unselfish" grouping. As explained at length above, some or all participating family members may actually be motivated to a greater or lesser degree by considerations of personal advantage rather than by other-regarding love and concern. But for the most part, family associations respond to supra-individual goals (kin selection). A variety of other communal associations ("brotherhoods")—social, religious, and the like—also exist, at least purportedly, to unite the members thereof in unselfish fellowship.

Economics, in contrast with other social sciences, has concentrated attention upon the "selfish" associations in the next line of the Table. These include *alliances* of all sorts: the firm in the realm of economics, the gang for criminal activity, political parties and other associations for achieving or

145 R. H. Coase, The Problem of Social Cost, 3 J. Law & Econ. 1 (1960).

TABLE 1
ACTING ENTITIES, UNITS, AND GROUPS

	ECONOMIC SYSTEM	BIOLOGICAL SYSTEM A	BIOLOGICAL SYSTEM B
AGENTS	Individuals	Organisms	Genes
COOPERATIVE GROUPS			
"Unselfish"	Families, "brotherhoods"	Reproductive associations	(None)
"Selfish"	Firms, parties and other political associations, gangs, exchange associations	Packs, mutualists	Organisms, chromosomes and other gene linkages
COMPETITIVE CLUSTERS	Industries, crafts and professions, other contending sets (of gangs, parties, nations, etc.)	Sexes, species, set of niche competitors	Set of alleles, of genotypes
UNIVERSAL GROUP	Society	Biota	Gene pool

exercising power. "Exchange associations" are links in the division of labor. Just as the "unselfish" associations are in fact not completely so, similarly the "selfish" combinations typically have and may indeed require a certain social cement in the form of feelings of fraternity and community (altruism). This cement is perhaps least binding in the case of exchange associations, but even there at least a simulation of uncalculated fellowship between the parties may be essential for good business. While the state or polity falls into the "selfish" grouping, its survival in the face of military competition probably requires a high degree of unselfish patriotic sentiment.

The next major heading represents "Competitive Clusters." The term, for lack of a better, is intended to represent aggregations of units that are mainly *striving against* rather than *cooperating with* one another. Here there may be no sense of actual association on the part of the participants, the cluster being merely a discrete *classification* as viewed by an observer. Such an aggregate of closely competing firms we call an industry, of competing workers a craft or profession, etc. We lack accepted single words for clusters of competing gangs, of competing parties and political associations, of competing nations, etc. (Sometimes we refer to them as the players in the political game, the diplomatic game, and so forth.) The members of cooperating groups may do *different* things, so as to complement one another; or they do the same thing, where scale economies make supplementation a more advantageous cooperation technique than complementation. But members of competitive clusters are trying to do the same thing in a rivalrous sense, in a

ECONOMICS FROM A BIOLOGICAL VIEWPOINT 49

context where the success of one entity to some extent precludes that of others.

Here again, the distinction is not always so sharp. Contending groups or individuals generally have some mutual interest in limiting at least the degree of competition. They are better able to find this opportunity for mutual gain if an element of "brotherhood" is thought to exist among the competitors. Trade unions (often actually called "brotherhoods") call on class sentiment to limit the competition among workers.

Finally, at the bottom line we have the "Universal Group"—society itself. Society as an entirety is a complex structure of cooperating and competing elements.

In the biological realm, as was indicated earlier, there are two interwoven *systems* of thinking—here simple denoted *A* and *B*. In *A* the organism is the fundamental unit, in *B* it is the gene. In system *A* the egg serves to reproduce the chicken, in system *B* the chicken is the means of reproducing the egg (that is, the gene). Genes are chemical units that have somehow evolved ways of reproducing themselves. (Not that they "want" to do so, of course, but rather that once self-reproduction somehow came about it tended to be selected by Nature for survival.) In system *A* there are "unselfish" (kin-selected) cooperative groupings like the family, here more abstractly called reproductive associations. But in system *B* there are no "unselfish" genes!

Now consider the "selfish" cooperative groupings of individual organisms in system *A*—packs or other alliances (within or between species) whose members gain by mutual association in feeding or defense or reproduction. The leading analog in system *B* is the *organism* itself. That is, the individual organism represents a kind of alliance of the various genes making up its genetic endowment! As a rather less important point, study of the details of the process of genetic reproduction reveals that the genes are themselves not isolated but are organized into chromosomes and other linkages whose prospects for reproduction are connected in various ways.

The most obvious instance of the "Competitive Cluster" category in system *A* is the species itself—regarded as the aggregate of its competing individual members. While competition is severest within a species, interspecific competition also occurs where the potential niches of different species overlap. Each *sex* also represents a competitive cluster (that is, all males compete against one another, as do all females) within a sexually reproducing species. In system *B* the set of competing alleles at a given locus, and the set of alternative genotypes, are instances of competitive clusters. Finally, the "Universal Group" is the entire biota in system *A*. In system *B* the gene pool represents the universe in which various forms of cooperation and competition may take place.

In Table 2 the chief point of interpretation to be emphasized is that the

50   THE JOURNAL OF LAW AND ECONOMICS

TABLE 2
PROCESSES AND RELATIONSHIPS

	ECONOMIC SYSTEM	BIOLOGICAL SYSTEM
OBJECTIVE FUNCTION	Subjective preferences ("tastes")	Reproductive survival ("fitness")
PRINCIPLE OF ACTION	Optimization [alternatively, "satisficing"]	"As if" optimization
OPPORTUNITIES	Production Exchange via market Crime, war Family formation	Exploitation of resources Mutualism Predation, war Reproduction
PRINCIPLE OF COMPETITIVE SELECTION	Economic efficiency	Superior "fitness"
PRINCIPLES OF EQUILIBRIUM		
a) Short-run	Markets cleared	?
b) Long-run	Zero-profit	Reproductive ratio = 1
c) Very long-run	Stationary state	Saturated environment
"PROGRESS"	Accumulation, technological advance	Evolution: improved adaptation via mutation, recombination, migration, drift, and behavioral adjustment
SOCIAL OPTIMALITY CONCEPTS	Pareto-optimality	None (?)

biological processes and mechanisms represent more general classes into which the economic ones fall as particular instances. Where standard economics takes the satisfaction of preferences as the primitive objective or "utility function" of the acting individuals, biological theory suggests that what seems like mere preference or taste evolves out of the objective dictates of reproductive survival. As to the principle of action or behavior, the process of calculated optimization postulated in standard economics can be regarded as a special instance of the uncalculated "as if" optimization dictated by the selective forces of Nature. The thrust of the "satisficing" controversy in descriptive economics is that, even in the economic sphere, explicit optimization cannot always serve as the principle of action.

The *opportunities* available to organisms in the biological realm can be categorized in ways that seem familiar to the economist. Exploitation of resources is akin to production; mutualism corresponds to exchange; predation and war have obvious analogs in human society. Biology's emphasis on reproduction corresponds to the range of choices involved in family formation in the social context.

In terms of selective processes at work, the biological environment chooses for superior fitness, the analog being superior economic efficiency in the processes studied by standard economics. However, since economic efficiency is not propagated by mechanisms closely analogous to inheritance in biology, the processes of competition in the two areas are not closely comparable.

Economics distinguishes three levels of equilibrium: (1) short-run exchange equilibrium (market-clearing); (2) long-run entry/exit equilibrium, in which there is no longer any net advantage from redirection of resources (zero-profit condition); and (3) a hypothetical very long-run stationary state where there is no longer any advantage to the formation of new resources (by accumulation). There seems to be no close analog in biology to the short-run concept. The equivalent of the long-run equilibrium condition of economics can be taken to be the biological situation where each type of population (on the organism level) or each type of allele (on the genetic level) has a reproductive ratio ("fitness") equal to unity. And one can also imagine a hypothetical very-long-run equilibrium condition in which the environment is so totally saturated as to leave no niche for the formation of new life entities.

"Progress" takes place in the economy in two main ways: accumulation of resources by saving and technological advance. In biology the analogous process is of course *evolution*, the improvement of adaptation to environment by a variety of processes.

Finally, we have the question of social optimality. In biology, the standard mechanistic view seems to leave no room for such a concept. In economics we have the one rather debatable, and in any case highly limited, criterion of Pareto-optimality. While Pareto-optimality is usually regarded as a normative concept, it does have positive content in one respect—that there is at least a weak tendency in the competitive economy to move toward Pareto-optimal outcomes. Despite the "teleological" ring of the argument, it is conceivable that a similar tendency, toward solving the Prisoners' Dilemma by arriving at cooperative rather than conflictual outcomes, may be operating, however weakly, in the biological realm.

VI. ECONOMY, BIOLOGY, AND SOCIETY

I have tried here to trace some of the implications of Alfred Marshall's view that economics is a branch of biology. Or, in more sweeping terms, of the contention that the social sciences generally can fruitfully be regarded as the sociobiology of the human species.[146] Yet, at the same time, it was suggested, we might well claim that certain laws of the economizing

---

[146] Compare Sociobiology, *supra* note 1, at ch. 27, and E. O. Wilson, Biology, *supra* note 1.

process—optimization on the individual level, and equilibrium on the societal level—apply to biology as well.[147] Viewed this way, economics can be regarded as the general field, whose two great subdivisions consist of the natural economy studied by the biologists and the political economy studied by economists proper.[148] Considerable light has been shed, I believe, upon many of the questions and results of the social sciences. These involve broad issues like the provenance of tastes (including, what is particularly essential for social processes, individuals' "taste" for *altruism*), the balance between optimization and selection in governing social outcomes, the forces favoring cooperation versus conflict as competitive strategies in social interaction, and the determinants of specialization in human productive activities. And some specific phenomena as well: the correlation of the male/female sex ratio with socioeconomic status, the recent tendency to have smaller numbers of "higher-quality" children, the predominance of small firms in transient economic environments, positive interest or time-preference, and minimum separation distances in locational or product-differentiation situations.

It was not very debatable, perhaps, that the sociobiological approach does have *some* utility for social science purposes. But how much? The central question is whether or not the human species has entered a new domain of experience where general biological laws will have only negligible relevance or have even been abolished by the unique developmental advances achieved by mankind. Among such might be included: (1) the transcending importance of cultural as opposed to genetic change; (2) the degree of intelligence and awareness, suggesting that man can henceforth regulate and control the evolutionary process by deliberate cultural and even genetic modifications of the human material itself—quite apart from operations on the environment; (3) the invention of weapons of intraspecies competition that threaten the survival of all mankind; and (4) what might hopefully be a countervailing factor, man's possession of moral, spiritual, and ethical values.

At this point it is possible only to pose the question, not to answer it. In terms of the proximate goal of research strategy, perhaps it is sufficient to say that the sociobiological approach holds out great hope for breaking down not only the "vertical" discontinuity between the sciences of human behavior and more fundamental studies of life but also the "horizontal" barriers among the various social studies themselves.

[147] See Martin L. Cody, *supra* note 15; David J. Rapport & James E. Turner, *supra* note 3.
[148] Michael T. Ghiselin, *supra* note 4.

[16]

The Origin of Predictable Behavior

By Ronald A. Heiner*

Despite vigorous counterargument by its proponents, optimization theory has been persistently attacked as an acceptable explanation of behavior. In one form or another, these attacks repeat the oldest critique of economics; namely, the ability of agents to maximize successfully. Over the years, this critique has taken various forms which include information processing limitations in computing optima from known preference or utility information, unreliable probability information about complex environmental contingencies, and the absence of a well-defined set of alternatives or consequences, especially in an evolving world that may produce situations that never before existed.

These complaints are not new to economics. Indeed, they have been present during the very intellectual sifting process that produced neoclassical optimization and general equilibrium theory. Thus, if we are to further elaborate this critique of conventional theory, the basic issue is whether there is anything new that is worthy of attention by someone well versed in standard tools and concepts. Are we simply advancing more refined or cleverly argued versions of older critiques, or extensions of them to areas not previously emphasized?

*Department of Economics, Brigham Young University, Provo, UT 84602. I am indebted to Axel Leijonhufvud for constant encouragement about applications to economics, and for numerous stylistic suggestions. Harold Miller helped familiarize me with a broad range of issues across the sociobiological, psychological, and behavioral science literatures. James Buchanan provided stimulating discussion about conceptual issues. I have also benefited from the advice and criticism of Armen Alchian, Ron Batchelder, Bruce Brown, Robert Clower, Daniel Friedman, Jack Hirshleifer, Kai Jeanski, Randy Johnson, Edward Leamer, Stephen Littlechild, John McCall, James McDonald, Richard Nelson, Gerald O'Driscoll, Dennis Packard, Clayne Pope, Lionello Punzo, Ezio Tarantelli, and Sidney Winter. Needless to say, these colleagues are not responsible for inadequacy in the conceptual framework or scope of ideas presented.

Such arguments would still represent an attack on the basic rationality postulate of economics (that agents are able to maximize), but without providing a clear alternative to traditional optimization theory. However plausible these arguments might be, ultimately they must be set aside by someone desiring a theoretical understanding of behavior, unless they lead to another modeling structure whose analytical ability can be explored and compared with existing optimization theory.

Another argument focuses on the desire to understand the "real" dynamic processes that actually generate observed behavior. In contrast, optimization is thought of as a surrogate theory based on false assumptions about agents' capacity to maximize. Thus, it can be defended only in terms of empirical testability, without really illuminating the underlying processes determining behavior.

Nevertheless, even if this view was fully accepted, it is unlikely by itself to cause a major shift away from conventional thinking. The reason is that evolutionary processes have long ago been interpreted as one of the key mechanisms tending to produce optimizing behavior; or conversely, optimizing models will predict the behavior patterns that will survive in an evolutionary process tending to select relatively superior performance.[1] The latter interpretation is in fact one of the dominant justifications for standard models against the criticism of unrealistic assumptions (i.e., the surviving agents of a selection process will behave "as if" they are able to maximize).[2]

[1] See in particular Armen Alchian's well-known 1950 paper, and also Sidney Winter, 1964, 1971; Jack Hirshleifer, 1977; Richard Nelson and Winter, 1974.

[2] A still used reference on the "as if" point of view is Milton Friedman's 1953 paper. Some recent journal illustrations are Benjamin Klein and Keith Leffler, 1981, p. 634; Richard Posner, 1980, p. 5; Hirshleifer, 1977, p. 50; Nelson, 1981, p. 1059. The ultimate extension of this view is to claim not that agents are able to maximize (select most preferred actions), but rather that any ob-

In spite of the above conclusions, I believe there is a viable alternative to standard models—one that directly comes to grips with the persistent critiques of economic theory and which broadens our analytical horizon to encompass a much wider range of phenomena.

In particular, I believe that observed regularities of behavior can be fruitfully understood as "behavioral rules" that arise because of uncertainty in distinguishing preferred from less-preferred behavior. Such uncertainty requires behavior to be governed by mechanisms that restrict the flexibility to choose potential actions, or which produce a selective alertness to information that might prompt particular actions to be chosen. These mechanisms simplify behavior to less-complex patterns, which are easier for an observer to recognize and predict. In the special case of no uncertainty, the behavior of perfectly informed, fully optimizing agents responding with complete flexibility to every perturbation in their environment would not produce easily recognizable patterns, but rather would be extremely difficult to predict. Thus, it is in the limits to maximizing that we will find the origin of predictable behavior.

If the view taken here is correct, it means that predictable features of behavior do not arise from optimizing with no uncertainty in choosing most preferred behavior; and furthermore, evolutionary selection processes will in general not produce approximations to optimizing behavior. Rather, predictable behavior will evolve only to the extent that uncertainty prevents agents from successfully maximizing.

In the following, I sketch the line of thought and the observations which have led me to this conclusion, and briefly outline the elements of a modeling structure that can be applied to a wide range of topics. A number of applications are presented to illustrate the range of issues unified by the analysis, which

is far broader than the reader is likely to anticipate without explicit examples.

I. Problems with the Methodological Arguments for Optimization

Optimizing with full ability to select most preferred behavior is rarely justified as an empirically realistic assumption. Rather, it is usually defended on methodological grounds as the appropriate theoretical framework for analyzing behavior. The chief defense is empirical fruitfulness in generating unfalsified predictions.

We might criticize this testability criteria with modern philosophy of science arguments.[3] Nevertheless, a long list of confirmed predictions would be persuasive evidence in favor of a theory. Yet, it is just here that we have a problem. Suppose we really asked to see the list of clearly implied, unambiguous predictions that have been derived from our basic optimization models.

The answer to this query, one that would be admitted by many practitioners in the field, is that at best we have developed a very short list. All sorts of behavior is consistent with or plausibly suggested by optimization models, yet still not predicted by them. For example, optimization models have never been able to imply the Law of Demand (buying less of a commodity when its price rises), which is probably the oldest and simplest behavioral regularity in economics. Of course, we can use the theory to argue it is unlikely that a negative income effect will outweigh the pure substitution effect, especially for goods that absorb a small fraction of a person's income.[4] The acceptance of this view is heavily influenced by our belief in the

---

[3] See for example, B. Caldwell, 1982; also Karl Popper, 1969; Imer Lakatos and Alice Musgrave, 1970.

[4] I was told in a graduate price-theory class by Armen Alchian that the only clear implication of consumer theory is that with more income, a consumer will buy more of at least something. Harold Demsetz, when informed of this story, responded by saying, "well then just define holding cash balances as saving, and we have no testable implications, just one mass of tautologies." See also the opening remarks of Kenneth Arrow, 1982, p. 1; and the closing remarks of Vernon Smith, 1982, p. 952.

---

served behavior is consistent with the maximization of some function. This latter formulation is probably incapable of either theoretical or empirical disproof (see Lawrence Boland, 1981).

562 *THE AMERICAN ECONOMIC REVIEW* *SEPTEMBER 1983*

empirical validity of the Law of Demand. Yet, regardless of how cleverly we interpret a Slutsky equation, no clear prediction is implied.

We could pursue a number of other examples, all of which suggest that conventional models have never really been fruitful in generating testable implications.[5] For this reason, I believe allegiance to these models is not grounded in the claim of empirical fruitfulness, despite the usual rhetoric that this is the case. Rather, it is based on a deeper methodological issue about the effect of dropping the basic rationality assumption.[6]

Think of this issue in the following terms. Standard choice theory tries to explain behavior by matching the "competence" of an agent with the "difficulty" in selecting most preferred alternatives. It assumes for the purpose of theoretical explanation that there is no gap between an agent's competence and the difficulty of the decision problem to be solved (hereafter called a "*C-D* gap").[7] On the other hand, the presence of a *C-D* gap will introduce uncertainty in selecting most preferred alternatives, which will tend to produce errors and surprises. Such mistakes are by their nature unpredictable and erratic. Yet, it is only the systematic elements of behavior that we can hope to scientifically explain and predict. Thus, in order to theoretically isolate the systematic tendencies in behavior, we must exclude a *C-D* gap, no matter how implausible or unrealistic this might be.[8]

This perspective has been a dominant factor in loyalty to traditional optimizing concepts. Nevertheless, I believe it is mistaken, and that essentially the opposite view is true. To see why, think of the above argument as an empirical hypothesis about the effect of "irrationality"; namely, that the additional uncertainty from a larger *C-D* gap will generate more errors and surprises, thus producing more irregularity and noise in behavior. There are numerous complicating factors about how to test this hypothesis, especially how to measure a person's *C-D* gap. We can avoid these problems by broadening our horizon to consider an interspecie comparison between humans and other animals. Here it is clear without detailed argument that the average *C-D* gap of other animals is larger than that of humans.[9] Yet when we observe nonhuman species, the overwhelming qualitative impression is not one of greater irregularity, but instead of greater rigidity and inflexibility of behavior. Pattern is not more

[5] Some other examples are: second Law of Demand, short- and long-run supply dynamics, risk aversion, time preference, self-interest, liquidity preference, expectation lag and adjustment structures, price-taking behavior, oligopoly strategic patterns, relative price vs. quantity elasticities, relative income-consumption elasticities, etc. The so-called "laws of supply and demand" have probably been the most empirically useful tools in economics (both in formulating simple hypotheses about market responses to parameter changes, and in providing the basic structural equation system used in modern econometric model building). Yet, these simple laws are not derivable from basic optimization concepts, and thus empirical analysis derived from them does not confirm these concepts.

[6] Without going into any details, I would also like to mention a large literature in behavioral psychology about the *matching law* (Richard Herrnstein, 1961, 1964, 1970), which has cast doubt on the validity of traditional maximization theory to explain behavior under certain reinforcement schedules. See P. de Villiers, 1977, for a summary of earlier experimental results, and for more recent experiments with human subjects, see C. M. Bradshaw, E. Szabadi, and R. Bevan, 1976; William Buskist and Harold Miller, 1981. For recent articles about the validity of maximization, see Herrnstein and Gene Heyman, 1979; Heyman and R. Duncan Luce, 1979; Howard Rachlin, John Kagel and R. C. Battalio, 1980; D. Prelec, 1982; and for recent experiments in which matching has dominated maximizing behavior, see Herrnstein and William Vaughan, 1980; Vaughan, 1981; John Mazur, 1981.

[7] Posing the problem in terms of a gap in an agent's decision competence relative to the difficulty of a decision problem was suggested to me by Axel Leijonhufvud.

[8] For a recent example of this view, see Jack Hirshleifer's 1980 price theory text, p. 9. A similar argument is used to justify "rational expectations" equilibria. See, for example, Robert Lucas, 1981, pp. 125, 223–24; and Robert Cooter, 1982b, p. 232.

[9] For analysis of cognative differences between humans and animals, and the evolution of intelligence, see M. Konner 1982, David Premack, 1983; P. Rozin, 1976; Carl Sagan, 1977; Harry Jerison, 1973; R. Masterton, William Hodos, and Jerison, 1976.

difficult but rather easier to notice in animals than in humans.

This qualitative difference between humans and other animals is obviously not new to us; it having long ago been given the capsulized description of "instinct." Still, I do not believe that we have recognized the significance of this general pattern for evaluating and constructing theoretical models of behavior. This pattern is telling us that it is not the absence of a C-D gap, but rather its presence which conditions regularity in behavior.

Why should this be the case? Think of an omiscient agent with literally no uncertainty in identifying the most preferred action under any conceivable condition, regardless of the complexity of the environment which he encounters. Intuitively, such an agent would benefit from maximum flexibility to use all potential information or to adjust to all environmental conditions, no matter how rare or subtle those conditions might be. But what if there is uncertainty because agents are unable to decipher all of the complexity of the environment (i.e., there is uncertainty due to a C-D gap)? Will allowing complete flexibility still benefit the agents? For example, if we could somehow "loosen up" the behavior of an organism without affecting its perceptual abilities, would it compete more effectively for food or mating partners than before?

I believe the general answer to this question is negative: that when genuine uncertainty exists, allowing greater flexibility to react to more information or administer a more complex repertoire of actions will not necessarily enhance an agent's performance. Even if we confine our attention to human behavior, we can find evidence for this proposition, especially in highly competitive situations with noticable elements of complexity relative to human information processing and other perceptual abilities.

For example, in sequential replication games of the basic prisoner's dilemma (see Robert Axelrod, 1980a), round robin competition identified the simplest strategy (the tit for tat strategy) as dominant over all of the others (submitted by persons in economics,

mathematics, psychology, political science, and sociology).[10] Moreover, the worst performance came from the strategy that specified the most "sophisticated" learning and probability adjustment process to guide its behavior.[11] Another example is the publishing history on strategies to win at blackjack. Earlier books emphasized sophisticated card-counting, bet-variation methods (see especially Edward Thorpe's book, *Beat the Dealer*). However, while no one has challenged the mathematical validity of these earlier more complex methods, their actual use resulted in worse performance by most persons attempting to use them (which generated sizable unexpected profits to the casinos).[12] As a result, later books have steadily evolved toward more rigidly structured methods (for example, two recent books are *No Need to Count* and *Winning Casino Blackjack for the Non-Counter*).[13]

Consider also Rubic's cube. There are over 43 trillion possible initial positions from which to unscramble the cube. Minimizing the number of moves to solve the cube would

---

[10] For a description of the tournament and its results, see Axelrod, 1980a. The top strategies were all variants of the simple tit for tat strategy, but none were able to beat the basic strategy (in particular, see pp. 8 and 18). When a second round of the tournament was run, tit for tat still won even though numerous more complex strategies were submitted (see Axelrod, 1980b). For recent analytical analysis on this issue, see David Kreps et al., 1982.

[11] Axelrod describes the worst of the submitted strategies in the first round:

This rule has a probability of cooperating, P, which is initially 30% and is updated every 10 moves. P is adjusted if the other player seems random, very cooperative, or very uncooperative. P is also adjusted after move 130 if the rule has a lower score than the other player. Unfortunately, the complex process of adjustment frequently left the probability of cooperation in the 30% to 70% range, and therefore the rule appeared random to many other players. [1980a, p. 24]

[12] For example, see Richard Canfield, 1979, pp. 19, 37–38, 144–47, 150.

[13] Some of the major books in order of publication are: Thorpe, 1962; Lawrence Revere, 1969; John Archer, 1973; Ian Anderson, 1975; Virginia Graham and C. I. Tulcea, 1978; Canfield, 1979; Leon Dubey, 1980; Avery Cardoza, 1981. See Canfield's book, especially pp. 11–12, 16–19, 37–38, 60–61, 62–65. See also Dubey, pp. 11–12, 17–19, 64, 165–66, 168, 172.

564   THE AMERICAN ECONOMIC REVIEW   SEPTEMBER 1983

require an extremely complex pattern of adjustment from one particular scrambled position to another. Yet, if mistakes are made in trying to select a short cut, the cube will remain unscrambled indefinitely. Consequently, cube experts have developed rigidly structured solving procedures that employ a small repertoire of solving patterns to unscramble the cube. These procedures follow a predetermined hierarchical sequence that is largely independent of the initial scrambled position.[14] However, they almost always require a much longer sequence of moves than the minimum number needed to unscramble the cube. Thus, they are not an approximation to the enormously complex behavior that would be exhibited by an omniscient agent who could immediately select the shortest sequence for each scrambled position. Note also that the information needed to behave in this fashion (present in the initially scrambled patterns on the face of the cube) is costless to observe and instantly available; one need only look at the cube while unscrambling it.

Finally, consider the research of Herbert Simon over a number of years,[15] which has shown that decision makers in a variety of contexts (including both individual and organizational behavior) systematically restrict the use and acquisition of information compared to that potentially available. For example, Simon's idea of "satisficing" represents a feedback mechanism between an internal target variable (called the "aspiration level") and the scope of information evaluated to implement that target. Over time, the feedback process will both guide and discipline the use of information and the resulting behavioral complexity that will evolve within a person or organization. Other learning,

cognitive processes, and decision algorithms can be similarly interpreted.

The above examples suggest that allowing flexibility to react to information or to select actions will not necessarily improve performance if there is uncertainty about how to use that information or about when to select particular actions. Thus, an agent's overall performance may actually be improved by restricting flexibility to use information or to choose particular actions.

II. How Uncertainty Generates Flexibility Constrained Behavior

The argument to this point has suggested that uncertainty due to a C-D gap may generate flexibility constrained behavior. The next step is to characterize more precisely how such uncertainty might produce this result. To do so, a simple "reliability condition" is developed that specifies when to allow or prohibit flexibility to select potential actions or to use information that might prompt particular actions to be chosen.

Two major classes of variables determine the uncertainty resulting from a C-D gap. The first are environmental variables (denoted by e) which determine the complexity of the decision problem to be solved by an agent (including the complexity of environmental situations potentially encountered; the relative likelihood of these situations; and the stability of the relationships that determine possible situations and their relative likelihood). The second are perceptual variables (denoted by p) which characterize an agent's competence in deciphering relationships between its behavior and the environment.[16] Thus, the p and e variables determine the "gap" between competence and difficulty (the C-D gap) which produces

---

[14]In following a typical set of instructions, one selects a side of the cube and begins by placing either its corner or its edge pieces in their proper positions; next, one places in sequence the pieces in the middle section; finally, one repositions the pieces on the remaining, opposite side of the cube (see Czes Kosniowski, 1981). Other similar procedures include D. Taylor, 1980; James Nourse, 1980; Patrick Bussert, 1981; B. W. Barlow, 1981.

[15]For example, Simon, 1955, 1959, 1969, 1976, 1978, 1979a; A. Newell and Simon, 1972.

[16]In economics, the p variables might describe mistaken perceptions about what is more preferred, information processing errors, unreliable probability information, etc.; while the e variables describe the complexity and volatility of both present and future exchange, legal, and political conditions. In biology, p might refer to the sensory and cognitive mechanisms of an organism, and e to the structure and stability of ecological relationships involving competition for food or mating partners.

uncertainty about how to use information in selecting potential actions. In general, there is greater uncertainty as either an agent's perceptual abilities become less reliable or the environment becomes more complex.

These relationships are formally represented as a vector-valued function, $U = u(\bar{p}, \overset{+}{e})$, which describes the structure of uncertainty from a *C-D* gap characterized by p and e. The signs above p and e signify that uncertainty is negatively related to an agent's perceptual abilities, and positively related to the complexity and instability of the environment.

Now consider a conceptual experiment about an agent initially limited to a fixed repertoire of actions, and ask whether allowing flexibility to select an additional action will improve the agent's performance. Under certain conditions, the new action will be more preferred than the other actions in the agent's repertoire (the "right" time to select the action), but otherwise it will be less preferred than one of those actions (the "wrong" time to select the action). Depending on the likelihood of different situations produced by the environment, the probabilities of the right or wrong time to select the action are written $\pi(e)$ and $1 - \pi(e)$, respectively.

Because of uncertainty, the agent will not necessarily select the new action when it is the right time to do so. The conditional probability of selecting the action when it is actually the right time is written $r(U)$, where the likelihood of so doing depends on the structure of uncertainty, $U = u(p,e)$. When this happens, the resulting gain in performance (compared to staying within the initial repertoire) is written $g(e)$, which depends on how the environment affects the consequences from different actions. Similarly, the conditional probability of selecting the new action when it is actually the wrong time is written $w(U)$, with consequent loss in performance of $l(e)$.

In the special case of no uncertainty, the new action would always be selected at the right time and never at the wrong time, so that $r = 1$ and $w = 0$. In general, however, the presence of uncertainty will imply $r < 1$ and $w > 0$.

We can intuitively measure the *reliability* of selecting a new action by the ratio r/w, which represents the chance of "correctly" selecting the action at the right time relative to the chance of "mistakenly" selecting it at the wrong time.[17] Greater uncertainty will both reduce the chance of correct selections and increase the chance of mistaken selections, thus causing the ratio r/w to drop (i.e., greater uncertainty reduces the reliability of selecting the new action).

Note also that $r(U)$ and $w(U)$ are not assumed to be known to an agent. The reason is that uncertainty produces mistakes about distinguishing the right from the wrong conditions to select an action, which distinction is necessary to determine the conditional probabilities of choosing an action under these two sets of conditions. For the same reason, the probability of the right situation to select an action, $\pi(e)$, may also be unknown to an agent. Thus, it is not assumed that an agent can tell whether a mistake has been made; nor are we necessarily dealing with situations where an agent consciously decides when to select an action. Rather, the more general issue is whether some process —conscious or not—will cause (or prevent) an "alertness" or "sensitivity" to information that might prompt selection of an action. For example, when will a person develop an alertness to potential information about whether to choose a particular action, or whether to modify a previous behavior pattern; or when will instinctive mechanisms in an organism precondition a sensitivity to certain environmental stimuli, while simultaneously blocking alertness to other potential stimuli.

---

[17] The probabilities r and w can also be interpreted using Type 1 and Type 2 errors used in statistical hypothesis testing. Let the null hypothesis represent the right situation to select an action (when it is more preferred); while the alternate hypothesis represents the wrong situation for selecting it. Thus, intuitively, Type 1 errors represent *excluded benefits* from failing to respond under the right conditions, while Type 2 errors refer to *included mistakes* from still responding under the wrong conditions. If we let t_1 and t_2 denote the respective probabilities of these errors, they characterize r and w by $r = 1 - t_1$, and $w = t_2$. Thus, r equals one minus the chance excluded benefits, and w equals the change in included mistakes.

Now, with the above components, we can formulate an answer to the question posed earlier: *when is the selection of a new action sufficiently reliable for an agent to benefit from allowing flexibility to select that action.*

To answer this question we must determine whether the gains $g(e)$ from selecting the action under the right conditions (when it is actually more preferred) will cumulate faster than the losses $l(e)$ from selecting it under the wrong conditions (when it is actually less preferred). Thus, combine the above elements in the following way. Right conditions occur with probability $\pi(e)$, which are correctly recognized with probability $r(U)$; so that the expected gain from allowing flexibility to select another action is $g(e)r(U)\pi(e)$. Similarly, the expected loss conditional on allowing the action to be selected is $l(e)w(U)(1-\pi(e))$. Accordingly, gains will cumulate faster than losses if $g(e)r(U)\pi(e) > l(e)w(U)(1-\pi(e))$. Hence, simple rearrangement yields the following *Reliability Condition*:

$$\frac{r(U)}{w(U)} > \frac{l(e)}{g(e)} \cdot \frac{1-\pi(e)}{\pi(e)}.$$

The left-hand side of the inequality is a *reliability ratio*, $r(U)/w(U)$, which measures the probability of "correctly" responding under the right circumstances relative to the probability of "mistakenly" responding under the wrong circumstances. The right-hand side of the inequality represents a minimum lower bound or *tolerance limit* (hereafter denoted simply by $T(e) = l(e)/g(e) \times (1 - \pi(e))/\pi(e))$, which a reliability ratio must satisfy. That is, $T(e)$ determines how likely the chance of selecting an action under the right conditions must be compared to the chance of selecting it under the wrong conditions before allowing flexibility to select that action will improve performance.

We can intuitively interpret the ratio $r(U)/w(U)$ as the "actual" reliability of selecting an action, in comparison to the minimum "required" reliability specified by the tolerance limit, $T(e)$. The components of the Reliability Condition summarize a potentially complex set of relationships between

an agent's repertoire and the structure of the environment.[18] Nevertheless, these relationships boil down to a conceptually simple answer about when to allow flexibility to select an additional action: *do so if the actual reliability in selecting the action exceeds the minimum required reliability necessary to improve performance.* Stated in its simplest notational form, this answer amounts to the condition, $r/w > T$.

The question which motivated this answer was phrased in terms of adding a new action to an agent's repertoire. However, once the Reliability Condition has been obtained we can also apply it to a range of further issues about when to allow or ignore particular actions. For example, it can be applied to dropping actions from a repertoire; namely, retain only those actions which satisfy $r/w > T$ compared to ignoring them.

We can also think of the Reliability Condition as solving a "decision" problem in which an agent determines what information he will allow to influence his behavior; or alternatively, as a "design" problem in engineering the appropriate information sensitivity of an agent. For each possible action, the Reliability Condition must be satisfied before allowing potential information to

---

[18]Both the agent's repertoire and the environment may contain a large number of possibilities, and the consequences from selecting an action may vary with different environmental situations. This will also complicate how to measure an agent's performance. Regardless of how performance is measured (for example, it may involve some kind of average over actions and/or environmental conditions), $g(e)$ and $l(e)$ still represent the gain or loss in performance from correct or mistaken selections, respectively; and $r(U)$, $w(U)$ still represent the conditional probabilities of these correct or mistaken selections. The probabilities $r(U)$ and $w(U)$ also result from a complex set of relationships that determine the source and likelihood of particular errors that interact to generate these probabilities. In addition, $l(e)$ and $g(e)$ may depend on an agent's internal components, such as the morphological attributes of an animal.

The objective of this paper is to develop only the bare essential modeling elements needed for a simple analytical solution, whose structure is invariant to the above-mentioned complications. In particular, the basic form of the Reliability Condition will remain the same. Much greater detail about the analytical structure, including extensive applications to economics and other fields, is now in progress.

prompt its selection. Those actions that can be guided with sufficient reliability are permitted; those that cannot are eliminated. In this way, an agent's outward behavior is determined by his response pattern to potential information.[19]

III. Four General Implications

Now that we have the Reliability Condition, its implications in four basic areas are briefly discussed.

A. Uncertainty Generates Rules Which are Adapted Only to Likely or Recurrent Situations

Note a simple but important feature of the tolerance limit. For any given l/g ratio, the likelihood of wrong to right conditions, $(1 - \pi)/\pi$, increases for smaller π; so that T also rises as the probability of right circumstances π decreases (see Figure 1). Thus, *an agent must be more reliable in selecting an action if the right situations for exhibiting it are less likely. Moreover, the required reliability quickly accelerates to infinity as the likelihood of right situations drops to zero.* Thus, for a given structure of uncertainty, $\mathbf{U} = u(\mathbf{p}, \mathbf{e})$, which determines the reliability of selecting a particular action (i.e., which determines the ratio $r(\mathbf{U})/w(\mathbf{U})$), the Reliability Condition will be violated for sufficiently small but positive, $\pi(\mathbf{e}) > 0$.

This intuitively means that to satisfy the Reliability Condition, an agent must ignore actions which are appropriate for only "rare" or "unusual" situations. Conversely, an agent's repertoire must be limited to actions which are adapted only to relatively likely or "recurrent" situations. Thus, a general characteristic of such a repertoire is that it ex-

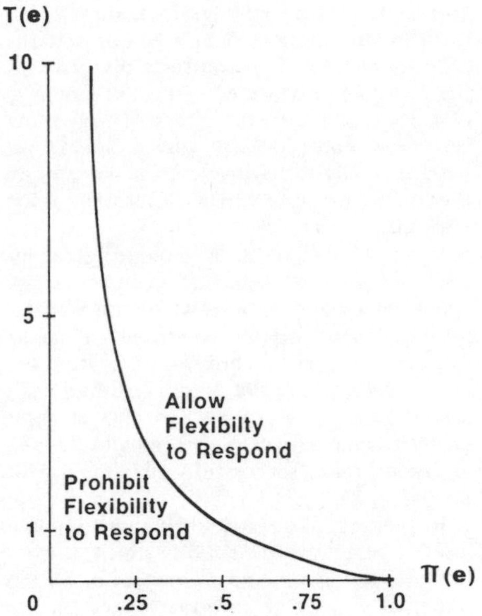

FIGURE 1

The curve shows how the tolerance limit $T(e)$ changes for a constant $l(e)/g(e)$ ratio (in this case $l/g = 1$) as the probability of right conditions π varies. Note how quickly T begins to rise as π drops below .25. The curve represents a boundary of minimum reliability that must be satisfied (i.e., $r/w > T$) before responding to information will enhance an agent's performance.

cludes actions which will in fact enhance performance under certain conditions, even though those conditions occur with positive probability, $\pi(\mathbf{e}) > 0$. We thus have a formal characterization of the pervasive association of both human and animal behavior with various connotations of "rule-governed" behavior, such as instinct, habits, routines, rules of thumb, administrative procedures, customs, norms, and so forth. All of these phrases refer to some type of rigidity or inflexibility in adjusting to different situations as a universal qualitative feature of behavior.

Therefore, since behavior patterns which satisfy the Reliability Condition must have this property, we will call them *behavioral rules* or simply *rules*. Note that we have been

---

[19]The relationship between information sensitivity and output complexity is also recognized in cybernetics; see Norbert Weiner, 1948, and W. Ashby, 1956. A reference in organizational behavior that refers to this is Barry Staw, Lana Sanderlands and Jane Dutton: "...a fundamental principle of cybernetics..., the number of output discriminations of a system (i.e., its behavioral repertoire) is limited by the variety of information inherent in its input" (1981, p. 517).

568   THE AMERICAN ECONOMIC REVIEW   SEPTEMBER 1983

able to derive the basic rigidity feature which justifies attributing to such behavior patterns the idea of rules. This contrasts sharply with the typical procedure of using the language of rules (often with the intent of suggesting certain connotations to the reader), yet without really justifying from a more basic theoretical structure why such terminology is appropriate.

If we use the jargon of standard economics, rule-governed behavior means that an agent must ignore actions which are actually preferred under certain conditions. Thus, as intuitively suggested above, the resulting behavior patterns are *not* an approximation to maximizing so as to always choose most preferred alternatives (i.e., behaving "as if" an agent could successfully maximize with no C-D gap).

In general, rules restrict behavior to only a limited repertoire of actions. Such restrictions do not assume an awareness of all the potential actions or information which are thereby implicitly ignored. Thus, no explicit decision about what potential actions to ignore is necessarily involved.

An agent need only be capable of determining when to select particular actions from a limited range of allowable alternatives. To do so does not require an ability to understand why the resulting behavior patterns evolved. This is obviously the case for animals, where we do not expect them to have an "intellectual awareness" of why they are programmed to exhibit certain behavior patterns. Yet even for humans, the general characteristic will be an inability to articulate a full understanding of why particular behavior patterns have arisen. This is implied even though human behavior is much more flexible than that of other species, and even though conscious mental processes are involved in most human behavior patterns.[20]

As a simple example involving human behavior, consider the solving methods for Rubic's cube mentioned above in Section I.

---

[20] For related comments about the legitimacy of standard psychotherapy practices, see Donald Campbell's 1975 presidential address to the American Psychological Association.

The environment represents all of the different scrambled positions or "situations" which might eventuate on the face of the cube, of which there are over 43 trillion. If each situation is produced by a simple random draw from the set of possible situations, the probability π of the right situation (the appropriate scrambled position) arising for any particular solving sequence is extremely low. Assuming the l/g ratio (resulting from unscrambling the cube in greater or lesser time, or number of moves) is not close to zero, the required reliability for selecting each of these sequences will also be very high. Without this ability, the repertoire of solving patterns must be severely restricted in order to satisfy the Reliability Condition, and structured so that their use is largely independent of particular scrambled positions (i.e., they are adapted only to the recurrent features of the environment).

B. *Selection Processes do not Simulate Optimizing Behavior*

Up to this point we have thought of performance simply in terms of an agent's "preferences" about the consequences of particular actions. Now generalize its meaning to represent any factor that determines whether behavior will continue or persist in the environment encountered by an agent. This might involve a preference evaluation, competition for profits or investment capital, or possibly biological determinants of physical survival or reproductive probability. Whatever the interpretation, we can apply the Reliability Condition to determine when allowing flexibility to use potential information or to select actions will improve rather than worsen performance.

Now suppose the actual process generating behavior is an evolutionary process that tends to select relatively superior performance at any point of time. From what has already been derived, this implies that such selection processes will tend to produce rule-governed behavior that is not an approximation to always selecting actions that maximize performance. Thus, in general, evolutionary processes will *not* generate simulations to optimizing behavior. Rather, they will tend to produce rules that systematically restrict the flexibility of behavior compared to that which would be exhibited by a full optimizer in the absence of uncertainty.

As mentioned earlier, this implication directly contradicts one of the dominant justifications for assuming agents are able to optimize. Predictable behavior is not an "as if" simulation to optimizing, but rather will evolve only to the extent that agent's are unable to maximize because of uncertainty.

Generalizing the meaning of performance also implies that we are not necessarily dealing with traditional economic agents, such as consumer, firm, worker, investor, etc. Rather, we can think of an agent as any system of interacting components. For example, a system might refer to biological entities such as individual organisms, species, ecological systems, or possibly to subsystems within organisms studied in physiology or molecular biology. Still other examples might be computers or other artificial cybernetic mechanisms.

Whatever the interpretation, the Reliability Condition characterizes when to allow flexibility to use information or select actions applicable to that interpretation. For example, we might apply it to the following situations: when is it the right time to unscramble Rubic's cube by starting from a middle section rather than from one of its outer sections; when is it the right time to purchase more of a particular commodity rather than other commodities; when is it the right time to search for additional price or quality information about potential future purchasing decisions; when is it the right time for an animal to deviate from its usual foraging strategies for food; when is it the right time to cooperate by helping other individuals (i.e., when is it the right time to be "altruistic" rather than "selfish");[21] when is it the right time to modify genetic information to perpetuate traits acquired in the lifetime of a

particular organism (i.e., when is it the right time to use "Lamarkian" genetic transmission);[22] or more generally, when is it the right time to use feedback from the environment to modify behavior (i.e., when is it the right time to "learn")?

C. Weak Selection Processes May Allow Dysfunctional Behavior to Persist

The preceding discussion implicitly assumed that selection processes would quickly eliminate relatively inferior performers. If this is actually the case, the Reliability Condition implies the evolution of behavioral rules that appropriately structure and limit the flexibility of behavior. The empirical examples that helped motivate the formal analysis also involved behavior produced in highly competitive conditions (i.e., biological competition for survival between nonhuman agents; strategies to win at blackjack, or in prisoner's dilemma games, or in Rubic's cube contests; organizations competing in exchange environments for profits or investment capital, etc.).

On the other hand, what if there is something about the environment that only sluggishly weeds out worse performers, or which only infrequently produces situations that severely punish vulnerable behavior. This possibility is fundamentally important when genuine uncertainty exists, because there is no magical element (empirically or in theory) to guarantee that only appropriately structured behavior will evolve. Indeed, the core assumption is literally the absence of ability to decifer all of the complexity of the environment; especially one whose very structure itself evolves over time.

Thus, consider an evolving world produced through a mixture of selective processes. These processes will have varying degrees of severity in reacting to differential performance between competing agents. Such a world will be a continual mixture of appropriately and inappropriately structured behavior. In some cases, weak selection processes may allow relatively dysfunctional

---

[21] Hirshleifer uses "recognition coefficients" (which represent particular examples of the $r(U)$ and $w(U)$ probabilities) to determine the reliability of helping strategies in identifying other agents with altruistic traits (1982, pp. 26–29). See also W. D. Hamilton, 1964; John Maynard Smith, 1964; Robert Trivers, 1971.

[22] On the "irreversibility" of genetic translation, see Jacques Monod, 1972, pp. 104–17.

behavior to persist: possibly with worse average performance than other agents; or with slowly dwindling performance over time; or with vulnerable performance that awaits only the next infrequent but severe test to challenge its further persistence in the environment.

This is clearly a different view from trying to comprehend the world as continually tending toward optimizing behavior. Indeed, we may be able to explain major features about the structure, occurrence, and error patterns of dysfunctional behavior. Only one class of possibilities is mentioned here, and briefly reconsidered at the conclusion of this paper. In particular, we can analyze the pattern of vulnerable behavior arising from political institutions, especially in the form of dysfunctional complexity in trying to manipulate the outcomes resulting from exchange competition. Specific instances of this issue have had a long history in economics about the scope of government regulation, and the debate over discretionary vs. rigid monetary policy.[23]

D. Greater Uncertainty will Cause Rule-Governed Behavior to be More Predictable

What is the effect of *greater* uncertainty on rule-governed behavior? In general, greater uncertainty (from either less reliable perceptual abilities or a more unpredictable environment) will both reduce the chance of recognizing the right situation to select an action, and increase the chance of not recognizing the wrong situation for selecting it. That is, greater uncertainty will both reduce $r(U)$ and increase $w(U)$, so that the reliability ratios, $r(U)/w(U)$, of particular actions will drop.

As these ratios drop, some of them may no longer exceed their respective tolerance limits, resulting in violations of the Reliability Condition. More violations will occur as uncertainty becomes more pervasive. Thus, greater uncertainty will cause behavioral rules to be more restrictive in eliminating particular actions or response patterns to potential information. This will further constrain behavior to simpler, less sophisticated patterns which are easier for an observer to recognize and predict. Therefore, *greater uncertainty will cause rule-governed behavior to exhibit increasingly predictable regularities, so that uncertainty becomes the basic source of predictable behavior*.

This is the most important implication of my analysis, one that has far-reaching implications across a diverse range of fields. It also has important implications for how we have been trying to model behavior. It implies that genuine uncertainty, far from being unanalyzable or irrelevant to understanding behavior, is the very source of the empirical regularities that we have sought to explain by excluding such uncertainty.[24] This means that the conceptual basis for most of our existing models is seriously flawed.

A major symptom of this has been the dominant tendency to model more complex decision problems by implicitly upgrading the competence of the agent to handle that complexity (so that traditional optimizing concepts can be used). For example, the number of decision alternatives or competing agents is increased, or complex probabilistic contingencies are introduced, or repercussions from future events are permitted, etc. Over the years this has resulted in the characterization of increasingly sophisticated,

---

[23]Another area involves differences in productivity between U.S. and Japanese industrial firms, because of differential ability either to manage a complex internal use of inputs, or to adjust to volatile external marketing conditions ("just in time" rather than "just in case" inventory management; greater employee discretion in production line monitoring; longer promotion, investment, and R&D planning horizons; etc.) See William Abernathy, Kim Clark, and A. Kantrow, 1981; Y. Mondon, 1981; Y. Sugimori, K. Kusunoki, and S. Cho, 1977; R. Clark, 1979; Anthony Athos and Richard Pascale, 1981; William Ouchi, 1981.

[24]The various authors that have emphasized the importance of uncertainty (for example, Frank Knight, 1921; the Australian view typified by F. A. Hayek, 1967, and Israel Kirzner, 1973; the subjectivist views of G. L. S. Shackle, 1969, 1972; etc.) have given the impression that genuine uncertainty and its effects cannot be represented with formal modeling tools. The approach suggested here is quite different: to harness the determinants of uncertainty in a modeling structure that characterizes regularity in behavior. Closely related ideas have also been recently analyzed by Richard Bookstaber and Joseph Langsam, 1983.

"optimal" behavior strategies, with little fruit in understanding observed behavior.

This trend is typified by recent Bayesian models of optimal risk behavior, which are synonymous with sophisticated continually updated response to new information. Some examples are optimal "search" models that specify various sequential strategies for job search, price or quality information, etc.[25] Yet, they bypass the issue that overides everything else: when to permit any search given the uncertainty in detecting whether the positive gains from efficient search strategies will outweigh the required search costs; especially when a diverse range of search opportunities might eventuate, and the timing of these future opportunities is also unknown.

IV. Explaining Predictable Behavior: Framework and Illustration

The reliability theory briefly outlined above can be applied to the full spectrum of cases produced by different structures of uncertainty. It thus represents a general framework for analyzing behavior under all of these possibilities. On the other hand, standard choice theory analyzes the special case where there is no uncertainty due to a C-D gap.[26]

The narrowness of standard optimizing concepts is evidenced in the dominant tend-

[25]See, for example, David Blackwell and M. A. Girshick, 1979; Thomas Ferguson, 1967; Peter Diamond and Michael Rothschild, 1978; Stephen Lippman and John McCall, 1979; Hirshleifer and John Riley, 1979.

[26]This conclusion also applies to the more recent models of behavior under uncertainty, which assume agents can infer reliable probabilities of future situations; and also recognize all possible events that might eventuate, or possible actions that might be useful to select. Such ability to comprehend the future is much more difficult than avoiding computational mistakes in a static world of known utility information over a fixed set of options. Consequently, these models are not moving closer but rather further away from dealing with genuine uncertainty due to a C-D gap. The reason is that in order to apply traditional optimizing concepts, the competence of the agent has been implicitly upgraded to handle the extra complexity resulting from an unpredictable future. On this issue, see the closing remarks of John Hey, 1979, pp. 232–34.

ency (even after years of extensive experience with conventional models) to steer away from incorporating genuine uncertainty into the analysis of behavior.[27] In contrast, the Reliability Condition directly harnesses the determinants of uncertainty to characterize regularity in behavior. This amounts to a reversal of the explanation assumed in standard economics, which places these determinants in the residual "error term" between observed behavior and the more systematic patterns claimed to result from optimization.

Thus, the idea of uncertainty as the source of predictable behavior is both a generalization and a major shift away from the explanatory framework of existing models, one that may be of importance to a number of fields. The following statements briefly summarize the major differences between the new framework (the economics of genuine uncertainty) and that of traditional optimization theory:

1) The basic theoretical objective is to understand the behavioral implications of genuine uncertainty, rather than the implications of maximizing for a given set of preferences or expectations. Genuine uncertainty results from a gap in an agent's decision competence relative to the difficulty in selecting more preferred alternatives, so that error and surprise cannot be avoided.

2) A wide range of factors contribute to uncertainty. In economics, these include cognitive limitations in processing given information or in interpreting potential information from the environment; vulnerable perceptions about preferences or expectations taken as given in traditional choice models; unreliable probability or expected utility information taken as given in standard risk-behavior theory. In addition, uncertainty may involve the ability to infer from past experience what was misunderstood that led to previous error; or the abil-

[27]For example, a recent statement by Lucas flatly concludes: "In situations of risk, the hypothesis of rational behavior on the part of agents will have usable content, so that behavior may be explainable in terms of economic theory.... In cases of uncertainty, economic reasoning will be of little value" (1981, p. 224; see also p. 223).

ity to identify potential actions which might be selected, or contingencies that might affect the consequences of future behavior.[28]

3) Optimizing with no uncertainty in choosing more preferred alternatives does not tend to produce systematic and stable regularity in behavior. Rather, it tends to destroy such regularity as successively more information can be reliably interpreted in guiding more complex behavior. This does not mean that formal optimization tools cannot be used, but rather that understanding how uncertainty affects behavior will systematically redirect the formulation of models and the questions to which they would be applied.

4) Predictable regularities of behavior are the manifestation of behavioral rules that represent patterns of behavior for which deviations exist that are preferred under certain conditions, but which are nevertheless ignored because of uncertainty in reliably interpreting potential information about when to deviate.

5) Intrinsic to behavioral rules is the ignoring or lack of alertness to potential information, the reaction to which would direct behavior into more complex deviations from such rules; even though such information may be costless to observe. Conversely, it is the alertness or sensitivity to information that determines the patterns and complexity of rules manifested in behavior. The Reliability Condition is a simple but general characterization of when greater flexibility to administer more complex behavior or to use more information will improve rather than worsen performance.

6) Behavioral rules not only involve outward symptoms of information sensitivity, but also internal mechanisms that generate such sensitivity. Thus, research in fields such as psychology, biology, and engineering has

direct bearing on the structure of such rules. In contrast, traditional economic models have largely ignored research in these and other fields.

To help see the range of issues unified by the above analytical framework, a few illustrations are briefly presented.

A. *The Consistency of Rule-Governed Behavior*

Traditional choice theory has tended to equate normative rationality with logical consistency of behavior, as described by various transitivity, intertemporal consistency, probability assessment, and other assumed conditions. For example, Jacques Drèze provides the following evaluation of the risk behavior axioms of standard expected utility theory:

> ... a consistent decision-maker is assumed always to be able to compare (transitively) the attractiveness of acts, or hypothetical acts and of consequences as well as the likelihood of events. These requirements are minimal, in the sense that no consistency of behaviour may be expected if any one of them is violated; *but they are very strong, in the sense that all kinds of comparisons are assumed possible, many of which may be quite remote from the range of experience of the decision-maker.* This is also the reason why the axioms have more normative appeal than descriptive realism; few people would insist on maintaining, consciously, choices that violate them, but their spontaneous behaviour may frequently fail to display such rigorous consistency.
>
> [1974, p. 11, emphasis added]

Drèze is quick to acknowledge and discount the descriptive validity of the expected utility axioms, but like many others he still feels secure in their normative validity in characterizing truly rational behavior under uncertainty.[29] Nevertheless, one might ask what

---

[28] The latter determinants have recently been described as particular types of uncertainty, such as parametric versus structural knowledge by Richard Langlois (1983) and "extended" uncertainty by Bookstaber and Langsam. They are extensions of the "unlistability problem" introduced by Shackle (1972). Whatever terminology or type of uncertainty is involved, we can characterize regularity in behavior depending on how each type of uncertainty affects the reliability of using information or selecting potential actions.

[29] See, for example, John von Neumann and Oskar Morgenstern, 1944, pp. 17–30; L. J. Savage, 1954, pp. 6–7, 19–21, 56–68, 82–84; Friedman and Savage, 1948.

would be the implication of a logically correct set of axioms (or a decision algorithm for search and learning behavior) *if obeying those axioms (or using the algorithm) would require the use and sensitive response to unreliable information* (for example, information remote from the range of experience of a decision maker)? To the extent this is the case, rule-governed behavior will ignore such axioms (or a decision algorithm) regardless of the logical properties violated in disobeying them.[30] Similar issues apply to traditional microeconomic theory. For example, what if preferences are less reliable for commodity bundles remote to a consumer's normal purchasing experience? Must we avoid this likely possibility in assuming fully connected preferences? Or is the violation of this assumption itself a major source of price-response regularities of consumers?

B. Social Institutions Evolve Because of Uncertainty

Neoclassical decision and general equilibrium models are typically without any explicit institutional structure, and have thus tended to direct attention away from questions about the evolution of particular forms of market organization and other social institutions.[31] In contrast, the Reliability Condition naturally suggests the systematic importance of such institutions to determine

the scope and complexity of exchange relationships, and other social interactions involving cultural norms, customs, and aggressive behavior.

In this regard, it is noteworthy that Schotter's recent book on the theory of institutions defines them in a manner immediately implied by the Reliability Condition: "A social institution is a regularity in social behavior that...specifies behavior in specific recurrent situations, and is either self-policed or policed by some external authority" (p. 11).

Thus, evolved institutions are social rule-mechanisms for dealing with recurrent situations faced by agents in different societies. That is, institutions are regularities in the interaction between agents that arise because of uncertainty in deciphering the complex interdependencies created by these interactions.[32] I will return to this topic in Section V below, which considers the evolution of legal and exchange institutions.

A persistent theme in human literature illustrates a closely related issue that has been largely ignored by traditional choice theory; namely, the attempt of individuals to constrain or bind the flexibility of their actions.[33] A famous example in *The Odyssey* describes Ulysses trying to prevent himself from responding to the allurement of certain sirens: "...but you must bind me hard and fast, so that I cannot stir from the spot where

---

[30]See Paul Slovic and Amos Tversky, 1974, Slovic and Sarah Lichtenstein, 1983; Dirk Wendt, 1975; D. Conrath, 1973; Detlof Winterfeldt, 1980; and for systematic empirical evidence see Daniel Kahneman and Tversky, 1979, 1981, 1982; Ward Edwards, 1962; William Fellner, 1961; R. M. Hogarth, 1975. Some recent attempts to modify standard expected utility theory by dropping the "independence" or "substitution" axiom include Mark Machina, 1982 (equivalence relationships to global risk-aversion axioms); Graham Loomes and Robert Sugden, 1982, 1983 (regret theory); and S. H. Chew and K. R. MacCrimmon, 1979a, b; Peter Fishburn, 1981; R. Weber, 1982 (*alpha*-utility theory).

[31]See the following diverse range of analytical perspectives, including Alchian, 1950; James Buchanan, 1975, 1977; Buchanan and H. G. Brennan, 1981; Ronald Coase, 1937; Carl Dahlman, 1980; Demsetz, 1967; Hayek, 1967, 1973; Menger, 1871, 1883; Nelson and Sidney Winter, 1982; Andrew Schotter, 1981; Joseph Schumpeter, 1942; Oliver Williamson, 1975, 1979, 1981.

[32]Consider a person within a complex interdependent society, where uncertainty in deciphering these interdependencies quickly increases as they widen beyond his immediate experience. The Reliability Condition implies that his behavior will quickly become insensitive to nonlocal social contingencies. If among such contingencies are effects on other individuals, this implies a relatively sensitive or "self-interested" motivation toward a person's own self (and family), and away from alertness or "sympathy" toward other persons. This implication underlies the ideas Adam Smith developed in the *Theory of Moral Sentiments*, published prior to the *Wealth of Nations*. See Coase (1976) for a number of passages from the *Theory of Moral Sentiments*; for example, Smith, 1969, pp. 321–23, 347–48, 109–10.

[33]See John Elster, 1979; R. H. Strotz, 1955; and N. Howard, 1971. Another classic moral dilemma of great literature poses the protagonist in a situation with abnormally convincing information that "right circumstances" are at hand to engage in behavior precluded by social or religious norms.

574   THE AMERICAN ECONOMIC REVIEW   SEPTEMBER 1983

you shall stand me...and if I beg you to release me, you must tighten and add to my bonds."

C. *Uncertainty and the Reliability of Expectations*

Both past and present economic models are crucially dependent on how they incorporate expectations in guiding behavior. Economists have been aware that beliefs about the future are often mistaken, and thus have been uneasy in both formulating and applying their models.[34] More recently, "rational expectations" models have attempted to resolve these problems by assuming that expectations correctly identify the mean and variance of stochastic variables that affect future environmental contingencies.[35] A key motivation for such models is to predict how "optimal" behavior will respond to changes in the structure of the environment, especially changes influenced by government policy. Yet, from a broader perspective, it is clear that most species that have evolved in nature exhibit relatively programmed behavior patterns that are highly insensitive to environmental changes, even if such rigidity results in their extinction. At best, such models could apply more broadly only by continually introducing specializing assumptions about the type of expectation "rationality" guiding the behavior of particular species.

Thus, in all of our existing models, either we are analyzing the maximizing response to possibly wrong expectations, or we avoid this issue by assuming expectations are reliable. In order to make progress in analyzing the role of expectations, we must understand how their use and formation are affected by genuine uncertainty in comprehending the future. For example, how reliable are agents' abilities to formulate beliefs about the future; and given the vulnerability of such beliefs, when will agents sensitively react to them, or when will they be alert to information that might prompt them to revise them?

D. *The Pattern of Behavioral Complexity Evidenced in Nature*

My departure from standard choice theory was suggested by the general pattern of animals having a larger $C-D$ gap than humans, yet regularity in their behavior is much more noticeable than for humans. The Reliability Condition implies a simple formal characterization of this overall pattern. Suppose we start with a given combination of the p and e variables, and consider a conceptual experiment where the e variables are held fixed, but the perceptual abilities of an agent are successively reduced compared to their initial effectiveness. This will increase the uncertainty in administering the initial behavioral repertoire, thus reducing the reliability ratios of particular actions. As already discussed, greater uncertainty will in general require a more inflexible structure of rules; that is, some of the actions in the initial repertoire must be excluded because their selection no longer satisfies the Reliability Condition.

Now apply this result to us as human observers watching other species with less reliable cognitive equipment than ourselves. We should notice a systematic pattern of greater rigidity and inflexibility in nonhuman species compared to our own behavior. This implication is testable to the extent that the effectiveness of different species' cognitive abilities can be independently measured from simply watching outward behavior (for example, relative brain to body mass). In addition, if we compare across a number of species, there should emerge a general pattern that correlates greater rigidity in behavior with less effective cognitive equipment.[36]

These implications characterize a pervasive qualitative pattern, one that is systematically evidenced in the comparative study of different species. Yet, they were obtained in a very simple way from the Reliability Condition. This is a significant indication that we are on the right track in understanding be-

[34] See John Hicks, 1935; Richard Muth, 1961; Axel Leijonhufvud, 1968, pp. 366–85, Rudiger Dornbusch and Stanley Fischer, 1978, pp. 270–75, 283–86.
[35] See for example, Thomas Sargent, 1979, and Lucas, 1981.

[36] For analysis of some of the more rigid, "forced" behavior movements of simple organisms, and other major instinctive patterns, see Roger Brown and Richard Herrnstein, 1975, pp. 23–31.

VOL. 73 NO. 4   HEINER: ORIGIN OF PREDICTABLE BEHAVIOR   575

havior, especially in developing a modeling structure that naturally suggests the very consideration of such questions.

E. Explaining Instinctive Behavior

The currently accepted explanation of instinctive rigidities is that they accomplish some function which is useful or adaptive most of the time for the natural environments in which they are exhibited.[37] But as already discussed, this feature is itself implied by the Reliability Condition; namely, that rule-governed behavior will ignore adjustment to unlikely contingencies, thus limiting response patterns to only the more probable or recurrent features of the environment. A number of implications concerning ecological structure, niches, extinction, etc., can also be derived (rather than simply described or assumed) from the analysis.

Explanation of specific behavioral rigidities can be obtained by using the Reliability Condition, $r/w > T$, with explicit variables and assumptions about an organism's perceptual components ($\mathbf{p}$) in terms of the sensory ($\mathbf{s}$) and cognitive ($\mathbf{c}$) attributes of particular organisms. In addition, we can introduce morphological ($\mathbf{m}$) attributes of organisms, along with the environmental variables ($\mathbf{e}$) which determine the structure of the environment. By understanding how these variables (denoted $\mathbf{z} = (\mathbf{s}, \mathbf{c}, \mathbf{m}, \mathbf{e})$) affect the reliability and tolerance limit components of the model, particular rule structures can be derived and compared with observed behavior of different organisms (including humans).

F. Brief Application to Imprinting

Consider very briefly the phenomenon of imprinting.[38] Suppose that responding to a particular pattern in the environment is crucial to an organism's survival (for example, following its parents). Suppose also that without highly developed cognitive mechanisms, if the organism did not initially know the particular pattern, then it could not reliably distinguish that pattern from a number of similar patterns (i.e., a newly born organism could not reliably distinguish its parents from similar adults); but given a specific reference pattern to "lock onto," it can reliably distinguish it from other similar patterns. However, if the wrong pattern is locked onto, the organism's survival would be severely jeopardized.

In particular, the probability of right circumstances π to lock onto a pattern is often a function of time since an organism's birth (for example, $\pi(t)$ is the chance of seeing only an organism's parents at time t since birth). Recalling that the required reliability (i.e., the tolerance limit T) will quickly increase as π drops to zero, we can derive the following two-stage behavioral process: stage one is a pattern-locking mechanism that reacts to whatever pattern first appears after the mechanism is initiated; while stage two is a resistance mechanism that severely constrains stage one to only certain sensitive periods for which the required reliability is very low (i.e., $\pi(t)$ is close to 1.0).

It can further be shown that the implied sensitive periods will be highly predictable across particular organisms of a species. In addition, comparative regularities across species in relatively sensitive learning periods can be derived. For example, we can characterize less rigidly patterned sensitivity phases in the development of human children in acquiring language, and the display of other cognitive skills.[39]

G. Punctuated Dynamics for Scientific Inquiry

The work of Thomas Kuhn (1962) (see also Popper, 1969; Lakatos and Musgrave,

---

[37] The classic reference on instinct is Nino Tinbergen, 1951 (for example, pp. 151–84, especially 156–57 and 152–53). Other references include John Alcock, 1979, pp. 57–76, 87–102; Brown and Herrnstein, 1975, pp. 31–59; William Keeton, 1980, pp. 490–512, especially 503, 494, 496, 498; Eric Pianka, 1978, pp. 82–86, 152–53.

[38] See Alcock, 1979, pp. 67–73; Keeton, 1980, pp. 498–500; Konrad Lorenz, 1981, pp. 259, 275–87; David McFarland, 1982, pp. 303–05; W. R. Hess, 1973.

[39] See for example, Alcock, 1979, pp. 73–79; E. Mavis Hetherington and Ross Park, 1979; R. Grinder, 1962; Lawrence Kohlberg, 1966, 1969; N. Chomsky, 1972; J. Piaget, 1947, 1952. For related material from ethology, see Lorenz, 1981.

576   *THE AMERICAN ECONOMIC REVIEW*   *SEPTEMBER 1983*

1970) has emphasized a systematic pattern of resistance in the behavior of scientists to quick and sensitive reaction to new ideas and theories. Yet, when sufficient anomalies and awkwardly interpreted evidence about a previous theory build up, a major shift in ideas (a "scientific revolution") will relatively quickly occur. This is an illustration of dynamic properties discussed below in Section VI. The Reliability Condition also implies other features in the behavior of scientists, such as: (a) resistance to accepting or using several competing theories unless there also exist easy to decipher (and reliable) criteria of when to switch between them; (b) similar resistance to incorporating new concepts or variables into accepted theories unless reliable criteria on how to use them are available (consider an economist's reaction to incorporating sociological variables into economic models); (c) differences in accepting and rewarding (salary, promotion, etc.) theoretical vs. empirical research in different fields depending on the reliability of observable data studied in those fields (for example, see Leijonhufvud's 1973 parody about "Life Among the Econ").[40]

H. *Uncertainty and Consensus in Social Judgments*

Finally, in the area of ethics and social policy, consider the theory of justice advanced by John Rawls (1971). Underlying his whole analysis is the recognition that if individuals have reliable information about their own future circumstances (will they be smart or resourceful, or have special educational opportunities, or own highly valued property, etc.), they will respond to such information in the way they view social policies and institutions that would affect their particular situations.[41] This will produce a wide diversity of opinions about how

to formulate and apply normative principles. Hence, in order to produce a highly uniform consensus or *regularity* in social judgments, Rawls introduced a pervasive uncertainty into the conceptual problem in the form of a "veil of ignorance." Such a procedure virtually eliminates reliable information (even in probabilistic form) about any particular individual's specific future circumstances that might eventuate depending on what principles are mutually agreed to by the whole group.[42] With a sufficient structure of uncertainty, individual judgments might be constrained to possibly a single, universally accepted principle of justice to guide social policy.

The important point is that the source of such a universal consensus, as well as the other behavior patterns discussed above, is uncertainty in using potential information about when to deviate from these regularities.

V. Application to Economic Modeling

In this section, the Reliability Condition is briefly applied to a few modeling issues in standard economics.

A. *Reluctance to Insure Against Rare Disasters*

Extensive empirical studies have shown that people are reluctant to insure themselves against large but rare disasters, in a manner that directly contradicts expected utility theory (see Howard Kunreuther et al., 1978). A recent statement by Kenneth Arrow summarizes the dilemma posed for standard "uncertainty" theory:

> A striking real life situation has given grounds for doubt about the validity of the expected utility hypothesis. Since 1969, the U.S. government has offered flood insurance at rates which are well below their actuarial value... Under the usual hypothesis of risk aversion, any

---

[40] Edward Leamer's work (1978) illustrates another issue about the reliability of model testing and formulation, which can be viewed as methodological rule-mechanisms to restrict "specification searches" used to claim empirical support for a theory. See Thomas Cooley and Stephen LeRoy (1981) for an application of Leamer's methodology to evaluating previous work on the demand for money.

[41] See Rawls, 1971, pp. 18–19, 137–38, 140, 149.

[42] See Rawls, 1971, pp. 150, 154–55. Notice in these passages how Rawls believes that a crucial feature of the veil of ignorance is the inability to formulate reliable probability information about the impact of social contingencies on particular individuals.

VOL. 73 NO. 4   HEINER: ORIGIN OF PREDICTABLE BEHAVIOR   577

individual should certainly be willing to undertake a favorable bet.... Yet, until the government increased the pressure by various incentives, very few took out this insurance.... The main distinguishing characteristic of those who took out flood insurance was acquaintance with others who took out insurance. This might be taken as an explanation in terms of information costs, but the information seems so easy to acquire and the stakes so large that this hypothesis hardly seems tenable.

[1981, p. 2]

In contrast, the above analysis immediately suggests that even costless information will be ignored if the behavior resulting from its use will not satisfy the Reliability Condition, (recall that solving procedures for Rubic's cube systematically ignore costless information available simply by looking at the cube while unscrambling it). The real issue is why are agents reluctant to engage in behavior that might be prompted by such information.

Consider a brief sketch of the insurance behavior phenomenon. As the probability, p, of a disaster goes to zero, the number of such extremely rare but conceivable events grows indefinitely large. Given any positive setup costs of insuring against each of these possibilities, the total insurance cost will eventually exceed a person's (finite) wealth. Thus, it is clearly not appropriate to insure against all of them. (What do we call someone who is constantly trying to protect against rare but serious sickness; and what would happen to total output net of the demand for medical services if everyone exhibited this propensity?)

The above argument implies that the probability of the right time to insure, π, is bounded by the ratio of a person's wealth to total insurance cost; so that π approaches zero as p approaches zero. Thus, the required reliability will steeply rise for sufficiently rare disasters (i.e., the tolerance limit T will begin to accelerate toward infinity as p approaches zero—see Figure 1).[43] Note also

that rare events are precisely those which are remote to a person's normal experience, so that uncertainty in detecting which rare disasters to insure against increases as p approaches zero. Such greater uncertainty will reduce the reliability of insurance decisions (i.e., reduce the ration r/w) as disasters become increasingly remote to a person's normal experience.

As a result of the above factors, the required reliability of when to insure increases sharply just when the actual reliability is dropping. Thus, at some point as p approaches zero, the Reliability Condition will be violated (i.e., T will rise above the falling r/w ratio). This implies people will switch from typically buying to typically ignoring insurance options, which is just the pattern documented in Kunreuther's 1978 study.

We can also show that after a person switches to ignoring insurance, he will be very reluctantly convinced to insure by any information source, *except those local to his normal experience* (for example, a neighbor, a relative, or an "acquaintance" as suggested in the above quotation). Note further that ignoring insurance does not necessarily mean a person consciously decides to ignore all the various potential insurance options—either those obtainable by contacting an insurance agent, or many other ones for which no market insurance is available.

This is a simple example of a more general implication: agents will only become alert or sensitive to information about options whose selection is reliable; or conversely, they will fail to become aware of information about options whose selection is unreliable. Another example of selective alertness to information is the use (or disuse) of marginal cost information to make production decisions, discussed next.

---

[43] Consider also very briefly the behavior of the l/g ratio of the tolerance limit. The loss l will be a negative function of the expected value of the disaster losses (denoted $E(p)$) relative to the expected value of the insurance costs (denoted $C(p)$); that is, l is a negative function of $E(p)/C(p) = v(p)$, denoted $l(v(p))$. Similarly, g is a positive function of $v(p)$, denoted $g(v(p))$. Now think of a sequence of actuarily fair or "pure" insurance options for which $v(p) \cong 1$. If the estimated $v(p)$ is close to zero, then the l/g ratio will not deviate substantially from $l(1)/g(1)$. When this result is coupled with a steeply rising $(1 - \pi(p))/\pi(p)$ ratio as $p \to 0$, we have the same acceleration implied for $T(p) \cong l(1)/g(1) \times (1 - \pi(p))/\pi(p)$.

B. *Spontaneous Alertness to Marginal Cost Information in Simple Production Environments*

A memorable episode in the history of economics was the marginalist controversy about whether businessmen use marginal cost calculations to guide their production decisions. The debate prompted Alchian to write "Uncertainty, Evolution, and Economic Theory" (1950). This was the article that first explicitly justified optimization theory as an explanatory tool to predict the outcome of selection processes (i.e., selection processes will produce simulations to optimizing behavior, which claim is contradicted by the above analysis). Regardless of how one views this debate, it is clear that businessmen typically do not use or are even aware of the kinds of marginal calculations discussed in standard production theory (this lack of awareness is itself an empirical regularity). But what would happen in a relatively simple production environment in which such information could be readily monitored and used with little uncertainty in directing production decisions?

The Reliability Condition implies the spontaneous development (without any special training in economic theory) of alertness and sensitive reaction to marginal cost information for sufficiently simple production environments. This will not be the usual situation, but are there cases that would naturally fit this hypothesis? An example is summarized in the following passage from Hirshleifer's price theory text:

> Electricity is typically generated by companies that operate a number of separate producing plants, with a transmission network providing connections to consumers as well as ties among the generating plants...the operating problem at any moment of time is to assign output most economically among the generating plants....
>
> Fred M. Westfield investigated the operating practices of a leading American electric utility. He discovered that this company employs a dispatcher to actually "assign the load" from moment to moment among the different plants. The dispatcher is guided by a Station-Loading Sliderule that shows what the economist would regard as the Marginal Cost function of each plant. By mechanically manipulating his Sliderule, the dispatcher automatically equates Marginal Cost for all plants in operation in such as way as to meet the total generation requirement....
>
> The company's method of division of output, and the Sliderule itself, were developed by engineers lacking the slightest acquaintance with economic theory. The company's engineers thus independently "discovered" Marginal Cost analysis.... [1980, pp. 286–87]

The engineers did not discover marginal cost analysis, but rather developed a way of reacting to what we as economists would call marginal cost information. Nevertheless, the development of a Station-Loading Sliderule is confirming evidence for the hypothesis of spontaneous sensitivity to marginal cost information in simple production environments. On the other hand, within standard price theory, it can only represent an isolated special case that illustrates a clearly noticeable use of such information.

C. *Uncertainty Implies "Corridor" Dynamics for Macroeconomic Shocks*

A major issue in macroeconomic theory has a direct parallel with the insurance behavior phenomenon discussed above. Instead of deciding whether to insure against various natural disasters, think of a repertoire of activities to prepare for the negative effects of macroeconomic "shocks"; or more generally, anything that produces a coordination failure in an economic system.

When will an economic system evolve so as to "self-insure" against these potential sources of unemployment and other symptoms of coordination failure? Costly shock-preparation activities are beneficial if they are appropriately timed to mitigate the effects of a shock, but otherwise there is a loss from the reduction in output otherwise attainable.

Now suppose, analogous to the insurance case, that there are different types of shocks, some more severe than others; where larger shocks are possible but less and less likely to happen. In addition, the reliability of detecting when and how to prepare for large shocks decreases as their determinants and repercussions are more remote to agents' normal experience.

In a similar manner to that discussed for the insurance case, we can derive that the economy's structure will evolve so as to prepare for and react quickly to small shocks. However, outside of a certain zone or "corridor" around its long-run growth path, it will only very sluggishly react to sufficiently large, infrequent shocks. This is essentially the "corridor hypothesis" for macroeconomic systems recently advanced by Leijonhufvud (1981, pp. 103–29).

In this paper, I have not gone into the specific microprocesses involved (individual agent behavior, intra- and intermarket structures, transmission mechanisms, etc.). Nevertheless, even without adding more specific assumptions we can still derive this general qualitative feature as a necessary consequence of uncertainty. Standard economic theory has been unable to do so, as summarized by Leijonhufvud:

> ...general equilibrium theorists have at their command an impressive array of proven techniques for modelling systems that "always work well". Keynesian economists have experience with modelling systems that "never work". But, as yet, no one has the recipe for modelling systems that function pretty well most of the time but sometimes work very badly to coordinate economic activities.   [1981, p. 103]

D. A Clear Prediction of the Law of Demand

Suppose consumers do not have well-defined preference relations, but instead must deal with uncertainty in trying to detect when to buy more or less of particular commodities. Myriad "internal" perceptual and "external" environmental factors come together to determine the relative value of particular commodities. In a prospective sense, there is no reliable information to compare all the margins of choice to calculate the most preferred response for each future situation. Rather, consumers must try to react appropriately to various influences that might prompt them to purchase more of particular commodities.

Now suppose the price of a commodity x rises. In order to benefit from continued purchases, the actual value of successive units of the commodity must exceed the now higher opportunity cost implied from the price increase. The likelihood of this situation arising is less than before, given the same structure of motivational influences affecting the value of x. Thus, the probability π of the right situation to buy more x is smaller. For the same reason, even when the right situation arises, the average excess of actual value over the higher price of x (denoted g) is less than before. In addition, the average loss from purchasing more x at the wrong time (denoted l) is now higher than before the price of x went up. Each of these factors will increase the required reliability for purchasing x (i.e., the tolerance limit for purchasing x, $T = (l/g)(1 - \pi)/\pi$, will rise).

Given that T has risen, *how is the consumer to change his behavior to be more reliable in purchasing x?* A general answer is suggested in an extensive literature in behavioral psychology about signal detection experiments.[44] The earliest experiments were similar to hearing tests where a person tries to detect the presence of a signal amid background noise (over a sequence of trials where the signal's occurrence is randomly distributed). A variety of other detection skills have been tested, which involve pattern recognition situations and various information processing and other cognative skills. All of the experiments exhibit a key feature: a person can increase the reliability of his detection behavior only by being more cautious in detecting the signals. That is, greater reliability requires a person to reduce the probabil-

---

[44]See David Green and John Swets, 1974; James Egan, 1975. A brief appendix on the signal detection experiments (plus some further material on reliability principles suggested by these experiments) is available on request from the author.

580 *THE AMERICAN ECONOMIC REVIEW* SEPTEMBER 1983

ity of reacting regardless of whether the signal is present or not. Note that reliability in these experiments is measured by the r/w ratio used in the Reliability Condition (and reported in graphical form with *ROC* curves).[45]

Now apply this principle to detecting when to buy more of a commodity x. A person can be more reliable in purchasing x only by reducing the probability that potential influences will successively prompt him into purchasing (whether they be internal promptings, advertising, behavior of other consumers, or whatever).

Thus, we have a simple two-step syllogism: *a higher price requires purchasing behavior to be more reliable, which can be achieved only by reducing the probability of purchase*. This implication is essentially the law of demand for consumer behavior, yet without any qualification for income effects; nor must we use complicated Slutsky derivations, or other technical maximizing conditions. To some of us, the logic involved might even seem "too simple" compared to our intellectual investment in n-dimensional consumer theory. Nevertheless, in its simplicity is a clear, unambiguous implication of the Law of Demand, which we have never been able to derive with traditional optimizing methods.[46]

E. *Evolution of Property Rights, Trading, and Market Structure*

Let me sketch a scenario about the evolution of an exchange system. Suppose initially

[45] *ROC* stands for "receiver operating characteristic"; see Green and Swets, pp. 31–34.
[46] The Reliability Condition also implies a number of other key empirical regularities that are not derivable from basic maximization theory (see fn. 5 above). Another implication is that behavior will be relatively sensitive to information that defines an agent's local frame of reference within the environment. This will produce "framing effects" studied by Kahneman and Tversky, and a number of other anomalies now widely recognized in the risk-behavior literature (see fn. 30 above). Still other examples include the "excessive reaction" of securities and futures markets to "current information"; the "tendency to ignore prior information" used in Bayesian probabilities; and the "insensitivity of judgments to sample size"; even by "professionally trained" econometricians (see Arrow, 1981, pp. 3–7).

that the reliable range of flexibility of agents' behavioral rules is more than sufficient to handle the complexity of the social environment (say in the primitive beginnings of human society). As a result, agent interactions evolve into more complex relationships in which the consequences from each agent's individual behavior depend on the actions of more and more other agents. In addition, the behavior of these other agents will become increasingly remote to the local experience of each agent as the network of social interdependencies broadens. Consequently, uncertainty in determining the consequences from selecting particular actions will successively increase for each agent in the society.

At some point, the evolution of more complex social interdependence will stop, unless social structures also evolve that reduce the scope of nonlocal information that individual agents must know to reliably forecast the consequences of their own behavior. (In more precise terms, the scope of information over which agents can reliably interpret successively narrows as the social environment becomes more complex.)

In general, further evolution toward social interdependence will require institutions that permit agents to know about successively smaller fractions of the larger social environment. That is, *institutions must evolve which enable each agent in the society to know less and less about the behavior of other agents and about the complex interdependencies generated by their interaction*.

One of the basic ways of accomplishing this is to divide up the decision authority to use resources so that only particular agents (or small groups of agents) have the right to control their use. With such a right-to-control institution, individual agents no longer have to know how other agents might use their "privately owned" resources. A whole range of factors that are within an agent's local experience can now be used to determine the consequences of particular use decisions. Two of the more important possibilities are decisions about whether to consume or delay the use of a resource, and about whether to transfer the right-to-control resources to other agents. Obtaining the right to control itself becomes valuable, given that only local information is now required to control the use of a resource.

In more basic terms, the question is whether agents will be willing to cooperate with each other through increasingly complex interdependencies that have the potential—if properly coordinated—to increase average output per agent. As the society becomes more complex, agents will cooperate only in ways that enable them to use increasingly local information to detect whether they will individually benefit. That is, they will exhibit a "propensity to cooperate" only in situations where increasingly local experience indicates a benefit—even if such restriction cuts off a whole range of benefits that might result from more subtly interconnected forms of cooperation. A major way of satisfying this restrictive criteria is to cooperate only in situations where agents immediately reciprocate the cooperative actions of each other, such that each perceives a net benefit based on his own self-evaluation of the forsaken and received items.

This form of reciprocation enables agents to decide based on immediately local experience about the results from cooperating. Thus, their tendency to cooperate in such situations will be relatively great compared to myriad other possibilities that would require the reliable use of more nonlocal information to avoid mistakes. (In more precise terms, we can show that the probability of agents cooperating in such situations will be much higher than for other forms of cooperation.) This limited tendency to cooperate can itself be regarded as a behavioral regularity, one that Adam Smith recognized as the "propensity to truck or barter." Notice also that such a propensity depends on a structure of property rights that enables agents' self-evaluations to determine the use of resources without knowing the behavior of other agents.

The above discussion is only a brief illustration of a large number of implications about legal and market institutions. These institutions will evolve so as to provide predictable opportunity for mutual reciprocation situations; and so as to reduce the scope and complexity of information that must be reliably interpreted for agents to benefit from

these situations. For example, a few implications include: a restriction to more centralized market organization and to financial instruments that enable agents to avoid knowing the particular circumstances, attributes, and identity of potential reciprocators and the items reciprocated; a severe restriction of futures markets and auction markets to certain strategic locations within a larger network of inventory markets structured so as to reduce price fluctuations;[47] and ownership structures that enable agents to avoid detecting whether continued reciprocation will be maintained, especially when this is necessary for particular reciprocators to realize longer term benefits or to prevent certain losses.[48] The essential factor in all of these institutional regularities is uncertainty in deciphering the complexity of the social environment.[49]

Finally, let me mention another key feature about the possibility of coordination failures. A complex cooperative system must somehow limit the occurrence of serious coordination failures. Nevertheless, its very complexity can evolve only to the extent that it enables agents to benefit without deciphering more than a tiny fraction of its overall structure. As a result, a complex system can-

---

[47]A few modern references on the above topics are: Alchian, 1969, 1977; Robert Clower, 1967; Clower and Leijonhufvud, 1975; Robert Jones, 1976; Seiichi Kawasaki et al., 1982; Lester Telser, 1981.

[48]The reliability model can be used both to predict the likelihood of opportunistic behavior (discontinuing reciprocation), and how the likelihood of such behavior affects the required reliability of various kinds of contractual arrangements. In many cases, the only solution is to structure ownership of assets in a way that eliminates having to detect when to engage in certain contracts. This will produce a stable regularity in contractual and market ownership patterns, which are also studied under the rubric of "transaction costs" (see Williamson, 1975, 1979, 1981, 1983; Benjamin Klein et al., 1978; also Alchian and Demsetz, 1972; Coase, 1937, 1960; Demsetz, 1969, 1967; Dahlman, 1980).

[49]Standard choice theory concentrates exclusively on the potential gains from trade (via Edgeworth exchange boxes, etc.), rather than on the effect of uncertainties created in trying to realize that potential. Consequently, we now have an elaborate general equilibrium theory of exchange which is devoid of the very institutional regularities necessary for complex exchange economies to evolve in the first place (see the epilogue of Vernon Smith, 1982, p. 952).

not prevent coordination failures that would require agents to understand a sizeable fraction of its complexity in order to avert them.

VI. Switching and Punctuation Dynamics

Recall the notation introduced above in Section IV, Part E, where $z = (s, c, m, e)$ represents an agent's sensory (s), cognitive (c), and morphological (m) components (hereafter denoted by $y = (s, c, m)$), along with the environmental variables e. Using these variables, we can analyze how uncertainty affects the dynamic response of behavioral rules, and how agents' internal components interact with each other and with the environment to generate evolutionary change in themselves and in the surrounding environment. Two key dynamic properties are conditioned by the transition point between satisfying or violating the Reliability Condition (i.e., the point at which $r/w = T$).

First: Changes in the environmental variables e may shift the reliability ratio r/w or the tolerance limit T of an action; causing them to "cross over" each other from their initial positions (i.e., shift r/w from below T to above it, or vice versa). If this happens, rule-governed behavior will switch from allowing to severely restricting that action. Thus, a relatively sudden "switching" between different behavior patterns may occur.

Second: If the reliability ratio of an action is initially bounded below its tolerance limit, then behavioral rules will prohibit that action. Now consider a small change in a particular component, $y^0 \in y$, which would shift r/w and T for such an action closer together, but not enough for them to cross over each other. So long as this is the case, there will be no change in an agent's behavior that might improve or worsen his performance, because the Reliability Condition for selecting that action is still violated. Suppose, however, that movement in some of the *other* z variables besides y^0 (which might include the e variables) shift r/w and T sufficiently for them to cross over each other.

At the point of transition, greater reliability from changes in y^0 will now allow selecting the action to improve an agent's performance; which may initiate evolutionary adjustment of y^0 in the appropriate direction. This means that the y attributes may exhibit relatively sudden increases or decreases in the speed of evolutionary change. Thus, evolutionary adjustment in the y attributes may be "punctuated" with a variety of sudden changes, especially as a large number of such attributes interact through an agent's behavioral rules, or the environment is itself influenced by the actions of other agents.

It is significant that a simple "crossover" mechanism will generate irregular dynamic movement in the outward behavior or internal attributes of an agent, and suggests an alternative to the recent attempts to account for such effects via catastrophe theory.[50] A recursive use of the Reliability Condition can also generate systematic hysteresis effects, in which the crossover point depends on the past history and direction of a variable's movement.[51]

A few examples to illustrate the above two dynamic properties are the following:

1) A number of implications characterize sudden switching of animal behavior between different actions, such as aggressive behavior in either attacking or retreating, or territorial behavior in either attack or defense strategies. A common example in economics involves switching between buying and selling strategies in financial markets, resulting in sudden movement in stock prices. In general, a wide range of behavior in economics is governed by such switching and hysteresis effects and has been obscured by the use of traditional optimization theory.

2) A specific economic illustration of the crossover mechanism is the "corridor hypothesis" for macroeconomic systems discussed above in Section V. Another example

---

[50] See E. C. Zeeman, 1977; Rene Thóm, 1975; David Berlinski, 1975; Hector Sussman, 1975.

[51] Consider very briefly a two-stage use of the Reliability Condition. First, $r/w = T$ is used to characterize a transition point between different behavior patterns. Second, introduce uncertainty about an agent trying to detect unstable shifts in this transition point. An agent may fail to switch once the transition point is reached, or he might mistakenly switch too early. A second application of the Reliability Condition implies that an agent will delay switching until he rarely switches too early; so that the observed switching point will shift depending on the action selected before the switch occurred.

VOL. 73 NO. 4   HEINER: ORIGIN OF PREDICTABLE BEHAVIOR   583

is a structure of expectation "stages" during inflations (ranging from initially "sluggish" to eventually "explosive" expectation adjustment), which contrasts with recent rational expectations modeling.[52]

3) Growing evidence supports the "punctuation hypothesis" recently advanced in evolutionary biology, which claims that irregular bursts in the pace of evolutionary change have produced speciation and macroevolution of dramatic morphological changes (see Stephen Gould and Niles Eldredge, 1977; Steven Stanley, 1979).

4) An example of the latter which has been of considerable interest is the dramatic expansion of the cerebrum responsible for the higher thought processes of humans. Of all the various y attributes, the cerebrum most directly tends to prompt increasingly sophisticated behavior patterns. Right situations for selecting particular actions within a behavioral repertoire will become increasingly rare as the complexity of that repertoire increases.[53] This will cause a steeply rising acceleration in the required reliability for selecting these actions. Thus, if the second dynamic property above ever triggers rapid expansion of the cerebrum, then its sudden leveling off at a larger size is also implied. This dynamic pattern has been of interest and puzzlement in the biology literature.[54]

VII. Hierarchical Structure and Evolution of Reliable Complexity

We can also characterize how uncertainty may generate hierarchical structures of increasingly flexible rules. Such rule-hierarchies have far reaching applications, some of which

are briefly discussed in the following remarks:

1) For example, consider a system of components that interact with each other at level v, while these interactions comprise a larger system that interacts within a surrounding environment at level $v + 1$. For simplicity, the relationship between a system and its subcomponents is functionally written, $s_{v+1}(s_v)$, where s_{v+1} denotes the system and s_v denotes its subcomponents. Thus, we have a recursive structure of rule-governed systems, $s_{v+1}(s_v)$, where each element of s_v is itself a system of components at the next lower level $v - 1$, denoted $s_v(s_{v-1})$.

2) Now, suppose that more simply structured subcomponents decrease the reliability of a system in administering more complex interactions with its environment. For example, such components might be more vulnerable in distinguishing nonlocal phenomena. For any given level of subcomponent structure, viable performance requires a minimum degree of behavioral rigidity. Thus no system composed of similarly structured components can allow greater flexibility without hindering its viability. Consequently, the only way more sophisticated behavior could arise from such systems is for a number of them to evolve into the subcomponents of a still larger system. Since the components of the larger system are recursively built up from smaller subsystems, additional structure may be permitted which enables them to reliably guide more complex behavior of a larger system. When this is possible, the behavior of the larger system can be less rigidly constrained than its component subsystems.

3) Recent discoveries in microbiology dramatically illustrate this implication. They show how molecular mechanisms direct the embryological unfolding of living systems. The essential feature of all of these mechanisms are large molecular structures (containing hundreds or thousands of atoms) that interact with each other literally by recognizing each other's shape. That is, they interact with noncovalent bonds which are very much weaker than the covalent bonds (i.e., the merging of electron clouds) of physical chemistry. Thus, stable bonding requires a relatively large surface closely matched to

[52] The explosive stage could refer to the final phase of a hyperinflation in which agent's expectations so quickly adjust that trying to counteract this reaction by further money supply acceleration will drive real balances toward zero.

[53] As an agent's behavior becomes more complex, each additional action must compete against more and more other actions. Thus, the likelihood of an additional action being more preferred than other actions is conditional on the behavioral complexity of an agent; and in general will decrease as the complexity of his repertoire increases.

[54] See, for example, Edward Wilson, 1975, pp. 547–50; Jerison, 1973, pp. 402–43; D. Pilbean, 1972.

the shape of another molecule (which large surfaces require many atoms within each molecule).[55] Molecular shape enables the precise calibration of "stereo-specific" bonding, which permits a much more complex structure of interaction possibilities than otherwise possible with the more rigid constraints of physical chemistry. Moreover, the precise recognition properties of stereo-specific bonding enables the reliable direction of complicated molecular mechanisms, as evidenced in the biochemistry of cell regulation and embryological processes.[56] The significance of this is summarized by Nobel Prize biochemist Jacques Monod:[57]

> [Stereo-specific bonding gave] molecular evolution a practically limitless field for exploration and experiment, [which] enabled it to elaborate the huge network of cybernetic interconnections which makes each organism an autonomous functional unit, whose performances appear to transcend the laws of chemistry if not to ignore them altogether. [1972, p. 78]

4) If the recursive structure, $s_{v+1}(s_v)$, is continued to higher or lower levels ($v+2$, $v+3,\ldots$; or $v-1, v-2,\ldots$) we obtain a hierarchical structure of increasingly sophisticated systems, where later stages are governed by successively more flexible rules. Such hierarchical structures represent a basic way systems conditioned by uncertainty can evolve into allowing successively more sophisticated behavior without hindering their viability in the process.

This pattern of hierarchical development is systematically evidenced in nature at a number of intertwining levels. For example, there are the invariable behavior patterns of atoms, which are composed of successively more basic subatomic particles; and which are themselves components of larger cosmological systems whose behavior is also synony-

mous with highly predictable laws.[58] Above this level, there is another hierarchy of organic molecules (discussed above) that eventually form components in living cells. Such cells in turn are subcomponents of still larger organs and tissues that permit relatively more flexible behavior of yet another hierarchy of increasingly sophisticated living organisms. Finally, there is the subtle, usually difficult to predict, behavior of humans and their social institutions. Looking back on this structure, the particular course of its evolution may be extremely improbable. Nevertheless, what did evolve has been through a hierarchical process from very predictable to relatively much less predictable phenomena.

5) Hierarchical structures may also have systematic importance in the design of cognitive and related (natural and artificial) learning processes.[59] For example, there may be

---

[55] See J. Monod, 1972, pp. 45–46.

[56] See J. Monod, 1972, chs. 4–7.

[57] For a recent more technical overview of the subject, see James Watson, 1976.

[58] The body of this paper has only briefly alluded to the physical sciences. At issue is whether the invariable regularities exhibited by natural phenomena can be regarded as "rule-mechanisms" to cope with extreme uncertainty in avoiding destabilizing interactions between the components of a system that might disintegrate its structure? More generally, what patterns of component interaction are viable in the sense of generating their own continuation, or the continuation of larger interactive patterns between components which are themselves systems? Many topics in the physical sciences could be discussed, but only three topics are mentioned here. First, we can analyze uncertainty in producing stable macrostructures to characterize relationships between the "particles" of matter and the "forces" that interconnect them. Second, we can consider uncertainty in maintaining the structural stability of tightly compacted systems to characterize symmetry properties, and other statistical regularities studied in quantum mechanics. Third, we can analyze the effects of violating the general relativity postulate of modern physics, especially about uncertainties in dealing with complex interdependencies permitted without the constraint of generally covariant interactions. On these three topics see respectively: P. C. W. Davies, 1979; J. P. Elliot and P. G. Dawber, 1979; Enrico Cantore, 1969; Albert Einstein, 1952, 1956.

Underlying these regularities is a persistent theme about the unity of science, as suggested in the following remark by Einstein: "The most incomprehensible thing about the universe is why it is so comprehensible." (See also the closing remarks of Kuhn's 1962 essay, p. 173.) The answer may lie in how extreme uncertainty affects the structure of self-continuing physical systems.

[59] See Simon, 1969, 1979a; Newell and Simon, 1972; J. R. Anderson, 1980; G. T. Miller et al., 1960.

resistance to knowledge not built up in recursive stages. For example, explicitly hierarchical methods have evolved in the above-mentioned strategy books on playing blackjack, and more recently on how to solve Rubik's cube.[60]

6) It has also been argued by Kohlberg, with extensive supporting experimentation, that the moral development of children as they mature into adults follows a highly patterned hierarchical structure of six stages. The first stage is guided by "blind obedience to rules and authority...," which proceeds though intermediate steps to stage six, which is "guided by self-chosen ethical principles."[61] A pattern of successively more complex moral judgments is clearly suggested in this hierarchy.

7) The viability of an evolving system, (for example an ecological system of organisms, or an exchange system of competing agents), which originates truly novel change (whose interactive possibilities are largely unrelated to the system's past history) may be quite sensitive to uncertainty in avoiding disruptive novelty. If this is the case, the very processes which generate and select such novelty will themselves be organized in a hierarchical structure of increasingly flexible rule-mechanisms. An important illustration is the structure of relationships that connect the rigidly patterned molecular design of DNA to the more visible interactions comprising natural selection.[62]

Other implications characterize the diversity and pace of novel change that can be reliably controlled by an evolving system. For example, a more rapid average pace is permitted as the reliability of selective processes increases. These implications underly the major differences in the qualitative nature and average speed of cultural compared to biological evolution.

VIII. Conclusion

I have argued that uncertainty is the basic source of predictable behavior, and also the main conditioning factor of evolutionary processes through which such behavior evolves. Uncertainty exists because agents cannot decipher all of the complexity of the decision problems they face, which literally prevents them from selecting most preferred alternatives. Consequently, the flexibility of behavior to react to information is constrained to smaller behavioral repertoires that can be reliably administered. Numerous deviations from the resulting behavior patterns are actually superior in certain situations, but they are still ignored because of uncertainty about when to deviate from these regularities.

In contrast, standard economics analyzes the special case of no uncertainty in selecting most preferred options. This way of understanding behavior forces the determinants of uncertainty into the residual "error term" between observed behavior and the more systematic patterns claimed to result from optimization. I am thus suggesting a reversal of the explanation assumed in standard economics: the factors that standard theory places in the error term are in fact what is producing behavioral regularities, while optimizing will tend to produce sophisticated deviations from these patterns. Hence, the

---

[60]A good example of a hierarchical method is Kosniowski, 1981, especially in contrast to David Singmaster, 1979 (called the "definitive treatise" by *Scientific American*), which follows a complex, cyclical development of ideas that switches back and forth between different parts of the book. Singmaster's book is also several times longer than later books (cited above in fn. 14), both in terms of number of words and notational density.

[61]See Kohlberg, 1976, pp. 30 and 32; and 1963, 1969.

[62]Consider the extreme uncertainty of tiny molecular structures directing the construction of living systems. Maurice Wilkin's 1953 paper (which accompanied Watson and Cricks' original paper in *Nature*) begins: "While the biological properties of deoxypentose nucleic acid suggest a molecular structure containing great complexity, X-ray diffraction studies described here show the basic molecular configuration has great simplicity" (p. 738). The Reliability Condition implies the opposite

presumption; namely, that precisely because DNA is the ultimate source of larger biological systems, whose complexity cannot be reliably manipulated from any interaction local to its tiny structure, its internal design must be both rigidly patterned and engineered to replicate virtually without guidance from its local chemical environment.

observed regularities that economics has tried to explain on the basis of optimization would disappear if agents could actually maximize.

Another basic conclusion is that appropriately structured behavioral rules will not necessarily arise. Rather, they will evolve to the extent that selection processes quickly eliminate poorly administered behavior. This will more likely occur when agents are involved in highly competitive interactions that themselves indirectly result from scarcity. However, if weak selection processes are present, relatively vulnerable or dysfunctional behavior may evolve.

One area of major normative significance is the development of human social institutions; in particular, political institutions that have the opportunity to influence the outcomes generated by exchange competition. This is especially important if human agents are able to foresee numerous potential cases where the cooperative results of exchange institutions could be improved, but without being able to reliably administer the additional complexity necessary to realize those improvements.

Think of this issue in terms of the Reliability Condition. People may be able to identify government actions where situations exist in which a society will benefit (i.e., the probability of right circumstances π for selecting these actions is positive). Nevertheless, they may be unable to administer these actions with sufficient reliability to benefit the society by adding them to the government's repertoire of authorized activities (i.e., $r/w < T$ even though $\pi > 0$). If this is the case, the society will benefit by appropriately limiting the scope and complexity of government behavior.

But how is such limitation to arise? It is here that we enter the area of "constitutionalism," defined broadly as the design of rule-mechanisms to restrict the flexibility of government to react to whatever influences might prompt it to engage in vulnerable activities. The writings of seventeenth- and eighteenth-century political philosophers and statesmen were primarily concerned with these issues. Out of their efforts came a number of features incorporated in

the United States Constitution, such as the separation of powers mechanism.[63]

On a wider scale, the history of civilization can be organized around a theme of groping for social rule-mechanisms.[64] Nevertheless, the understanding of such mechanisms is only in its rudimentary beginnings; and in the last hundred years, the general trend has been away from these topics—especially for analysts trained in mainstream economic theory.[65] The reason is that mainstream theories have systematically directed attention away from the study of processes that limit flexibility to choose potentially preferred actions. A refocusing of research on such processes—with the appropriate analytical framework to guide us—may have practical consequences for the viability of existing institutions.

---

[63] The basic source materials on these issues are the Federalist Papers by Hamilton and Jefferson (for example, numbers 10, 47, 48, 51). For a modern reference, see Martin Diamond, 1981.

[64] The often seemingly bizarre practices of religion and cultural ritual may also represent the design technologies of social rules crucial to the coordination and intensification of social bonds. For some interesting readings about ritual, symbolism, and comparative religion, see William Lessa and Evon Vogt, 1979, and M. Gluckman, 1962.

[65] Notable exceptions to this general trend are the writings of Buchanan and Hayek (see fn. 31 above).

REFERENCES

Abernathy, William J., *The Productivity Dilemma: Roadblock to Innovation in the Automobile Industry*, Baltimore: Johns Hopkins University Press, 1978.

_____, Clark, Kim and Kantrow, A., "The New Industrial Competition," *Harvard Business Review*, September-October 1981, *59*, 68–81.

Alchian, Armen A., "Uncertainty, Evolution and Economic Theory," *Journal of Political Economy*, June 1950, *58*, 211–21.

_____, "Information Costs, Pricing and Resource Unemployment," *Western Economic Journal*, June 1969, 7, 109–28.

_____, "Why Money?," *Journal of Money*,

Credit, and Banking, February 1977, 9, 133–40.

_____ and Demsetz, Harold, "Production, Information Costs, and Economic Efficiency," American Economic Review, December 1972, 62, 777–95.

Alcock, John, Animal Behavior: An Evolutionary Approach, Sunderland: Sinauer Associates, 1979.

Aldrich, R., Organization and Environments, Englewood Cliffs: Prentice-Hall, 1979.

Alexander, Richard, Darwinism and Public Affairs, Seattle: University of Washington Press, 1979.

_____ and Borgin, G., "Group Selection, Altruism, and the Levels of Organization of Life," Annual Review of Ecology and Systematics, September 1978, 9, 449–75.

Anderson, Ian, Turning the Tables on Las Vegas, New York: Harper & Row, 1975.

Anderson, J. R., Cognitive Psychology and Its Implications, San Francisco: W. H. Freeman, 1980.

Archer, John, The Archer Method of Winning at 21, Hollywood: Wilshire Book Company, 1973.

Arrow, Kenneth J., "Risk Perception in Psychology and Economics," Economic Inquiry, January 1981, 20, 1–9.

_____, "Vertical Integration and Communication," Bell Journal of Economics, Spring 1975, 6, 173–83.

Ashby, W., An Introduction to Cybernetics, New York: Wiley, 1956.

Athos, Anthony G. and Pascale, Richard T., The Art of Japanese Management, New York: Simon & Schuster, 1981.

Axelrod, Robert, (1980a) "Effective Choice in the Prisoner's Dilemma," Journal of Conflict Resolution, March 1980, 24, 3–25.

_____, (1980b) "More Effective Choice in the Prisoner's Dilemma," Journal of Conflict Resolution, September 1980, 24, 379–403.

Barlow, B. W., The Cube: A Short and Easy Solution, Salt Lake City: Hawkes Publishing, 1981.

Berlinski, David, "Mathematical Models of the World," Synthese, August 1975, 31, 211–27.

Black, M. R. and Taylor, H., Unscrambling the Cube, Burbank: Zephyr Engineering Design, 1980.

Blackwell, David and Girshick, M. A., Theory of Games and Statistical Decisions, New York: Dover, 1979.

Bookstaber, Richard and Langsam, Joseph, "Coarse Behavior and Extended Uncertainty," Working Paper 83–1, Graduate School of Management, Brigham Young University, 1983.

Boland, Lawrence, A., "On the Futility of Criticizing the Neoclassical Maximization Hypothesis," American Economic Review, December 1981, 71, 1031–36.

Bradshaw, C. M., Szabadi, E. and Bevan, R., "Behavior of Humans in Variable-Interval Schedules of Reinforcement," Journal of the Experimental Analysis of Behavior, September 1976, 26, 135–41.

Brown, Roger and Herrnstein Richard, Psychology, Boston: Little-Brown, 1975.

Buchanan, James M., Freedom in Constitutional Contract, College Station: Texas A&M University Press, 1977.

_____, The Limits of Liberty: Between Anarchy and the Leviathan, Chicago: University of Chicago Press, 1975.

_____ and Brennan H. G., Monopoly in Money and Inflation, London: Institute for Economic Affairs, 1981.

Buskist, William F. and Miller, Harold L., Jr., "Concurrent Operant Performance in Humans: Matching When Food is the Reinforcer," Psychological Record, January 1981, 31, 95–100.

Bussert, Patrick, You Can Do the Cube, New York: Puffin Books, 1981.

Cagan, Phillip, "The Monetary Dynamics of Hyperinflation," in M. Friedman, ed., Studies in the Quantity Theory of Money, Chicago: University of Chicago Press, 1956.

Caldwell, B., Beyond Positivism: Economic Methodology In the Twentieth Century, London: Allen & Unwin, 1982.

Campbell, Donald C., "On the Conflicts Between Biological and Social Evolution and Between Psychology and Moral Tradition," American Psychologist, December 1975, 30, 1103–26.

_____, "Downward Causation in Hierarchi-

588   THE AMERICAN ECONOMIC REVIEW   SEPTEMBER 1983

cally Organized Biological Systems," in F. J. Ayala and T. Dobzhausky, eds., *Studies in the Philosophy of Biology*, New York: Macmillan, 1974.

Canfield, Richard A., *Blackjack: Your Way to Riches*, Secaucus: Lyle Stuart, Inc., 1979.

Cantore, Enrico, *Atomic Order: An Introduction to the Philosophy of Microphysics*, Cambridge: MIT Press, 1969.

Cardoza, Avery D., *Winning Casino Blackjack for the Noncounter*, Santa Cruz: Cardoza School of Blackjack, 1981.

Carter, C. F. and Williams, B. R., *Industry and Technical Progress: Factors Governing the Speed of Application of Science*, New York: Oxford University, 1957.

Cavelli-Sforza, L., and Feldman, Marcus, *Cultural Transmission & Evolution: A Quantitative Approach*, Princeton: Princeton University, 1981.

Chandler, Alfred D., *Strategy and Structure: Chapters in the History of Industrial Enterprise*, Cambridge: MIT Press, 1962.

_____, *The Visible Hand: The Managerial Revolution in American Business*, Cambridge: Belknap Press, 1977.

Cheung, Steven, "Transactions Costs, Risk Aversion, and the Choice of Contractual Arrangements," *Journal of Law and Economics*, April 1969, *12*, 23–42.

Chew, S. H. and MacCrimmon, K. R., (1979a) "Alpha-Nu Choice Theory: A Generalization of Expected Utility Theory," Working Paper No. 669, University of British Columbia, 1979.

_____ and _____, (1979b) "Alpha Utility Theory, Lottery Composition, and the Allais Paradox," Working Paper No. 686, University of British Columbia, 1979.

Chomsky, N., *Language and Mind*, New York: Harcourt, Brace & Jovanovich, 1972.

Clark, R., *The Japanese Company*, New Haven: Yale University Press, 1979.

Clower, Robert W., "The Keynesian Counterrevolution: A Theoretical Appraisal," in F. Hahn and F. Brechling eds., *The Theory of Interest Rates*, London: Macmillan, 1965.

_____, "A Reconsideration of the Microfoundations of Monetary Theory," *Western Economic Journal*, December 1967, *6*, 1–8.

_____ and Leijonhufvud, Axel, "The Coordination of Economic Activities: A Keynesian Perspective," *American Economic Review Proceedings*, May 1975, *65*, 182–88.

Coase, Ronald H., "The Nature of the Firm," *Economica*, November 1937, *4*, 386–405.

_____, "The Problem of Social Cost," *Journal of Law and Economics*, October 1960, *3*, 1–44.

_____, "Adam Smith's View of Man," *Journal of Political Economy*, October 1976, *19*, 529–46.

Cohen, Michael D. and Axelrod, Robert, "Coping with Complexity: The Adaptive Value of Changing Utility," *American Economic Review*, forthcoming.

Conner, M., *The Tangled Wing: Biological Constraints on the Human Spirit*, New York: Basic Books, 1982.

Conrath, D., "From Statistical Decision Theory to Practice: Some Problems with the Transition," *Management Science*, April 1973, *19*, 873–94.

Cooley, Thomas F. and LeRoy, Stephen F., "Identification and Estimation of Money Demand," *American Economic Review*, December 1981, *71*, 825–44.

Cooter, Robert, (1982a) "The Cost of Coase," *Journal of Legal Studies*, January 1982, *11*, 1–34.

_____, **Marks, Stephen and Mnookin, Robert,** (1982b) "Bargaining in the Shadow of the Law: A Testable Model of Strategic Behavior," *Journal of Legal Studies*, June 1982, *11*, 225–52.

Dahlman, Carl, *The Open Field System and Beyond*, Cambridge: Cambridge University Press, 1980.

Davies, P. C. W., *The Forces of Nature*, Cambridge: Cambridge University Press, 1979.

Demsetz, Harold, "Information and Efficiency: Another Viewpoint," *Journal of Law and Economics*, April 1969, *12*, 1–22.

_____, "Toward a Theory of Property Rights," *American Economic Review Proceedings*, May 1967, *57*, 347–59.

de Villiers, P., "Choice in Concurrent Schedules and a Quantitative Formulation of the Law of Effect," in W. K. Honig and J. E. R. Standdon, eds., *Handbook of Operant Behavior*, Englewood Cliffs: Prentice-Hall, 1977, 233–87.

Diamond, Martin, *The Founding of the Democratic Republic*, Itasca: Peacock, 1981.

Diamond, Peter and Rothschild, Michael, *Uncertainty in Economics*, New York: Academic Press, 1978.

Dornbusch, Rudiger and Fischer, Stanley, *Macro-Economics*, New York: McGraw-Hill, 1978.

Drèze, Jacques H., "Axiomatic Theories of Choice, Cardinal Utility, and Subjective Probability," a review in his *Allocation Under Uncertainty: Equilibrium and Optimality*, New York: Wiley, 1974, 1–23; reprinted in P. Diamond and M. Rothschild, eds., *Uncertainty in Economics*, New York: Academic Press, 1978, 37–57.

Dubey, Leon B., Jr., *No Need to Count: A Practical Approach to Casino Blackjack*, San Diego: A.S. Barnes & Co., 1980.

Edwards, Ward, "Subjective Probabilities Inferred from Decisions," *Psychological Review*, March 1962, *69*, 109–35.

Egan, James P., *Signal Detection Theory and ROC Analysis*, New York: Academic Press, 1975.

Einstein, Albert, *The Meaning of Relativity: Including the Relativistic Theory of the Non-Symmetric Field*, Princeton: Princeton University Press, 1956.

_____, *The Principle of Relativity*, New York: Dover, 1952.

Elliot, J. P. and Dawber, P. G., *Symmetry in Physics*, Vols. 1; 2, London: Macmillan, 1979.

Elster, John, *Ulyssess and the Sirens*, Cambridge: Cambridge University Press, 1979.

Fellner, William, "Distortion of Subjective Probabilities as a Reaction to Uncertainty," *Quarterly Journal of Economics*, November 1961, *75*, 670–90.

Ferguson, Thomas S., *Mathematical Statistics: A Decision Theoretic Approach*, New York: Academic Press, 1967.

Fishburn, Peter C., "Transitive Measurable Utility," Discussion Paper No. 224, Bell Laboratories, 1981.

Fischer, Stanley, "Long Term Contracts, Rational Expectations, and the Optimal Money Supply Rule," *Journal of Political Economy*, February 1977, *85*, 191–206.

Friedman, Milton, "The Methodology of Positive Economics," in his *Essays in Positive Economics*, 1953; reprinted in W. Breit and H. M. Hochman, eds., *Readings in Microeconomics*, New York: Holt, Rinehart & Winston, 1968, 23–47.

_____, *A Program for Monetary Stability*, New York: Fordham University Press, 1969.

_____ and Savage, L. J., "The Utility Analysis of Choices Involving Risks," *Journal of Political Economy*, August 1948, *56*, 279–304.

Gibson, J., "The Theory of Affordances," in R. E. Shaw and J. Bransford, eds., *Perceiving, Acting, and Knowing*, Hillsdale: Lawrence Erlbaum Assoc., 1977.

Gluckman, M., *Essays on the Ritual of Social Relations*, Manchester: Manchester University Press, 1962.

Gould, Stephen J. and Eldredge, Niles, "Punctuated Equilibria: The Tempo and Mode of Evolution Reconsidered," *Paleobiology*, January 1977, *3*, 115–51.

Graham, Virginia L. and Tulcea, C. Ionescu, *A Book on Casino Gambling*, New York: Pocket Books, 1978.

Green, David M. and Swets, John A., *Signal Detection Theory and Psychophysics*, New York: Robert Kriegur, 1974.

Grinder, R., "Parental Childrearing Practices, Conscience, and Resistance to Temptation of Sixth-Grade Children," *Child Development*, December 1962, *33*, 802–20.

Hahn, Frank, *On the Notion of Equilibrium in Economics*, Cambridge: Cambridge University Press, 1973.

Hamilton, W. D., "The Genetical Evolution of Social Behavior," *Journal of Theoretical Biology*, 1964, *7*, 1–17.

Hayek, F. A., *Studies in Philosophy, Politics, and Economics*, Chicago: University of Chicago Press, 1967.

_____, *Law, Legislation, and Liberty*, Chicago: University of Chicago Press, 1973.

Heiner, Ronald A., "A Theory of Predictable Behavior: Application to Insurance Behavior Anomolies," Department of Economics, Brigham Young University, February 1982.

Heisenberg, Werner, *The Physical Principles of the Quantum Theory*, New York: Dover, 1949.

590   THE AMERICAN ECONOMIC REVIEW   SEPTEMBER 1983

Herrnstein, Richard J., "On the Law of Effect," *Journal of the Experimental Analysis of Behavior*, November 1970, *13*, 243–66.

_____, "Relative and Absolute Strength of Response as a Function of Frequency of Reinforcement," *Journal of the Experimental Analysis of Behavior*, 1961, *4*, 267–72.

_____, "Secondary Reinforcement and Rate of Primary Reinforcement," *Journal of the Experimental Analysis of Behavior*, January 1964, *7*, 74–91.

_____ **and Heyman, Gene M.**, "Is Matching Compatible with Maximization in Concurrent Variable Interval, Variable Ratio?," *Journal of the Experimental Analysis of Behavior*, March 1979, *31*, 209–23.

_____ **and Vaughan, W.**, "Melioration and Behavioral Allocation," in J. E. R. Staddon, ed., *Limits to Action: The Allocation of Individual Behavior*, New York: Academic Press, 1980, 143–76.

Hess, W. R., *Imprinting: Early Experience and the Developmental Psychobiology of Attachment*, New York: Van Nostrand 1973.

Hetherington, E. Mavis and Park, Ross D., *Child Psychology: A Contemporary Viewpoint*, 2d ed., New York: McGraw-Hill, 1979.

Hey, John D., *Uncertainty in Microeconomics*, New York: New York University Press, 1979.

Heyman, Gene M. and Luce, R. Duncan, "Operant Matching is not a Logical Consequence of Maximizing Reinforcement Rate," *Animal Learning and Behavior*, May 1979, *7*, 133–40.

Hicks, John, "A Suggestion for Simplifying the Theory of Money," *Economica*, February 1935, *2*, 1–19.

Hirshleifer, Jack, "Evolutionary Models in Economics and the Law: Cooperation Versus Conflict Strategies," *Research in Law and Economics*, 1982, *4*, 1–60.

_____, "Economics from a Biological Viewpoint," *Journal of Law and Economics*, April 1977, *20*, 1–54.

_____, *Price Theory and Applications*, 2d ed., Englewood Cliffs: Prentice-Hall, 1980.

_____ **and Riley, John**, "The Analytics of Uncertainty and Information," *Journal of Economic Literature*, December 1979, *17*, 1375– 421.

Hoffman, Eric and Spitzer, Mathew, "The Coase Theorem: Some Experimental Tests," *Journal of Law and Economics*, April 1982, *25*, 73–98.

Hogarth, R. M., "Cognitive Processes and the Assessment of Subjective Probability Distributions," *Journal of the American Statistical Association*, June 1975, *70*, 271–94.

Holmes, Warren G. and Sherman, Paul W., "Kin Selection in Animals," *American Scientist*, January-February 1983, *7*, 46–56.

Howard, N., *Paradoxes of Rationality*, Cambridge: MIT Press, 1971.

Jerison, Harry, *Evolution of the Brain and Intelligence*, New York: Academic Press, 1973.

Jones, Robert, "On the Origin and Development of Media of Exchange," *Journal of Political Economy*, August 1976, *84*, 757–76.

Judson, Horace F., *The Eighth Day of Creation*, New York: Simon & Schuster, 1979.

Kahneman, Daniel and Tversky, Amos, "Prospect Theory: An Analysis of Decision Under Risk," *Econometrica*, March 1979, *47*, 263–91.

_____ **and** _____, "The Framing of Decisions and the Psychology of Choice," *Science Magazine*, January 30, 1981, *211*, 453–58.

_____ **and** _____, "The Psychology of Preferences," *Scientific American*, January 1982, *246*, 160–73.

Kawasaki, Seiichi, McMillan, John and Zimmerman, Klaus F., "Disequilibrium Dynamics: An Empirical Study," *American Economic Review*, December 1982, *72*, 992–1004.

Keeney, Ralph L. and Raiffa, Howard, *Decisions with Multiple Objectives: Preference and Value Tradeoffs*, New York: Wiley, 1976.

Keeton, William, *Biological Science*, 3d ed., New York: Norton, 1980.

Kirzner, Israel M., *Competition and Entrepreneurship*, Chicago: University of Chicago Press, 1973.

Klein, Benjamin, Crawford, Robert and Alchian, Armen, "Vertical Integration, Appropriable Rents, and the Competitive Contracting Process," *Journal of Law and Economics*, October 1978, *21*, 297–326.

_____ **and Leffler, Keith**, "The Role of Market Performance in Assuring Contractual Performance," *Journal of Political*

Economy, October 1981, *89*, 810–34.

Knight, Frank, *Risk, Uncertainty and Profit*, Boston: Houghton Mifflin, 1921.

Kohlberg, Lawrence, "Stage and Sequence: The Cognitive-Developmental Approach to Socialization," in D. A. Goshn, ed., *Handbook of Socialization Theory and Research*, New York: Rand McNally, 1969, 347–480.

_____, "The Development of Children's Orientation Toward Moral Order: Sequence in the Development of Moral Thought," *Vita Humana*, January 1963, *3*, 11–33.

_____, "The Domain and Development of Moral Judgment: A Theory and Method of Assessment," in his et al., eds., *Assessing Moral Judgment States: A Manual*, New York: Humanities Press, 1976, 14–45.

_____, "Cognitive Stages and Preschool Education," *Human Development*, January 1966, *9*, 5–17.

_____, "Justice as Reversibility," in P. Laslett and J. Fishkin, eds., *Philosophy, Politics, and Society*, New Haven: Yale University Press, 1979.

Konner, M., *The Tangled Wing: Biological Constraints on the Human Spirit*, New York: Basic Books, 1982.

Kosniowski, Czes, *Conquer that Cube*, Cambridge: Cambridge University Press, 1981.

Kreps, David et al., "Rational Cooperation in the Finitely Repeated Prisoner's Dilemma," *Journal of Economic Theory*, August 1982, *27*, 245–52.

Kuhn, Thomas, *The Structure of Scientific Revolutions*, Chicago: University of Chicago Press, 1962.

Kunreuther, Howard et al., *Disaster Insurance Protection*, New York: Wiley, 1978.

Kydland, Finn E. and Prescott, Edward C., "Rules Rather Than Discretion: The Inconsistency of Optimal Plans," *Journal of Political Economy*, June 1977, *85*, 473–91.

Lakatos, Imer and Musgrave, Alice, *Criticism and the Growth of Knowledge*, Cambridge: Cambridge University Press, 1970.

Langlois, Richard, "Internal Organization in a Dynamic Context: Some Theoretical Considerations," Economic Research Report No. 83–04, C. V. Starr Center for Applied Economics, New York University, January 1983.

Leamer, Edward, "'Explaining Your Results' As Access Biased Memory," *Journal of the American Statistical Association*, March 1975, *70*, 88–93.

_____, *Specification Searches: Ad-Hoc Inference With Nonexperimental Data*, New York: Wiley, 1978.

Leblebici, Huseyin and Salanik, Gerald R., "Effects of Environmental Uncertainty on Information and Decision Processes in Banks," *Administrative Science Quarterly*, December 1981, *26*, 578–96.

_____ and _____, "Stability in Interorganizational Exchange: Rulemaking Processes of the Chicago Board of Trade," *Administrative Science Quarterly*, June 1982, *27*, 227–42.

Leibenstein, Harvey, "Allocative Efficiency vs. X-Efficiency," *American Economic Review*, June 1966, *56*, 392–415.

Leijonhufvud, Axel, *On Keynesian Economics and the Economics of Keynes*, New York: Oxford University Press, 1968.

_____, *Information and Coordination*, New York: Oxford University Press, 1981.

_____, "Life Among the Econ," *Western Economic Journal*, September 1973, *11*, 327–37.

Lessa, William and Vogt, Evon, *Reader in Comparative Religion: An Anthropological Approach*, New York: Harper & Row, 1979.

Levins, Richard, *Evolution in Changing Environments*, Princeton: Princeton University Press, 1968.

Lippman, Stephen and McCall, John, "The Economics of Job Search: A Survey," *Economic Inquiry*, June 1979, *14*, 155–89.

Loomes, Graham and Sugden, Robert "Regret Theory: An Alternative Theory of Rational Choice Under Uncertainty," Department of Economics Working Paper, University of Newcastle-upon-Tyne, 1982.

_____ and _____, "A Rationale for Preference Reversal," *American Economic Review*, June 1983, *73*, 428–32.

Lorenz, Konrad, *The Foundations of Ethology*, New York: Springer-Verlag, 1981.

Lucas, Robert E., Jr., "An Equilibrium Model of the Business Cycle," *Journal of Political Economy*, December 1975, *83*, 1113–44.

_____, "Expectations and the Neutrality of Money," *Journal of Economic Theory*, April

1972, *4*, 103–24.

_____, "Rules, Discretion, and the Role of the Economics Advisor," in S. Fischer, ed., *Rational Expectations and Economic Policy*, Chicago: University of Chicago Press, 1980, 199–210.

_____, *Studies in Business Cycle Theory*, Cambridge: MIT Press, 1981.

Lumsden, Charles J. and Wilson, Edward O., *Genes, Mind, & Culture: The Coevolutionary Process*, Cambridge: Harvard University Press, 1981.

McFarland, David, *The Oxford Companion to Animal Behavior*, New York: Oxford University Press, 1982.

Machina, Mark, "Expected Utility Analysis Without the Independence Axiom," *Econometrica*, March 1982, *50*, 277–323.

March, James G., "Bounded Rationality, Ambiguity, and the Engineering of Choice," *Bell Journal of Economics*, Autumn 1978, *9*, 587–608.

Masterton, R., Hodos, William and Jerison, Harry, *Evolution, Brain, and Behavior: Persistent Problems*, New York: Wiley, 1976.

Maynard Smith, John, "Group Selection and Kin Selection," *Nature*, March 14, 1964, *201*, 1145–47.

Mayr, Ernst, *Populations, Species, and Evolution*, Cambridge: Belknap, 1970.

_____ and Provine, W., *The Evolutionary Synthesis: Perspectives on the Unification of Biology*, Cambridge: Harvard University Press, 1980.

Mazur, John E., "Optimization Theory Fails to Predict Performance of Pigeons in a Two-Response Situation," *Science*, September 1981, *214*, 823–5.

Menger, Carl, *Principles of Economics*, (1871), trans. by James Dingwall and Bert F. Hozelitz, eds., New York: New York University Press, 1981.

_____, *Problems In Economics and Sociology*, (1883), trans. by F. J. Nock, Urbana: University of Illinois Press, 1963.

Michaels, C. F. and Carello, C., *Direct Perception*, Englewood Cliffs: Prentice-Hall, 1981.

Miller, G. T., Galanter, E. and Pribram, K. H., *Plans and the Structure of Behavior*, New York: Holt, 1960.

Miller, James G., *Living Systems*, New York:

McGraw-Hill, 1978.

Mondon, Y., "What Makes the Toyota Production System Really Tick," *Industrial Engineering Magazine*, January 1981, *17*, 37–46.

Monod, Jacques, *Chance and Necessity*, New York: Random House (Vintage Books), 1972.

Montgomery, Viscount, *A History of Warfare*, Cleveland: World Publishing, 1968.

Montross, L., *War Through the Ages*, New York: Harper & Brothers, 1960.

Muth, Richard, "Rational Expectations and the Theory of Price Movements," *Econometrica*, July 1961, *29*, 315–35.

Nelson, Richard, "Research on Productivity Growth and Productivity Differences: Dead Ends and New Departures," *Journal of Economic Literature*, September 1981, *19*, 1029–64.

_____ and Winter, Sidney, *An Evolutionary Theory of Economic Capabilities and Behavior*, Cambridge: Harvard University Press, 1982.

_____ and _____, "Neoclassical Versus Evolutionary Theories of Economic Growth," *Economic Journal*, December 1974, *84*, 886–905.

Newell, A. and Simon, Herbert, *Human Problem Solving*, Englewood Cliffs: Prentice-Hall, 1972.

Nourse, James G., *The Simple Solution to Rubik's Cube*, New York: Bantam Books, 1980.

Okun, Arthur M., "Inflation: Its Mechanics and Welfare Cost," *Brookings Papers on Economic Activity*, 2: 1975, 351–401.

_____, *Prices and Quantities: A Macroeconomic Analysis*, Washington: The Brookings Institution, 1981.

Ouchi, William, *Theory Z*, New York: Avon Publishers, 1981.

Pauli, Wolfgang, *Theory of Relativity*, New York: Dover, 1981.

Phelps, Edmond, "Okun's Micro-Macro System: A Review Article," *Journal of Economic Literature*, September 1981, *19*, 1065–73.

Piaget, J., *The Psychology of Intelligence*, London: Routledge & Kegan Paul, 1947.

_____, *The Origins of Intelligence*, New York: International Universities Press,

1952.

Pianka, Eric R., *Evolutionary Ecology*, 2d ed., New York: Harper & Row, 1978.

Pilbean, D., *The Ascent of Man: An Introduction to Human Evolution*, New York: Macmillan, 1972.

Popper, Karl, *Conjectures and Refutations: The Growth of Scientific Knowledge*, 3d ed., rev., London: Routledge & Kegan Paul, 1969.

_____, *The Logic of Scientific Discovery*, New York: Basic Books, 1959.

Posner, Richard, *Economic Analysis of Law*, 2d ed., Boston: Little-Brown, 1977.

_____, "A Theory of Primative Society, With Special Reference to Primative Law," *Journal of Law and Economics*, April 1980, *23*, 1–54.

Prelec, D., "Matching, Maximizing, and the Hyperbolic Reinforcement Feedback Function," *Psychological Review*, March 1982, *89*, 189–230.

Premack, David, *The Mind of an Ape*, New York: Norton, 1983.

Priest, George L., "The Common Law Process and the Selection of Efficient Rules," *Journal of Legal Studies*, January 1977, *6*, 65–83.

Rachlin, Howard, Kagel, John H. and Battalio, R. C., "Substitutability in Time Allocation," *Psychological Review*, July 1980, *87*, 355–74.

Rawls, John, *A Theory of Justice*, Cambridge: Harvard University Press, 1971.

Revere, Lawrence, *Playing Blackjack as a Business*, Secaucus: Lyle Stuart, Inc., 1969.

Roughgarden, Jeffrey D., "Reasons and Rules in Choice: A Framework for Analysis," Department of Engineering Economics Systems, Stanford University, December 1982.

Rowan, B., "Organizational Structure and the Institutional Environment: The Case of Public Schools," *Administrative Science Quarterly*, June 1982, *27*, 259–79.

Rozin, P., "The Evolution of Intelligence and Access to the Cognative Unconscious," in J. A. Spague and A. N. Epstein, eds., *Progress in Psychobiology and Physiological Psychology*, Vol. 6, New York: Academic Press, 1976, 245–80.

Sagan, Carl, *The Dragons of Eden*, New York: Random House, 1977.

Samuelson, Paul A., *Foundations of Economic Analysis*, Cambridge: Harvard University Press, 1947.

Sargent, Thomas J., *Macroeconomic Theory*, New York: Academic Press, 1979.

_____, (1976a) "A Classical Macroeconometric Model for the United States," *Journal of Political Economy*, March-April 1976, *84*, 207–37.

_____, (1976b) "The Observational Equivalence of Natural and Unnatural Rate Theories of Macroeconomics," *Journal of Political Economy*, May-June 1976, *84*, 631–40.

_____ and Wallace, Neil, "'Rational' Expectations, the Optimal Monetary Instrument, and the Optimal Money Supply Rule," *Journal of Political Economy*, April 1975, *83*, 241–54.

Savage, L. J., *The Foundations of Statistics*, New York: Wiley, 1954.

Schelling, Thomas C., *Micromotives and Macrobehavior*, New York: W. W. Norton, 1978.

Schotter, Andrew, *The Economic Theory of Social Institutions*, New York: Cambridge University Press, 1981.

Schumpeter, Joseph, *Capitalism, Socialism, and Democracy*, New York: Harper & Brothers, 1942; Harper Colophon Edition, 1976.

Seligman, Martin E. P., "On the Generality of the Laws of Learning," *Psychological Review*, September 1970, *77*, 406–18.

Shackle, G. L. S., *Decision, Order, and Time in Human Affairs*, 2d ed., Cambridge: Cambridge University Press, 1969.

_____, *Epistemics and Economics: A Critique of Economic Doctrines*, Cambridge: Cambridge University Press, 1972.

Simon, A. and Sikossy, L., *Representation and Meaning: Experiments With Information Processing Systems*, Englewood Cliffs: Prentice-Hall, 1972.

Simon, Herbert, "A Behavioral Theory of Rational Choice," *Quarterly Journal of Economics*, February 1955, *69*, 99–118.

_____, *Administrative Behavior: A Study of Decision-Making Processes in Administrative Organization*, 2d ed., New York: Macmillan, 1959.

_____, *The Sciences of the Artificial*, Cambridge: MIT Press, 1969.

594 THE AMERICAN ECONOMIC REVIEW SEPTEMBER 1983

_____, "From Substantive to Procedural Rationality," in S. Latsis, ed., *Method and Appraisal in Economics*, Cambridge: Cambridge University Press, 1976, 129–48.

_____, *The New Science of Management Decision*, Englewood Cliffs: Prentice-Hall, 1977.

_____, "On How to Decide What to Do," *Bell Journal of Economics*, Autumn 1978, 9, 494–507.

_____, (1979a) *Models of Thought*, New Haven: Yale University Press, 1979.

_____, (1979b) "Rational Decision Making in Business Organizations," *American Economic Review*, September 1979, 69, 493–513.

Singmaster, David *Notes on Rubik's Magic Cube*, Hillside: Enslow, 1979.

_____ and Frey, Alexander H., Jr., *Handbook of Cubic Math*, Hillside: Enslow, 1982.

Slovic, Paul and Tversky, Amos, "Who Accepts Savage's Axiom," *Behavioral Science*, November 1974, 19, 368–73.

_____ and Lichtenstein, Sarah, "Preference Reversals: A Broader Perspective," *American Economic Review*, September 1983, 73, 596–605.

Smith, Adam, *The Theory of Moral Sentiments*, (1759), New Rochelle: Arlington House, 1969.

Smith, Vernon L., "Microeconomic Systems as an Experimental Science," *American Economic Review*, December 1982, 72, 923–55.

Sowell, Thomas, *Knowledge and Decisions*, New York: Basic Books, 1980.

Stanley, Steven M., *Macroevolution: Pattern and Process*, San Francisco: W. H. Freeman, 1979.

Staw, Barry, Sanderlands, Lana and Dutton, Jane, "Threat Rigidity Effects in Organizational Behavior: A Multilevel Analysis," *Administrative Science Quarterly*, December 1981, 26, 501–24.

Stigler, George, J., "The Economics of Information," *Journal of Political Economy*, June 1961, 69, 213–25.

Strotz, R. H., "Myopia and Inconsistency in Dynamic Utility Maximization," *Review of Economic Studies*, November 1955, 23, 165–80.

Sugimori, Y., Kusunoki, K. and Cho, S., "Toyota Production System and Kanban System: Materialization of 'Just in Time' Production and 'Respect for Human' System," *International Journal of Production Research*, December 1977, 15, 553–64.

Sussman, Hector J., "Catastrophe Theory," *Synthese*, August 1975, 31, 229–70.

Taylor, D., *Mastering Rubik's Cube*, New York: Holt, Rinehart & Winston, 1980.

Telser, Lester, "Why Are There Organized Futures Markets?," *Journal of Law and Economics*, April 1981, 24, 1–22.

Thòm, Rene, *Structural Stability and Morphogenesis*, Reading: W. A. Benjamin, 1975.

Thorpe, Edward, O., *Beat the Dealer: A Winning Strategy for the Game of Twenty-One*, New York: Vintage Books, 1962.

Tinbergen, Nino, *The Study of Instinct*, London: Oxford University Press, 1951.

Toates, Fredric, *Animal Behavior: A Systems Approach*, New York: Wiley, 1980.

Tobin, James, "Are New Classical Models Plausible Enough to Guide Policy?," *Journal of Money, Credit and Banking*, November 1980, 12, 788–99.

Trivers, Robert L., "The Evolution of Reciprocal Altruism," *Quarterly Review of Biology*, March 1971, 46, 35–58.

Tversky, Amos, "Intransitivity of Preferences," *Psychological Review*, January 1969, 76, 31–48.

Ullman-Margalitt, Edna, *The Emergence of Norms*, New York: Oxford University Press, 1978.

Varian, Hal R., "Catastrophe Theory and the Business Cycle," *Economic Inquiry*, January 1979, 17, 14–28.

Vaughan, William, "Melioration, Matching, and Maximization," *Journal of the Experimental Analysis of Behavior*, September 1981, 36, 141–49.

von Neumann, John and Morgenstern, Oskar, *Theory of Games and Economic Behavior*, Princeton: Princeton University Press, 1944.

Watson, James, D., *Molecular Biology of the Gene*, 3d ed., Menlo Park: W. A. Benjamin, 1976.

Weber, R., "The Allais Paradox, Dutch Auctions, and Alpha-Utility Theory," J. L. Kellogg Graduate School of Management Working Paper, Northwestern University, 1982.

Weiner, Norbert, *Cybernetics*, Cambridge: MIT Press, 1948.

Weintraub, E. Roy, "The Microfoundations of Macroeconomics: A Critical Survey," *Journal of Economic Literature*, March 1977, *15*, 1–23.

Wendt, Dirk, "Some Criticism of Stochastic Models Generally Used in Decision Making Experiments," *Theory and Decision*, May 1975, *6*, 197–212.

White, Andrew D., *Fiat Money Inflation in France*, New York: D. Appleton-Century, 1933; Los Angeles: Pamphleteers, Inc., 1945.

Wilkins, Maurice, "Molecular Structure of Deoxypentos Nucleic Acids," *Nature*, April 1953, *171*, 738–40.

Williamson, Oliver E., *Markets and Hierarchies: Analysis and Antitrust Implications*, New York: The Free Press, 1975.

_____, "Transactions-Cost Economics: The Governance of Contractual Relations," *Journal of Law and Economics*, October 1979, *22*, 233–61.

_____, "The Modern Corporation: Origins, Evolution, Attributes," *Journal of Eco-nomic Literature*, December 1981, *19*, 1537–68.

_____, "Credible Commitments: Using Hostages to Support Exchange," *American Economic Review*, September 1983, *73*, 519–40.

Wilson, Edward O., *On Human Nature*, Cambridge: Harvard, 1978.

_____, *Sociobiology: The New Synthesis*, Cambridge: Belknap, 1975.

Winter, Sidney G., "Economic 'Natural Selection' and the Theory of the Firm," *Yale Economic Essays*, May 1964, *4*, 225–72.

_____, "Satisficing, Selection, and the Innovating Remnant," *Quarterly Journal of Economics*, May 1971, *85*, 237–62.

_____, "Optimization and Evolution," in R. H. Day and R. Groves, eds., *Adaptive Economic Models*, New York: Academic Press, 1975.

Winterfeldt, Detlof, "Additivity and Expected Utility in Risky Multi-Attribute Preferences," *Journal of Mathematical Psychology*, February 1980, *21*, 66–82.

Zeeman, E. C., *Catastrophy Theory*, New York: Addison-Wesley, 1977.

C
Experimental Economics

[17]

Journal of Economic Literature
Vol. XX (June 1982), pp. 529–563

The Expected Utility Model: Its Variants, Purposes, Evidence and Limitations

By PAUL J. H. SCHOEMAKER

Graduate School of Business
University of Chicago

The author would like to express his appreciation to David Brée, Victor Goldberg, Paul Kleindorfer, Roger Kormendi, Michael Rothschild, and the anonymous referees for their helpful comments on earlier drafts of this article. Additionally, his colleagues in the Center for Decision Research at the University of Chicago, especially Hillel Einhorn, Robin Hogarth and J. Edward Russo, are acknowledged for stimulating discussions on the present topic. Funding for this review was received from the Graduate School of Management in Delft and the Erasmus University of Rotterdam, both in the Netherlands. Their support is much appreciated.

I. *Introduction*

IT IS NO EXAGGERATION to consider expected utility theory the major paradigm in decision making since the Second World War. It has been used prescriptively in management science (especially decision analysis), predictively in finance and economics, descriptively by psychologists, and has played a central role in theories of measurable utility. The expected utility (EU) model has consequently been the focus of much theoretical and empirical research, including various interpretations and descriptive modifications as to its mathematical form. This paper reviews the major empirical studies bearing on the EU model. Although previous reviews of decision making have covered some of this research (e.g., Ward Edwards, 1961; Gordon Becker and Charles McClintock, 1967; Amnon Rapoport and Thomas Wallsten, 1972; Paul Slovic et al., 1977; Robert Libby and Peter Fishburn, 1977; Charles Vlek and Willem Wagenaar, 1979; and Hillel Einhorn and Robin Hogarth, 1981), few have attempted to organize the relevant evidence around the different purposes served by the EU model. Similarly, there has been no systematic examination of the way various descriptive extensions of expected utility theory relate to their progenitor, or of how the current normative variant differs from its historical roots.

In addressing these issues, the present paper first discusses various EU modifications. Special attention will be given to the types of cardinal utility used in various models, as well as the manner in which probabilities are incorporated. Thereafter four conceptually different purposes of the EU model are identified, namely: descriptive, predictive, postdictive and prescriptive. The types of evidence relevant in testing the model's adequacy for each purpose are discussed. Building on these distinctions, the empirical evidence is then divided into four clusters centering around tests of the axioms, field research, information processing studies, and recent findings on context effects. Although the review covers considerable ground, its focus is on major studies; it does not provide a comprehensive discussion of all relevant research. Moreover, the focus is on individual decision making rather than the behavior of firms or markets. It shows that at the individual level most of the empirical evidence is difficult to reconcile with the principle of EU maximization. Whereas the simplicity of EU theory, especially its mathematical tractability, may make it a very attractive model for purposes of social aggregation, its structural validity at the individual level is questionable. As such, a separate section is devoted to important behavioral decision aspects that are currently ignored in EU theory. Finally, the discussion section synthesizes the divergent strands of research touched upon, with an eye to future roles of the EU model.

II. *Expected Utility Variants*

Expected utility models are concerned with choices among risky prospects whose outcomes may be either single or multidimensional. If we denote these various (say n) outcome vectors by $\bar{x}_i$ and denote the n associated probabilities by p_i such that $\sum_{i=1}^{n} p_i = 1$, we then generally define an EU model as one which predicts or prescribes that people maximize

$\sum_{i=1}^{n} F(p_i) U(\bar{x}_i)$. The key characteristics of this general maximization model are: (1) a holistic evaluation of alternatives,[1] (2) separable transformations on probabilities and outcomes, and (3) an expectation-type operation that combines probabilities and outcomes multiplicatively (after certain transformations).

Within this general EU model different variants exist depending on (1) how utility is measured, (2) what type of probability transformations $F(\cdot)$ are allowed, and (3) how the outcomes $\bar{x}_i$ are measured. In this section we examine some of the major variants, including their extra-mathematical interpretations. We start with some background information on EU theory as traditionally understood. Thereafter the neoclassical notion of cardinal utility is compared with the modern day one. Special attention is given to the ways in which EU theory can be cardinal. Finally the concept of probability is discussed, both in terms of its ontology and its treatment in various EU models. The section concludes with a summary table listing the major EU variants.

a. *Background Information*

The mathematical form of expected utility theory goes back as far as Gabriel Cramer (1728) and Daniel Bernoulli (1738), who sought to explain the so-called Petersburg paradox. The issue they addressed was why people would pay only a small dollar amount for a game of infinite mathematical expectation. This well-known game involves flipping a fair coin as many times as is necessary to produce "heads" for the first time. The payoff of this experiment depends on the number

---

[1] A holistic model is one in which the attractiveness of an alternative is evaluated independently of the other alternatives in the choice set. In contrast, a non-holistic or decomposed model directly compares alternatives, e.g., one dimension at a time, without assigning a separate utility level to each.

of tosses required to get heads. Say this number is n, the payoff will then be \$$2^n$, which means the game has many possible outcomes, namely: \$2, 4, 8, . . . , 2^n, with probabilities $\frac{1}{2}, \frac{1}{4}, \frac{1}{8}, . . . , (\frac{1}{2})^n$, respectively. Interestingly, the expected monetary value (EV) of this gamble is infinite,

since $\sum_{n=1}^{\infty} (\frac{1}{2})^n 2^n = \infty$.

To explain why most people value this infinite EV game below \$100, or even \$20, Bernoulli proposed that people maximize expected utility rather than expected monetary value. The utility function $U(x)$ he proposed was logarithmic, exhibiting diminishing increases in utility for equal increments in wealth.[2] Bernoulli then proceeded to show that for a logarithmic function the game's expected utility, i.e., $\Sigma(\frac{1}{2})^n \log_e(2^n)$, is indeed finite.[3] However, he did not address the issue of how to measure utility, nor why his expectation principle would be rational. As such, Bernoulli's theory is mostly a descriptive model, even though the expectation principle at the time may have enjoyed much face validity normatively. It was not until John von Neumann and Oskar Morgenstern (1944) that expected utility maximization was formally proved to be a rational decision criterion, i.e., derivable from several appealing axioms. In their own words they "practically defined numerical utility as being that thing for which a calculus of expectations is legitimate"

(1944, p. 28). In this sense, von Neumann-Morgenstern (NM) utility theory is quite different from Bernoulli's conceptualization. Moreover NM utility applies to any type of outcomes, money being a special case.

Specifically, von Neumann and Morgenstern proved that five basic axioms imply the existence of numerical utilities for outcomes whose expectations for lotteries preserve the preference order over lotteries: i.e., greater expected utility corresponds to higher preference. Their utility function is unique up to positive linear transformations, meaning that if the function $U(x)$ represents a person's risk preferences then so will $U^*(x)$ if and only if $U^*(x) = aU(x) + b$ for numbers $a > 0$ and b. Jacob Marschak (1950) reformulated the NM axioms and proof, and proposed them as a definition of rational behavior under risk. In light of later discussions, the NM axioms are informally stated below.

1. Preferences for lotteries L_i are complete and transitive. Completeness means that for any choice between lotteries L_1 and L_2 either L_1 is preferred to L_2 (denoted $L_1 > L_2$), $L_2 > L_1$ or both are equally attractive. Transitivity implies that if $L_1 \geqslant L_2$ and $L_2 \geqslant L_3$ then $L_1 \geqslant L_3$ (where $\geqslant$ denotes "at least as preferred as").

2. If $x_1 > x_2 > x_3$, then there exists some probability p between zero and one such that the lottery
   $\begin{smallmatrix} p \\ 1-p \end{smallmatrix}\begin{smallmatrix} x_1 \\ x_3 \end{smallmatrix}$ is as attractive as receiving x_2 for certain.

3. If objects x_1 and x_2 (being either risky or riskless prospects) are equally attractive, then lottery
   $\begin{smallmatrix} p \\ 1-p \end{smallmatrix}\begin{smallmatrix} x_1 \\ x_3 \end{smallmatrix}$ and lottery $\begin{smallmatrix} p \\ 1-p \end{smallmatrix}\begin{smallmatrix} x_2 \\ x_3 \end{smallmatrix}$ will also be equally attractive (for any values of p and x_3).

---

[2] The exact function proposed by Bernoulli was $U(x) = b\log[(a + x)/a]$. Note that $dU(x)/dx = b/(a + x)$, which is inversely proportional to wealth. Also, $d^2U(x)/dx^2 < 0$. Bernoulli's logarithmic function was later suggested by Gustav Fechner (1860) for subjective magnitudes in general.

[3] A proof of the convergence of this infinite series is offered in my book on expected utility experiments (1980, p. 12). Note that the certainty equivalence of this game, i.e., the amount ce for which $U(ce) = \Sigma(\frac{1}{2})^n U(2^n)$, will be finite for many other concave utility functions as well, although not for all. The same holds for the maximum bid (m) one would pay for the Petersburg game, which is determined from the equation $U(0) = \Sigma(\frac{1}{2})^n U(2^n - m)$.

4. Consider the lotteries $L_1 \overset{p}{\underset{1-p}{\diagdown}} \overset{x_1}{\diagdown} x_2$

and $L_2 \overset{q}{\underset{1-q}{\diagdown}} \overset{x_1}{\diagdown} x_2$ which differ only
in probability. If $x_1 > x_2$ then the
first lottery (L_1) will be preferred
over the second (L_2) if and only
if $p > q$.

5. A compound lottery (i.e., one
whose outcomes are themselves
lotteries) is equally attractive as the
simple lottery that would result
when multiplying probabilities
through according to standard
probability theory. For example,
lottery

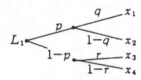

should be as attractive as

$$L_2 \overset{pq}{\underset{\underset{(1-p)(1-r)}{(1-p)r}}{\overset{p(1-q)}{\diagup}}} \begin{matrix} x_1 \\ x_2 \\ x_3 \\ x_4 \end{matrix}$$

The above axioms are sufficient to guarantee that there exists a utility index such
that the ordering of lotteries by their expected utilities fully coincides with the
person's actual preferences.[4] Note that
utility, in the NM context, is used to *represent* preferences whereas in neoclassical
theory it *determines* (or precedes) preference. Since $U(x)$ is unique up to positive
linear transformation one is free to choose

both the origin and the unit of measurement of the utility scale. For example, we
may arbitrarily place the origin at $10 (i.e.,
$U(10) = 0$), and set $U(10,000)$ equal to say
100 utiles. Given these two reference
points, the utility index is constructed
from such simple questions as: "What
amount for certain is equally attractive as
a 50–50 lottery offering $10 or $10,000?"
Say the answer is x^*, we then compute
$U(x^*)$ as being equal to $.5U(10) +$
$.5U(10,000) = 50$ utiles. As long as the reference lottery contains amounts for which
the utilities are known, new utility points
can be obtained through which a utility
function may then be interpolated.

An important concept in EU theory is
that of risk aversion. If some gamble is
less (or more) preferred than its expected
monetary value for sure, the preference
is said to be risk-averse (or risk-seeking).
A concave utility function implies risk-
averse preferences for lotteries within the
range of concavity: i.e., their certainty
equivalences will be less than their expected monetary values. Kenneth Arrow
(1971) and John Pratt (1964) proposed as
a local measure of risk-aversion for $U(x)$
the negative ratio of the second to first
derivative, i.e., $-U''(x)/U'(x)$. This measure is invariant under linear transformation, and assumes a constant value for linear and exponential utility functions. As
such it captures the important EU property that risk preferences derived from
exponential (or linear) utility functions are
not affected by changes in the person's
wealth position.[5]

---

[4] A highly readable proof of this important theorem was provided by William Baumol (1972, p. 548–
51). Alternative sets of axioms, resulting in the same
general theorem, have been presented by Israel N.
Hernstein and John Milnor (1953), Leonard Savage
(1954), Duncan Luce and Howard Raiffa (1957), John
Pratt, Raiffa and Robert Schlaifer (1964) and Peter
Fishburn (1970).

[5] Further discussions of expected utility theory,
particularly from an applied perspective, can
be found in Raiffa (1968) and in Chapter 4 of
Ralph Keeney and Raiffa (1976). In subsequent
chapters these authors extend the one-dimensional
theory to n-dimensions, in which case the determination of $U(x_1, x_2, \ldots, x_n)$ is considerably more
complicated. Also, the concept of risk-aversion is less
well-defined in the multiattribute case (Scott Richard,
1975).

Schoemaker: The Expected Utility Model   533

b. *Types of Cardinal Utility*

As Peter Fishburn (1976) has noted, the concept of cardinal utility has psychological, empirical as well as measurement-theoretic aspects which together with such related terminology as "measurable," "additive," "determinate," "intensive," and "linear" utility has given rise to considerable confusion as to its precise meaning. The term "cardinal utility" goes back to John R. Hicks and R. G. D. Allen (1934) who argued that only ordinal preference was needed in economic theory, thereby dispensing with neoclassical utility (Vivian Walsh, 1970). Cardinal utility in the neoclassical context refers to strength of preference, i.e., to statements about intensity as well as direction of preference. From a measurement-theoretic viewpoint, cardinal utility has a rather different meaning, referring to the allowable transformations of the underlying measurement scale. If the scale is unique up to at least linear transformation, it constitutes cardinal or so-called strong measurement (S. S. Stevens, 1946). Common examples are temperature and weight measures which constitute interval and ratio scales respectively. From a measurement perspective NM utility theory is cardinal in that its utility scale has interval properties. However, from a preference perspective, NM utility theory is ordinal in that it provides no more than ordinal rankings of lotteries.

The cardinal nature of NM theory must thus be interpreted carefully. Even though NM utility functions are interval scales, implying that the ratios of utility differences are invariant under linear transformations, it does not follow that if $x_1 > x_2 > x_3 > x_4$ and $u(x_1) - u(x_2) > u(x_3) - u(x_4)$, the change from x_2 to x_1 would be more preferred than the change from x_4 to x_3 (Duncan Luce and Raiffa, 1957, p. 32). Thus NM utility should *not* be interpreted as measuring strength of prefer-ence under certainty, being quite different in this regard from neoclassical cardinal utility (George Stigler, 1950).[6] One reason is that preferences among lotteries are determined by at least two separate factors; namely (1) strength of preference for the consequences under certainty, and (2) attitude toward risk. The NM utility function is a compound mixture of these two, without direct resort to interval comparisons or strength of preference measures. As a preference theory, it is wholly ordinal. Nevertheless it *implicitly* assumes that a neoclassical type of utility exists, otherwise it would not be possible psychologically to determine the certainty equivalence of a lottery. An interesting analysis as to the connection between ordinal and cardinal utility was offered by Eugene Fama (1972). Since some economists consider intensity of preference meaningless (Charles Plott, 1976, p. 541), putatively because it cannot be measured from revealed preferences, it merits closer examination.

One approach is to view strength of preference as an intuitive psychological primitive. For instance, most people would consider it meaningful to say that the increase in pleasure due to adding milk to one's coffee is of a lower magnitude than the pleasure increment associated with a sizable salary raise. Similarly, someone might note that the last hour on some trip was more tiring than the first. Indeed, in psychological scaling experiments subjects routinely make interval comparisons involving such quantities as loudness, weight, temperature, and brightness (Stevens, 1957). Usually, subjects' perceptions of the interval differ-

---

[6] Consequently, the notion of marginal utility has a rather different meaning in NM theory as well. In classical economics marginal utility refers to pleasure increments under certainty. In NM theory it refers to "the marginal rate of substitution between x and the probability of winning the prespecified prize of the standard lottery ticket" (Baumol, 1972, p. 548).

ences correspond very closely (in the curve fitting sense) to the true underlying scale, after appropriate logarithmic or power transformations. The latter are necessary as the human response system tends toward relative rather than absolute judgments (Gustav Fechner, 1860). It is thus a small leap to presume a similar judgment capability for strength of preference, even though objective verification is not yet possible.

Gerard Debreu (1959), D. Scott and Patrick Suppes (1958), Ragnar Frisch (1964), Frantz Alt (1971), and others, proposed various axiomatizations of such a strength of preference measures under certainty, which we shall denote by $v(x)$. Its essential property is that the function provides ordinal preference as well as an ordering on differences (under certainty). Thus, $v(x_1) > v(x_2)$ implies that x_1 is preferred to x_2, and $v(x_1) - v(x_2) > v(x_3) - v(x_4)$ implies that the value difference between x_1 and x_2 is greater than that between x_3 and x_4 (where x_3 is preferred to x_4). David Krantz, et al., (1971, pp. 145–50) review the formal properties of this so-called positive-difference structure. Operationally, it may rely on the so-called midpoint scaling technique, which requires respondents to split intervals into equally valued increments (Warren Torgerson, 1958).

A different measurement approach is to infer $v(x)$ from revealed preferences, provided certain conditions hold. By introducing a second attribute, say y, it may be asked how much of y_0 (the initial y endowment) the respondent would give up to go from x_2 to x_1. From such willingness-to-pay questions a multidimensional interval-scaled function $W(x, y, z)$ can be constructed via conjoint measurement (Luce and John Tukey, 1964), with z denoting the set of other relevant attributes. If $W(x, y, z)$ is separable in x, meaning it can be written as $f(v(x), w(y,z))$, and if $\delta W/\delta x$ is independent of y and z, then

$v(x)$ may be considered an intrinsic preference measure for x. These conditions are met, for example, if $W(x, y, z)$ is additive, i.e., expressable in the form $v(x) + w_1(y) + w_2(z)$. However, a *direct* empirical test that $\delta W/\delta x$ is independent of y and z may require another (i.e., nontradeoff) measure of strength of preference (David Bell and Raiffa, 1979). If so, we are back to our first approach, leaving introspection as the only likely way out of this vicious circle (Fishburn, 1970, p. 82). Various other operational measures exist for intensity of preference, which were recently examined by John Hauser and Steven Shugan (1980). Their study consists of theoretical and empirical analyses, with a focus on marketing applications.

There are several advantages in distinguishing cardinal utility measures constructed under certainty, denoted $v(x)$, from those constructed under risk, denoted $u(x)$. First, it emphasizes that there exist different types of cardinal utility, even within each category, which only have to be related monotonically. (See Amos Tversky, 1967, for empirical examples.) Second, by examining $u(x) = f(v(x))$, an Arrow-Pratt type measure of *intrinsic* risk aversion may be defined and empirically measured, namely $-f''(v(x))/f'(v(x))$ (Bell and Raiffa, 1979). Third, the construction of $u(x)$ may be simplified by first examining the nature of $v(x)$, especially in the case of multiattribute utility. For example, Detlof von Winterfeldt (1979) proved that $u(x_1, \ldots, x_n)$ must be either linearly, logarithmically or exponentially related to $v(x_1, \ldots, x_n)$ in case the former is additive and the latter multiplicative (see also: James Dyer and Rakesh Sarin, 1979a). Similar relationships between riskless and risky cardinal utility were recently examined by Bell and Raiffa (1979) and Dyer and Sarin (1982) for one-dimensional cases (see also: Sarin, 1982). Dyer and Sarin (1982) proposed a fourth reason

Schoemaker: The Expected Utility Model   535

for separating $v(x)$ and $u(x)$: namely, group decision making. In an organizational context it may be desirable only to have members' inputs regarding their $v(x)$ functions, but not their risk attitudes (which might be centrally determined). Finally, cardinal utility under certainty may be useful for welfare theory (Dyer and Sarin, 1979b), although it seems to suffer as well from impossibility theorems (T. Schwartz, 1970).

The distinction between $v(x)$ and $u(x)$, denoting cardinal preference scalings under certainty and risk, respectively, is often overlooked or has been a source of considerable confusion, even among experts. During the beginning of the 1950s, *The Economic Journal* and *Econometrica* published a variety of articles debating the cardinality of NM utility (e.g., Herman Wold, 1952 and Armen Alchian, 1953). Amid considerable confusion, lucid analyses were offered by Robert Strotz (1953), Daniel Ellsberg (1954) and John S. Chipman (1960). Ellsberg compared how such classical utilitarians as William Stanley Jevons, Carl Menger, Leon Walras or Alfred Marshall might have predicted choice under risk with the approach taken by NM. The difference lies in the way the utility function is constructed: namely, under certainty or risk. Which expectation model will predict better is an empirical question. An important difference, however, is that the $E[v(\bar{x})]$ model has no normative justification other than its face validity, whereas the $E[u(\bar{x})]$ model derives from a set of appealing decision axioms. It is my interpretation that Bernoulli proposed the $v(x)$ type expectation model, although he never explicitly addressed the measurement question.

The above discussion on cardinal utility was provided because, even today, the distinction between $v(x)$ and $u(x)$ is often unrecognized. Textbooks in economics and management science occasionally discuss the NM function as if it only measured

intrinsic pleasure under conditions of certainty. For example, a concave $u(x)$ might erroneously be interpreted as implying that equal increments in money (under certainty) contribute to utility at a decreasing rate. Of course, $v(x)$ is confused here with $u(x)$. Apart from textbook confusions, the above distinction is occasionally not recognized in research designs. For example, in a study of simulated real-life decisions, such as whether or not to enroll in a Ph.D. program, Thomas Bonoma and Barry R. Schlenker (1978) considered subjects suboptimal if they did not maximize $\Sigma\ p_i v(x_i)$; what these authors should have tested, in making such normative evaluations of risky choices, is whether $\Sigma\ p_i u(x_i)$ was maximized.

To summarize, $v(\bar{x})$ was defined as an interval-scaled utility measure constructed under conditions of certainty, similar to neoclassical utility except that no ratio properties are presumed. In contrast, $u(\bar{x})$ is a cardinal NM utility measure derived from preferences among lotteries. These two utility functions only need to be monotone transforms of each other. Thus when presented with different commodity bundles $\bar{x}_i$ under certainty, $v(\bar{x})$ and $u(\bar{x})$ should yield the same ordering for a person satisfying the axioms underlying either construct. However, when presented with risky prospects $\bar{x}_i$ the formally correct ordering is determined from $E[u(\bar{x}_i)]$, which will generally differ with that obtained from $E[v(\bar{x}_i)]$ unless $v(x)$ is a linear transform of $u(x)$. Finally to obtain an interval ranking of the risky prospects $\bar{x}_i$, the $E[u(\bar{x}_i)]$ could be inverted into their certainty equivalents CE_i which might then be interval ranked by computing $v(CE_i)$.

c. The Concept of Probability

Other potentially confusing aspects of the expected utility model concern the treatment of probabilities. In the NM axiom system probability is considered a

536   *Journal of Economic Literature, Vol. XX (June 1982)*

primitive whose values are objectively given. Empirically, however, the notion of probability is problematic, both philosophically as well as practically. To illustrate this let us briefly identify four major schools of probability and their limitations. The first is the classical view of Pierre La-Place (1812), who defined probability as the number of elementary outcomes favorable to some event divided by the total number of possible elementary outcomes. Since these elementary outcomes must all be equally likely (i.e., have the same probability), LaPlace's definition suffers from circularity. Moreover, this view cannot easily handle infinite outcome spaces, and is practically limited to well-structured uncertainties.

Jacques Bernoulli (1713), a relative of Daniel, had earlier evaded this circular definition by distinguishing the concept from its measurement. He defined probability as a "degree of confidence" which for a given event may vary from person to person. Nevertheless, he considered the art of guessing (*Ars Conjectandi*) to consist of precise estimation of unknown probabilities, for instance by studying objective frequencies. This frequency approach was later placed on an axiomatic footing by John Venn (1866), Hans Reichenbach (1935), and Richard Von Mises (1957, 1964) who defined probability as the limiting value of the percentage of favorable outcomes in an infinite sequence of independent replications. The limitations of this view are at least three-fold. First, probability is never exact numerically, being at best a large sample estimate. Second, it is often unclear what sample space to use. For instance, when taking a plane trip is the objective probability of crashing determined by all previous flights, or only those by that carrier, with that type of airplane, in that season, etc.? Third, the notion of exact replication is problematic. If a coin toss is replicated perfectly, it should always yield the same outcome.

This raises questions about the locus of uncertainty; i.e., whether it is internal or out in the world. The answer depends on one's world-view; for some people determinism may rule out true randomness (its only source being imperfect knowledge), whereas others might argue in favor of irreducible uncertainty: e.g., Heisenberg's uncertainty principle in physics (R. B. Lindsay, 1968).

A third attempt to define probability objectively is the so-called logical school of John Maynard Keynes (1921) and Harold Jeffreys (1948). These authors argued that a given set of evidence bears a logical, objective relationship to the truth of some hypothesis (e.g., someone being guilty), even when the evidence is inconclusive. Probability measures the strength of this connection as assessed by a rational person. Since all three of the above views have appealing aspects various attempts have been made to reconcile them. Rudolf Carnap (1962, 1971) developed a formal theory of a coherent learning system (along Bayesian lines), which merges objective and subjective views. Glenn Shafer (1976) on the other hand, proposed a reconciliation by formally distinguishing different types of probability, emphasizing the essential difference between aleatory probability and degree of belief. This latter epistemic concept is fundamental to the subjectivists, the fourth school to be mentioned.

The subjective or personal school of probability was primarily developed by Frank Ramsey (1931), Bruno de Finetti (1937, 1974), Leonard Savage (1954), and Pratt, Raiffa and Schlaifer (1964). In their view, probabilities are degrees of beliefs, applicable to both repetitive and unique events such as a third world war. For a given set of hypotheses, any assignment of subjective probabilities is permissible in principle, provided some consistency requirements are met. In contrast to other schools, these conditions are viewed as suf-

Schoemaker: The Expected Utility Model   537

ficient (as well as necessary), without additional restrictions being imposed for logical or empirical reasons. The main consistency axiom of subjective probability theory is coherence (de Finetti, 1937). Informally, it requires that for a given belief system, it should not be possible for a clever bookmaker to lay multiple fair bets so that the bookmaker wins under all possible outcomes. This axiom (together with some others) implies that the probabilities of elementary events sum to one, and that conjunctive and disjunctive events follow the product and addition rules respectively. As such, subjective probabilities are mathematically indistinguishable from other types of probability. The subjective school developed measurement procedures for the simultaneous estimation of utility and probability as based on revealed preferences (Donald Davidson and Suppes, 1956).

The important point is that probability is not a simple construct (Henry Kyburg and Howard Smokler, 1964). Its measurement is obviously difficult in real-world settings, but may even be so in simple games of chance (Davidson, Suppes and Sidney Siegel, 1957). To distinguish subjective from objective probability, it shall be denoted by $f(p)$. The $f(\cdot)$ transformation signals that the probabilities to be used in EU model may differ from the stated or objective ones assumed by the researcher. However, not all $f(p_i)$ transformations satisfying the properties of probability (such as $\Sigma\ f(p_i) = 1$) should be viewed as degrees of belief. In the literature, $f(p_i)$ transformations have been proposed to reflect risk-taking attitudes (Jagdish Handa, 1977), to explore symmetry between the probability and outcome component in expectation models (Hans Schneeweiss, 1974), to reflect probability and/or variance preference (Edwards, 1954a and 1954b), or simply to fit data under the assumption that preferences are non-linear in probability (John Quig-

gin, 1980). Although these various models are commonly referred to as Subjective Expected Utility theory (SEU), the $f(p_i)$ transformation may not strictly be degree of belief measures.

Apart from transformations that do preserve the properties of mathematical probability, various theories exist where this requirement is relaxed. In Table 1 such probability transformations are denoted by $w(p_i)$, and will be called decision weights. To quote Daniel Kahneman and Tversky (1979, p. 280), "decision weights are not probabilities: they do not obey the probability axioms and they should not be interpreted as measures of degree of belief." In prospect theory (Kahneman and Tversky, 1979) decision weights are aimed at reflecting the impact of events on the overall attractiveness of gambles. As such they are monotonic with probability, but not necessarily linear.

To summarize, there are several ways that utility and probability have been treated in EU models. Systematic combining of the different transformations discussed yields nine EU variants, which are shown in Table 1 together with their names and main originators.[7] Note that this table focuses on the allowable probability and outcome transformations of the various models. However, there are other differences as well. For example, in prospect theory the outcomes x_i are defined on changes in financial position rather than on final asset position. Moreover, in descriptive models the outcome space may include such dimensions as regret, justifiability of one's choice, etc. Most of the models listed were advanced as descriptive ones, with the exception of von Neumann-Morgenstern and Savage. It is

---

[7] The subjective expected utility (SEU) model is also encountered outside the context of monetary bets. Victor Vroom's (1964) expectancy theory of work motivation shows formal parallels to EU theory, as do theories in learning, attitude formation, and personality development (Edward Lawler, 1973).

538   *Journal of Economic Literature, Vol. XX (June 1982)*

these normative variants, especially NM theory, we henceforth refer to when speaking of EU theory:

TABLE 1

NINE VARIANTS OF THE
EXPECTED UTILITY MODEL

1.	$\Sigma\ p_i x_i$	Expected Monetary Value
2.	$\Sigma\ p_i v(x_i)$	Bernoullian Expected Utility (1738)
3.	$\Sigma\ p_i u(x_i)$	von Neumann-Morgenstern Expected Utility (1947)
4.	$\Sigma\ f(p_i) x_i$	Certainty Equivalence Theory (Schneeweiss, 1974; Handa, 1977; de Finetti, 1937)
5.	$\Sigma\ f(p_i) v(x_i)$	Subjective Expected Utility (Edwards, 1955)
6.	$\Sigma\ f(p_i) u(x_i)$	Subjective Expected Utility (Ramsey, 1931; Savage, 1954; Quiggin, 1980)
7.	$\Sigma\ w(p_i) x_i$	Weighted Monetary Value
8.	$\Sigma\ w(p_i) v(x_i)$	Prospect Theory (Kahneman and Tversky, 1979)
9.	$\Sigma\ w(p_i) u(x_i)$	Subjectively Weighted Utility (Uday Karmarkar, 1978)

Note: $v(x)$ denotes an interval scaled utility measure constructed under certainty; $u(x)$ denotes one constructed via lotteries.

III. *Purposes of the EU Model*

Generally, it would be inappropriate to assess the acceptability of an optimality model without an explicit prior statement of its purposes. If models are defined as simplified representations of reality, they should not and cannot always be true. Models, by their nature, balance costs such as complexity, prediction error, domain specificity, with various benefits such as simplicity, prediction power, generality, etc. Consequently, we should evaluate a model according to its stated objectives. We shall distinguish four essentially different purposes that the EU model can serve.

First, EU theory may be used *descriptively* to model the decision processes underlying risky choice. Descriptive models are concerned with, and tested by more than prediction alone. Evidence concerning the validity of the underlying axioms would be relevant, as would the manner in which information is processed. The latter may include: (1) how stimuli are attended to, encoded and stored; (2) how information is searched for and retrieved from memory, (3) how stimuli are aggregated or decomposed (i.e., comprehended and integrated), and (4) how value conflicts are resolved when choice is exercised (James Bettman, 1979).

A second usage, dominant in economics and finance is to view the EU model as *predictive* or *positivistic*. Realism of its axioms and postulated computational mechanism are not important within the positivistic view. What matters is whether the model offers higher predictive accuracy than competing models of similar complexity. According to Milton Friedman (1953) and Fritz Machlup (1967), two leading exponents of the positivistic view, (economic) theories should be tested on their predictive ability rather than the descriptive validity of their assumptions. Hence direct violations of EU axioms are not particularly disturbing. What counts is whether the theory, in its capacity of an "as if" model, predicts behavior not

Schoemaker: The Expected Utility Model   539

used in the construction of the model. In that case, empirical findings of field studies and realistic laboratory studies are especially relevant. However, in such studies the evidence counter to EU theory can often be refuted because it is indirect.

For instance, in field studies assumptions need to be made about the values of various parameters (e.g., costs, tax rates, probabilities, etc.) as well as the form of $U(x)$. If the data are inconsistent with certain of these prior assumptions, another set of parameters can usually be found, ex post facto, that fit the data better. To illustrate, when Peter Pashigian, Lawrence Schkade and George Menefee (1966) concluded that consumers did not act in accordance with EU theory because they bought expensive low-deductible policies for collision in automobile insurance, John Gould (1969) countered that the data were in fact consistent with certain types of sufficiently risk-averse exponential utility functions. The presumed incompatibility only applied to quadratic and logarithmic utility functions. The question therefore arises, within the positivistic view, to what extent the EU hypothesis is falsifiable. The most irrefutable evidence, which directly concerns the axioms, is discounted in positive economics. On the other hand, the evidence that is admissible (e.g., actual decision making in the real world) often suffers from lack of controls, multiple interpretations, and measurement problems regarding key constructs (e.g., probabilities). Some examples are provided later in the context of the capital asset pricing model in finance and studies on the effect of pension plans on private savings.

Nevertheless, the distinguishing feature of a positive theory is that it yields hypotheses that are falsifiable in principle: i.e., they meet Karl Popper's (1968) so-called demarcation criterion. The latter requires that a theory specifies clearly and a priori the conceivable empirical results which

support it and those which refute it (without the latter set being empty). To distinguish between those researchers who allow falsification of the EU model in principle, and those who regard the optimality of economic behavior as an essentially unfalsifiable meta-postulate, we might distinguish a third purpose of EU models, which I shall refer to as *postdictive*. The essential premise of the postdictive EU view is that all *observed* human behavior is optimal (in the EU sense), *provided* it is modeled in the appropriate manner. Seeming suboptimalities are explained, ex post facto, by introducing new considerations (e.g., costs, dimensions, constraints, etc.) that account for the anomalies, so as to make them optimal. From this perspective, satisficing (Herbert Simon, 1955) is just a more general type of optimizing, including such factors as the cost of information, decision time, constraints, and cognitive effort. It is the latter degrees of freedom, however, that may make the postdictive approach tautological: i.e., non-empirical and non-falsifiable (for a different view see Lawrence Boland, 1981).

Many economists have acknowledged the postdictive perspective in economics, some with sorrow and some with pride. For instance, Tibor Scitovsky (1976) remarked that the concept of utility maximization "set back by generations all scientific inquiry into consumer behavior, for it seemed to rule out—as a logical impossibility—any conflict between what man chooses· to get and what will best satisfy him" (p. 4). Gary Becker (1976) on the other hand views this as a strength; he acknowledges the potential for tautology or circularity in economics, especially if unobservable transaction costs are permitted ex post: "of course, postulating the existence of costs closes or 'completes' the economic approach in the same, almost tautological, way that postulating the existence of (sometimes unobserved) uses of energy completes the energy system and preserves the law of the conservation of energy . . . the critical question is whether a system is completed in a useful way" (p. 7), i.e., whether it yields "a bundle of empty tautologies" or provides the basis for predicting behavioral responses to various changes.

The challenge of the postdictive view is to look at the available data in a coherent way that highlights the optimality of human behavior (e.g., Becker, 1976). Whether such an exercise is trivial or a masterly craft depends on the degrees of freedom one allows. The possible respecifications of a particular model are of course not arbitrary and must gain the approval of fellow practitioners. Furthermore, most model respecifications imply testable predictions. However, if these testable predictions were also not to hold, additional respecifications would be sought until all relevant past (i.e., observed) behavior would be accounted for as indeed being optimal. It is in this sense that the perspective is ex post. A major limitation of the postdictive view is that ex post empirical models may have limited refutation power regarding the corresponding theoretical ex ante model. The Sharpe-Lintner capital asset pricing model in finance (see Fama, 1976) is a case in point. Its main hypothesis of a linear relationship between a security's return and the market's return has evoked numerous empirical studies. However, this hypothesis presumes that the market portfolio has minimum variance for its level of expected return (i.e., is mean-variance efficient). Since the market portfolio includes all assets (financial and otherwise) it is in reality unknowable, making empirical tests very difficult if not impossible (Richard Roll, 1977).

This is not to say, however, that closed systems are without merit. The postdictive view resembles the natural sciences in their ex post search for optimality principles, some of which have proved most valuable. For instance, when Pierre Fermat suggested (c. 1650) that light travels the path of the shortest distance in time, he not only derived Willebrord Snel's refraction law in optics (which was his original intent), but also suggested a host of new hypotheses quite unrelated to the refraction law. Many of these hypotheses were subsequently verified empirically, dealing with relative velocities of light in different media and the behavior of light in convergent lenses. Two centuries later, William Hamilton generalized and elevated the least effort principle to a cornerstone theorem in theoretical physics. Similarly, in biology optimality principles abound, ranging from homeostasis (i.e., minimization of the divergence between actual and desired states) to optimal adaptation (Robert Rosen, 1967; M. Cody, 1974 or J. Maynard Smith, 1978). Elsewhere I examined optimality principles in more detail (1982), and concluded that their main advantages are: (1) elegance, (2) parsimonious summary of empirical knowledge, and (3) high metaphoric value in generating new hypotheses. The disadvantages, on the other hand, are that the optimality approach (1) encourages search for confirming rather than disconfirming evidence, (2) often fails to acknowledge its ex post nature, and (3) may be more reflective of analytical than empirical truths. Thus, when sociobiology (Edward Wilson, 1975) broadly claims to have established that the existing structures in human and animal societies benefit the stronger genes, Richard Lewontin (1979) justifiably highlights the difficulty of defining such key terms as "favorable traits," "ecological niche" and "strong genes," independently of knowing evolution's outcomes. Similarly, when economics expands its claim of optimal choice behavior into new and broad domains of human activity (e.g., Gary Becker, 1976), or even animal behavior, the tautological nature of these models (in the sense of ad hoc, ex post rationalization) may well increase accordingly.[8] It is beyond our scope to examine further the merits of positivistic and postdictive perspectives as they entail complex epistemological issues. Penetrating analyses on this topic were recently offered in books by Alexander Rosenberg (1975) and Mark Blaug (1980).

Finally, there exists a fourth perspective according to which EU theory is a *prescriptive* or *normative* model. Decision analysts and management scientists (implicitly) assume that human behavior is generally suboptimal. Their goal is to improve decisions (prescriptive), for instance by using EU theory (normative). If so, the theory serves to advise which alternative(s) to select in complex decision situations on the basis of the decision maker's basic tastes and preferences. As outlined earlier these basic risk preferences are captured through a NM utility function. The complex options are then rank-ordered on the basis of expected utility.

Each of the four EU purposes discussed above has its constituents, who would interpret empirical evidence on the EU model differently. For instance, evidence on axioms is relevant to the descriptive and prescriptive usages whereas predictions, preferably about real-world behavior, matter to the predictive or postdictive views. A complicating feature of the EU model as employed in economics and finance (e.g., Peter Diamond and Rothschild, 1978) is that the assumption of EU maximization may have the following three important qualifiers. First, the theory is usually restricted to decisions that

are important economically. Evidence on hypothetical decisions might thus be dismissed on grounds of having no significant economic consequence to the decision maker. Second, since the concern in economics is with market rather than individual behavior, only those individuals trading at the margin need to be EU maximizers. For instance, in busy traffic only a small portion of highway drivers need to change from slower to faster lanes (a type of arbitrage) for the lanes to move at the same speed eventually. Thus it often requires only a few rational persons for the market as a whole to behave rationally. Third, in economics, EU maximization is mostly assumed in *competitive* environments, where feedback enables people, over time, to improve their behavior. Hence, some history of learning and struggle for economic survival are often assumed for the EU model as used in finance and economics (Alchian, 1950; Sidney Winter, 1964 and 1971).

IV. *Empirical Evidence*

In recognition of the various purposes served by EU models, the present overview of empirical evidence is organized around four different approaches. Although some research studies could properly be discussed under several of these, they are mostly treated under just one category.

a. *Tests of EU Axioms*

The first EU axiom has two components: (1) for any choice people have a definite preference (including indifference), and (2) preferences are transitive. In one of the first empirical tests of the EU model (1951) Frederick Mosteller and Philip Nogee found, however, that subjects on repeated measures of preference would not always give the same answers. They subsequently conducted their research assuming stochastic rather than deterministic

---

[8] This is not to say that economic animal experiments advance non-falsifiable hypotheses. For instance, Raymond Battalio, et al. (1981) found in their experiments that pigeons engaged in insufficient substitution when compared to the Slutsky-Hicks theory. However, in some respecified model the observed behavior might well be "optimal." My concern is with the meta-postulate that all animal behavior is in some sense optimal, as this may lead to empirically vacuous theories.

preferences. Concerning the transitivity axiom, Tversky (1969) examined some conditions under which it might be violated. The axiom has a deterministic and stochastic form: in the former it states that $A > B$ and $B > C$ implies $A > C$. In its (weak) stochastic form it asserts that if the probability that $A > B$, denoted $P(A > B)$, is at least ½, and $P(B > C) \geq$ ½, then $P(A > C) \geq$ ½. Violations of stochastic transitivity cannot be attributed to *random* error.

In two separate experiments, one dealing with gambles, the other with college applicant decisions, Tversky (1969) showed systematic and predictable violations of weak stochastic transitivity. The violations are likely to occur if subjects use evaluation strategies involving comparisons within dimensions: e.g., first comparing price, then quality, then size, etc. The strategy Tversky examined is the so-called additive difference model in which an alternative $\bar{x} = (x_1, \ldots, x_n)$ is preferred to $\bar{y} = (y_1, \ldots, y_n)$ if and only if $\sum_{i=1}^{n} \phi_i[u_i(x_i) - u_i(y_i)] \geq 0$. The u_i functions measure the subjective values of the various attributes, and the ϕ_i are increasing continuous functions determining the contribution of each subjective difference within dimension i to the overall evaluation of the alternatives. Tversky proved analytically that for $n \geq 3$, transitive choices are guaranteed under the additive difference rule if and only if the ϕ_i are linear, which is a rather severe restriction.

The second EU axiom (combined with that of transitivity) implies that a lottery offering outcomes A and B should have an attractiveness level intermediate to those of A and B. This in-betweenness property was experimentally tested by Clyde Coombs (1975). Subjects were asked to rank three gambles A, B, and C in order of attractiveness, where C was a probability mixture of A and B. For ex-

ample, if A offers a 50–50 chance at $3 or $0, and gamble B offers a 50–50 chance at $5 or $0, then a 40–60 mixture of A and B, called gamble C, would offer outcomes of $5, $3 and $0 with probabilities .3, .2 and .5 respectively. According to the EU axioms, gamble C should be in-between A and B in terms of attractiveness. In evaluating these three gambles, subjects can give six possible rankings, which Coombs reduced to three basic classes, namely monotone orderings (ACB or BCA), folded orderings (CAB or CBA), and inverted orderings (ABC or BAC). Only the first of these, the monotone ranking, is consistent with EU. Of the 520 rank-orderings Coombs examined, 54 percent were monotone, 27 percent folded, and 19 percent inverted, suggesting that nearly half the subjects violated the in-betweenness axiom. Similar violations had been observed earlier by Becker, Morris de Groot, and Marschak (1963).

The third axiom, which assumes invariance of preference between certainty and risk when other things are equal, was examined by Kahneman and Tversky (1979) as a generalization of Maurice Allais' (1953) well-known paradox. They observed a so-called certainty effect according to which outcomes obtained with certainty loom disproportionately larger than those which are uncertain. As an example, consider the following two-choice situations:

Situation A:	(1a)	a certain loss of $45.
	(2a)	a .5 chance of losing $100 and a .5 chance of losing $0.
Situation B:	(1b)	a .10 chance of losing $45 and a .9 chance of losing $0.
	(2b)	a .05 chance of losing $100 and a .95 chance of losing $0.

Most subjects preferred (2a) to (1a) and (1b) to (2b) which violates EU since the former implies that $U(-45) < .5U(-100)$

Schoemaker: The Expected Utility Model 543

+ $.5U(0)$, whereas the latter preference implies the reverse inequality. To see why this preference pattern violates the third EU axiom, note the following relationship between situations A and B:

$$(1b) = \begin{array}{c} .1 \swarrow (1a) \\ .9 \searrow 0 \end{array} \qquad (2b) = \begin{array}{c} .1 \swarrow (2a) \\ .9 \searrow 0 \end{array}$$

In prospect theory, Kahneman and Tversky (1979) provide several additional examples of this certainty effect, which they explain as the result of probability distortions.

A related experiment on the effect of certainty vs. uncertainty was performed by Ellsberg (1961); however, his focus was on the probability dimension. He showed that people dislike ambiguity as to the exact level of the probability of winning (p_i). The essential finding was that subjects look at more than the expected value of such a probability, when given some prior distribution as to its levels. This sensitivity to other moments is contrary to EU theory for which only $E(\bar{p}_i)$ matters.[9] The Allais and Ellsberg paradoxes can both be shown to entail a violation of an alternative type of EU axiom, called Savage's independence or sure-thing principle (1954). This axiom holds that if two lotteries have an identical probability and payoff branch, the levels of this payoff and probability should not affect people's choice between the lotteries.

The above violations particularly raise questions about the fifth EU axiom, i.e., the assessment of compound lotteries. Direct evidence of its violation was offered

by Maya Bar-Hillel (1973) who found that people tend to overestimate the probability of conjunctive events and underestimate the probability of disjunctive events. In her experiment subjects were presented with three events on which they could bet:

1. A simple event: drawing a red marble from a bag containing 50 percent red and 50 percent white marbles.
2. A conjunctive event: drawing a red marble 7 times in succession, with replacement, from a bag containing 90 percent red marbles and 10 percent white marbles.
3. A disjunctive event: drawing a red marble at least once in 7 successive tries, with replacement, from a bag containing 10 percent red marbles and 90 percent white marbles.

The majority preferred bet 2 to bet 1. Subjects also preferred bet 1 to bet 3. The probabilities of the three events, however, are .50, .48 and .52 respectively. These biases can be explained as effects of anchoring: i.e., the stated probability of the elementary event (.1 in the disjunctive case) provides a natural starting point from which insufficient adjustment is made to arrive at the final answer.

A sixth postulate, not formally part of NM utility theory, is the traditional risk-aversion assumption in economics and finance, particularly for losses (Friedman and Savage, 1948; Arrow, 1971; Isaac Ehrlich and Becker, 1972; J. Marshall, 1974; Martin Bailey et al., 1980). Recent laboratory studies, however, seriously question this pervasive assumption (also see, Harry Markowitz, 1952). For instance, John Hershey and Schoemaker (1980) found that less than 40 percent of their subjects would pay $100 to protect against a .01 chance of losing $10,000. Similar refusals to accept actuarially fair insurance were uncovered by Paul Slovic et al. (1977), Kahneman and Tversky (1979), Schoemaker and Howard Kunreuther (1979), and Fishburn and Gary Kochenberger (1979). Dan Laughhunn et al. (1981) found

[9] A normative reply to the Ellsberg paradox can be found in Raiffa (1961), Harry Roberts (1963), and Jacques Drèze (1974). Other discussions of the Ellsberg experiment and related paradoxes (e.g., Allais) are contained in William Fellner (1961), Selwyn Becker and Fred Brownson (1964), Karl Borch (1968), Kenneth MacCrimmon (1968), Frank Yates and Lisa Zukowski (1976), MacCrimmon and Stig Larsson (1979), and Soo-Hong Chew and MacCrimmon (1979b).

executives to be risk-seeking when presented with gambles having outcomes below target return levels (e.g., breakeven returns on investments). However, when the gambles involved ruinous losses, the executives were often risk-averse.

b. *Field Studies*

From a positivistic viewpoint the above evidence may be of limited interest. For instance, economists might argue that although subjects may behave non-optimally in hypothetical and unrepresentative experiments, in the real world, where decisions do matter, people will in fact maximize expected utility.

Real-world data on insurance against flood and earthquake insurance, however, suggest a different conclusion (Dan Anderson, 1974). In spite of Federal subsidies of *up to 90 percent* for flood insurance (this past decade), Kunreuther et al. (1978) found that the majority of eligible homeowners in flood plains were uninsured. One obvious reason could be that people's perceptions of the probability and magnitude of loss, or their perceptions as to the cost of insurance, differed from the actuarial figures used by the government. To test whether homeowners were *subjectively* rational, Kunreuther et al. interviewed 2,000 homeowners in flood plains and 1,000 homeowners in earthquake areas to obtain subjective estimates of these figures. Many respondents, over one-half, were ill-informed on the availability of insurance against these hazards. Of those who were aware, however, many acted contrary to subjective EU maximization (around 40 percent for flood and 30 percent for earthquake insurance), assuming a marginal tax rate of 30 percent and plausible degrees of risk aversion. The study also controlled for people expecting post-disaster relief aid from federal, state or local agencies. Results found by Kunreuther et al (1978) thus seriously question people's ability to process information on

low probability, high loss events. (See also Kunreuther, 1976). A similar conclusion emerges from the low demand for crime insurance (Federal Insurance Administration, 1974), and people's general reluctance to wear seat belts in automobiles (L. Robertson, 1974).[10]

Although the above results imply risk-seeking for losses (within the EU model), in other domains of insurance people appear highly risk-averse. As mentioned earlier, Pashigian et al. uncovered a strong preference for expensive low deductible automobile insurance. Similarly, Robert Eisner and Strotz (1961) showed that although flight-insurance is considerably more expensive than regular life-insurance, there exists a strong demand for the former. Indeed, flight insurance is one of the few coverages which is actually "bought" (i.e., the consumer rather than insurance agent initiates the purchase).

The above examples suggest that people sometimes ignore low probability events, whereas at other times they focus on the loss dimension. They question whether people are as coherent and consistent as EU maximization implies, highlighting the importance of psychological factors in economic behavior (George Katona, 1975). An interesting illustration of the need to include psychological factors was offered by Katona (1965). He examined whether working people who expect retirement income from pension plans placed more or less funds into private savings (e.g., deposits with banks and savings institutions, bonds or stocks) than working people who are not covered by such pension plans. Private pension plans, which were relatively unimportant in 1945, ex-

---

[10] An intriguing economic explanation for this was offered by Sam Peltzman (1975). His data show that the effects of legally mandated installation of various automobile safety devices are offset by increased risk-taking by drivers (e.g., not wearing seatbelts), supporting the notion that drivers determine their own, individually optimal, risk exposure.

panded so much that in 1965 almost one-half of all privately employed workers in the U.S.A. were covered (in addition to almost universal social security coverage). Hence, it presented a unique opportunity for a field study on the effect of private pension plans on discretionary savings, particularly as coverage by these pension plans was largely a function of the type of employment rather than the result of deliberate action to obtain such coverage.

At the outset two alternative hypotheses were formulated. The first derived from traditional economic theory, and suggested that increased "forced savings" (via private pension plans) would *reduce* voluntary savings, other things being equal. The alternative to this "substitution effect" hypothesis was that increased forced savings would lead to *increased* voluntary savings because of aspiration level adjustments and goal gradient effects.[11] Comparisons between "the average savings ratios of the people covered and people not covered under a private pension plan—paired so as to make them similar in many (socio-economic) characteristics—indicated that the former saved more than the latter" (Katona, 1965, p. 6). These real-world results seem to support an aspiration level and goal gradient hypothesis rather than the traditional economic substitution effect.[12]

[11] The level of aspiration effect, as initially studied by Kurt Lewin (see A. Marrow, 1969, pp. 44–46), states that people raise their sights (i.e., aspirations) with success and lower them with failure. The goal gradient effect refers to a well-known phenomenon in which effort is intensified the closer one gets to a goal.

[12] Martin Feldstein questioned this interpretation on grounds of ignoring that "workers who are covered by pensions have an incentive to retire earlier than they otherwise would" (1974, p. 907). He presented time-series data suggesting that public social security depressed personal savings by 30 to 50 percent. Corrections to these analyses by Dan Leimer and Selig Lesnoy (1980), however, found no systematic reduction. A later study by Feldstein (1978) on the effect of private pension programs similarly

c. Information Processing Research

One explanation of the above evidence is that people are intendedly rational, but lack the mental capacity to abide by EU theory. This view is corroborated by artificial intelligence research on human perception, recognition, information storage and information retrieval. The bounded rationality view (Simon, 1955) of humans is that of an information processing system which is very narrow in its perception, sequential in its central processing, and severely limited in short-term memory capacity (George Miller, 1956; Simon and Allen Newell, 1971). This limited information processing capacity compels people to simplify even simple problems, and forces them to focus more on certain problem aspects than others (i.e., anchoring). Such adaptation implies sensitivity to the problem presentation, as well as the nature of the response requested. For instance, Joshua Ronen (1973) found that simply interchanging the two stages of a lottery affected preferences (e.g., a .7 chance at a .3 chance of getting $100 was more attractive to subjects than a .3 chance of getting a .7 chance at $100).

Several other studies on gambles also indicate that people adapt their information processing strategy to the specifics of the task. For instance, Slovic and Sarah Lichtenstein (1968a) compared the relative importance of gambles' dimensions using two different response modes. They constructed so-called duplex gambles which contain a separate gain and loss pointer. Such a gamble is fully characterized by four risk-dimensions: namely, a probability of winning (Pw), an amount to be won (Aw), a probability of losing (Pl), and an amount of loss (Al). Using sev-

showed no adverse effects on saving, and possibly an increase. Further evidence bolstering Katona's interpretation derives from a study by Diamond (1977) demonstrating that people do not save enough (by objective standards).

eral such gambles, the following regression model was tested (per subject) $y = w_0 + w_1 Pw + w_2 Aw + w_3 Pl + w_4 Al$, where the dependent variable y represented dollar bids for one group, and rankings on some interval scale for another group of subjects. In the bidding task the dollar dimensions (Aw and Al) received significantly more weight than in the ranking task. Apparently subjects adapt their information processing strategies to the response mode: when dollar bids are required dollar dimensions become more salient.

An important issue raised by this study concerns the exact nature of human information processing. Someone might object that Slovic and Lichtenstein (1968a) presupposed a linear regression model (i.e., the above equation) whereas subjects in fact may have processed the moments (i.e., expected value, variance, etc.) of the gamble (as an EU maximizer would).[13] Indeed, several (earlier) studies of gambles support such a moment view, suggesting that expected value and variance are very important (Edwards, 1954b; Coombs and Dean Pruitt, 1960; Lichtenstein, 1965; Norman Anderson and James Shanteau, 1970). The relevant question, therefore, is what results a direct comparison would show.

Two such direct tests were conducted. In another study, Slovic and Lichtenstein (1968b) compared bids between gambles whose stated risk-dimensions (i.e., Pw, Aw, Pl and Al) were identical but whose variances were different. The bids for such gambles did not differ significantly (within a pair). Conversely, John Payne and My-

ron Braunstein (1971) compared equivalent duplex gambles whose stated risk-dimensions differed, but whose moments were identical. This time subjects were not indifferent between the gambles in a pair. Hence, the available data on duplex gambles support the risk-dimension model rather than the moment or EU view. For a review see Payne, 1973. Coombs and Paul Lehner (1981) concluded that the moment model also fails as a descriptor of risk *perceptions* (as opposed to preference).

Additional evidence for these conclusions derives from the so-called preference reversal phenomenon. Harold Lindman (1971) showed that subjects might prefer gamble A to B when given a direct choice but, at the same time, place a lower reservation price on gamble A than on gamble B when assessed separately. In direct choice subjects focus mostly on the probability of winning, whereas in naming reservation prices the amount of winning is more salient. Such response-induced preference reversals were also demonstrated by Lichtenstein and Slovic (1971) in comparing bids with choices, and have been replicated with real gamblers in Las Vegas (Lichtenstein and Slovic, 1973). Since such reversals may be counter to EU theory or any other holistic choice model, David Grether and Plott (1979) carefully replicated the effect while controlling for such economic explanations as income effects, real vs. hypothetical payoffs, hidden incentives, strategic misrepresentation, etc. None of these hypotheses, however, offered an adequate explanation of the preference reversal phenomenon.

The above results suggest that various choice phenomena cannot be understood or predicted without a detailed understanding of the way information is processed. A natural representation for information processing models are flow-charts, in which components of the alternatives

---

[13] For example, if the utility function is linear, only expected value matters. If it is quadratic, both mean and variance are important (H. Levy and Harry Markowitz, 1979). More generally, however, any well-behaved utility function (i.e., one whose derivatives exist and are finite) can be expanded into a Taylor series, whose expected utility is a function of the moments of the gamble (Jack Hirshleifer, 1970; David Baron, 1977).

Schoemaker: The Expected Utility Model   547

are compared sequentially, either against each other (Payne and Braunstein, 1971) or against an external reference point. For example, Kunreuther's 1976 sequential model of flood insurance purchase starts with concern about the hazard. If the probability of loss is below some threshold level, insurance will not be considered seriously, irrespective of the loss and premium (Slovic, et al., 1977).

d. *Context Effects*

Additional complexities in choice behavior stem from the role of context. The latter refers to the script, verbal labels, social dimensions, information displays, and response modes of a decision problem. Since EU theory focuses on the underlying structure of choices, as modeled by "rational" outside observers, it is largely insensitive to such contextual differences.

Recent studies by Schoemaker and Kunreuther (1979), and Hershey and Schoemaker (1980) uncovered an interesting context effect concerning the wording used in describing decision alternatives. To illustrate, consider the following two formulations for presenting a choice between a sure loss and a probabilistic one:

Gamble formulation:	1a.	A sure loss of $10.
	1b.	A 1 percent chance of losing $1,000.
Insurance formulation:	2a.	Pay an insurance premium of $10.
	2b.	**Remain exposed to a hazard of losing $1,000 with a 1 percent chance.**

According to EU theory the gamble and insurance formulations involve identical choices between $U(w_0 - 10)$ on the one hand, and $[.01\,U(w_0 - 1,000) + .99\,U(w_0)]$ on the other. Psychologically, however, these two choice situations are quite different. Of 42 subjects, 56 percent preferred the sure loss when presented in the gambling formulation versus 81 percent in the insurance formulation. Hershey and

Schoemaker (1980) demonstrated this discrepancy also with other probability and loss levels. The effect was strongest for probability and loss levels representative of insurable hazards (e.g., low probabilities and moderate to large losses). Furthermore, wherever the difference was statistically significant ($p < .05$), the insurance formulation evoked greater risk aversion than did the gamble formulation. Possible reasons for this particular context effect are that different psychological sets are evoked (Robert Abelson, 1976). For example, societal norms about prudent behavior may play a role in the insurance context. Alternatively, different reference points may be used, giving the impression that something is gained in the insurance formulation. Finally, other dimensions may be at play besides money, reflecting the various connotations of insurance such as an assumed administrative cost of filing a claim, less than perfect certainty that repayment will indeed occur in case a legitimate loss is incurred, or regret. However, the first two of these concerns would argue against buying insurance. Regret considerations on the other hand might favor insurance, as the insurance formulation implies that one will know whether or not the loss occurred. Note that this is not implied in the gamble formulation.

Another good example in which isomorphic problems are judged differently was provided by Tversky and Kahneman (1981). Imagine that the U.S. is preparing for the outbreak of an unusual Asian disease, which is expected to kill 600 people. Two alternative programs to combat the disease have been proposed. Assume that the consequences are as follows:

| A: | If program A is adopted exactly 200 will be saved. |
| B: | If program B is adopted, there is a ⅓ probability that 600 people will be saved, and a ⅔ probability that no people will be saved. |

When this choice was given to 158 subjects, the majority (76 percent) preferred program A. A similar group of 169 subjects were also given the same choice, but in slightly altered form as follows:

A': If program A is adopted exactly 400 people will die.

B': If program B is adopted there is a ⅓ probability that nobody will die, and ⅔ probability that 600 people will die.

Although formally equivalent to the earlier formulation, this time only 13 percent preferred program A. This example illustrates how changes in wording can affect the reference point used to evaluate outcomes.

It is a complex issue as to whether context effects are counter to EU theory. Ex post many might fit the model by including additional dimensions, constraints or different reference points. For instance, Bell (1980, 1982) successfully explained such EU anomalies as the Allais paradox, violations of dominance, risk-seeking for losses, preference reversals etc., by introducing regret as the second dimension in a two-attribute expected utility model. Similar ingenious regret explanations were offered by Graham Loomes and Robert Sugden (1981), who suggest that the utility of an object may well be different when it is chosen than when it is received as a gift. Although such EU extensions are intriguing, the EU model does not offer a rich descriptive theory of problem representation and will therefore not easily predict new context effects. The latter requires a better psychological understanding of decision making in general, an issue we turn to next.

V. *Psychological Aspects*

The failure of EU theory as both a descriptive and predictive model stems from an inadequate recognition of various psychological principles of judgment and choice. Underlying most of these is a general human tendency to seek cognitive simplification. In this section, five psychological aspects are discussed that are particularly germane to risky choice.

First, most decisions are made in *decomposed* fashion using *relative* comparisons. Evaluations of multidimensional alternatives are seldom holistic in the sense of each alternative being assigned a separate level of utility. It is cognitively easier to compare alternatives on a piece-meal basis, i.e., one dimension at a time. Two types of such approaches might be distinguished. In the first, alternatives are compared against a preset standard and eliminated if they fail to measure up. If it is required that *all* attributes meet certain minimum standards, the model is conjunctive.[14] If satisfaction of at least one dimensional standard is sufficient, the model is disjunctive. For example, Melvin W. Reder (1947) found that investment projects are often eliminated from consideration because the probability of ruin exceeds some critical level (i.e., a disjunctive rejection rule). Additional examples are discussed and cited by Roger Shepard (1964), Einhorn (1970, 1971) and Libby and Fishburn (1977).

In the second type, no preset standards are used; instead the alternatives are compared directly (in a decomposed manner). One such approach is elimination-by-aspects, a type of lexicographic model.

In contemplating a dinner at a restaurant, for example, the first aspect selected may be sea food: this eliminates all restaurants that do not serve acceptable sea food. Given the remaining

---

[14] This model is non-compensatory in that failure to meet a minimum level on one dimension cannot be compensated for by "surpluses" on others. A good example is the satisficing model associated with Simon's (1955) theory of bounded rationality. In this model, search among alternatives is terminated once a solution is found that satisfies all preset constraints. Examples of such satisficing behavior in organizational contexts were examined by James March and Simon (1958), Richard Cyert and March (1963), Charles Lindblom (1964) and more recently March and Johan Olsen (1976).

alternatives, another aspect—say a price level—is selected, and all restaurants that exceed the selected price level are eliminated. The process continues until only one restaurant that includes all the selected aspects remains [Tversky, 1972, p. 349].

Another lexicographic model was proposed by Payne and Braunstein (1971) in their study of pairs of duplex gambles. Subjects first compared probabilities. If the difference was sufficiently large a choice would be made on this basis alone. If not, dollar dimensions would be considered. A detailed review of lexicographic models can be found in Fishburn (1974).

An alternative approach is Tversky's (1969) additive difference model mentioned earlier (p. 542). Empirical evidence for this compensatory model comes from several marketing studies involving binary product choices. J. Edward Russo and Barbara Dosher (1981) used eye-fixation sequences (i.e., whether subjects examined information across rows or columns) as well as verbal protocols to demonstrate that subjects first estimate utility differences within dimensions and then combine these estimates across dimensions. Small differences are often ignored. Similar results were reported by Willem Van Raaij (1977), who examined consumer information-processing strategies under various task structures. The prevalence of such decomposed evaluation strategies raises serious doubts about EU theory's holistic approach.

A second important principle of choice is that *decision strategies vary with task complexity*. As Payne (1976) showed, when alternatives and dimensions are numerous, subjects tend to use conjunctive and lexicographic models as initial screening rules. With fewer attributes, holistic evaluations are more probable. However, with just two alternatives and many different attributes the additive difference model is predominant. The idea of variable strategies and mixed scanning was also

proposed by Amitai Etzioni (1967), and Irving Janis and Leon Mann (1977). Interesting evidence comes from studies on decision time and task complexity by Charles Kiesler (1966), who examined how much time children took in choosing one piece of candy from four alternatives. Surprisingly, the decision times were *shorter* when all four pieces were about equally attractive than when two were attractive and two unattractive! This finding suggests a greater motivation to be optimal with simple than with complex choices. Such aspiration shifts are likely to affect decision strategies markedly (Hogarth, 1975b) in ways counter to EU theory.

A third important principle of choice is that of *isolation*. According to EU theory, decision making requires a portfolio perspective (Markowitz, 1952). For instance, a decision concerning a particular insurance policy would, in theory, depend on all other risks one faces. However, people may not approach decisions in this comprehensive way, and simply treat problems in isolation. Tversky and Kahneman (1981) demonstrated that violations of first-order stochastic dominance can be induced easily because of isolation.[15] Another example they discuss concerns the treatment of a $20 loss. Say that in one scenario you purchase a $20 theater ticket, which you then lose while waiting in the lobby. Would you buy a new ticket? In the other scenario you are about to purchase this same theater ticket, but upon opening your wallet you discover that $20 is missing. Would you still buy the ticket? Because of the way people partition decision contexts, the $20 loss seems less relevant to the second than to the first choice.

---

[15] A random variable $\tilde{x}$ is said to stochastically dominate another different random variable $\tilde{y}$ to the first degree (or order) if the cumulative probability function of $\tilde{x}$ nowhere exceeds that of $\tilde{y}$. If so, the expected utility of $\tilde{x}$ will be higher than that of $\tilde{y}$ for any monotonic utility function (Joseph Hadar and William Russell, 1969).

Of course, in both scenarios the choice is either not to go to the theater and be $20 poorer or to go and be $40 poorer. Similar isolation effects are demonstrated in prospect theory (Kahneman and Tversky, 1979) concerning windfall profits, and in Schoemaker (1980) with insurance.

The fourth principle to be mentioned concerns the role of *reference points* and *aspiration levels*. Although EU theory suggests that alternatives are evaluated with respect to their effects on final wealth levels, it is cognitively easier to assess options in terms of gains and losses relative to some reference point (Simon, 1955). This target point will often be the status quo, but might also be a target return level, or an aspired future wealth position. Importantly, risk-taking attitudes are likely to be quite different above versus below this reference point. For instance, in prospect theory $v(x)$ is assumed to be convex for losses and concave for gains (Kahneman and Tversky, 1979). In risk-return models, risk is often related to the probability and consequences of failing to meet a target return level (Fishburn, 1977). Similarly, return may be related to above target probabilities and consequences (Duncan Holthausen, 1981). Although such two-parameter models are descriptively appealing (G. Shackle, 1952), they are theoretically incompatible with EU maximization.

An experimental test of aspiration level effects was offered by Payne et al. (1980, 1981) who examined binary choices of students and managers between three-outcome gambles whose expected values were equal. In each pair, the outcomes of the second gamble all fell within the range of the first. By adding a constant amount to all outcomes, the pairs were translated through the origin to different degrees. Such translations commonly induced changes in preferences, especially if they were such that in one gamble all outcomes were positive (or negative)

while in the other gamble there were mixed outcomes. Since at least two general reversals were observed under this design, it would be difficult to explain these results by postulating inflection points in the NM utility function. Instead, these data (especially Payne et al., 1981) point toward strong aspiration level effects. Also see Arthur Williams, 1966.

Another descriptive model that explicitly incorporates the aspiration level concept was proposed by Coombs and Lily Huang (1970). In this so-called portfolio theory, an optimal risk level is assumed for every level of expected value. Gambles of equal expected value are judged in terms of their deviations from this optimal risk level. Hence if two gambles A and B, having equal expected values, are combined into a probability mixture called gamble C, then the new gamble could be closer in risk to the optimal level than either A or B. This model could thus explain the types of the inverted ordering discussed earlier (pp. 542).

An interesting everyday example of inappropriate reference points was offered by Tversky and Kahneman (1981). Suppose you are about to purchase an electronic calculator for $25 and then learn from your friend that exactly the same calculator is for sale at $20 five blocks away. Would you leave the store and go to the cheaper one? Now imagine the same scenario except you are buying a stereo set for $500, and then your friend tells you it is for sale at $495 five blocks away. Would you go this time? Although the crucial question in both cases is whether or not you would walk five blocks for $5, the first saving of 20 percent seems much more attractive than the second which is only 1 percent. Hence, instead of looking at final asset positions, people's reference dimension is percent savings. Pratt, David Wise and Richard Zeckhauser (1979) found field-evidence for this effect in price differences of highly similar

Schoemaker: The Expected Utility Model   551

consumer products across stores. The price variance increased markedly with price level, but was fairly constant when expressed as a percentage of price.

Often reference point effects underlie sunk-cost fallacies and failures to treat opportunity costs as being real. As an illustration, consider the following actual example offered by Richard Thaler:

> Mr. R bought a case of good wine in the late 50's for about $5 a bottle. A few years later his wine merchant offered to buy the wine back for $100 a bottle. He refused, although he never paid more than $35 for a bottle of wine [1980, p. 43].

Although such behavior could be rationalized through income effects and transaction costs, it probably involves a psychological difference between opportunity costs and actual out-of-pocket costs.

Finally, there is a fifth major factor that underlies EU violations, namely the psychology of probability judgments (Hogarth, 1975a). We shall briefly touch on three aspects: (1) the impact of objective (or stated) probabilities on choice, (2) quantitative expressions of degrees of beliefs through subjective probabilities, and (3) probabilistic reasoning, particularly inference.

A general finding of subjective expected utility research is that subjective probabilities relate non-linearly to objective ones (e.g., Edwards, 1953; 1954a). Typically, the subjective probability curves overweigh low probabilities and underweigh high ones (Wayne Lee, 1971, p. 61). For example, Menahem Yaari (1965) explained the acceptance of actuarially unfair gambles as resulting from optimism regarding low-probability events, as opposed to convexities in the utility function. Although the evidence is inconclusive as to the general nature of probability transformations, particularly with respect to its stability across tasks and its dependence on outcomes (Richard Rosett, 1971), R. W. Marks, 1951, Francis Irwin, 1953, and Slo-

vic, 1966 found that subjective probabilities tend to be higher as outcomes become more desirable (i.e., a type of wishful thinking). Furthermore, subjective "probabilities" often violate mathematical properties of probability (Kahneman and Tversky, 1979). In such cases we refer to them as decision weights $w(p)$, as noted earlier.

In expressing degrees of confidence probabilistically, other biases are encountered. A robust result is that people are generally overconfident. For instance, if one were to check out all instances where a person claimed 90 percent confidence about the occurrence of events, typically that person would be correct only about 80 percent of the time (Lichtenstein, et al., 1981). This same bias manifests itself in subjective confidence intervals, which are typically too tight (M. Alpert and Raiffa, 1981). Many biases in subjective probability judgments stem from the type of heuristics (i.e., simplifying rules) people use to estimate relative likelihoods. For instance, a doctor may judge the likelihood of a patient having disease A versus B solely on the basis of the similarity of the symptoms to textbook stereotypes of these diseases. This so-called representativeness heuristic, however, ignores possible differences in the a priori probabilities of these diseases (Kahneman and Tversky, 1972). Another common heuristic is estimation on the basis of availability (Tversky and Kahneman, 1973). In judging the chances of dying from a car accident versus lung cancer, people may base their estimates solely on the frequencies with which they hear of them. Due to unrepresentative news coverage in favor of car accidents, these estimates will be systematically biased (Lichtenstein et al., 1978). Finally, people suffer from a serious hindsight bias resulting in suboptimal learning. Events that did (not) happen appear in retrospect more (less) likely than they did before the outcome was known. Baruch Fischhoff (1975) explains this phenomenon as due to reconstructive memory. Once new information is received it is combined with older information, making the latter irretrievable by itself.

A third area where probabilities are improperly estimated is Bayesian inference in well-structured tasks. Two somewhat opposite phenomena are encountered depending on the context. One is conservatism (Edwards, 1968) according to which new information is underweighted in the revision of opinions (e.g., in poker chip experiments). It reflects an anchoring onto the old information with insufficient adjustment in the direction of the new information. The other phenomenon involves ignorance of stated prior probabilities, similar to the earlier example of disease A vs. B. One psychological explanation is that people's heuristic for assessing the relevance of information is based on its causal relationship (Tversky and Kahneman, 1980). This would explain why most people consider the probability of a daughter having blue eyes, given that her mother has blue eyes, to be higher than the probability of a mother having blue eyes, given that her daughter has blue eyes. However, assuming that successive generations have the same incidence of blue eyes, these probabilities are the same.

Perceptions regarding causal connections may similarly explain people's general insensitivity to prior probabilities, the causality of which is often unclear. For instance, in judging the probability that a taxi involved in some city accident was blue rather than green, subjects focused entirely on the reliability of the eye-witness testimony while ignoring the explicitly stated information that only 10 percent of the taxis in the city were blue. However, when Bar-Hillel (1980) rephrased the problem by saying that although there were as many blue as green cabs in the city, only 10% of the taxis involved in past accidents were blue, this prior information received considerable

weight. Even though this problem is statistically identical to the earlier version, emphasizing the causal connection of the prior probabilities to the event of interest markedly improved subjects' posterior probabilities (as judged from Bayes' theorem). The above examples underscore that subjective probabilities commonly violate basic statistical principles, thereby invalidating axiom five in NM utility theory as well as Savage's SEU axioms.

VI. *Conclusions*

The research reviewed in this article suggests that at the individual level EU maximization is more the exception than the rule, at least for the type of decision tasks examined. To assess the role of EU theory more generally, e.g., for future decision models, we next examine the evidence from each of the four perspectives identified at the beginning of the paper.

As a descriptive model seeking insight into how decisions are made, EU theory fails on at least three counts. First, people do not structure problems as holistically and comprehensively as EU theory suggests. Second they do not process information, especially probabilities, according to the EU rule. Finally, EU theory, as an "as if" model, poorly predicts choice behavior in laboratory situations. Hence, it is doubtful that the EU theory should or could serve as a general descriptive model. However, there may be exceptions. For well-structured repetitive tasks, with important stakes, and well-trained decision makers, EU maximization may well describe the actual decision process, e.g., oil-drilling decisions. Indeed, in large organizations where computers are used and highly trained managers operate, the EU model might be explicitly followed. However, even under such favorable circumstances, problem definitions and solutions can be plagued by sunk-cost fallacies, isolation effects, and asymmetrical treat-

Schoemaker: The Expected Utility Model 553

ments of opportunity and out-of-pocket costs. As Thaler (1980) argues, these biases afflict organizational as well as individual decision making.

From a positivistic perspective, the interpretation of evidence counter to EU theory is more complicated. A well-known example of Friedman and Savage (1948) notes that complex equations of rigid body mechanics and plane geometry may offer excellent predictions of the manner in which expert billiard players take their shots, even if these players are totally ignorant of such equations. The reason is that the geometric model captures well what the players try to do. Since they are experts, years of training and feedback have led to heuristics that closely approximate optimal behavior. Four conditions, however, make this analogy of limited value to economic behavior. First, most people are not experts in economic matters (Thaler, 1980). Second, learning from feedback is not a simple or automatic activity in daily decision making. Uncertainty, environmental instability, improper assessment frameworks, and lack of insight into one's decision rules are all serious obstacles to learning from experience (Einhorn, 1980). Third, the optimality of economic behavior in real-world settings is often difficult to assess without specific knowledge of the person's utility function, the particular problem perception, and the rationality criteria being pursued (March, 1978). Finally, even if the EU model did predict well (while its assumptions are wrong) the notion that only prediction matters is epistemologically quite unappealing (Paul Samuelson, 1963). For instance, it would be interesting to know what makes the model so robust under misspecification (Robyn Dawes, 1979).

A second reaction, from a positivistic economic perspective, is to note that individual biases and differences may not matter in aggregate behavior. For example, Stigler and Becker (1977) argued that peo-ple may usefully be treated as similar in basic tastes and preferences, both across time and persons. Moreover, market mechanisms may be presumed to correct misperceptions and individual decision biases. However, not necessarily. Paul Kleindorfer and Kunreuther (1982) examined analytically the effect of probability misinformation (by firms and consumers) on insurance markets. Using Rothschild's and Joseph Stiglitz' (1976) solution to the adverse selection problem (i.e., allowing insurers to offer varying dollar premiums as a function of total coverage), they established various conditions under which the market fails. Pratt, Wise and Zeckhauser's 1979 study on price differences among highly similar consumer products also demonstrates a failure of the market to correct individual biases. Finally, Thomas C. Schelling (1978) discusses many other examples of "irrational" macro behavior, such as drivers incurring a thirty minute delay to have a one-minute peek at some highway accident. The point to be made is that the connection between micro and macro behavior is too complex to argue that at higher levels of social aggregation individual biases generally wash out or self-correct.

As a third discussion point, let us examine the view that hypothetical and "artificial" laboratory experiments have limited implications for economic theory. Sociological research (H. Schuman and M. P. Johnson, 1976) indeed underscores the consideration that intentions (i.e., hypothetical choices) cannot be mechanically substituted for, or assumed to be generally highly correlated with, actual behavior. In the context of gambles, however, several empirical studies by Nathan Kogan and Michael Wallach (1967) and Slovic (1969) on the effect of hypothetical vs. real payoffs suggest that cognitive processes and decisions do not differ considerably between these two conditions. Indeed, I know of *no evidence* that suboptimal laboratory behavior improves when committing subjects financially to their decisions. For example, Lichtenstein and Slovic (1973) found similar biases and inconsistencies in their Las Vegas replications with real gamblers (who played with their own money for large stakes), as they had earlier found with college students who had provided hypothetical judgments (Lichtenstein and Slovic, 1971). Similarly, Grether and Plott's (1979) recent replication of the so-called preference reversal phenomenon, using gambles with real money, revealed similar, and at times greater inconsistencies than under the hypothetical condition. From these studies, it appears unlikely that the subjects in the experiments discussed would come closer to optimal EU behavior when making decisions for real. The failure to optimize appears to be cognitive (i.e., related to the way problems are structured and what decision strategies are used) rather than motivational (i.e., the amount of mental effort expended). This brings us to the charge that laboratory experiments tend to be artificial, which is confused here with being unrepresentative (Karl Weick, 1967). Behavior in the laboratory is as real as other forms of behavior. If economic theory is proposed as a general model of scarce resource allocation, it should apply to experimental settings as well (Vernon Smith, 1976). Indeed, the burden of proof should be on those wishing to exclude laboratory behavior from economic theory rather than on those who want to include it.

From a postdictive perspective, the EU violations discussed would all be considered illusory. It would be argued that the examples cited *appear* to violate the EU model because of improperly specified costs and benefits. The ensuing rationalization would focus on *hidden* costs, incentives, dimensions and constraints. For instance, intangible cognitive costs might be introduced, even with justification (e.g., Steven Shugan, 1980). However, to mount an elaborate rescuing mission along this line may be self-defeating. The postdictive view is particularly prone to fall prey to a methodological sunk-cost fallacy. Having invested heavily in complex deductive structures, with wide domains of applicability and mathematically elegant decision models that allow for easy aggregation across people, it is a natural tendency to patch up the theory cosmetically. A better alternative is to examine closely the type of anomalies reported, and the cognitive reasons underlying them. Although cognitively realistic choice models may be task dependent and presented in process or flow-chart form, they can often be approximated holistically (Einhorn et al., 1979). For instance, a chess program that provides a cognitive representation of some human chess master might be approximated by a set of functions that are to be maximized. Once such optimality-based approximations are obtained they can be connected with traditional economic theory. The point is that modifications to economic theory (while retaining some sort of optimality) should be based on cognitive insights (see Roy Lachman, Janet Lachman, and Earl Butterfield, 1979 for a review) rather than ad hoc rationalization or mathematical expedience.

Finally, there is the prescriptive or normative perspective. At first glance, the numerous EU violations cited strengthen the case for formal decision analysis as a way of circumventing and supplementing the suboptimal nature of intuitive, unaided decision making. However, there are two related implications we should consider. First, some of the biases described (particularly regarding the axioms) may be so basic that they render the normative theory inoperational. Second, persistent violations of the EU model may raise questions as to its normative validity.

Regarding the operationality issue, an important difficulty concerns the con-

Schoemaker: The Expected Utility Model   555

struction of NM utility functions. As Cornelius Van Dam (1973) and Karmarkar (1978) have shown, 50–50 reference lotteries will often lead to a different NM utility function than, for example, would result if 30–70 lotteries had been used. Furthermore, as shown in Hershey and Schoemaker (1980) and Tversky and Kahneman (1981), subtle changes in the context or framing of a problem may lead to different preferences (see also Don Wehrung et al., 1980). Thus the question arises which context measures the "true" risk-taking attitude (Jim Barnes and James Reinmuth, 1976, and Hans Binswanger, 1980) or more fundamentally, whether there really exist basic tastes and preferences that are compatible with the EU axioms. A recent study by Hershey, Kunreuther and Schoemaker (1982), focusing on response mode biases, probability distortions, translation effects, risk transfer asymmetries and context effects, suggests that the answer to the latter question is no.[16]

One solution many normative theorists (e.g., Keeney and Raiffa, 1976) would recommend is to explain to the decision maker his or her inconsistencies and see if a revision of preference(s) is desired. For instance, MacCrimmon (1968) found that executive subjects would often change their choices when made aware of violations of normative postulates (e.g., those of Savage, 1954). However, social pressure and conformity tendencies may have confounded these results. In a follow-up study, Slovic and Tversky (1974) controlled for these influences. As mentioned earlier, they tested Savage's independence principle by presenting subjects

with the Allais (1953) and Ellsberg (1961) paradoxes. Once subjects had made their choices, they were then given a prepared, authoritative argument against their particular choice (i.e., either Allais' position or that of Savage). After reflecting on these arguments, the subjects were subsequently asked to reconsider their choice. Except for a few individuals, *most* subjects did *not* change their preferences, many of which were in violation of Savage's independence principle. Indeed, even among experts these paradoxes evoked considerable debate concerning the normative acceptability of the EU postulates (e.g., Samuelson, 1952; Allais, 1953; Savage, 1954; Raiffa, 1961; and Ellsberg, 1961 and 1963), which brings us to the second normative implication.

As MacCrimmon and Larsson (1979) noted: "since many careful, intelligent decision makers do seem to violate some axioms of expected utility theory, even upon reflection of their choices, it does seem worthwhile exploring this third option of considering modifications of the standard theory" (p. 83). In this vein Chew and MacCrimmon (1979a and 1979b) recently proposed an alternative generalized EU model, in which the substitution axiom is considerably weakened. Mark Machina (1982) showed that the major economic concepts and tools of EU analysis do not depend on the independence axiom. As an alternative route, Loomes and Sugden (1981) proposed to drop the transitivity axiom, both descriptively and normatively. Finally Fishburn (1981) recently developed an alternative preference representation that utilizes neither the transitivity nor the independence axiom.

Apart from modifications to the normative model two other options were presented by MacCrimmon and Larsson (1979), namely: (1) to maintain that one's choices are valid and that the assumptions or axioms do not apply in the given case, or (2) to change one's choices to conform

---

[16] Recent experiments suggest that the mathematical EU form of separable $f(p)$ and $U(x)$ transformations is questionable (John Lynch, 1979 and Lehner, 1980). Rather than reflecting risk-attitude indirectly in $U(x)$, it is proposed that the utility function explicitly incorporates probability, i.e., $EU = \Sigma f(p_i) U(x_i, p_i)$.

with the axioms. Let us examine the former, which can be interpreted in two ways: (1) someone disagrees with the probabilities used in showing violations of EU, or (2) the notion of objective risk is rejected, and hence the problem representation is disputed. Regarding the first one, objective probabilities exist only in *hypothetical* situations (and even this is disputable). In reality they are estimated and subjective. Since legitimate differences may exist among people in their subjective probabilities for the same event, violations of EU may be difficult to prove other than in hypothetical choice situations.

More basically, however, someone could refute a particular problem representation. For example, in the previously discussed context effect (Hershey and Schoemaker, 1980), the insurance formulation elicited more risk averse behavior than did the gamble formulation. However, this apparent EU violation might be explained by assuming that the outcome space is different in the insurance formulation. Since problem representation is inherently a subjective matter, it is subject to only limited normative evaluation (L. Jonathan Cohen, 1981). Indeed, there exists no general normative theory as to how problems should be defined, or how language and context should be encoded.[17] Moreover, someone might fundamentally question the meaningfulness of the notions of probability and risk. As noted earlier, there exist difficult, unresolved philosophical problems in the area of probability (Arthur Burks, 1977). To quote

West Churchman (1961, p. 139): "almost everyone knows what it means to say that an event is only probable—except those who have devoted their lives to thinking about the matter." Historically, probability is a relatively recent formal construct (Ian Hacking, 1975), which lacks primary sensory evidence as to its existence. As such it might be viewed as an invention rather than a discovery. Note in this regard the finding by Lawrence Phillips and C. N. Wright (1977) that the Chinese are less likely than the English to view the world probabilistically. Hence, an extreme but tenable attitude is to view the EU model as an interesting theoretical construction which is useless for real-world decision-making.

In conclusion, we have attempted to review recent evidence concerning the EU model from four different perspectives. Although the evidence and associated interpretations have been critical as to the model's usefulness, it must be emphasized that much of the research would not have resulted without the existence of EU theory in the first place. As such, the model has yielded deeper insights and more refined questions, both descriptively and normatively, concerning decisions under risk. It has revealed that people perceive and solve problems differently, and has offered a framework and language in which to discuss these differences. Our intellectual indebtedness to the EU model is thus great, although its present paradigmatic status (in certain fields) should be questioned. Nevertheless, until richer models of rationality emerge, EU maximization may well remain a worthwhile benchmark against which to compare, and toward which to direct, behavior. On the other hand, it is likely that today's paradoxes and persistent EU violations hold the seed of future normative as well as descriptive theories of choice. After all it was a paradox (Bernoulli, 1738) that gave birth to the current normative model.

[17] Churchman (1971) discusses various philosophical approaches to defining rationality and structuring inquiry systems concerning the nature of the world. A strong prior commitment to axiom systems, as in the EU model, is a Leibnitzian approach. If the formal model is correct, this strategy would be highly effective; if wrong, however, its costs could be considerable due to delayed detection of misspecifications. A more prudent strategy is the dialectical approach of Hegel or Kant (see Richard Mason and Ian Mitroff, 1973).

REFERENCES

ABELSON, ROBERT P. "Script Processing in Attitude Formation and Decision Making," *Cognition and social behavior.* Edited by JOHN S. CARROLL AND JOHN W. PAYNE. Hillsdale, N.J.: L. Erlbaum, 1976, pp. 33–45.

ALCHIAN, ARMEN A. "Uncertainty, Evolution and Economic Theory," *J. Polit. Econ.*, June 1950, *58*, pp. 211–21.

———. "The Meaning of Utility Measurement," *Amer. Econ. Rev.*, Mar. 1953, *43*, pp. 26–50.

ALLAIS, MAURICE. "Le Comportement de l'Homme Rationnel Devant le Risque: Critique des Postulats et Axiomes de l'École Américaine," *Econometrica*, Oct. 1953, *21*(4), pp. 503–46.

ALPERT, M. AND RAIFFA, HOWARD. "A Progress Report on the Training of Probability Assessors," *Judgment under uncertainty: Heuristics and biases.* Edited by DANIEL KAHNEMAN, PAUL SLOVIC, AND AMOS TVERSKY. New York: Cambridge Univ. Press, 1981.

ALT, FRANTZ. "On the Measurement of Utility," *Preference, utility and demand; a Minnesota symposium.* Edited by J. S. CHIPMAN ET AL. New York: Harcourt Brace Jovanovich, 1971.

ANDERSON, DAN R. "The National Flood Insurance Program—Problems and Potentials," *J. Risk Ins.*, Dec. 1974, *41*(4), pp. 579–99.

ANDERSON, NORMAN H. "Functional Measurement and Psychophysical Judgment," *Psych. Rev.*, 1970, *77*, pp. 153–70.

——— AND SHANTEAU, JAMES C. "Information Integration in Risky Decision Making," *J. Exper. Psych.*, 1970, *84*, pp. 441–51.

ARROW, KENNETH J. *Essays in the theory of risk-bearing.* Chicago: Markham, 1971.

BAILEY, MARTIN L.; OLSON, MANCUR AND WONNACOTT, PAUL. "The Marginal Utility of Income Does Not Increase: Borrowing, Lending, and Friedman-Savage Gambles," *Amer. Econ. Rev.*, June 1980, *70*(3), pp. 372–79.

BAR-HILLEL, MAYA. "On the Subjective Probability of Compound Events," *Organ. Beh. H.*, June 1973, *9*(3), pp. 396–406.

———. "The Base-Rate Fallacy in Probability Judgments," *Acta Psych.*, 1980, *44*, pp. 211–33.

BARNES, JIM D. AND REINMUTH, JAMES E. "Comparing Imputed and Actual Utility Functions in a Competitive Bidding Setting," *Decision Sciences.* Oct. 1976, *7*(4), pp. 801–12.

BARON, DAVID P. "On the Utility Theoretic Foundations of Mean-Variance Analysis," *J. Finance*, Dec. 1977, *23*(5), pp. 1683–97.

BATTALIO, RAYMOND C.; KAGEL, JOHN H.; RACHLIN, HOWARD ET AL. "Commodity-Choice Behavior with Pigeons as Subjects," *J. Polit. Econ.*, 1981, *89*(1), pp. 67–91.

BAUMOL, WILLIAM J. *Economic theory and operations analysis.* Englewood Cliffs, N.J.: Prentice-Hall, 1972.

BECKER, GARY S. *The economic approach to human behavior.* Chicago: Univ. of Chicago Press, 1976.

BECKER, GORDON M.; DE GROOT, MORRIS H. AND MARSCHAK, JACOB. "An Experimental Study of

Some Stochastic Models for Wagers," *Behavioral Science.* 1963, *8*(3), pp. 199–202.

——— AND MCCLINTOCK, CHARLES G. "Value: Behavioral Decision Theory," *Ann. Rev. Psych.* 1967, *18*, pp. 239–68.

BECKER, SELWYN W AND BROWNSON, FRED O. "What Price Ambiguity? Or the Role of Ambiguity in Decision-making," *J. Polit. Econ.* Feb. 1964, *72*, pp. 62–73.

BELL, DAVID E. "Decision Regret: A Component of Risk Aversion?" Working Paper 80–56, Grad. School of Bus. Admin., Harvard Univ., June 1980.

———. "Regret in Decision Making under Uncertainty," *Operations Research*, Forthcoming.

——— AND RAIFFA, HOWARD. "Marginal Value and Intrinsic Risk-Aversion," Working Paper 79–65, Grad. School Bus. Admin., Harvard Univ., Oct. 1979.

BERNOULLI, DANIEL. "Specimen Theoriae Novae de Mensura Sortis," *Commentarri Academiae Scientiarum Imperialis Petropolitanae* 1738, *Tomus V*, pp. 175–92. Translated by LOUISE SOMMER as "Expositions of a New Theory on The Measurement of Risk," *Econometrica*, Jan. 1954, *22*, pp. 23–26.

BERNOULLI, JACQUES. *Ars conjectandi*, 1713. Translated into German by R. HAUSSNER as "Wahrscheinlichkeitsrechnung," *Ostwald's Klassiker der Exakten Wissenschaften*, No. 107 and 108. Leipzig: W. Englemann, 1899.

BETTMAN, JAMES R. *An information processing theory of consumer choice.* Reading, Mass.: Addison-Wesley, 1979.

BINSWANGER, HANS. " 'Attitudes Toward Risk' Experimental Measurement in Rural India," *Amer. J. Agr. Econ.* Aug. 1980, *62*(3), pp. 395–407.

BLAUG, MARK. *The methodology of economics.* N.Y.: Cambridge Univ. Press, 1980.

BOLAND, LAWRENCE A. "On the Futility of Criticizing the Neoclassical Maximization-Hypothesis," *Amer. Econ. Rev.* Dec. 1981, *71*(5), pp. 1031–36.

BONOMA, THOMAS V. AND SCHLENKER, BARRY R. "The SEU Calculus: Effects of Response Mode, Sex, and Sex Role on Uncertain Decisions," *Decision Sciences*, 1978, *9*(2), pp. 206–27.

BORCH, KARL H. *The economics of uncertainty.* N.J.: Princeton Univ. Press, 1968.

BURKS, ARTHUR W. *Chance, cause, reason: An inquiry into the nature of scientific evidence.* Chicago: The Univ. of Chicago Press, 1977.

CARNAP, RUDOLF. *Logical foundations of probability.* Second edition. Chicago: Univ. of Chicago Press, 1962.

———. "A Basic System of Inductive Logic, Part I," *Studies in inductive logic and probability.* Vol. I. Edited by RUDOLF CARNAP AND RICHARD C. JEFFREY. Berkeley: Univ. of Calif. Press, 1971, pp. 33–1650.

CHEW, SOO-HONG AND MACCRIMMON, KENNETH R. "Alpha-Nu Choice Theory: A Generalization of Expected Utility Theory." Working paper 669, Univ. of British Columbia, Vancouver, Canada, 1979a.

——— AND MACCRIMMON, KENNETH R. "Alpha Utility Theory, Lottery Composition, and the Allais Paradox." Working Paper, Faculty of Commerce and Business Administration, Univ. of British Columbia, Vancouver, Canada, Sept. 1979b.

CHIPMAN, JOHN S. "The Foundations of Utility," *Econometrica*, Apr. 1960, *28*, pp. 193–224.

CHURCHMAN, C. WEST. *Prediction and optimal decision; philosophical issues of a science of values.* Englewood Cliffs, NJ: Prentice Hall, 1961.

_____ *The design of inquiring systems; basic concepts of systems and organization.* New York: Basic Books, 1971.

CODY, M. "Optimization in Ecology," *Science*, 1974, *183*, pp. 1156–64.

COHEN, L. JONATHAN. "Can Human Irrationality Be Experimentally Demonstrated?" *The Behav. & Brain Sci.* (4) 1981. pp. 317–70.

COOMBS, CLYDE H. "Portfolio Theory and the Measurement of Risk," in *Human judgment and decision processes.* Edited by MARTIN F. KAPLAN AND STEVEN SCHWARTZ. New York: Academic Press, 1975, pp. 63–86.

_____ AND HUANG, LILY C. "Tests of a Portfolio Theory of Risk Preference," *J. Exp. Psych.* 1970, *85*(1), pp. 23–29.

_____ AND LEHNER, PAUL E. "An Evaluation of Two Alternative Models for a Theory of Risk," Working Paper, Dept. of Psychology, Univ. of Michigan, Ann Arbor, 1981.

_____ AND PRUITT, DEAN G. "Components of Risk in Decision Making: Probability and Variance Preference," *J. Exp. Psych.* 1960, *60*, pp. 256–77.

CRAMER, GABRIEL. Letter to Nicolas Bernoulli, a cousin of Daniel (see Bernoulli 1738, above).

CYERT, RICHARD M. AND MARCH, JAMES G. *A behavioral theory of the firm.* Englewood Cliffs, NJ: Prentice-Hall, 1963.

DAVIDSON, DONALD AND SUPPES, PATRICK. "A Finistic Axiomatization of Subjective Probability and Utility," *Econometrica*, 1965, *24*, pp. 264–75.

_____ AND SIEGEL, SIDNEY. *Decision making: an experimental approach.* Stanford, Calif.: Stanford Univ. Press, 1957.

DAWES, ROBYN M. "The Robust Beauty of Improper Linear models in Decision Making," *Amer. Psych.* July 1979, *34*(7), pp. 571–82.

DEBREU, GERARD. *Theory of value: An axiomatic analysis of economic equilibrium.* New York: Wiley, 1959.

DE FINETTI, BRUNO. "La Prevision: Ses Lois Logiques, Ses Sources Subjectives," *Annales de l'Institut Poincaré*, 1937, *7*, pp. 1–68.

_____ *Theory of Probability: A Critical Introductory Treatment.* Vol. 1. Translated by ANTONIO MACHI AND ADRIAN SMITH. N.Y. Wiley [1970], 1974.

DIAMOND, PETER A. "A Framework for Social Security Analysis," *J. Public Econ.*, Dec. 1977, *8*(3), 275–98.

_____ AND ROTHSCHILD, MICHAEL. *Uncertainty in economics: Readings and exercises.* New York: Academic Press, 1978.

DRÈZE, JACQUES H. "Axiomatic Theories of Choice, Cardinal Utility and Subjective Probability: A Review," *Allocation under uncertainty: Equilibrium and optimality.* Edited by JACQUES H. DRÈZE. New York: Wiley, 1974, pp. 1–23.

DYER, JAMES S. AND SARIN, RAKESH K. "Measurable Multi-attribute Value Functions," *Operations Res.* 1979a, *27*(4), pp. 810–22.

_____ AND SARIN, RAKESH K. "Group Preference Aggregation Rules Based on Strength of Preference," *Manage. Sci.* 25(9), 1979b, pp. 822–32.

_____ AND SARIN, RAKESH K. "Relative risk aversion." *Manage. Sci.*, forthcoming.

EDWARDS, WARD. "Probability Preferences in Gambling," *Amer. J. Psych.*, 1953, *66*, pp. 349–64.

_____ "Probability Preferences Among Bets with Differing Expected Values," *Amer. J. Psych.* 1954(a), *67*, pp. 55–67.

_____ "Variance Preference in Gambling," *Amer. J. Psych.*, 1954(b), *67*, pp. 441–52.

_____ "The Prediction of Decisions Among Bets," *J. Exper. Psych.*, 1955, *50*, pp. 201–14.

_____ "Behavioral Decision Theory," *Ann. Rev. Psych.*, 1961, *12*, pp. 473–98.

_____ "Conservatism in Human Information Processing," *Formal representation of human judgment.* Edited by BENJAMIN KLEINMUNTZ. New York: Wiley, 1968, pp. 17–52.

EHRLICH, ISAAC AND GARY S. BECKER. "Market Insurance, Self-Insurance, and Self-Protection," *J. Polit. Econ.*, July/Aug. 1972, *80*(4), pp. 623–48.

EINHORN, HILLEL J. "The Use of Nonlinear, Noncompensatory Models in Decision Making," *Psych. Bull.*, 1970, *73*(3), pp. 221–30.

_____ "Use of Nonlinear, Noncompensatory Models as a Function of Task and Amount of Information," *Organ. Beh. H.*, Jan. 1971, *6*(1), pp. 1–27.

_____ "Learning From Experience and Suboptimal Rules in Decision Making," in *Cognitive processes in choice and decision behavior.* Edited by THOMAS S. WALLSTEN. Hillsdale, NJ: L. Erlbaum, 1980, pp. 1–20.

_____ AND HOGARTH, ROBIN M. "Behavioral Decision Theory: Processes of Judgment and Choice," *Ann. Rev. Psych.* 1981, *32*, pp. 53–88.

_____; KLEINMUNTZ, DON H. AND KLEINMUNTZ, BENJAMIN. "Linear Regression and Process-Tracing Models of Judgment," *Psych. Rev.*, 1979, *86*(5), pp. 465–85.

EISNER, ROBERT AND STROTZ, ROBERT H. "Flight Insurance and the Theory of Choice," *J. Polit. Econ.*, Aug. 1961, *69*, pp. 355–68.

ELLSBERG, DANIEL. "Classic and Current Notions of 'Measurable Utility'," *Econ. J. 64*, Sept. 1954, pp. 528–56.

_____ "Risk, Ambiguity and the Savage Axioms," *Quart. J. Econ.*, Nov. 1961, *75*, pp. 643–69.

_____ "Risk, Ambiguity and the Savage Axioms: A Reply," *Quart. J. Econ.* May 1963, *77*, pp. 336–41.

ETZIONI, AMITAI. "Mixed Scanning: A Third Approach to Decision-Making," *Public Admin. Rev.*, Dec. 1967, *27*, pp. 385–92.

FAMA, EUGENE F. "Ordinal and Measurable Utility," *Studies in the theory of capital markets.* Edited by MICHAEL C. JENSEN. Praeger 1972, pp. 125–45.

Schoemaker: The Expected Utility Model 559

_____ Foundations of finance. New York, NY: Basic Books, 1976.

FECHNER, GUSTAV T. Elemente der Psychopsysik. Vol. 1. Leipzig: Breitkopf and Harterl, 1860. Translated by H. E. ADLER, D. H. HOWES AND E. G. BORING. New York: Holt, Rinehart and Winston, 1966.

FEDERAL INSURANCE ADMINISTRATION. Full insurance availability. Washington, D.C.: U.S. Dept. of Housing and Urban Development, 1974.

FELDSTEIN, MARTIN. "Social Security, Induced Retirement, and Aggregate Capital Accumulation," J. Polit. Econ. Sept./Oct. 1974, 82(5), pp. 905–26.

_____ "Do Private Pensions Increase National Savings?" J. Public Econ., Dec. 1978, 10(3) pp. 277–93.

FELLNER, WILLIAM. "Distortion of Subjective Probabilities as a Reaction to Uncertainty," Quart. J. Econ., Nov. 1961, 75, pp. 670–89.

FISCHHOFF, BARUCH. "Hindsight is not Equal to Foresight: The Effect of Outcome Knowledge on Judgment Under Uncertainty," J. Exp. Psych. H. Aug. 1975, 104(1), pp. 288–99.

FISHBURN, PETER C. Utility theory for decision making. New York: Wiley, 1970.

_____ "Lexicographic Orders, Utilities and Decision Rules: A Survey," Manage. Sci., July 1974, 20 pp. 1442–71.

_____ "Cardinal Utility: An Interpretive Essay," Rivista Int. Sci. Econ. Com., 1976, 23(12), pp. 1102–14.

_____ "Mean-Risk Analysis with Risk Associated with Below-Target Returns," Amer. Econ. Rev., Mar. 1977, 67(2), pp. 116–26.

_____ "Nontransitive Measurable Utility." Economics Discussion Paper No. 209, Bell Laboratories, Murray Hill, NJ, Sept. 1981.

_____ AND KOCHENBERGER, GARY A. "Two-Piece Von Neumann-Morgenstern Utility Functions," Decision Sciences, Oct. 1979, 10(4), pp. 503–18.

FRIEDMAN, MILTON. Essays in positive economics. Chicago: Univ. of Chicago Press, 1953.

_____ AND SAVAGE, LEONARD J. "The Utility Analysis of Choices Involving Risk," J. Polit. Econ., Aug. 1948, 56, pp. 279–304.

FRISCH, RAGNAR. "Dynamic Utility," Econometrica, July 1964, 32, pp. 418–24.

GOULD, JOHN P. "The Expected Utility Hypothesis and the Selection of Optimal Deductible for a Given Insurance Policy," J. Bus., Apr. 1969, 42(2), pp. 143–51.

GRETHER, DAVID M. AND PLOTT, CHARLES R. "Economic Theory of Choice and the Preference Reversal Phenomenon," Amer. Econ. Rev., Sept. 1979, 69(4), pp. 623–38.

HACKING, IAN. The emergence of probability. Cambridge, Mass.: Cambridge Univ. Press, 1975.

HADAR, JOSEPH AND RUSSELL, WILLIAM R. "Rules for Ordering Uncertain Prospects," Amer. Econ. Rev., Mar. 1969, 59(1), pp. 25–34.

HANDA, JAGDISH. "Risk, Probabilities, and a New Theory of Cardinal Utility," J. Polit. Econ., Feb. 1977, 85(1), pp. 97–122.

HAUSER, JOHN R. AND SHUGAN, STEVEN M. "Intensity Measures of Consumer Preference," Opera-

tions Research, Mar.-Apr. 1980, 28(2), pp. 278–320.

HERNSTEIN, ISRAEL N. AND MILNOR, JOHN. "An Axiomatic Approach to Measurable Utility," Econometrica, Apr. 1953, 21, pp. 291–97.

HERSHEY, JOHN C. AND SCHOEMAKER, PAUL J. H. "Risk-Taking and Problem Context in the Domain of Losses—An Expected Utility Analysis," J. Risk Ins. 1980, 47(1), pp. 111–32.

_____; KUNREUTHER, HOWARD AND SCHOEMAKER, PAUL J. H. "Sources of Bias in Assessment Procedures for Utility Functions," Manage. Sci., forthcoming.

HICKS, JOHN R. AND ALLEN, R. G. D. "A Reconsideration of the Theory of Value," Economica, Feb. 1934, Part 1, pp. 52–75, and May 1934, Part II, pp. 196–219.

HIRSHLEIFER, JACK. Investment, interest and capital. Englewood Cliffs, NJ: Prentice-Hall, 1970.

HOGARTH, ROBIN M. "Cognitive Processes and the Assessment of Subjective Probability Distributions," J. Amer. Statist. Assoc., June 1975a, 70(350), pp. 271–94.

_____ "Decision Time as a Function of Task Complexity," in Utility, probability and human decision making. Edited by DIRK WENDT AND CHARLES VLEK. Dordrecht-Holland: D. Reidel, 1975b, pp. 321–38.

HOLTHAUSEN, DUNCAN M. "A Risk-Return Model with Risk and Return Measured as Deviations from a Target Return," Amer. Econ. Rev. 1981, 71(1), pp. 182–88.

IRWIN, FRANCIS W. "Stated Expectations as Functions of Probability and Desirability of Outcomes," J. Personality, 1953, 21, pp. 329–35.

JANIS, IRVING L. AND MANN, LEON. Decision making: A psychological analysis of conflict, choice and commitment. New York: Free Press, 1977.

JEFFREYS, HAROLD. Theory of probability. Second edition. Oxford: Clarendon Press, 1948.

KAHNEMAN, DANIEL AND TVERSKY, AMOS. "Subjective Probability: A Judgment of Representativeness," Cognitive Psychology, July 1972, 3(3), pp. 430–54.

_____ "Prospect Theory: An Analysis of Decision Under Risk," Econometrica, 1979, 47(2), pp. 263–91.

KARMARKAR, UDAY S. "Subjectively Weighted Utility: A Descriptive Extension of the Expected Utility Model," Organ. Beh. H. 1978, 21(1), pp. 61–72.

KATONA, GEORGE. Private pensions and individual savings. Monograph No. 40, Survey Research Center, Institute for Social Research, The University of Michigan, 1965.

_____ Psychological economics. New York Elsevier, 1975.

KEENEY, RALPH L. AND RAIFFA, HOWARD. Decisions with multiple objectives: Preferences and value tradeoffs. New York: John Wiley, 1976.

KEYNES, JOHN MAYNARD. A treatise on probability. London: Macmillan, 1921.

KIESLER, CHARLES A. "Conflict and Number of

Choice Alternatives," *Psychological Reports,* 1966, *18*(2), pp. 603–10.

KLEINDORFER, PAUL R. AND KUNREUTHER, HOW-ARD. "Misinformation and Equilibrium in Insurance Markets," *Issues in pricing and regulation.* Edited by J. FINSINGER. Lexington Books, forthcoming.

KOGAN, NATHAN AND WALLACH, MICHAEL A. "Risk Taking as a Function of the Situation, the Person, and the Group," *New directions in psychology.* Vol. 3. New York: Holt, Rinehart and Winston, 1967, pp. 111–278.

KRANTZ, DAVID H.; LUCE, DUNCAN R., SUPPES, PATRICK ET AL. *Foundations of measurement.* Vol. I. *Additive and polynomial representations.* New York: Academic Press, 1971.

KUNREUTHER, HOWARD. "Limited Knowledge and Insurance Protection," *Public Policy,* Spring 1976, *24*(2), pp. 227–61.

———; GINSBERG, RALPH; MILLER, LOUIS, ET AL. *Disaster insurance protection: Public policy lessons.* New York: Wiley, 1978.

KYBURG, HENRY E. AND SMOKLER, HOWARD E. *Studies in subjective probability.* New York: Wiley, 1964.

LACHMAN, ROY; LACHMAN, JANET L. AND BUTTERFIELD, EARL C. *Cognitive psychology and information processing; An introduction.* Hillsdale, NJ: L. Erlbaum, 1979.

LAPLACE, PIERRE S. *A philosophical essay on probabilities.* Translated by F. W. TRUSCOTT AND F. L. EMORY. New York: Dover, 1951.

LAUGHHUNN, DAN J.; PAYNE, JOHN W. AND CRUM, ROY L. "Managerial Risk Preferences for Below-Target Returns," *Manage. Sci.* forthcoming.

LAWLER III, EDWARD E. *Motivation in work organizations.* Monterey, Calif.: Brooks/Cole, 1973.

LEE, WAYNE. *Decision theory and human behavior.* New York: Wiley, 1971.

LEHNER, PAUL E. "A Comparison of Portfolio Theory and Weighted Utility Models of Risky Decision Making," *Organ. Beh. H.* Oct. 1980, *26*(2), pp. 238–49.

LEIMER, DAN R. AND LESNOY, SELIG D. "Social Security and Private Saving: A Reexamination of the Time Series Evidence Using Alternative Social Security Wealth Variables." Working Paper 19, Social Security Admin., U.S. Dept. of Health, Education and Welfare, Nov. 1980.

LEVY, H. AND MARKOWITZ, HARRY M. "Approximating Expected Utility by a Function of Mean and Variance," *Amer. Econ. Rev.,* June 1979, *69*(3), pp. 308–17.

LEWONTIN, RICHARD C. "Sociobiology as an Adaptationist Program," *Behavioral Science,* 1979, *24,* pp. 5–14.

LIBBY, ROBERT AND FISHBURN, PETER C. "Behavioral Models of Risk-Taking in Business Decisions: A Survey and Evaluation," *J. Acc. Res.* Autumn 1977, *15*(2), pp. 272–92.

LICHTENSTEIN, SARAH. "Bases for Preferences among Three-Outcome Bets," *J. Exp. Psych.* 1965, *69*(2), pp. 162–69.

———; FISCHHOFF, BARUCH AND PHILLIPS, LAW-

RENCE D. "Calibration of Probabilities: The State of the Art to 1980," *Judgment under uncertainty: Heuristics and biases.* Edited by DANIEL KAHNEMAN, PAUL SLOVIC AND AMOS TVERSKY. NY: Cambridge Univ. Press, 1981.

LICHTENSTEIN, SARAH AND SLOVIC, PAUL. "Reversals of Preference between Bids and Choices in Gambling Decisions," *J. Exp. Psych.* 1971, *89*(1), pp. 46–55.

——— "Response-Induced Reversals of Preference in Gambling: An Extended Replication in Las Vegas," *J. Exp. Psych.* 1973, *101*(1), pp. 16–20.

———, FISCHHOFF, BARUCH ET AL. "Judged Frequency of Lethal Events," *J. Exp. Psych.* 1978, *4*(6), pp. 551–78.

LINDBLOM, CHARLES E. "The Science of Muddling Through," in *The making of decisions: a reader in administrative behavior.* Edited by WILLIAM J. GORE AND J. W. DYSON. New York: Free Press, 1964.

LINDMAN, HAROLD R. "Inconsistent preferences among gambles," *J. Exp. Psych.* 1971, *89*(2), pp. 390–97.

LINDSAY, R. B. "Physics—To What Extent is it Deterministic?," *Amer. Scientist,* 1968, *56,* pp. 93–111.

LOOMES, GRAHAM AND SUGDEN, ROBERT. "Regret Theory: An Alternative Approach to Rational Choice Under Uncertainty." Unpublished paper, Univ. of Newcastle. Newcastle upon Tyne, England, 1981.

LUCE, R. DUNCAN AND RAIFFA, HOWARD. *Games and decisions.* New York: Wiley, 1957.

——— AND TUKEY, JOHN W. "Simultaneous Conjoint Measurement: A New Type of Fundamental Measurement," *J. Math. Psych.* 1964, *1,* pp. 1–27.

LYNCH, JOHN G. "Why Additive Utility Models Fail as Descriptions of Choice Behavior," *J. Exp. Soc. Psych.* 1979, *15,* pp. 397–417.

MACCRIMMON, KENNETH R. "Descriptive and Normative Implications of Decisions Theory Postulates," in *Risk and uncertainty: Proceedings of a conference.* Edited by KARL BORCH AND JAN MOSSIN. London: St. Martin's Press, New York: Macmillan, 1968, pp. 3–23.

——— AND LARSSON, STIG. "Utility Theory: Axioms versus 'Paradoxes'," *Expected utility and the Allais Paradox.* Edited by MAURICE ALLAIS AND OLE HAGEN. Dordrecht, Holland: D. Reidel, 1979, pp. 333–409.

MACHINA, MARK J. " 'Expected Utility' Analysis without the Independence Axiom," *Econometrica.* forthcoming.

MACHLUP, FRITZ. "Theories of the Firm: Marginalist, Behavioral, Managerial," *Amer. Econ. Rev.* Mar. 1967, *57*(1), pp. 1–33.

MARCH, JAMES G. "Bounded Rationality, Ambiguity, and the Engineering of Choice," *Bell J. Econ.* 1978, *9*(2), pp. 587–608.

——— AND OLSEN, JOHAN P. ET AL. *Ambiguity and choice in organizations.* Bergen, Norway: Universitetsforlaget, 1976.

——— AND SIMON, HERBERT A. *Organizations.* New York: John Wiley, 1958.

MARKOWITZ, HARRY M. "The utility of wealth," *J. Polit. Econ.* Apr. 1952, *60*(2), pp. 151–58.

—— "Portfolio Selection," *J. Finance,* Mar. 1952, 1, pp. 77–91.

MARKS, R. W. "The Effect of Probability, Desirability, and 'Privilege' on the Stated Expectations of Children," *J. Personality,* 1951, *19,* pp. 332–51.

MARROW, A. J. *The practical theorist: The life and work of Kurt Lewin.* New York: Basic Books, 1969.

MARSCHAK, JACOB. "Rational Behavior, Uncertain Prospects, and Measurable Utility," *Econometrica,* Apr. 1950, *18*(2), pp. 111–41.

MARSHALL, J. "Insurance as a Market in Contingent Claims: Structure and Performance," *Bell J. Econ. Manage. Sci.* Autumn 1974, *5,* pp. 670–82.

MASON, RICHARD O. AND MITROFF, IAN I. "A Program for Research on Management Information Systems," *Manage. Sci,* 1973, *19*(5), pp. 475–87.

MAYNARD SMITH, J. "Optimization Theory in Evolution," *Annual Rev. of Ecology and Systematics,* 1978, *9,* pp. 31–56.

MILLER, GEORGE A. "The Magical Number Seven, Plus or Minus Two; Some Limits on our Capacity for Processing Information," *Psych. Rev.* 1956, *63*(2), pp. 81–97.

MOSTELLER, FREDERICH AND NOGEE, PHILIP. "An Experimental Measurement of Utility," *J. Polit. Econ.* Oct. 1951, *59*(5), pp. 371–404.

PASHIGIAN, B. PETER; SCHKADE, LAWRENCE AND MENEFEE, GEORGE H. "The Selection of an Optimal Deductible for a Given Insurance Policy," *J. Bus.* Jan. 1966, *39*(1), pp. 35–44.

PAYNE, JOHN W. "Alternative Approaches to Decision Making Under Risk: Moments Versus Risk Dimensions," *Psych. Bull.* 1973, *80*(6) pp. 439–53.

—— "Task Complexity and Contingent Processing in Decision Making: An Information Search and Protocol Analysis," *Organ. Beh. H.* 1976, *16*(2), pp. 366–87.

—— AND BRAUNSTEIN, MYRON L. "Preferences Among Gambles with Equal Underlying Distributions," *J. Exp. Psych.* 1971, *87*(1), pp. 13–18.

——; LAUGHHUNN, DAN J. AND CRUM, ROY L. "Translation of Gambles and Aspiration Level Effects in Risky Choice Behavior," *Manage. Sci.* 1980, *26*(10), pp. 1039–60.

——; LAUGHHUNN, DAN J. AND CRUM, ROY L. "Further Tests of Aspiration Level Effects in Risky Choice Behavior," *Manage. Sci.,* Aug. 1981, *27*(8), pp. 953–58.

PELTZMAN, SAM. "The Effects of Automobile Safety Regulation," *J. Polit. Econ.* Aug. 1975, *83*(4), pp. 677–725.

PHILLIPS, LAWRENCE D. AND WRIGHT, C. N. "Cultural Differences in Viewing Uncertainty and Assessing Probabilities," in *Decision making and change in human affairs.* Edited by HELMUT JUNGERMANN AND GERARD DE ZEEUW. Dordrecht, Holland and Boston: D. Reidel, 1977, pp. 507–19.

PLOTT, CHARLES R. "Axiomatic Social Choice Theory: An Overview and Interpretation," *Amer. J. Polit. Sci.* Aug. 1976, *20*(3), pp. 511–96.

POPPER, KARL R. *Conjectures and refutations: The growth of scientific knowledge.* New York, NY: Harper and Row, 1968.

PRATT, JOHN W. "Risk Aversion in the Small and in the Large," *Econometrica,* Jan., April 1964, *32,* pp. 122–36.

——; RAIFFA, HOWARD AND SCHLAIFER, ROBERT. "The Foundations of Decisions Under Uncertainty: An Elementary Exposition,"*J. Amer. Statist. Assoc.* 1964, *59.*

——; WISE, DAVID AND ZECKHAUSER, RICHARD. "Price Differences in Almost Competitive Markets," *Quart. J. Econ.* May 1979, *93*(2), pp. 189–211.

QUIGGIN, JOHN "A Theory of Anticipated Utility." Unpublished Manuscript, Canberra City, Australia: Bur. of Agri. Econ. 1980.

RAIFFA, HOWARD. "Risk, Ambiguity and the Savage Axioms: Comment," *Quart. J. Econ.* Nov. 1961, *75,* pp. 690–94.

—— *Decision analysis: Introductory lectures on choice under uncertainty.* Reading, Mass: Addison-Wesley, 1968.

RAMSEY, FRANK P. *The foundations of mathematics.* New York: Harcourt Brace, 1931.

RAPOPORT, AMNON AND WALLSTEN, THOMAS S. "Individual Decision Behavior," *Ann. Rev. Psych.* 1972, *23,* pp. 131–75.

REDER, MELVIN W. "A Reconsideration of the Marginal Productivity Theory," *J. Polit. Econ.,* Oct. 1947, pp. 450–58.

REICHENBACH, HANS. *The theory of probability.* Second edition. Translated by E. H. HUTTON AND M. REICHENBACH. Berkeley: Univ. of Calif. Press, [1935] 1949.

RICHARD, SCOTT F. "Multivariate Risk Aversion, Utility Independence and Separable Utility Functions," *Manage. Sci.* 1975, *22*(1), pp. 12–21.

ROBERTS, HARRY. "Risk, Ambiguity and the Savage Axioms: Comment," *Quart. J. Econ.,* 1963, *77,* pp. 327–36.

ROBERTSON, L. "Urban area safety belt use in automobiles with starter interlock belt systems: A preliminary report." Washington, D.C.: Insurance Institute for Highway Safety, 1974.

ROLL, RICHARD. "A Critique of the Asset Pricing Theory's Tests; Part I: On Past and Potential Testability of the Theory," *J. Finan. Econ.* Mar. 1977, pp. 129–76.

RONEN, JOSHUA. "Effects of Some Probability Displays on Choices." *Organ. Beh. H.,* Feb. 1973, *9*(1) pp. 1–15.

ROSEN, ROBERT. *Optimality principles in biology.* London: Butterworths, 1967.

ROSENBERG, ALEXANDER. *Micro economic laws: A philosophical analysis.* Univ. of Pittsburgh Press, 1976.

ROSETT, RICHARD N. "Weak Experimental Verification of the Expected Utility Hypothesis," *Rev. Econ. Stud.,* Oct. 1971, *38*(116), pp. 481–92.

ROTHSCHILD, MICHAEL AND STIGLITZ, JOSEPH E. "Equilibrium in Competitive Insurance Markets: An Essay on the Economics of Imperfect Information," *Quart. J. Econ.,* Nov. 1976, *90*(4), pp. 630–49.

RUSSO, J. EDWARD AND DOSHER, BARBARA A. "Cognitive Effort and Strategy Selection in Binary Choice," Working Paper, Univ. of Chicago. Grad. School of Bus., May 1981.

SAMUELSON, PAUL A. "Probability, Utility, and the Independence Axiom," *Econometrica*, Oct. 1952, *20*(4), pp. 670–78.

_____. "Discussion: Problems of Methodology," *Amer. Econ. Rev.*, 1963, *53* (supplement), pp. 227–36.

SARIN, RAKESH K. "Strength of Preference and Risky Choice," *Operations Research*, forthcoming.

SAVAGE, LEONARD J. *The foundations of statistics.* New York: Wiley, 1954.

SCHELLING, THOMAS C. *Micromotives and macrobehavior.* New York: Norton, 1978.

SCHNEEWEISS, HANS. "Probability and Utility—Dual Concepts in Decision Theory," *Information, inference and decision.* Edited by Guenter Menges. Dordrecht, Holland: D. Reidel 1974, pp. 113–44.

SCHOEMAKER, PAUL J. H. "The Role of Statistical Knowledge in Gambling Decisions: Moment vs. Risk Dimension Approaches," *Organ. Beh. and H.*, 1979, *24*(1), pp. 1–17.

_____. *Experiments on decisions under risk: The expected utility hypothesis.* Boston, Mass.: Nijhoff Publishing Co., 1980.

_____. "Optimality as a Positive Heuristic of Science: An Epistemological Analysis," *The quest for optimality.* Edited by JAN BERTING, JEAN H. PAELINCK AND PAULUS H. VOSSEN. Sussex, England: Gower Pub. Co., forthcoming.

_____ AND KUNREUTHER, HOWARD C. "An Experimental Study of Insurance Decisions," *J. Risk Ins.*, Dec. 1979, *46*(4), pp. 603–18.

SCHUMAN, H. AND JOHNSON, M. P. "Attitudes and Behavior," *Ann. Rev. Soc.*, 1976, *2*, pp. 161–207.

SCHWARTZ, T. "On the Possibility of Rational Policy Evaluation," *Theory and Decision*, 1970, *1*, pp. 89–106.

SCITOVSKY, TIBOR. *The joyless economy.* Oxford Univ. Press, 1976.

SCOTT, D. AND SUPPES, PATRICK. "Foundational Aspects of Theories of Measurement," *J. Symbolic Logic*, 1958, *23*, pp. 113–28.

SHACKLE, G. L. S. *Expectation in economics.* Second edition. England: Cambridge Univ. Press, 1952.

SHAFER, GLENN. *A mathematical theory of evidence.* Princeton, NJ: Princeton Univ. Press, 1976.

SHEPARD, ROGER N. "On Subjectively Optimum Selections Among Multi-Attribute Alternatives," in *Human judgments and optimality.* Edited by MAYNARD W. SHELLY AND GLENN L. BRYAN. New York: Wiley, 1964, pp. 257–81.

SHUGAN, STEVEN M. "The Cost of Thinking," *J. Consumer Research*, Sept. 1980, *7*(2), pp. 99–111.

SIMON, HERBERT A. "A Behavioral Model of Rational Choice," *Quart. J. Econ.*, Feb. 1955, *69*, pp. 174–83.

_____ AND NEWELL, ALLEN. "Human Problem Solving: The State of the Theory in 1970," *Amer. Psych.*, 1971, *26*(2), pp. 145–59.

SLOVIC, PAUL. "Value as a Determiner of Subjective Probability," *IEEE Transactions on Human Fac-* tors in Electronics, Mar. 1966, *HFE-7*(1), pp. 22–28.

_____. "Differential Effects of Real versus Hypothetical Payoffs on Choices Among Gambles," *J. Exp. Psych.*, 1969, *80*(3), pp. 434–37.

_____; FISCHHOFF, BARUCH AND LICHTENSTEIN, SARAH. "Behavioral Decision Theory," *Ann. Rev. Psych.*, 1977, *28*, pp. 1–39.

_____, ET AL. "Preference for Insuring against Probable Small Losses: Insurance Implications," *J. Risk Ins.* 1977, *44*(2), Pp. 237–58.

_____ AND LICHTENSTEIN, SARAH. "The Relative Importance of Probabilities and Payoffs in Risk Taking," *J. Exp. Psych.* Nov. 1968a, *78*(3, Part 2), pp. 1–18.

_____ AND LICHTENSTEIN, SARAH. "Importance of Variance Preferences in Gambling Decisions," *J. Exp. Psych.* 1968b, *78*(4), pp. 646–54.

_____ AND TVERSKY, AMOS. "Who Accepts Savage's Axiom?" *Behavioral Science.* 1974, *19*(6), pp. 368–73.

SMITH, VERNON L. "Experimental Economics: Induced Value Theory," *Amer. Econ. Rev.*, May 1976, *66*(2), pp. 274–79.

STEVENS, S. S. "On the Theory of Scales of Measurement," *Science*, 1946, *103*, pp. 677–80.

_____. "On the Psychophysical Law," *Psych. Rev.*, 1957, *64*(3), pp. 153–81.

STIGLER, GEORGE J. "The Development of Utility Theory," *J. Polit. Econ.* Aug. 1950, *58*, Part I, pp. 307–27 and Oct. 1950, *58*, Part II, pp. 373–96.

_____ AND BECKER, GARY S. "De Gustibus Non Est Disputandum," *Amer. Econ. Rev.*, Mar. 1977, *67*(2), pp. 76–90.

STROTZ, ROBERT H. "Cardinal Utility," *Amer. Econ. Rev.* May 1953, *43*(2), pp. 384–97.

THALER, RICHARD. "Toward a Positive Theory of Consumer Choice," *J. Econ. Beh. Organ.* 1980, *1*(1), pp. 39–60.

TORGERSON, WARREN S. *The theory and measurement of scaling.* New York: Wiley, 1958.

TVERSKY, AMOS. "Additivity, Utility and Subjective Probability," *J. Math. Psych.*, 1967, *4*(2), pp. 175–201.

_____. "Intransitivity of Preferences," *Psych. Rev.* 1969, *76*(1), pp. 31–48.

_____. "Choice by Elimination," *J. Math. Psych.* Nov. 1972, *9*(4), pp. 341–67.

_____ AND KAHNEMAN, DANIEL. "Availability: A Heuristic for Judging Frequency and Probability," *Cognitive Psychology*, 1973, *5*(2), pp. 207–32.

_____ AND KAHNEMAN, DANIEL. "Causal Schemas in Judgments under Uncertainty," *Progress in social psychology.* Edited by MARTIN FISHBEIN. Hillsdale, NJ: L. Erlbaum Associates, 1980, pp. 49–72.

_____ AND KAHNEMAN, DANIEL. "The Framing of Decisions and the Psychology of Choice," *Science* 1981, *211*, pp. 453–58.

VAN DAM, CORNELIUS. *Beslissen in onzekerheid.* Leiden, The Netherlands: H. E. Stenfert Kroese, 1973.

VAN RAAIJ, WILLEM F. *Consumer Choice Behavior: An Information Processing Approach.* Ph.D. The-

An *Information Processing Approach*. Ph.D. Thesis. Tilburg University, The Netherlands, 1977.

VENN, JOHN. *The logic of chance*. Third edition. London and New York: Macmillan, [1866] 1888.

VLEK, CHARLES AND WAGENAAR, WILLEM A. "Judgment and Decision Under Uncertainty," in *Handbook of psychonomics*. Vol. 2. Edited by J. A. MICHON, E. G. EIJKMAN AND L. F. W. DEKLERK. Amsterdam: North-Holland, 1979.

VON MISES, RICHARD. *Probability, statistics and truth*. Second edition. Prepared by HILDA GEIRINGER. London: Allen and Unwin. [1928] 1957.

———. *Mathematical theory of probability and statistics*. New York and London: Academic Press, 1964.

VON NEUMANN, JOHN AND MORGENSTERN, OSKAR. *Theory of games and economic behavior*. Second edition. Princeton, NJ: Princeton Univ. Press, [1944] 1947.

VROOM, VICTOR H. *Work and motivation*. New York: Wiley, 1964.

WALSH, VIVIAN CHARLES. *Introduction to contemporary microeconomics*. New York: McGraw-Hill, 1969, 1970.

WEHRUNG, DON A.; MACCRIMMON, KENNETH R. AND BROTHERS, K. M. "Utility Measures: Comparisons of Domains, Stability, and Equivalence Procedures." Working Paper 603, Faculty of Commerce and Business Admin., Univ. of British Columbia, 1980.

WEICK, KARL E. "Organizations in the Laboratory," *Methods of organizational research*. Edited by VICTOR H. VROOM. Pittsburgh: Univ. of Pittsburgh Press, 1967.

WILLIAMS, C. ARTHUR JR. "Attitudes Toward Speculative Risks as an Indicator of Attitudes Toward Pure Risks," *J. Risk Ins.*, Dec. 1966, *33*(4), pp. 577–86.

WILSON, EDWARD O. *Sociobiology: The new synthesis*. Cambridge, MA: Harvard Univ. Press, 1975.

WINTER, SIDNEY G. "Economic 'Natural Selection' and the Theory of the Firm," *Yale Econ. Essays*, 1964, *4*, pp. 225–72.

———. "Satisficing, Selection and the Innovative Remnant," *Quart. J. Econ.*, May 1971, *85*(2), pp. 237–61.

WINTERFELDT, DETLOF VON. "Functional Relationships Between Risky and Riskless Multiattribute Utility Functions." Soc. Sci. Res. Report *79*(3), Univ. of S. Calif., Dec. 1979.

WOLD, HERMAN. "Ordinal Preferences or Cardinal Utility?," *Econometrica*, Oct. 1952, *20*(4), pp. 661–64.

YAARI, MENAHEM E. "Convexity in the Theory of Choice Under Risk," *Quart. J. Econ.*, May 79, 1965, pp. 278–90.

YATES, J. FRANK AND ZUKOWSKI, LISA G. "Characterization of Ambiguity in Decision Making," *Behavioral Sci.* 1976, *21*(1), pp. 19–25.

[18]

Journal of Economic Perspectives— Volume 3, Number 1 — Winter 1989 — Pages 151–169

Theory, Experiment and Economics

Vernon L. Smith

I t is now over thirty years since research was initiated in the laboratory experimental study of market behavior and performance.[1] This essay provides my interpretation of what the implications of this type of work are for the study of economics. The essay is not intended as a systematic survey of the field, although examples will be cited where appropriate and necessary. The reader can find the associated references in more general surveys (E. Hoffman and M. Spitzer, 1985; C. Plott, 1979, 1982, 1986a, 1986b; V. Smith, 1976, 1980, 1982a, 1982b, 1986).

Experimentation and Economics

Economics as currently learned and taught in graduate school and practiced afterward is more theory-intensive and less observation-intensive than perhaps any other science. I think the statement that "no mere fact ever was a match in economics for a consistent theory" accurately describes the prevailing attitude in the profession (Milgrom and Roberts, 1987, p. 185). This is because the training of economists conditions us to think of economics as an *a priori* science, and not as an observational science in which the interplay between theory and observation is paramount. Conse-

---

[1] My first supply and demand experiment was done in January 1956, but others were involved at about the same time or earlier. Among the pioneering contributors to experimental economics were a number of scholars in the United States and Germany, many of whom were working quite independently without knowledge of each other's almost simultaneous work: E. Chamberlin (Harvard), A. Hoggatt (Berkeley), H. Sauermann and R. Selton (Germany), M. Shubik (Yale), S. Siegle and L. Fouraker (Pennsylvania State) and J. Friedman (Yale).

■ *Vernon L. Smith is Professor of Economics and Research Director, Economic Science Laboratory, University of Arizona, Tucson, Arizona.*

quently, we come to believe that economic problems can be understood fully just by thinking about them. After the thinking has produced sufficient technical rigor, internal coherence and interpersonal agreement, economists can then apply the results to the world of data.

But experimentation changes the way you think about economics. If you do experiments you soon find that a number of important experimental results can be replicated by yourself and by others. As a consequence, economics begins to represent concepts and propositions capable of being or failing to be demonstrated. Observation starts to loom large as the centerpiece of economics. Now the purpose of theory must be to track, but also predict new observations, not just "explain" facts, *ex post hoc*, as in traditional economic practice, where mere facts may be little more than stylized stories. The professional problem is for the theorist to recognize and respond to this purpose, and to undertake the arduous and challenging task of theory development disciplined by ongoing empirical studies. As Einstein put it, "[T]his theory is not speculative in origin; it owes its invention entirely to the desire to make physical theory fit observed fact as well as possible... the justification for a physical concept lies exclusively in its clear and unambiguous relation to facts that can be experienced." But this process is not tautological so long as every time new data motivates an extension in theory, the new theory can be confronted with new field or laboratory observations, and this confrontation yields at least some victories some of the time.

In any confrontation between theory and observation the theory may work or fail to work. When the theory works it becomes believable in proportion to its predictive "miracle," instead of only respectable in proportion to its internal elegance or its association with authority. But when it works, you lean mightily upon the theory with more challenging "boundary" experiments designed to uncover the edges of validity of the theory where certainty gives way to uncertainty and thereby lays the basis for extensions in the theory that increase its empirical content. When the theory performs well you also think, "Are there parallel results in naturally occurring field data?" You look for coherence across different data sets because theories are not specific to particular data sources. Such extensions are important because theories often make specific assumptions about information and institutions which can be controlled in the laboratory, but which may not accurately represent field data generating situations. Testing theories on the domain of their assumptions is sterile unless it is part of a research program concerned with extending the domain of applications of theory to field environments.

When the theory fails to work in initial tests, the research program is essentially the same. This is because all theories can be expected to be more or less improvable, and statistical tests of theories, whether the results are initially "falsifying" or not, are simply the means to motivate extensions in theory. Better theory that narrows the distance between theory and observation is always welcome.

From the perspective of experimental methodology, this scenario is what the profession of economics is all about. But it is not always what we economists do very well as a profession, because our publishing incentives are not always compatible with this research paradigm.

What Is There in a Theory to Test?

As is well known, when economists test a theory we make direct comparisons between observations and the predictions of the theory. But what precisely among the elements of a theory do we test when we make these comparisons? To answer this underlying question, it is instructive to distinguish among the following three ingredients of a theory: environment, institution and behavior.

The *environment* consists of the collection of all agents' characteristics; that is, tastes and technology, which in traditional economics are represented by utility or preference functions, resource endowments and production or cost functions. In reduced form these characteristics are the individual demand (willingness-to-pay) and supply (willingness-to-accept) schedules. The *institution* defines the language (messages or actions) of communication; examples include bids by buyers, offers by sellers, acceptances by either, and the characteristics of the commodity. The institution also specifies, either formally as on an organized exchange or informally by tradition, the order in which economics agents move, or that there is no order (moves are free form), and the rules under which messages become contracts and thus allocations. For example, in most retail markets the sellers first post their offer prices, then buyers scan, search and perhaps accept offers for stated quantities. The organized commodity and stock markets use variations on the oral double auction; buyers and sellers freely announce price-quantity bids and offers. A contract occurs when a buyer accepts a seller's offer or a seller accepts a buyer's bid. Consequently, the institution specifies the rules, terms or conditions under which components of market demand make contact with components of market supply to produce binding allocations.

Finally, *behavior* is concerned with agent choices of messages or actions given the agent's characteristics (environment) and the practices (institutional rules) relating such choices to allocations. Theories introduce assumptions about agent behavior: that agents maximize utility, profit or expected utility, that common information yields common expectations, that agents make choices as if they are risk averse, that expectations adjust using Bayes rule, that transactions costs (the cost of thinking, deciding, acting) are negligible.[2] Theories of behavior make predictions about messages—the bid(s) that an agent will submit at a sealed bid auction, the price that will be posted by an oligopolist, the reservation price below which a price searching agent will buy, and so on. Messages are not outcomes; they translate into outcomes depending upon the allocation and cost imputation rules of the institution.

---

[2]The distinction between that which we label "behavior" and that which is called an "agent's characteristic" (environment) will not, nor need it be, *a priori*. Part of the function of experiments is to increase our understanding of the issues involved in being or not being able to make this distinction. For example, is risk aversion an agent characteristic or an element of behavior embedded in his choices? It is both, but can we separate them in the context of experiments? It is yet to be shown empirically that we can operationalize this separation. See Cedric Smith's proposal (discussed below) to risk neutralize subjects by paying them in lottery tickets.

In laboratory market experiments, we test the theory's assumptions about agent behavior. How? Laboratory market experiments begin with an experimental design which seeks to control the environment using the techniques of induced valuation, and to control the institution by defining the language and the rules under which experimental subjects will be allowed to trade.[3] With these controls we narrow the interpretation of inconsistency between predictions and observations so that the burden of inconsistency is borne by the behavioral assumptions of the theory. When the experimental observations are consistent with a theory we have our first evidence that the theory—as implemented by the particular environment and institution that was used—has predictive power. If the theory was explicit about the institution (for example, specified a sealed-bid discriminative auction), but made very general assumptions about the environment (for example, Q units offered to $N > Q$ unit bidders), then it is natural to direct the research exercise to variations on the original experimental environment. If the theory was not explicit about the institution (the strong interpretation is that the theory claims to be institution-free, but more likely the demands of tractability led the theorist to make simplifying institutional assumptions), then a reasonable research objective is to explore experimental designs that vary the institution. In this way one lays a foundation of empirical results that can motivate accommodating extensions in the original theory.

The above interpretation of experimental tests of a theory can be contrasted with tests based only on field data. In the latter case the economist has no independent control over the environment and the institution; as a result, the process is a *composite test* of the theory's assumptions about the environment, the institution and agent behavior. If the theory passes the test, it may be because all elements of the theory are "correct," or because "incorrect" elements of the theory had offsetting effects that could not be identified by the test. If the theory fails, the economist cannot know which of its elements accounted for the falsifying outcome.

When various operational forms of a theory are not falsified by laboratory data, we can say that the theory's assumptions about behavior are supported given the environment and institution posited by the theory and the experiment. But we are not finished. Often the theory will specify a particularly simple artificial institution which may fail to coincide with any that we observe in the field: for example, that firms choose price and/or quantities, and that buyers fully reveal demand. These institu-

---

[3] Value is induced on buyer i by assigning him/her values $V_i(1) \geq V_i(2) \geq \cdots \geq V_i(Q_i)$ for successive units $1, 2, \ldots, Q_i$, and guaranteeing to i that he/she will be paid in cash the difference between the assigned value, and the corresponding realized price paid in the market, $V_i(q_i) - Pq_i$, for each unit purchased, q_i. If $U_i(\cdot)$ is i's unobserved monotone increasing utility of money, then i is motivated to buy an additional unit at any price below its assigned value. The valuation schedule thus becomes the individual's maximum willingness-to-pay for the item. Similarly, a supply schedule is induced upon sellers by assigning them individual "costs" for successive units and paying in cash the difference between the realized prices received and the assigned costs. This procedure easily generalizes to induce utility $U_i[V'(X_i, Y_i)]$ on two "commodities" (X_i, Y_i) with the dollar valuation function $V'(X_i, Y_i)$. The environment is defined and controlled by the collection of all assigned value (cost) schedules. The institution is controlled by defining the manner in which individuals interact to yield exchange prices and contracts.

tional assumptions can be reproduced in the laboratory, with real reward-motivated people as firms and simulated demand-revealing buyers. But it is a one-sided partial equilibrium theory of the firm and its market. This modelling tradition has carried over into contemporary game-theoretic theories of behavior in industrial organization.[4] In recent extensions of search theory it is assumed that firms quote prices, knowing search behavior, and this generates an equilibrium-predicted price distribution. These models can be tested using artificial institutions that impose the conditions postulated by the theories. But the observed institution is free-form so that firms may quote prices while learning about the search behavior of buyers, and simultaneously the latter may choose their search behavior while learning about the prices set by firms. In these examples the experiments are constrained by the (message space) *limitations of the theories* that are tested, *not by limitations in the experimental methodology*. In fact, the easiest experiment is to put no restrictions on the price setting-searching process.

Much of the experimental literature is guided by nothing more sophisticated than the static theory that markets will clear. However, this body of literature has sought to break through the boundaries created by the current limitations of theory, and to establish a less restrictive empirical foundation for theory improvement. One such example is the large literature on the double "oral" auction trading institution, various forms of which are used in the organized stock, commodity, currency and interest rate futures markets. In this institution the messages are bids by buyers, offers by sellers and acceptances by either. There are some rules, such as that all-or-none bids are prohibited, and that a new bid must provide better terms than a standing bid. But beyond these the institution is free-form and is similar to modelling a *two-sided* search equilibrium market. Sellers announce and modify offer prices, while learning about the acceptance behavior of buyers. Simultaneously, the latter choose their acceptance behavior while learning about the prices announced by sellers. Buyers also announce bid prices, and sellers are free to accept such prices. Until recently (in the work of Easely and Ledyard, Wilson and Friedman) this institution has been beyond our analytical efforts. Yet to date no other trading institution studied in the laboratory has exceeded its capacity to exhaust the gains from exchange, or exceeded its speed of convergence to competitive equilibria.

Although this discussion has emphasized laboratory experiments, what I say applies also to field empirical research. Natural experiments occur all the time, and it would be desirable to develop a professional readiness to seize upon these occasions. When Mt. St. Helens started to quiver, it was quickly peppered with geologists and instruments collecting the data that can only be generated during the reactivation of a volcano. By comparison, the tradition of direct observation in economics appears weak; our training does not seem to include the techniques, nor develop the alertness, to respond to contemporary or historical empirical opportunities. One need not romanticize the techniques of other sciences, or exaggerate their applicability to

[4]Several experimental studies suggest that market behavior may be different when there are real buyers than when one simulates a revealed demand schedule in response to seller decisions.

economics, to recognize that economists could benefit from a stronger passion and curiosity for the microeconomics of how things work.[5]

Experiments, Institutions and Economic Theory

Since it is impossible to test a theory using experimental market data without specifying an institution, the experimental study of allocation processes forces an institutional and informational mode of thinking into every research design. People have to know what the message space is, who can move when, (as in posted price institutions), or that moves are unrestricted (as in oral double auction institutions), who knows what, when, and how their message decisions generate allocations, cost imputations and net returns. Experimentalists were therefore primed to welcome, and their research has been much influenced by, the *institution-specific theory* that began to develop about 1960.

The important thing we have learned from these theories, and from many of the experiments testing them, is that *institutions matter*.[6] This is because agent incentives in the choice of messages (like bids) are affected by the institutional rules that convert messages into outcomes (like whether the high bidder wins an auction and pays the amount of the high bid or the amount of the second highest bid). In pre-1960 theory, by contrast, allocations were derived directly from the environment using ad hoc assumptions about demand revelation, or "price taking" behavior, by agents. Figure 1 illustrates the different ways of thinking. Experiments now address the question of how different institutions affect the incentive to reveal demand and supply. Thus the double oral auction elicits effective full revelation of demand and supply, but everyone in the market is a price maker as well as a price taker. Pre-1960 economic theory was totally unprepared for this kind of result.

Several questions can be raised concerning this dichotomy between institution-free and institution-specific theory. For example: doesn't the above definition of an institution preclude the possibility that any theory be institution-free? The answer is that a theory can be considered institution-free if it can be shown that the allocations it predicts are the same for all members of some class of institutions. An example is the theory of the four standard auctions: the English ascending price auction, in which the prices increase until only one bidder is left; the Dutch descending price auction, in

[5]An example of what I mean is the opportunistic response of Deacon and Sonstelie (1985) to an unusual natural experiment in which federal regulations temporarily constrained a few California stations to sell gasoline at prices less than those at other stations. Of course queues formed at the lower price stations. The authors put together a survey research program which was applied to both the high-price and low-price outlets which enabled them to measure the characteristics of respondents in the two situations, estimate the welfare cost of a market-wide ceiling on gasoline prices, and estimate the value of time spent in queues.
[6]The influential early contributions to this new conception of theory include Vickrey's (Nash-Harsanyi) models of the four standard auctions, Hurwicz's more abstract "mechanism" theory, and Shubik's emphasis on the extensive form game representation of microeconomics. Since that time there has been an increased development (particularly in bidding, information, and price search theory) of models that show how prices and allocations can or might be generated out of the internal processes of an institutionally mediated information exchange system. These theories have allowed institutions to slip unannounced back into economics, but now as an integral part of theorizing.

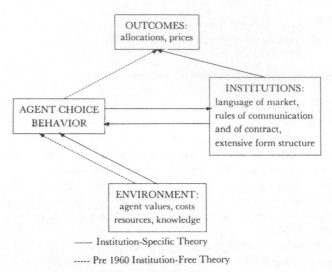

Fig. 1. Institutions in economic theory

which prices fall until some bidder bids; the first price sealed bid auction, in which the high bidder wins and pays his bid; and the second price sealed-bid auction, in which the high bidder wins but pays the amount of the second highest bid. These institutions are all equivalent if the environment is one in which all agents are risk neutral. The English and second price auctions are equivalent and the outcomes are all the same regardless of the risk attitude of agents. The Dutch and first price auctions are equivalent whatever the risk attitude of agents, but the outcomes (except in the risk neutral case) are distinct from those in the English and second price auctions. The experimental data tend to support the equivalence between English and second price auctions; do not support the equivalence of all four auctions (people do not behave as if risk neutral), and do not support the equivalence of Dutch and first price auctions.

Experimental methods can be used to test hypotheses about why certain institutions survive in the economy. Laboratory experiments enable economists to evaluate the performance characteristics of alternative institutions in controlled value-cost environments. These performance measures include: efficiency, speed of convergence, price stability, extent of price discrimination, responsiveness to changes in the environment, and so on. Dutch auctions are less efficient but faster (as implemented in the field), than English, first price, or second price auctions. This difference may account for the tendency to use Dutch auctions for selling perishables such as cut flowers, produce and fish. Posted price institutions are less efficient and yield higher selling prices than oral double auction institutions; but in the former price policy can be centralized, negotiation (a transactions cost) avoided and the products vended do not have to be standardized. These data can provide the basis for more complete theories of markets in which the institution is a variable and whose predictions can be tested with field observations across markets organized under different institutions of exchange.

There now exist many examples of continuing research programs in which theory has been sufficiently institution-rich to allow direct tests of the behavioral assumptions of the theory. I will discuss the first of two such examples in some detail to illustrate how a dialogue between testing and theory development can proceed using the trichotomy: environment, institution and behavior.

The first example involves Vickrey's risk neutral Nash equilibrium model of the first price sealed bid auction, which has stimulated an extensive study of bidding behavior in private value auctions by Cox, Smith and Walker (1988). (In a private value auction, each agent has a distinct value for the item.) Vickrey's theory assumes that each of N bidders, i, derives utility $u = v_i - b_i$ if i is the high bidder with bid b_i and i's value for the auction objective is v_i. Note that all bidders are identical except for their values, v_i. Vickrey also assumed that the v_i are distributed as a rectangular distribution. Each bidder knows N and his/her own value, but only the distribution of all others values. Given this environment Vickrey deduced the equilibrium bid function $b_i = (N - 1)v_i/N$; that is, all individuals are predicted to bid the same fraction, $(N - 1)/N$, of their respective values.

We first found that about 92 percent of the subjects bid too high to be consistent with the Vickrey model; that is, they bid on the risk averse side of Vickrey's linear bid function. I often encounter the argument that the amounts of money used in laboratory experiments are "too small" for subjects to show risk averse behavior. But there is no theorem stating how small is "locally" in the phrase "locally linear." A lot of data from quite different experimental markets shows systematic deviations from risk neutral predictions. These data are given coherence by the hypothesis that subjects are risk averse.

Our experiments also found that the relationship between bids and values tends to be systematic for each individual, but to differ across individuals. This result is inconsistent with the hypothesis that individuals have identical risk aversion.[7] Given these empirical results, we derived a new theoretical model based on the assumption that each bidder has constant relative risk averse utility from winning the auction with a particular bid given a particular private value of the prize. This model was consistent with the highly linear distinct bidding behavior of subjects. It can be shown that this is the *only* utility model which predicts that bids in relation to value will not be affected if the payoffs are increased by any multiple. We reran some of the

---

[7]A comprehensive survey of bidding theory (McAfee and McMillan, 1987) contains only one paper which admits of an environment in which agents may have differing nonlinear utility functions. Yet here is a critique of the above experimental results: "Of course, we don't have to go to an experimental situation to refute the hypothesis that individuals have the same degree of risk aversion!" Two comments are in order. First, if there is a widespread consensus on this "stylized fact" how come so many bidding models assume it away? I would suggest that the requirements of tractability, and the incentive to publish, loom large in charting this "low-apple-picking" course of least resistance. Otherwise, why do theory that assumes to be true that which we "know" to be false? Second, our auction experiments reject the hypothesis that people have the same degree of risk aversion, but a valuable field study by Binswanger (1980, p. 395), framed within the context of choice among uncertain prospects, found that "at high payoff levels, virtually all individuals are moderately risk-averse with little variation according to personal characteristics. Wealth tends to reduce risk aversion slightly, but its effect is not statistically significant."

experiments but tripled the payoffs, and observed no significant change in the relationship between an individual's bid and his/her value.[8]

Our model, however, implies linear homogeneous bid functions, and some 22 percent of the fitted linear individual bid functions had intercepts significantly different from zero. We hypothesized that the positive intercepts were due to a utility of winning in addition to the utility of the surplus won, while the negative intercepts were due to a threshold income necessary to provide positive utility. Does our *ex post facto* attempt to explain these nonzero intercepts increase empirical content? Yes; the new model is testable in that it implies that paying winning subjects a cash lump sum in addition to the auction surplus will increase their estimated linear bid function intercepts. Similarly, charging winning subjects a lump sum is predicted to decrease these intercepts. These new implications are not falsified by the indicated new experiments.

Despite this deepening chain of empirical successes, like *all* theory, this class of models is not without some unresolved empirical anomalies. For example, many years ago it was pointed out (C. Smith, 1961, pp. 13–14) that one could induce risk neutral behavior on risk averse expected utility maximizing agents. Instead of paying them cash for the outcomes of their decisions you give them chances, or lottery tickets, on a fixed reward if they win, and a smaller amount if they lose. This makes expected utility linear in outcomes whatever the utility of money function, and subjects are predicted to bid as if risk neutral in lottery tickets. However, this prediction is clearly falsified by auction experiments using this environment. It seems likely that it is the compound probability axiom of expected utility theory that fails in this application.[9]

---

[8]I have been asked: "How do you react to criticisms which say that from market data we can reject the assumption of constant relative risk aversion? We can look at how individuals change their portfolio with wealth, and it does not conform even to a much looser specification of the utility function? Why test a theory which has been rejected by market data?" Here are my reactions: (1) We can't reject the theory from this kind of market data. That data tells us how portfolios change with some measure of "wealth," confounded with changes in time, income, expectations, information, unmeasured probability assessments, and so on *ad infinitum*. We can't learn what we want to know from this sort of exercise independently of more rigorous tests, although market evidence and experimental evidence can illuminate each other. (2) Constant relative risk averse utility has been reported to do well in accounting for U.S. Treasury bill dealers' behavior (Wolf and Pohlman, 1983) both as elicited and as observed in bidding, but the constant relative risk averse coefficient shows greater risk aversion for actual bids than for the (Kahneman and Tversky) hypothetical assessments. (3) Non-constant relative risk averse utility cannot account for first price auction bidding behavior because the latter appears not to change when we triple payoffs. (4) Constant relative risk averse utility need not be valid over the entire interval of positive income to yield predictive accuracy over the relevant range of observations. Probably no functional form will be satisfactory everywhere.

[9]This interpretation raises the question, "If the compounding axiom fails, what does it imply about individual behavior? You can't have an important prediction of the theory rejected and still accept the theory." It is correct to say that not all observed behavior is consistent with expected utility maximization, but it is incorrect to say that you cannot therefore accept the theory. You can accept it, indeed you have little choice, until a better theory emerges. Theories are not accepted because all tests have failed to refute them. Lakatos (1978, pp. 4–5) wrote, "...scientists talk about anomalies, recalcitrant instances, not refutations...When Newton published his *Principia* it was common knowledge that it could not properly explain even the motion of the moon; in fact, lunar motion refuted Newton. Kaufman, a distinguished physicist, refuted Einstein's relativity theory in the very year it was published." People accept theories, in spite of anomalies, because they account for some evidence, and in particular are able to predict novel, even

In any case these results should alert scholars to the hazards of applying this procedure and assuming that their subjects are rendered neutral to risk. Any test of a theory which applies this procedure is necessarily a joint test of Smith's hypothesis and the theory; if the hypothesis fails to test out, the test of the theory is open to doubt. But even if C. Smith's hypothesis had been consistent with these tests, the exercise has limited transfer value in natural field and laboratory environments if real people are risk averse in the rewards that mediate their choices. If this is the case one must sooner or later confront the empirical demand for theories based on heterogeneous risk averse agents.

The second example is one in which the demand for new theory requires more than modifications that introduce individual differences in risk aversion. This is the extensive study of common value auctions by J. Kagel and D. Levin (1986) showing that subjects generally do not satisfy the predictions of a particular risk neutral Nash model of bidding. In this environment (see Thaler in the Winter 1988 issue of this journal for a discussion and a different interpretation) subjects do not know the common value of the item when they bid; but they each have an independent unbiased sample ("signal") which is positively related to true value. Unless one's bid is suitably discounted, as in this Nash model, the high bidder tends to be the one with the most optimistic sample estimate of value, and is said to be a victim of the "winner's curse." In small groups (3–4) experienced subjects make consistently positive profits and bid closer to the Nash prediction than the "winner's curse" prediction. (Profits are about 65 percent of the Nash prediction so that even here there appears to be room for theory improvement by appropriately introducing risk aversion). However, bids are found to increase with the number of bidders in larger groups (6–7), and contrary to this theory, experienced subjects suffer losses and bankruptcies. These data suggest that, *ceteris paribus*, the theory needs extensions that make the number of active bidders endogenous, and which predict equilibrium adjustment over time through some exit (entry) survival process. This is implied by the fact that the endogenous forces tending to vary N frustrated the Kagel-Levin attempt to fix N as a treatment variable in the larger groups. But the theory under test assumes that N is given. The data suggest an alternative zero profit market clearing model (it might be formulated as a Nash model) with N as a variable, in which entry would occur for $N = 3$ or 4 and exit when $N = 6$ or 7, yielding an equilibrium industry size, $N^* = 5$, for the parameters used by Kagel and Levin. One would seek a model in which N^* is a function of parameters characterizing the environment and, in

---

stunning, facts that cannot be accounted for by alternative theories. Newton's theory enabled Halley to make the stunning prediction that a certain comet would return in seventy-two years, as indeed it did, and Einstein's theory made the stunning prediction that a star's light was bent by the gravitational pull of the sun. Vickrey's model, suitably modified for heterogeneous risk averse bidders, rather astoundingly, I would say, accounts for and predicts the behavior of naive reward-motivated subjects in a first price auction. What alternative theory shows a comparable capacity to organize this immense data set?

addition to explaining the Kagel-Levin results, would lead to new testable implications.

Noncooperative Equilibrium Theory and Experiment

Two prevailing criticisms about noncooperative (Nash) equilibrium theory require modification in the light of experimental evidence.

First, it is widely believed that the concept of a noncooperative Nash equilibrium is "inherently" unsatisfactory because of its strong (or unrealistic) information requirements that each agent must know the preferences of all other agents.

Second, noncooperative equilibrium concepts are of questionable value because there are so many different such concepts leading to distinct theoretical implications; even with any given concept, such as Nash-Harsanyi, there are sometimes multiple solutions that leave open the question of a criterion for choosing among them.

The first criticism does not reflect the experimental results from many different environments which support noncooperative theory. The second criticism reflects a mode of thinking that excludes the prospect that a theory might be taken seriously enough to test it.

There are now numerous experimental studies based on noncooperative equilibrium concepts in which the results support the proposition that such equilibria are *more* likely to obtain under the minimal information requirement that no agent knows the preferences (or in an experiment, the payoffs used to induce preferences) of any other agent, and are *less* likely to obtain, or take longer to obtain, under the complete information conditions that critics argue are needed for equilibrium.

Fouraker and Siegel provided the first evidence on this point a quarter of a century ago in their classic work on bargaining behavior. Their bilateral bargaining, repeat transaction experiments were run under both complete and incomplete information. In these experiments, the seller chooses a price message, followed by the buyer choosing a quantity message, so that the noncooperative message equilibrium corresponds to the monopoly price and quantity. With incomplete information, eight of nine observations support a Nash outcome, and one supports the competitive equilibrium. With complete information 11 of 21 observations support a Nash noncooperative equilibrium, while 10 support competitive. Similarly, in their Cournot quantity message triopoly markets, support for Nash was 15 of 33 under complete information, 20 of 33 under incomplete. Finally, in their Bertrand price message markets, Nash was supported in 17 of 17 duopoly pairs under incomplete information, but only 11 of 17 under complete information. Another example based on large group double auction markets is discussed in the next section.

Two rudimentary fallacies underlie the criticism that the Nash equilibrium is not useful because it requires full information. First, *theorists* have to assume complete information in order to calculate a noncooperative equilibrium. But it does not follow that agents either require such information, or would know how to make the calculations if they had the information. An equilibrium is a state, and analysts can ask whether a market tends to settle upon that state independently of the process used to calculate the state.

The second fallacy is that if agents have complete information, why should they use it to identify a noncooperative equilibrium? With complete information one can also identify more lucrative cooperative outcomes, and this is precisely the way real people deviate from Nash in most of the above experiments. Subjects are not so irrational as to satisfy "rational" models of behavior when it is contrary to their self-interest!

As theorists, we have been lax in the assumptions we make as to what follows from the state of common knowledge. First, what can objectively exist—say, in an experiment—is a state of common information, which is not the same thing as common knowledge or *expectations*. Real people have their own diverse ideas as to the knowledge implications of common information. Second, people have their own agenda as to what it is rational to expect and do given common information, and their presuppositions need not accord with economists' presumptions about rational behavior.

The second major criticism of the concept of noncooperative equilibrium, that there are so many such concepts all with different theoretical implications, is symptomatic of a research program which attempts to answer scientific questions independently of observations. The obvious criterion in most sciences for selecting among alternative theoretical predictions is empirical, not *a priori*. One can design experiments capable of yielding results that may support any of the theoretical predictions, then see if the data "select" (are closer to) one among the competitors. Multiple theoretical predictions are exactly what the experimentalist likes to see in any science.

Concepts of noncooperative equilibrium have performed well in a large number of experimental markets—better than they have had a right to perform given that they were never intended to be tested, and that their acceptability is judged on internal rather than empirical criteria. Furthermore, the nonuniqueness of Nash equilibrium concepts (and even of equilibria) is a strength, not a weakness. When one concept fails empirically (as in common value auctions with N fixed and certain) there may be other formulations that do not contradict observation.

Laboratory Experiments, Psychology and Economics

The considerable literature that has developed using experimental methods has examined many of the mainstream issues in microeconomic theory and is helping to illuminate an increasing number of applied economic questions. If one seeks common general themes in this literature, particularly concerning behavior, I see three such empirical propositions, with far-reaching implications for how economists think about economics and how we interpret, and perhaps do, theory. The first proposition is that economic agents do not solve decision problems by thinking about them and calculating in the same way as economists. Second, from this first proposition it should not be presumed that economic agents will fail to get the "right" answers in the context of markets: namely, the answers that are predicted by market theories. The experimental evidence is often consistent with the predictions of market theories. Third, economists have little in the way of formal understanding of how people are able to get the "right" answers without consciously performing our logic and calculations.

Experimentalists in both psychology and economics have provided overwhelming evidence in market experiments, in informal subject debriefing, and in choice surveys, that supports the first proposition. The second receives support from hundreds of supply and demand, oligopoly, bargaining and other experiments stretching back three decades in the work of many experimental economists and the psychologist S. Siegel. The third proposition calls attention to the lack of a satisfactory analytical-empirical integration of two bodies of evidence: one relating to the introspective and sometimes actual cash motivated responses of people in surveys soliciting choices among alternatives; the other to cash motivated choices in the context of repetitive market exchange.

Several psychologists (Edwards, Kahneman, Lichtenstein, Slovic, Tversky) and economists (Allais, Ellsberg) have pioneered the development of experimental designs for collecting evidence on hypothetical and actual individual choice behavior. This evidence generally tends to be inconsistent with expected utility theory, and with some of the fundamental behavior hypotheses in the theory of demand (Kahneman, Knetsch and Thaler, 1986; Knetsch and Sinden, 1984), such as the opportunity cost principle, and the implication of demand theory that there should exist only "small" differences between willingness-to-pay and willingness-to-accept. Some of this work has been replicated using cash payoffs and the conclusions (preference or demand theory is violated) are not changed. Although replication using cash payoffs (where this has not been done) is certainly needed, I think it is a mistake to assume that the economist's paradigm will somehow be rescued in the context of these particular experimental designs, if experimenters would just pay money.

Given the high replicability of most of these studies, I think further such replications are of marginal value. What would be of much greater value is research directed at closing two gaps: the gap between decision theory and decision behavior, and the gap between evidence concerning how people think about economic questions and evidence concerning how people behave in experimental markets. Closing these gaps is crucial if we are not to get stuck on a research plateau. This is because it is clear from the work of Lakatos and other philosopher-historians of science that "there is no refutation without a better theory" (Lakatos, 1978, p. 6). Scientists in all disciplines simply ignore falsifying evidence until new and better theory emerges. Theory selection is based on opportunity cost, not absolute falsificationist standards.

There are two distinct paths whereby the distance between decision theory and behavior can be narrowed. The first lies in the empirical interpretation of expected utility theory: What are the prizes as perceived by the decision maker?

Almost uniformly we economists have assumed *a priori* that the objects to which the axioms of utility theory "should" apply are different amounts of wealth. Psychologists have followed this tradition in their empirical interpretation of data on choice behavior. For example, Kahneman and Tversky have a class of decision problems in which the observations are consistent with expected utility theory if the utility function is S-shaped and is applied not to wealth, but to changes in wealth (income) from a reference point representing the individual's current wealth state. This curve describes risk seeking behavior below the reference point, and risk averse behavior above. But this result does not violate the theory. The axioms of the theory do not tell us what the prizes are. The theory simply postulates objects that can be preference ordered. It is an extra-theoretical subsidiary hypothesis to assert that these objects are amounts of final wealth measured in some particular way. Empirical evidence going back 35 years to H. Markowitz has suggested that the theory does much better if the prizes are changes in wealth, not absolute wealth. Selecting among hypotheses that are subsidiary to the axioms of a theory, but essential to its empirical interpretation, ought to be one of the more important functions of experimental methods.

In our application of utility theory to a risk averse model of the first price auction discussed earlier, we explicitly apply it to income because subjects participate in a sequence of auctions, with each auction representing a potential increment of wealth for each bidder. It is this form of the theory that organizes the data. This interpretation is consistent with other experimental evidence, and with the observed tendency of gamblers to make repetitive small stakes bets, as against a single bet wagering one's entire gambling budget.

Also in the auction example, notice that when we encountered linear empirical bid functions with nonzero intercepts, instead of dumping all utility theory forthwith, we asked whether it was possible to redefine the prizes so as to account for this contrary evidence, but in a way that was testable. The modified utility function has the Kahneman-Tversky S-shape, but with a "reference point" whose position varies with individual characteristics. The point to be emphasized is not that we have shown that prize reinterpreting extensions of expected utility theory will always work, but that they work in the context of auctions. Furthermore, such extensions in one context may be applicable in others, increasing coherence.

The second path in bringing together decision theory and behavior is to modify the axioms. Chew and Machina have done this expertly with various modifications of independence. These modifications account for some but not all of the violations. The Chew-Machina modifications accommodate Allais-type violations, and under certain conditions, preference reversals[10]; they provide new testable propositions not deducible from expected utility theory, and thereby yield an increase in empirical content. For a comprehensive discussion of these developments, see Machina (1987).

The fact that expected utility theory is consistent with some of the empirical evidence, especially when reinterpreted in terms of the prizes, and when extended along more fundamental Chew-Machina lines, argues strongly against any serious

---

[10]A preference reversal occurs when a subject says that he prefers *A* to *B* (or *B* to *A*) and that his willingness-to-pay (or willingness-to-accept) for *A* is less (greater) than that for *B*. A great many subjects' choices exhibit such reversals when *A* and *B* are different gambles (or different dividend paying assets). It should be added that the Chew-Machina modifications can accommodate preference reversals if they are the result of violations of the independence axiom. This is implied by the contributions of Holt and Karni and Safra. However the experimental tests by Cox and Epstein (1987) support the proposition that preference reversals are not due to violations of independence.

proposal to abandon it. At this juncture there is no alternative so that to abandon it is to substitute the void for a foundation of sand. The predictions of the theory and its extensions are noncontroversial, and it provides a powerful problem solving heuristic (Lakatos, 1978). Without this theory we have several empirical regularities whose predictive power in new situations is a function of the experience and opinion of the observer. There is a world of difference between having a theory whose predictions for all parameterizations are noncontroversial and having names to assign to certain empirical regularities.

How do we close the second gap, between the psychology of choice and agents' economic behavior in experimental exchange markets? The introspective empirical results make it clear that people's choices violate such basic tenets of demand theory as opportunity cost considerations and the approximate equality between willingness to accept and willingness to pay.[11] I think we economists need to accept these replicable empirical results as providing meaningful measures of *how people think about economic questions.* For their part, psychologists need to accept the dominating message in experimental research on the performance of a wide variety of bidding, auctioning and customer (posted price) markets: markets quite often "work" in the sense that over time they converge to the predictions of the economist's paradigm.[12] The few studies that simultaneously measure what people *say* (as questionnaire respondents), and what people subsequently *do* in experimental markets, confirm both kinds of evidence (Coursey, Hovis and Schulze, 1987; Knez and Smith, 1987). That is, the introspective responses of those subjects replicate the similar results of psychologists, but the responses are not necessarily consistent with the subjects' own subsequent market convergence behavior over time.[13] I suggest that we assume that these two bodies of evidence correctly measure the thoughtful choices and revealed actions of

[11]It should be emphasized that what is at stake here is the traditional utility-based theory of excess demand functions whose validity or falsity is separable from the theory of markets. The observation that willingness-to-accept exceeds willingness-to-pay, and that this is due to "loss aversion," implies that excess demand functions are discontinuous at the initial endowment. This means that gains from exchange are predicted to be lower than the prediction of the standard utility analysis. But market theory begins with postulated demand functions, which need not come from a utilitarian theory of demand. The Swedish economist Gustav Cassel argued that market theory should only begin with market demand and supply because the utilitarian derivation of market behavior was doomed to fail. Markets can be doing their thing whether or not demand theory is of any relevance to expressed demand.

[12]A new example of the discrepancy between behavior in one-shot choice experiments and behavior in markets is in the study of experimental markets for insurance by C. Camerer and H. Kunreuther (1987). Choice experiments often show evidence of violating expected utility theory when low probability significant loss events are involved. Camerer and Kunreuther study double auction markets for insurance contracts with these characteristics, and conclude that there is nothing special about risky losses in the range of parameters they study using this particular trading institution.

[13]In Knez and Smith (1987) we solicited willingness-to-pay and willingness-to-accept responses from potential buyers and sellers for two assets with known probability distributions of dividends. In subsequent double auction trading of these assets 40 percent of the buyers and 34 percent of the sellers announced bids or offers that violated their earlier stated responses. Furthermore, the stated preferences of subjects between the two assets changed considerably after experiencing market trading in them. From these results one should not conclude that the original hypothetical measures were wrong, but that people adapt their beliefs in the light of market experience. Here the incidence of "irrationality" is fairly common in the measures of what people think, but rare in their actual transactions. Only 3 of 146 transactions violated rational principles.

human subjects in these contexts. Reconciling these two sets of observations might be accomplished along the following lines.

People have their own homegrown beliefs about how markets work, or should work. (This is why economic concepts are difficult to teach to beginners.) Their questionnaire responses reflect these beliefs, which are often couched in terms of "fairness" criteria. Also, their initial behavior in a market may reflect these beliefs. But over time their behavior adapts to the incentive properties of markets as often (but certainly not always) represented in the standard economic analysis or its extensions.

It seems to me that we are confronted with two experimental research programs both of which have weak theoretical underpinnings. The economist's maximizing paradigm often performs well in predicting the equilibrium reached over time in experimental markets, but this theory is not generally able to account for short-run dynamic behavior, such as the contract price paths from initial states to final steady states. Similarly, the psychologist's "reference frame" descriptive paradigm performs well in explaining subject introspective responses, and their short-run, or initial, decision behavior, but it provides no predictive theory of reference frame adjustment over time. In fact, the statement (Kahneman, Knetsch and Thaler, 1986, p. 731) "that they (people) adapt their views of fairness to the norms of actual behavior" can be interpreted as a description of what is observed in experimental markets.

Initial choices may reflect all manner of beliefs and expectations, but if these choices are not sustainable in a market clearing or a noncooperative equilibrium, subjects adapt their expectations and behavior until they attain such an equilibrium. For example, it has been demonstrated that in an experimental design in which all the exchange surplus is captured by the buyers, convergence to the competitive equilibrium is slower and more erratic under complete (all values and costs are common knowledge) than under incomplete (values and costs are private) information (C. Smith, 1982, pp. 945–946). The condition of complete information gives the freest play to expectations based on social norms and beliefs. The latter are often inconsistent with equilibrium and retard full convergence until traders learn to adapt their beliefs about what they think "ought" to occur to what is attainable and can be sustained. Real people abandon their *a priori* beliefs when they find that their interest is poorly served by such beliefs. Under incomplete information people have little contextual basis for applying their *a priori* beliefs, and can be presumed to be more accepting of the behavior that sustains equilibrium. For the theorist, perhaps one way to model these phenomena in common information environments is to introduce agent *uncertainty about the behavior* of other agents.[14] Now the theory will no longer predict that agents will come off the blocks straight into full rational expectations equilibrium. But as people adapt, and behavioral uncertainty is reduced, the theory can account for equilibrium convergence under some learning scenarios. This accords with observed price bubbles in experimental asset markets. With increasing subject experience

---

[14] For example, in the various decision problems presented to subjects (see Kahneman, Knetsch and Thaler (1986) and the literature they cite) about 20 to 40 percent of the subjects respond with answers consistent with standard economic reasoning, while the majority responds contrarily, using "fairness" or other "nonrational" criteria.

the incidence of bubbles decreases and prices tend to converge to intrinsic dividend value.

The proposition that people adapt their beliefs about markets to the incentives of markets may also apply to disparate bodies of evidence on opportunity cost and sunk cost. Survey instruments show that, contrary to standard economic analysis, people do not ignore sunk costs and do not treat opportunity costs as equivalent to out-of-pocket costs. These concepts have not been generally examined in experimental markets. However, in my joint work with A. Williams and J. Ledyard in double auction trading with three commodities and two markets, the results fail to falsify the opportunity cost principle. In this environment each demand function depends on the prices of both commodities, and therefore willingness-to-pay in each market is based on foregoing the opportunity to buy an additional unit in the alternative market. These markets converge to the competitive equilibrium, supporting the effectiveness of opportunity cost in this context.

In general, one might think of changes in the reference frame or norms of behavior over time as being induced by the invisible reality of opportunity costs, entry or exit, and the irrelevance of sunk costs. Adaptation, where it is observed, may therefore be forced and agents need not have a cognitive grasp of the causes that are driving changes. Such a model implies sluggish nonoptimal intertemporal adjustment. If some agents (20 to 40 percent) are aware of the effects of opportunity cost, the effects of entry and exit, and the irrelevance of sunk costs, they may approximate optimal adjustment over time, and expedite the adjustment of the less perceptive agents.

Postscript

Experimentalists in economics frequently encounter an argument that proceeds roughly as follows: (a) If a theory is well articulated with clearly stated assumptions, and if there are no errors in the logic and the mathematics; then, (b) certain correct conclusions follow from the theory. So (c), what is there in a theory to test? The punch-line (c) often comes out in other forms without the conditionals (a) and (b) being stated. For example, when the data are consistent with the predictions of a theory, it is sometimes said that the results are not interesting because they merely confirm what economists already knew (or teach?), which seems to suggest that "truly" authoritative theory cannot be doubted seriously. When the data are inconsistent with the predictions of theory it is not uncommon to assert that there must be "something" wrong with the experiments.

Such objections are not without precedent in the history of any science. They tend to impose a double standard: if your theory says that the world is flat, then the tendency of some travelers to be "lost" (they never return home) is taken as evidence that they fell off the edge, while the fact that other travelers return home is interpreted to imply that they did not travel far enough to fall off the earth's edge. Similarly, my experience has been that questions about experimental procedure are more likely to be raised when the results appear to disconfirm accepted theory than when they appear to confirm such theory. However, if one wants to gain a greater understanding of economic phenomena, the most productive knowledge-building attitude is to be skeptical of *both the theory and the evidence*. This is likely to cause you to seek improvements in both the theory and the methods of testing.

One often hears it said that there is "too much theory spinning" or "not enough empirical work" in economics. Neither of these complaints adequately targets our professional weaknesses. Empirical studies would certainly benefit from more theory built directly on observed institutional processes. But not every testable theory may be worth laboratory testing. We need to think ahead to the domain of applicability of such efforts to field environments and institutions. Similarly, we could benefit from an increase in the kind of empirical research, both laboratory and field, that identifies and collects new data sources under the control and responsibility of the scientist; research that seeks to establish, rigorously, those empirical regularities worthy of stimulating deeper theoretical treatment. But we are particularly weak in ongoing research programs in which there is a progressive dialogue between theory development and particular results from laboratory and field tests; that steadily increase the empirical content of theory; and that build usable knowledge and a deeper understanding of things. The process will sometimes yield lags in empirical research, but just as often lags in theory. As the physicist Steven Weinberg described a similar situation in particle physics recently: "[T]here is not one iota of direct experimental evidence for supersymmetry, yet we study it because it looks so much like the sort of theory we would like to believe in. This is symptomatic of the terrible state we are in... The salvation of elementary particle physics is, at least for the moment, in the hands of the experimentalists."

In economics the tendency of theory to lag behind observation seems to be endemic, and, as theorists, few of us consider this to be a "terrible state." But as noted by Lakatos (1978, p. 6), "where theory lags behind the facts, we are dealing with miserable degenerating research programmes."

Theory should be ever more demanding of our empirical resources. Simultaneously, data should be ever more demanding of the empirical relevance of theory and of the theorist's expertise in working imaginatively on problems of the world, rather than on stylized problems of the imagination.

■ *I am grateful for research support from the National Science Foundation and from the Sloan Foundation to the University of Arizona, Economic Science Laboratory. I wish also to express my thanks to J. Cox, D. Kahneman, M. Machina, D. McCloskey, C. Shapiro, J. Stiglitz, T. Taylor and R. Thaler for dozens of pages of commentary on earlier drafts of this essay. I have attempted to incorporate their many valuable comments into the final version. That the final result is an improvement is as certain as is my failure to do as well as I would have liked. Words, pictures and formulas cannot convey a lifetime of experiences under the able tutoring of one's experimental subjects.*

References

Binswanger, Hans P., "Attitudes Toward Risk: Experimental Measurement in Rural India," *American Journal of Agricultural Economics*, August 1980, *62*, 395–407.

Camerer, Colin, and Howard Kunreuther, "Experimental Markets for Insurance," Department of Decision Sciences, University of Pennsylvania, July 1987.

Coursey, Don, John Hovis, and William Schulze, "On the Supposed Disparity Between Willingness-to-Accept and Willingness-to-Pay Measures of Value," *Quarterly Journal of Economics*, August 1987, *102*, 679–690.

Cox, James, Vernon Smith, and James Walker, "Theory and Individual Behavior of First Price Auctions," *Journal of Risk and Uncertainty*, March 1988, *1*, 61–99.

Cox, James C., and Seth Epstein, "Preference Reversals Without the Independence Axiom," Department of Economics, University of Arizona, Discussion Paper No. 87-10, Sept. 1987.

Deacon, Robert, and Jon Sonstelie, "Rationing by Waiting and the Value of Time: Results from a Natural Experiment," *Journal of Political Economy*, August 1985, *93*, 627–647.

Hoffman, Elizabeth, and Matthew L. Spitzer, "Experimental Law and Economics," *Columbia Law Review*, June 1985, *85*, 991–1036.

Kagel, John, and Daniel Levin, "The Winner's Curse and Public Information in Common Value Auctions," *American Economic Review*, December 1986, *76*, 894–920.

Kahneman, Daniel, Jack Knetsch, and Richard Thaler, "Fairness as a Constraint on Profit Seeking: Entitlements in the Market," *American Economic Review*, September 1986, *76*, 728–741.

Knetsch, Jack, and John Sinden, "Willingness to Pay and Compensation Demanded: Experimental Evidence of An Unexpected Disparity in Measures of Value," *Quarterly Journal of Economics*, August 1984, *99*, 507–521.

Knez, Marc, and Vernon Smith, "Hypothetical Valuations and Preference Reversals in the Context of Asset Trading." In Roth, Alvin, ed., *Laboratory Experiments in Economics: Six Points of View*. Cambridge: Cambridge University Press, 1987, pp. 131–154.

Lakatos, Imre, *The Methodology of Scientific Research Programmes*. Vol 1. Worrall, J., and G. Currie, eds. Cambridge: Cambridge University Press, 1978.

Machina, Mark J., "Choice Under Uncertainty: Problems Solved and Unsolved," *Journal of*

Economic Perspectives, Summer 1987, *1*, 121–154.

McAfee, R. Preston, and John McMillan, "Auctions and Bidding," *Journal of Economic Literature*, June 1987, *25*, 699–738.

Milgrom, Paul, and John Roberts, "Information Asymmetries, Strategic Behavior, and Industrial Organization," *American Economic Review*, May 1987, *77*, 184–193.

Plott, Charles R., "The Application of Laboratory Experimental Methods to Public Choice." In Russell, C. S., ed., *Collective Decision Making: Applications from Public Choice Theory*. Baltimore: Johns Hopkins University Press, 1979, pp. 137–160.

Plott, Charles R., "Industrial Organization Theory and Experimental Economics," *Journal of Economic Literature*, December 1982, *20*, 1485–1527.

Plott, Charles R. (a), "Laboratory Experiments in Economics: The Implications of Posted-Price Institutions," *Science*, 9 May 1986, *232*, 732–738.

Plott, Charles R. (b), "Rational Choice in Experimental Markets," *Journal of Business*, October 1986, *59*, S301–S327.

Smith, Cedric, "Consistency in Statistical Inference and Decision," *Journal of the Royal Statistical Society*, Ser. B, 1961, *23*, 1–25.

Smith, Vernon L., "Bidding and Auctioning Institutions: Experimental Results." In Amihud, Y., ed., *Bidding and Auctioning for Procurement and Allocation*. New York: New York University Press, 1976, pp. 43–64.

Smith, Vernon L., "Relevance of Laboratory Experiments to Testing Resource Allocation Theory." In Kmenta, J., and J. Ramsey, eds., *Evaluation of Econometric Models*. New York: Academic Press, 1980, pp. 345–377.

Smith, Vernon L. (a), "Reflections on Some Experimental Market Mechanisms for Classical Environments." In McAlister, L., ed. *Choice Models for Buyer Behavior*. Greenwich: JAI Press, 1982, pp. 13–47.

Smith, Vernon L. (b), "Microeconomic Systems as an Experimental Science," *American Economic Review*, December 1982, *72*, 923–955.

Smith, Vernon L., "Experimental Methods in the Political Economy of Exchange," *Science*, 10 October 1986, *234*, 167–173.

Thaler, Richard H., "Anomalies: The Winner's Curse," *Journal of Economic Perspectives*, Winter 1988, *2*, 191–201.

Wolf, Charles, and Larry Pohlman, "The Recovery of Risk Preferences from Actual Choices," *Econometrica*, May 1983, *51*, 843–850.

D
Constitutional Economics

[19]

CONSTITUTIONAL POLITICAL ECONOMY, VOL. 1, NO. 1, 1990

THE DOMAIN OF CONSTITUTIONAL ECONOMICS*

James M. Buchanan**

Constitutional political economy is a research program that directs inquiry to the working properties of rules, and institutions within which individuals interact, and the processes through which these rules and institutions are chosen or come into being. The emphasis on the choice of constraints distinguishes this research program from conventional economics, while the emphasis on cooperative rather than conflictual interaction distinguishes the program from much of conventional political science. Methodological individualism and rational choice may be identified as elements in the hard core of the research program.

Introduction

Richard B. McKenzie introduced the term *constitutional economics* to define the central subject matter of a Heritage Foundation conference that he organized in Washington, D.C., in 1982. In his fortuitous addition of the adjective *constitutional* to the familiar disciplinary base, McKenzie provided precisely the combination of meaning that was needed to identify and to isolate a research program that had emerged as an integral, but distinguishable, part of the subdiscipline of public choice over the three decades of the latter's existence. The term *Constitutional Politics* calls attention to the relevant subject phenomena but fails to convey the relevance and applicability of economics, as a disciplinary base, in the examination and evaluation of the foundational rules of social order. By borrowing McKenzie's term, I was then able to suggest, and later to write, an extended entry on *constitutional economics* for *The New Palgrave* (1987). With these beginnings, the ongoing research program (which is readily translatable into the more inclusive *constitutional political economy*) attained full semantic legitimacy in the 1980's. The journal, *Constitutional Political Economy* becomes the institutionalized complement.

This paper describes the domain of the still-emerging research program, the boundaries of which must be considered to be sufficiently

*Paper prepared for Liberty Fund Symposium on "German Ordnungstheorie and American Constitutional Economics" Bonn, 3-6 June 1989.

**Professor of Economics; Center for Study of Public Choice, George Mason University, Fairfax, Va. 22030. USA

CONSTITUTIONAL POLITICAL ECONOMY

provisional to allow for analytical developments along any of several now-predictable dimensions. My first task is to clarify the separate parts of the name itself, and to distinguish the usage of the partial terms from other applications. *Constitutional* economics must be shown to be different from *non-constitutional*, *orthodox* or *standard* economics. At the same time, constitutional economics must be shown to be different from constitutional politics as the latter may be commonly understood. Sections I and II are designed to accomplish this task. My second task is to place or to locate constitutional political economy within a more inclusive intellectual tradition, and in particular in relation to classical political economy and contractarian political philosophy (Section III). My third self-assigned task, attempted in Section IV, is to expose for criticism and to defend the central philosophical presuppositions upon which the whole constitutional economics enterprise rests. Section V introduces some of the more controversial issues concerning the role that perception, vision, and belief must play in constitutional economics, as in other areas of social inquiry. And I should note that some of the arguments advanced in this section may be viewed as personally idiosyncratic, even by some of my fellow constitutional political economists. It is also here that nonsympathetic critics may suggest, appropriately, that in some ultimate sense the whole enterprise is normative. This normative grounding must not, however, be used to deny the relevance of the wholly positive analyses that consists of comparing alternative structures from within the perspective defined by the hard core of the research program. The whole inquiry involves the study of rules, how rules work and how rules might be chosen. But any such effort may be meaningless without some stipulation of the game that rules are to describe.

I. Constitutional and Non-constitutional Economics

There is a categorical distinction to be made between constitutional economics and non-constitutional, or ordinary, economics, a distinction in the ultimate behavioral object of analytical attention. In one sense, all of economics is about choice, and about the varying and complex institutional arrangements within which individuals make choices among alternatives. In ordinary or orthodox economics, no matter how simple or how complex, analysis is concentrated on choices made *within* constraints that are, themselves, imposed exogenously to the person or

2

THE DOMAIN OF CONSTITUTIONAL ECONOMICS

persons charged with making the choice. The constraints that restrict the set of feasible choice options may be imposed by nature, by history, by a sequence of past choices, by other persons, by laws and institutional arrangements, or even by custom and convention. In the elementary textbook formulation of demand theory, for example, the individual consumer-purchaser confronts a range of goods available at a set of prices, but is restricted by the size of the budget. This budget is not within the choice set of the consumer-purchaser during the period of choice under scrutiny. Indeed it would seem unnatural or bizarre, within the mind-set fostered by ordinary economics, to consider the prospect that an individual might deliberately choose to constrain or limit the set of available choice options. Within this mind-set, the utility of the chooser is always maximized by allowing for choices over the whole range allowed by the exogenously determined constraints.

It is precisely at this critical point that constitutional economics, in its most inclusive definition, departs from the conventional framework of analysis. Constitutional economics directs analytical attention to the *choice among constraints*. Once stated in this fashion, economists will recognize that there is relatively little in their established canon that will assist in analyzing choices of this sort. To orthodox economists, only the elementary reality of scarcity makes choice necessary; without scarcity there would be no need to choose. And it would appear to be both methodologically and descriptively absurd to introduce the artificial creation of scarcity as an object for behavioral analysis. Such bedrock conservatism presumably explains much of ordinary economists' inattention and disinterest in constitutional questions, at all levels.

If we move beyond the models of orthodox economics, however, even while remaining at the level of individual behavior, we observe that individuals do, in fact, choose their own constraints, at least to a degree and within some limits. Within recent decades, a few innovative thinkers from economics and other social sciences have commenced to study the choice processes that are involved here (Elster, Schelling, Shefrin, Thaler). The *economics of self control* has reached the status of a respectable, if minor, research program, which may be destined to become more important in this era of emphasis on diet, exercise, health, and the environment. We must surely be sufficiently catholic to allow analysis in this *individual constitutional economics* to qualify for inclusion in the domain.

3

CONSTITUTIONAL POLITICAL ECONOMY

As they carry on within their own guaranteed private spaces, however, individuals would presumably subject themselves to a relatively small set of prior constraints. Individuals basically *trust themselves* to choose rationally when confronted with the externally imposed constraints that are dictated in their historically emergent conditions. If the choice among constraints, in all its complexity, is limited to the economics of self-control, or stated conversely, to the economics of temptation, there might be little to be gained in delineating a constitutional economics enterprise.

It is essential to acknowledge, near the outset of discussion, that individuals choose to impose constraints or limits on their own behavior primarily, even if not exclusively, as a part of an *exchange* in which the restrictions on their own actions are sacrificed in return for the benefits that are anticipated from the reciprocally extended restrictions on the actions of others with whom they interact along the boundaries of private spaces and within the confines of acknowledged public spaces. That is to say, a domain of constitutional economics would exist even if individuals, in their private spaces, chose never to impose constraints on their own behavior. Note that by interpreting the individual's choice of a generalized constraint that restricts the actions both of others and himself (herself) as a part of a reciprocal exchange, we have moved toward the familiar domain of orthodox economics. So interpreted, the individual who joins in a collective decision to impose a generally applied constitutional rule is not, at base, acting differently from observed behavior in a setting that involves giving up one desired good, apples, for another desired good, oranges. In the latter example, we can, without violating the meaning of words, say that the individual chooses to constrain or to limit, the potential consumption of apples in exchange for the expanded opportunity to consume oranges. Expressed in this way, all that is required is that we classify the restrictions on others' actions as *goods* in the individual's preference function along with the more natural classification or restrictions on his (her) own actions as *bads*.

In this simplistic and individualistic perspective, the choice of a reciprocally binding constraint by individuals who are related one to another in an anticipated set of interactions becomes fully analogous to trade in ordinary goods and services, and, so treated, becomes quite different from the choice of a self-imposed constraint in the much more difficult economics of self-control, briefly discussed above.

4

THE DOMAIN OF CONSTITUTIONAL ECONOMICS

Why have the practitioners of orthodox economics seemed so reluctant to extend analysis to include the reciprocal exchanges of liberties that are central to the domain of constitutional economics?

I can advance several related reasons. Economists, along with their peers in the other social sciences as well as other academic disciplines have had no difficulty, through the ages, in implicitly classifying restrictions on some of the activities of some persons in the body politic to be *good*. But the classification procedure has been quite different from the subjective evaluations presumed to be embodied in individuals' preference functions. The nonconstrained voluntary behavior is not classified to be *bad* because an individual simply disprefers such behavior in the ordinary way. Some such behavior is deeded to be bad, and hence its rectification to be good, on the basis of an externally-derived criterion of *goodness* or *truth*. The attributes or qualities of goodness and/or badness applied to actions of persons are treated as if they are intrinsically public, in the Samuelsonion taxonomic sense. An action cannot, properly, be adjudged to be good by one person without an implied generalization of such judgment to other persons. In this conceptualization, persons must, ideally, be brought into agreement on some ultimate classification of actions through a process that resembles scientific discourse. Agreement does not emerge from a trading process where different interests are essentially compromised, with each party reckoning to enjoy some benefits while suffering some sacrifice of preferred position.

In some respects, it is surprising that economists have 'jumped out' of their own analytical framework so readily when they consider the possible imposition of generalized constraints on behavior. They have expressed little curiosity in deriving justification for such constraints from a calculus of individual interests. Economists have, instead, been willing intellectual captives of idealistic political philosophers, and they have readily embraced variants of the Platonic and Hegelian mind-sets. Amartya Sen's usage of the term *meddlesome preferences* (Sen: 1970), by sharp contrast with such terms as *merit goods* and *merit wants*, tends to focus analysis back toward a straight-forward calculus of interest and away from non-individualistic attributes of either goods or actions.

A second, and related, reason for economists' general failure to use the exchange setting when they consider the possible imposition of generalized constraints on individual behavior lies in the methodological dominance of the maximization paradigm. In the latter, *the economic*

5

CONSTITUTIONAL POLITICAL ECONOMY

problem is defined as one of allocating scarce means (resources) among alternative ends. Choice is made necessary by the scarcity of means, and that which is desired (utility) is maximized when like units of resources yield equivalent returns in all uses to which they are put. In this elementary formulation, emphasis is almost exclusively placed on the choices that are made within the scarcity constraints that are, themselves, presumed to be beyond the scope for chooser selection. There is little or no attention paid to the identification of the choosing unit in this abstracted definition, and this feature allows for a relatively unnoticed transference of analysis from individual choice to *social* or *collective* choice on the basis of some implicit presumption that collectivities choose analogously to individuals.

This shift from individual to supraindividual choice was supported, and indirectly justified, by the emergence of macroaggregation and macroeconomic theory and policy during the early decades of the post-Robbins half century. Target levels of macroaggregates (national product, rates of growth, levels of employment) were established to be objectively *good* and to serve as guideposts for choices to be made by collective entities (governments) subject only to the constraints imposed by natural scarcities and technological limits. By some implicit extension of the model for individual choice behavior, constrained only by external forces, governments came to be viewed romantically and were deemed capable of achieving the *good*, as defined for them by the economists and other social philosophers. Microeconomists had long been ready at hand to proffer policy advice to governments concerning ways and means to promote greater overall economy efficiency.

A third reason for economists' general failure to extend their analytical apparatus to the derivation of institutional-constitutional structure is to be found in their presumption that structural constraints are not, themselves, subject to deliberative choice, and, hence, to change. Economists have not neglected to recognize the relevance of institutional rules in affecting patterns of human behavior. Property-rights economics, in particular, (Alchian: 1977), has opened up a research program that concentrates attention directly on the effects of alternative structures. For the most part, however, the emphasis here is on existing arrangements rather than on the comparative analysis involved in extension to structures that might be designed and implemented.

Constitutional economics differs from nonconstitutional or orthodox economics along each of the dimensions that may be inferred from the

6

THE DOMAIN OF CONSTITUTIONAL ECONOMICS

reasons for neglect detailed above. Analysis is consistently individualistic, in the several senses that are relevant. The derivation of institutional constraints is based on a calculus of individual interests, which, in turn, requires the introduction and use of an exchange paradigm as opposed to the idealists' search for the unique *good*. Furthermore, there is no extension of the choice calculus from the individual to collectivities, as such. Collective *choice* is factored down into the participatory behavior of individual members. Finally, emphasis is centered directly on the selection of rules, or institutions, that will, in turn, limit the behavior of the persons who operate within them. Institutions, defined broadly, are variables subject to deliberative evaluation and to explicit choice (Buchanan and Tullock: 1962).

As noted, at one extreme constitutional analysis may be applied to the individual in total isolation, who may act solely in private space. At the other extreme, constitutional analysis is applied to the whole set of persons who make up the membership of the polity. This subcategory of research emphasis is the most familiar, since the very word *constitutional* tends to convey political connotations. The derivation of constraints on government does, indeed, occupy much of our attention. But the inclusive domain of constitutional economics also includes the derivation, analysis of, and justificatory argument for rules that constrain both individual and collective behavior in a wide array of membership groupings, larger than the one-unit limit but smaller than the all-inclusive limit of the whole polity. Clubs, trade unions, corporations, parties, universities, associations—these, and many more, exist and operate under constitutions that are amenable to scientific inquiry.

II. Constitutional *Economics* and Constitutional *Politics*

In Section I, I have attempted to distinguish between *constitutional* and *non-constitutional* economics. I propose, in Section II, to distinguish between constitutional *economics* and constitutional *politics*, as the latter term may be generally and wisely interpreted. As I have noted, most constitutional inquiry and analysis is concentrated at the level of the politically-organized collectivity and is, in this sense, political. The distinction to be emphasized, however, is one of perspective rather than one that relates directly to either the form of organization or to the type of activity. If an exchange rather than a maximizing paradigm is taken to be descriptive of the inclusive research program

7

CONSTITUTIONAL POLITICAL ECONOMY

for the discipline, then *economics* involves inquiry into *cooperative* arrangements for human interaction, extending from the simplest of two-person, two-good trading processes through the most complex quasi-constitutional arrangements for multi-national organizations. As noted in Section I, orthodox economics has rarely been extended to noncommercial or political activity, as such, but the exchange perspective readily allows this step to be taken.

The cooperative perspective, however, must be categorically distinguished from the contrasting *conflictual* perspective, which has been applied, almost automatically, to all political interactions, whether or not these are classified as constitutional. It will be useful here to examine the differences between the cooperative and the conflictual perspectives more carefully. The very term *politics* tends to conjure up a mental image of potential conflict among those persons who are members of the politically-organized community. This conflict may be interpreted to be analogous to scientific disputes, in which separate participants or groups seek to convince one another of the *truth* of their advanced propositions. The age-old tradition of idealism in political philosophy conceives of all of politics in this light and, as noted earlier, the dominance of this model of politics has tended to discourage economists from political extensions of the exchange or cooperative paradigm. But, even if the teleological interpretation is rejected, politics may seem, by its very nature, to involve conflict between and among individuals and groups within a polity.

From the institutionally-determined characteristics of collective decisions, the characteristics that dictate mutual exclusivity among the alternatives for selection (only one candidate can be electorally chosen) imply some ultimate division of the membership into two subsets, *winners* and *losers*. This perspective almost directly suggests that politics is primarily if not exclusively a distributional game or enterprise, a process that involves transfers of value (utility) among and between separately identified coalitions of persons.

Note that the predominance of the distributional elements in the conflictual model of politics need not imply that the game be zero sum, although this limiting case may be useful for some analytical purposes. Conflictual politics may be positive, zero, or negative sum, as gains and losses are somehow aggregated over all participants (members). And this seems to be the natural model for analyzing politics so long as rules for reaching collective decisions require less than full agreement. If a

8

THE DOMAIN OF CONSTITUTIONAL ECONOMICS

majority, whether simple or qualified, is allowed to be decisive and impose its will on a minority, then the observed opposition of the minority to the alternative preferred by the majority can be taken to indicate that members of the minority expect to suffer utility losses, at least in a lost-opportunity sense. In this model of conflictual politics, which appears to be descriptive of ordinary political activity, there seems to be no direct way of introducing a cooperative interpretation. A necessary condition for cooperation in social interaction is the prospect for positive expected gains by all parties, or, in the gainer-loser terminology, the prospect that there be no net losers. At a first descriptive cut, this condition seems to be foreign to the whole political enterprise.

It is precisely at this point, however, that constitutional politics, or politics at the constitutional level of choices among alternative sets of basic rules or constraints, rescues the cooperative model, at least in some potential explanatory and normative sense. As it operates and as we observe it to operate, ordinary politics may remain conflictual, in the manner noted above, while participation in the inclusive political game that defines the rules for ordinary politics may embody positively valued prospects for all members of the polity. In other words, constitutional politics does lend itself to examination in a cooperative analytical framework, while ordinary politics continues to lend itself to analysis that employs conflict models of interaction.

Generalized agreement on constitutional rules that allow for the reaching of ordinary collective decisions by means that do not require general agreement is surely possible, as is empirically demonstrated in the context of almost all organizations. The analytical-scientific inquiry that involves comparisons of the working properties of alternative sets of rules along with the examination of processes through which agreement on rules may be attained defines the domain of primary concern. The usage of the terminology *constitutional economics* or *constitutional political economy* rather than the somewhat more accurate *constitutional politics* is prompted by the linkage in scientific heritage between *economics* and *cooperation*, by the inference of the appropriateness of the exchange as opposed to the conflict paradigm.

III. The Intellectual Traditions of Constitutional Political Economy

In Sections I and II, I have attempted to set the research program in constitutional political economy apart from ongoing programs within

9

CONSTITUTIONAL POLITICAL ECONOMY

the interrelated and more inclusive disciplines of economics and political science. It would be totally misleading, however, to infer from my discussion that this research program has emerged full blown, as if divorced from any traditions of intellectual inquiry. As I have noted, constitutional economics, in its modern variant, did indeed blossom only in the second half of this century. But the program was not based either on a new scientific discovery, at least as usually defined, or on a new set of analytical tools. Constitutional political economy is best interpreted as a re-emphasis, a revival, a re-discovery, of basic elements of earlier intellectual traditions that have been set aside, neglected, and sometimes forgotten in the social sciences and social philosophy.

These traditions are those of classical political economy and contractarian political philosophy. It will be useful to discuss each of these traditions briefly.

Classical political economy, represented especially in the works of Adam Smith, was directed toward offering an explanation and understanding of how an economy (set of markets) would work without detailed political interventions and control. Smith's aim was to demonstrate that the *wealth* of the nation would be larger under a regime of minimal politicization than under the alternative closely controlled mercantilist regime. And the whole thrust of the argument was to the effect that all groups in the economy and especially the laboring classes, could be expected to share in the benefits promised upon the shift in regimes. The emphasis was on the generalization of expected gains over all persons and classes. The suggested change in the structure, or basic rules, that depoliticization involves was, therefore, within the feasible limits of potential agreement by all parties. The normative focus, again especially in Adam Smith, was not explicitly distributional. Only with the Marxian extensions of Ricardo's abstract analysis did interclass conflict enter into classical attention.

It is also important to recognize that the Smithean emphasis was not allocational in the modern economists' meaning of this term. The analysis was not designed to show that economic resources would be more effectively allocated to higher valued uses under a market than under a politicized regime, as measured by some external and objective standard of value. The aim was, instead, to show that the market order would allocate resources such that the evaluations (preferences) of individuals would be more fully satisfied, *regardless of what these evaluations might be*. In terms of his familiar example of the butcher,

10

THE DOMAIN OF CONSTITUTIONAL ECONOMICS

Smith's lesson was to show that self-interest in the marketplace works to supply meat for supper, provided that meat is what consumers want. There is no implication here that self-interest in the marketplace works to supply meat because meat is valuable in some nutritional sense as defined by experts.

So interpreted, therefore, Adam Smith's enterprise falls squarely within the domain of constitutional political economy. In a strictly positive sense, his analysis described both how the existing regime worked and how an alternative regime might work. And, since the alternative seemed to generate more wealth to all parties, as measured by their own standards, the normative extension of the positive analysis was quite straightforward. In this extension, the object upon which collective attention must be placed is the set of rules or constraints within which persons behave in their capacities as consumers-buyers and producers-sellers. The laws and institutions that define the economic-political order become the variables subject to possible adjustment and reform.

I have, in the immediately preceding paragraphs, selected elements from the tradition of classical political economy that seem to provide precursory foundations for the modern research program in constitutional political economy. My treatment would surely be accused of bias, however, if I failed to indicate the presence of considerable ambiguity and confusion in the philosophical underpinnings of the classical economics enterprise. An interpretation of that enterprise in terms of classical utilitarianism would be quite different from my own; this alternative interpretation would stress quite separate elements of the tradition. The interpersonal comparability and aggregate measurability of utility were not explicitly rejected by the classical economists and, in a selected reading, these may be attributed, as presumptions, to their analyses. In this case, the whole enterprise becomes precursory to he maximizing rather than to the exchange paradigm in economics, with both allocational and distributional implications, and with a wholly different avenue for moving from the individual to the collective levels of choice. The categorical distinction between choices among rules and choices within rules all but disappears in the utilitarian configuration.

The elements of Adam Smith's intellectual enterprise become directly precursory to he research program in constitutional economics only when these laments are imbedded within the tradition of contractarian political philosophy, the tradition that was developed prior to but

11

CONSTITUTIONAL POLITICAL ECONOMY

became competitive with and quite different from classical utilitarianism. From the 17th century, from the works of Althusius, Hobbes,
Spinoza, and Locke in particular, attempts were made to ground justificatory argument for state coercion on agreement by those individuals
who are subject to coercion. This intellectual tradition invented the
autonomous individual by shucking off the communitarian cocoon. The
assignment to the individual of a capacity for rational independent
choice, as such, allowed a *science* of economics and politics to emerge,
a *science* that embodied a legitimatizing explanation for the emergence
of and existence of the state. In agreeing to be governed, explicitly or
implicitly, the individual exchanges his own liberty with others who
similarly give up liberties in exchange for the benefits offered by a
regime characterized by behavioral limits.

The contractarian logic leaves open any specification of the range
and scope for agreed-on coercive authority. The early contractarians
and notably Hobbes, had no understanding of the efficacy of market
order, as it might function under the umbrella of the protective or
minimal state. This understanding was provided only in the 18th century, and was fully articulated only in the great work of Adam Smith.
Classical political economy, as appended to the contractarian intellectual foundations, allowed the development of a scientifically-based analysis aimed at comparing alternative structures of political-legal order,
analysis that could introduce and use principles of rational choice
behavior of individuals and without resort to supra-individualistic
norms. Utilitarianism also rejected all supra-individual norms, as such,
and grounded all norms in a calculus of pleasure and pain. Nonetheless,
this Benthamite intrusion created ambiguity in the efforts to add up
utilities over persons. In this way, the contractarian justification derived
from conceptual agreement was obscured, and the way was opened for
a non-transcendental utilitarian supercession of individualistic norms.
The contractarian philosophical basis upon which classical political
economy should have been exclusively developed was, at least partially, undermined and neglected for almost two centuries, only to be
rediscovered in the research program of constitutional economics.

IV. The Hard Core and its Critics

Throughout this paper I have referred to constitutional economics
or constitutional political economy as a *research program*, thereby

12

THE DOMAIN OF CONSTITUTIONAL ECONOMICS

deliberately using the Lakatosian classification. In this scheme, there exist elements in the hard core of the program that are rarely, if ever, challenged by those scholars who work inside the intellectual tradition defined by the program. These central elements are taken as presuppositions, as relatively absolute absolutes, and, as such, they become, themselves, the constraints (the constitution) within which the scientific discourse is conducted. External intellectual challenges to the whole enterprise tend to be directed at these elements in the core of the program. The ongoing research within the constraints can, of course, proceed without concern for these external criticisms, but practitioners need to be aware of the core-imposed limits on the persuasive potential of the internalized analytical exercise.

For constitutional economics, the foundational position is summarized in *methodological individualism*. Unless those who would be participants in the scientific dialogue are willing to locate the exercise in the choice calculus of individuals, *qua* individuals, there can be no departure from the starting gate. The autonomous individual is a *sine qua non* for any initiation of serious inquiry in the research program. Individual autonomy, as a defining quality, does not, however, imply that the individual chooses and acts as if he or she exists in isolation from and apart from the community or communities of other persons with whom he or she may be variously associated. Any form of community or association of individuals may reflect some sharing of values, and, further, any individual's formation of values may be influenced by the values of those with whom he or she is variously associated in communities. The communitarian challenge to methodological individualism must go beyond the claim that individuals influence one another reciprocally through presence in communities. The challenge must make the stronger claim that individuation, the separation of the individual from community is not conceptually possible, that it becomes meaningless to think of potential divergence between and among individual interests in a community. Stated in this way, it is evident that methodological individualism, as a presupposition of inquiry, characterizes almost all research programs in economics and political science; constitutional economics does not depart from its more inclusive disciplinary bases in this respect.

The communitarian critique does not often appear in such blatant guise. For constitutional economics, in particular, the critique apparently leaves the individualistic postulates unchallenged, while either

13

CONSTITUTIONAL POLITICAL ECONOMY

implicitly or explicitly asserting the existence of some supraindividual-istic source of evaluation. Individual evaluations are superseded by those emergent from God, natural law, right reason, or the state. This more subtle stance rejects methodological individualism, not on the claim that individuation is impossible, or that individual evaluations may not differ within a community, but rather on the claim that it is normatively improper to derive collective action from individual evaluations. To the communitarian who posits the existence of some supraindividualistic value scale, the whole analysis that builds on a base of an individualistic calculus can only be useful as an input in schemes of control and manipulation designed to align individualized preferences with those orderings dictated by the overarching norms for the community.

Concomitant with methodological individualism as a component of the hard core is the postulate of rational choice, a postulate that is shared over all research programs in economics. The autonomous individual is also presumed to be capable of choosing among alternatives in a sufficiently orderly manner as to allow a quality of rationality to be attributed to observed behavior. For constitutional economics, the capacity for rational choice is extended to include a capacity to choose among constraints, both individually and collectively applied, within which subsequent choices may be made.

Rationality implies that choices may be analyzed as if an ordering of alternatives exists, arrayed in accordance with some scalar of *preferred-ness*. We may, but need not, use the term utility to designate that which the individual calls upon to make up the ordinal ranking. At the analytical level, there is no need that the ranking correspond with any array of the choice alternatives that may be objectively measurable by some outside observer. The test for individual rationality in choice does require, however, the minimal step of classifying alternatives into *goods* and *bads*. The central rationality precept states only that the individual choose more rather than less of goods, and less rather than more of bads. There is no requirement that rationality dictates choice in accordance with the individual's economic interest, as this might be measured by some outside observer of behavior.

The individualistic postulate allows the interests or preferences of individuals to differ, one from another. And the rationality postulate does not restrict these interests beyond the classificatory step noted.

14

THE DOMAIN OF CONSTITUTIONAL ECONOMICS

Homo economicus, the individual who populates the models of empirical economics may, but need not, describe the individual whose choice calculus is analyzed in constitutional political economy. When selecting among alternative constitutional constraints, however, the individual is required to make some predictions about the behavior of others than himself. And, in such a setting, there is a powerful argument that suggests the appropriateness of something akin to the *homo economicus* postulate for behavior. (Brennan and Buchanan: 1985)

I have briefly discussed the individualistic and the rationality presuppositions for the research program. These elements are not controversial and if they would be listed as components of the hard core both by practitioners and critics of constitutional economics. A less obvious element that is, however, equally fundamental involves the generalization of the individualistic and the rationality postulates to *all* persons in the political community. All individuals must be presumed capable to make rational choices among alternatives in accordance with individually autonomous value scales. And this generalization does not allow derivation of collective action, whether or not directed toward choices among constraints, from individual evaluations on anything other than an *equal weighting*. To introduce a weighting scheme through which the evaluation of some persons in the community are deemed more important than other persons would require resort to some supraindividualistic source, which is, of course, ruled out by adherence to the individualistic postulate. In this sense the whole of the constitutional economics research program rests squarely on a *democratic* foundation.

The identification of the elements in the hard core of the research program in constitutional economics allows for the simultaneous identification of its vulnerabilities. As noted, critics who call upon extraindividual sources of value cannot participate in the ongoing dialogue, nor can those skeptics who refuse to apply models of rational choice to the behavior of individuals as autonomous actors. To this point in its development, the program is vulnerable also in its failure to address the issue of defining membership in the community of persons over whom the postulates are to be applied. Who is to count as an autonomous individual? How are children to be treated, and at what age or stage of development does childhood cease and full membership in community granted? How are the mentally and emotionally incompetent to be handled, and who is to decide who is incompetent? Is the community considered to be open to potential entrants?

15

CONSTITUTIONAL POLITICAL ECONOMY

These and related issues are relevant for inquiries in constitutional economics, but the program, by its nature, cannot address them readily. The starting point for analysis is a set of autonomous individuals, either already organized or potentially organizable in a political unit. Once the set is initially defined, the program can be extended to include examination and analysis of how the defined community itself addresses such issues. But the initial definition lies beyond the boundaries of any analytical construction within the program, as such.

V. Perception, Vision and Faith

Nietzsche used the metaphor of viewing the world of reality through differing windows (Kaufman 1950: 61), and Ortega y Gasset went so far as to define ultimate reality itself as a perspective (Ortega y Gasset 1961: 45). In a sense, any research program involves a way of looking at, and thereby imposing an order on, that which is perceived. This characterization applies particularly to any program in social science, where the ultimate object of inquiry is behavior in a social interaction process. I have on several occasions referred to the *constitutional perspective*, which I have acknowledged to be different from other perspectives that might be used in examining and evaluating the interaction of individuals in social and/or political settings. This elementary fact that perspectives differ, or may differ, raises difficult issues in epistemology that cannot be ignored.

Consider, first, perception at its simplest level. Presumably, individuals are sufficiently alike, one to another, biologically that we see, hear, taste, smell, and feel physical phenomena similarly if not identically. We all see a wall as a barrier to movement, and no one of us makes an attempt to walk through walls. Someone who failed to perceive a wall as the others of us would be classified to be abnormal in at least one of the basic perceptual senses. As phenomena come to be increasingly complex, however, individuals may come to differ in their perceptions, despite the fact that, biologically, they continue to possess the same perceptual apparatus. Elementary sense perception must be accompanied by imaginative constructions that require some mental processing before a basis for evaluation, and ultimately for action, can be established.

As phenomena increase in complexity, the imaginative elements in perception increase relative to those that emerge directly from the

16

THE DOMAIN OF CONSTITUTIONAL ECONOMICS

senses. In this progression from the simple to the complex, the similarity in perceptions among persons must decrease. What may be called the *natural* way of observing phenomena fades away at some point along the spectrum. Individuals may then be brought into agreement on that which they observe only by entry into some sort of association of shared values or norms, which members, either explicitly or implicitly, choose. This statement may seem contradictory when first made; it may seem to state that persons choose how they see reality. But the statement becomes less challenging to ordinary notions when we replace *see* with *think about*.

I have been accused of committing the naturalistic fallacy, in some of my own works, of failing to respect properly *the fact—value, positive—normative* distinction, and, hence, of deriving the *ought* from the *is*, at least implicitly. I submit, however, that my critics mount such charges only because of their own confusion about the nature of perception of complex phenomena. If there exists no *natural* way of observing reality, some evaluation and choosing process is a necessary complement to the imaginative step that allows apparent chaos to be converted into order. We select the *is* that defines the hard core of our research program, and this holds true whether or not we are professional scientists. Within this *is*, we can adhere strictly to the precepts laid down for positive analysis. But the normative implications that may be drawn are, indeed, derivative from the chosen perceptive framework, and could not, or would not, be otherwise available.

Constitutional economics is a domain of inquiry and discourse among scientists who choose to perceive social interaction as a set of complex relationships, both actual and potential, among autonomous persons, each of whom is capable of making rational choices. The domain, as such, cannot be extended to include inquiry by those who choose to perceive social interaction differently. There is simply no common basis for scientific argument, and ultimately agreement, with those who choose to perceive social interaction either in purely conflictual or purely idealistic visions. These visions are, indeed, alternative 'windows' on the world. And the process through which individuals choose among such windows remains mysterious. How can empirical evidence be made convincing when such evidence must, itself, be perceived from only one vantage point at a time? The naivete of modern empirical economists in this respect verges on absurdity.

17

CONSTITUTIONAL POLITICAL ECONOMY

When all is said and done, *Constitutional Economics*, for me, must be acknowledged to rest upon a precommitment to, or a faith in if you will, man's cooperative potential. Persons are neither bees in hives, carnivorous beasts in a jungle, nor angels in God's heaven. They are independent units of consciousness, capable of assigning values to alternatives, and capable of choosing and acting in accordance with these values. It is both physically necessary and beneficial that they live together, in many and varying associations and communities. But to do so, they must live by rules that they can also choose.

REFERENCES

Alchian, A. (1977) *Economic Forces at Work*. Indianapolis: Liberty Press.

Althusius, J. (1932) *Politica Methodica digesta*. (Ed. by C. J. Friedrich) Cambridge: Harvard University Press.

Brennan, G. and Buchanan J. (1985) *The Reason of Rules*. Cambridge: Cambridge University Press.

Buchanan, J. (1987) "Constitutional Economics," *The New Palgrave*. London: Macmillan.

Buchanan J. and Tullock, G. (1962) *The Calculus of Consent*. Ann Arbor: University of Michigan Press.

Elster, J. (1979) *Ulysses and the Sirens*. Cambridge: Cambridge University Press.

Hobbes, Th. (1943) *Leviathan*. London: Everymans Library.

Kaufman, W. (1950) *Nietzsche*. Princeton: Princeton University Press.

Locke, J. (1955) *Second Treatise of Civil Government*. Chicago: Gateway.

McKenzie, R. (ed) (1984) *Constitutional Economics*. Lexington, MA: Lexington Books.

Ortega y Gasset, J. (1961) *Meditations on Quixote*. New York: Norton.

Schelling, Th. (1978) "Egonomics, or the Art of Self Management". *American Economic Review* 68: 290-294.

Sen, A. K. (1970) "The Impossibility of a Paretian Liberal". *Journal of Political Economy* 78: 152-157.

Smith, A. (1979) *The Wealth of Nations*. Oxford: Clarendon Press.

Spinoza, B. (1854) *A Treatise in Politics*. London: Holyoake. (Trans. by William McCall)

Thaler, R. and Shefrin H. M. (1981) "An Economic Theory of Self-Control". *Journal of Political Economy* 89: 392-406.

18

Name Index

The International Library of Critical Writings in Economics

International Trade
J. Peter Neary

The Foundations of Public Finance
Peter Jackson

Labor Economics
Orley Ashenfelter

International Finance
Robert Z. Aliber

Welfare Economics
William J. Baumol and Janusz A. Ordover

Agricultural Economics
G.H. Peters

The Theory of Inflation
Michael Parkin

The Economics of Information
David K. Levine and Steven A. Lippman

Analytical Marxism
John E. Roemer

The Theory of the Firm
Mark Casson

The Economics of Inequality and Poverty
A.B. Atkinson

Implicit Contract Theory
Sherwin Rosen

Business Cycle Theory
Finn E. Kydland

The Economics of Housing
John M. Quigley

The Economics of Institutions
G.M. Hodgson

Population Economics
Julian L. Simon

The Economics of Crime
Isaac Ehrlich

The Economics of Integration
Willem Molle